Public Speaking
and
Civic Engagement

J. Michael Hogan
Penn State University

Patricia Hayes Andrews
Indiana University

James R. Andrews
Indiana University

Glen Williams
Southeast Missouri State University

PEARSON

Boston ■ New York ■ San Francisco
Mexico City ■ Montreal ■ Toronto ■ London ■ Madrid ■ Munich ■ Paris
Hong Kong ■ Singapore ■ Tokyo ■ Cape Town ■ Sydney

Editor-in-Chief, Communication: Karon Bowers
Associate Development Editor: Jenny Lupica
Series Editorial Assistant: Jessica Cabana
Marketing Manager: Suzan Czajkowski
Production Supervisor: Liz Napolitano
Editorial Production Service: Marty Tenney, Modern Graphics, Inc.
Composition Buyer: Linda Cox
Manufacturing Buyer: JoAnne Sweeney
Electronic Composition: Modern Graphics, Inc.
Photo Researcher: Rachel Lucas
Cover Designer: Kristina Mose-Libon

For related titles and support materials, visit our online catalog at *www.ablongman.com*.

Between the time website information is gathered and then published, it is not unusual for some sites to have closed. Also, the transcription of URLs can result in typographical errors. The publisher would appreciate notification where these errors occur so that they may be corrected in subsequent editions.

Library of Congress Cataloging-in-Publication Data

Public speaking and civic engagement / J. Michael Hogan . . . [et al.].
  p. cm.
Includes bibliographical references and index.
ISBN 13: 978-0-205-56298-5
ISBN-10: 0-205-56298-1
1. Public speaking. 2. Persuasion (Rhetoric) I. Hogan, J. Michael, 1953–

PN4129.15.P832 2008
808.5'1—dc22

2007038996

Printed in the United States of America
10 9 8 7 6 5 4 3 2 1   RRD-OH   11 10 09 08 07
Credits appear on page 519, which constitutes an extension of the copyright page.

BRIEF CONTENTS

CONTENTS

PART IV
Types of Public Speaking

In our democratic society, we have both a right and a responsibility to participate in civic affairs. An important part of that participation is speaking in public. Engaged citizenship means voicing our opinions, sharing our insights and ideas, persuading those with differing points of view, and deliberating in groups. In short, being an engaged citizen means *communicating* with others, and this book can help you learn how to communicate effectively and responsibly.

Our Approach and Themes

Three convictions guided our writing of *Public Speaking and Civic Engagement*:

- We believe that public speaking is not only a valuable personal skill but also an important part of engaged citizenship in a democracy. You will deliver many speeches in your life, but the most important will be those you deliver as a citizen.
- We approach public speaking as a collaborative partnership between the speaker and the audience. No speaker can succeed alone—the audience is crucial to the planning, delivery, and outcome of the speech.
- We view public speaking as more than a set of performance skills. Truly effective public speakers have ideas or information worth communicating. They think critically and reason soundly, and they are motivated by a commitment to the good of the community.

The Centrality of Civic Engagement

Preparing a classroom speech should be no different from planning a speech to present at a business conference or at a town hall meeting. The classroom is a public space, and your fellow students are citizens. You should treat a speech to your classmates as seriously as you would a speech to any other group of co-workers or citizens.

In treating public speaking as a form of civic engagement, this book will encourage you to develop an ethic of active participation. It will urge you to read widely and reflectively, and it will hold you responsible for becoming well informed on your topic. As you begin to seek out opportunities to speak in public, you will learn to listen critically, yet approach others in a spirit of mutual respect and cooperation. You will learn to speak persuasively, but you also will be encouraged to join *with* your fellow citizens in a spirit of inquiry and common cause. As you work with others in seeking solutions to your common problems, you will come to understand what it means to deliberate "in good faith."

The emphasis on civic engagement makes this book different from many public speaking books. Some books treat public speaking as a tool of personal success—a skill that you need to "beat the competition" or climb the ladder of success. We approach public speaking as something more than that. Emphasizing ethical and civic concerns, we view public speaking as an essential tool of democratic citizenship. Protected by the First Amendment to our constitution, our "free speech" distinguishes us from citizens of totalitarian states and empowers us to govern ourselves. In this book, speech is treated as a means for defining our purposes and identity as a nation, discussing the choices we face, and resolving the differences and disagreements among us. Even ceremonial speeches are treated as important expressions of our democratic culture and traditions. Your course in public speaking may well contribute to your personal and professional success. But in the final analysis, the best reason to study public speaking is so that you can participate in the civic life of your community and nation. In other words, your course in public speaking is part of your education for citizenship.

The Speaker-Audience Partnership

This book does not treat the audience as something to be manipulated, but rather as an active partner in the public speaking process. From the earliest stages of planning a speech to the question-and-answer period that may follow, your listeners will be important to your success. You need to consider your listeners' needs and interests in tandem with your own. You need to ask, What are my listeners' priorities and concerns? How can I persuasively advance my own ideas while still respecting their values and beliefs? Am I open to being influenced by my audience even as I try to persuade them? What can I do to promote a genuine spirit of democratic deliberation in which my audience and I have a shared interest in discovering common ground?

When considering your audience, it is important to recognize that our society is more diverse than ever before. Your audience may consist of people of all genders, races, and religions. It may even include people from other parts of the world. At the very least, your audience will have widely varying interests and values and hold differing political opinions. Respecting this diversity is crucial to connecting with your audience. In this book, we recognize the challenges of communicating in an increasingly diverse society, yet we also stress the need for people to come together in a spirit of dialogue and collaboration if we hope to solve our common problems.

Respecting the speaker-listener partnership is more than a practical necessity; it is an ethical obligation. Ethical speakers keep in touch with the audience's needs, concerns, and welfare, even as they pursue their own purposes in speaking. In *Public Speaking and Civic Engagement*, we treat the speaker-listener partnership as both a practical necessity and an ethical responsibility.

The Plan of the Book

The theme of civic engagement is integrated throughout this book. We begin by illuminating the relationship between public speaking and civic engagement, addressing ethical concerns and reflecting on the challenges of listening critically and addressing diverse audiences. Then we move step-by-step through the process of preparing a speech, devoting chapters to generating ideas for your speeches, investigating your topic, and supporting and organizing your speech. Next we focus on language and delivery, emphasizing the importance of the words you use and your methods of oral and visual presentation. Finally, we consider the major types of speeches—informative, persuasive, and ceremonial—and the challenge of speaking and deliberating in groups. Different instructors may choose to assign chapters in a different order, and the book allows for that flexibility.

Public Speaking in a Democratic Society

Chapters 1–5 are devoted to the role of public speaking in a democratic society. They address overarching concerns in public speaking and articulate our philosophical perspective on public speaking as civic engagement.

Chapter 1 reflects on the problem of civic alienation in America, as well as the promise of a renewed commitment to engaged citizenship. It explains the connections between public speaking and democratic citizenship in the rhetorical tradition, and it considers the unique challenges of communicating in the twenty-first century. Finally, it outlines the characteristics of the responsible citizen-speaker in our technologically advanced and increasingly diverse democratic society.

Chapter 2 establishes an ethical framework for public speaking. After examining why some people may be "turned off" by politics, we explore various ways that individuals can become involved in civic affairs. We also consider some of the major ethical issues in public speaking, such as plagiarism and ghostwriting. The chapter concludes by reflecting on the meaning of deliberating "in good faith" and on the problem of demagoguery in the media age.

Chapter 3 presents an overview of the key principles involved in preparing to speak with commitment and confidence. We examine the importance of the speaker-listener partnership and present a collaborative, audience-centered view of public speaking. We also explore strategies for understanding and managing communication apprehension. The chapter concludes by emphasizing how a sincere commitment to one's purpose as a speaker contributes to the ability to speak with confidence.

Chapter 4 focuses on the responsibility of the engaged citizen to be an active, well-informed, and critical listener. The chapter points to a respectful attitude as the foundation of the speaker-listener partnership and considers some of the barriers to effective listening. It concludes with some specific guidelines for enhancing your critical thinking and listening skills, including note taking, developing visual literacy, and suspending judgment.

Chapter 5 examines the diversity of audiences in our modern democratic society. It emphasizes the importance of understanding listener needs and values and suggests ways to adapt to audiences while maintaining the integrity of your own ideas and convictions. It distinguishes between universal listener values and those that differ across demographic dimensions, such as age, race, and gender. The chapter concludes by introducing tools for analyzing audiences, including administering an audience survey, and by offering suggestions for adapting to audiences without stereotyping.

Developing Your Speech

In Chapters 6–10, we turn to the more specific steps in preparing a speech. While continuing to emphasize the theme of civic engagement, the chapters address everything from selecting a topic to organizing your ideas and preparing an outline.

Chapter 6 focuses on how to select topics that reflect both your own interests and important public concerns. We emphasize the need to choose topics that engage your listeners and address substantive issues of importance to the community. Stressing the importance of having a clear purpose when you speak, we conclude by offering specific guidelines for crafting and testing thesis statements for your speech.

Chapter 7 examines the process of conducting responsible and productive research. The chapter describes the creative enterprise of building a speech, doing careful research through the Internet and the library, and interviewing for information. In acknowledging the need for thorough, thoughtful, and diversified research, we consider how this process might even challenge the speaker's own thinking. The chapter concludes with tests for evaluating information and guidelines for quoting and citing sources.

Chapter 8 examines the ways speakers make their ideas believable, understandable, and persuasive through the ethical and effective use of supporting material. We discuss specific ways of supporting ideas with evidence, and we introduce a variety of tests for analyzing the quality of your evidence. We also consider ways to make evidence more compelling to listeners. The chapter concludes with tips for critically evaluating evidence from various sources.

Chapter 9 emphasizes the importance of sound organization and offers guidance on evaluating the quality of ideas. We cover the basic principles of organization and introduce a wide variety of ways that ideas may be organized, ranging from categorical to problem-solution to narrative patterns. The chapter illustrates transitions and transitional devices that can contribute to the coherence and clarity of your speech. We conclude with a detailed discussion of various strategies for introducing and concluding speeches.

Chapter 10 discusses working, formal, and keyword outlines that may be used at various stages of the speech preparation process. We also cover the basic principles of outlining and offer specific guidance for developing both the formal and the keyword outlines. Finally, the chapter provides extended examples of the different types of outlines for speeches that emphasize civic engagement topics.

Presenting Your Speech

Chapters 11–13 of the book focus on the effective presentation of the speech, specifically style and delivery. While we do not consider style and delivery more important than the substantive content of speeches, we recognize that the use of language and how a speech is presented can have an enormous impact on its success.

Chapter 11 addresses the ethical and appropriate use of language. We explore the ways that language conveys ideas and actually may complement one's arguments. The chapter also considers how a speaker's style—especially the choice and use of language—can advance the audience's understanding and conviction. We examine some ways to make your language interesting and engaging for listeners, including the use of figurative language and rhetorical questions. The chapter concludes by emphasizing the importance of language that is appropriate to the situation, gender inclusive, and ethical.

Chapter 12 considers the characteristics of effective delivery. We emphasize that even good ideas may not be understandable or convincing if they are poorly presented. At the same time, we distinguish between "sounding good" and "being sound." The chapter examines the basic principles of good delivery, with an emphasis on effective extemporaneous speaking. We also consider other styles of delivery, including manuscript, memorized, and impromptu speeches. The chapter concludes by acknowledging the importance of the question-and-answer period as an opportunity for respectful and mutually beneficial dialogue.

Chapter 13 explores ways of using presentational aids to support ideas visually. We examine the ways in which visual arguments are constructed and how visual aids can sometimes distort and mislead. The chapter considers the basic functions of presentational aids and offers guidelines for their preparation and use by speakers—as well as their evaluation by listeners. We explore high-tech and low-tech options, paying special attention to computer-generated slideshows. We conclude with a discussion of ethical concerns in the use of presentational aids.

Types of Public Speaking

In Chapters 14–18, we turn our attention to the specific types of speeches we give as citizens in a democracy. In each chapter, we consider the purposes and context of each type of speech and offer tips for delivering ethical and effective speeches of each type.

Chapter 14 discusses speaking to inform. We define informative speeches as those that seek to educate or enlighten audiences rather than take sides in a public controversy. The chapter identifies the functions and types of informative speeches, and we illustrate specific patterns of organization that are especially well suited to informative speaking. The chapter concludes by considering how informative speeches can help listeners become better educated and more discerning citizens.

Chapter 15 defines "public controversy" and discusses how public controversies invite persuasive speaking. We revisit what it means to deliberate in good faith and distinguish among three types of persuasive issues: fact, value, and policy. Considering two of the so-called "modes of proof," the chapter then discusses how to strengthen your ethos, or ethical proof, and concludes by considering the techniques and ethics of appealing to audience emotions.

Chapter 16 continues our consideration of persuasive speaking by reflecting on the last mode of proof: logos, or logical argument. Exploring what it means to make a reasonable, logically compelling argument, we begin by distinguishing between persuasion and demagoguery in a free society, then explore the components of a sound argument. We also identify four different types of reasoning: inductive, deductive, causal, and analogical. The chapter concludes by identifying and discussing a number of common fallacies of reasoning and evidence.

Chapter 17 considers speaking on special occasions. We begin by discussing the important functions of ceremonial speaking in a democratic society. We then describe the specific types of ceremonial speeches, defining the purposes and common themes of each. We reflect on the role of ceremonial speaking in articulating and reinforcing social values, and we discuss the importance of language and delivery in such speeches. The chapter concludes by considering what makes some ceremonial speeches "eloquent" and by offering tips for delivering such speeches from manuscript.

Chapter 18 focuses on speaking and deliberating in groups. We examine the importance of communicating with others in groups in community and organizational settings. We point to the need for respectful dialogue in public deliberation, along with the potential benefits and challenges of deliberating in groups. The chapter highlights group structures that encourage dialogue, such as study circles and National Issues Forums. We explore some of the factors that influence effectiveness in group deliberations. The chapter concludes by briefly discussing formal group presentations, such as panels and symposia, and by offering some guidelines for participating effectively in all kinds of groups.

Special Features

Public Speaking and Civic Engagement offers a number of distinguishing features designed to make the book an engaging teaching and learning tool.

A Unique Approach

A strong introductory chapter establishes the unique framework of the book by highlighting the connections between public speaking and democratic citizenship. From the start, students are encouraged to think of public speaking not just as a tool of personal success, but also as a way to serve others in a democratic society. A stand-alone chapter on ethics follows, reinforcing the theme that public speaking entails certain responsibilities beyond one's personal interests: the responsibility to become well-informed on your topic, for example, and to deliberate in good faith. The book includes chapters on all the topics typically addressed in a public speaking textbook, including communication apprehension, audience analysis, organization, and style. Yet throughout the book, the focus on civic engagement is sustained by an emphasis on the ethics as well as the techniques of public speaking and by historical and contemporary examples of both responsible and irresponsible speakers.

Among the unique chapters of the book are those discussing the various *types* of public speaking. Distinguishing persuasive from informative speaking in terms of the situations that "invite" persuasion, the book defines "public controversy" and not only discusses what makes for effective proof but also distinguishes between responsible and "demagogic" persuasion. The book also offers the first serious treatment of ceremonial speaking as a mode of civic engagement and community building, and its chapter on communicating in groups focuses on town hall meetings and other civic forums. In these chapters and throughout the book, the emphasis is not only on how to prepare a good speech, but also on the importance of being a committed and responsible speaker. That is what makes this book unique: it combines sound instruction in the techniques of public speaking with a sustained emphasis on the ethics of speech and the role of public speaking in our democratic society.

Focus on Civic Engagement

Every chapter provides boxed special features showcasing real-world examples of politicians, celebrities, students, and ordinary citizens who have made a difference by speaking out or otherwise getting involved in their communities. These stories about real people—young and old, famous and not-so-famous—are designed both to illustrate course concepts and to inspire students to get involved themselves.

Focus on Civic Engagement

Defining Leadership in a New Way

Getting people to travel from one fixed point to another is what the work of leadership is about. It takes no leadership to get teachers to support higher teacher salaries or Sierra Club members to oppose the destruction of forests or national parks. They don't have to traverse any distance to arrive at such positions, because these are the positions they're starting from in the first place. But it does take leadership to convert conservative business leaders into supporters of federally funded school lunch programs and breakfast programs, or to persuade financially stretched taxpayers to support funding for the arts.

If you accept the above definition of leadership as true, several other truths are inherent in it.

One of these sample truths follows:

. . . The most effective leaders do not concentrate all their energies on addressing and organizing those who agree with them, but rather on building bridges to those who disagree and winning them over to their point of view. Advocacy is not advocacy when aimed at those who share your views. This is redundancy. The key to solving most problems is in building a larger consensus than previously existed for a solution.

The definition concludes with a discussion of how leaders use persuasion:

Leaders employ a variety of tactics to move their followers. They give speeches, tell stories, make reasoned arguments, serve as examples, and conduct symbolic acts. All of these tactics are designed to do one thing: persuade. Persuasion is most successful when it shows how the recommended course of action is in one's self-interest. The intersection of self-interest and a larger public interest is where leaders stake their claim.

In the larger context of the book, Shore suggests that leadership is as much about consensus building as winning arguments. He also believes that leadership potential resides within many citizens, who can truly make a difference in their communities.

Source: Bill Shore, *The Cathedral Within: Transforming Your Life by Giving Something Back* (New York: Random House, 2001), 182–84.

Key Concepts Highlighted

Extended examples of key concepts such as ethos, advocacy, visual literacy, critical listening, fallacies, ethics, and differences in cultural values are illustrated through a special "highlighting" feature in every chapter.

Highlighting Source Accuracy

Beware of Wikipedia

Wikipedia is a free online encyclopedia that started in 2001. Its content is written collaboratively by users around the globe.

- The site is called "wiki," meaning that anyone with Web access can add to, correct, or amend it by clicking on an edit function.
- The site had 25.6 million visitors in a single month in 2006, making it the 18th most popular site on the Internet.
- Due to the nature of the site, a sobering possibility for misinformation and vandalism exists.
- Already, political operatives have covertly rewritten—or defaced—candidates' biographical entries to make their boss look good, or to make the opponent look ridiculous. Altering senators' ages, entering highly personal information, and posting damaging "jokes" are just a few of the problematic practices that have surfaced.
- Experts in communication technology believe that the sheer size of Wikipedia and the huge number of entries make it impossible to monitor or police it in any effective way.

Source: "Wikipedia: An Online Encyclopedia Being Used for Political Tricks," *Bloomington Herald-Times* (April 30, 2006), D3.

Annotated Speeches

Nearly half of the book's chapters conclude with an annotated speech that offers critical commentary and analysis. Each speech deals with a substantive issue and provides a real-world illustration of civic engagement. The speakers include both political figures and ordinary citizens and they date from the founding of our nation to today's debate over the war in Iraq.

To Those Whom Much Is Given

HONORING OUR OBLIGATIONS AS AMERICANS

Rebecca W. Rimel,
President and CEO, The Pew Charitable Trusts

Rebecca Rimel, CEO and president of The Pew Charitable Trusts, gave this speech on September 30, 2003, to a group of civic-minded citizens and philanthropists belonging to the organization Town Hall Los Angeles. Her goal was to get more people involved in a variety of civic actions—from voting to volunteering—and to encourage young people to become engaged, as well.

Delivered to the Town Hall Los Angeles, Los Angeles, California, September 30, 2003

Good afternoon and thank you for that truly generous and gracious introduction. I trust you know how fortunate you are to live in this town and to have an organization like Town Hall Los Angeles. Any city in America would truly feel blessed to gather together this number of people with the energy, enthusiasm and commitment you have to making your community a better place. You have extraordinary philanthropists in this town, many of them here today. It's particularly nice to be able to see some old friends: Wallace Annenberg and Norman Lear, who's committing his life now to getting us all back and involved in the future of our country.

"To those whom much is given, much is expected." Each and every one of us has been blessed with tremendous resources and opportunities. As a result, much is expected of us. We are called upon to give back to our community, to our country and to our shared civic life. Many think that America is at a crossroads—and I believe our individual and collective involvement will be key in determining its future.

IN ADAPTING TO HER IMMEDIATE AUDIENCE, MS. RIMEL RECOGNIZES BY NAME TWO VERY ACTIVE AND WELL-KNOWN PHILANTHROPISTS IN THE AUDIENCE. ACKNOWLEDGING THESE RESPECTED LEADERS—GENERALLY ASSOCIATED WITH DIFFERENT POLITICAL VIEWS—SIGNALS HER IMPARTIAL STANCE, AS WELL AS HOLDING UP MODELS FOR HER AUDIENCE TO EMULATE. IT IS IMPORTANT THAT HER AUDIENCE NOT SEE HER AS A SPOKESPERSON FOR A PARTICULAR PARTY OR CAUSE, SO SHE REINFORCES HER NONPARTISANSHIP BY ASSURING LISTENERS THAT SHE HAS NO POLITICAL AGENDA.

I am addressing you today as business and community leaders. As men and women who have achieved positions of privilege and power. I am addressing you as Americans. Too often, especially in challenging times, such as those we now face, we forget the blessings we enjoy in this country. We often fail in our obligations to nurture the institutions and democratic principles that assure us those blessings. It's in vogue right now to criticize the U.S. foreign policy—our leaders and our government.

I'm not here to echo those complaints or refute them. I have no political agenda. What I'd like to do however is convince you of three critical factors that will play a pivotal role in our future. First, America's stature and leadership is in question—just when we've become the world's sole super power. That said, the greatest threat we confront is our own apathy and that of our youth. Joining in this criticism won't stem these dangerous trends. Whether you agree or disagree with the direction of your country, your state or your community, it's time for us to get off the bench and back into the game. Working together we can make a difference in America's future.

What brings me to these conclusions is the information provided and the advocacy undertaken by our many partners at The Pew Charitable Trusts. We work in areas as diverse as culture and religion and address topics ranging from the environment to health care. However, we have one overriding objective—to advance the debate on the issues that matter to the long-term health and happiness of the American people and our global neighbors.

One of our primary roles is to provide fact-based information in the public interest. But we do more than inform at the Trusts. Once the facts are clear and irrefutable, we also educate, enable, and, when the facts beg for it, advocate for change—even fight for it. At the Pew Trusts, we engage the most talented experts to provide credible, nonpartisan, balanced research and inform and facilitate the public debate on some of the most pressing issues affecting the health of our nation.

BY REFERRING TO THE CAREFUL AND EXPERT RESEARCH CARRIED OUT BY HER ORGANIZATION, THE SPEAKER BUILDS CREDIBILITY WITH HER AUDIENCE AND AGAIN STRESSES THE GOAL OF EDUCATING ABOUT ISSUES AND ADVOCATING ON BEHALF OF SOUND SOLUTIONS ON THE BASIS OF THE FACTS, NOT BECAUSE OF ANY IDEOLOGICAL BIAS.

Issues like bio-engineered food and its impact on the economy, the environment and our public health . . . global warming and how we can promote policies and practices that will protect our planet . . . under-aged drinking and how we can stop the marketing of alcohol to our youth . . . and how we can ensure that quality, early education is available for all children from the age of three. We fight with facts to advance these and other issues—to improve life for our citizens.

With that in mind, let me address the first concern I want to share today: that America is losing its luster, both domestically and globally. This is not my personal observation; it is the chief finding of a major global public opinion poll commissioned by The Pew Research Center for the People and the Press. Chaired by former secretary of state Madeleine Albright the Project last year surveyed 38,000 individuals in 44 nations, including such "hard-to-interview" places as China. Libya and Angola. In a second survey, they polled 16,000 people in 20 countries and the Palestinian Authority. The results show a stunning disconnect between how Americans perceive themselves and their government and how the rest of the world perceives us. America's image has taken a beating in recent years—among longtime NATO allies, in developing countries, in Eastern Europe, and—most dramatically—in Muslim societies. Since 2000, favorability ratings for the U.S. have fallen in 19 of 27 countries where benchmark data was available.

While people around the world embrace things American—including our economic and democratic ideals—they condemn U.S. influence on their way of life. Hollywood is the perfect example. While it does seem contradictory, people in most countries say they enjoy the movies, music and TV that this town exports, but they dislike the spread of U.S. ideas and customs. Even among our strongest allies, anti-American sentiment is growing.

To me, the most frightening finding of all is our image in most of the Muslim world. Negative views of the U.S. among Muslims are wide and deep—from the Middle East to Indonesia to Nigeria. In fact, over 80 percent of Palestinians and Jordanians express disdain toward the U.S.—our leaders and, yes, our citizens. In a town that understands the power of ratings, think about this: A 37 point drop in favorability in Turkey, and in Egypt, only six percent of the population has a kind thing to say about us. The post-Cold War reality is this: Old friends who need us less, like us less, especially in Western Europe, and we're failing to win new friends as well.

CAREFULLY SUPPORTING HER ARGUMENTS WITH HARD DATA, MS. RIMEL POINTS OUT SERIOUS PROBLEMS THAT MEMBERS OF HER AUDIENCE CERTAINLY CARE ABOUT SINCE THEY TOUCH BOTH THEIR PRIVATE LIVES AND THEIR ECONOMIC OR BUSINESS INTERESTS.

Perhaps the most disheartening finding, however, is that we as Americans are clueless. Our own opinion of ourselves is—shall we say—highly inflated and strikingly at odds with the rest of the world. Americans think the U.S. takes into account other countries' interests when crafting foreign policy. Eighty percent of us believe it is a good thing that our ideas and customs are spreading around the world, but we appear insensitive to the cultures and priorities of our global neighbors.

The bar is set high for the U.S., as it should be. We're the big kid in the canoe—the only big kid in the canoe these days. We exercise dominant influence on global affairs, and we need to step up to the obligations that come with that influence. It's time to accept the full weight of responsibility that comes with our privileged position. I know working together we can respond.

Make no mistake—we are a blessed nation and must remember: To those whom much is given, much more is expected. We need to do more to reduce carbon dioxide and other greenhouse gases that contribute to global warming. We must move now to save the world's oceans from destruction. If not, the impact will be profound. We must work to improve the quality of life for all the world's citizens if we are to have peace and prosperity.

THE REPETITION OF "TO THOSE WHOM MUCH IS GIVEN, MUCH MORE IS EXPECTED" THROUGHOUT HER SPEECH IS A WAY OF EMPHASIZING THE PRIVILEGED POSITION OF HER AUDIENCE MEMBERS AND REINFORCES THE NOTION THAT WITH POWER AND PRIVILEGE COMES RESPONSIBILITY.

Pedagogical Features in Each Chapter

Within the text, we provide a variety of pedagogical features that clarify and reinforce the material or summarize key points. Specifically, each chapter contains:

- A *Chapter Survey* to overview key topics addressed in the chapter.
- *Learning Objectives* to give students learning goals against which they can measure their personal progress.
- *Previews* to give readers a map of the material in each section of the chapter.
- *Real-world examples* to illustrate, highlight, and clarify principles discussed.
- A *Summary* to reiterate the chapter's core concepts.
- *Questions for Review and Reflection* to help students review the ideas presented in each chapter and to assist them in test preparation.

At the end of the book, a *Glossary* defines key terms and technical language appearing throughout the book. Further *Questions for Application and Analysis* can be found in the Instructor's Manual.

Service-Learning Resources

For those interested in approaching the course from a service-learning perspective, the Instructor's Manual includes a sample syllabus for a service-learning approach to public speaking. The manual also suggests activities and assignments for a service-learning approach to the course and provides a list of organizations, websites, and other resources on service learning.

Instructor Supplements

Instructor's Manual and Test Bank

Authored by Glen Williams, Southeast Missouri State University, this detailed Instructor's Manual addresses such key topics as: what it means to be a teacher, the defining qualities of effective teaching, course and lesson planning, teaching methods, testing and evaluation, the role of feedback, classroom management, and professional development. The Instructor's Manual also provides a chapter-by-chapter guide to the textbook and provides time-tested activities, sample syllabi, and class assignments. In addition, the Test Bank portion of the manual contains numerous multiple choice and essay questions. The test bank provides questions that engage the entire cognitive domain, from the very basics of recall and comprehension to application, analysis, and evaluation. This variety allows each instructor to create exams of varying types and differing degrees of difficulty. The multiple choice, true/false and essay questions are rated on a scale of 1 to 3, making question selection easy. Answers for each question are given along with the page number where they can be found within the book.

Available only online on our Instructor's Resource Center at www.ablongman .com/irc (please contact your Pearson representative for an access code).

TestGen EQ: Computerized Test Bank

The user-friendly interface enables instructors to view, edit, and add questions, transfer questions into tests, and print tests in a variety of fonts. Search and sort features allow instructors to locate questions quickly and arrange them in preferred order. Available only online on our Instructor's Resource Center at www.ablongman .com/irc (please contact your Pearson representative for an access code.

The Public Speaking and Civic Engagement Blog

Maintained by the authors, this site (**www.personal.psu.edu/jimh32/blogs/ civicengagement**) offers a forum for people teaching public speaking. Regular posts by authors update the text material, give suggestions for how professors might use the Instructor's Manual and provide additional resources for teaching public speaking. Professors can also visit the site to participate in an online discussion where they can post comments, offer their own ideas, or simply get in touch with the authors of the text.

PowerPoint Presentation Package

Created by Glen Williams, Southeast Missouri State University and Michael Simmons, Southeast Missouri State Unviersity, this text-specific package consists of a collection of lecture outlines and graphic images keyed to every chapter in the text. Available only online at our Instructor's Resource Center at www.ablongman.com/irc (please contact your Pearson representative for an access code).

Public Speaking and Civic Engagement Speeches DVD

The video clips featured on this DVD include a unique blend of speeches and presentations that feature a civic engagement theme. Speeches include: nonprofit leaders speaking as advocates for their agencies, citizens speaking out at a public hearing, panelists responding to audience questions, professionals and concerned citizens speaking to inform and persuade, and students speaking on topics related to civic engagement. These can be assigned for out-of-class work or used in the classroom to illustrate key concepts. Many of these speeches also are featured in the MySpeechKit that accompanies this text. Please contact your Pearson representative for details.

MySpeechKit (www.myspeechkit.com)

MySpeechKit is an interactive and instructive online solution for introductory public speaking. Designed to be used as a supplement to a traditional lecture course, MySpeechKit includes book-specific learning objectives, chapter summaries, flashcards and practice tests, as well as web links, an outlining wizard, media clips and interactive activities to aid student learning and comprehension. Also included in MySpeechKit is Research Navigator, a valuable tool to help students conduct online research. **Access code required and comes automatically packaged with new copies of this text.**

Teacher Training Video

This video, introduced by author Jim Andrews, contains 14 different triggers that present an array of teaching challenges, including how to deal with challenges to authority and grade complaints, to questions of how to offer feedback, how to stimulate classroom discussion, and how to deal with communication apprehension.

The accompanying Supervisor's Manual, written by authors Glen Williams and Patricia Hayes Andrews (available only online with an access code at www.ablongman.com/irc), offers an extensive guide to the video, including background for each trigger, suggestions for how to introduce each one, post-viewing questions for reflection, and some suggested points that might be made by course directors as they lead TAs in discussion. The manual also contains additional materials for instructor training, including an orientation schedule and other sections on such topics as: the role of the course director, leadership styles, effectively administering exams, and other matters that would be of special interest or concern to course directors and department heads.

Student Supplements

VangoCard for Public Speaking

Colorful, affordable, and packed with useful information, Pearson's VangoCards make studying easier, more efficient, and more enjoyable. Course information is distilled down to the basics, helping you quickly master the fundamentals, review a subject for understanding, or prepare for an exam. Because it is laminated for durability, you can keep this VangoCard for years to come and pull it out whenever you need a quick review. **May be packaged with this text upon request; contact your Pearson representative for details.**

MySpeechKit (www.myspeechkit.com)

MySpeechKit is an interactive and instructive online solution for introductory public speaking. Designed to be used as a supplement to a traditional lecture course, MySpeechKit includes book-specific learning objectives, chapter summaries, flashcards and practice tests, as well as web links, an outlining wizard, media clips and interactive activities to aid student learning and comprehension. Also included in MySpeechKit is Research Navigator, a valuable tool to help students conduct online research. **Access code required and comes automatically packaged with new copies of this text.**

A&B Public Speaking Study Site, accessed at www.abpublicspeaking.com

This website features public speaking study materials for students, including flashcards and a complete set of practice tests for all major topics. Students also will find web links to sites with speeches in texts, audio, and video formats, as well as links to other valuable sites.

ResearchNavigator.com Guide: Speech Communication

This updated booklet, by Steven L. Epstein of Suffolk County Community College, includes tips, resources, and URLs to aid students conducting research on Pearson Education's research website, www.researchnavigator.com. The guide contains a student access code for the Research Navigator database, offering students free, unlimited access to a collection of more than 25,000 discipline specific articles from top-tier academic publications and peer-reviewed journals, as well as the *New York Times* and popular news publications. The guide introduces students to the basics of the Internet and the World Wide Web, and includes tips for searching for articles on the site, and a list of journals useful for research in their discipline. Also included are hundreds of web resources for the discipline, as well as information on how to correctly cite research. The guide is available packaged with new copies of the text.

Acknowledgments

We are indebted to many individuals who provided encouragement, support, and inspiration for us as we undertook this writing project. We extend our special thanks to the undergraduates at Indiana University, Southeast Missouri State University, and at Penn State University, whose enthusiasm for our approach to public speaking was unwavering, and to the graduate students at these schools, whose passion for critical pedagogy and civic engagement led to provocative discussions and, in some cases, to exciting new ideas.

We also wish to thank a number of undergraduate and former or current graduate students and colleagues who either directly contributed to the book or served as reviewers of earlier versions of the manuscript:

Rukhsana Ahmed, Ohio University
Kevin J. Ayotte, California State University, Fresno
Diane M. Badzinski, Bethel College
Kristin M. Barton, Florida State University
Sean Beppler, Syracuse University
Jennifer A. Bieselin, Florida Gulf Coast University
LeAnn M. Brazeal, Kansas State University
Nanci M. Burk, Glendale Community College
Lynn Borich, Missouri State University
Ellen R. Cohn, University of Pittsburgh
Linda Czuba Brigance, State University of New York at Fredonia
Donnette Dennis-Austin, Broward Community College
Cynthia Duquette Smith, Indiana University
Michael Eaves, Valdosta State University
Lyn J. Freymiller, Pennsylvania State University - University Park
Grace Giorgio, University of Illinois
John Gore, Ivy Tech State College

Gary Hiebsch, College of the Ozarks
Patricia S. Hill, Ph.D., The University of Akron
Mark E. Huglen, University of Minnesota, Crookston
Daisy L. Johnson, Heartland Community College
Katerina Katsarka Whitley, Appalachian State University
Rick Lindner, Georgia Perimeter College
Rick Maxson Ph.D., Drury University
Richard McGrath, Central College
Steve E. Martin, Ripon College
Lisa M. Orick-Martinez, Central New Mexico Community College
Dean A. Pape, Ripon College
Shawn J. Parry-Giles, University of Maryland
Claire H. Procopio, Baton Rouge Community College
Jody M. Roy, Ripon College
Shawn Spano, San Jose State University
Sanda Tomuletiu, Duquesne University
Mary E. Triece, University of Akron
Esin C. Turk, Mississippi Valley State University
Karrin Vasby Anderson, Colorado State University
Alaina M. Winters, Heartland Community College

We also want to extend our appreciation toward those individuals who assisted with the supplement preparations for this text: Bob Clubbs, Jo Mueller, Kristen Sanchez, and Michael Simmons. Claudia Reudiger and Michelle Dubaj, both librarians at Southeast Missouri State University, should also be acknowledged for their feedback on chapter research.

Finally, we are grateful for those who were our inspiration and mentors: the late Gayle Compton, Donald Zacharias, the late J. Jeffery Auer, and the late Robert G. Gunderson—all gifted and caring teachers and engaged citizens of their communities. Through actions and words, they taught us the meaning and importance of being engaged citizens in a democracy.

We want too to extend our thanks to the staff at Allyn and Bacon, especially Karon Bowers, our Editor-in-Chief, who had the courage to move forward with our project, who listened to our concerns, who challenged our thinking, and who always made suggestions that enhanced the quality of our work.

In 1952, William Norwood Brigance, Professor of Speech at Wabash College, published his ground-breaking text, *Speech: Its Techniques and Disciplines in a Free Society*. In it, he wrote:

"Democracy and the system of speechmaking were born together. Since that early day we have never had a successful democracy unless a large part, a very large part, of its citizens were effective, intelligent, and responsible speakers. Today, as twenty-three centuries ago, a system of speechmaking is imperative for preserving democracy."

Brigance's philosophy inspired our writing of *Public Speaking and Civic Engagement*, and it is to his memory that we dedicate this book.

CHAPTER 1

Public Speaking and Democratic Citizenship

CHAPTER SURVEY

Public Speaking and Civic Engagement

The Rhetorical Tradition

Communication Challenges of the Twenty-first Century

The Responsible Citizen-Speaker

CHAPTER OBJECTIVES

After studying this chapter, you should be able to

1. Discuss some of the challenges facing our democratic system.

2. Describe how the rhetorical tradition relates to civic engagement.

3. Identify some of the challenges of speaking and listening in the modern age.

4. Describe some of the legal and ethical obligations of the responsible citizen-speaker.

What does it mean to be a citizen in a democracy? For some, it means voting in elections, donating money to political candidates, or making "statements" about their political views by displaying bumper stickers or yard signs. For others, citizenship means something less political, like volunteering to help others in their community, raising money for a worthy cause, or joining with neighbors to clean up a local park. Whatever citizenship means to you, it involves meeting with others to share common concerns, exchange ideas, and make decisions about issues of concern to the community. In other words, being a citizen means *communicating* with others. Throughout history, the ability to communicate effectively has not only been the mark of great leaders, but also an important skill for ordinary citizens.

This book is dedicated to helping you become a better speaker—*and* a better citizen. It offers practical advice about preparing and delivering speeches in a variety of public settings. Beyond that, it discusses the responsibilities of citizenship, including your ethical obligations to respect the opinions of others and to participate in ongoing deliberations over matters of public importance. In the process, we will introduce you to a number of people—both famous and not-so-famous—who have made a difference by "speaking out." We also will teach you how to recognize and resist the techniques of demagogues and propagandists—those who use the power of speech to manipulate and deceive others. When you complete your course in public speaking, it is our hope that you will have the confidence and skills necessary to participate fully in our democratic system. But more than that, we hope that you will have an *ethical* commitment to participating *responsibly*.

Public Speaking and Civic Engagement

Preview. *As you read this, you may be a full- or part-time student, a business major, a pre-med student, or a student who hasn't yet decided on a major. You are many other things as well. You are a daughter or a son; you may be a single parent, a United Methodist, a part-time employee, a tennis player, a movie buff, a sports fan, or a camp counselor. We all play many different roles in life, but we also have one thing in common: we are all citizens in a democracy. Our country's fate depends on how well—or how poorly—we perform that role. As citizens, we have a responsibility to become involved in the civic life of our communities. Public speaking is among the most important skills of citizenship, and your effectiveness as a speaker can make a real difference in your own life and in the life of your community.*

At the close of the twentieth century, some feared that Americans had forgotten how to be good citizens. According to some observers, our American democracy had become threatened by widespread alienation from the civic life of both our local communities and the nation. Summarized in a best-selling book, Robert D. Putnam's *Bowling Alone: The Collapse and Revival of American Community*, this threat to democratic governance was seen both in familiar ways, such as low turnout among voters, and in less obvious ways, including sharp declines in newspaper readership and participation in voluntary associations. The challenges to our democracy appeared considerable and the statistics sobering. But is the American democracy really in decline? And, if so, what can we do to revive civic participation and democratic deliberation?

The Challenges of Democratic Citizenship

First, the bad news. Voter turnout in presidential elections has declined steadily over the last half century, despite greatly relaxed voter registration requirements, "motor voter" laws, and massive get-out-the-vote campaigns. In 1960, more than 63 percent of eligible Americans voted in the federal elections; by 1996, that figure had dropped to 49.1 percent. The figures were up slightly in the 2000 election, to about 51 percent, and in 2004 more than 55 percent of eligible citizens voted.[1] Still, the United States continues to trail all but a handful of the world's democracies in the proportion of its citizens who bother to vote.[2] The problem has been particularly evident among young people. Since the 26th Amendment lowered the voting age to 18 in 1971, turnout among people aged 18–24 has steadily declined, from about 50 percent in 1972 to only 32 percent in the 1996 election and 36.5 percent in 2000.[3]

Other indicators of civic engagement have also shown disturbing declines. The number of people under 35 who read a newspaper daily, for example, dropped from two-thirds in 1965 to one-third in 1990, and this was not, as some suggested, a reflection of young people turning to new media. As David Mindich has noted, young people are "tuning out" the news altogether, including TV news and even Internet sources of news and information.[4] In addition, the number of people attending political meetings or working for a political party has declined by more than half since the 1970s. Between 1973 and 1994, the number of Americans who attended even *one* public meeting in the previous year decreased by about 40 percent. This means that about 16 million fewer Americans participated in public meetings in the 1990s than 20 years earlier.[5]

In a nation that prides itself on free speech, the most discouraging trends concern how Americans publicly express themselves. According to Roper surveys, there have been steady declines over the last several decades in the number of people signing petitions, writing letters to their elected representatives or local newspapers, giving speeches at meetings and political rallies, or writing articles for a magazine or newspaper. The proportion of the American public who engaged in *none* of these civic activities rose by nearly one-third through the 1970s and 1980s. By the mid-1990s, 32 million fewer Americans were involved in these sorts of activities than was the case just two decades earlier. In 1973, most Americans participated in at least one of these forms of civic expression. By 1994, most Americans did not engage in *any* of them. Significantly, the forms of civic engagement that have declined most are those involving collaborating or talking with others, such as giving and listening to speeches at public meetings.[6]

Americans actually donate *more* money to political and civic causes today than ever before, and the *Encyclopedia of Associations* reports that the number of nonprofit organizations in America doubled from 1968 to 1997, increasing from 10,299 organizations to 22,901.[7] Yet these statistics only seem to confirm that Americans are becoming *spectators* rather than *participants* in public life. For many Americans, "getting involved" means writing a check, and most of those checks go to organizations not in our local communities, but in Washington, D.C. What that means is that they are not organizations of ordinary citizens. Rather, they are paid professionals whose business is to raise and spend money on behalf of special interests. They do not promote *public* deliberation but its opposite: they bombard the nation with direct mail, TV, and Internet ad campaigns that substitute for the voice of the people.

All this has important implications for our public deliberations. With the proliferation of special-interest groups, the rhetoric of slogans and sound bites has displaced the collective voice of ordinary people debating matters of public importance. Principled leadership has given way to appeals shaped by polling and focus groups, and we see more and more of the techniques of the propagandist and the demagogue in our mainstream political talk. In political campaigns, what Bill Clinton called the "politics of personal destruction" prevails; while, in legislative debates, negotiation and compromise have given way to ideological posturing and gridlock. Everywhere, we hear more combative or confrontational rhetoric as people shout each other down, distort each other's positions, or hurl wild accusations at one another. Scholars and politicians alike have lamented this loss of civility and substance in our nation's political talk. But the real losers are the citizens, whose voices have been squeezed out of the public dialogue by the polarizing voices of professional activists.[8]

Now for the good news. As we begin the twenty-first century, there are hopeful signs of a rebirth of civic engagement in America. Ironically, the terrorist attacks of

A crowd of young people participate in a "Vote or Die" rally at Miami Dade Community College in October of 2004. The rally, featuring hip hop performer Sean "P. Diddy" Combs and other celebrities, reflected increased participation among young people in the presidential election of 2004.

September 11, 2001, brought many Americans together in a common cause, inspiring millions to contribute to relief and charity efforts or even to volunteer for military service. As Putnam observed, the 9/11 attacks at least "interrupted" the downward trend in "political consciousness and engagement," with the public's interest in political affairs rising to levels "not seen in at least three decades."[9] This spike in political awareness was also evident in the 2004 elections, in which Americans voted at the highest rate since 1968. According to some estimates, about 15 million *more* Americans voted in 2004 than in the 2000 presidential election.[10] In 2004, young voters also turned out in numbers not seen in more than a decade. According to the Center for Information and Research on Civic Learning and Engagement (CIRCLE), turnout among voters between ages 18 and 24 increased by about 5.8 percent in 2004, rising to 42.3 percent from just 36.5 percent in the 2000 election."[11]

Some of the credit for these positive signs must go to the many schools or charitable foundations and civic groups that have launched new initiatives to stimulate participatory democracy. After documenting the problem in *Bowling Alone*, for example, Robert Putnam founded the Saguano Seminar, which is an ongoing initiative of the John F. Kennedy School of Government at Harvard University concerned with developing "far-reaching, actionable ideas to significantly increase Americans' connectedness to one another and to community institutions."[12] At the University of Texas, the Annette Strauss Institute for Civic Participation has a similar mission: "(1) to conduct cutting-edge research on how civic participation, community understanding, and communication are undermined or sustained, and (2) to develop new programs for increasing democratic understanding among citizens."[13] Another initiative, Project Pericles, provides funding to colleges across the nation to improve their community-service efforts and to "make civic engagement a part of the curriculum in every department."[14] And at the nearly 1,000 colleges and universities affiliated with Campus Compact, more than 1.7 million students have been involved in learning about ethics and effective communication while participating in a variety of civic and community-service projects.[15]

New technologies also hold promise of reinvigorating grassroots democracy in America. During the 2004 primary elections, for example, Democratic presidential hopeful Howard Dean used the Internet to mobilize thousands of young people never before involved in a presidential campaign, and a variety of other politicians and political activists have also used the Internet to organize and mobilize like-minded citizens. Web logs, or "blogs," have become an important forum for political news and debate, often attracting people not otherwise interested in political discussions. E-mail and chat rooms also have become forums for democratic deliberation, and there are indications that at least some young people are turning to the Web more frequently for political news and information.[16]

Yet new technologies in and of themselves cannot solve all our problems. Although the Internet has great potential, it also has made it easier for extremists to spread their messages of hate, and some Internet users seem to have withdrawn into a "virtual" world of bizarre conspiracy theories and political hoaxes. Many Internet users visit only those websites that confirm their existing opinions, thus avoiding information that might challenge their thinking. It is important to remember that when television was first invented, it too was touted as a magical new tool of civic engagement and democratic deliberation. Instead, it became what former

Participants in the 2006 Penn State Interfraternity/Panhellenic Dance Marathon hold up cards bearing the grand total of money raised during that year's "Thon": $4,214,748.18.

FCC chairman Newton N. Minow famously described as a "vast wasteland"—a bleak landscape of mindless entertainment programming with very little news and political information.[17] If new technologies are to promote democratic deliberation, we must *learn* to use them wisely. We must learn to be critical consumers of information we find on the Internet and other new media, and we must insist on responsible use of these new technologies. In the years to come, Internet literacy—the ability to distinguish between good and bad information on the information superhighway—will become a critical skill. In the Information Age, it is more important than ever that citizens know how to distinguish between responsible and irresponsible speech.

The Engaged Citizen

What does it mean to be a responsible citizen? And what can *you* contribute to the revival of participatory democracy in America? We've already suggested part of the answer: *get involved*, whether that means voting in the next presidential election, speaking out at a local "town hall" meeting, or volunteering to help the less fortunate in your community. This book will not only remind you why it's important to get involved, but also help you develop some of the skills you need to participate effectively. It also will help you understand what it means communicate *ethically* in a democracy. The responsible citizen is not just an effective communicator but one with a strong code of ethics.

Many people engage in civic activities to build their resumés—it looks good on a college or job application to be "involved" in one's community. But civic involvement is more than simply a way to advance your career. It also is a commitment—a commitment to a cause or activity that both gives you personal satisfaction and helps make your community a better place to live. Wherever you get involved—in your school, at your place of work, in your town, or in a broader national or even international arena—you should think beyond your own personal interests to the good you can do by working with others. The benefits of responsible citizenship are shared benefits. Everyone is better off when you take the initiative to organize support or raise money for a worthy cause. *Somebody* has to take the lead in making our communities better places to live. Why not you?

However you choose to serve, you *can* make a difference. Young people sometimes think they have little power to change the world. Yet by working together, even busy college students can make important contributions. At Penn State University, for example, the largest student-run charitable organization in the world raises money to fight childhood cancer with an annual dance marathon. "Thon," as it is popularly called, involves hundreds of students in a variety of activities, ranging from publicity efforts to the care and feeding of the dancers themselves. Thon even has a communications committee for "Penn State students with a passion for spreading the word." To date, this group of involved students has raised more than $46 million to combat pediatric cancer. In 2007 alone, Thon raised more than $5.2 million.[18]

A smaller-scale example of how just a few students can make a difference comes out of a service-learning class taught by one of the authors of this book. The theme of the class was "Homelessness and Poverty in Our Community." Several students volunteered to work at a day shelter for the homeless. A group assignment in the class was to examine in depth one problem faced by those they met at the shelter. This group learned that dental care was a serious issue for many poor people. For some, it even became an obstacle to finding a job. The group studied the issue, presented a Community Action Group Symposium to their classmates, and followed up with letters to large companies asking for donations of dental hygiene products. Most companies did not respond, but one did: the John O. Butler Company of Chicago. By donating 450 toothbrushes and two cases of toothpaste to the shelter, the company helped not only adults, but also many children whose parents could not afford to buy them these basic dental care items.

The responsible citizen not only helps others, but also strives to be well informed and thoughtful. In a democracy, you have a right to your opinion. Yet the responsible citizen recognizes the difference between an informed and carefully considered opinion and one grounded in ignorance or prejudice. The responsible citizen forms opinions based on careful investigation and thoughtful evaluation of the evidence. The responsible citizen bases his or her convictions on a careful survey of the facts, the testimony of credible experts or witnesses, or firsthand experience. The responsible citizen does not simply *assert* his or her "right" to an opinion, but rather *earns* that right by developing an *informed* opinion. If you choose to participate in civic affairs, you must first have the intellectual, ethical, and practical knowledge needed to act as a *responsible* citizen in a democracy. Those skills have been taught since ancient times, and they have been handed down to us in what scholars call the "rhetorical tradition."

The Rhetorical Tradition

Preview. *"Rhetoric" is an ancient discipline concerned with the techniques and ethics of speech. There are three traditions of scholarship and teaching in rhetoric that focus on the knowledge and skills necessary for democratic citizenship:*

- *the tradition of rhetorical theory that dates back to ancient Greece and Rome*
- *the tradition of rhetorical criticism, which emphasizes the critical analysis of public discourse in all its various forms*
- *the tradition of historical studies in public address, which focuses on the lessons we might learn from the speakers, speeches, social movements, and persuasive campaigns of the past*

The scholarly traditions of rhetorical theory, criticism, and public address have something important to contribute to our understanding of public speaking and civic engagement. In recognizing rhetoric as one of the oldest scholarly traditions, we realize that the ability to communicate in public has long been considered an important part of democratic citizenship. By learning to speak in public, and by developing our skills at evaluating the speeches of others, we develop what might be called civic literacy.

Responsible Speaking

The study of speech dates back to ancient times, with some of the great Greek and Roman thinkers, including Aristotle and Cicero, counted among the earliest rhetorical theorists. In the classical tradition, personal ethics and civic virtue were the cornerstones of rhetorical education. Cicero, for example, saw rhetoric as more than simply a collection of techniques used to persuade an audience. He saw rhetoric as the expression of civic morality and broad learning.[19] The Roman rhetorician Quintilian described the ideal orator as "a good man skilled in speaking"—with the emphasis on the "good man."[20] Quintilian's ideal orator was more than an effective platform speaker. He was, first and foremost, a good citizen—a civic leader, a lover of wisdom and truth, a sincere advocate of worthy causes, and a servant of the community. For both Cicero and Quintillian, responsible orators promoted the common good, not just their own selfish interests.

We must acknowledge the greater challenges of public speaking in the United States today. Unlike the ancient Greeks, we live in a diverse, multicultural society, and we must take account of changing social values, new information technologies, and the realities of the Consumer Age. But that does not mean we cannot still strive to be responsible speakers; that is, people who assume the responsibilities of leadership, tell the truth, believe sincerely in our causes, and serve our communities. In the modern world, it is more important than ever that we rise above our own selfish interests and promote the common good. If we hope to resolve the difficult problems of the twenty-first century, we must learn to deliberate *together* and reconcile our diverse and competing interests.

The classical rhetorical tradition still has something important to teach us: that public speaking in a democratic society must be grounded in a strong code of ethics and a commitment to the common good. The classical tradition suggests an approach to public speaking that emphasizes not the techniques of manipulation, but rather the character and civic virtues of the speaker and the shared interests of speakers and listeners. Now more than ever, citizens must be able both to promote their own ideas effectively and to deliberate with others in search of solutions to our common problems. That requires that we embrace the virtues of Quintilian's ideal orator and *demand* such virtues in all who aspire to leadership. And that is where the second tradition of scholarship and teaching in rhetoric, the tradition of rhetorical criticism, comes in.

Thinking Critically

Today, citizens must be more than skilled speakers. They also must have the skills necessary to evaluate the messages of others. Every day we are faced with choices that can affect our lives, and it is important that we learn to *think critically* about those choices. In the marketplace, we have so-called consumer watchdogs who warn us against false advertising and defective products. But in the "marketplace of ideas," we must learn to think for ourselves and be on guard against attempts to manipulate or deceive us.

During presidential campaigns, newspapers and television news programs present ad watches, which evaluate the truth and accuracy of political campaign commercials. Similarly, editorial columnists frequently evaluate major political speeches, such as the president's annual State of the Union address. At colleges and universities, professional rhetorical critics publish detailed evaluations of major speeches and debates, and some comment on important speeches in the popular media. The interested citizen might consult all of these sources in deciding whether to accept or reject the claims in a political ad or speech. But often we must render judgments on the spot, without the benefit of research or time for reflection. In the day-to-day world of democratic life, we all must be "citizen-critics,"[21] ready and able to make our own judgments about who deserves to be believed—and why.

By studying public speaking, you are developing your own ability to communicate effectively and learning how to recognize misleading arguments, faulty reasoning, or inadequate evidence in other people's speeches. "Demagogues," or speakers who employ "highly suspect means in pursuit of equally suspect ends,"[22] abound in our media-saturated world. So it is important that we, as citizens, recognize and resist their attempts to mislead us. Should we believe that speaker who insists that the U.S. government was actually behind the 9/11 terrorist attacks? What about that politician who claims he knew nothing about those illegal campaign contributions? And what about that preacher who insists that all "good Christians" must vote for a particular candidate? Studying the principles and methods of public speaking can help you decide how to respond to such appeals. It can help you distinguish between a reasonable argument and an attempt to deceive or manipulate.

Obviously, it is not possible that everything you read or hear is true, especially when so many messages are contradictory. Consider, for example, the debate over the Atkins Diet. Enough people were convinced of its effectiveness to create, for a time, a new fad in the food industry: "low-carb" eating. At the same time, however, some nutritionists, physicians, and physical trainers warned of health risks associated with low-carb diets. How would *you* go about sorting out the competing claims of advocates on both sides of this debate? How would you evaluate all the contradictory testimonials, statistics, and other forms of evidence?

Or consider another issue—the proposal for a national sales tax. Proponents will argue that this tax would simplify the tax structure and impose exactly the same burden on all citizens. Those opposed to such a tax insist that it is grossly unfair, placing the greatest burden on those who can least afford to pay. Again, whom should you believe? And how do you evaluate the arguments on both sides of the issue? Students of public speaking learn to take nothing at face value. Becoming a citizen-critic means learning how to investigate claims, weigh evidence, and come to reasoned conclusions based on a careful examination of the arguments on all sides of an issue.

In a democracy, citizens must know not only how to communicate well but how to critically evaluate the speaking of others. It is not enough that we speak responsibly; we also must demand that *all* who speak in public live up to high ethical standards, promoting not just their own self-interests but the common good. Critical listening and thinking are no less central to the rhetorical tradition than the skills of preparing and delivering a speech. If democratic deliberation is to lead to sound collective judgment, we all must learn to be more critical consumers of public discourse.

Lessons of the Past

Finally, a healthy democratic republic requires a common store of historical and political knowledge. It requires appreciation for the well-crafted argument and the eloquent speech, as well as an understanding of the American rhetorical tradition and our unique history as a deliberative democracy. In short, it requires some measure of historical and civic *literacy*. Unfortunately, as Bruce Cole of the National Endowment for the Humanities has noted, Americans have forgotten much of their own country's history, and this historical amnesia clouds our vision of the future. "We cannot see clearly ahead if we are blind to history," Cole argues, for "a nation that does not know why it exists, or what it stands for, cannot be expected to long endure." Combating this collective amnesia requires careful study of our own history and political traditions. As Cole concludes: "We must recover from the amnesia that shrouds our history in darkness, our principles in confusion, and our future in uncertainty."[23]

One of the best ways to learn about our past is to study the great speakers and speeches of American history. The most basic principles of our government were forged by speakers who assumed the responsibilities of leadership and put the public good ahead of their own personal opinions and interests. During our Constitutional Convention, for example, Benjamin Franklin admitted that he had personal reservations about the proposed U.S. Constitution. Nevertheless, he consented to ratification "because I expect no better, and because I am not sure that it is not the best. The opinions I have had of its errors I sacrifice to the common good."[24] Similarly, Abraham Lincoln is remembered as a great president because of his lofty, magnanimous speeches in the closing days of the Civil War. Putting that terrible tragedy in perspective and beginning a process of national healing, Lincoln used his second inaugural address to urge "malice toward none" and "charity for all." Pledging to "bind up the nation's wounds" and care for those who had "borne the battle," Lincoln pointed the way to "a just and lasting peace among ourselves and among all nations."[25]

Many of the issues and controversies debated in the early years of our republic are still with us today. Past debates shape the way we think about our own times. The great controversy over slavery and the rights of freed African Americans after the Civil War echo in today's debates over racial discrimination and affirmative action. In the nineteenth century, Susan B. Anthony's demand for women's suffrage laid the groundwork for today's debates over gender equality. Debate over the Pure Food and Drug Act of 1906 foreshadowed today's arguments over genetically engineered foods, food additives, and labeling requirements. We may think we live in an unprecedented age of scientific and technological progress, yet many of the challenges we face today have roots deep in our past.

By studying the great speakers and speeches of the past, we learn not only about the origins of contemporary controversies but about the principles of public advocacy and democratic deliberation. By examining the speeches of the great African American abolitionist Frederick Douglass, for example, we can learn how appeals to "higher law" can motivate us to live up to our national ideals. By studying the inaugural addresses and fireside chats of Franklin Roosevelt, we can witness the power of speech to boost morale and promote sacrifice for the common good. By reflecting on how our ancestors debated controversies over America's role in the world or our economic and social policies, we can learn how to disagree while still working together toward common goals. American history is, in large measure, a history of people who made a difference by "speaking out." We can learn about our past from those voices, but also about how to deliberate today's challenges more productively.

America has always had its share of propagandists and demagogues. Yet we can learn from them, too, as the rhetorical theorist Kenneth Burke suggested in a study of Adolph Hitler. By studying the rhetoric of Hitler, Burke wrote, we can "discover what kind of 'medicine' this medicine-man . . . concocted," so that we know "what to guard against" in our own country.[26] How have cult leaders like Jim Jones or David Koresh persuaded their followers to sacrifice everything, even their lives, for some imagined reward in the hereafter? How have groups like the Ku Klux Klan manipulated hatred and bigotry to promote their racist agendas? How have demagogues like Joseph McCarthy exploited our fears to increase their own personal power? By studying the techniques of demagogues like these, we can learn to guard against demagogues in the future.

Today, we continue to witness the power of public speaking to inspire and unify us—or to polarize and divide. Speaking at the National Cathedral only three days after the 9/11 attacks, President George W. Bush sought to comfort a grieving nation, to honor the heroes who saved lives, and to urge the nation to embrace its "responsibility to history." Quoting Franklin Delano Roosevelt, the president celebrated what FDR called the "warm courage of national unity" and assured us that America would prevail against the "enemies of freedom."[27] Yet just two years later, actor Tim Robbins complained of a "chill wind" in America and accused Bush of silencing debate with a rhetoric of "fear and hatred."[28] According to Robbins, the unity forged in the aftermath of 9/11 was an illusion, and the War on Terrorism a threat to our freedoms. In his view, the War on Terrorism was just an excuse to silence dissent.

The American news media, of course, thrives on political conflict. Rarely do we hear from speakers who propose compromise or voice respect for their political opponents. Political talk shows also seem to encourage people to take extreme positions, to shout at one another, or to call each other names. Even comedian Jon Stewart, host of *The Daily Show*, has complained of the "partisan hackery" that substitutes for real debate on TV talk shows. During an appearance on CNN's *Crossfire* in 2004, Stewart complained that such shows "hurt America" and reminded hosts Tucker Carlson and Paul Begala of their "responsibility to public discourse." "You're doing theatre, when you should be doing debate," Stewart concluded.[29] The president of CNN, Jonathan Klein, apparently agreed. Shortly after Stewart's appearance, Klein canceled *Crossfire*, stating that he agreed "wholeheartedly" with Stewart.[30]

We all should join Jon Stewart in denouncing those speakers who hurt our democracy. As citizen-critics, we need to speak out against those who engage in reckless or divisive political speech. We need to hold all who speak in public to a higher standard. For self-government to succeed, we need more than a shared understanding of our history and traditions. We also need a common commitment to what political commentator E. J. Dionne has called "serious speech"—speech motivated by a search for "truth"; speech designed not just to defeat political adversaries but to aid citizens in their common search for understanding; speech that *engages* citizens in a continuous and ongoing effort to balance worthy but competing values, to mediate conflicts, to resolve disputes, and to solve problems.[31] The American rhetorical tradition is rich in such speech, so we have much to learn by studying the speakers, speeches, and debates of the past. By studing past speeches, we can learn much about the ideas that have shaped our nation's history and gain a better appreciation for "serious speech."

Focus on Civic Engagement

Voices of Democracy: The U.S. Oratory Project

In an educational project funded by the National Endowment for the Humanities, "Voices of Democracy: The U.S. Oratory Project," teachers and students will soon be able to study great speeches and debates online. In addition to texts and audio/visual clips of each speech featured, the website will include biographical and historical information, interpretations of each speech, and teaching/learning materials that explore each speech's historical significance and contemporary relevance. By visiting the site, you will be able to learn about important "moments" in U.S. history when "speaking out" really made a difference. You also might learn more about the importance of getting involved and the principles of effective and ethical public speaking. Voices of Democracy will open to the public in the summer of 2008, online at www .voicesofdemocracy.com.

Communication Challenges of the Twenty-first Century

Preview. *Communication is an integral part of our lives, occurring in a wide variety of settings. Public speaking has always been crucial in the conduct of human affairs and has a direct bearing on our own successes—in personal relationships, at school and work, in our community, and in various groups to which we belong. In the contemporary world, the ability to communicate effectively has become more important than ever.*

This book aims to help you develop your abilities as an effective and responsible speaker in a democratic society. We focus on speaking in public, although the principles we stress here apply to other communication situations as well. Speaking with others in any context can be challenging, but speaking in public means assuming a leadership role. Perhaps you will be asked to report to your dorm on the results of a new recycling program, or you might someday urge fellow members of a service organization to help raise funds for a local children's hospital. Or perhaps you will find yourself addressing a town hall meeting on tax relief or aid for education. At some point in your life, you might even appear on a national or international stage, addressing some great issue such as globalization or human cloning. Whatever the setting, your success as a citizen—and as a leader—will depend on your ability to communicate effectively.

Sometimes, the situation that motivates you to speak out is ordinary though personally important: think of the time, for example, that you sought to persuade your friends to support some cause important to you. Or perhaps you have found yourself stifled by a domineering member of a group project at school—and finally felt the need to make your feelings known. In a job interview, you might be forced to speak when the recruiter asks you the question, "What are your strengths and weaknesses?" Or in your job you might be called on to address a group of co-workers, clients, or customers. Whatever your career, you will at some point need to voice your needs, desires, beliefs, or opinions. We communicate—and we react to communication by others—every day, no matter what our role or station in life.

Speaking in public, of course, presents a special challenge. It arouses our anxiety more than any other communication situation. If we hope to share our ideas or to influence others, we must overcome our anxieties about speaking in public. As citizens in a democracy, it is especially important that we develop the confidence to voice our opinions. In a democracy, citizens afraid to speak out have no say in the decisions that affect their lives.

The Importance of Public Speaking

Throughout your life, public speaking will be important to your personal success. The ability to express yourself clearly and effectively will help you now, as a student, as well as later in life, as a professional and a citizen. As a student, the principles you learn in your public speaking class can help you improve your written communications—your term papers and essay exams, for example. Furthermore,

more and more colleges and universities are requiring oral presentations in courses as diverse as marketing, biology, history, and foreign languages. Some colleges and universities are even requiring students to demonstrate proficiency in oral communication before they graduate.[32]

Good communication skills also have become increasingly important in the workplace. Surveys reveal that most of us experience problems at work arising from poor communication. Many employees wish that their co-workers could communicate more effectively.[33] Employers and professional groups increasingly emphasize the importance of effective communication, and many now offer courses or training workshops to bolster communication skills.[34] Although administrators, board directors, and chief executive officers have always given speeches, employees at all levels are called on to speak in today's workplace. Organizations of all types are downsizing, eliminating many middle managers.[35] As this happens, managerial work is being carried out by employees throughout the organization. A team leader may be called on to present the group's ideas to those higher up in the organization. Successful professionals, whether they work in business, health care, education, law, or government, will inevitably be required to speak in public.

Effective public speaking is more than an important job skill, however. Throughout history, public speaking has been taught as an essential part of education for citizenship. In a democracy, you have the *right* to speak. Yet without proper training, that right is worthless. If you hope to participate fully as a citizen, you need to learn *how* to speak with confidence and skill.

Many of the greatest leaders in history have felt a responsibility, even a special *calling*, to "speak out." In the early nineteenth century, for example, abolitionist Angelina Grimké literally risked her life as she traveled about the country speaking out against slavery. More than once, hostile mobs threatened Grimké or tried to break up her meetings. In the late nineteenth and early twentieth centuries, William Jennings Bryan, Theodore Roosevelt, and many others went on public speaking tours of exhausting dimensions to promote the great movements for populist and progressive reform. In the 1930s, Franklin Delano Roosevelt used his oratorical skills to give hope and inspiration to millions of Americans caught in the Great Depression, while Winston Churchill did the same for the British people during the darkest days of World War II. In the 1960s, Martin Luther King Jr.'s powerful voice became the driving force behind a civil rights movement that dramatically transformed America, and Jesse Jackson and others have carried on the fight for racial justice since King's death.

Today, the ability—and the inspiration—to "speak out" in public remains the hallmark of effective political or social leadership. Yet you do not have to be an important political figure or the leader of a great social movement to make a difference by speaking out. In the mid-1990s, Doris Haddock, an 85-year-old great-grandmother from New Hampshire, took it upon herself to do something about the corruption of the American political process by big money. Testing both her public speaking skills and her physical endurance, "Granny D" took her case for campaign finance reform on the road, speaking to thousands of her fellow citizens as she, quite literally, walked across America.

Focus on Civic Engagement

"Granny D" Gets Involved

In 1995, a newly proposed law regulating campaign financing, the McCain-Feingold bill, failed to win congressional approval. In New Hampshire, 85-year-old Doris Haddock decided to do something about it. Incensed that some congressional leaders had stated that the American public didn't care about the issue, Haddock—or "Granny D," as she became known—decided on a dramatic gesture to attract attention to the issue and gain support for reform.

After getting into shape by taking long walks around her home town of Dublin, New Hampshire, Granny D set out to walk across the country to rally support for campaign finance reform. On January 1, 1999, she began her walk in Pasadena, California. By the time she arrived in Washington, D.C., on February 29, 2000, she was 90 years of age and had walked 3,200 miles. In Arizona, she was hospitalized for dehydration and pneumonia. Near the end of her journey, she faced heavy snows and had to cross-country ski for 100 miles between Cumberland, Maryland, and Washington.

All along the way Granny D gave speeches and urged public support for campaign finance reform. When she reached the nation's capital, she was met by more than 2,000 people, including representatives of various reform groups and several members of Congress. Many of these supporters walked the final miles with her.

Granny D is widely credited with helping to push the final bill into law. Al Gore, in adopting a finance reform plank in his campaign platform during the 2000 presidential election, credited Senator John McCain, former senator Bill Bradley, and Granny D.

Granny D continues to speak out. In a speech at the Kennedy School of Government in 2003, she

Doris Haddock, better known as "Granny D," talks about campaign finance at the Statehouse in Concord, New Hampshire, on April 20, 2000. Haddock, of Dublin, New Hampshire, walked from California to Washington, D.C., to promote campaign finance reform.

launched a drive to register more working women to vote. And in 2004, when it became apparent that New Hampshire's incumbent senator would run unopposed, Granny D announced her candidacy for the U.S. Senate.

The text of a speech given by Doris Haddock to the freshman class of Franklin Pierce College follows this chapter. Its theme is the importance of involvement in civic affairs.

Source: http://grannyd.com.

So what *are* the communication skills that we need as students, workers, and citizens? They include not only the ability to speak in front of an audience but the ability to perform well in interviews and group discussions and the critical-thinking skills needed to evaluate the messages of others. As a student, your professor may ask you to lead a class discussion one day—for 20 percent of your grade. As a worker, you might find yourself addressing your fellow employees, negotiating with your boss, or interviewing prospective clients. As a citizen, you might one day appear before the local school board to oppose cutbacks in extracurricular programs or to advocate new classroom facilities. Whatever the situation, the ability to speak effectively is an important skill that you will need throughout your life. The ability to speak well is more than just a job skill; it is an essential qualification for democratic citizenship. Responsible citizens do more than just vote every four years. They also speak out on issues of concern to their communities and the nation.

Public speaking, in short, is an important part of citizenship. It plays an important role in our education and in the workplace, and it sustains our democratic way of life. Public speaking creates opportunities for us to share our knowledge, life experiences, and ideas with others, and it allows us to get feedback on our ideas. Whenever you speak in public, you will grow from the experience, developing more confidence and respect for differing points of view. This textbook will teach you both basic principles and specific strategies for communicating more effectively. It also will highlight ethical considerations in public speaking, and it will help you become a better informed, more critical consumer of other people's messages.

Speaking and Listening Today

Speakers today face different challenges from speakers in the past. While we still speak face-to-face, we communicate today in a wide variety of technological and social contexts, all of which have altered *how* we communicate and *how* we debate and decide important public issues. Many speeches today are electronically mediated. In addition, the audiences we address are far more diverse than those addressed by our parents or grandparents. In the nineteenth century, many considered it scandalous to address what was then called a promiscuous audience—an audience composed of both men and women. Today, we routinely address audiences that include a wide diversity of people from different races and ethnic groups, socioeconomic backgrounds, and religious and moral traditions. Via the Internet, we can even speak to global audiences. Obviously, times have changed, and one-size-fits-all speeches will no longer do.

Electronic media have extended the reach of speakers, but they also have posed new challenges and problems. They have even changed the very way we speak, rendering the passionate, arm-waving style of an earlier era obsolete. Most of today's speakers use a more conversational style, a style that one rhetorical scholar has even labeled "effeminate." According to Kathleen Hall Jamieson, this effeminate style—a style that emphasizes storytelling, self-revelation, and emotional appeals—is a natural response to the intimacy of television. On television, we see speakers close up, as if they are sitting in our own living rooms. We would be shocked to hear them yell and pound on a podium as they spoke to us. On television, the more successful speakers are those who have a relaxed, conversational style, tell good stories, and communicate with us personally. On television, the best speakers are those who seem to talk *with* us, not *at* us.[36]

Former president Ronald Reagan—known as the Great Communicator—was a master of this "effeminate" style. On TV, Reagan communicated warmth and personal charisma, smiling and nodding his head, telling stories, and generally talking with his TV audiences as if he were sitting in their own living room. His personal anecdotes were legendary, and he used self-deprecating humor to good effect. To millions of Americans, Reagan seemed like an ordinary American—just "one of us."

Another former president, Bill Clinton, likewise connected personally with voters via television. After a disastrous debut speech at the Democratic National Convention in 1988, Clinton restrained his tendency toward long-winded policy addresses and instead took a lesson from Reagan: talk *with*, not *at* your audience. With his voice full of emotion, Clinton told those struggling economically that he could "feel their pain," and he reassured many black Americans of his commitment to racial justice. Unlike some politicians, Clinton never looked wooden or stiff when speaking on television. To the contrary, he looked relaxed and confident, communicating sincerity as he spoke.

Of course, we must always be on guard against politicians who might deceive or manipulate us with a slick speaking style. As citizen-critics, we need to recognize that politicians carefully cultivate their TV images and that sometimes we can be distracted from the real issues at hand. We also must guard against being sidetracked by irrelevant concerns blown out of proportion by media coverage. In the 1992 presidential debate, for example, the first President Bush looked at his watch while challenger Bill Clinton spoke, suggesting that he was uncomfortable with the town hall–style format of the debate. Based largely on this nonverbal behavior, many pundits declared Bush the loser without even analyzing the substance of the debate. Similarly, Vice President Al Gore was said to have lost the 2000 presidential debate because he sighed audibly and looked disapprovingly at his opponent, George W. Bush. Again, the debate's so-called winner was declared not on the basis of his arguments, but because of allegedly rude and patronizing nonverbal signals.

These examples point to the challenge many politicians face in trying to get their message across in today's political environment. The news business is highly competitive, and journalists tend to prefer the striking or dramatic story that can be simply told. "If it bleeds, it leads," as the old saying goes. This is especially true of television news, where the desire for compelling visuals often overrides more important concerns. On television news, complex issues are rarely discussed in depth. Speakers on television talk in slogans and sound bites, oversimplifying complex issues and reducing them to simplistic, black-and-white terms. Speaking about his support for the War in Iraq during the 2004 presidential campaign, Senator John Kerry was quoted as saying "first I voted for it and then I voted against it." Kerry apparently was trying to explain a complicated parliamentary maneuver during the Senate debate. On television, however, the sound bite only reinforced his image as a "waffler."

As citizens, we are challenged to go beyond the sound bites and media spin to evaluate messages critically. We need to look beyond mere appearances—and even beyond what respected journalists or political commentators tell us. As citizens, we are called on to make our own judgments, and we should take responsibility for educating ourselves about important issues. To be a responsible citizen is to be an *informed* and *critical* consumer of public communication. It means making an effort to understand the motives of speakers, evaluating their evidence and reasoning, and suspending judgment until we are fully informed. It means being fair-minded and respectful toward those who disagree, and it means being sensitive to the advantages some advocates have because they have more resources or greater media access.

Another major challenge faced by speakers today is the growing diversity of audiences. We live in a world where men and women of all ages, races, religions, and educational backgrounds must come together to resolve problems. During the 1980s, immigrants accounted for more than one-third of U.S. population growth, and our increasing cultural diversity can now be seen in all regions of the country.[37] An overwhelming 92 percent of Americans recognize that the United States is now made up of many different cultures.[38]

Whether you make a speech in your classroom or to a community group, your audience will undoubtedly be more diverse than it would have been even a decade ago. You can't assume that all of your listeners will be like you, sharing the same values, beliefs, and experiences. All listeners won't view fraternities and sororities the same way you do. All listeners won't trust the police to protect them. All listeners will not agree that the measure of success in life is the amount of money one makes. And not all listeners will define the term *family values* the same way. Indeed, some listeners may completely reject your most cherished principles and values.

Does that mean we can no longer discuss important issues and find common ground in our diverse, multicultural society? Let's hope not! The growing diversity of American society makes it more important than ever that we learn how to communicate both effectively and responsibly. We may be a more diverse nation today, but we still face many of the same problems and share common dreams and aspirations. If we hope to sustain America's great experiment in democratic government, we must learn to resolve our competing interests and work together for the common good.

The Responsible Citizen-Speaker

Preview. *In a democracy, every speaker should be committed to communicating responsibly. Responsible speakers examine their own motives. They insist on accuracy and are concerned with the ways in which they acquire and present information. They see human communication as respectful dialogue and strive to live up to the legal and ethical standards of the larger community.*

As a speaker, you hope to influence your audience. Like any speaker, you hope your audience will respond positively to your ideas and proposals. Yet that does not mean you should be willing to say *anything* to "win the day." Nor does it mean that you should shamelessly pander to your audience. As we suggested earlier, the ideal orator of classical times was not just an *effective* public speaker, but one who communicated *responsibly*. But what does that mean—to communicate "responsibly"? And what are the responsibilities of the citizen-speaker in the modern world?

First, you have a responsibility to speak honestly and truthfully, with a genuine concern for the well-being of your audience and your community. Responsible communication is not just something you tack on to the end of your speech. Rather, it must grow out of your own character and personal virtues, and it must reflect the core values of your community. Responsible speakers remain true to their own principles but are bound by the legal and ethical standards of the broader community. Inevitably, you will face ethical dilemmas as a public speaker—a conflict, for example, between a principle you hold dear and a more expedient or profitable course of action. How well you resolve such dilemmas will determine your success not only as a public speaker, but also as a citizen.

Fundamental to responsible communication is a commitment to the pursuit of truth and respectful dialogue. We live in a society that allows freedom of expression and relies on public deliberation as a means of resolving controversies. To opt out of that process is to shirk one's responsibilities as a citizen. The right of free speech in a democratic society carries with it certain responsibilities: a responsibility to speak the truth as you know it, for example, and a responsibility to speak without prejudice or malice toward others.

Characteristics of the Responsible Citizen-Speaker

Responsible speakers examine their own motives, and they do not slant the truth just to "win" an argument. Responsible speakers insist on accuracy—they tell the audience what they believe to be true based on their own research and reflection. Responsible speakers are committed to communication as a transactional dialogue; they honor the right of their listeners to raise questions, suggest alternatives, or even disagree. Responsible speakers carefully research their topics and are sensitive to the ways in which they present their information. They consider the audience's rights, needs, and values. Finally, responsible speakers do not pander. They might compromise on some issues, but they do not abandon their core beliefs in order to win. You want to be an effective speaker, but not at the cost of your principles and ideals. In a democracy, truly successful speakers articulate their own views effectively, but they also listen to others and combine their own intellectual and creative resources with those of their fellow citizens. In the final analysis, that is what democracy is all about: citizens deliberating *together* with a view toward arriving at good collective decisions.

Public speaking is an ancient art, because citizens have always needed to *learn* the habits and practices of democratic deliberation. It is our hope that you will tackle the challenge of becoming both an effective and a responsible public speaker—a twenty-first century version of the ideal orator of the classical rhetorical tradition.

Legal and Ethical Issues in Public Speaking

Imagine having to speak to an audience you know to be opposed to your ideas. How far will you go to win their agreement? Suppose you have to speak on the same topic to several different audiences, each with different concerns. How will your basic message vary as you move from one audience to another? Or perhaps you are making a persuasive presentation to potential customers or clients. If you

Students gather outside the Supreme Court in Washington, D.C., to support affirmative action during a demonstration in April 2003. The Court was hearing a case involving the admissions policies of the University of Michigan.

land this "deal"—if they buy your product, invest in your idea, or sign your contract—your career will take off. How far are you willing to go in order to make that deal? Will you still present your case fairly, with a balanced concern for your audience's needs as well as your own? Or will you resort to misleading statements or attack the competition in order to persuade your audience?

Every day, we see politicians and other public advocates wrestle with these questions. During presidential campaigns, we hear about "battleground states," but there are many battlegrounds in contemporary culture and politics. On any number of social and political issues, we hear voices from the far ends of the political spectrum: Ann Coulter on the right, for example, or Michael Moore on the left. Some public figures, such as Howard Stern, even push the boundaries of decency and good taste. Still others, such as white supremacist Matthew Hale, openly preach hate and advocate violence. So where do we draw the line? What are the limits of free speech in America? And who has the power to define those limits? We have laws against slander and libel, of course, and the Supreme Court has ruled that speech that threatens public safety is outside the protections of the First Amendment. Yet controversies remain. To what extent, for example, should the Federal Communications Commission be able to regulate what we see on television or hear on the radio? Should a city government be allowed to close an art exhibit that it deems pornographic? Do "pro-life" activists have a First Amendment right to advocate violence against doctors who perform abortions? All of these questions point to difficult dilemmas for our free society.

Generally, we all recognize that there must be limits to free speech. By law, for example, we do *not* have a First Amendment right to slander or threaten others, nor do we have a right to incite mob violence. Beyond these legal limitations, however, there are few clear guidelines for responsible democratic speech. As a result, all public speakers must make choices. As a public advocate, will you resort to name-calling or appeals to fear in order to win an argument? Will you attempt to prevail by labeling your opponents "ignorant" or "radical," or by trying to scare your audience into agreeing with your position? Or will you show respect for your listeners by grounding your speech in the best available information, supporting it with sound evidence and reasoning, and acknowledging the legitimacy of opposing points of view?

Issues that matter to people should be explored in depth, not clouded by language that dismisses rather than engages the arguments of the opposition. In the heat of political battle, some speakers might be tempted to exaggerate their case, to state mere opinions as fact, or to make promises they cannot keep. Yet, in the end, those who resort to such methods cheat not only their audiences but themselves. We can all think of times when irresponsible speakers have carried the day. Eventually, however, most have been exposed as demagogues, denounced by their fellow citizens, and discredited in history.

You might not think it matters much what you talk about in your public speaking classroom, or how you go about communicating your ideas there, as long as you meet the requirements of your assignment. The classroom is a public forum, however, and communicating responsibly *is* part of your assignment. Your instructor may assign different types of speeches, and each may emphasize different aspects of the speaking process. But whatever your assignment, you should choose a topic of real significance and do your best to live up to the standards of the responsible citizen-speaker. Giving a poorly prepared or deceptive speech cheats both you and your audience of the opportunity to confront real issues and to engage in serious discussion of the challenges we face.

In the next chapter, we will discuss at greater length the ethical dimensions of public speaking, considering in particular the ethical principles important in public speaking, the relationship between ethical and effective communication, and some very practical problems you will face—such as plagiarism—as you prepare yourself to speak. As you prepare for your first public speaking assignment, do not forget: the truly successful citizen-orator is both an effective speaker *and* a good citizen.

Summary

- The engaged citizen "gets involved," strives to be well informed and thoughtful, and speaks out on matters of civic concern.
- The tradition of scholarship and teaching in rhetoric emphasizes the knowledge and skills necessary for democratic citizenship.
  - Theories of rhetoric dating back to ancient Greece and Rome have stressed the ethics of public speaking and civic virtue.

- Rhetorical criticism teaches us to be citizen-critics; that is, to carefully evaluate the arguments and evidence we hear in speeches or in the mass media.

- By studying the great speakers and speeches of the past, we can learn about American history and about the principles and traditions of democratic deliberation.

- In our increasingly diverse, mass-mediated society, the ability to communicate effectively has become more important than ever.

  - Public speaking skills are crucial to success in the workplace and in your role as a citizen.

  - Electronic media have created new challenges for speakers and changed the character of our public discourse.

  - The growing diversity of our society challenges speakers to understand and adapt to different cultures.

- The responsible citizen-orator is committed to honesty, respects his or her audience and the process of deliberation, and understands the legal and ethical constraints upon free speech in a democratic society.

QUESTIONS FOR REVIEW AND REFLECTION

1. How is public speaking related to "civic engagement"? Offer some concrete examples.
2. What evidence suggests that Americans have become less politically involved or community spirited? Do you believe that Americans are less engaged than in the past? Alternatively, can you think of ways that citizens have become *more* civically engaged in recent years?
3. On your campus, what activities, clubs, or other special opportunities invite students to participate in civic affairs? Offer at least three examples.
4. How is the rhetorical tradition relevant to concerns with civic engagement? What kinds of knowledge and skills can be learned from the rhetorical tradition?
5. What are the communication skills that are most important in the twenty-first century? Is public speaking more or less important today than it was, say, 100 years ago?
6. In what ways has public speaking been important historically? Other than those listed in the book, offer at least one example of a public speaker who has had a significant impact on his or her community, state, nation, or the world.
7. How have mass media (and television, in particular) altered the way we deliver speeches? What makes a speaker effective on television?
8. What are the characteristics of the responsible citizen-speaker? What are some of the legal and ethical constraints on speakers in a democracy?

ENDNOTES

1. See Infoplease, "National Voter Turnout in Federal Elections: 1960–2000," www .infoplease.com/ipa/A0781453.html (accessed August 11, 2006).
2. Center for Voting and Democracy, "International Voter Turnout, 1991–2000," www .fairvote.org/turnout/intturnout.htm (accessed May 13, 2005).
3. Center for Voting and Democracy, "Youth (Non-)Voters," www.fairvote.org/turnout/ youth_voters.htm (accessed May 13, 2005).

4. David T. Z. Mindich, *Tuned Out: Why Americans under 40 Don't Follow the News* (New York: Oxford University Press, 2005), esp. 18–33.

5. Robert Putnam, *Bowling Alone: The Collapse and Revival of American Community* (New York: Simon and Schuster, 2000), 32–43.

6. Putnam, 43–45.

7. Putnam, 49.

8. See James Davidson Hunter, *Culture Wars: The Struggle to Define America* (New York: Basic Books, 1991), 135–70.

9. Robert Putnam, "Bowling Together," *The American Prospect*, February 11, 2002, 20–22.

10. Committee for the Study of the American Electorate, "President Bush, Mobilization Drives Propel Turnout to Post-1968 High," News Release, November 4, 2004, www .fairvote.org/reports/CSAE2004electionreport.pdf (accessed May 13, 2005).

11. Center for Information and Research on Civic Learning and Engagement, "Youth Voting in the 2004 Election," Fact Sheet, November 8, 2004 (updated January 25, 2005), www .civicyouth.org/PopUps/FactSheets/FS-PresElection04.pdf (accessed May 13, 2005).

12. "The Saguano Seminar: Civic Engagement in America," www.ksg.harvard.edu/saguaro/ (accessed May 13, 2005).

13. See "Our Purpose," *The Strauss Report: A Publication of the Annette Strauss Institute for Civic Participation*, 2005–2006 edition, n.p.

14. Jeffrey R. Young, "Persuading Students to Care: Eugene Lang's Program Aims to Prod Colleges into Encouraging Civic Involvement," *Chronicle of Higher Education*, April 11, 2003, A47.

15. See Campus Campact, "About Us," www.compact.org/ (accessed May 9, 2005); and Carolina Center for Public Service, "The Public Service Scholars Program," www.unc .edu/cps/scholars/ (accessed May 9, 2005).

16. A recent study done at UCLA found that more than 55 percent of Internet users aged 18 to 34 obtain news online in a typical week, and a Nielson/NetRatings study showed that traffic to the 26 most popular sites in 2003 grew by 70 percent from May 2002 to October 2003. Pew Charitable Trust, Media Fact Sheet, March 2004, www.pewtrusts. com (accessed August 25, 2005).

17. Minow's speech to the National Association of Broadcasters, May 9, 1961, www .historychannel.com/speeches/archive/speech_194.html (accessed August 15, 2005).

18. *THON, 2004*, www.thon.org (accessed July 10, 2004).

19. Cicero, *De Oratore, Books I and II*, trans. E. W. Sutton and H. Rackham (New York: Loeb Classical Library, 1959); see also Anthony Everitt, *Cicero: The Life and Times of Rome's Greatest Politician* (New York: Random House, 2001), 179–80.

20. Quintilian, *Institutes of Oratory*, trans. J. S. Watson (London: G. Bell & Sons, 1913), 2:391.

21. See Rosa A. Eberly, *Citizen Critics: Literary Public Spheres* (Urbana: University of Illinois Press, 2000).

22. Stephen R. Goldzwig, "A Social Movement Perspective on Demagoguery: Achieving Symbolic Realignment," *Communication Studies* 40 (1989): 202–28. For Aristotle's classical definition see William A. Dunning, "The Politics of Aristotle," *Political Science Quarterly* 15 (1900): 273–307.

23. Bruce Cole, "Our American Amnesia," *Wall Street Journal*, June 11, 2002, www .wethepeople.gov/newsroom/wsjarticle.html (accessed May 11, 2005).

24. Benjamin Franklin, "On the Constitution," in *A Choice of Worlds: The Practice and Criticism of Public Discourse*, ed. James R. Andrews (New York: Harper and Row, 1973), 100.

25. Abraham Lincoln, "Second Inaugural Address," in *American Voices: Significant Speeches in American History, 1640–1945*, ed. James R. Andrews and David Zarefsky (New York: Longman, 1989), 294–96.

26. Kenneth Burke, *The Philosophy of Literary Form* (Baton Rouge: Louisiana State University Press, 1941), 191.

27. George W. Bush, "President's Remarks at National Day of Prayer and Remembrance," Office of the Press Secretary, the White House, news release, September 14, 2001, www .whitehouse.gov/news/releases/2001/09/20010914-2.html (accessed October 10, 2005).

28. Tim Robbins, "'A Chill Wind is Blowing': Transcript of the Speech Given by actor Tim Robbins to the National Press Club in Washington, D.C., on April 15, 2003," www .commondreams.org/views03/0416-01.htm (accessed May 13, 2005).

29. Cable News Network, *Crossfire*, October 15, 2004.

30. Bill Carter, "CNN Will Cancel 'Crossfire' and Cut Ties to Commentator," *New York Times*, January 6, 2005, C5.

31. E. J. Dionne Jr., *They Only Look Dead: Why Progressives Will Dominate the Next Political Era* (New York: Touchstone Books, 1997), 261.

32. See "Integrity in the Curriculum: A Report to the Academic Community," Association of American Colleges, Washington, D.C., 1985; see also the National Communication Association's *Spectra* (March 1995): 9, for a summary of the findings of a Department of Education study of the communication skills that faculty, employers, and policymakers believe are critical for college graduates.

33. David A. Whetten and Kim S. Cameron, *Developing Management Skills*, 6th ed. (Englewood, Cliffs, NJ: Prentice Hall, 2005); Dan B. Curtis, Jerry L. Winsor, and Ronald D. Stephens, "National Preferences in Business and Communication Education," *Communication Education* 38 (1989): 6–15.

34. See, for example, "Speak for Success" and "Advanced Presentations Workshop," published for the American Bar Association (Boston: Speech Improvement Company, n.d.). We might also note that many self-help books offer advice on how to improve one's communication skills. Although the advice might not always be sound, the existence of such books suggests that many people recognize the need to improve their communication skills.

35. David L. Bradford and Allan R. Cohen, *Power Up: Transforming Organizations through Shared Leadership* (New York: John Wiley and Sons, 1998); and Peter F. Drucker, "The Coming of the New Organization," *Harvard Business Review* 66 (1988): 45–53.

36. Kathleen Hall Jamieson, *Eloquence in an Electronic Age* (New York: Oxford UP, 1988), 67–89.

37. Sally J. Walton, *Cultural Diversity in the Workplace* (New York: Irwin Professional Publishing, 1994).

38. Pew Hispanic Center/Kaiser Family Foundation, *The 2004 National Survey of Latinos: Politics and Civic Participation*, July 2004, 73.

DORIS "GRANNY D" HADDOCK

*Since becoming famous for her cross-country walk in support of campaign finance reform in 1999–2000, Doris "Granny D" Haddock has published a memoir (*You're Never Too Old to Raise a Little Hell*), led voter registration campaigns, and delivered dozens of speeches at political rallies and on college campuses. In this speech, she offers the incoming freshmen at Franklin Pierce College some sage advice on life, the world around them, and their obligations as citizens in a democracy.*

September 5, 2003

To the Freshman Class at Franklin Pierce College, New Hampshire

Thank you.

It is a great pleasure to grow old and to be asked to dispense advice and to not have to follow it oneself. In that department, let me urge you to go to bed early, get up at dawn, keep well ahead of your studies, stay well behind your credit limit, refrain from smoking and drinking and wild living. I give you that advice, not because I have ever followed it myself, but because life's pleasures are all the more delicious if an old lady has told you to do otherwise.

GRANNY D OPENS ON A HUMOROUS NOTE, ESTABLISHING HER ETHOS AS A REBEL.

The fact is, life is a feast of great pleasures and we are rude to our Creator if we do not partake of the beauty and fun and pleasure of this life. So I do hope you will take care of yourself and that you will mind your schedules to the extent that you will not always be behind and worried and stressed and missing out on the joy all around you. The captain of a well-run ship can afford the time to enjoy the breeze and the view. Be that to your own life, starting with college. It is a challenge, I know, but if you keep at it, you will get the hang of living well in this life.

HERE SHE USES THE METAPHOR OF A "WELL-RUN SHIP" TO EMPHASIZE HER POINT.

You will see that some of the students around you are forever behind and worried, and others seem on top of it and have a smile. Your choice, indeed. The moment of truth is when you are tempted away from your resolve. Will you be a person of strong character? Here is the test of it: a person of character stays true to a task, long after the passing of the mood in which that resolution was made. Watch for that: Your conscious overview of your daily life can guide you toward improvements that will strengthen your hold on life and its happiness. Let me warn you more specifically that problems like depression and chronic procrastination are always a good excuse for a visit to the health center, where you can get very useful help. The brain is no less fixable an organ than the stomach, and we do get our aches and pains and should go for help sooner rather than later.

IN THIS PARAGRAPH, SHE URGES THE STUDENTS TO TAKE CARE OF BOTH THEIR MENTAL AND PHYSICAL HEALTH.

Now, that is all boilerplate advice. Let me tell you something more interesting. You come into college with the expectation of learning many new things—of becoming an expert in many areas. But there is one area where you are already the expert, and where the professors and the other old birds are not. Young people bring something special and, if you are not fully aware of this superior quality, you might waste it unknowingly.

HERE SHE CELEBRATES YOUTH, NOTING THAT YOUNG PEOPLE HAVE "SOMETHING SPECIAL," A FRESH "VIEW OF THE WORLD."

I am not speaking of your athletic or more personal areas of strength and stamina, though I am sure you are very impressive to watch in action. I am speaking of your view of the world, which in many ways is superior to the view seen by older eyes.

Trust your sensibilities toward justice and fairness and toward the environment and peace. Understand that your value judgments in these areas are better because they have not been beaten down or crusted over. Information overload can make us insensitive. While your eyes are wide open—and so also your heart—trust what you see. Do not hang back from involvement in addressing the problems of the world, waiting to become an expert. You are expert enough. You are our annual re-supply of new eyes and fresh hearts to give our sorry species its best hope for improvement and survival. Take your part in the great dramas and the great struggles now still in their opening acts in this world. It is the part where you storm on stage with a confused but mischievous look and the audience cheers you madly. Don't wait to know the part too well, or the moment will pass without you.

What is your passion? There is a place for you in that passion. Or are you drifting, looking for your passion? Let your curiosity lead you to it. Trust the force of that curiosity—it is a lighted way for you, and just for you. Be brave when your curiosity takes you to places you would rather not go—it knows what it is doing and it has served you well for much longer than you can possibly imagine.

Look around every now and then and wonder what all this life is about. Whom is served by all this life? Whom does life serve? Life serves life, and we are happiest and at our best when we let our full life force—indeed our divine life force—rise within us as we engage our lives in service to the world, to the life around us. We are happiest when we are serving life and adding to its health and bounty. We are simply made that way—made for cooperation and joining of every kind.

This is an extraordinary time you have chosen to come. What an amazing world! The young woman college student in Iran, wearing her Levi's under her burka, is your sister and your friend. The farmer in Central America who is trying to get a fair price for his coffee beans so that he can build a better house for his children is your uncle and a man you deeply respect. The Navajo woman who is fighting for the right to stay on land that has been her family's for generations is your grandmother, and she needs your help.

It is not too much. It is all quite beautiful. Cast your heart into this world right now, for your eyes and your heart are open and your senses of justice and fairness and your sense of the right thing to do by the planet that sustains us are fully matured and at their perfect moment to give hope and progress to the world. Don't save yourselves for later; spend yourselves today in love, and your investment will come back to you a hundredfold if you survive.

Most of the social progress of the past hundred years has come from college students demanding a better world.

A good friend of mine was flying across the U.S. this past week and his seat-mates were a young man and woman from Iran. The man was a naturalized U.S. citizen. The young woman had come here more recently. She told my friend how she had grown up under the artillery barrages of the Iran-Iraq War. She described how the Iranians saw that war: that the Americans had built up the Shaw's army to be among the strongest in the region, but that when he was toppled by the Ayatollah, the U.S. then armed Saddam Hussein in Iraq and encouraged him to take down the Iranian army a few notches. It was in that game that she found herself as a child target of artillery. My friend asked her if she did not resent Americans for that time in her young life. She said that she tried not to hold Americans responsible for the actions of their government, as she hoped she wouldn't be held responsible for the actions of the Iranian government. She said that Americans seemed so kind and so unaware of what was being done in their names around the world, and she said she thought it must be like being the children in a family where the daddy is a monster—their lives are comfortable, but they know there is something wrong. They do not ask too many questions because they love their way of life. She said that she did not like to tell Americans about all that she knew, because it was kind of a shame to wake them up to all this when their lives were so cluelessly blissful—her words.

Well, she was wrong on many counts. As citizens of a democratic republic, we are indeed responsible for what our nation does in our name. And it is no discourtesy to help us be the awakened citizens we must be.

America is a great country and we love it. We love this planet, too. And you young people here today are the bright eyes that must be the open and awake eyes, though still full of joy and honor, love and mischief, duty and courage to serve life in a time when life is challenged by its old foes: fear and hate and ignorance.

Be you a great brotherhood and sisterhood of love and action. Arrange your personal lives so that you have the time and resources to take your part on this great stage. And smile the smile of the peaceful warrior whose weapons are love and light, and ever more love and more light.

Thank you and good luck this great scholastic and political year.

If it gets too crazy, come down to my porch in Dublin and we'll talk it over —if I'm not away on some adventure of my own. Call first.

Thank you very much.

Source: Used by permission of Granny D. Haddock.

GRANNY PROFESSES HER LOVE FOR HER COUNTRY AND FOR THE "PLANET, TOO."

CONCLUDING WITH A CALL TO ACTION, GRANNY URGES THE STUDENTS TO GET INVOLVED, PLAYING THEIR PART ON THE "GREAT STAGE" OF CIVIC LIFE AND BECOME A "PEACEFUL WARRIOR" WHOSE WEAPONS ARE "LOVE AND LIGHT."

CHAPTER 2

The Ethical Public Speaker

CHAPTER SURVEY

The Engaged Citizen

Getting Involved in Politics

The Ethics of Public Speaking

Deliberation and Demagoguery in the Media Age

CHAPTER OBJECTIVES

After studying this chapter, you should be able to

1. Explain what it means to be an engaged citizen.

2. Describe various ways to become involved in civic affairs.

3. Identify some important ethical issues in public speaking.

4. Define *plagiarism* and *ghostwriting*.

5. Explain what it means to deliberate in good faith.

6. Define *demagoguery* and describe some of the characteristics of the demagogue.

Following World War I, a young artillery officer named William Norwood Brigance returned from the battlefields of France to teach high school speech and history. In 1922, he began a 38-year career teaching speech and coaching debate at Wabash College, a small liberal arts college in Crawfordsville, Indiana. Brigance earned his doctoral degree while on sabbatical from Wabash in 1929–30—the first Ph.D. in speech ever granted by the University of Iowa. By that time, he already had published more than a dozen scholarly articles and two books, all written during the summers, when he had time off from teaching.

Brigance's career at Wabash spanned some of the most turbulent times in our nation's history. The 1930s, of course, brought the Great Depression, which left millions of Americans broke and out of work. Then came Adolph Hitler, World War II, and the horrors of the Nazi concentration camps. Throughout the 1950s and 1960s, the Cold War kept Americans on edge, with a whole generation of Americans growing up under the shadow of the atomic bomb. Brigance, like many Americans of his day, worried about America's future. Yet he also had faith in the American people.

Brigance's teaching and scholarship emphasized the need for every citizen in a democracy to be an "effective, intelligent, and responsible" speaker. A "system of speechmaking" was "imperative for preserving democracy," he wrote, for in the modern world there were only two kinds people: "Those who in disagreements and crises want to *shoot* it out, and those who have learned to *talk* it out." If America hoped to remain a "government by talk," Brigance wrote, it needed *leaders* who spoke "effectively, intelligently, and responsibly," informing people about the challenges they faced and inspiring them to get involved. In addition, it needed to assure that all citizens had "an equal right" to be heard and to hear "both sides of every public question." Finally, it needed "popular intelligence," or a citizenry trained both to speak and to "listen and judge." In troubling times, Brigance concluded, these were the "conditions" that were essential to the "survival of democracy" itself.[1]

Brigance epitomized what former *NBC Nightly News* anchor Tom Brokaw called America's "greatest generation."[2] Like many in his day, he talked less about the *rights* than about the *responsibilities* of citizenship, reminding his fellow Americans of their duties as citizens. According to Brigance, nobody was *born* with the right of free speech. One had to *earn* that right by becoming well informed and respecting the rules and traditions of democratic debate. As Brigance explained:

> We are beset by choices and temptations. We are haunted by shadows of fear. We listen to speakers, then, because we hope they will throw light on our problems, temptations, and fears. We listen because we hope they will give us new information, new ideas, or will simply water and cultivate old ideas. We listen because we want to be given encouragement, to renew our faith, to strengthen our determination.

In Brigance's view, we all have a right to hear speeches "worth listening to," and speakers who fail to deliver "useful goods" deserve to be "put out of business."[3]

Today, it seems, there is less speech "worth listening to." On radio and TV, speakers seem more concerned with scoring political points than delivering "useful goods," and our public debates have become overheated, polarized, and unproductive. Some even fear that, as a nation, we have lost that sense of *duty* and *service* that characterized Brigance's generation. Yet many Americans, including many young people, still get involved in politics or public service. As citizens in a democracy, we have an *ethical* responsibility to speak out on matters of public importance and to become involved in the civic life of our communities and nation.

The Engaged Citizen

Preview. *Citizenship entails responsibilities as well as rights, most notably the responsibility to get involved. There are many different ways to participate in civic life, and more and more young people today are doing so through political and volunteer activities.*

We began this book with an important question: What does it mean to be a citizen in a democracy? For some, as we noted, citizenship means paying one's taxes or voting in elections. For others, it means volunteering to help the less fortunate or raising funds for a worthy cause. However you define it, citizenship entails an *ethical* commitment to working with others to make our communities better.

As we noted in the last chapter, the good citizen gets involved, whether that means participating in politics or engaging in public service. The ways to do this are as diverse as the American population itself. In Foxborough, Massachusetts, a local resident named Phillip Henderson organized a group of neighbors to fight plans by a fast-food chain to build a new franchise on an environmentally sensitive site. Henderson's group, the Quality of Life Committee, fought for seven years to stop the development. They finally prevailed, and the disputed land is now part of a 19-acre protected wetland and wildlife preserve.[4] In Washington State, a similar scenario played out as Pete Knutson, the owner of a small family fishing operation, organized an unlikely alliance of working-class fishermen, middle-class environmentalists, and Native Americans to protect salmon fisheries in the Pacific Northwest. Standing up against powerful special interests, Knutson's alliance pushed for cleaner streams, enforcement of the Endangered Species Act, and an increased flow of water over regional dams to help boost salmon runs. When the special interests pushed for new regulations that would have put small family fishing operations out of business, Knutson and his supporters defeated the effort in a statewide referendum.[5]

"Getting involved" is not just something older Americans do. All across America, college and even high school students have been making a difference by participating in civic or service activities. In one survey of people between the ages of 18 and 30, two-thirds of the respondents said that they had volunteered their time, joined a civic or service organization, or advocated some public cause in the past three years. Some 75 percent of these young people indicated an interest in tutoring or mentoring others, and majorities also expressed interest in helping to build affordable housing for low-income people, promoting access to health care and social services, educating others about environmental conservation, or assisting with local homeland security.[6] In another survey in 2002, the Center for Information and Research on Civic Learning and Engagement (CIRCLE) found that while few young

Americans participated in traditional politics, many *had* found ways to get involved in other sorts of civic activities. When asked whether they personally had walked, run, or bicycled for a charitable cause," for example, some 40.8 percent of young respondents said they had participated in such an event. More than half also reported that they had boycotted some product "because of the conditions under which it was made."[7]

Many college students are even giving up their spring breaks to help others. According to Break Away, a nonprofit group that organizes "alternative" spring breaks, 30,000 students spent their vacations in 2003 building homes, tutoring inner-city kids, or participating in other sorts of volunteer or community service. In 2002, for example, some 300 students from James Madison University participated in 30 different spring break service programs, ranging from trail and campground projects in national parks to working with at-risk youth in Washington, D.C. Each spring dozens of students from the University of Southern California travel to a Navajo reservation in Utah to paint houses, while other USC students have built furniture for a new school in Guatemala or planted trees on Isla Mujeres, near Cancún, Mexico. During spring break 2005, some 80 students from Slippery Rock University worked with homeless people in Atlanta, ran youth programs in inner-city Baltimore, tutored high school dropouts in Denver, or helped rebuild homes destroyed by hurricanes in Florida. "It's just a really great way to spend your spring break," said Laura Creamer, a 21-year-old

Focus on Civic Engagement

Students against Breast Cancer

What motivates young people to get involved? For Erica Pamenta and Sarah Costello, it was knowing somebody who was diagnosed with breast cancer. Erica, a biology major at Rutgers University, sought a way to participate in the fight against breast cancer after her best friend's mother was diagnosed with the disease. Sarah, a political science major at Ramapo College, also became concerned about breast cancer while still in high school—after her own mother was diagnosed with the disease.

Even as busy college students, Erica and Sarah have continued their fight against breast cancer. At Rutgers, Erica organized a Relay for Life to benefit the American Cancer Society (ACS), while Sarah worked to establish a student chapter of the ACS's Cancer Action Network. The two students go to different schools, but they are partners in a common cause: raising money for the Susan G. Komen foundation, which for more than 20 years has been a leader in the fight against breast cancer.

"Cancer is not a pleasant topic and many people do not want to talk about it," Erica observed while taking a break from her busy schedule. According to Sarah, the hardest thing about mobilizing other students is getting their attention in the first place: "You need to create an interest, a passion, for high school or college students to become involved." Both students developed their public speaking skills through participation in high school forensics, and both have found those skills invaluable as they spread the word about breast cancer—a disease that kills an estimated 40,000 women annually in the United States alone and is the second-leading cause of cancer deaths among women worldwide.

For more information, visit the Susan G. Komen foundation at www.komen.org. Also see "Imaginis: The Breast Health Resource," http://imaginis.com/breasthealth/statistics.asp (accessed November 5, 2005).

More than 2,000 people, including 300 breast cancer survivors, participated in this three-day fund-raising event in Santa Barbara, California.

English major at Agnes Scott College, who was among the 10,000 students taking part in Habitat for Humanity's spring break program. "It's a really great experience to help someone out who's less fortunate."[8]

By volunteering to work in a soup kitchen or to help clean up a park, you can have an immediate, tangible impact. Perhaps that explains why so many young people prefer community service over more "traditional" political activities such as circulating petitions or supporting political candidates. According to a survey in 2000, nearly three-quarters (73 percent) of college students have participated in some kind of volunteer work, but barely a third of college students voted in the 1998 national elections. Perhaps you view politics as too negative or less effective than community service.[9] But if you really hope to make a difference, you cannot ignore politics.

Getting Involved in Politics

Preview. *As citizens in a democracy, we have a responsibility not only to vote but to participate in the processes of democratic deliberation and decision making. Some people are more passionate about politics than others, but every citizen has a right to be heard. However you get politically involved, you can make a difference by speaking out.*

Many Americans say they're "turned off" by politics. But if you really hope to make a difference, you need to be politically engaged. Many of the problems we face today are, at bottom, *political* problems. Why do we have homeless citizens? Perhaps it is because our elected leaders have not made affordable housing a high priority. Why do we need volunteers to build trails or to help clean up our national parks? Again, the answer involves politics: our elected officials have chosen *not* to fund such projects with taxpayer dollars. If you have ever tutored inner-city kids, perhaps you've wondered how our public schools could do a better job teaching at-risk children. Or perhaps you've visited a nursing home and wondered what more we could do to care for our senior citizens. All of these problems are *political* problems; all require *political* solutions.

Involvement in politics can take many forms—beyond just voting or supporting political candidates. Some people support political groups that share their general philosophy, like MoveOn.org or Focus on the Family. Others dedicate their time or money to particular causes, like protecting the environment or improving public schools. Still others attend protest rallies or boycott companies that they consider socially irresponsible. Whatever your interests, you can find ways to "make your voice heard." Whether you prefer traditional or unconventional ways of expressing your political views, you *can* make a difference.

Getting involved in politics does *not* mean that you must talk in the loud, combative style of some political activists. As political scientist Morris P. Fiorina has observed, our democracy has been "hijacked" by political activists who have a much more aggressive style than the rest of us: "They are completely certain of their views; they are right and their opponents are wrong." Moreover, some of these activists view all who disagree not just as misguided or misinformed, but as "corrupt, stupid, evil, or all three."[10] Most Americans are not so sure of themselves, nor do they view all who disagree with their opinions as stupid or evil. Most Americans take moderate, middle-of-the-road positions, even on hot-button issues such as abortion and gun control. They want no part of the so-called culture wars that have divided and polarized the "political class." For most of us, politics is not about defeating some enemy but about finding solutions to our common problems.

All this is not to say that we should ignore or silence those who feel passionate about politics. Devoted political activists—even those who sociologist Eric Hoffer once called "true believers"[11]—have played an important role in American history, giving voice to the powerless and calling attention to injustices long ignored. Many of the most important social and political reforms in U.S. history—the abolition of slavery, woman suffrage, and environmental protection, to name just a few—were brought about by passionate activists who, at one time, many considered too radical. Indeed, our nation's founders were radicals, as were many later activists we now consider heroic, such as abolitionist Wendell Phillips, woman suffrage activist Susan B. Anthony, or civil rights leader Martin Luther King Jr.

Still, democracy is about *majority* rule, and the loud, passionate voices of a few should never be allowed to drown out the quieter, more moderate voices of the vast majority of Americans. Nor should we *have* to shout or make a scene in order to be heard. When loud, angry voices prevail, compromise and consensus building become more difficult. As Fiorina suggests, the "less intense and less extreme" voices of the majority should be given *at least* as much weight as those of the political activists. Not only would that "lower the decibel level of American politics," it would also focus attention on more "mainstream concerns."[12]

Whatever your own political views, you have the right to speak out. At the same time, you have an *ethical* obligation to respect the right of others to be heard. You also have an obligation to speak honestly, to know what you're talking about, and to remain open to changing your mind when confronted with compelling arguments. Good citizens keep up with current events and pride themselves on having informed opinions. They take advantage of opportunities to learn more about the issues, and they carefully weigh all the arguments before forming their own opinions. They may feel strongly about their views, but they also respect the opinions of others. Good citizens—people of good will—can and will disagree about politics, sometimes passionately. But they remain committed to free and open debate and to resolving their differences through democratic processes.

As a citizen in a democracy, you have an ethical obligation to become informed about news and events before voicing your political opinions.

Perhaps by speaking out, you will someday influence the decision of your local school board or city council. Or by discussing political issues with your neighbors, maybe you will contribute to a change in public opinion on an issue that matters to you. You might even change the minds of your classmates when you give a speech in class. Whatever the results of your participation, it is important—both to you and to our democracy—that you get involved. But before you do, you should reflect on your *ethical* responsibilities as a speaker. Those responsibilities, like the study of speech itself, date back to the earliest democracies of the ancient world.

The Ethics of Public Speaking

Preview *Your ethical responsibilities as a public speaker must be kept in mind at every stage of the speech-making process, from your decision to speak out in the first place to the choices you make as you research, prepare, and deliver your speech. Not only must your goals be ethical, but you have a responsibility to speak honestly and to take responsibility for what you say.*

At the time of our nation's founding, the classical rhetorical tradition—with its emphasis on moral character and civic virtue—was the foundation of our educational and political culture. "To the revolutionary generation," as historian Gordon Wood has explained, "rhetoric lay at the heart of an eighteenth-century liberal education," and the ability to speak effectively was "regarded as a necessary mark of a gentleman and an indispensable skill for a statesman, especially for a statesman in a republic."[13] Since that time, we have lost touch with the classical tradition, and demagoguery—deceptive or manipulative speech—has become more commonplace in our civic life. Today we have no formal "code of conduct" for those who speak in public, and new technologies and the growing diversity of our culture have created new challenges.

Yet if we hope to resolve our political differences through discussion and debate, we need shared ethical principles—some "rules of the game"—to guide our deliberations. And the foundational principles of the classical tradition can still provide guidance. Like the ancient rhetoricians, we can still demand truth from those who speak in public, and we can insist on sound evidence and reasoning. We can still uphold high moral standards for all who speak in public, and we can honor and celebrate those speakers who display civic virtue. In the modern world, it has become harder than ever to distinguish truth from disinformation, disinterested advice from attempts to mislead. Yet the ethics of public speaking have remained essentially unchanged for more than 2,000 years. Today, as in ancient times, we still expect public speakers to be honest and accountable for what they say.

Ends and Means in Public Speaking

Perhaps it goes without saying that ethical public speakers do not pursue unethical goals. We might all agree, for example, that Adolph Hitler was wrong to advocate genocide, whatever his rationale. Yet questions of ethics are rarely that clear-cut. For one thing, speakers often face ethical *dilemmas*, or situations in which they must choose between the lesser of two evils. In addition, *circumstances* sometimes affect the ethics of public speaking, complicating the speaker's choices by clouding the ethical issues involved.

Many speakers face ethical dilemmas arising out of their professional obligations. Lawyers, for example, may find themselves assigned to defend clients whom they believe are guilty. What are their ethical obligations in that situation? They are professionally committed to defending their clients. Yet they are also ethically bound to tell the truth. Similarly, people in advertising or public relations often face ethical dilemmas when asked to represent products or companies that they do not personally endorse. What would *you* do if asked to develop an advertising campaign for a product that you considered harmful to the environment or dangerous to consumers? As a public relations consultant, would you work for a company that you felt exploited its workers?

Sometimes the ethics of your goals as a speaker might depend, at least in part, on the circumstances. Ordinarily, for example, we might consider it unethical to advocate violence or war. Yet most cultures recognize a right of self-defense, and some religions have a "just war" doctrine that specifies the circumstances under which war might be morally justified.[14] Within the Catholic Church, for example, war is considered morally legitimate only when the cause is just, all other means of resolving the conflict have been exhausted, and the resort to arms does not threaten to do even greater harm than whatever provoked it. If these and other conditions have been met, Catholics can, in good conscience, support a resort to arms. Yet it is always debatable whether these conditions have been met, which is why Catholics may still disagree over whether a particular war is just. The same is true of most other ethical guidelines. Changing circumstances—and, in some cases, ambiguities in the ethical code itself—always leave room for debate.

If the ethical implications of your goals as a speaker are debatable, that is all the more reason to give them careful thought.

- Are your purposes consistent with prevailing social norms or the religious beliefs of your audience?
- By speaking out, would you be violating your own personal ethics?
- Are you willing to stick to your own ethical principles at the risk of offending your audience?
- What, exactly, *are* the ethical standards of your community or the larger culture?

These are important questions, and they ought to be asked every time you speak in public. Yet it is not enough to have ethical *goals*. Ethical issues arise at every stage of the speech-making process, and you must take them into account every step of the way.

Honesty and Accountability

Your most basic ethical obligation as a public speaker is to tell the truth and take responsibility for what you say. You also have an ethical obligation to give credit where credit is due for ideas or language that you borrow from others. No doubt you recognize that principle from your other classes; you probably have been taught the meaning of the word plagiarism and told to cite your sources. Yet honesty and accountability in public speaking are more than just academic requirements. They suggest a broader commitment to intellectual honesty and social responsibility—a commitment that we should demand of *all* who speak in public.

Plagiarism

In a survey of 4,500 high school students in 2002, some 75 percent admitted to cheating in school, with more than half admitting to plagiarizing work they found on the Internet. Even more troubling, some did not see anything wrong with cheating. "What's important is getting ahead," said one student at George Mason High School in Falls Church, Virginia. "In the real world, that's what's going to be going on."[15] Unfortunately, cheating already has become a way of life for this student, and she no doubt will continue to cheat—at least until she gets caught. Other students do not cheat intentionally, instead committing plagiarism "accidentally." Cheating results not only from the attitude that "getting ahead" is more important than honesty but from simple carelessness or confusion over what constitutes academic dishonesty.

So what exactly *is* plagiarism? According to Northwestern University's "Principles Regarding Academic Integrity," plagiarism may be defined as "submitting material that in part or whole is not entirely one's own work without attributing those same portions to their correct source."[16] At first glance, this definition makes plagiarism a simple matter: you should never "borrow" all or even part of your speech from somebody else—at least not without acknowledging your sources. Yet the issue is complicated by gray areas in our definitions of plagiarism, as well as by confusion over when and how to cite your sources in an *oral* presentation. Thus, it is important that you have a clear understanding not only of what constitutes plagiarism, but also of how to avoid inadvertent plagiarism when preparing and delivering a speech.

Students sometimes take shortcuts in their speech class that constitute obvious and deliberate plagiarism. You are obviously guilty of plagiarism if you take your whole speech from a file at your fraternity house, for example, or if you buy your speech from an Internet site that sells ready-made papers and speeches. You are also guilty of plagiarism if you "cut and paste" all or part of your speech from Internet sources. But what if you "borrow" just a few quotations from that same source? Or what if you just paraphrase an article you read, borrowing some information and ideas but putting them into your own words? Does that constitute plagiarism? Here is where misunderstanding the rules might result in accidental plagiarism.

In a term paper, of course, you use quotation marks or indented block quotes to indicate passages that you took verbatim from others. But how do you indicate quoted material in a speech? Some people *say* "quote" and "unquote" to signify that they are quoting, but that can become annoying if overused. A better way is to use phrasing, structural strategies, and/or vocal inflections to indicate quoted material. Notice, for example, how the following passage is structured to signal where the quoted passage begins and ends: "Theodore Roosevelt stated his approach to American foreign policy in simple terms when he said: 'Speak softly but carry a big stick.' In saying this, Roosevelt actually took a middle ground between the imperialists and the isolationists of his day."

In a speech, of course, you can't cite your sources in parentheses, footnotes, or endnotes. So how *do* you "footnote" a speech? The answer is simple: you must cite your sources *in the text of the speech itself*. Even if your instructor requires that you turn in a list of sources for your speech, you should get into the habit of citing your sources orally and saying something to establish their credibility. As we will discuss in Chapter 15, your *ethos* or credibility as a speaker depends in part on how the audience perceives the credibility of your sources. Speakers who quote well-qualified sources impress us with their research; those who cite questionable sources or no sources at all damage their own ethos.

Paraphrasing refers to putting the ideas or insights of others into your own words. When paraphrasing, you should strive for language that differs significantly from the original. Yet that still doesn't excuse you from giving credit for ideas or insights that are not your own. You need not document your own unique insights or conclusions, nor do you need to cite sources for what can be considered common knowledge or generally accepted facts. Yet how do you know when you have a genuinely original idea? And what constitutes common knowledge? Here is a useful rule of thumb: when in doubt, cite your sources.

If you find yourself tempted to take your speech off the Internet, remember that new technologies have not only made it easier to cheat; they also have made it easier to *catch* cheaters. Many teachers now use Internet search engines, or websites like Turnitin.com, in their fight against plagiarism. At Turnitin.com, papers are checked against several massive databases, including more than 4.5 billion websites, more than 10 million student papers already submitted to the site, and millions of published articles in ProQuest, a full-text academic search engine. Within seconds, Turnitin.com returns an "Originality Report" highlighting possible instances of plagiarism and linking those passages to their sources. Although Turnitin.com is used mostly by teachers to detect and deter plagiarism, students also can use the site to learn more about how to paraphrase and cite their sources properly.[17]

Plagiarism can cost you much more than a good grade on your speech. At Penn State University, for example, penalties for plagiarism range from warnings, grade penalties, or academic probation to expulsion from the university. In the fall of 2000, Penn State even adopted a new XF grade to indicate failure of a course because of academic dishonesty. In 2001–02, there were 268 cases of alleged academic dishonesty at Penn State, up from just 51 the year before. Out of those students, five ended up with an XF grade on their permanent records. About half of those accused of academic misconduct failed the assignment in question, while about 30 percent received an F in the course.[18] Other schools also have toughened up their penalties for plagiarism. Some have even rescinded degrees or expelled students from honorary societies like Phi Beta Kappa after discovering later that the students had plagiarized academic work.[19]

Beyond the classroom, plagiarism can have serious, real-world consequences. In 1988, for example, Joseph R. Biden, a U.S. senator from Delaware, was forced to withdraw from the race for the Democratic presidential nomination when an opposing campaign released a videotape showing him repeating passages stolen from a speech by British Labour Party leader Neil Kinnock. Later, reporters discovered a number of similar incidents in Biden's past, including other plagiarized speeches and accusations of plagiarism against Biden in law school.[20] More recently, Republican Nevada governor Jim Gibbons, when he was a congressman, delivered a hard-hitting attack on liberals at a Lincoln Day dinner in Elko, Nevada, including this stinging shot at the music and film industries: "I say we [tell] those liberal, tree-hugging, Birkenstock-wearing, hippie, tie-dyed liberals to go make their movies and music and whine somewhere else." Unfortunately for Gibbons, it soon came out that he had stolen almost his entire speech from a copyrighted address delivered in 2003 by Alabama state auditor Beth Chapman. "Not only is it a bad speech," commented one Democratic party leader, "it's a bad, stolen speech."[21]

Among those whose reputations have been damaged by accusations of plagiarism are such well-known figures as the Reverend Martin Luther King Jr. and historians Stephen Ambrose and Doris Kearns Goodwin. In these cases, the plagiarism may have been unintentional, but the accusations nevertheless proved embarrassing. At other times, the plagiarism is obviously deliberate, as in the case of a young *New York Times* reporter named Jayson Blair. Blair's blatant use of stolen and fabricated stories led to his own resignation and to the resignations of two high-ranking editors at the *Times*.[22] Plagiarism is *not* just something that you worry about in college. In the "real world," the penalties for plagiarism are severe and the consequences can be devastating.

Ghostwriting

Presenting somebody else's words or ideas as your own is not always unethical. Since ancient times, ghostwriters, or professional speechwriters, have helped others write their speeches. Today ghostwriting is considered an inevitable (if not fully understood) part of our political and corporate culture. Many political and business leaders are simply too busy to write their own speeches. The president of the United States employs a whole team of researchers and speechwriters. Generally, we do not consider this unethical, so long as the speaker takes full responsibility for his or her words.

The earliest ghostwriters actually helped make democracy possible. Assisting citizens as they prepared speeches for the deliberative and legal assemblies of the Greek city-state, the first ghostwriters also *taught* the art of public speaking. Subsequently, ghostwriting "proliferated through the ages," and today almost every speech by a major political, business, or academic leader is "written by someone else."[23] America's first president, George Washington, had a speechwriter: Alexander Hamilton. So, too, have many other presidents, including some whom we consider among our greatest presidential orators: Franklin Delano Roosevelt, for example, and John F. Kennedy.[24] Even the "Great Communicator," Ronald Reagan, employed not only a ghostwriter but a whole team of researchers and writers to help prepare his speeches. One of those writers, Peggy Noonan, wrote many of Reagan's most famous lines.[25] Still, we remember those famous words as the words of Ronald Reagan.

When does ghostwriting become unethical? According to Craig R. Smith, a speechwriter for both President Gerald Ford and the Chrysler Corporation's Lee Iacocca, ghostwriting becomes unethical when the use of a speech writer is "hidden from the audience." According to Smith, if "someone who uses a ghostwriter denies it," then they are "lying and acting unethically." Beyond that, Smith holds ghostwriters to the same ethical standards he would hold any writer or speaker to: if their speeches are "purposefully deceptive," then they are unethical. Comparing ghostwriters to lawyers, Smith denies that it is unethical for ghostwriters to "write against their personal convictions." Just as lawyers sometimes defend people they think are guilty, a speechwriter might defend an idea simply to assure that it gets "fair play in the marketplace of ideas." Smith has never done that himself, but for practical, not ethical reasons: "I personally don't do it because I don't write as effectively when I'm writing about an idea I don't believe in."[26]

Today, ghostwriters rarely hide their role in the speech-making process. To the contrary, some presidential speechwriters have become celebrities in their own right, writing best-selling memoirs or achieving fame in politics, journalism, or even popular entertainment. Among the former presidential speechwriters who have become well-known celebrities are William Safire, Patrick Buchanan, television personality

Highlighting Ghostwriting

George W. Bush and the "Axis of Evil"

On January 29, 2002, George W. Bush delivered what is typically a routine speech: his State of the Union address to Congress. On this occasion, however, America was at war in Afghanistan and was preparing to extend the War on Terrorism to Iraq and possibly other nations. In the president's own words, the United States was prepared to take the fight against terrorism to any nation known to "harbor terrorists."

Planning for Bush's 2002 State of the Union address began in late December 2001, when presidential speechwriter Michael Gerson began soliciting suggestions from dozens of people across the government. He gave one of his assistants in the presidential speechwriting office, David Frum, a difficult task: develop justifications for expanding the War on Terrorism. As Frum recalls in his memoir, *The Right Man*, he began by rereading a speech that he had last read on September 11, 2001: Franklin Roosevelt's War Address after the Japanese attack on Pearl Harbor in 1941. He began to see parallels between the Axis Powers in World War II—Japan, Nazi Germany, and Italy—and the terrorist states that now threatened America. The result was a memo to Gerson in which Frum labeled Iraq, Iran, and North Korea a new "axis of hatred." As Frum recalls, he expected his "radical" memo to be ignored. Instead, Gerson not only em-

braced the idea but added "the theological language that Bush had made his own since September 11," changing "axis of hatred" to the "axis of evil."

The result was a passage in Bush's State of the Union address that provoked great controversy: "States like these, and their terrorist allies, constitute an axis of evil, arming to threaten the peace of the world. By seeking weapons of mass destruction, these regimes pose a grave and growing danger. . . . The United Sates of America will not permit the world's most dangerous regimes to threaten us with the world's most destructive weapons." To some, this language seemed clear evidence of the administration's plans to invade other countries, and a little more than a year later the United States did, in fact, invade Iraq.

George Bush did not invent the phrase "axis of evil," but by uttering those words in his State of the Union address he made them his own. Moreover, he took full responsibility for the language even before he delivered the speech. As Frum writes: "Bush read the speech closely. He edited it in his own bold hand. He understood all its implications. He backed them with all the power of his presidency."

Source: David Frum, *The Right Man: The Surprise Presidency of George W. Bush* (New York: Random House, 2003), 224–45.

Ben Stein, and presidential press secretary Tony Snow. Some still question the ethics of speechwriters profiting from inside accounts or going directly from the White House into journalism. Generally, however, we respect speechwriters who are honest about what they do.

The role of research and new technologies in speechwriting raises additional ethical concerns. With polling and focus groups, speechwriting teams can now create what one scholar has described as "quantitatively safe" speeches,[27] or speeches scientifically designed to offend nobody. Through research, ghostwriters also can test which arguments or evidence the public will find convincing or determine which emotional appeals will best move the public. Famous for such research, former Clinton advisor Dick Morris has described a process called triangulation, in which polling data was used to position Clinton in the most politically advantageous positions.[28] Morris denies that he was a spin doctor who distorted the truth or manipulated public opinion. But the use of polling to craft presidential messages raises new concerns that, rather than leading or educating, politicians merely "pander" to public opinion.[29]

Political ghostwriters are quick to defend their craft as a noble and worthy profession. Some college students even aspire to careers as professional speechwriters. What is the best preparation for such a career? According to Noonan, "communications majors" do *not* make the best speechwriters, but by that she means journalism or mass communications majors who neglect the study of history, literature, and other liberal arts.[30] Ghostwriter Craig R. Smith clarifies Noonan's point, suggesting that aspiring speech writers *should* major in rhetoric or *speech* communication, where they study not only the practical arts of argumentation and style but the history of great speeches, critical theory and methods, and the liberal arts. According to Smith, the "rhetorically trained ghost" puts out "a much better product" than one without such training. By studying rhetoric, students learn how to clearly "state the case and prove it."[31]

President Bush delivering his 2002 State of the Union address, in which he labeled North Korea, Iraq, and Iran an "axis of evil" and warned that their pursuit of weapons of mass destruction posed a "grave and growing danger."

As you study the American rhetorical tradition, you'll learn that public speaking is *not* just about "winning" debates. It is also about leadership, public service, and respect for our traditions of free speech and democratic deliberation. The great speakers in history are not those who have successfully manipulated public opinion. To the contrary, we most remember those who have educated and inspired their audiences, such as Abraham Lincoln and Franklin D. Roosevelt. To be sure: unethical demagogues have sometimes risen to power in American politics. In the long run, however, history honors those who use the power of public speaking not to deceive or manipulate but to serve the public good.

Deliberation and Demagoguery in the Media Age

Preview *Those who speak in public need not be objective, or free of all personal opinions and biases, but they do have an obligation to be well informed and fully prepared. In most respects, the rules of ethical speech have not changed since ancient times, although unethical speech, or demagoguery, has assumed new forms in the modern world.*

As the late U.S. senator Daniel Patrick Moynihan used to say, we are all entitled to our own opinions, but not to our own facts.[32] What Moynihan meant, of course, is that we should never twist the truth or invent facts just to win a debate. As public speakers, we have an ethical obligation both to speak honestly and to make the necessary effort to gather reliable information about our topic. We also have an obligation to remain open to other points of view and to respect those who may disagree with our opinions. Democratic deliberation is not about winning and losing. It is about joining with other citizens in a search for solutions to our common problems.

Perhaps you've heard the expression "deliberating in good faith." What does that mean? Does it mean that we must always strive to be objective? The answer is no. Nobody is completely objective. Nor are we expected to deny all our subjective reactions and personal experiences when we participate in public debate. We all have religious beliefs, political biases, and social values that influence our opinions. As a speaker, nobody expects you to erase your past, nor do audiences demand that you deny your own beliefs and values, however controversial they may be. To the contrary, democratic deliberation is all about airing those differing opinions. It is about reconciling our disagreements through discussion and debate. Your fellow citizens do not expect you to be perfectly objective, but they do expect you to make good arguments in support of your opinions. That means providing sound reasoning and evidence to back up your views. If citizens are unwilling to consider opposing points of view or become too closed-minded to be swayed by compelling evidence, then democratic deliberation breaks down.

In many situations, you will be *expected* to take sides on a controversial issue. If, for example, you plan to speak on HMOs and the decline of health care in America, your audience will expect to hear you denounce HMOs and advocate some alternative system for funding health care in America. Yet that does not mean that you will simply announce your opposition to HMOs and wait for your audience to shout its approval. You must provide *reasons* for your opinion and *evidence* to back it up. Nor does taking a stand on a controversial issue mean that, once you deliver your speech, you should close your mind to the possibility of changing your own opinion. Ethical speakers avoid allowing their existing opinions to blind them to new information, and they remain open to persuasion by advocates with different points of view. Once you have carefully researched and prepared your speech, you may be confident that your conclusions are both thoughtful and fair. Yet down the road, you might need to reevaluate your opinion in light of new information or changing circumstances.

As a public speaker in a democratic society, you have an ethical obligation to be well informed and fully prepared. Speaking in public is not like casual conversation, where you just "bounce a few ideas" off a friend. It is a *formal presentation*, often in a setting where people have gathered to discuss issues crucial to their own lives and communities. In such a setting, you owe it to your listeners to investigate your topic carefully and to provide information that is relevant, reliable, and up-to-date. More than that, you should organize and deliver that information in the most effective manner possible. Being fully prepared means more than developing an informed opinion—although that is a crucial first step. It also means carefully organizing your ideas, choosing the right language to express them, and supplying solid evidence to back up them up. It may even mean preparing visual aids to help your audience understand the information, and it should always include rehearsing the timing and delivery of your speech.

The ethics of democratic deliberation rest upon the fact that when you speak in public, you ask your fellow citizens not only for their time and attention, but also for their trust. And so you have an ethical obligation to contribute something useful to their deliberations—to deliver useful goods, as Brigance put it. Perhaps you can contribute some fact that others have overlooked. Or maybe you have a unique way of looking at a problem or some new ideas for solving an old problem. Whatever your contribution, you should investigate your topic thoroughly, consider all sides of the issue, and make sure that you have your facts straight. As Moynihan reminded us, you have a right to your own opinion, but not to your own facts.

Demagoguery and the Ethics of Emotional Appeal

As Charles Lomas observed in *The Agitator in American Society*, "demagoguery" is one of those words that is loosely thrown around in American politics and is "difficult to define."[33] To the Greeks who invented the word, a "demagogue was simply a leader of the people." Yet even in ancient Greece the term implied deceit and manipulation, with Euripides describing the demagogue as "a man of loose tongue, intemperate, trusting to tumult, leading the populace to mischief with empty words."[34]

Today, we use the term *demagogue* to describe speakers who deceive or manipulate their audiences, usually by provoking strong emotional responses. In a widely cited study, for example, historian Reinhard Luthin defined the demagogue as a "mob-master" who, with "considerable histrionic variety and always noisily," seeks to "whip up and intensify the emotions, the prejudices and the passions, of the voting public." According to Luthin, the demagogue is long on "gasconade and bluster" but short on "public service and constructive thinking."[35]

Demagogues typically appeal to the darker emotions, such as fear, anger, or hatred. During the Great Depression, for example, Huey P. Long, a U.S. senator from Louisiana, exploited the fears and hopelessness of many Americans by offering a quick fix to America's economic woes: a vague, utopian plan to "share the wealth." Similarly, Senator Joseph McCarthy became a household name in the 1950s by exploiting fears of communism and the uncertainties of the cold war era. Accusing high-ranking government officials and even U.S. military leaders of "selling out" to the enemy, McCarthy's reckless accusations were later proven unfounded, but for a time he whipped the entire country into an anticommunist frenzy.

Of course, not all appeals to emotions are, in and of themselves, unethical. Emotions play an important role in all aspects of our lives. As speakers, we must recognize that people get excited, upset, or angry about issues that concern them. Emotions are also a powerful motivator. If you want your audience to *do* something, you simply cannot ignore the role of emotions in human behavior. Many speakers use emotional appeals to move people to do good—donate time or money to a charitable cause, for example, or fight for better schools in their community. Actor Michael Douglas uses emotional appeals to persuade us to help children affected by the AIDS epidemic in Africa. The Red Cross uses emotional appeals to solicit aid for victims of hurricanes and other natural disasters. The Veterans of Foreign Wars appeal to our emotions when they call on us to "support our troops." Appeals to emotions take many forms, and they are not *all* demagogic. If your goals

Senator Huey P. Long addressing students at Louisiana State University in Baton Rouge on November 12, 1934. Long's flamboyant speaking style mesmerized audiences, yet many considered him a demagogue because of his emotional appeals and his utopian plan to "Share the Wealth." Long was assassinated the following year by the son-in-law of a political rival and died at the age of 42.

are ethical and you are honest in what you say, there is nothing inherently wrong with appealing to emotions.

Yet emotional appeals should never *substitute* for sound, well-supported arguments, and as speakers we need to give careful thought to when—and under what circumstances—emotional appeals might be appropriate. In addition, we need to recognize that *some* forms of emotional appeal are, almost by definition, unethical. Name-calling, for example, is a kind of emotional appeal that is always unacceptable. By calling people derogatory names rather than responding to their arguments, you demean, degrade, or even dehumanize others. In the hands of the demagogue, name-calling is *designed* to do just that—short-circuit the reasoning process by demeaning those with different points of view. Thus, the demagogue might characterize all feminists as man-haters or all evangelical Christians as religious fanatics. This sort of name-calling is not only intellectually dishonest; it silences others and undermines democratic debate.

Finally, there are a number of specific rhetorical techniques that scholars have long associated with demagoguery. According to J. Justin Gustainis, demagogues not only employ excessive emotional appeals and name-calling, they focus attention on their own personalities rather than the issues, oversimplify complex matters, and make specious, or logically fallacious, arguments. Like emotional appeals, none of these tactics is *necessarily* demagogic. Political candidates, for example, may emphasize their personal qualifications for office, and speakers sometimes oversimplify complex issues for uninformed or uneducated audiences. Demagogues, however, *habitually* use such tactics, and they do so to promote their own selfish interests, not the public good. In other words, demagogues deceive and manipulate others to promote *themselves*, and in the process they rarely show "concern for the truth."[36]

However offensive they may be, even demagogues enjoy the protections of the First Amendment. Direct incitements to violence go beyond the bounds of free speech, but even the most offensive forms of name-calling and stereotyping are generally considered protected speech under our Constitution. In recent years, a number of colleges and universities have banned what has been termed "hate speech" on campus, but these speech codes rarely stand up in court. Nor do libel and slander laws offer much protection against even the most vicious personal attacks on public figures. Perhaps that helps to explain why our political campaigns have become so nasty. Inevitably, some will exploit our right to free speech to engage in unethical practices.

In an era of rapid technological and social change, the ethics of public speaking have become even more complicated. Hate speech has found a new home on the Internet, where its sources can remain anonymous and unaccountable. Meanwhile,

Highlighting Ethical Communication

1. Do not use false, fabricated, misrepresented, distorted, or irrelevant evidence to support arguments or claims.

2. Do not intentionally use unsupported, misleading, or illogical reasoning.

3. Do not represent yourself as informed or an expert on a subject when you are not.

4. Do not use irrelevant appeals to divert attention or scrutiny from the issue at hand. Among the appeals that commonly serve such a purpose are "smear" attacks on an opponent's character; appeals to hatred or bigotry; derogatory insinuations, or innuendoes; God and devil terms that cause intense but unreflective positive or negative reactions.

5. Do not ask your audience to link your idea or proposal to emotion-laden values, motives, or goals to which it is actually not related.

6. Do not deceive your audience by concealing your real purpose, self-interest, the group you represent, or your position as an advocate of a viewpoint.

7. Do not distort, hide, or misrepresent the number, scope, intensity, or undesirable features of consequences or effects.

8. Do not use emotional appeals that lack a supporting basis of evidence or reasoning, or that would not be accepted if the audience had time and opportunity to examine the subject themselves.

9. Do not oversimplify complex, gradation-laden situations into simplistic, two-valued, either-or polar views or choices.

10. Do not pretend certainty when tentativeness and degrees of probability would be more accurate.

11. Do not advocate something in which you do not believe yourself.

Source: Richard L. Johannesen, *Ethics in Human Communication*, 4th ed. (Prospect Heights, IL: Waveland Press, 1996), 287–88. Reprinted by permission of Waveland Press. All rights reserved.

our society grows more diverse every day, complicating our efforts to identify shared ethical standards. Yet the basic principles of ethical speech—honesty, accountability, good faith, and commitment to the larger "public good"—remain as relevant today as they were more than 2,000 years ago. It is up to us—each and every one of us— to speak out against demagoguery and contribute something positive and constructive to our public deliberations. As William Norwood Brigance put it, we should all insist upon speech "worth listening to"—speech that serves democracy by delivering "useful goods."

Summary

- Democratic citizenship entails responsibilities as well as rights, including the responsibility to "get involved."
  - For some, getting involved might mean supporting political candidates.
  - For others, getting involved means volunteering to help others in their community or "speaking out" on the issues of the day.

- Civic engagement involves *communicating* with others, so it is important that citizens in a democracy learn *how* to communicate both effectively and ethically.
- Your ethical responsibilities as a public speaker should be kept in mind at every stage of the speech-making process.
  - The ethical speaker pursues worthy goals.
  - The ethical speaker is honest and accountable, avoiding plagiarism and taking full responsibility for words spoken in public.
- The basic rules of ethical speech have not changed since ancient times, although demagoguery has assumed new forms and the ethical issues relating to speech have been complicated by technological and social change.
  - The ethical speaker deliberates "in good faith" and is well informed and fully prepared.
  - The ethical speaker avoids the techniques of the demagogue and never substitutes appeals to the emotions for sound, well-supported arguments.
  - The ethical speaker uses the power of speech to enlighten and inspire his or her fellow citizens and to serve the public good.

QUESTIONS FOR REVIEW AND REFLECTION

1. What, in your opinion, are the most important responsibilities of citizenship in a democracy? What does it mean to "get involved" as a citizen, and what sorts of involvement are most satisfying or effective?
2. What are the most important ethical concerns surrounding public speaking in a democracy? What does it mean to speak "ethically"? How, if at all, have the ethical considerations in public speaking changed over time?
3. How would you define the term *plagiarism*, and what are the differences between deliberate and "accidental" plagiarism?
4. What ethical concerns, if any, are raised by the practice of ghostwriting? Is ghostwriting always unethical, or is it unethical only under certain circumstances? How might we distinguish ethical from unethical ghostwriting?
5. What does it mean to deliberate in "good faith"? Does deliberating in good faith mean being completely objective? Can you be passionate about your political views and still deliberate in good faith?
6. Define *demagoguery*. How does demagoguery relate to the use of emotional appeals? Is it always demagogic to appeal to your audience's emotions? How, if at all, would you distinguish between ethical and unethical emotional appeals? Beyond emotional appeals, what other techniques in public speaking are associated with demagoguery?

ENDNOTES

1. William Norwood Brigance, *Speech: Its Techniques and Disciplines in a Free Society*, 2nd ed. (New York: Appleton-Century-Crofts, 1961), 1, 4–5.
2. Tom Brokaw, *The Greatest Generation* (New York: Random House, 1998).
3. William Norwood Brigance, *Speech Communication*, 2nd ed. (New York: Appleton-Century-Crofts, 1955), 2–3.

4. Judith Forman, "Grass-Roots Activism Is Thriving; Causes Differ, but Aim Is Better Communities," *Boston Globe*, November 1, 2001, 1.

5. Paul Rogat Loeb, *Soul of a Citizen: Living with Conviction in a Cynical Time* (New York: St. Martin's Press, 1999), 4–6, 199–200.

6. Peter D. Hart and Mario A. Brossard, "A Generation to Be Proud Of," *Brookings Review* 20 (Fall 2002): 36–37.

7. Michael Olander, "How Young People Express Their Political Views," Center for Information and Research on Civic Learning and Engagement, *Fact Sheet*, July 2003, www.civicyouth.org/research/products/fact_sheets.htm (accessed August 23, 2005).

8. See Eleni Berger, "Students Look beyond the Beach for Spring Break," CNN.com, March 12, 2003, www.cnn.com/2003/TRAVEL/02/27/spring.service/; "Students Battle Hunger, Poverty in Alternative Spring Break," *JMU News*, www.jmu.edu/jmuweb/general/news/general_20023114231.shtml (accessed August 23, 2005); Jane Engle, "For This Party over Spring Break, Bring Your Own Hammer," *LATimes.com*, February 20, 2005, www.latimes.com/travel/la-tr-insider20feb20,1,2302870.column (accessed August 23, 2005); Karl E. Schwab, "80 SRU Students to Spend Spring Break Offering Community Service across U.S.," *SRU News*, www.sru.edu/pages/10651.asp (accessed August 23, 2005).

9. See Tobi Walker, "The Service/Politics Split: Rethinking Service to Teach Political Engagement," *PS: Political Science and Politics* 33 (September 2000): 646–49.

10. Morris P. Fiorina, *Culture War? The Myth of a Divided America* (New York: Pearson, 2005), 102.

11. Eric Hoffer, *The True Believer* (New York: Harper and Brothers, 1951).

12. Fiorina, *Culture War?* 111.

13. Gordon S. Wood, "The Democratization of the American Mind," in *Leadership in the American Revolution* (Washington, DC: Library of Congress, 1974), 70.

14. See Alexander Moseley, "Just War Theory," *Internet Encyclopedia of Philosophy*, www.utm.edu/research/iep/j/justwar.htm (accessed November 3, 2005).

15. Kathy Slobogin, "Survey: Many Students Say Cheating Is OK," *CNN.com*, April 5, 2002, archives.cnn.com/2002/fyi/teachers.ednews/04/05/highschool.cheating/index.html (accessed August 23, 2005).

16. "How to Avoid Plagiarism," www.northwestern.edu/uacc/plagiar.html (accessed November 3, 2005).

17. See the home page for Turnitin.com, www.turnitin.com/static/home.html (accessed September 9, 2005).

18. Jeremy R. Cooke, "More Cheaters Found, XF Grade on the Rise," *The DigitalCollegian*, January 20, 2003, www.collegian.psu.edu/archive/2003/01/01-20-03tdc/01-20-03dnews-02.asp (accessed November 3, 2005).

19. See Ronald B. Standler, "Plagiarism in Colleges in U.S.," www.rbs2.com/plag.htm (accessed August 4, 2005).

20. See Jim Geraghty, "Biden Time," *National Review*, January 22, 2003, www.nationalreview.com/comment/comment-geraghty012203.asp (accessed October 13, 2005).

21. Erin Neff, "Gibbons' Speech Plagiarism: 15 Paragraphs Came from Copyrighted Talk by Alabama Woman," *Las Vegas Review-Journal*, March 4, 2005 www.reviewjournal.com/lvrj_home/2005/Mar-04-Fri-2005/news/25992087.html (accessed October 13, 2005).

22. Rose Arce and Shannon Troetel, "Top New York Times Editors Quit," *CNN.com*, March 1, 2004, www.cnn.com/2003/US/Northeast/06/05/nytimes.resigns/ (accessed October 13, 2005).

23. Lois Einhorn, "Ghostwriting: Two Famous Ghosts Speak on Its Nature and Its Ethical Implications," in *Ethical Dimensions of Political Communication*, ed. Robert E. Denton Jr. (New York: Praeger, 1991), 115.

24. Kennedy's speechwriter, Theodore C. Sorensen, not only wrote speeches but served as one of Kennedy's closest and most trusted advisers. Sorensen later wrote a best-selling biography of the 35th president. See Theodore C. Sorensen, *Kennedy* (New York: Harper and Row, 1965).

25. See Peggy Noonan, *What I Saw at the Revolution: A Political Life in the Reagan Era* (New York: Ivy Books, 1990).

26. Einhorn, "Ghostwriting," 127–30.

27. See Wynton C. Hall, "The Invention of 'Quantifiably Safe Rhetoric': Richard Wirthlin and Ronald Reagan's Instrumental Use of Public Opinion Research in Presidential Discourse," *Western Journal of Communication* 66 (2002): 319–46.

28. Dick Morris, *Behind the Oval Office: Getting Reelected against All Odds* (Los Angeles: Renaissance Books, 1999).

29. For a review of the literature and a discussion of the debate surrounding these issues, see J. Michael Hogan et al., "Report of the National Task Force on the Presidency and Public Opinion," in *The Prospect of Presidential Rhetoric*, ed. and James Arnt Aune and Martin J. Medhurst (College Station: Texas A&M University Press, 2007).

30. Noonan, *What I Saw at the Revolution*, 73.

31. Einhorn, "Ghostwriting," 135–40.

32. Qtd. in Fiorina, *Culture War?* ix.

33. Charles W. Lomas, *The Agitator in American Society* (Englewood Cliffs, NJ: Prentice Hall, 1968), 18.

34. Qtd. in T. Harry Williams, *Huey Long* (New York: Knopf, 1969), 411.

35. Reinhard H. Luthin, "Some Demagogues in American History," *American Historical Review* 57 (1951): 22, 45.

36. J. Justin Gustainis, "Demagoguery and Political Rhetoric: A Review of the Literature," *Rhetoric Society Quarterly* 20 (1990): 155–61.

ON THE CONSTITUTION

Benjamin Franklin
The Constitutional Convention,
Philadelphia, September 1787

> *The two speeches that follow have similar themes despite the fact that one was given at the very beginning of our development as a nation while the other was delivered over two hundred years later. Both speeches argue that the critical role of citizens in a democracy is to engage in reasoned discourse. Franklin and Clinton urge citizens to set aside their personal goals for the public good. They don't expect everyone to agree and they do expect conflict, but conflict that is resolved through compromise and a willingness to listen to and evaluate fairly the ideas and arguments of others. Both speeches make the case for deliberating in good faith.*

Beginning on May 25 and lasting throughout the hot Philadelphia summer, delegates to a convention called to amend the old form of government, the Articles of Confederation, produced an entirely new constitution for the young country. The debates had been long and arduous: small states and large states wrestled over proportional representation; Northern and Southern states had differing views over counting the slave population; delegates coming from agricultural states saw the world differently from financiers and those who represented merchants' interests. Opinions varied widely on the issues of the power of the central government in relation to the states and the strength of the chief executive. The document that finally emerged, the Constitution of the United States, was the result of careful deliberation that led most of the delegates to approve a document that none found exactly to his liking. Just before the signing, the 81-year-old Benjamin Franklin, aside from George Washington the most distinguished delegate attending the convention, urged all parties to put aside personal and regional interests and join in approving the compromises for the good of the country.

Mr. President:

I confess that there are several parts of this constitution which I do not at present approve, but I am not sure I shall never approve them; for having lived long, I have experienced many instances of being obliged by better information, or fuller consideration, to change opinions even on important subjects, which I once thought right, but found to be otherwise. It is therefore that the older I grow, the more apt I am to doubt my own judgment, and to pay more respect to the judgment of others.

Most men indeed as well as most sects in Religion, think themselves in possession of all truth, and that wherever others differ from them it is so far error. Steele, a Protestant, in a Dedication tells the Pope, that the only difference between our Churches in their opinions of the certainty of their doctrines is, the Church of Rome is infallible and the Church of England is never in the wrong. But though many private persons think almost as highly of their own infallibility as of that of their sect, few express it so naturally as a certain French lady, who in a dispute with her sister, said "I don't know how it happens, Sister but I meet with no body but myself, that's always in the right. "Je ne trouve que moi qui aie toujours raison."

In these sentiments, Sir, I agree to this Constitution with all its faults, if they are such; because I think a general Government necessary for us, and there is no form of Government but what may be a blessing to the people if well administered, and believe farther that this is likely to be well administered for a course of years, and can only end in Despotism, as other forms have done before it, when the people shall become so corrupted as to need despotic Government, being incapable of any other.

I doubt, too, whether any other convention we can obtain, may be able to make a better Constitution. For when you assemble a number of men to have the advantage of their joint wisdom, you inevitably assemble with those men, all their prejudices, their passions, their errors of opinion, their local interests, and their selfish views. From such an assembly can a perfect production be expected? It therefore astonishes me, Sir, to find this system approaching so near to perfection as it does; and I think it will astonish our enemies, who are waiting with confidence to hear that our councils are confounded like those of the Builders of Babel; and that our States are on the point of separation, only to meet hereafter for the purpose of cutting one another's throats.

Thus I consent, Sir, to this Constitution because I expect no better, and because I am not sure, that it is not the best. The opinions I have had of its errors, I sacrifice to the public good. I have never whispered a syllable of them abroad. Within these walls they were born, and here they shall die. If every one of us in returning to our Constituents were to report the objections he has had to it, and endeavor to gain partisans in support of them, we might prevent its being generally received, and thereby lose all the salutary effects and great advantages resulting naturally in our favor among foreign Nations as well as among ourselves, from our real or apparent unanimity.

Much of the strength and efficiency of any Government in procuring and securing happiness to the people, depends, on opinion, on the general opinion of the goodness of the Government, as well as well as of the wisdom and integrity of its Governors. I hope therefore that for our own sakes as a part of the people, and for the sake of posterity, we shall act heartily and unanimously in recommending this Constitution (if approved by Congress and confirmed by the Conventions) wherever our influence may extend, and turn our future thoughts and endeavors to the means of having it well administered.

On the whole, Sir, I can not help expressing a wish that every member of the Convention who may still have objections to it, would with me, on this occasion doubt a little of his own infallibility, and to make manifest our unanimity, put his name to this instrument.

RESPONSIBLE CITIZENSHIP AND COMMON GROUND

President William J. Clinton

Georgetown University, July 6, 1995

After the 1994 elections, the new Congress was under the sway of the new Speaker of the House, Newt Gingrich, a fiercely partisan Republican who was just as fiercely denounced by Democrats. As the Congress moved quickly to pass legislation, Republican leaders seemed to imply that the President was irrelevant. For their part, partisan Democrats disdained Clinton's efforts at accommodation and complained that he didn't put up a determined enough fight against the Republicans. The political atmosphere was becoming increasing combative. It was in this context that Bill Clinton deplored the mean-spirited tone of public discourse and urged "conversation . . . not combat."

Today I want to have more of a conversation than deliver a formal speech about the great debate now raging in our nation, a conversation not so much about *what* we should do, but about *how* we should resolve these great questions, here in Washington and in communities all across our country. I want to talk about the obligation of citizenship imposed on the President and people in power and upon all Americans to find common ground.

Politics has become more and more fractured and pluralized, just like the rest of our lives. It's exciting in some ways. But as we divide into more and more sharply defined organized groups around more and more stratified issues, as we communicate more and more with people in extreme rhetoric through talk radio, mass mailings or sometimes semi-hysterical telephone messages right before elections, or 30-second ads designed far more to inflame than to inform, as we see politicians actually getting language lessons on how to turn their adversaries into aliens, it is difficult to draw the conclusion that our political system is producing the sort of discussion that will give us the kind of results we need.

One great debate we're having, for example, is about the nature and role of government. If we want to maintain a public response, there must be a relentless effort to change but not to eviscerate the government. We have tried weak government, nonexistent government, in a complex industrial society where powerful interests that are driven only by short-term considerations call all the shots. We tried it decades and decades ago. It didn't work out very well. It didn't even produce a very good economic policy. It had to do with the onset of the Depression.

On the other hand, we know that an insensitive, overly bureaucratic, yesterday-oriented, special-interest-dominated government can be just as big a nightmare. We've done what we could to change that. The government has 150,000 fewer people working today than it did when I took office. We've gotten rid of thousands of regulations and hundreds of programs. We've dramatically improved government efficiency. We have a few shining stars like the Small Business Administration, which today has a budget that's 40 percent lower than it was when I took office, that's making twice as many loans, has dramatically increased the loans to women and minorities, has not decreased loans to white males and hasn't made a loan to a single unqualified person.

We can do these things—and it's not an "either/or." You don't have to choose between being personally right and having common goals. The important thing is not whether I'm right or my opponents are—the important thing is *how* we are going to resolve this debate.

I believe—and you've got to decide whether you believe this—that a democracy requires a certain amount of common ground. I don't believe you can solve complex questions like this at the grass-roots level or at the national level or anywhere in between if you have too much extremism of rhetoric and excessive partisanship. Times are changing too fast. We need to keep our eyes open. We need to keep our ears open. We need to be flexible. We need to have new solutions based on old values.

We can't get there unless we can establish some common ground. And that seems to me to impose certain specific responsibilities on citizens and on political leaders.

Let me say what those responsibilities are. They may be painfully self-evident, but I don't think they're irrelevant. Every citizen in this country has got to say, "What do I have to do for myself or my family, or nothing else counts?" The truth is that nobody can repeal the laws of the global economy, and people who don't have a certain level of education and skills are not going to be employable in good jobs with long-term prospects. That's just a fact.

The truth is that if every child in this country had both parents contributing to his or her support and nourishment and emotional stability and education and future, we'd have almost no poor kids, instead of having over 20 percent of our children born in poverty.

The second thing is: More of our citizens have got to say, "What should I do in my community?" You know, it's not just enough to bemoan the rising crime rate or how kids are behaving and whatever—that's just not enough. It is not enough. Not when you have example after example from this LEAP Program, the "I Have a Dream" Program, to the world-famous Habitat for Humanity Program, to all these local initiatives that are now going around the country, revolutionizing slum housing and giving poor, working people decent places to live; to the work of the Catholic social missions in Washington, D.C., and other places.

People have to ask themselves: "What should I be doing through my church or my community organizations?" People who feel very strongly about one of the most contentious issues in our society, abortion, ought to look at the United Pentecostal Church. They'll adopt any child born, no matter what race, no matter how disabled, no matter what their problems are. There is a positive, constructive outlet for people who are worried about every problem in this country if they will go and seek it out. And there is nothing the government can do that will replace that kind of energy.

Are we making good decisions? Do we approach these decisions in the right frame of mind? Do we have enough information? Do we know what we're doing? I can tell you, the American people are hungry for information. When I announced my balanced budget and we put it on the Internet, there were a few hours when we were getting 50,000 requests an hour. The American people want to know these things.

So I say to every citizen, do you have the information you need? Do you ever have a discussion with somebody who is different from you? Not just people who agree with you but somebody who's different. Do you ever listen to one of those radio programs that has the opposite point of view to yours, even if you have to grind your teeth? And what kind of language do you use when you talk to people who are of different political parties with different views? Is it the language of respect or language that sees a suspect? How do you deal with people? This is a huge thing.

Thomas Jefferson said he had no fear of the most extreme views in America being expressed with the greatest passion as long as reason had a chance. Citizens have to give reason a chance.

What do the political leaders have to do? I would argue four things. Number one, we need more conversation and less combat. Number two, when we differ we ought to offer an alternative. Number three, we ought to look relentlessly at the long-term and remind the American people that

HERE CLINTON ARGUES THAT DEMOCRACY THRIVES ON REASONED ARGUMENT AND SHARED VALUES, NOT THE EXCESSES OF PARTISANSHIP.

CLINTON GIVES CONCRETE EXAMPLES OF THE WAYS IN WHICH CIVIC ENGAGEMENT WILL CONTRIBUTE TO THE PUBLIC DIALOGUE IN WAYS THAT IGNORING OR COMPLAINING ABOUT THE STATE OF AFFAIRS CAN NOT.

CLINTON MAKES THE POINT THAT BEING A GOOD CITIZEN MEANS BEING WELL INFORMED AND LISTENING TO THOSE WHO DON'T SHARE YOUR VIEWS.

CLINTON ACKNOWLEDGES THAT HE AND OTHER LEADERS HAVE SPECIAL RESPONSIBILITIES IN ESTABLISHING COMMON GROUND.

the problems we have developed over a long period of years. And, number four, we shouldn't just berate the worst in America, we ought to spend more time celebrating the best.

Those are things that I think I should do and I think every other leader in this country ought to do.

Americans don't want "just say no" politics. If they can get the truth, they'll make the right decision 99 times out of 100. And we have to offer an alternative. And so do they. We all should. When we differ, we should say what we're for, not just what we're against.

Look for the long-term... Our job is not to get reelected, it's to think about the long-term because the problems are long-term problems.

President Havel said in his Harvard commencement speech, "The main task of the present generation of politicians is not to ingratiate themselves with the public through the decisions they take or their smiles on television. Their role is something quite different—to assume their share of responsibility for the long-range prospects of our world, and thus, to set an example for the public in whose sight they work. After all, politics is a matter of serving the community, which means that it is morality in practice."

Maybe the most important thing is, we should not just condemn the worst, we ought to find the best and celebrate it, and then relentlessly promote it as a model to be followed. You know, I kept President Bush's Points of Light Foundation when I became President.

And we recognize those people every year because I believe in that. I always—I thought that was one of the best things he did. But I tried to institutionalize it in many ways. That's what AmeriCorps is all about. The national service program gives young people a chance to earn money for college by working in grass-roots community projects all across the country. I was in Texas the other day walking the streets of an inner city and a girl with a college degree from another state was there working with welfare mothers because she was raised by a welfare mother who taught her to go to school, work hard, and get a college degree, and she did.

We have to find a way to systematically see these things that work sweep across this country with high standards and high expectations and break through all this bureaucracy that keeps people from achieving. We can do that.

Now, I believe, obviously, that my New Covenant approach is better than the Republican Contract approach to deal with the problems of middle class dreams and middle class values. But when I ran for this job I said I wanted to restore the American Dream and to bring the American people together. I have now come to the conclusion, having watched this drama unfold here and all around our country in the last two and a half years, that we cannot do the first unless we can do the second. We can't restore the American Dream unless we can find some way to bring the American people closer together. Therefore, how we resolve these differences is as important as what specific positions we advocate.

I think we have got to move beyond division and resentment to common ground. We've got to go beyond cynicism to a sense of possibility. America is an idea. We're not one race. We're not one ethnic group. We're not one religious group. We do share a common piece of ground here. When you read the Declaration of Independence and the Constitution, and you'll find that this country is an idea. And it is still going now in our 220th year because we all had a sense of possibility. We never thought there was a mountain we couldn't climb, a river we couldn't ford, or a problem we couldn't solve.

We need to respect our differences and hear them, but it means instead of having shrill voices of discord, we need a chorus of harmony. In a chorus of harmony you know there are lots of differences, but you can hear all the voices and we can hear the notes we have in common. And that is important.

And we've got to challenge every American in every sector of our society to do their part. We have to challenge each other in a positive way and hold accountable people who claim to be not responsible for any consequences of their actions that they did not specifically intend—whether it's in government, business, labor, entertainment, the media. None of us can say we're not accountable for our actions because we did not intend those consequences, even though we made some contribution to them.

You know, Oklahoma City took a lot of the meanness out of America. It gave us a chance for more sober reflection. It gave us a chance to come to the same conclusion that Thomas Jefferson did in his first inaugural. Thomas Jefferson was elected the first time by the House of Representatives in a bitterly contested election in the first outbreak of completely excessive partisanship in American history. In that sense, it was a time not unlike this time. And Jefferson said: "Let us unite with our heart and mind. Let us restore to social intercourse that harmony and affection without which liberty and life itself are but dreary things."

In our hour of the greatest peril and the greatest division when we were fighting over the issue which we still have not fully resolved, Abraham Lincoln said, "We are not enemies but friends. We must not be enemies."

My friends, amidst all our differences, let us find a new, common ground.

Thank you very much.

Clinton closes by referring to the bombing of the Murrah Federal Building in Oklahoma City, then quotes from Thomas Jefferson and Abraham Lincoln, reinforcing his theme that the American "idea" stretches from the founding to the present.

CHAPTER 3

Preparing to Speak with Commitment and Confidence

CHAPTER SURVEY

Public Speaking as Civic Engagement

Preparing Yourself to Speak

Speaking with Confidence

CHAPTER OBJECTIVES

After studying this chapter, you should

1. Understand the meaning and importance of collaborative communication.

2. Be able to explain the nature and significance of the speaker-listener partnership.

3. Know the key principles involved in preparing yourself to speak.

4. Understand how to deal with communication apprehension while preparing yourself to speak with confidence.

Public Speaking as Civic Engagement

Preview. *Communication models stress that the aim of communication is to get a response from an audience. As a form of civic engagement, however, public speaking is audience centered and assumes an equal, collaborative partnership between the speaker and listeners. For a speech to be truly successful, the audience as well as the speaker should derive some benefit from the exchange.*

Some view communication as a one-way street. If the speaker gets what he or she is after, according to this view, the speech is effective. But that's only part of the picture. In a democratic society, the true value of a speech must be judged by the outcome for all parties involved in the communication process: the speaker *and* the listeners. In addition, a speech should be judged by its larger contributions to society. Does it contribute something useful to public discussion? Does it help the community resolve important controversies, or does it motivate members of the community to do good things?

To communicate effectively, you must respect your listeners' needs, sensitivities, and rights. You must know something about their predispositions, tastes, prejudices, capabilities, and knowledge. If you hope to get a response from your listeners, you need to consider what characteristics they share as a group and what qualities individual members bring to the public speaking situation. Seeing public speaking as a mutually beneficial experience for both speaker and listener means that taking advantage of an audience—getting them to do something that is harmful to them, buy something that is useless, or act in some destructive way—should never be your goal. Public speaking is a way of promoting the public good, and as such, it must occur within an ethical framework.

The Speaker-Listener Partnership in a Democratic Society

More than 40 years ago, communication scholar David Berlo, in his groundbreaking book *The Process of Communication*, argued that all communication, including public speaking, should be viewed as a process.[1] That process is a two-way, reciprocal exchange in which speaker and listeners exchange messages and negotiate meanings. In other words, the speaker, while primarily a sender, is also a receiver who should make adjustments based on the messages that come back from the audience. Listeners, while primarily receivers, are not passive—they send information about their reactions to the speaker. (See Figure 3.1.)

This view of communication fits well within a broader perspective on public speaking as civic engagement. As a public speaker in a democratic society, your goal should never be to manipulate your audience just to get your way. Rather, your aim should be to join *with* your fellow citizens in deliberating about the best solutions to our common problems. During a question-and-answer period, for example, audience members might ask questions, state their disagreement with the arguments you've advanced, or suggest alternatives to your proposals. As a speaker, you should recognize this exchange as an opportunity to learn more about your audience's concerns and reactions to your speech. It is an opportunity to contemplate new information and/or a new perspective.

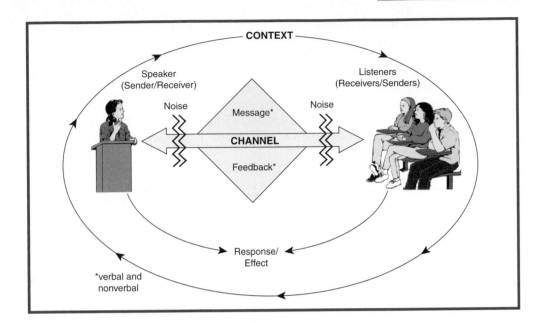

Figure 3.1
An Audience-
Centered
Communication
Model

This process, this exchange, must also be understood in light of the various challenges it presents. For example, sometimes messages flow smoothly. At other times, noise—any kind of interference, from a squeaky microphone to hostile attitudes—may intervene to distort or interrupt the message flow. A hot, stuffy room will offer a greater challenge to a speaker than a comfortable setting. Furthermore, all of us filter messages though our own beliefs and values. We understand, believe, or act based partly on our own experiences, the values we hold, our age or sex, or our cultural practices. These factors will be discussed in detail in Chapter 5, where we consider audience analysis and adaptation. For now, just remember that the situation in which you speak and the backgrounds and interests of the listeners can influence the way a message is received. A good speaker will anticipate the nature and extent of these influences.

This process must also be understood in light of situational factors. Speeches always take place in a context. If you were a student at Tulane University or the University of New Orleans, the economic impact of hurricanes would be an inherently more interesting topic to you than it would be to a student at the University of Wisconsin. If a fellow student was attacked at night while walking across campus, the issue of safety would undoubtedly concern you and other students in your audience. If environmental activists have tried to stop logging in a nearby state forest by spiking trees or sabotaging equipment, you might expect students on your campus to have some understanding of radical environmentalism. In short, *where* and *when* you speak make a big difference. A speech must be designed not only for a specific audience, but also for a particular historical, political, or social context.

Viewing public speaking from a process perspective and as a part of human affairs yields important lessons. Both speakers and listeners must be involved in the communication process, and both also have some larger responsibilities to the community. Speakers have an obligation to address serious matters of public concern, while listeners have the responsibility to listen attentively and to critically yet fairly evaluate the speaker's ideas and proposals. If the speaker has been successful, both the speaker and the listeners will benefit.

Much the same might be said about the speaker-listener relationship. If you give your listeners information they can use, then they will trust you to do the same on other occasions. Public speaking should be viewed as a shared experience with positive results for all parties. As rhetorical scholar William Norwood Brigance once observed, we all have a right to free speech, but we also have a responsibility to deliver *"useful goods to the listener."*[2]

Public speaking, in short, connects the speaker to the audience in an ongoing, collaborative partnership. It is not just something that you do *to an audience*, but rather something that depends on the active participation *of* the audience in the communication process.

Preparing Yourself to Speak

Preview. *The overview of the basic principles of public speaking that follows will be developed in detail throughout the rest of this book. These principles will guide you in selecting a topic, establishing credibility, analyzing the audience, discovering relevant material, fashioning arguments, delivering the speech, and determining the audience response.*

This book is designed to help you acquire the abilities you need to speak. But, first, you must have some *reason* to speak. In your public speaking class, you may speak because you've been given an assignment to do so. In life outside the classroom, however, the need to speak goes deeper than that: it is part of your responsibilities as a citizen in a democracy. Our history is filled with examples of people who felt the need to speak out, including some who risked their lives by doing it. William Lloyd Garrison, the fiery nineteenth-century abolitionist, for example, spent much of his life speaking out against slavery, often facing hostile mobs and threats against his life. More than 30 years before the Civil War, Garrison described his determination to end slavery in the first issue of his famous abolitionist periodical, the *Liberator*: "I am in earnest—I will not equivocate—I will not excuse—I will not retreat a single inch; and I will be heard!"[3] Few of us are as passionately involved with an issue as William Lloyd Garrison. But as citizens in a democracy, we all have the right and the responsibility to speak out on matters of public concern.

Once you have made the decision to speak, you might think that the next step is to write the speech itself. But what about preparing *yourself* to speak? This is not just a trick of words. It is important to think about what *you* need to do to get ready to give a speech. Preparing yourself to speak means, first, making the decision to speak in public, then learning about the principles of effective and ethical public speaking.

Know Yourself

You are your most important asset as a public speaker. Your own beliefs, ability, knowledge, and potential are the foundation on which any speech is built. However, very few people have speeches in their heads just waiting to be delivered. Getting ready to give a speech is hard work; it involves study, research, reflection, and a desire to contribute to the public dialogue. It begins with what you know and care about. In Chapter 6 we examine ways to develop significant topics. The key word here is *significant*. Your speeches ought to be about things that matter, things that are important on your campus or in your community, things that affect you and your audience locally, nationally, or globally.

Many students react initially by thinking they don't have anything to talk about. But you should start with what is important to you—such as how the knowledge you will gain as a student of literature or history, or as a prospective teacher, lawyer, computer specialist, or manager will impact you and others, what problems you and your friends face as you try to get an education, or what the future holds for you and your audience in a globalizing world filled with both opportunities and serious dangers. When you turn your attention to such matters, you will begin to generate ideas for issues that you can address in your speeches.

Although you might first canvass your own interests and concerns in deciding what to talk about, you also need to think about another dimension of yourself: your credibility. We've all heard the expression "If you could only see yourself as others see you." As a speaker, you need to do just that—to try to see yourself as others do. We use the word *ethos*, a concept developed more than 2,000 years ago by the philosopher-rhetorician Aristotle, to describe how an audience perceives the character, intelligence, and motives of a speaker.

Shuttle commander Eileen Collins would likely be very effective when talking about space travel because she is recognized by listeners as an expert.

Some speakers have a well-established ethos related to their expertise or experiences. When Dwight Eisenhower ran for president in 1952 and promised to bring the Korean conflict to an end, people believed him because he had led the allied armies that defeated Nazi Germany in World War II. When space shuttle commander Eileen Collins talks about the hazards of space travel, lay audiences are inclined to accept her views. These advantages of reputation, however, are not afforded to most of us. What you do to prepare for your speech and what you do during the speech itself will most affect how the audience perceives you. Being well prepared lets the audience know that you take them and your topic seriously and are in command of the facts. Being able to communicate directly and easily with your audience reassures them that you can be trusted. In short, in preparing yourself to speak, you must consider how you will be perceived and what you might do to improve your own ethos.

Know Your Audience

Speeches are delivered to specific audiences, and you must consider that audience's needs, interests, beliefs, and knowledge. Your knowledge of yourself must be supplemented by knowledge about those who will be listening to what you have to say.

Knowing your audience makes it possible to adapt to their special needs or interests. If you wished to critique plans to reform Social Security that included allowing contributions to be invested in the stock market, for example, you might emphasize different points, depending on the age of the audience. If talking to people about to retire, you might emphasize the immediate impact of the reform proposal on benefit payments. If, on the other hand, you are talking to an audience of college students, you might emphasize instead the long-term solvency of the system—whether Social Security will still be there for them when they retire in 40 or 50 years. This doesn't mean you would ignore the impact of the plan on age groups not represented in your audience, but only that the emphasis would change as you adapt to your listeners. Further, the United States is a country that encompasses people from many different cultures, not all of whom have the same priorities, the same values, the same experiences, or the same set of normative behaviors.

It would, however, be foolish to assume that everyone belonging to a particular demographic group, such as older people or college students, will react in exactly the same way to a particular message. But it is possible to make limited generalizations about listeners based on their group characteristics. We'll take this up in detail in Chapter 5, but the point made here is that you must consider carefully the characteristics of the audience that are relevant to the speech and take this understanding into account.

Adapting to your audience does not mean pandering to what your listeners might *want* to hear. For example, in 1950 the virulent anticommunism spurred on by the Republican senator from Wisconsin, Joseph McCarthy, led to vicious, unsubstantiated personal attacks on politicians, governmental officials, and other public figures, seriously threatening freedom of speech and political association. Criticism of McCarthyism was, however, considered very dangerous, possibly leading to the destruction of one's career and personal life. It was in such an atmosphere that Senator Margaret Chase Smith of Maine rose in the Senate to introduce "A Declaration of Conscience." "I speak," she told her colleagues, "as a Republican. I speak as a woman. I speak as a United States Senator. I speak as an American." In spite of the risk of political backlash, she asserted that "those of us who shout the loudest about Americanism in making character assassinations are all too frequently those who, by our own words and acts, ignore some of the basic principles of Americanism: The right to criticize; the right to hold unpopular beliefs; the right to protest; the right of independent thought. The exercise of these rights," she went on to say, "should not cost one single American citizen his reputation or his right to a livelihood nor should he be in danger of losing his reputation or livelihood merely because he happens to know someone who holds unpopular beliefs."[4] Senator Smith did not succeed in stopping Senator McCarthy and his supporters from their campaign of character assassination; it wasn't until four years later that the Senate for-

Senator Margaret Chase Smith of Maine reminded her audience of basic values as she stood up against character assassination and reckless charges made by Senator McCarthy and his followers.

mally censured McCarthy. But in making her case, Smith reminded her audience of basic values that they shared and offered hope to those who wished to restore civility in public discourse.

As a speaker, you never set out to deliberately alienate your audience. In speaking your mind, however, you *will* sometimes tell an audience something they don't especially want to hear. It is important, of course, that controversial ideas be presented respectfully and supported with convincing arguments and strong evidence. When presenting unpopular ideas, your persuasive challenge becomes greater.

Know the Situation

The setting for a speech can significantly influence how your audience responds to you. You may be speaking in a comfortable or an uncomfortable physical setting. Or you may be close to your audience or separated from them by an orchestra pit. You may be speaking directly to them or using a microphone. You may be talking to them first thing in the morning or right after lunch. Your audience may be there because they are interested in what you have to say or because their attendance is required. It is to your advantage to know in advance something about the setting in which you will be speaking so that you can anticipate potential problems and capitalize on advantages that the setting might afford.

One of the most dramatic examples of the use of a setting by a speaker occurred shortly after Woodrow Wilson was elected president in 1912. What we now refer to as the State of the Union address was, at the time, called the "annual message." Since Thomas Jefferson's day, this message had been written out by the president, then sent to Congress, where it was read aloud by a clerk. It usually did not generate much excitement. Wilson decided to break with precedent and appear in person before a Joint Session of Congress to deliver his annual message. While some deplored the break with tradition, Wilson's speech captured national attention and generated so much excitement that every president since has followed his example.[5]

In addition to the setting, the temporal context of your speech will influence how it is received. Consider how much the events of September 11, 2001, changed the context for George W. Bush's speeches. After the terrorist attacks, political disagreements suddenly seemed petty, and some even thought it disrespectful or unpatriotic to criticize the commander-in-chief. President Bush's speeches, at least for a time, received more respectful and less partisan attention. By 2004, however, the context had changed again. In the midst of an election year, people again felt free to criticize the president on such issues as the War in Iraq and the state of the economy. In retrospect, some even felt free to criticize how Bush had responded to the terrorist attacks.

On a smaller scale, you face the challenge of recognizing and adapting to what is going on in your listeners' world. Imagine, for example, that you are giving a class presentation on the role of government in student aid. The student newspaper has just published a story detailing proposed cuts in student aid programs. It is likely that your audience will be aware of this turn of events and will be listening for what you have to say about it. Before you speak, you need to be aware of what is happening in your audience's immediate world that is relevant to your topic.

Aim for Audience Response

Think about the model of communication we presented earlier in the chapter. As a speaker, your goal is to bring about some specific response from your audience. This principle is fundamental to everything else you will learn about public speaking, although it does *not* mean that you will resort to any means necessary to get that response. Still, knowing specifically what you want the audience to believe or do will help you determine what ideas to include in your speech. Do you want your audience simply to understand a concept or to take a specific action? For example, if you were giving a speech about UNICEF, you could explain how and why it was founded, and you could describe the Trick-or-Treat for UNICEF and the UNICEF greeting cards programs—this might help listeners gain a better general understanding of what UNICEF is. If, however, you were to ask for donations, listeners would want to know how their money will be spent. In this case, the speaker might spend much less time on such background information and concentrate instead on the disastrous famine and fatal epidemics in Africa, explaining how they affect young people, and describing in specific detail what UNICEF is doing to help hungry, sick, and dying children there.

One of the first things you should do in preparing yourself to speak is to determine your specific purpose as precisely as possible, since it will affect all your other choices. That choice should be realistic, yet that does not mean you should never think big or take a long-range view. Elizabeth Cady Stanton, who organized the first women's rights convention in Seneca Falls, New York, in 1848, advocated that women should have the same rights as men, including the right to vote. It would be another seventy years before women could vote in national elections, but Stanton at least raised the issue in 1848 and started a national debate over women's rights.[6]

There may be times when you will realize that your views are not widely accepted and that it is unrealistic to think you can change people's minds overnight. In such situations, you might aim for a more modest response—to get your listeners to admit that there is some problem that needs to be addressed, or to get them at least thinking about an issue that concerns you.

Discover Relevant Material

As you begin to work on your chosen speech topic, you will most likely have some information already in your head. You may be building on your knowledge of the stock market, the frustrations with the educational system that led your family to choose homeschooling, or your experiences when volunteering at a shelter for battered women. But even with this kind of initial experience or knowledge, you will have to learn a great deal more to become a credible speaker. Once you have decided on the specific purpose for your speech, you will still need to explore other sources of information and supporting material to back up your ideas. It is especially important to realize that in the process of learning more about your topic, you might even change your position. As you do research, you may find that some of your preconceptions are wrong, or at least questionable. As a public speaker you should always be open to the possibility that your own views may change.

It is always important to craft specific purposes that will help you connect directly with your audience and that reflect your own beliefs.

Gathering pertinent information may begin with reading about an issue in a general news magazine, such as *Time* or *Newsweek*. These will give you a broad overview and offer multiple perspectives. You also might search for materials on the World Wide Web, although you need to be careful when using information from the Web. Since it is relatively easy to post material, many websites present highly biased or even totally false information, rumors, or unsubstantiated gossip. Even the names of websites can be misleading. If, for example, you were to come upon www.martinlutherking.org, you might think you have found a good source of biographical information about the famous civil rights leader. In fact, that site is hosted by Stormfront, a white-supremacist hate group. The Southern Poverty Law Center has described this site as "the first major hate site on the Internet . . . created by former Alabama Klan leader Don Black in 1995."[7] Unless you know an online source to be highly reliable (a government bureau, the *New York Times* or the *Wall Street Journal*, or a professional journal, for example), it is best to confirm information through other sources. Of course, you can always find reliable articles, books, and government publications in your campus or local public library. You may also want to interview experts, depending on the subject of your speech. Experts can be quoted as sources, and often they can direct you to additional resources. Whatever sources you use, they must be authoritative, reliable, and correctly cited, as we will discuss further in Chapters 7 and 8. The importance of using reliable sources and the criteria for judging websites are also discussed in that chapter.

Any topic of importance calls for research. All speakers, no matter how knowledgeable, can benefit from learning more about their topic. Obviously some will need to engage in more research than others, but few can talk "off the top of their head" and hope to be effective.

Present a Reasonable Argument

When you have decided what you hope to accomplish in your speech, you will need to set about framing ideas and finding material that supports those ideas and builds a reasonable argument. You should seek information that will connect your topic with your audience's feelings, needs, and emotions—what is often referred to as *pathos*—and that makes logical sense. Remember that public speaking is a process: your purpose may change as you gather more information. As you learn more, however, what you hope to accomplish will become clearer.

Consider the following example of how to develop an argument. You are about to cast a vote in presidential elections for the first time. As you try to sort out the issues and where the candidates stand, you realize that there are a lot of things going on in the campaign that do not really encourage you to think for yourself. You would like to look at the issues and decide which person and/or party would exert the best leadership. There are a lot of irrelevant appeals for your vote, however, and a lot of misinformation has been disseminated. You might wonder, for example, why you should vote for a candidate because you are urged to do so by your favorite rock star or country music singer. You see the media paying a lot of attention to personal accusations and to who is ahead in the latest polls. Much of what the candidates say about education or jobs is ignored by the media. You see 15- or 30-second ads that offer slogans and assertions with nothing to back them up. This state of affairs seems to you to trivialize the electoral process. As you mull this over, you determine that you want to talk about presidential campaigns and, more specifically, about media coverage and advertising in presidential campaigns. Finally, you shape this into a specific purpose—specifically describing the response you want from your audience: *I want my audience to look critically at the political information presented to them during presidential campaigns and to work harder to become well-informed voters.*

You then ask yourself, Why do I believe this is so? Why should my audience agree with me? By answering these questions, you begin to form main ideas—ideas that will be convincing—such as the following:

- Relying on the advice of others can be a mistake.
- Campaign ads may be technically true but still be very misleading.
- Campaign news focuses on polls and other aspects of the "horse race" rather than on the issues.

As you then set about studying the topic, these ideas may be modified or new ones might emerge. As you conduct research, you will find specific data or relevant information that will help you make these ideas more convincing to your audience—that is, you collect supporting material. You might support your first idea, for example, by

- describing the lack of credentials and expertise among well-known celebrities who have been politically active
- quoting from real political experts on the content and effects of political ads and news coverage
- uncovering for your audience the sponsors of campaign material that is hostile to one candidate or the other and explain those sponsors' stake in the election

This process helps you build your argument. As you begin to find relevant material, this material helps you refine your ideas and provides data to make those ideas more convincing to your audience. Consulting several different kinds of sources and always looking for differing perspectives will help you build the strongest, most compelling argument possible.

Give Your Message Structure

Well-organized speeches make it easy for the audience to follow the speaker's argument. They help the audience remember what has been said, and they give clear and convincing reasons for responding as the speaker wishes. If your audience perceives that you are disorganized—if they cannot follow your ideas—they will have trouble accepting your information and arguments and may doubt your credibility.

For an audience to follow your ideas, your speech must have structure. Your ideas must relate to one another logically. Taken together, they must present a coherent case in support of your argument. In an introduction, you will need to plan ways in which you can relate your topic to an audience, gain their attention and interest, and establish your own credibility. Usually you would include a preview and state your thesis. The body of your speech, built around main ideas supported with evidence, needs to be planned carefully. You can help listeners move with you smoothly from one idea to the next by devising strong transitions between your ideas and selecting places where it makes sense to summarize what has already been said. Finally, your conclusion, as the last word to the audience, will repeat the thesis of your speech, summarize your main ideas, and leave listeners with a memorable quotation or anecdote or challenge them to act.

The speech must form a pattern that is clear to your audience. Using a meaningful pattern of organization helps the audience take mental notes as you speak and remember what you have said. Your organizational pattern also makes clear to them how everything in the speech fits together, points to the desired response, and contributes to your ethos as a speaker. The many patterns available to you will be discussed in more detail in Chapter 9, but an example of a short speech that illustrates a simple organizational structure appears in Highlighting Organization.

Highlighting Organization

SPECIFIC PURPOSE: I WANT MY AUDIENCE TO UNDERSTAND HOW THE USE OF EMINENT DOMAIN ILLUSTRATES THE PROBLEM OF CONFLICTING INDIVIDUAL VERSUS COMMUNITY RIGHTS.

THESIS STATEMENT: THE GOVERNMENT'S USE OF EMINENT DOMAIN RAISES QUESTIONS OF HOW TO PROTECT INDIVIDUALS WHILE FURTHERING COMMUNITY GOALS.

INTRODUCTION

I expect that there aren't many people who don't know how the Michael Jackson trial came out a few years ago. And I suppose most of us would be able to identify what celebrity movie stars are getting together or breaking up. If you watch television—the morning shows, the evening news, the talk shows—you learn a lot about famous people and their public and private lives. You also get some information on politics or international affairs. But how about eminent domain? Even if you do understand what it is, do you get very excited about it? Probably not. Well, it interests me because it has affected people close to me, and it could affect you and your family or friends. The use of eminent domain raises serious issues about how individual rights conflict with community goals. Today I'd like to tell you how I got interested in this problem, identify some of the issues it raises, and explain why there are no easy answers.

BODY

I. I became interested in eminent domain for personal reasons.
   A. Eminent domain is the right of public bodies (like the city council) to condemn and buy property, even if the owner does not want to sell. A Supreme Court decision in 2005 gave cities broad power in exercising eminent domain.
   B. My grandparents live on a farm that was far out of the city when they first moved in, but it is now within the city limits and the council is considering allowing the school board to acquire property (including that belonging to my grandparents) to build a new regional school. My grandparents don't want to sell their land and move from the house where they've always lived. So the eminent domain story that took about 30 seconds to report on in the nightly news has a real impact on people that I care about.

Speak Directly with Your Audience

The language you use and the way you use it can have a great impact on your audience and the way it responds to your speech. By choosing language suitable to the audience and the occasion, and by developing a conversational and direct speaking style, you will promote understanding and belief on the part of the audience. Suitable language keeps both the audience and your purpose in mind. It is language that is precise, clear, interesting, and appropriate to the situation in which your speech takes place. Beginning speakers sometimes believe that public speaking always demands formal language, with the result that their speeches sound stiff. We have often had the experience of talking with a student who describes a particular event or personal experience in an animated and natural way, then recounts the same story in a stiff, awkward way when speaking to an audience.

It may help to think of public speaking as an enlarged conversation with friends. Speaking to an audience is not the same as a casual conversation. After all, you plan a speech in advance, and it is more carefully organized than casual remarks. In a speech, you also should avoid language that is *too* informal, such as the "fillers" we sometimes use in casual conversation—the "likes" and the "you knows" that clutter

TRANSITION: SINCE I DO CARE ABOUT MY GRANDPARENTS, I'M CONVINCED THAT THE LAW OF EMINENT DOMAIN IS WRONG, RIGHT? WELL, MAYBE NOT.

II. The use of eminent domain raises serious questions that I have to think about no matter how it affects me personally.
   A. I love my grandparents, but I have to wonder if their property rights outweigh the need to provide up-to-date facilities that will help children learn.
   B. On the other hand, I worry about whether the price paid to owners will fairly compensate them for the loss of their property—including the emotional cost.
   C. I know that this law will affect a lot of people other than my own grandparents, and the law can be used to make way for Wal-Marts or strip malls. I'm not sure that this will always be in the public interest.

III. I raise these questions because this issue illustrates that, even if there are no simple solutions, there are problems that we have to face in our communities.
   A. I'm concerned about individual rights—my grandparents' and all those who might be forced to sell property they want to keep.
   B. But I'm also aware that there are needs that, if met, will produce benefits for the entire community, such as building good public schools.
   C. Basically, I believe that we need to question easy solutions to problems—I recognize that, while the law could be good for a community, it could be abused for the profit of a few and not for the community as a whole.

CONCLUSION

By the way, I don't much care for Michael Jackson, but I do like music. I'm not into celebrity watching, but I enjoy adventure movies and am really into special effects. More important, however, I believe that I—all of us, really—need to understand that news stories that seem to get only passing attention may mean a lot to all of us. I admit that I don't have a lot of answers. But in the days ahead in this course I'll be searching for some answers as I prepare speeches that examine the big question that underlies this issue and a lot of others that face us today. It's a big question that matters a lot to me: How can the rights of the community and the rights of individuals be reconciled? I hope that together, in this class, we might begin to answer it.

everyday speech. Yet the same conversational style that you use in conversing with friends may be perfectly appropriate in most public speaking situations. In addition, many of the personal experiences and stories you talk about with your friends might well work in your speech, depending on the topic.

Of course, all situations do not call for the same style of delivery. Some formal occasions may call for manuscript speaking, in which you read a carefully prepared speech to an audience. At other times you may be asked to speak on the spur of the moment, with little or no time for preparation; this is called impromptu speaking. On rare occasions, you may be expected to memorize your whole speech. Most often, however, you will be speaking extemporaneously—that is, with careful preparation but with minimal notes and a less formal, more direct, and audience-centered delivery.

No matter how much work you put into preparing yourself to speak, what the audience finally sees and hears will determine their response. The best delivery does not call attention to itself; you don't want the audience to pay more attention to *how* you talk than to *what* you have to say. Good delivery, in most of the contexts in which you will speak, should be conversational and relaxed. If the delivery is good, listeners can hear and understand what you say and will not find themselves distracted by mannerisms, inappropriate language, or an overly dramatic presentation.

The overview of principles we have been discussing in this section will help you become an effective speaker and an engaged citizen. While they will be developed in more detail in the rest of this book, they can serve as the foundation on which you can begin now to prepare yourself to speak.

One other important factor needs to be considered at the outset. The prospect of getting up in front of an audience can make anyone nervous. The degree of nervousness may vary from person to person, but feeling apprehensive is normal and to be expected. This is something a speaker must face and deal with; in the next section we offer some practical advice on how to do just that.

Speaking with Confidence

Preview. *Everyone experiences communication apprehension. It order to deal with it, you will need to understand what communication apprehension is, ways to manage it, and how it can benefit you.*

No one was more universally admired than our nation's first president, George Washington. Yet this heroic figure was extremely nervous when delivering his first inaugural address. One senator who attended the ceremony observed that this "great man was agitated and embarrassed more than ever he was by the leveled canon or pointed musket."[8] His successor, the second president of the United States, was also terrified about delivering his inaugural address. After a sleepless night, John Adams felt ill and was afraid he might faint during his speech. He was so scared that he told his wife, Abigail, he was "in great doubt whether to say anything" at all "besides repeating the oath."[9]

Understanding Communication Apprehension

When even national heroes suffer from communication apprehension, it is not surprising that the rest of us become nervous when asked to speak in public. In one famous survey, it was discovered that people are more afraid of public speaking than they are of dying.[10] Comedian Jerry Seinfeld joked about this finding:

> According to most studies, people's number one fear is public speaking. Number two is death. Death is number two. Does that seem right? That means to the average person, if you have to go to a funeral, you're better off in the casket than doing the eulogy.[11]

However humorous this may sound, doctors at the Duke University Medical Center consider public speaking sufficiently stressful that they include it on a list of "mental stress tests." Physicians use these tests in identifying those most at risk for future heart problems.[12] For many people, then, fear of public speaking is no laughing matter.

Whether you call it speech anxiety, stage fright, or communication apprehension, you need to understand this phenomenon for several reasons.[13] Not only can it become a significant barrier to your personal success, but it can rob you of your voice as a citizen. Indeed, if you are afraid to speak out, you *have* no voice in our democratic system.

Communication scholar James McCroskey, who has studied communication apprehension for more than 30 years, defines it as "an individual's level of fear or anxiety associated with either real or anticipated communication with another person or persons."[14] Most of us experience only mild to moderate communication apprehension; but for some, speaking anxiety can be quite severe—so severe, in fact, that they may avoid speaking at all.[15] Fortunately, we can all learn to better manage our fears of public speaking.

Managing Communication Apprehension

Great leaders find ways to overcome their fear of speaking, no matter how momentous the occasion or how high the stakes. In 1859, for example, Abraham Lincoln faced the biggest

Lincoln was such a successful speaker because he prepared carefully and spoke with conviction about matters of significance.

challenge of his young political career when he was invited to speak at the Cooper Union in New York City, a traditional proving ground for presidential candidates. Self-educated and with a "rough and tumble" style,[16] Lincoln was hardly known as a great orator. Yet now his whole future—indeed, the future of the nation—rested on this single speech. A successful speech would make him a leading candidate for president; a poorly received speech could doom his career. As his law partner, William H. Herndon, recalled, "No former effort in the line of speech-making had cost so much time and thought as this one."[17] In the end, that effort paid off. After putting off the sponsors long enough to carefully research and prepare his remarks, Lincoln delivered a tremendously successful speech—a speech that Harold Holtzer aptly characterized in the subtitle of his book *Lincoln at Cooper Union: The Speech That Made Abraham Lincoln President.*

How did Lincoln do it? Part of the answer, of course, lies in the extra time he took to research and prepare his speech. But just as important was his firm conviction that he was *right* in taking the position he took: that the Republican Party should oppose the further spread of slavery in America. In other words, Lincoln was thoroughly prepared and firmly *believed* in what he said, and those are the most critical factors in dealing with communication apprehension.

Sometimes speakers do not seem particularly invested in their topics. Perhaps they view the speech as merely a course requirement or an unpleasant task they must perform for their job. So they select their topic casually, giving very little thought to its importance to them or whether the audience might find it interesting. At other times, speeches fail because of inadequate preparation. Inadequate preparation may stem from a failure to find and focus the speech topic early enough, or it could involve problems finding relevant or current information. Still other speakers suffer from a general tendency to procrastinate, putting things off until the last minute. Either of these problems—lack of commitment to your topic or inadequate preparation—may contribute to communication apprehension. This leads to the two most fundamental principles in combating communication apprehension: addressing substantive issues to which you are committed and being well prepared.

Address Substantive Issues to Which You Are Committed

A genuine commitment to your topic can help you overcome the anxiety you might have about speaking in public, since you are more likely to speak with confidence if you are addressing a topic that really matters to you and your audience. As part of a community forum on health care, for example, an ER doctor might speak out on the critical importance of finding ways to care for the uninsured—perhaps arguing that universal health insurance would assure that everyone who needed health care would get it and thereby create a more humane society. A student whose roommate has been attacked outside the school library might make an impassioned plea to a group of campus administrators, asking them to fund more lighting, police patrols, and campus escort services. Because of the commitment of these speakers to their topics, any communication apprehension they may have felt at the start of their speeches would likely fade as they focused on their arguments and the importance of persuading their audiences.

Be Well Prepared

There is no better psychological defense for dealing with communication apprehension than honestly being able to say to yourself that you *are* well prepared. You have selected a topic of interest and value to you as well as your audience. You have done your homework, perhaps even conducting an audience survey. You have devoted significant time and effort to gathering information and to broadening your understanding of the subject. You have carefully organized your speech into a clear, coherent, and unified whole. You have practiced by going over your speech—aloud—several times, timing yourself and fine-tuning your ideas. You have asked friends for feedback. You feel confident that there is very little more you could have done to prepare for your speech.

Reminding yourself of your careful preparation can be reassuring and even liberating as you grapple with feelings of anxiety. Your delivery will reflect your careful preparation, and the audience will sense that you have worked hard out of respect for their time and attention. Also remember that your audience *shares* responsibility for the success of your speech. You have a right to expect that. Just as you have prepared well and met your responsibilities as a speaker, your audience, too, has a responsibility to listen carefully and constructively to what you have to say.

Focus on Civic Engagement

Speaking with Conviction

A small community in southern Indiana had begun to experience a serious problem with homelessness and poverty. Although there were three shelters for housing the poor at night, during the day they wandered the streets—trying to find jobs, food, and warmth.

One woman, Shirley, had once worked as the director of a day shelter for the poor when she resided in Arizona. Now she was convinced that such a shelter was urgently needed in her new hometown in Indiana. She decided to approach the administrative board of the church to which she belonged. Her goal was to persuade them to donate some space in the church's basement, which had a kitchen and restroom facilities, as well as a large dining hall, so that a day center for the poor could be established. As she prepared her presentation, she pored over figures on homelessness and poverty—studying the trends and looking specifically at how and why the problem had grown in Indiana. She reflected on her experiences in Arizona and reread some books on poverty by such experts as Ruby Payne and David Shipler. She carefully organized her information and arguments and practiced her speech aloud several times. She also knew her audience very well, since they were all fellow members of her church. As a result, she was able to anticipate some of the kinds of questions and concerns they would likely bring to the meeting. How could the church afford it? What would be the risks? How might other citizens in the community react? How would this endeavor affect church membership?

On the day of her speech, Shirley felt somewhat anxious. She knew she had to wait until the board's evening meeting to make her presentation, and the day ahead loomed long. She maintained her routine that day—eating lightly but well, taking a brisk walk, and then practicing her speech one last time. She reminded herself of the gravity of the problem. She thought about the human beings she had encountered—each with a different story—those striving to get their lives back on track following a period of incarceration, the women who were escaping abusive relationships, the mentally ill who needed structure and regular medication, and the children who had never known a home. Armed with her convictions, her painstaking preparation, and her deep desire to connect with the audience, Shirley walked toward the boardroom, determined to speak as convincingly as possible on behalf of those who could not speak for themselves. She still felt some level of anxiety, but she felt a far greater desire to share her convictions and ideas—and hopefully, ultimately, to move her audience to action.

Source: Personal narrative of one volunteer, Bloomington, IN, June 2005. For sources that informed this woman's knowledge about poverty, see Ruby K. Payne, *A Framework for Understanding Poverty* (Highlands, TX: Aha! Process, 1996), and David K. Shipler, *The Working Poor: Invisible in America* (New York: Alfred A. Knopf, 2004).

The best way to reduce speech anxiety is to address topics that genuinely concern you and to be well prepared for your presentation. In addition, you might employ a variety of other strategies for managing communication apprehension. As you give more speeches, you will no doubt find strategies that work especially well for you. For now, however, let's examine some of the specific strategies that experienced speakers have found helpful for dealing with communication apprehension.[18]

Develop a Positive Attitude

What do you think of when you imagine yourself making a speech? Do you picture yourself stumbling over your own words, dropping your note cards, or freezing as you attempt to respond to a listener's question? Research has clearly shown that people with high speech anxiety tend to have more negative thoughts before the delivery of a speech than people who are comfortable speaking.[19] It stands to reason, then, that developing more positive thoughts may help in managing or reducing anxiety.

When you dread making a speech, when you think of it as a burden or something that you "have to do" for a class or for your job, you are more likely to develop severe communication apprehension. What if you learned to view it differently: as an opportunity to change minds, to share what you know, or to make a real difference in the community where you live? The principle here is simple: speakers who anticipate success rather than failure suffer less apprehension about speaking.

Practice Your Speech

Ideally, you should practice over a period of a few days, not a few hours. It is always a mistake to put off rehearsing your speech until the last minute. Prepare your speech well in advance and give yourself ample time to practice. You may be able to get a friend or a few friends to listen to your speech. Practicing early and often is the key here. No one can tell you exactly how many times to practice or what techniques might work best for you. As you give more speeches over time, you will learn what approach works best for you.

Anticipate the Speech Situation

There are times in life when it is nice to be surprised, but before or during a public speech is not one of them. As we have said before, effective speakers know their audiences. Gathering information about your audience and the speaking situation *before* you speak helps you to focus on the audience right from the start. Whenever someone invites you to make a speech, try to obtain as much information as you can. If you are addressing a community group that holds regular meetings, ask permission to attend one of those meetings, to get a feel for the room and the typical audience, and to note how they interact. If the organization has a website, you will also want to visit that, and you can ask the person who invited you to speak to respond to a few questions before the speech. Figure 3.2 provides some basic questions that you might want to ask about your audience and the speech situation.

Practice Active Listening

Active listening can be a powerful tool for managing communication apprehension.[20] Rarely do you make a speech under circumstances in which you arrive, immediately stand up and talk, then quickly depart. More likely, your speech will be part of a longer program, meeting, or banquet, and others will speak before you. Listening closely to those speakers will draw your attention away from your own anxieties and may even give you ideas about last-minute changes to your own speech. In your speech class, you will be listening to other speakers before and after you make your speech. Instead of fretting over your notes, strive to listen carefully to those who speak before you. You might learn something, and

---

Figure 3.2

Collecting Information about Your Audience

Some Guiding Questions

1. Does the audience expect me to address a particular aspect of a topic?

2. What is the audience composition?
   a. audience size
   b. age (range and distribution)
   c. sex (mixed or largely same sex)
   d. race/ethnicity
   e. values (religious, political, economic, etc.)

3. What is the speaking environment like?
   a. size and arrangement of room
   b. availability of podium, blackboard, flip chart, microphone
   c. degree of formality
   d. location of building (do I need to get a map?)
   e. parking issues?

4. Are there any time constraints?

5. Will questions follow the speech?

6. What is the anticipated length of the entire meeting? When should I arrive?

7. Can I arrive early or check out the setting ahead of time?

---

hopefully you also will find yourself a bit more relaxed when it is your turn to speak. In addition, you might be able to reference something in another speech that complements your own in some way.

Exercise for Relaxation

If you feel tense and nervous before you speak, you can do some simple physical exercises to relax. One excellent way to relax is by breathing deeply. Deep breathing allows you to take in a large quantity of air, giving you a good supply of oxygen and the potential for enhanced vocal control. You will also want to breathe deeply before you speak and to continue breathing deeply and regularly *while* you are delivering your speech for better vocal support and ongoing relaxation.

Isometric exercise, which involves tensing and then relaxing specific muscles, can also be a useful relaxation technique. Try clenching and unclenching your fists, pressing your legs firmly together and then relaxing them, or squeezing the palms of your hands together as if you were trying to flatten a piece of clay. Alternatively, you can push your leg, arm, or foot against some immovable object, such as a wall, table, or even the podium. After you have pressed firmly, release the muscle, relaxing it as completely as possible. These isometric exercises are subtle—you can do them without being noticed, even in the middle of your speech. They can also be used before and after the speech.

Finally, performing *aerobic exercise* before your speech can help reduce communication apprehension. Aerobic exercise, such as walking, jogging, running, or swimming, is not only good for your cardiovascular system and general well-being, it also helps reduce tension and brings communication apprehension into a manageable range.

Acknowledge the Potential Benefits of Moderate Communication Apprehension

Some people have serious problems with speech anxiety and are virtually incapacitated by their fear of speaking.[21] Most of us, however, can learn to manage our speech anxiety, and experienced speakers even find ways to channel their nervous energy in positive directions. They are able to do this, in part, because they have developed specific techniques that work for them. Some speakers, for example, begin their speaking day with meditation, prayer, a two-mile run, or a quiet walk. Everyone will benefit from getting a good night's rest and eating a light, nutritious meal before making a speech. Wearing comfortable clothes that make you feel good about yourself also will contribute to a positive mental attitude. What is important is to learn what helps *you* most in managing your feelings of anxiety.

In most speaking situations, however, a little anxiety can be a *good* thing, for that little spurt of adrenaline can energize your mind and body, keep you alert, and perhaps even contribute to a more dynamic delivery. As you gain experience as a public speaker, you will become more comfortable and confident standing up before an audience, and eventually you might even come to anticipate and welcome that adrenaline rush that we all feel when we speak in public.

Maintain a Sense of Perspective

No matter how well you prepare for any speech, bad things can happen. The microphone may fail. The person who introduces you may mispronounce your name. You may get something under your contact lens, or drop one of your note cards. By preparing well you can reduce the likelihood that something will go wrong, but you will never have complete control over the situation. Do not be intimidated by that fact. The unpredictability is what makes public speaking both challenging and interesting.

You need to maintain a sense of perspective. Prepare well, do your best, be flexible, and pay attention to feedback from your listeners. Even if, in your judgment, your entire speech goes badly—that is, *you* feel disappointed in your performance—you should view it as a learning experience. Concentrate on what you learned. Get ready to have another go at it. No matter how brilliantly or poorly you think you performed, it is important that you view each speech as a chance for personal growth. If you are truly committed to speaking out, you *will* have other opportunities to speak on the subject.

By employing any or all of these strategies for managing communication apprehension, you *can* become a more poised and confident speaker.

Summary

- A speech is successful only if it benefits both speaker and audience.
- You must have a collaborative approach to preparing and presenting your speech.
- Basic principles for preparing yourself to speak:
  - examining your own knowledge, ability, beliefs, and potential (*know yourself*)
  - discovering the audience's needs, interests, beliefs, and knowledge (*know your audience*)
  - understanding how the setting and other outside factors may influence the speech (*know the situation*)
  - devising a clear purpose that reflects the desired response (*aim for audience response*)
  - exploring potential sources of information (*discover relevant material*)
  - using language and delivering the speech in a manner suitable to the audience and the occasion (*speak directly with your audience*)
  - practicing a well-prepared presentation frequently enough to give yourself oral command of the speech (*develop confidence through practice*)
- Understanding what communication apprehension is and how to manage it will help you gain confidence.
  - Communication apprehension is a normal reaction to speaking in public.
  - Commitment to your topic and thorough preparation are fundamental to building your confidence.
  - A positive attitude, practice, anticipating the situation, listening actively, exercise, acknowledging the benefits of apprehension, and maintaining a sense of perspective will also help you overcome apprehension.

QUESTIONS FOR REVIEW AND REFLECTION

1. Explain the significance of the speaker-listener partnership. Offer one example of how the speaker and listener are mutually interdependent.
2. What are the most important things you will do to prepare yourself to speak responsibly and ethically?
3. In your view, are any of these elements more important than others? Why or why not?
4. As you learn to give speeches, what do you imagine will be your greatest challenge? How might you begin to grapple with it?
5. What is meant by communication apprehension?
6. This book suggests that commitment and preparation are the most significant factors in reducing communication apprehension. Do you agree or disagree? Explain.

ENDNOTES

1. The process perspective is widely referred to as the "transactional perspective." David K. Berlo, *The Process of Communication* (New York: Holt, Rinehart and Winston, 1960).

2. William Norwood Brigance, *Speech: Its Techniques and Disciplines in a Free Society*, 2nd ed. (New York: Appleton-Century-Crofts, 1961), 20.

3. Cited by James Brewer Stewart, *Wendell Phillips: Liberty's Hero* (Baton Rouge: Louisiana State University Press, 1986), 46.

4. Margaret Chase Smith, "A Declaration of Conscience," Washington, D.C., June 1, 1950, http://gos.sbc.edu/s/chasesmith.html (accessed August 29, 2005).

5. Robert Alexander Kraig, *Woodrow Wilson and the Lost World of the Oratorical Statesman* (College Station: Texas A&M University Press, 2004), 131–33.

6. See Karlyn Kohrs Campbell, *Man Cannot Speak for Her: A Critical Study of Early Feminist Rhetoric*, 2 vols. (New York: Praeger, 1989), 51–58.

7. T. K. Kim, "Electronic Storm: Stormfront Grows a Thriving Neo-Nazi Community, 2005, www.splcenter.org/intel/intelreport/article.jsp?aid=551 (accessed August 20, 2005).

8. James Thomas Flexner, *George Washington and the New Nation: 1783–1793.* (Boston: Little, Brown, 1969), 188.

9. Letter to Abigail Adams, March 17, 1797, in *John Adams: A Biography in His Own Words*, ed. James Bishop Peabody (New York: Harper and Row, 1973), 359.

10. "What Are Americans Afraid Of?" *Bruskin Report* 53 (July 1973): 8.

11. Jerry Seinfeld, *SeinLanguage* (New York: Bantam Books, 1993), 120.

12. "Mental Stress Test Indicator of Future Cardiac Problems," *Bloomington Herald-Times* (June 5, 1996), A6.

13. A great deal of research during the past three decades has focused on communication apprehension. See, for example, James C. McCroskey, "Oral Communication Apprehension: A Summary of Recent Theory and Research," *Human Communication Research* 4 (1977): 78–96. More recent articles include Ralph R. Behnke and Chris R. Sawyer, "Milestones of Anticipatory Public Speaking Anxiety," *Communication Education* 48 (1999): 165–72; Behnke and Sawyer, "Public Speaking Anxiety as a Function of Sensitization and Habituation Processes," *Communication Education* 53 (2004): 164–73; Amy M. Bippus and John A. Daly, "What Do People Think Causes Stage Fright? Naive Attributions about the Reasons for Public Speaking Anxiety," *Communication Education* 48 (1999): 63–72; and Rebecca B. Rubin, Alan M. Rubin, and Felecia F. Jordan, "Effects of Instruction on Communication Apprehension and Communication Competence," *Communication Education* 46 (1997): 104–114.

14. McCroskey, "Oral Communication Apprehension," 78.

15. James C. McCroskey and Virginia P. Richmond, "The Impact of Communication Apprehension on Individuals in Organizations," *Communication Quarterly* 27 (1979): 55–61.

16. Waldo W. Braden, *Abraham Lincoln: Public Speaker.* (Baton Rouge: Louisiana State University Press, 1988), 3.

17. Harold Holtzer, *Lincoln at Cooper Union: The Speech That Made Abraham Lincoln President* (New York: Simon and Schuster, 2004), 28.

18. See Joe Ayres, "Speech Preparation Processes and Speech Apprehension," *Communication Education* 45 (October 1996): 228–35, for an interesting study on how the nature of speaking preparation is vital to the quality of the speech as delivered.

19. Joe Ayres and Tim Hopf, *Coping with Speech Anxiety* (Norwood, NJ: Ablex, 1993), 5–21.

20. In the interpersonal communication and interviewing literature, *active listening* refers to a listening approach in which the listener participates in the conversation by summarizing, paraphrasing, and occasionally interrupting the speaker with clarifying, supportive questions. We are using the term in a different way here.

21. James McCroskey, *An Introduction to Rhetorical Communication*, 7th ed. (Boston: Allyn and Bacon, 1997), 39–61.

The Listener as Engaged Citizen

CHAPTER SURVEY

The Importance of Effective Listening

Understanding Barriers to Good Listening

Guidelines for Improving Listening

CHAPTER OBJECTIVES

After studying this chapter, you should be able to

1. Describe the importance of effective listening to the speaker-listener partnership.

2. Embrace your responsibility to listen critically yet respectfully.

3. Identify the major barriers to effective listening.

4. List strategies for improving listening.

5. Apply the listening guidelines in this chapter.

Listening is an important communication skill—in the classroom, in professional life, and in our communities. Listening well—attentively, actively, respectfully, and critically—is not only an essential part of effective communication but an important responsibility of citizenship in a democracy. As we listen closely to others, we become better informed, more discerning consumers of information and ideas, and more likely to make judicious decisions about who to vote for, what causes to invest in, and what courses of action to pursue.

Studies show that we typically spend about 70 percent of our waking hours in some form of communication: participating in meetings, exchanging ideas and information, attending presentations, talking on the telephone, and so forth.[1] Much of this communication involves listening. Research shows that the average person on the job spends 40 percent of his or her time listening.[2] Author Stephen Covey argues that effective listening is one of the "seven habits of highly effective people."[3] We value those who are good listeners, and we aspire to be good listeners ourselves.

Regardless of your chosen occupation, listening well will be important to you. The intelligent doctor listens carefully to patients' complaints before diagnosing the causes of their illnesses. Investment counselors listen to clients' financial goals before suggesting an investment strategy. Assembly-line workers and construction workers must listen to and master safety regulations if the company or crew is to remain accident-free. When members of the Academy of Certified Managers were asked to list the skills most crucial for managerial ability, "active listening" was rated number one.[4] In another survey, 170 businesspeople were asked to describe the communication skills that they considered most important; listening was ranked first.[5] Across diverse occupations and situations, good listening is crucial.

Yet effective listening can be a challenge. Listening expert Ralph Nichols estimates that the average white-collar worker listens at about a 25 percent efficiency level.[6] This figure is supported by research showing that immediately following a 10-minute presentation, a typical audience member recalls only about 50 percent of the information presented. After 48 hours, the recall level drops to 25 percent. In addition, poor listeners often *overestimate* how effectively they listen, assuming that poor listening is someone else's problem.[7]

Of course, statistics on listening can be misleading. Sometimes we may listen carefully because we know we are going to be evaluated on how much we can remember. Or it may be that a speaker's information is especially relevant or important to us. On other occasions, we might barely pay attention at all because we do not agree with the speaker or because we are distracted by other thoughts. Whatever the circumstances, we can all benefit from becoming better listeners.

The Importance of Effective Listening

Preview. *Listening may serve varied purposes—ranging from enjoyment to the critical assessment of ideas. When we listen well, we are likely to experience an array of positive outcomes, including more knowledge and awareness of the world around us, a clearer sense of ourselves, improved* *interpersonal relationships, and enhanced public speaking skills. In addition, our willingness to listen is crucial to our role as engaged citizens in a deliberative democracy. As citizens, we have an obligation to listen to our fellow citizens and to give their views respectful consideration.*

Diverse Purposes for Listening

Depending on our goals, we may approach listening differently in differing situations.[8] Sometimes we may *listen for appreciation*, like when we listen to good music. We do not expect to be analytical or critical; we are simply listening for enjoyment. On other occasions, we may engage in *empathic listening*, or listening just to show our support and understanding for the feelings of another person. By doing so, we may hope to strengthen our relationships with other people or demonstrate that we care. By making everybody feel valued, listening empathically may also build greater cohesiveness within civic and professional groups as we deliberate with others in an effort to make decisions for the common good, as we will discuss at greater length in Chapter 18.

As citizens, we are most likely to engage in *informational* or *critical* listening. In informational listening, we seek to take in information accurately and expand our knowledge about a subject. We want to understand and remember what we are hearing. In critical listening, we aim to *analyze* and *evaluate* the speaker's message. In both kinds of listening, we make judgments about the message's relevance, accuracy, timeliness, and validity. In many instances, informational listening serves as the foundation for critical listening.

Positive Outcomes of Effective Listening

There are plenty of good reasons for becoming a better listener. Whether in the classroom, the workplace, or the community, we can all benefit from enhanced listening skills. Indeed, our society as a whole benefits when respectful, careful listening becomes a shared goal.[9] Here are just a few of the reasons we should all work to become better listeners:

- *Listening carefully helps us become better informed.* Many of our ideas come from listening to others. Whether in a group discussion, watching the news, or listening to a formal speech, we can learn information that will help us to make more informed decisions. Students who are good listeners usually perform better in their classes. Citizens who are good listeners become better informed voters and tend to participate more actively in civic life.
- *Listening to others is part of our responsibility as citizens in a democratic society.* When we listen closely to others' arguments, we show respect for their views and are able to respond more thoughtfully and intelligently to their concerns. By listening carefully as others share their ideas, we also communicate a desire for dialogue and collaboration. By behaving respectfully and attentively while others are speaking, we demonstrate our faith in the democratic process and our conviction that the views of every citizen deserve a respectful hearing.

- *Listening gives us a clearer sense of who we are and what we value.* Listening allows us to compare and contrast our own beliefs and values with those of our fellow citizens. By listening to others, we get a better sense of who we are and how our views compare to those of others. If we find that our views are out of the mainstream, we may want to ask, What influences or life experiences have shaped my unique perspective on this issue? Why might others have developed a different point of view?

- *Good listening helps us develop and sustain better interpersonal relationships.* Listening to others shows that we care about them. Furthermore, good listening is often reciprocated. When we show that we care by listening carefully to the problems, perspectives, and ideas of others, they are more likely to give our views full and fair consideration.

- *By becoming better listeners, we can become better speakers.* By carefully observing how others communicate, we can learn to communicate more effectively ourselves. Moreover, listening carefully helps us to better understand our audiences. By listening to what our audience members say about themselves—by interacting with them before or after a speech—we can gather information that will help us frame our own ideas and arguments.

In short, effective listening is an ethical responsibility for citizens in a democratic society and a practical imperative for anyone who hopes to communicate effectively.

Preparing for Critical Listening: Our Responsibility as Citizens

If we are to listen effectively, we must possess sufficient information and knowledge to comprehend and assess the ideas of others. If we plan to attend a community forum on affordable housing, for example, we should know something about the topic in advance. How expensive is housing in our community? How does our community compare with surrounding communities? If our housing has become unaffordable, what might account for that? What options do we have for creating more affordable housing? And who needs to be involved in addressing the problem? These are only a few of the questions that the thoughtful citizen might ask even *before* attending the presentation.

In your public speaking classroom, you may not know much about some of the topics your classmates will address. Even so, you should make an effort to be as well informed as possible. Get into the habit of reading a good newspaper and watching the news on television. Make an effort to talk about important public issues with your classmates. By becoming more knowledgeable about a wide array of local, state, national, and international issues, you can become a better listener and a more informed citizen.

As we become better informed, we are better able to distinguish fact from opinion, assess the quality of a speaker's ideas and arguments, and pose thoughtful questions. Listeners who are uninformed have difficulty distinguishing sound and useful information from that which is irrelevant, invalid, or unreliable. Sometimes poorly prepared listeners may not be able to grasp a speaker's arguments at all.

Focus on Civic Engagement

National Issues Forums

- National Issues Forums (NIF) is a nonpartisan, nation-wide network of locally sponsored public forums for the consideration of public policy issues. It is rooted in the simple notion that people need to come together to reason and talk—to deliberate about common problems.
- By offering citizens a framework for discussing important issues, the NIF network helps the public take an active role in democratic deliberation. As the NIF website notes, "The health of this nation's democratic enterprise depends on the active participation of responsible citizens who take the initiative to deliberate about public policy choices and to set the public agenda."
- NIF forums are organized by civic, service, and religious organizations, as well as by libraries, colleges, universities and high schools, literacy and leadership programs, prisons, labor unions, and senior groups. NIF participants vary in age, race, ethnicity, gender, economic status, and geographic location.

- These forums focus on such issues as health care, immigration, Social Security, or ethnic and racial tensions—at a national, state, or community level. The forums provide a way for people of diverse backgrounds and experiences to seek a shared understanding of the problem and to search for common ground for action. Citizens who have attended a forum often decide to continue to work together to try to solve problems in their community.
- Forums range from large group meetings similar to New England town hall meetings to study circles held in public places or in people's homes on an ongoing basis. In each context, citizens are called on to function as *good critical listeners* and as active participants and problem solvers.
- To read more about NIF, turn to Chapter 18 of this book.

Source: National Issues Forums Institute, "The Forums," www.nifi.org (accessed February 22, 2007).[10]

Clearly, there are both personal advantages and social benefits to good listening. When *both* speakers and listeners are well informed, democratic deliberation works better and the prospects for constructive problem solving are enhanced.

Understanding Barriers to Good Listening

Preview. *Most of us underestimate the kind of effort it takes to learn to listen effectively. We want to listen well but often fail to recognize the barriers we will first need to conquer if we hope to become better listeners. Most of these barriers are grounded in our attitudes toward listening, as well as in certain deficiencies in our listening behaviors. As we learn to identify and understand the sorts of barriers that impede our ability to listen effectively, we will soon recognize that good listening is an acquired skill that requires us to work at it and to want to do it well.*

Passivity Syndrome

Many of us are vaguely aware of the statistics on poor listening and simply assume that they do not apply to us. We think listening is easy, at least for us! After all, we have been listening since we were born, and as students we listen for many hours every day. Perhaps we feel that we already know all there is to know about listening. Or maybe we feel that the primary responsibility for good listening rests with the speakers. As long as we show up, we believe that we have done our part, and it is up to speakers to *make* us want to listen. If they fail, too bad for them, we think.

This line of reasoning—known as the *passivity syndrome*—is rooted in a view of public speaking as a one-way street. In this view, the speaker acts and the listener re-acts; the speaker controls the communication process, while the listener remains es-sentially passive. At a conscious level, few of us want to admit that, as listeners, we are overly compliant, easily manipulated, or uninvolved in the communication process. Yet that is precisely what happens if we allow ourselves to be passive listen-ers. If we listen passively, we give up control.

The principle that *should* influence our approach to listening is simple: *listening is an active process*.[11] Anyone can make us hear just by turning up the volume. But no one can make us *listen*. We have to *want* to listen, and we have to be willing to work at it. Speakers can encourage us to listen by presenting their ideas effectively. But if they do not—even if their performance is disappointing in some way—that does not let us off the hook. No speaker is perfect; nearly all will need our goodwill and understanding. When we attend a public talk, we hope to learn, to grow, to be stimulated, or perhaps to discover new strategies for solving a community problem. If we come away empty-handed, we must share some of the blame. If we hope to derive some benefit from listening, we must do our part. We must get actively in-volved in the communication process by listening more carefully. Later in the chap-ter, we will offer tips for active listening.

Mental Games

Listening is more difficult when a speaker challenges our existing beliefs or values. We prefer listening to speakers whose thinking is consistent with our own.[12] If a speaker challenges our worldview, we may try to avoid listening altogether, or we might be jarred into defensiveness. It can be difficult to listen to a speaker who ar-gues that Wal-Mart exploits its female employees if you are a male who has worked for Wal-Mart for 10 years and been promoted three times. It can be painful to listen to a speaker discuss the dangers of smoking when you happen to be a smoker. Or perhaps you feel so passionately about the issue of gay marriage that you immedi-ately turn off anybody who disagrees with your views.

Sometimes we try simply to escape from distressing communication. We have seen members of our family turn off the TV in disgust when a politician they dislike begins to speak. Others may utter disrespectful comments or otherwise "talk over" a speaker they do not want to hear. When attending a live speaking event, we rarely encounter such avoidance behaviors. Few listeners get up and walk out during a speech. Even so, it is always possible to turn off a speaker mentally. We may *pretend to listen* to a speaker without really listening at all. Instead, we may fantasize, reflect on our day, or think about our plans for later that evening. When we do this, we are not only being disrespectful to the speaker, but also robbing ourselves of an oppor-tunity to learn something new.

When we become defensive about something we hear, we typically engage in *mental argument*, silently refuting the ideas of a speaker. This is somewhat preferable to pretending to listen, but mental argument is not the same as listening. As we concentrate on refuting the speaker's ideas, we often lose the thread of the argument. When the speech is finished, we may not recall the speaker's whole argument because we were too busy coming up with our own reservations and counterarguments. It is hardly surprising, then, that during question-and-answer periods, those who oppose the speaker's position often ask questions that reveal that they were not listening closely to the speech.

As effective and ethical listeners, we should allow the speaker to state his or her whole case before we jump to conclusions. We should give every speaker a fair and honest hearing before raising whatever objections we might have. It is perfectly acceptable to disagree with points made by the speaker, but during the speech itself, you might just note those points and continue listening. After you have listened to the speaker's whole argument, you are in a better position to respond to those ideas with which you disagree.

Unfortunately, too many public advocates today simply refuse to listen to others. On political talk shows, for example, we frequently see speakers interrupt or shout down those who disagree with their views, apparently thinking this is how you "win" a debate. While these sorts of "debates" might be entertaining to some, they are hardly models of effective and constructive listening. If democratic deliberation is to lead to sound collective decisions, we need to listen to one another without becoming combative or defensive. Genuine listening means listening actively with an open mind and respect for those who might disagree with us.[13]

Public discussion of important issues undermines democratic deliberation when speakers are combative and confrontational, hoping to score points rather than listen to different points of view.

Short Attention Span

How long can you listen to someone speak without starting to fidget or finding that your mind is wandering? Can you easily listen to your professor's 45-minute lecture and remain focused and attentive throughout? If you can, you have an excellent attention span.

Modern technology has changed significantly the way we listen and what we listen to. In the age of television and the Internet, senatorial candidates could not even imagine arranging a series of seven political debates each lasting about three hours. Yet that is exactly what happened in the mid-nineteenth century in the famous Lincoln-Douglas debates in Illinois. A "sustained public discussion" of serious issues could hardly take place in an era of 30-second commercials and call-in talk radio.[14] Audiences of those days, used to long speeches, sermons, and lectures, were prepared to listen to Daniel Webster speak for hours when commemorating the landing of the Pilgrims or debating on the floor of the Senate.[15] The most famous preacher of the nineteenth century, Henry Ward Beecher, delivered countless provocative and entertaining lectures that drew huge crowds for a lively evening's entertainment.[16]

Many people believe that our attention spans are simply not as good, or as long, as they used to be. Today we seem to demand shorter messages—preferably no more than a few minutes. Teaching experts increasingly advise instructors to break their lectures into small chunks, with no chunk lasting longer than 15 minutes.[17] Some believe that television viewing has contributed to our shorter attention spans, making us used to watching only 10 or 12 minutes of a program at a time, with periodic breaks for commercials or station identification.[18] In addition, television, radio, video games, instant messaging, text messaging, and newspapers give us much of our information in sound bites or sidebars, which provide the gist of a story without requiring that we read or listen to the whole thing.

In the classroom, a teacher might accommodate our short attention span by stopping for discussion, showing video clips, interjecting exercises, and so forth. But other speaking contexts do not lend themselves as readily to these kinds of variations. In fact, in most public speaking situations (other than workshops), we would be surprised if the speaker stopped from time to time to ask *us* questions or broke us into small groups for discussion.

As listeners, we need to work at overcoming our own short attention spans. We need to accept that we will sometimes be expected to listen to talks that run 30 minutes or more, and that we need to work at remaining attentive in such situations. If we find ourselves fading in and out during a speaker's presentation, we need to catch ourselves, refocus our attention, and practice some of the techniques of active listening discussed later in this chapter. Good listening does not just happen. We must make an effort to overcome our short attention spans and become better listeners.

Stereotyping

In the early twenty-first century, we thankfully have left behind many sexual, cultural, racial, religious, and ethnic stereotypes. Even so, not all stereotypes have disappeared. Although racial and gender stereotypes have been discredited in recent years, even well-meaning people sometimes still stereotype older people, people with disabilities, or people from particular geographical regions. In many situations, stereotypes remain a barrier to good listening.

The *American Heritage Dictionary* defines *stereotype* as "a conventional, formulaic, and oversimplified conception or image."[19] When stereotyping, we observe a few members of a particular category (African American males, Asians, older women, homosexuals, and so forth) and draw conclusions about all others belonging to that same category. The difference between making a generalization about a group of individuals and stereotyping them is that, in stereotyping, we leave no room for individual differences. We believe that every individual will fit the same mental mold we have created for the group.

Stereotyping represents a problem in many realms of life, and it can greatly interfere with our ability to listen effectively. When we are preoccupied with a speaker's gender, race, age, or other characteristic, we are focusing on dimensions that may have little or nothing to do with his or her message. We are not focusing fully on the information and ideas being communicated. For example, suppose you were listening to a speech that addressed the problem of the glass ceiling, an invisible barrier of prejudices and discrimination that allegedly hampers women's ability to rise to the top of business and professional organizations. Would you listen to that speech carefully and with an open mind if you already had stereotyped the speaker as a radical feminist?

In examining our tendency to stereotype speakers, it may be useful to think about how you would feel if others stereotyped you. Consider making a list of your personal qualities, organizational memberships, and other characteristics. What sorts of stereotypes might be associated with those traits? More important, in what ways do you believe you *differ* from those stereotypes? Suppose, for example, that you are a white male, a former Boy Scout, a Baptist, and lifelong resident of Alabama. Does that mean you fit the stereotype of a "southern redneck"? Of course not. Perhaps you drive a Volvo, not a pickup truck, and you might even be a liberal Democrat. Whether it is true or not that *most* people with all those characteristics are very conservative, *you* are unique and you undoubtedly resent being stereotyped.

As you think through this kind of exercise, you might reach some of these conclusions:

- Stereotypes abound.
- It is easier to think about stereotyping someone else than it is to examine how others might stereotype you.
- Stereotypes may have some truth in them. You probably found that you have some things in common with your own stereotype.
- Yet stereotypes are ultimately misleading. Everybody is unique, and nobody perfectly fits the stereotypes that might be applied to them.

In all communication situations—and public speaking is no exception—we need to respect each person's uniqueness as an individual.

Distractions

Sometimes, as audience members, we behave as if we can listen only when the situation enables us to do so. We may become very sensitive to distractions in our surroundings, using them as easy excuses for our inability to listen. Perhaps we sit in the last row and then complain about the speaker's voice not carrying very well. We sit by an open window and find ourselves distracted by a lawn mower, the shouts of children, or the beauty of the view. We tell ourselves that we had every intention of listening carefully but fell prey to distractions.

There are times, of course, when speeches are presented in listener-challenging contexts. Distractions are often real as well as imagined. In most instances, however, we can overcome situational distractions if we really want to. For instance, one of the authors of this book attended the March on Washington in August of 1963, at which Dr. Martin Luther King Jr. delivered his famous "I Have a Dream" speech. King delivered his speech out of doors—standing in front of the Lincoln Memorial and addressing a crowd of thousands. For any member of the audience, the distractions were numerous—sweltering heat, an emotion-charged crowd, and, for most, an enormous distance between speaker and audience. And yet, somehow, everyone listened with rapt attention and departed with a renewed commitment to fighting for the civil rights of African Americans. Clearly, few speaking situations are so dramatic. Yet, in most public speaking situations, we have the ability to receive the speaker's message *if* we are determined and motivated to exert the effort required to listen.

Dr. Martin Luther King Jr.'s message was so powerful that he was able to engage his audience despite the enormous crowd and the great distance between him and his listeners.

In addition to the surrounding environment, sometimes speakers themselves present distractions. Most public speakers are "on display" before they make their speeches. Seated at a luncheon table or on a speaker's platform, they can be viewed before speaking to the audience. Thus there is plenty of time for listeners to look at them and form early, and often stereotypic, impressions. For example, what might you conclude about a speaker who wore sandals and casual attire at an event where everyone else was dressed formally? How might a speaker's weight, build, or personal attractiveness influence the way you react? Obviously, to some extent, your reaction will depend on the topic and situation. For example, the speaker's weight might seem irrelevant if he is speaking about adult literacy, but might well seem pertinent if he is addressing the growth in diabetes among young people in the United States.

The point is that some of our initial impressions of a speaker will be based, in part, on physical appearance. In fact, without additional information, appearance may be the sole basis for early judgments. Some listeners, for example, might be impressed by a speaker who appears in an Armani suit; they might be disposed to suspend their critical faculties and more readily believe what he says because he looks successful. If we allow ourselves to react only on the basis of first impressions, however, we have judged the speaker as if he were a contestant in a beauty pageant. What is critical, then, is to recognize the first impression for what it is—and not allow ourselves to hear only what reinforces our first impression.[20]

It is true, of course, that nonverbal communication is important and cannot be ignored, but what we observe with the eyes is only the beginning. We are there to listen to the speaker's complete presentation. Only then, on the basis of what we have heard and observed, can we formulate a reasonable reaction to the speaker and the speech.

Finally, we need to recognize that any *visual image* can distract us from listening closely. In some cases, it may function as a powerful means of influencing our ideas and behavior, even when we are unaware of its impact. Even the colors used in some visuals can elicit feelings or establish moods—and may influence the way we feel about what the speaking is saying.[21] Communication scholar Kathleen Jamieson has argued that, especially in *persuasive* messages, images often *substitute* for words.[22] As discerning audience members, we must view visual messages as critically as we do verbal ones by asking ourselves how and in what ways what we are *seeing* is influencing our thoughts, feelings, and beliefs. We will return to the subject of visual images in later chapters of the book.

Let us now lay out the tactics, most of which we have alluded to in the preceding pages, that should form your listening strategy. Effective listening provides the foundation for critical and constructive thinking and offers a powerful tool for anyone who wishes to function as a contributing member of a democratic society in which citizens exchange information and ideas and gather together to deliberate about ideas and courses of action.

Guidelines for Improving Listening

Preview. *Effective listening requires considerable effort. As we learn to improve our listening skills, we will need to consider our attitudes and predispositions, as well as to discover some of the things we can do to enhance our listening effectiveness. Above all, we must remind ourselves of our ethical responsibility as citizens to approach listening seriously, to listen to others attentively, critically, and constructively, and to practice listening as an active process.*

In an ideal world, all speakers would be well prepared, articulate, and knowledgeable. They would strive to involve us intellectually and emotionally. They would deliver their presentations with passion and conviction and present clear and forceful arguments. These speakers would attempt to minimize distractions in the speaking environment. They would structure their remarks logically and emphasize main ideas through their delivery, language, and strategic use of presentational aids. They also would listen carefully when audience members questioned them after the speech, and they would respond thoughtfully and respectfully to each question. We know, of course, that not all speakers meet this ideal. Because of this, your listening responsibilities may be demanding.

The guidelines that follow will assist you in listening more effectively. Some suggest specific behaviors you might employ, while others focus more on the expectations and attitudes you have as a listener.

Remind Yourself of the Importance of Listening

Because good listening does require effort, it is easy to become lazy and minimize its importance. So we need to remind ourselves often of how much we can learn, how we can benefit, by becoming better listeners. If you catch your mind wandering while listening to a speech, remind yourself that every speech has the potential to broaden your knowledge, teach you something important, or give you insight into people you also might address someday.

Remember Your Responsibilities as a Citizen

The U.S. Constitution protects the right to free speech, but the rights and responsibilities of citizenship extend to listening as well as speaking. If democracy is to work, those who ultimately make the decisions—the citizens themselves—must be critical, well-informed listeners. Effective listening is a must for all who aspire to be responsible and engaged citizens.

Come Prepared to Listen

Before you attend a speech or community forum, read as widely as you can on the topic. Formulate some tentative questions. Give some thought to your existing views and any potential biases you might have toward the speaker or topic. Commit yourself to listening with an open mind. Recognize the effort it will take to listen carefully and promise yourself that you will make that effort.

Be Prepared to Offer Feedback

In many speaking contexts, you will have the opportunity to ask questions and offer feedback after the speaker is finished talking. Knowing that you may be expected to react verbally to a speaker may help you focus your attention and listen especially carefully and critically. You will want to ask intelligent, appropriately challenging questions and offer relevant comments that engage the substance of the speech.

Making comments may be optional in many speech settings, whereas in the classroom your instructor may ask that you regularly participate in offering feedback. You may be invited to offer commentary on overall strengths and areas for improvement, or to focus on a particular aspect of a speech (such as the speaker's organization or use of supporting material). You may give your feedback orally or in writing. Some of your feedback may take the form of questions.

Understand Your Identity as a Listener

We all bring who we are to a speaking situation, and who we are colors how we interact with the speaker. Your background, your personal characteristics, and the roles you play in life all contribute to certain predispositions and biases that will influence your reactions. No one can totally eliminate bias, but you can, through self-analysis, discover some of the forces at work in your own listening behaviors. Only by understanding yourself—what you bring to a speaking situation and who you are in relation to it—will you be able to listen in a critical yet fair-minded way.

Listen with a Purpose

The speaker has a purpose in getting up to talk. As audience members we, too, should have a purpose, whether that purpose is to learn, to evaluate, or to prepare for our own speech before the same audience. Do you want simply to gather information from a speech? Or do you hope to better understand an opposing point of view? Are you interested in relating the topic to your life or in preparing to speak out yourself on the topic the speaker is addressing?

Your purposes may evolve as you listen. You may begin by thinking you just want information about a problem, such as global warming. But as you listen, you may decide that you want to get involved—to do something to address the problem. By listening purposefully, you can respond to the message on your own terms while still maintaining a healthy respect for the speaker's position and purpose.

Understand the Setting

As we pointed out earlier, the setting of a speech imposes certain restrictions and expectations on a speaker. A political candidate who has bought 30 seconds of radio time is very limited in what he or she can say. A speaker at an outdoor rally works under different constraints than one in a lecture hall. When you listen, be aware of how the particular setting may be affecting the speaker's efforts. If the speaker is given little time to speak, for instance, you might be less critical if his or her main points are not fully developed. If the speaker had no time to prepare, you might forgive minor errors or an unpolished style. The circumstances under which the speaker prepared and delivered the speech should always be taken into account.

Understand the Speaker's Intended Audience

Sometimes a speaker's words are aimed at more than one audience. For example, at a large state university, a series of racially motivated incidents resulted in several protest demonstrations and rallies on campus. At these rallies, students spoke to an audience of their peers—their immediate audience. However, these students also knew that members of the press were present. Through the press, the speakers hoped to send powerful persuasive messages to a wider target audience composed of campus and community leaders. The types of appeals speakers make, or the types of arguments they advance, may be puzzling to listeners who do not consider who the target audience might be.

Consider the Speaker's Purpose

Understanding what the speaker hopes to accomplish by speaking helps prepare us to listen effectively. Speakers do not always make their purpose clear, and some may even intend to mislead the audience. If a speech is poorly structured, it may not be easy to identify the speaker's goal or purpose. Knowing something about the setting, the speaker, and the general nature of the topic may help us identify the speaker's goal. Once we think we discern the basic purpose of the speech, we are in a better position to make judgments about the quality of the ideas and information that follow.

Examine the Impact of the Speaker's Ethos

Often when we listen to a speech, we have some initial perceptions of the speaker's credibility. If we are not careful or honest with ourselves, we may find ourselves overly influenced by *who* the person is rather than *what* he or she says in the speech.

If, for example, you do not like the speaker, then face up to that fact. You might be tempted to fool yourself into believing that your personal opinion of the speaker has nothing to do with your assessment of her or his ideas or proposals. But the real reason might be that you just do not *want* to believe anything this speaker has to say. If the matter is not of vital importance, it may not matter whether your judgment is biased by your opinion of the speaker. But suppose it is a very serious matter that could affect your health or the well-being of your community. Separating your personal views of the speaker from your assessment of his or her message *can* be vital.

Practice Critical Listening as an Active Process

All the guidelines we have presented point to the hard work that must go into preparing yourself to listen effectively. Here are some more specific and practical tactics that you can use to become a more active and engaged listener.

Communicate Nonverbally

Use nonverbal communication to show the speaker that you are actively listening. When you look at the speaker or lean forward as he or she talks, you show your interest in the speech. You also might smile or nod your head in agreement to show the speaker that you are interested, engaged, or even endorse his or her point of view. Through your facial expressions, you can show interest, agreement, confusion, or concern.[23]

As we have stressed throughout the book, effective communication demands thoughtful, responsible, and active participation by all those involved in the process. When you are an audience member, you have a *responsibility* to offer feedback. After the speech, you can ask questions and make comments, but during the speech, most of your feedback will be nonverbal. Based on your nonverbal feedback, the speaker can begin to process your concerns, clarify points of confusion, or anticipate issues or objections that you might raise after the speech. In this way, you, as a listener, can show that you are an active partner in the communication process.

Take Notes as You Listen

Effective note taking can help you follow the speech and record critical information and ideas for later use.[24] Because note taking requires some action on your part, it also can help keep you engaged in active listening.[25] In taking notes, you might want to jot down a basic outline of the speech, as well as specific questions you will want to ask after the speech. You also might make note of any statistics, facts, or particular examples that you want to remember.

Note taking consumes time, so it can slow down our thinking and help synchronize our listening with the tempo of the speaker.[26] Finally, note taking helps us to remember. Our notes can help us ask better questions after the speech and provide us with some recorded information to ponder and possibly use in the future. Some researchers argue it is not until *after* a speech is over that we typically process most of the ideas and information we gathered while listening to a speech. A good set of notes can help in this process of analysis and reflection.[27] See *Highlighting Note Taking* for advice on the note-taking process.

Critically Examine the Speaker's Evidence and Reasoning

As you identify main ideas, pay attention to the evidence used by the speaker to support them. Did the speaker cite credible sources of information? Were the statistics used clear and meaningful in helping you grasp the magnitude of the problem? To what extent did the speaker rely on personal experiences and opinions? If the speaker leaned heavily on personal knowledge, were you convinced that his or her personal experiences were sufficient proof?

You will also want to consider the quality of the speaker's reasoning. Did the speaker seem to jump to any conclusions too quickly, or with too little evidence? Did he draw any analogies or comparisons that did not make sense? Did she attack someone personally instead of responding to his arguments? Were you urged to do something simply because a lot of other people are doing it? There may be plenty of good reasons for doing as the speaker suggests, but you need to focus on the reasoning in the speech itself. Can it withstand critical scrutiny? In taking notes, jot down important evidence and arguments that you want to remember, and make note of any information or conclusions that you doubt or have questions about.

As a good critical thinker, you need to be reflective—about your own ideas and those of others. When a speaker advances a claim, you will want to ask, What is he basing this on? Why should I believe what she is saying? You will also want to distinguish fact from opinion and unstated assumptions from explicit claims. If you are well versed on the speaker's topic (and if you are well-read in general), you will be better able to think critically about how problems are framed and whether proposed solutions appear sound.

Minimize Distractions

Do all you can to stay focused on the speech. Note taking will help. Arriving early enough to get a good seat will help, too. Beyond that, put distractions—whether they come from the speaker or from the environment—in perspective. Remind yourself that your purpose is *not* to offer a critique of the speaker's gestures or hairstyle,

Highlighting Note Taking

Suggested Strategies

- *Write down those ideas and key points that are most important*. You cannot write down everything the speaker says. Focus instead on jotting down the thesis and main ideas.
- *Use keywords to record main ideas*. Attempting to write down every word is inefficient and likely impossible. Routinely omit articles (*the, a, an*), many prepositions, and some verbs. Just make sure you retain the *sense* of the idea being communicated.
- *Abbreviate and use symbols whenever possible*. Some of these may be unique to you. So long as you understand them, you will be fine. For example, in taking notes on a speech on civic engagement, you might simply write *CE* in place of *civic engagement. Comm. App.* might be used to designate *communication apprehension*. More common symbols might include *w* (for *with*), *w/o* (for *without*), = (for *equal*), > (for *more than*), or < (for *less than*).

- *Organize your notes as a rough outline of the speech*. Once you have identified major headings, you can also record substantiating material. Leave room in the left-hand margin and between items in your notes so that you can add things as the speaker presents them. Do not concern yourself with following a formal outlining format. Nearly any format will work, so long as you are able to distinguish main ideas from supporting (subordinate) material.
- *Use your notes to help you evaluate the speech*. Your notes serve two purposes: recording the speaker's ideas and assessing their quality. If you feel a main idea is unsubstantiated, you might write (perhaps in a different color) "weak support" next to the recorded idea. If you think of a specific question or concern, jot that down as well.

nor to do an acoustical analysis of the room. Rather, you are there to listen to the ideas and information advanced by the speaker and to react as intelligently and thoughtfully as you can.

Remember, too, that the visual aspects of a speaker's presentation may influence the way you react. Good listeners will not allow visual images to distract them from the substance of the speaker's message. Some scholars believe that the ability to think discerningly about visual images, or so-called *visual literacy*, is a crucial skill in an increasingly visual world.[28]

Suspend Judgment

You should suspend final judgment of a speech until the speaker is finished. As you listen, you will, of course, make some judgments. You will react to each argument; you will scrutinize every piece of evidence. You will assess and reassess your perceptions of the speaker's ethos—his or her intentions, integrity, and competence— throughout the speech. As a responsible listener, however, you should strive for some measure of open-mindedness. Give the speaker a fair and reasonable chance.

Whatever your ultimate reaction to the speech, it should come at the *end* of the speaker's presentation. Better yet, wait until you have heard the speaker's responses to questions from the audience to decide what you think of the speech. Sometimes speakers will clarify and illuminate their main ideas as they address

Highlighting Visual Literacy

The Visual Dimension of Critical Listening

Veteran journalist Gregg Hoffmann argues that visual literacy is a "requirement for clear thinking in the 21st century." He writes:

- Two photos likely will become symbolic of the Elian Gonzalez story. First is the Associated Press photo of the federal marshal, dressed in riot gear, demanding the boy be turned over. Second is the photo of the boy smiling at his father. People on both sides of the issue point to those photos to support their contentions.
- You can see "what happened" in a photo or video, most people would argue. "A picture is worth a thousand words" is a widely accepted statement. Words are another person's abstraction of what happened, but a photo captures reality.
- But does it? Is a photo or video simply a mirror of reality, or is it a product of certain premises and processes that then make it susceptible to manipulation? A photo or video grows from a point of view,

or a set of premises. The photographer will select his subject, to a large degree, to represent his or her own world view, or to meet what is perceived as the preferences of an audience.

- A skilled photographer can capture your senses and then craft the photo or video in such a way that you leap from that sensory level to very high, abstract levels. So, we see the photo of the federal officer and Elian and jump to thoughts of fascism. Or, we see the smiling Elian with his father and jump to thoughts of family values.
- In political propaganda, advertising, and other media products, we see these attempts to foster such leaps all the time. The intent is *not* to have the viewer logically analyze or think about the image. The intent is to capture the viewer's senses and then evoke certain emotions and thoughts.

Source: Reprinted with permission of the author and the Institute of General Semantics, publishers of *ETC: A Review of General Semantics.*

These two very different photos illustrating the Elian Gonzalez story evoke contrasting reactions. They show how visual depiction can neutralize logical analysis to capture viewers' emotions and direct their thoughts.

listener concerns. The point here is simple: we owe it to every speaker to suspend judgment until we have heard everything he or she has to say about their topic. A good critical listener is interested in hearing the most complete version of the speaker's arguments and ideas before rendering a judgment.

Summary

- Effective listening is an important communication skill. In virtually any context—whether professional, personal, or community life—listening well is highly valued. Yet as we know from research into the listening process, most of us usually do not listen very carefully.

- We listen for a variety of purposes, some of which do not require much effort.
  - Sometimes we listen merely for pleasure or to provide a "sympathetic ear" to a friend or co-worker.
  - Other times, we may seek information or need to critically evaluate the ideas of others. In those situations, it is important that we listen carefully and actively evaluate the information that we hear.

- There are many excellent reasons for striving to improve our listening skills.
  - By becoming better listeners, we can improve our interpersonal relationships and become better speakers ourselves.
  - We also can learn a great deal from listening well, both about the world and about ourselves.
  - As citizens in a democracy, we need to listen carefully to others as we participate in public deliberations. By listening actively and respectfully to our fellow citizens, we can improve the quality of discussion and debate in our democratic society and, hopefully, make better collective decisions.

- Unfortunately, there are many barriers to effective listening.
  - Some listeners take a passive approach to listening, assuming that it is the speaker's job to keep them interested.
  - Other listeners may try to avoid information that they do not want to hear, or perhaps they become defensive when a speaker disagrees with their existing opinions.
  - Short attention spans contribute to poor listening, and stereotypes can still get in the way of effective listening.
  - A variety of physical and mental distractions can prevent us from listening effectively. Perhaps we are distracted by the speaker's appearance or mannerisms, or by other visual images he or she presents during the talk. Whatever the distraction, it detracts from our ability to really "hear" what is said.

- With genuine desire and effort, all of us can learn to become better, more engaged listeners.

- Remind yourself of the importance of listening, especially in a democratic society, and come prepared to listen without allowing your own personal biases to get in the way.

- Try to understand the speaker's purposes and how the setting or intended audience might have affected the speaker and the speech.

- Actively and critically *engage* the speaker, giving nonverbal feedback and perhaps taking notes while evaluating the ideas and evidence presented in the speech itself.

QUESTIONS FOR REVIEW AND REFLECTION

1. Why is listening effectively so important?
2. How would you describe the listening effectiveness of most people?
3. Describe several different reasons for listening. Give an example of each.
4. How is effective listening related to good citizenship in a democratic society?
5. What positive outcomes are associated with listening effectively?
6. Describe your understanding of critical listening as an *active* process.
7. Name at least five problems that audience members often experience when listening to a public speech. Give an example of each.
8. List at least five ways that audience members can improve their listening skills. Why is each potentially valuable?
9. In your past experiences as a listener (in your classroom, profession, or community), what have been your greatest listening challenges? Provide examples of each. What have you done to address these challenges?

ENDNOTES

1. See, as examples, Deborah Borisoff and M. Purdy, eds., *Listening in Everyday Life: A Personal and Professional Approach*, 2nd ed. (Lanham, MD: University Press of America, 1997); Ralph G. Nichols and L. A. Stephens, "Listening to People," *Harvard Business Review* 60 (1990): 95–102; and David A. Whetten and Kim S. Cameron, *Developing Management Skills*, 6th ed. (Englewood Cliffs, NJ: Prentice Hall, 2005).

2. Madelyn Burley-Allen, "Listen Up," *HR Magazine* (November 2001): 115–20.

3. Stephen Covey, *The Seven Habits of Highly Effective People* (New York: Golden Books, 1997).

4. Samuel L. Becker and L. R. Ekdom, "The Forgotten Basic Skill: Oral Communication," *Association for Communication Bulletin* 33 (1980): 12–15. In addition, an excellent source of information about all aspects of listening is the website of the International Listening Association, http://www.listen.org.

5. Vincent DiSalvo, et al., "Communication Skills Needed by Persons in Business Organizations," *Communication Education* 25 (1976): 269–75.

6. Ralph G. Nichols, "Listening Is a 10-Part Skill," *Nation's Business* 75 (1987): 40; and Andrew D. Wolvin and Carolyn Gwynn Coakley, *Listening*, 5th ed. (Dubuque, IA: Brown and Benchmark, 1996).

7. Ralph G. Nichols, *Are You Listening?* (New York: McGraw-Hill, 1957), 1–17; and Judi Brownell, *Listening: Attitudes, Principles, and Skills*, 3rd ed. (Boston: Allyn and Bacon, 2006).

8. The International Listening Association defines *listening* as "the process of receiving, constructing meaning from, and responding to spoken and/or nonverbal messages."

9. See, for example, Kay Lindahl, *The Sacred Art of Listening* (Woodstock, VT: Skylight Paths Publishing, 2002).

10. Periodically, the NIF publishes reports to communicate the outcomes of forums held across the nation about a particular issue. These publications can be accessed online at www.nifi.org/reports/issues. Sample report titles include "Examining Health Care: What's the Public Prescription?" "Terrorism: What Do We Do Now?" "Protecting Our Rights: What Goes on the Internet," "The National Piggybank: Does Our Retirement System Need Fixing?" "Mission Uncertain: Reassessing America's Global Role," and "The Troubled American Family: Which Way Out of the Storm?"

11. Carl Rogers and Richard E. Farson, "Active Listening," in *Organizational Communication*, 2nd ed., ed. Stewart D. Ferguson and Sherry Ferguson (New Brunswick, NJ: Transaction, 1988), 319–34.

12. Joseph A. DeVito, *The Interpersonal Communication Book*, 10th ed. (Boston: Allyn and Bacon, 2003), 64.

13. For an extended discussion of these ideas, see Susan Bickford, *Listening, Conflict, and Citizenship: Dissonance Democracy* (Ithaca, NY: Cornell University Press, 1996).

14. David Zarefsky, *Lincoln Douglas and Slavery: In the Crucible of Public Debate* (Chicago: University of Chicago Press, 1990), x.

15. See Robert Remini, *Daniel Webster: The Man and His Time* (New York: Norton, 1997), esp. chap. 9, "The Plymouth Oration," 178–87, and chap. 18, "The Webster-Hayne Debate," 312–31.

16. Debby Applegate, *The Most Famous Man in America: The Biography of Henry Ward Beecher* (New York: Doubleday, 2006), esp. 215–19.

17. Joan Middendorf and Alan Kalish, "The Change-up in Lectures," *National Teaching and Learning Forum* 5, no. 2 (1996): 1–4.

18. Peter J. Frederick, "The Lively Lecture: 8 Variations," *College Teaching* 34, no. 2 (1986): 43–50; and A. H. Johnstone and F. Percival, "Attention Breaks in Lectures," *Education in Chemistry* 13 (1976): 49–50.

19. *The American Heritage College Dictionary*, 3rd ed., s.v. "Stereotype."

20. We know, for example, that interviewers form early impressions of job applicants, rarely changing their judgments after the first five minutes. See Robert W. Eder and Michael M. Harris, eds., *The Employment Interview Handbook* (Thousand Oaks, CA: Sage Publications, 1999); and Charles B. Stewart and William B. Cash, *Interviewing: Principles and Practices*, 10th ed. (New York: McGraw-Hill, 2003).

21. Paul Martin Lester, *Visual Communication: Images with Messages* (Belmont, CA: Wadsworth Thomson Learning, 2000).

22. Kathleen H. Jamieson, *Eloquence in an Electronic Age* (New York: Oxford University Press, 1988), 114–17.

23. Carol A. Carrier, "Note-Taking Research: Implications for the Classroom," *Journal of Instructional Development* 6, no. 3 (1983): 19–25; and J. L. Fisher and M. B. Harris,

"Effect of Note Taking and Review on Recall," *Journal of Educational Psychology* 65 (1973): 321–25.

24. Burley-Allen, 119–20; and "Train Yourself in the Art of Listening," *Positive Leadership* (July 1998): 10.

25. See K. Bosworth and J. Hamilton, eds., *Critical Thinking and Collaborative Learning: Underlying Processes and Effective Techniques* (San Francisco: Jossey-Bass, 1994); Rosabeth Moss Kanter, "Thinking across Boundaries," *Harvard Business Review* 68 (1990), editor's foreword; and S. Holly Stocking et al., *More Quick Hits: Successful Strategies by Award-Winning Teachers* (Bloomington: Indiana University Press, 1998), esp. "Fostering Critical and Creative Thinking," 40–57.

26. Research has shown that the average speaker talks at a rate of 125 words per minute, while listeners' minds race along at speeds of 400 to 500 words a minute. See Patricia Hayes Andrews and John E. Baird Jr., *Communication for Business and the Professions*, 8th ed. (Long Grove, IL: Waveland Press, 2005), 238–42; and Wolvin and Coakley, 12–15.

27. For recent insights on note taking, see Rick Reis, Stanford Learning Lab, "Tomorrow's Professor Message #163: More Effective Note-Taking Strategies," http://sll.stanford.edu/projects/newtomprof/postings/163.html (accessed August 20, 2006); and Rick Reis, Stanford Learning Lab, "Tomorrow's Professor Message #172: Teaching Students to Take Better Notes," http://sll.stanford.edu/projects/tomprof/newtomprof/postings/172.html (August 23, 2006).

28. B. A. Chauvin, "Visual or Media Literacy?" *Journal of Media Literacy* 23, no. 2 (2003): 119–28.

Diverse Audiences in a Democratic Society

CHAPTER OBJECTIVES

After studying this chapter, you should be able to

1. Explain the role and significance of audience analysis in public speaking.

2. Describe the diverse audience characteristics you need to consider as you prepare to deliver a speech.

3. Identify individual and communal needs and values.

4. Know how to gather information about an audience, including conducting an audience survey.

5. Implement strategies for ongoing adaptation.

Audiences often come together to hear about matters of importance to them. Issues can be relevant in different ways to different people. A new interstate highway, for example, might not come anywhere near a person's property, but that person may still be vitally interested because of the possible impact on the environment or the economy. And, as you can imagine, environmentalists, real estate developers, and union members will likely have conflicting goals and opinions. Sometimes audiences will come to learn more about an issue, while others will show up because they already have strong views. On some occasions an audience might be required to attend, as in your public speaking class or in a job training program, for example.

As a responsible speaker and listener, you try to recognize your own biases and understand how they can affect your judgment. It is not easy to keep an open mind, but that is what citizenship is about—reaching informed decisions. Your audience will be diverse, but you will still want to consider what characteristics they share as a group and what qualities they, as individuals, bring with them to the speaking situation. Based on the information you uncover, you will then be challenged to adapt what you have to say to your listeners.

Understanding Diverse Audiences

Preview. *As a responsible speaker, you must think carefully and analytically about your listeners. You and the members of your audience form a partnership, since the goal of public speaking is mutual betterment. Knowing something about your listeners will affect how you frame and deliver your message, and there are a number of factors to consider when analyzing your audience.*

Table 5.1

AUDIENCE DEMOGRAPHICS

- Age
- Gender
- Race and ethnicity
- Intercultural factors
- Religion
- Geographic/cultural environment
- Education
- Occupation or profession
- Economic status

Many elements go into making people who they are. These factors can influence the way people see events and how important they consider an issue, which in turn can mold their values, determine how attentive they will be to a speech, or suggest whether they will accept or reject change. Table 5.1 lists some audience demographics that every speaker must consider.

Of course, making a comprehensive list of audience characteristics can seem overwhelming, and you can never expect to know everything about your audience. To prepare for a speech, however, you must know as much as you can about your listeners and the ways in which their views might differ from your own.

One thing to keep in mind as we discuss audience characteristics is that these demographics represent *tendencies*, not absolute predictors of behavior. Advertisers, for example, study demographics very carefully and try to promote their products in publications, TV shows, and websites that will reach the particular group they wish to target. This does not mean, of course, that all teenage women read *Seventeen* or that those who do will all respond to a given ad the same way. Nor will every member of the American Association of Retired Persons (AARP) be interested in long-term-care insurance. As we pointed out in Chapter 4, to overgeneralize is to stereotype, that is, to assume that all people belonging to the same group will respond in the same way. However, just as it would be ridiculous to run Miracle Ear ads on MTV or ads for Rollerblades on reruns of the *Lawrence Welk Show*, it would be foolish to disregard the tendencies of certain groups to share characteristics that have the potential to influence their responses to messages. Nevertheless, too much reliance on assumed demographics can lead to faulty assumptions and missed opportunities, as the Highlighting Stereotyping suggests.

Age

The age of audience members will influence the way they receive messages. Some might argue that age is mostly a state of mind rather than a physical fact. Even so, our age often influences the sorts of experiences we have and the issues that most concern us.

The Role of Experience

Being "young" or "old" means, in part, living through different times. Although two people of exactly the same age can have widely divergent experiences, passing through a time in which certain events take place influences the way we feel about those events, as well as the way we perceive later events. Today's students, with different experiences, may look back on World War II or the turbulent 1960s as ancient history. Their views have been shaped by the terrorist attacks of September 11, 2001, not by the Japanese attack on Pearl Harbor or the antiwar protests of the Vietnam era. By 2025, another generation of college students will come of age with no memory of planes crashing into the World Trade Center or the devastation of Hurricane Katrina in 2005. The point, of course, is that the shared experience of a generation unquestionably affects its outlook. That is just one reason that you, as a speaker, must take your audience into account.

Audience members who are over forty years old are more likely to be married, have children, and own homes than are audience members who are under twenty years of age. Each generation will have danced to different music, watched different

Highlighting Stereotyping

Recently *Time* magazine reported on a book written by former aides to Bill Clinton and George W. Bush that asserts that Democrats might be wrong in their assumption that the growing megachurches are staunchly Republican. Their analysis of 2004 exit polls "found that Protestant suburbanites who attend church at least weekly are 49 percent Democrat or independent and 39 percent believe in gay rights. 'Democratic leaders should stop stereotyping and start targeting,'" the authors write.

Source: "A Prayer for the Dems," *Time*, September 11, 2006, 24.

movies, admired different political leaders, and used different technologies during their formative years. Because all of these experiences shape how people will respond as audience members, they need to be taken into account.

Matters of Immediate Concern

Matters of immediate concern may be different for different age groups. On the most basic, practical level, getting a job, keeping a job, and living comfortably in retirement would be matters of concern for three different age groups. Put another way, issues have *saliency*, or great personal relevance or importance, partly because of age. In recent debates over modifying Social Security, for example, older people tended to be more suspicious of changes in the program, since they anticipated relying on Social Security benefits in the immediate future, while younger people tended to be more supportive of changes that they thought might benefit them in the long run.[1] To take another example, many older Americans voiced strong negative opinions about the new Medicare prescription programs introduced in 2006, while college students are understandably more concerned with cuts in the student loan program.

Age and Values

Shared experiences, social mores, and personal concerns related to age all have their impact on values. Recent research demonstrates, for example, that a generation who has lived through hard economic times is more likely to value security and stability than a generation that has experienced little threat to their material well-being. Generally, older groups who value stability will tend to be more resistant to change, while younger people are usually more adventuresome and willing to take risks. Likewise, older groups are more likely to value tradition and conformity than are younger age groups.[2]

Further, while younger listeners will likely be very concerned about how civic issues directly affect them, older audiences may respond more to appeals emphasizing the well-being of children or future generations. In the Highlighting Age and Values box that follows, note how Lonnie Bristow, a former president of the American Medical Association, urged an older audience to accept the AMA's plan to reform Medicare—for their grandchildren's sake.

Gender

While anatomy defines our sexual identity—whether we are male or female—*gender* identity is more complex. Differences and similarities in the way men and women behave, what they value, and what they believe, are shaped in large measure by social norms and expectations that will vary according to the culture with which one identifies and that will change over time and place. There was a time in the nineteenth-century, for example, when it was considered scandalous for a woman to speak in public and when a man who took care of children would have been viewed as unnatural. In the twenty-first-century United States, however, behaviors that society assigns to men and women are much more flexible. That is not as true, however, in all parts of the world where what men and women wear, how they relate to each

Highlighting Age and Values

Well, without going so far as to even hint that any of us in this room today are "elderly," let me say that your support is critical. If you agree with me and America's physicians that the program now being considered by Congress is best for patients, best for the generations to follow, and, yes, best for doctors, too, then speak out.

If I've done my job of "selling it here," then help us sell it everywhere. Write. Call. FAX. Send e-mail. Whenever it's possible, actually visit your Senators and Representatives. Let them know you support the AMA's plan to transform Medicare. Tell them you want it for today, sure. But tell them that—even more important— you want it for tomorrow. For your children's sake. For your grandchildren's sake . . .

I'm reminded of something I saw last night when I was driving home—here at Rossmoor. I turned a corner and my headlights shined [sic] on three deer. A stag, a doe, and a fawn.

You know what their first instinct was? No. They didn't run. That was their second act. The first thing that the stag and the doe did was turn so that their bodies shielded the fawn from the approaching harm. And that's what every older generation does. We shield our young from harm. We protect the generation we're leaving behind. It's an instinct as primal as food and shelter and warmth.

And that's what is being asked of us today. We are like those deer. . . . We are harvesting the accumulated wisdom and knowledge of a lifetime and sharing it with those who have it in their power to enact change to help the generations to come. To protect the generations to come. It is our time.

Source: Lonnie R. Bristow, "A Time for Every Season: Medicare and Tomorrow's Generations," *Vital Speeches of the Day* 62 (December 15, 1995), 136.

---

other, and what they can and cannot do in public is much more prescribed. Gender, then, is "socially constructed," which is to say that male and female identity is determined by what the culture deems appropriate actions, attitudes, and roles for each sex.

The Influence of Socialized Gender Roles

As men and women in our society move beyond prescribed gender roles and attitudes, expectations of how listeners will respond have begun to change. One can no longer assume that women will want to hear about fashion and that men will want to hear about sports. Jokes that portray women as vain, silly, or nagging are in bad taste everywhere, as are those that portray men as insensitive, arrogant, tough, and unfeeling.[3]

Even though artificial gender roles exert less influence in the United States now than in the past, the gender composition of the audience remains an important concern for speakers. A listener's gender may have an impact on his or her outlook and experiences. For example, gay women and men with longtime partners will encounter far greater barriers in adopting a child or obtaining housing than will a traditional married couple. Single women and widows have more difficulty obtaining credit than do single men and widowers. Furthermore, men's and women's tastes and interests still differ in our culture, and popular culture still reflects gender differences. Movie producers target some films at female audiences (so-called *chick-flicks*, for example) and others at males (war movies, for example).

As with age, gender may influence how salient a particular topic might be. Certain health concerns are obviously of differing importance: women will be more attuned to problems related to breast cancer, while men are more concerned with prostate cancer. More women still tend to be caregivers than men and are thus likely to be more attentive to topics related to that subject. Thoughtful speakers will give serious attention to how the issues they address or the plans they advocate may affect men and women differently.

Gender Stereotypes

Although all of the above is true, it is also good to remind ourselves that no category—such as sex, age, or race—automatically predetermines an individual listener's responses, interests, or life experiences.

Common assumptions based on the speaker's knowledge of listeners' sexual orientation provide an enlightening illustration. Homosexuals, for example, regardless of stereotypes, do not tend to work in certain industries. A survey of more than 4,000 gay men and lesbians conducted by Overlooked Opinions, a Chicago market-research firm, reported that 40 percent more homosexuals are employed in the finance and insurance industries than in the entertainment and arts industries, and 10 times as many homosexuals are in the computer industry as in the fashion industry. There are also more homosexuals working in science and engineering than in social services.[4]

In addition, we should not assume that because an issue is a "women's issue," for example, that male listeners cannot be motivated to care about it, or act to address it. A *good* speaker should be able to persuade an audience of women *and* men to partici-

Men and women, people of different ages and races, can be brought together to fight for common causes, as in this American Cancer Society Rally for Life.

pate in a breast cancer walk. Similarly, a student speaker ought to be able to raise his classmates' awareness of the problem of sexual assault on campus, and perhaps even convince them to take part in a "Take Back the Night" march—either by participating directly in the march or by walking on the sidelines and distributing flyers.

While the distinction between generalizing and stereotyping is sometimes hard to make, stereotyping is generally harmful. The feminist movement of the last half century should have taught us all one truth: although men and women do have concerns and experiences that are unique to their sex, there are also aspirations, attitudes, and aptitudes that are common to all humans and cannot be attributed to people strictly on the basis of gender. The advocate who would inspire, engage, and motivate listeners must be sensitive to both differences and commonalities across genders.

Race and Ethnicity

At one time, it was generally believed that Americans were a homogeneous people. The myth was that we arrived as immigrants and then emerged from the "melting pot" of U.S. culture with a distinctively American character. Of course, there may be certain ways of looking at things that are especially or even uniquely American. In recent years, however, we have come to realize that the melting-pot concept is not quite accurate. Within the broader culture, there exist varied subcultures that continue to differ. Although people who fall within these various groupings share characteristics with the general U.S. culture, they may have marked differences that could affect their responses to spoken messages.

Race

Race is determined not only by biological, genetic, or inherited factors, but is also a product of politics, social definitions, and personal preferences.[5] Nevertheless, people define themselves as part of a particular race and see the world through African American, Asian American, or Caucasian eyes. Understanding how race may be operating in a public speaking situation is very important.

Over time, we have come to realize that, as each race has its own integrity, each also has its own perceptions and problems. Recognizing these racial influences is not racism. Racism, the belief in the superiority of one race that leads to prejudice, antagonism, and fears directed toward other races, denies the essential humanity of those who are different and thus severely limits the potential for communicating successfully. Racists can talk effectively only to other racists. Those who appreciate the distinctions between people of different races are better equipped to talk effectively with diverse audiences. For example, speakers must understand that African Americans and white Americans have different histories and cultural experiences in the United States. Communication between these different races can be extremely complicated and, too often, fraught with distrust.[6] Affirmative action in the workplace, for example, may cause some white listeners to fear that their jobs will be sacrificed to make room for unemployed blacks. The administration of justice might be viewed with great skepticism by urban African Americans who have had bad experiences with white police.

At the everyday level in which most of us live, successful communication across races, while sometimes difficult, does occur every day.[7] A speaker simply must be sensitive to the racial influences operating in listeners' attitudes and approaches to issues.

Ethnic Origins

The forebears of most Americans came from someplace else. With the exception of Native Americans, people emigrated from other countries to America beginning in the seventeenth century, and they are still arriving today. Depending partly on when they arrived, partly on their habits and tastes, and partly on where they settled, the outlook of these immigrants has been colored by their own national history, customs, and experiences. Since listeners identify with their own heritage, speakers should realize that issues that seem to directly affect the mother country may shape the reactions of those who identify with a particular national group. An Irish American, for example, is likely to be interested in the fate of Northern Ireland and to have strong opinions about political and religious disputes in that country.

A culture's particular viewpoints and values can influence even its transplanted citizens and their descendants. There are, for example, different expectations among ethnic groups with regard to taking care of parents in their old age. As a study by the AARP concluded, parents of Asian and Hispanic heritage still expect their family members to participate in their care, whereas non-Hispanic Caucasian parents are more likely to view living with their children as a sign of failure. Unlike some other ethnic groups, they expect a mix of personal attention and community services as they age.[8]

One of the most significant problems plaguing the world today is ethnocentrism, the belief that one's own ethnic heritage is superior to all others. The results of such feelings can range from exclusion ("We don't associate with *those* people.") to the outright warfare that has recently torn apart countries in the Balkans and the Middle East. What is important to speakers is that they respect differences in customs, practices, and beliefs grounded in ethnic origins and take them into account when preparing to speak to ethnically diverse audiences.

Intercultural Factors

Beyond ethnic differences among different groups in this country, those who grow up in cultures outside the United States may hold values and exhibit behaviors that vary widely from Americans' values and behaviors. Scholars may not agree on whether differences should be attributed to dissimilar social and religious practices or languages or geography or ways of thinking. Yet most agree that the differences are very real. Some of the most recent studies have implications for the ways people communicate with each other, how they judge speaker credibility, and how they react to arguments opposing their own views. For example, in a recent study, student subjects were asked to analyze a conflict between mothers and daughters. "American subjects quickly came down in favor of one side or the other. Chinese subjects were more likely to see merit in both sides, commenting, for example, 'Both the mothers and the daughters have failed to understand each other.'"[9] There are many other examples. While Americans view time as a commodity, something that can be spent, saved, or wasted, other cultures may view time as better spent in cultivating interpersonal relationships than in "getting right down to business." While Americans tend to be individualistic and value privacy, group-oriented cultures more readily associate privacy with loneliness and isolation. Future-oriented Americans who expect things to get better will not view the past the way traditional societies do. In cultures where subtlety and indirection are valued, what Americans see as open and honest can be viewed as blunt and insensitive.[10] Many intercultural differences may affect the ways individuals communicate.[11]

The point to be drawn from a consideration of cultural differences, both within American subcultures and across international lines, is that all of us—in the classroom and in the community—need to make strenuous and sincere efforts to work together and communicate effectively to bridge cultural divides and identify and achieve mutual goals.

Religion

Perhaps it is less accurate to talk of religious cultures than of religious beliefs that are associated with diverse cultures. In any case, a listener's religion, or a lack of religious beliefs, can influence that listener's reception and evaluation of a speech. On some issues, certain religious groups tend to take uniform stands. While some Catholics may not support antiabortion legislation, most would, for example, tend personally to oppose abortion; Jews tend to favor strong U.S. support of Israel; Quakers generally oppose war of any kind.

Religion can also have other kinds of influences on audience members. Some religions stress obedience and conformity, whereas others emphasize individualistic participation. Some religions stress personal salvation and hold political or social issues to be beyond any religious concerns. Others insist that all matters affecting human beings should be of concern to the church, including political and social behavior. Church teachings can make a difference in the way people respond to a speech. Fundamentalists, for example, may be more open to messages that reflect conservative policies and values than to liberal religious views.[12]

Conventional wisdom once advised public speakers to avoid talking about religion. Many instructors advise students not to choose religious topics since they may be considered too personal or potentially explosive. If you *do* choose to talk about an issue related to religion, you must realize that your assumptions about what is "true" and what sources are "authoritative" may not be shared by those in your audience who hold different religious beliefs.

Religious differences, however, are reflected in many social and political controversies. In our time, many bitter divisions over social issues, such as abortion, stem cell research, and gay marriage, grow from varying interpretations of religious doctrines and moral principles. That should not make it impossible, however, for those on different sides of religious controversies to talk with each other and find common ground. Early in 2004, for example, Senator Hillary Clinton spoke to an abortion rights group and expressed the need to recognize and respect their differences. This effort to engage an issue of civic importance in a cooperative way is illustrated in the report on her speech in the *Focus on Civic Engagement*.

Focus on Civic Engagement

Seeking Common Ground

Senator Hillary Rodham Clinton said on Monday that the opposing sides in the divisive debate over abortion should find "common ground" to prevent unwanted pregnancies and ultimately reduce abortions, which she called a "sad, even tragic choice to many, many women."

In a speech to about 1,000 abortion rights supporters near the New York State Capitol, Mrs. Clinton firmly restated her support for the Supreme Court's ruling in *Roe v. Wade*, which legalized abortion nationwide in 1973. But then she quickly shifted gears, offering warm words to opponents of legalized abortion and praising the influence of "religious and moral values" on delaying teenage girls from becoming sexually active. "There is an opportu-

nity for people of good faith to find common ground in this debate—we should be able to agree that we want every child born in this country to be wanted, cherished and loved," Mrs. Clinton said. . . .

Mrs. Clinton called on abortion rights advocates and anti-abortion campaigners to form a broad alliance to support sexual education—including abstinence counseling, family planning, and morning-after emergency contraception for victims of sexual assault as ways to reduce unintended pregnancies.

Source: "Clinton Seeking Shared Ground Over Abortions," by Patrick D. Healy, *The New York Times*, January 25, 2005, A 17. Used by permission of The New York Times.

Geographic/Cultural Environment

Where a listener lives can make a difference in how he or she reacts to a public speech. Even though people might come from the same part of the country, their outlooks can differ depending on the kind of community with which they identify. Newark, New Jersey, is not the same as Franklin, New Jersey; Chicago, Illinois, is not the same as Peoria, Illinois; and Dallas, Texas, is not to be confused with College Station, Texas.

People who have grown up in rural areas may develop different habits and lifestyles from those who have grown up in the city. Muggings, commuting on unreliable trains, or moving at a frantic pace may be unimaginable to the rural resident, whereas the city dweller imagines that the dullness and lack of stimulation in the country would bore him or her to death. Sometimes the reverse is true: the excitement of the city lures one, and the longed-for peace and safety of the country lures the other. Each group will also have a specific set of problems. To urbanites, the following questions might be most important: How do we reduce crime? How do we improve mass transit? How do we keep food prices down? By contrast, the residents of a farming community will be more troubled by these questions: How do we save the family farm? How do we reduce property taxes? How do we keep grain prices at a high level?

It is also true that different sections of the country have, through the course of our history, developed unique ways of looking at things. Easterners, westerners, southerners, southwesterners, and midwesterners have different ethnic mixes in their populations, different industries, different religious views, and different approaches to social and political problems. Westerners, for example, are proud of their rugged, independent individualism; New Yorkers value their cultural and artistic sophistication; and many Sunbelt communities are proud of their climates and reputations as safe, comfortable places for older citizens to live.

Education

Education provides us with specific knowledge, ways to solve problems rationally, awareness of the choices open to us, and ways of evaluating the best choices to make. To be truly engaged, you must be as informed as possible on issues of civic concern. Being an informed citizen is fundamental to being an effective speaker.

Acquired Knowledge

The educational level of a listener—his or her acquired knowledge—influences reactions to messages. You might be giving a speech on emergency preparedness to a junior high school assembly and a speech on the same topic to a college group. What each group would expect from a speaker, what they might already know, and what they would be prepared to understand would be different. Even first- and second-year college students would likely differ in their levels of sophistication and their knowledge needs; and both groups will likely differ in these respects from college seniors.

Education versus Training and Intelligence

It is important to distinguish between education and training. Many people are *trained*, but they are not necessarily *educated*. They may have a specific skill but not much general information, or perhaps they have not had much experience in life. One's training may range from relatively simple skills, such as driving a bus, to more complex ones, such as performing vascular surgery. But a mastery of skills does not necessarily produce an educated person.[13] Training should not be confused with education, nor should education be confused with intelligence. Some very intelligent people have had little formal education, just as some who have attended good universities are not exceptionally bright.

Nevertheless, without embracing stereotypes, you can still expect most educated listeners to be more critical and to have more information about certain topics. For example, it would be hard to help an audience understand the accomplishments or failings of George W. Bush's presidency if they had little knowledge of political, social, and economic events in the United States at the beginning of the twenty-first century. A persuasive speech aimed at convincing the audience that global warming is responsible for recent natural disasters may be grounded in certain assumptions about what the listeners already know. As with all the characteristics we have been talking about, the precise role education plays in public speaking depends on the specifics of the situation.

The Educated Response

How well audience members have been educated will determine not only whether they are familiar with your speech topic but whether they can intelligently evaluate the message. One speaker may claim that present health-care plans are inadequate to meet the needs of low-income families. Another may claim that voting for a particular candidate will improve your economic situation. Educated listeners should be in a good position to evaluate such claims. They should have specific facts at their disposal and should have had previous intellectual experiences that relate to the message.

Suppose, for example, that you hear someone argue that force must be used in response to a foreign-policy crisis. And suppose they back up that claim by comparing the current situation with the situation Americans faced in the 1940s when confronted by Nazi Germany. If, as an educated person, you take the time to think, you will not just agree automatically because you know Nazism was evil. You will ask questions about the legitimacy of the comparison. You will demand that the speaker *prove* to you that the situation before World War II was really similar to the present situation.

As you judge the speaker's argument, you will apply principles you have learned and knowledge you have acquired. If you find the speaker unconvincing, and if you cannot fully test the argument by your own knowledge and experience, you will suspend judgment. You will wait and see—listen to other arguments, read more material, and assemble more facts—before you reach a judgment. You will be acting as an educated person. We will discuss how to evaluate claims in more detail in Chapter 16.

Occupation or Profession

The job you have can make a difference in the attitudes you hold and the way in which you grasp specific information. When people receive public messages, they sometimes ask themselves, How is this going to affect me? When discussing the problem of how to improve our schools, for example, a travel agent may be uneasy about the suggestion that schools be kept open all year, since that could mean that

Sharing common occupations may cause listeners to see issues in a way especially related to their professional problems and interests.

people might cancel vacations, while parents who believed that this would improve their children's education would look favorably on the idea.

Attitudes and Skills

The occupations we hold make us feel differently about the world around us. Teachers, doctors, construction workers, dancers, postal clerks, and lawyers all deal with specific sets of problems. The constant practice of these problem-solving skills is what establishes people as experts. When experts function as listeners, they bring a whole set of competencies and attitudes with them to a speaking situation. An engineer, for example, will respond to technological information as a specialist, and the speaker must be aware of this. Professional experience also will affect responses to issues. Recently, an insurance company covering a large number of university employees informed its clients that anesthesiologists at the local hospital had withdrawn from the plan. Policyholders were asked to consider a medical center fifty miles away for elective surgery. Many policyholders initially saw this as a greedy move on the part of the doctors. A clinical psychologist with a private practice argued, however, that most health-care providers were dissatisfied with the insurance company. She sympathized with the anesthesiologists. In this case, health-care providers viewed this issue from a perspective strongly influenced by their professions.

Perceptions of Relevance

Finally, one's job or profession will affect one's perspective. Consider the issue of capping medical malpractice suits. It is abundantly clear that physicians and their professional associations and lawyers and their organizations are diametrically opposed on this issue. Clearly, doctors want caps and lawyers do not. There will be arguments presented by both sides that focus on the rights and protection of consumers, but their respective occupational interests and goals influence each group.

Likewise, listeners will be influenced by their special job-related concerns. Take health care; most people agree that everyone should have some kind of coverage. Nevertheless, small-business owners might be alarmed by proposals that would require all employers (no matter how few employees they have) to share health insurance costs for their workers. Those who work for insurance companies would be concerned about their loss of business if health costs were largely assumed by the government. Physicians would object to plans that give insurance companies the power to decide whether or not particular medical procedures may be performed. Employees are likely to be dubious about health insurance proposals that would cause them to pay higher individual premiums and absorb higher deductibles. If a speaker fails to anticipate and prepare for responses stemming from different occupational perspectives, his or her good idea might be impossible to sell.

Economic Status

The income of listeners may influence their response. Again, the extent to which this factor is important and the precise ways in which it might affect listener responses depend on the speaker's subject and purpose. The topic of a message may naturally interest some income groups and not others. A speech on tax shelters, for example, might have limited appeal to low-income listeners. By the same token, those with high incomes may not be interested in a speech on needs-based tuition assistance.

How groups think their income level compares with that of others may have profound effects on the communication process. People in the middle-income group, for example, may see themselves as overburdened with taxes and yet excluded from the benefits of social welfare. Such people may look on many social programs with the jaundiced eye of those who expect to foot the bill.

Professional persuaders, such as advertisers, go to great lengths to target their messages to particular income groups. They carefully choose a mailing list (such as American Express cardholders) that will put their material in the hands of those who can afford to buy their product. They carefully choose magazines in which they advertise, the time slots for their television ads, and the kinds of radio stations that will air their ads. They are concerned with many factors besides income, but they want to reach people who can afford to buy their products.

The extent of financial resources available to listeners will surely help determine their receptiveness to any proposals that involve acquiring or spending money. The wise speaker will try to anticipate how listeners' income might influence their response to his or her message.

In addition to the specific characteristics that distinguish listeners, it is also important to remember that all of us—no matter who we are or what we do—have fundamental human needs that have to be met and common values that we all embrace.

Identifying Individual Listener Needs and Values

Preview. *Like all people, audience members have fundamental needs. Maslow's hierarchy provides an excellent conceptual framework for understanding those shared needs—physical well-being, safety and security, love and belonging, esteem, and self-actualization.*

So far, we have considered the ways that audience members may differ among themselves and how speakers need to acknowledge those differences in analyzing and adapting messages to their listeners. Yet whatever differences listeners may bring to the speech situation, they still share certain universal human needs.

In a groundbreaking work, psychologist Abraham H. Maslow described basic human needs in terms that help us understand and develop tactics for listener involvement.[14] As illustrated in Figure 5.1, Maslow presented the needs in a hierarchy, noting that some needs are more basic than others. For instance, if listeners are extremely hungry, they may not be all that concerned about protecting the environment, dealing with campus safety, or even finding a job. Once their hunger is satisfied, however, they may become very interested in such issues.

Satisfying Basic Physiological Needs

People have physiological needs. Basic to all human life is the need to be physically secure. We all need food and drink, clothing, shelter, and sexual gratification if we want to feel comfortable and avoid the discomforts of pain, sickness, injury, and so

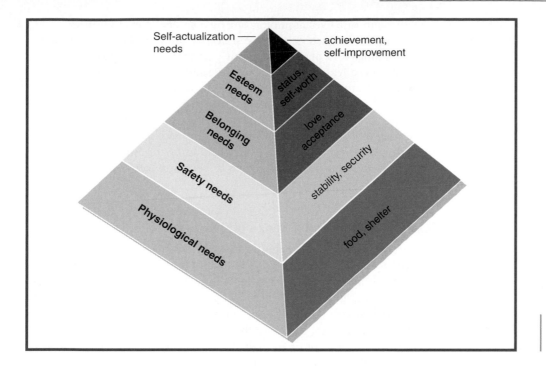

Figure 5.1
Maslow's
Hierarchy

on. These needs are considered to be basic because, in a sense, they preempt all other needs if they are not met. Long ago, groups such as the Salvation Army, community kitchens, and faith-based groups recognized that those who are in the deepest and most serious distress can hardly be called on to live up to their full potential as human beings when their most basic needs are not being met. And so, such organizations provide food, clothing, and shelter and only then make an appeal to people to fulfill other kinds of needs.

Most of the audiences you will talk with, however, will have had their basic needs met. Freed from the preoccupation of satisfying those needs, most listeners will be more successfully engaged by appealing to their "higher" needs.

Ensuring Listeners' Personal Safety

We all desire a secure world. A certain amount of routine, order, and predictability protects us from dangerous, surprising, and unfamiliar situations that threaten our safety. There are routine ways in which safety is guaranteed in any organized society. We have police to protect us from crime; we have fire departments to protect us from disaster; and we have many agencies dedicated to ensuring that gas lines do not blow up, electric wires do not break, buildings do not crumble beneath our feet, and highways do not disintegrate under our automobiles. There is a defense establishment designed to protect us from potential enemies abroad, and government bureaus to protect us from being poisoned at home. Our safety is the concern of many people and groups.

Most of us go through our lives assuming our own safety. It is only during crises, such as war or natural disasters, that we seriously question how safe we are. Nevertheless, there are times and places where our personal safety appears to be seriously threatened, and these fears may influence an audience. No one in the United States today, for example, can be completely free of the fear of terrorism. Supporters of the Patriot Act consistently argued that it was necessary to keep us all safe. Those who would modify the act had the burden of proving that we could be safe while simultaneously preserving our cherished civil liberties. Any speaker who wants information to be understood, action to be taken, or beliefs to be modified would be well advised to consider how such purposes will meet the very important safety needs of the audience.

Reinforcing Feelings of Love and a Sense of Belonging

Once safety needs are satisfied, people begin to think of other needs, such as belonging needs, or the need to be loved by others. The love that exists between individuals—a parent and a child, a husband and a wife, committed partners—fulfills a very important human need. In a larger sense, there is a distinct human need to be loved or at least to be accepted, wanted, or welcomed into groups. People join clubs, maintain close family or ethnic ties, associate themselves strongly with a church or religious movement, or take great pride in their patriotic feelings toward their country. All these associations help them meet their need to be accepted and cared for. Successful speakers understand and often engage this need.

In his speech accepting the Republican nomination for president in 1988, George H. W. Bush stressed the connectedness of all Americans, depicting "diversity spread like stars, like a thousand points of light in a peaceful sky."

In his 1988 acceptance speech, George H. W. Bush, the newly nominated Republican candidate for president, attempted to convey a sense of belonging as he stressed the importance of volunteerism. Describing the United States as "a nation of communities, of thousands and tens of thousands of ethnic, religious, social, business, labor union, neighborhood, regional and other organizations, all of them varied, voluntary, and unique," Bush appealed to individuals who might not have felt very important on their own: "This is America: the Knights of Columbus, the Grange, Hadassah, the Disabled American Veterans, the Order of Ahepa, the Business and Professional Women of America, the union hall, the Bible study group, LULAC, Holy Name—a brilliant diversity spread like stars, like a thousand points of light in a broad and peaceful sky."[15]

Listeners are likely to be more emotionally involved when they believe that a speaker is advocating a proposal that will be of direct benefit to those whom they love, reduce their feelings of isolation, or contribute to their sense of belonging.

Helping Listeners Feel Confident and Appreciated by Others

In addition to a sense of belonging, people want to feel that they have some worth and importance. People like to feel that they control their destiny, that they are not constantly under the thumb of other people, and that others recognize them as being good or important human beings. This need is frequently exploited as it is translated into a desire for status, or a desire to be better than other people. No doubt, it is the basis of much advertising that would have us believe that smoking a certain type of cigarette, driving a certain type of car, or wearing a certain brand of shoes will help us acquire status. These kinds appeals to status are aimed more at achieving the communicator's personal goals than advancing the cause of the community. On the other hand, when people feel oppressed or neglected, or when they feel that they are of no account, their need to feel confident and valuable may be the most basic need to be met before they can be expected to act.

Helping Listeners Realize Their Own Potential

When people possess self-esteem and know that others respect them, they can begin to think about self-fulfillment. The self-actualization need, as Maslow calls it, recognizes that human beings want to realize their own potential; they want to make the most of themselves. Not everyone, of course, has the same goals or the same ambition. For some, it may be to seek their own material gain. But for someone who cares about the community in which she or he lives, realizing one's own potential may mean helping to improve the lives of their fellow citizens.

Most people will strive to better themselves throughout life and will never be completely self-actualized. Nevertheless, the speaker who realizes that people *want* to achieve the full extent of their capabilities will appeal to this very important need. Of course, not all listeners will define self-fulfillment in the same way. Some might be more attuned to their own spirituality than to community needs, while others may seek a sense of empowerment through their work. The distinguished preacher David Owen played on a Hindu notion to differentiate between the agitated "Little" or "Surface Self" and the serene "Big" or "Deep Self," pointing to self-actualization in posing the question, "Which of ourselves shall we become?" In a sermon given in 2002, Owen addressed the question this way:

> Say that we are faced with a fork in the road. We could go to the right or the left. This could be true in any situation. It might be that we are faced with a tough business decision. It might be we are tempted to stray from the path of faithfulness in a love relationship. As a campaigning politician, we may discover that we are fading in the polls and have to decide whether we will launch an untrue and unfair attack on our opponent. . . . If we stay on the surface, we are likely to be driven by . . . the many shallow voices that our culture keeps beaming toward us. On the other hand, when we know that we have both a Surface Self and a Deep Self, we could stop to ask, "What does my Deep Self want in this situation? What would I do if I were to be faithful to my Big Self? If we ask ourselves what our Deep Self wants, and give it time to answer, our Deep Self will usually tell us.
>
> The disclaimer here is that getting in touch with our Deep Selves takes time, especially if we have been living too long on the surface of things. But if we take time on a regular basis, the yapping of our Surface Self begins to fade, and the wisdom and serenity of our Deep Self begins to emerge. Our life is elevated and we *become ourselves more and more*, when we make our Deep Self our daily companion and friend.[16]

Identifying Audience Values

When you analyze an audience by cataloging listener characteristics and identifying their needs, you are doing so, in part, to uncover audience values. You are especially interested in looking for areas of agreement (as well as potential conflict), and you will want to think about how listeners' value priorities might shape the way you approach your speech. For certain audiences, patriotic values may be extremely important; for others, the desire to get ahead or to advance their education might take precedence.

All of us possess a network of interlocking values, some of which conflict with others. For example, Americans tend to admire individualism, yet we also recognize the need for teamwork.[17] We may profess the golden rule—do unto others as we would have them do unto us—while also valuing a competitive spirit. We hear of the "work ethic," the "business ethic," and the "Puritan ethic," all of which denote different sets of values at work in our society. Your job as a responsible speaker will be to determine, as a result of your careful consideration of your audience, what values are relevant to the issue you are discussing.

Once you have considered your audience's values, you should reflect on how those values translate into specific attitudes and beliefs. For instance, you may determine that both you and your listeners greatly value integrity and responsibility. Yet in an election year, you may discover that your listeners distrust the political candidate you are supporting. Whereas you see the candidate as honest, experienced, and trustworthy, your listeners see her as unqualified or dishonest or untrustworthy. In this case, you would not try to change listener values (which you share). Instead you would try to convince them that they have misjudged your candidate. Perhaps they believe that women in general are poorly suited for high-level leadership positions. Or maybe they believe that your candidate's background has not prepared her for the office she seeks. Or maybe they do not like your candidate's record on environmental protection, which is a real priority for them. Whatever the nature of their objections, you need to understand those objections before you can adapt your speech to your audience. Perhaps you can establish common ground by emphasizing the values you share. Then you can try to change their beliefs and attitudes toward your candidate.

Identifying Communal Needs and Values

Preview. *Listeners are usually members of a variety of communities. The groups and organizations your listeners belong to and identify with will have an impact on their response to your speeches.*

What group affiliation is uppermost in the minds of your listeners? A single listener may belong to the American Baptist Church, the Democratic Party, the Parent Teacher Organization, the American Bar Association, and the Executive Board of the United Way. These affiliations will almost certainly influence how listeners respond to a speech.

Membership in groups that are important to listeners will influence how they react to messages that are salient to those groups.

The Saliency of Key Group Memberships

Some memberships may be more important than others. When you attend a meeting of a particular group (a fraternity, a political club, the Boys and Girls Club, or the Future Farmers of America), the reasons for being in that organization may be very important to you at that moment. You hear and respond to messages as a member of that group. At other times, and in other contexts, the goals of that group may seem less relevant.

It is difficult, and not really necessary, to keep any one membership foremost in all our decisions. Whether we are active Democrats or Republicans will hardly matter as we decide which toothpaste to buy. However, there are times when membership in a particular group is so important that all other concerns are subordinated.[18] Certain Evangelical Christian (pro-life) groups on one side and the National Organization of Women (pro-choice) on the other have diametrically opposed views on abortion. There will be members of each group to whom this matter is so important that they will subordinate all other issues to this one and will end up voting for or against a political candidate because of his or her position on this single issue. Such a dedicated member may ignore the candidate's stand on the economy, foreign affairs, or the environment. Issues that might seem crucial to others will become less significant because identification with the member's group goals is so strong that everything else pales in comparison. In some measure the groups one identifies with defines who one is, so group membership must be taken into account in any public speech.

Complicating the speaker's task is the fact that important issues force us to consider several demographic categories. Consider, for example, poverty. The latest statistics from the Census Bureau show how it relates to gender and age: poverty affects children under 18 years old more than any other age group, and women typically have principal responsibility for children. Poverty is also a matter of race and ethnicity: 24.7 percent of blacks and 21.9 percent of Hispanics are below the poverty line, while non-Hispanic whites represent only 8.6 percent of the poor population.[19] Furthermore, while the number of people living in poverty has decreased slightly in recent years, the number of people in *extreme* poverty (those with incomes at less than half the poverty level) has increased.[20] When you consider the effects that poverty can have on the cost of social programs, health care, and educational opportunities, one can easily imagine that this issue affects everybody. Yet, a good speaker will still reflect on how poverty especially affects different groups and adapt accordingly.

A further complication arises when two groups to which one belongs or whose goals one supports come into conflict. In Florida, for example, some lawmakers were distressed when two organizations whose aims they supported clashed over proposed legislation. A bill backed by the National Rife Association to make it a felony for an employer to prohibit employees from bringing guns to work was strongly opposed by the Chamber of Commerce. A legislator who gets the highest ratings from both associations admitted that "it's very awkward for me."[21] In such conflicting situations, speakers will have to take listeners' conflicting loyalties into account.

It should be clear by now that it is important to design your speech for the specific audience you will address. As a responsible citizen, you should focus your attention on your audience so that you can solicit a response that achieves your purpose and contributes to the welfare of the community. To connect your message with your listeners, you begin by analyzing the situation and the audience. In order to adapt your message to the particular circumstances you will face, you need to gather as much information about your specific audience as you can.

Gathering Information for Audience Adaptation

Preview. *There are different ways of collecting information about your audience. Information can be gathered by conducting research on the Internet, through interviewing, and with an audience survey. You should continuously assess the audience before, during, and after the speech.*

Gathering information about your audience is extremely important. First, as a responsible speaker, you will want to know how your ideas might best serve the needs of your listeners. Second, as we pointed out earlier in this chapter, there is little chance of achieving your own goals if you do not have relevant information about your audience. Now the question is, How do you go about getting the information you need?

Internet Research

You can learn much about the organization or group by conducting research on the Internet. Suppose you represented a campus group that wanted to promote discussion of an issue relevant to its interests and goals (e.g., national trends in tuition costs, immigration laws and international students, regulation of off-campus housing). If you wanted to engage other students, you might go to the appropriate student government or student organization website to gather information. If, for example, you were starting to plan such an event at Indiana University you could start at the Union Board home page, where you would gather information on meeting times and contact persons for such committees as the Colloquium Committee, which sponsors faculty-led lectures and seminars, the Debates and Issues Committee, which organizes live debates, or the Lectures Committee, which engages outside speakers with special expertise.[22]

Interviewing for Information

A good way to begin gathering information about an audience is to interview the person who asked you to speak. Usually this contact person is a member of the group or organization that you will address and can tell you much about the audience. Your goal is to find out as much as you can about the audience—their experiences, level of knowledge, values and interests, and the particular speaking situation.[23] Regardless of the specific topic, here are some of the questions you might want to ask:

- How diverse is the audience in terms of age, sex, and other characteristics?
- How many listeners will likely be present when I speak?
- Could you describe the room where I'll be speaking?
- How knowledgeable is the audience about my topic?
- What relevant experiences might audience members have had?
- How likely are they to be open to the sort of information I'm discussing or the proposal I'm making?
- Are there likely to be great differences of opinion or experience within the audience? If so, explain.
- How much time is available for my presentation?
- Will there be a question-and-answer period after the speech?

Of course, you will want to adapt this basic interviewing format to the specific situation.

Still other avenues for collecting information about the audience exist. For instance, you might consider attending a meeting of the group that you will address and learn for yourself about their concerns, interests, and values. This strategy is practical only if you have the time and the opportunity. Your contact person should prove helpful in arranging this.

Administering an Audience Survey

You might also construct and administer an audience survey, with the permission of the contact person and the cooperation of the group, aimed at gathering insights into the same sorts of issues. This approach to gathering information can be especially valuable in your own public speaking class. Your public speaking instructor might even require you to design and administer a brief questionnaire, giving you the opportunity to learn more about your fellow students.

Although survey construction can be fairly complicated, you can learn to design a very basic questionnaire that will serve as a valuable analytical tool.[24] Following are some principles to follow as you design your audience survey:

- *Use the survey to collect relevant demographic information about the audience.* For some topics, for instance, you may want to know the age or major of your audience. For others, you may want to know about their political affiliation or religion.
- *Use different kinds of questions to gather the kind of information you need.*[25] Some questions may ask audience members to check the appropriate answer from among several choices. Others may ask them to write a few sentences.
- *Limit your audience survey to a few good questions that can be answered in a short period of time.* This way, respondents will be more willing to participate and are more likely to provide you with accurate and better-developed responses. If listeners take the questionnaire home, they will be more inclined to complete and return the survey if it is not too long and complicated.
- *Be sure to use the results of the survey as you craft your speech and adapt your message to your audience.* Administering an audience survey is not just an academic exercise. It is one of the most direct means available of finding out about your audience's knowledge, opinions, and values. Allow your listeners to remain anonymous as they complete the survey. They are more likely to respond with candor if they do not have to identify themselves.

When you conduct an audience survey, you may choose to probe listener attitudes regarding a specific topic, or you may survey their beliefs and values more generally.

Devising Good Questions for an Audience Survey

Whether you are interviewing for information or constructing an audience questionnaire, you should include both closed and open questions (see Chapter 7). Closed questions yield limited information, while open questions may be hard to tabulate and are more time-consuming to complete. The key is balance.[26]

There is no magic formula for constructing an audience survey, but here are some tips to guide you:

- *Begin the survey with closed, fixed-choice questions relevant to your topic to collect basic demographic and other factual information.* For example:

What is your class standing?

Freshman _____ Sophomore _____ Junior _____ Senior _____
Are you registered to vote?
Yes _____ No _____ Not sure _____
If you are registered to vote, are you registered as a(n):
Democrat _____ Republican _____ Independent _____ Other _____
Do you drive or would you consider driving an SUV?
Yes _____ No _____ Maybe _____
Do you like to walk?
Frequently _____ Sometimes _____ Not much _____

Through these kinds of questions, you can collect "bottom-line" information very quickly. However, the responses give you no insight into how strongly listeners identify with the choices they make. For example, one person might be registered as an Independent but consistently vote for candidates from one party.

■ *Use scale questions to acquire more precise information from respondents or to gain an understanding of how firmly committed they are to their opinions and beliefs.* For example:

How many news broadcasts do you typically watch or listen to each week?
Seven or more _____ Five or six _____ Three or four _____
One or two _____ None _____

Indicate the extent to which you agree or disagree with the following statements:
I believe that a flat tax of 15 percent for everybody would be the fairest tax.
Strongly agree _____ Somewhat agree _____ Somewhat disagree _____
Strongly disagree _____ Not sure _____
I read a newspaper or news magazine, print or online.
All the time _____ Most of the time _____ Rarely _____
Never _____ Not sure _____

Scale questions allow you to gather more precise information and to measure degrees of commitment.

■ *You will also want to include some open questions on your survey to provide greater depth of response.* For instance:

How do you feel about the proposal to make this campus pedestrian-only by the year 2003?

In your view, why do so few U.S. citizens vote in the presidential elections?

Through open questions, you give the audience the freedom to respond as they choose. By examining their responses, you may grow to better understand *why* they believe as they do and how they justify their actions and opinions. At the same time, you may find that some listeners will give you irrelevant information and some will simply refuse to write out a response. When used in combination with other questions, however, open questions should enrich your survey's results.

- *Finally, avoid leading or loaded questions.* Make sure you phrase your questions with neutrality and objectivity so that you do not lead respondents to a particular answer. If you were giving a speech about drinking on campus, you might ask this question on your audience survey: "Describe your drinking habits." A leading version of the same question might read, "Describe the last time you drank excessively." The second version assumes that the respondent does in fact drink excessively. By contrast, the first version invites the respondent to describe an array of behaviors ranging from complete abstinence to extreme drinking. All survey questions should be written in the most neutral way possible.[27]

Table 5.2 is an example of an audience survey used by one public speaking student who was interested in giving a persuasive speech on vegetarianism. She initially planned to try to get her audience to agree with her that vegetarianism was both ethically and morally preferable to eating meat.

After studying the following results of her survey, she decided to change her basic approach.

1. Definitions of vegetarianism varied widely among audience members. About one-third believed that a person is a vegetarian if he or she does not eat red meat. Two class members believed that all vegetarians do not eat any animal products (such as milk or eggs). The speaker knew that she would have to take some time early in the speech to clarify her definition of vegetarianism.

Table 5.2

SAMPLE AUDIENCE SURVEY ON VEGETARIANISM

1. Please check the categories that most accurately describe you:
   Sex: Male _____ Female _____
   Major: Liberal arts _____ Business _____ Health-care professions _____ Music _____
   Engineering _____ Other _____

2. How would you define vegetarianism?

3. Are you a vegetarian?
   Yes _____ No _____

4. Do you have a close friend or relative who is a vegetarian?
   Yes _____ No _____ Not sure _____

5. Do you agree or disagree with the following statement?
   Vegetarians can enjoy a nutritious and flavorful diet.
   Strongly agree _____ Somewhat agree _____ Undecided _____ Somewhat disagree _____
   Strongly disagree _____

6. If you are a vegetarian, please explain your reasons for becoming one.

7. In your view, what are the main reasons that people choose to become vegetarians?

2. Only 2 students (other than the speaker herself) out of a class of 24 students were vegetarians. In addition, 6 other students, or 25 percent of the class, said that they had a vegetarian friend or relative. The speaker realized that she could not count on much direct experience among the audience.

3. The reasons the 2 students gave for becoming vegetarians were primarily related to their own health rather than moral objections to consuming meat.

4. Sixty percent of the class did not believe that vegetarians can enjoy a healthy, flavorful diet.

5. Students tended to view vegetarians as having taken a rather extreme approach to a healthy diet. Some cited dangers. Out of the class, 2 or 3 seemed hostile toward vegetarians—one calling them "kooks" and another referring to them as "granola." In general, men were more negative than women. Nearly 70 percent of the women discussed animal rights as one reason for vegetarianism. Students' majors seemed unrelated to their responses.

The speaker's own commitment to vegetarianism grew from a deep ethical conviction regarding animal rights. Based on the survey results, however, she felt that converting this particular audience to her point of view would be unrealistic, given their initial views and the short time available for persuading them. Instead, she decided to make them aware of the problems (both to animals and humans) associated with factory farms (with a specific focus on poultry farms). She would acknowledge inhumane killing, but she would go beyond that to discuss dangerous working conditions, the extreme poverty of the workforce, and the unsanitary conditions under which the chickens are bred, fed, and killed—making them unsafe for consumers. As a result of her survey, then, she had devised a more modest but potentially attainable goal: her specific purpose was to get her audience to purchase only free-range chickens—for the welfare of the workers, the animals, and the consumers.

Had the speaker not conducted the audience survey and had she given her original speech, she surely would have been doomed to failure. As it was, her speech was extremely well received, and five or six students said that they were going to purchase only free-range chickens in the future.

The audience survey is an extremely helpful tool that enables a speaker to gather the kind of information he or she needs to adapt a message to the concerns, experiences, and priorities of an audience.

Thus, through various avenues—using the resources available to you through the Internet, the community, your contact person, and the group itself—you should be able to craft your speech with a clear sense of your audience.

Ongoing Strategies for Audience Adaptation

Preview. *Sometimes we may assume that audience analysis is done only before the day of the speech. Of course, much analysis will be done in advance. But a resourceful speaker can continue to assess and adapt to the audience immediately before, during, and even after a speech.*

Many speeches are made in the context of conferences, public meetings, and other ongoing events. When you arrive at a conference or meeting room and begin to interact with the audience before your speech, you may learn a good deal about their interests and priorities. If you wish to be heard during the time allotted for public input at a city council meeting, attend one beforehand or, if possible, watch a few meetings on your local community-access channel. Get to the meeting early and observe the gathering audience. You may discover that the audience looks a little different from what you had imagined. They may be younger, they may sound more conservative, or they may express interests you had not learned about in advance. Based on what you learn immediately preceding the speech, you may choose to make minor adjustments in your presentation.

It is even possible to adapt to your audience *while* you are speaking. To some extent, all effective speakers do this. If they sense that the audience is bored by too much background information, they may cut some material and move on to the next point. They may use more humor if the audience seems to enjoy it, or they move closer to listeners and speak more informally if they sense that the podium is creating a barrier. Finally, based on your perceptions of how much you are "on target" with your planned remarks, you may choose to shorten your speech so that you can devote more time to the audience's concerns during a question-and-answer period.

Audience analysis and adaptation is an ongoing process. From the moment you learn you are to make a speech until the moment you stop interacting with listeners, you can continue to learn more about them and make appropriate adjustments in your strategy, style, and response. And from this experience, you may reflect on what you have learned, how your speech was received, and what you would like to change if you were to give it again. This kind of reflective analysis will help you grow as a public speaker.

Summary

- In analyzing an audience, you seek to learn all that you can about listener values, beliefs, and attitudes.
  - A speaker-listener partnership with mutual benefits is central to the success of any public speaking venture.
  - Consider the sources of listeners' diversity while remaining mindful of the needs and values they likely share.
- Audiences are rarely homogeneous; avoid overgeneralizing or stereotyping listeners.
- In analyzing your audience, consider such diverse factors as
  - age
  - gender
  - race and ethnicity
  - intercultural factors
  - religion
  - education
  - occupation

- geographic/cultural environment
- economic status

- Recognize that there are some universal human needs that all listeners share: basic physiological needs, as well as the need for safety and security, love and belonging, esteem, and self-actualization.

- Consider the communal needs and values of audiences related to the groups with which they identify and the relevance of these associations to your topic.

- Gather specific information about your listeners by exploring the Internet, interviewing persons relevant to your speaking situation, observing the audience in their natural environment, or conducting an audience survey.

- Since audience adaptation is an ongoing process, you can make adjustments immediately preceding and even during the speech, as you assess, watch, listen, and reflect on the communication experience.

QUESTIONS FOR REVIEW AND REFLECTION

1. What is your understanding of the meaning of *audience adaptation*?
2. What are some key situational factors you will want to consider as you analyze your audience and anticipate the speaking situation? Consider the topic you plan to use for your next speech. Which of these situational factors might be especially important in this speaking context?
3. What are the major stereotypes associated with the following groups: football players, sorority members, accountants, lawyers, and college professors? For each category, offer at least one example of someone you know who violates the stereotype.
4. What are the major audience characteristics you ought to consider when planning a speech? Why is each important?
5. Think of a topic that you believe might be a good one to use in your public speaking class based on your interests and your perceptions of your fellow classmates' interests and values. How could this topic be adapted to a significantly older audience?
6. In your view, are there any topics that would be of greater interest to women than to men? How about the opposite? How might you broaden the appeal of a topic that you associate with either sex?
7. How might the location or geography of your hometown affect the kinds of issues that people who live there are interested in?
8. As a person who is currently in the role of college student, what are some topics that are of interest to you? Now imagine that you are pursuing the occupation of your choice in the future (attorney, teacher, salesperson, or computer analyst, for example). What sorts of topics would likely interest you as a member of that occupational group?
9. The following are some possible speech topics:
   a. gun control
   b. exercising for fitness
   c. finding the career that's right for you
   d. how to excel as a first-year college student
   e. the health-care crisis

f.   alternative energy sources

g.   pain management

h.   becoming a volunteer for the local humane society

Of those needs described in Maslow's hierarchy, which ones would you probably want to consider in speaking about each of these topics? Why would those needs be especially important?

10. Besides conducting a survey, what are some other audience-adaptation methods you can use before, during, and after you make a speech?

ENDNOTES

1. In February 2005, 46 percent of all age groups combined polled by the Pew Charitable Trust favored private accounts, while those in the 18–29 age group approved the plan by 66 percent. (Support, however, especially among younger persons, did dwindle considerably in later polls, particularly among those who were most knowledgeable about the plan.) The Pew Charitable Trust, "Public Divided on Alaska Drilling, as Well as Social Security," March 24, 2005, www.pewtrusts.com/pdf/PRC_approvalrating_0305.pdf (accessed October 12, 200)].

2. LESS Eunet (2005), "Human Values," http://essedunet.nsd.uib.no/opencms.war/opencms/ess/en/topics/1/2/2.html (accessed January 5, 2006).

3. See A. Cann and W. D. Siegfried, "Sex Stereotypes and the Leadership Role," *Sex Roles* 17 (1987): 401–08.

4. T. A. Stewart, "Gay in Corporate America," *Fortune* (December 6, 1991), 43–56.

5. Richard D. Alba, *Ethnic Identity: The Transformation of White America* (New Haven, Conn.: Yale University Press, 1990).

6. See L. Barna, "Stumbling Blocks in Intercultural Communication," in *Intercultural Communication: A Reader*, ed. L. Samovar and R. Porter, 322–30 (Belmont, CA: Wadsworth, 1988). Barna has found that individuals are often so steeped in their own culture that they do not recognize how it influences their thinking, views, beliefs, norms, and values, and they assume that others think, perceive, and value things similarly.

7. To help all communicators better understand and communicate with one another, researchers have studied how people in racially mixed groups interact. See, for example, Melanie Booth-Butterfield and Felecia Jordan, "Communication Adaptation among Racially Homogeneous and Heterogeneous Groups," *Southern Communication Journal* 54 (Spring 1989): 253–72.

8. Sheel Pandya, AARP Public Policy Institute, "Racial and Ethnic Differences among Older Adults in Long Term Care Service Use," June 2005, www.aarp.org/research/longtermcare/trends/fs119_ltc.html (accessed February 15, 2006).

9. Erica Goode, "How Culture Molds Habits of Thought," *New York Times* (August 8, 2000), D1 and D4.

10. Ohio State University Extension Fact Sheet: Family and Consumer Sciences, "Appreciating Other Cultures," n.d., http://ohioline.osu.edu/shy-fact/5000/5202.html (accessed June 15, 2004).

11. Lustig and Koester, *Intercultural Competence*, note several value differences between those of different cultures. For instance, they point out that "the fast, hectic pace of European Americans, governed by clocks, appointments, and schedules, has become so commonly accepted that it is almost a cliché. The pace of life in cultures such as India,

Kenya, and Argentina and among African Americans is less hectic, more relaxed, and more comfortably paced" (104).

12. Arnold D. Hunt, Marie T. Crotty, and Robert B. Crotty, eds., *Ethics of World Religions*, rev. ed. (San Diego: Greenhaven Press, 1991).

13. See *Integrity in the College Curriculum: A Report to the Academic Community* (Washington, DC: Association of American Colleges, 1985) for a discussion of how all students need a broad-based liberal arts education in place of more narrow, specialized training.

14. Abraham H. Maslow, *Motivation and Personality* (New York: Harper and Row, 1954).

15. George Bush, "Acceptance of the Republican Nomination for President," in *Contemporary American Voices*, ed. James R. Andrews and David Zarefsky, 389 (New York: Longman, 1992).

16. David Owen, "Little Big Self," *Wending Our Way: Reflections on the Journey* (Indianapolis: North United Methodist Church, 2002): 89, 91.

17. James R. Andrews, "Reflections of the National Character in American Rhetoric," *The Quarterly Journal of Speech* 57 (October 1971): 316–24.

18. George Cheney, "On the Various and Changing Meanings of Organizational Membership: A Field Study of Organizational Identification," *Communication Monographs* 50 (1983): 342–62; and George Cheney and Phillip K. Tompkins, "Coming to Terms with Organizational Identification and Commitment," *Central States Speech Journal* 38 (1987): 1–15.

19. "Poverty: 2004 Highlights," U.S. Census Bureau, August 30, 2005, www.census.gov/hhes/www/poverty/poverty04/pov04hi.html (accessed January 5, 2006).

20. "Why Are People Homeless?" National Coalition for the Homeless, September 2002, www.nationalhomeless.org/publications/facts.html (accessed February 12, 2006).

21. Barbara Liston, "Caught in a Gunfight," *Time*, February 20, 2006, 17.

22. "Union Board," Indiana University, February 2006, http://imu.indiana.edu/union_board/committees.html (accessed August 15, 2006).

23. There are many excellent books on interviewing. See, for example, Jeanne Tessier Barone and Jo Young Switzer, *Interviewing Art and Skill* (Boston: Allyn and Bacon, 1995); Arnold B. Kanter, *The Complete Book of Interviewing: Everything You Need to Know from Both Sides of the Table* (New York: Times Books, 1995); and Charles J. Stewart and William B. Cash Jr., *Interviewing: Principles and Practices*, 11th ed. (Boston: McGraw-Hill, 2006).

24. Priscilla Salant, *How to Conduct Your Own Survey* (New York: Wiley, 1994).

25. Jeane M. Converse and Stanley Presser, *Survey Questions: Handcrafting the Standardized Questionnaire* (Newbury Park, CA: Sage, 1986); see also Floyd J. Fowler Jr., *Survey Research Methods* (Newbury Park, CA: Sage, 1993), for an excellent discussion of how to construct survey questions.

26. Stanley L. Payne, *The Art of Asking Questions* (Princeton, NJ: Princeton University Press, 1980). Also see Robert W. Eder and Michael M. Harris, eds., *The Employment Interview Handbook* (Thousand Oaks, CA: Sage, 1999); even though this book is focused on the employment interview, it contains an excellent section on questioning as related to structured and unstructured interviews (143–216).

27. For additional information about survey construction, see Paul Rosenfeld, Jack E. Edwards, and Marie D. Thomas, "Improving Organizational Surveys," *American Behavioral Scientist* 36 (1993): 414–26; and Sam G. McFarland, "Effects of Question Order on Survey Responses," *Public Opinion Quarterly* 45 (1981): 208–15.

HONORING OUR OBLIGATIONS AS AMERICANS

Rebecca W. Rimel,
President and CEO, The Pew Charitable Trusts

> *Rebecca Rimel, CEO and president of The Pew Charitable Trusts, gave this speech on September 30, 2003, to a group of civic-minded citizens and philanthropists belonging to the organization Town Hall Los Angeles. Her goal was to get more people involved in a variety of civic actions—from voting to volunteering—and to encourage young people to become engaged, as well.*

Delivered to the Town Hall Los Angeles, Los Angeles, California, September 30, 2003

Good afternoon and thank you for that truly generous and gracious introduction. I trust you know how fortunate you are to live in this town and to have an organization like Town Hall Los Angeles. Any city in America would truly feel blessed to gather together this number of people with the energy, enthusiasm and commitment you have to making your community a better place. You have extraordinary philanthropists in this town, many of them here today. It's particularly nice to be able to see some old friends: Wallace Annenberg and Norman Lear, who's committing his life now to getting us all back and involved in the future of our country.

"To those whom much is given, much is expected." Each and every one of us has been blessed with tremendous resources and opportunities. As a result, much is expected of us. We are called upon to give back to our community, to our country and to our shared civic life. Many think that America is at a crossroads—and I believe our individual and collective involvement will be key in determining its future.

I am addressing you today as business and community leaders. As men and women who have achieved positions of privilege and power. I am addressing you as Americans. Too often, especially in challenging times, such as those we now face, we forget the blessings we enjoy in this country. We often fail in our obligations to nurture the institutions and democratic principles that assure us those blessings. It's in vogue right now to criticize the U.S. foreign policy—our leaders and our government.

I'm not here to echo those complaints or refute them. I have no political agenda. What I'd like to do however is convince you of three critical factors that will play a pivotal role in our future. First, America's stature and leadership is in question—just when we've become the world's sole super power. That said, the greatest threat we confront is our own apathy and that of our youth. Joining in this criticism won't stem these dangerous trends. Whether you agree or disagree with the direction of your country, your state or your community, it's time for us to get off the bench and back into the game. Working together we can make a difference in America's future.

What brings me to these conclusions is the information provided and the advocacy undertaken by our many partners at The Pew Charitable Trusts. We work in areas as diverse as culture and religion and address topics ranging from the environment to health care. However, we have one overriding objective—to advance the debate on the issues that matter to the long-term health and happiness of the American people and our global neighbors.

One of our primary roles is to provide fact-based information in the public interest. But we do more than inform at the Trusts. Once the facts are clear and irrefutable, we also educate, enable, and, when the facts beg for it, advocate for change—even fight for it. At the Pew Trusts, we engage

IN ADAPTING TO HER IMMEDIATE AUDIENCE, MS. RIMEL RECOGNIZES BY NAME TWO VERY ACTIVE AND WELL-KNOWN PHILANTHRO-PISTS IN THE AUDIENCE. ACKNOWLEDGING THESE RESPECTED LEADERS—GENERALLY ASSOCIATED WITH DIFFERENT POLITICAL VIEWS—SIGNALS HER IMPARTIAL STANCE, AS WELL AS HOLDING UP MODELS FOR HER AUDIENCE TO EMULATE. IT IS IMPORTANT THAT HER AUDIENCE NOT SEE HER AS A SPOKESPERSON FOR A PARTICULAR PARTY OR CAUSE, SO SHE REINFORCES HER NON-PARTISANSHIP BY ASSURING LISTENERS THAT SHE HAS NO POLITICAL AGENDA.

BY REFERRING TO THE CAREFUL AND EXPERT RESEARCH CARRIED OUT BY the most talented experts to provide credible, nonpartisan, balanced research and inform and facilitate the public debate on some of the most pressing issues affecting the health of our nation.

Issues like bio-engineered food and its impact on the economy, the environment and our public health . . . global warming and how we can promote policies and practices that will protect our planet . . . under-aged drinking and how we can stop the marketing of alcohol to our youth . . . and how we can ensure that quality, early education is available for all children from the age of three. We fight with facts to advance these and other issues—to improve life for our citizens.

With that in mind, let me address the first concern I want to share today: that America is losing its luster, both domestically and globally. This is not my personal observation; it is the chief finding of a major global public opinion poll commissioned by The Pew Research Center for the People and the Press. Chaired by former secretary of state Madeleine Albright the Project last year surveyed 38,000 individuals in 44 nations, including such "hard-to-interview" places as China. Libya and Angola. In a second survey, they polled 16,000 people in 20 countries and the Palestinian Authority. The results show a stunning disconnect between how Americans perceive themselves and their government and how the rest of the world perceives us. America's image has taken a beating in recent years—among longtime NATO allies, in developing countries, in Eastern Europe, and—most dramatically—in Muslim societies. Since 2000, favorability ratings for the U.S. have fallen in 19 of 27 countries where benchmark data was available.

While people around the world embrace things American—including our economic and democratic ideals—they condemn U.S. influence on their way of life. Hollywood is the perfect example. While it does seem contradictory, people in most countries say they enjoy the movies, music and TV that this town exports, but they dislike the spread of U.S. ideas and customs. Even among our strongest allies, anti-American sentiment is growing.

To me, the most frightening finding of all is our image in most of the Muslim world. Negative views of the U.S. among Muslims are wide and deep—from the Middle East to Indonesia to Nigeria. In fact, over 80 percent of Palestinians and Jordanians express disdain toward the U.S.—our leaders and, yes, our citizens. In a town that understands the power of ratings, think about this: A 37 point drop in favorability in Turkey, and in Egypt, only six percent of the population has a kind thing to say about us. The post-Cold War reality is this: Old friends who need us less, like us less, especially in Western Europe, and we're failing to win new friends as well.

Perhaps the most disheartening finding, however, is that we as Americans are clueless. Our own opinion of ourselves is—shall we say—highly inflated and strikingly at odds with the rest of the world. Americans think the U.S. takes into account other countries' interests when crafting foreign policy. Eighty percent of us believe it is a good thing that our ideas and customs are spreading around the world, but we appear insensitive to the cultures and priorities of our global neighbors.

The bar is set high for the U.S., as it should be. We're the big kid in the canoe—the only big kid in the canoe these days. We exercise dominant influence on global affairs, and we need to step up to the obligations that come with that influence. It's time to accept the full weight of responsibility that comes with our privileged position. I know working together we can respond.

Make no mistake—we are a blessed nation and must remember: To those whom much is given, much more is expected. We need to do more to reduce carbon dioxide and other greenhouse gases that contribute to global warming. We must move now to save the world's oceans from destruction. If not, the impact will be profound. We must work to improve the quality of life for all the world's citizens if we are to have peace and prosperity.

HER ORGANIZATION, THE SPEAKER BUILDS CREDIBILITY WITH HER AUDIENCE AND AGAIN STRESSES THE GOAL OF EDUCATING ABOUT ISSUES AND ADVOCATING ON BEHALF OF SOUND SOLUTIONS ON THE BASIS OF THE FACTS, NOT BECAUSE OF ANY IDEOLOGICAL BIAS.

CAREFULLY SUPPORTING HER ARGUMENTS WITH HARD DATA, MS. RIMEL POINTS OUT SERIOUS PROBLEMS THAT MEMBERS OF HER AUDIENCE CERTAINLY CARE ABOUT SINCE THEY TOUCH BOTH THEIR PRIVATE LIVES AND THEIR ECONOMIC OR BUSINESS INTERESTS.

THE REPETITION OF "TO THOSE WHOM MUCH IS GIVEN, MUCH MORE IS EXPECTED" THROUGHOUT HER SPEECH IS A WAY OF EMPHASIZING THE PRIVILEGED POSITION OF HER AUDIENCE MEMBERS AND REINFORCES THE NOTION THAT WITH POWER AND PRIVILEGE COMES RESPONSIBILITY.

Clearly, the rest of the world believes we are failing to live up to our leadership and steward-ship responsibilities as the most powerful and affluent nation. That should trouble and sadden us all, but should serve as a clear and compelling call to action.

However, Americans today—unlike our forefathers—often take for granted the democratic ideals that others admire and are willing to die for. The growing disengagement of Americans—par-ticularly our young people—has been well documented. Just a couple of facts: Only a third of eligi-ble Americans under 25 voted in the last Presidential election. Imagine only forty-five percent of those under 25 even bothered to register to vote. Fifty percent say voting is not important. Even more than that say they have no impact on their community. Forty percent never volunteer—for absolutely anything.

At a time when our global power is at an all-time high, civic participation has hit an all-time low. If current trends continue, only one in five voters under 30 will cast a ballot in 20 years. Its no exaggeration to say that the future health of our democracy hangs in the balance.

The second point I want to make today is that the gravest threat to our way of life may not lie outside our borders . . . but rather inside the apathetic hearts and cynical minds of a checked out citizenry. One of our founding family members, J. Howard Pew, gave a speech in 1953, during a hot period in the Cold War, which still resonates today. And I quote:

"We are constantly being alerted to the dangers of subversive activity at work in our land, but a far greater danger lurks in what has been called subversive inactivity. No subversive forces can ever conquer a nation that has not first been conquered by subversive inactivity on the part of the citizenry, who have failed in their civic duty and in service to their country. As freedom is our most precious national asset, I am convinced that apathy—indifference—is our greatest national sin."

We inherited a great democracy. Shame on us if we take it for granted. Let's remember: To those whom much is given, much is expected. Our government not only invites participation, it feeds on it. Four decades of declining voter turnout must be stopped. The target of our efforts has to be young Americans. I believe they are ready to accept our invitation into the public square. Historically, young Americans have energized civic life. All of the major social and political movements—women's rights, civil rights, human rights—were fueled by the idealism, voices and action of the young. Agree or dis-agree with their agenda, you can't debate the force and impact of their passion.

But today, far too many young Americans are checked out—proud to be civic slackers. And they are not checking back in as they grow older. We need their enthusiasm, insights, intellect and commitment if we are going to address the issues that will define our future. It's said all the time that children are our future. The vibrancy of our democracy rests with the generation coming of age in it. Young people who participate learn to build instead of berate. They learn to commit instead of complain. They learn to defend what they believe in, rather than attack what they don't understand.

Kids in college today see an electoral system that is badly broken, where one person does not equal one vote—where special interests with deep pockets hold all the cards. Is it any wonder that our young people are so disgusted and disenfranchised? We've told them over and over that their voice isn't heard and their vote doesn't count.

Is it any surprise that the American public believes that big money can elect a candidate, big money can remove someone from office and big money can influence those in office and drive pub-lic policy in this country? Since the late 1980s, the rules governing campaign financing have become totally ineffective. The cost of running for office and the amount of time spent raising money is stag-gering. The work we have supported documents a shift in power away from the individual and into the hands of organized special interests. Knowing this, why wouldn't Americans silence their voice and shelve their vote? However, there are some positive signs of change.

After years of effort with little progress, campaign finance reform took a huge leap forward with the passage of the McCain-Feingold bill. As we all know, a final decision on the legislation is imminent from the Supreme Court. In addition, there is an open question as to whether the Federal Election Commission is ready, willing and able to enforce the legislation.

Campaign finance reform is a good "case study" of The Pew Trusts' approach to our work. I noted earlier that we see ourselves as an honest broker of information in the public interest, but that we often take our role further once the facts are clear and irrefutable. We also educate, enable, and when the information begs for it, advocate for change—even fight for it.

Campaign finance reform is an issue where my organization has advocated for the public interest. Over the past seven years, we have funded efforts to shine a bright light on the flow of money into and throughout campaigns, whether tracking television advertising dollars, "soft money" contributions or state campaign contribution disclosures. Our grantees educated and advocated as the bills moved to the floors of both the Senate and House and, upon passage, to Committee. Throughout the debates, the reform argument drew heavily on the facts, figures and research compiled by at least ten of our partners. Now that this landmark legislation is being challenged, we're supporting an aggressive strategy to make sure the "people's voice" is heard and that the challenges to dilute the legislation are defeated.

Some of our most important and influential partners are in your hometown. USC's Annenberg School for Communication effectively campaigned for a revamped Federal Election Commission with the "teeth" and the "bite" to really enforce our laws on campaign financing. UCLA's School of Law is grading the campaign finance disclosure systems in all 50 states. Major state loopholes exist which undermine the very integrity of our system. I stand here embarrassed to say that the great state of Pennsylvania received an "F" finding itself in the company of Iowa, Mississippi, New Hampshire, Vermont and several others. You can feel somewhat better—California received a passing grade of "C." Without transparency and trust in our electoral system, we'll never bring the public—young or old—back to the voting booths.

I've used this as an example of how all of us here can all bring our influence, our intellect and our investments to bear on a critical issue by providing accurate, timely information. by leveraging resources, and by bringing the best ideas and influence to move the needle on problems that matter to the health of our civic life.

At The Pew Trusts, our investments are not an act of charity. We invest for leverage and work to return results. There's a sense out there—at least in some part earned—that foundations are some sort of ATM in the sky. You figure out the right button to push, and they cough out the cash. I'm afraid that's wrong. We approach our work more like strategic investors, looking to reap the maximum benefit from our time, talent and capital. Like any business, we seek a return on our investment, except, in our case, it is measured not in dollars, but rather positive, powerful change in the public interest.

I mentioned three factors in my opening, and I'll close with the most important: With our country facing turmoil both at home and abroad, it's time for American citizens to get off the bench and back into the game. Because as you and I both know, to those whom much is given, much is expected.

Martin Luther King, Jr., once observed that "the ultimate measure of a man is not where he stands in moments of comfort and convenience, but where he stands at times of challenge and

131

controversy." With the scars of September 11th still fresh in our hearts and the weight of world opinion pressing down upon us, it's too easy to let cynicism and helplessness rule. While the challenges are enormous, recognizing our limits is no excuse to embrace them. Rather, it is a mandate to answer the call. Americans will fight for their rights, and we should do no less in honoring our responsibilities.

If you vote, I applaud you. Next time, bring a young person with you. Ask their view—you may be surprised and better informed for it. Volunteer in a classroom. E-mail a Senator. Learn about the issues that affect you and your community, and most importantly, act on them. Idealism needs an anchor, and aspiration needs accountability. If democracy is to thrive, we need the people sitting in this room, citizens and leaders from every walk of life with the clout and confidence to speak truth to power—to call all citizens to live up to our civic and global responsibilities.

California leads the nation. You are playing a key role in guiding America's future—on issues ranging from education to environment, on topics as critical as tolerance and diversity. As you go, so goes the nation. No other city in America plays a more important role in shaping the hearts and minds of our citizens, so you—individually and collectively—matter—and matter a lot. So let's all get informed, get involved and get invested. Because to those whom much is given, much, much more is expected.

Source: From "To Those Whom Much Is Given: Honoring Our Obligation as Americans." Speech by Rebecca W. Rimel, Town Hall, Los Angeles, CA, September 30, 2003. Used by permission.

WHILE MANY IN THE AUDIENCE MIGHT CONSIDER THEMSELVES "ENGAGED," AND ALL ARE LIKELY TO HAVE VOTED, MS. RIMEL POINTS OUT MANY OTHER WAYS THEY CAN BE INVOLVED IN SHAPING THE FUTURE. FINALLY, SHE SPECIFICALLY NOTES THE IMPORTANCE OF CALIFORNIA IN GENERAL, AND LOS ANGELES IN PARTICULAR, IN LEADING THE NATION.

Developing Significant Topics

CHAPTER OBJECTIVES

After studying this chapter, you should be able to

1. Generate significant speech topics.

2. Revise and narrow your topic.

3. Determine how ethical considerations affect your choice of a topic.

4. Understand what is meant by a general purpose.

5. Distinguish among the goals of informative, persuasive, and ceremonial speeches.

6. Devise a good specific purpose for your speech.

7. Write a clear thesis statement.

After giving a poor speech, a student came to talk to his instructor and told this story. Two weeks before he was scheduled to give a five- to seven-minute informative speech, David had not yet chosen a topic. He admitted that he was clueless. As he sat in his political science class, he had a bright idea. His professor was explaining how a president is elected in the United States. David had taken several pages of notes and read two chapters on the subject. That seemed to him to be a lot of information. Why not, David thought, just summarize his notes and develop a short speech? He felt great relief as he decided to speak about presidential elections.

Although David's choice of a speech topic may seem sensible, it was not. Randomly choosing a topic can prove disastrous. In this situation, his choice was random because it was inspired by convenience and not by the demands of the communication setting. For one thing, his topic was too broad to be addressed adequately in the available time. The information was much too technical to be useful to David's listeners. In short, David had a difficult time because he did not choose a topic that took into account his audience's knowledge and interests. This "boiled-down" version of a lecture failed to connect with his public speaking classmates.

To make matters worse, David had not taken the time to come up with a clear focus for his speech. He thought only about his general purpose—talking about presidential elections—instead of the specific ideas he wanted his audience to understand. Beginning with his own interests, coupled with important issues of the day, David should have asked himself, What do I care about that would be significant and interesting to this audience? Many worthy topics might have emerged from this kind of reflection. David might have chosen to speak about political action committees, campaign finance reform, or the evolution of the national party conventions. These topics might have grown out of what David already knew something about, but they also should have been fashioned to connect with the interests and needs of the audience. Naturally, David would have to do additional research to address these topics intelligently. He also would need to think more specifically about how he hoped to influence the audience's behavior and thinking. In short, David still needed to go through the process of refining and narrowing his topic, by considering both the general purpose of his speech and the specific response he wanted from his audience.

Finding a Suitable Topic

Preview. *As you start thinking about a topic, first focus your attention on what you know and care about. Taking an inventory of your personal concerns and their relationship to community issues, your intellectual and educational interests, your career goals, and your leisure activities will help you come up with good speech topics. These interests represent a starting point for considering matters of significant public concern that you are motivated to learn more about.*

Deciding what to talk about may or may not be one of your initial concerns as a speaker. In some situations, the topic of your speech will be predetermined. You may be invited to talk because of your expertise or experience, and the invitation determines the topic. If, for example, you have been especially active in an environmental group, you may be asked to speak at a service club about environmental problems in your community. Or perhaps the Student Association at your school distributes funds to campus organizations, and you have been chosen to speak as an advocate for your group. Sometimes the situation determines the topic, as when you attend a public meeting to speak for or against a specific proposal. Many times, however, you will be asked to determine your own topic. Your public speaking class is one such situation. In most cases, you will be assigned only a *type* of speech and you will choose the topic. Your task, then, will be to find the right topic—one that is important, fits with your interests, meets the needs of the situation, and positively impacts your listeners.

Early in your public speaking class, you may be assigned a very specific topic that does not require much preparation or specialized knowledge, just to help you get comfortable speaking before a group. You may be asked to give a short speech describing a person you admire, for example, or a speech introducing yourself or a classmate. Normally, however, you will have to choose your own topic, whether speaking in or outside your class. In most cases, neither circumstances nor setting nor audience demands will determine your specific topic. It will be up to you to choose the best topic.

What Matters to You?

A good way to start thinking about a topic is by thinking about yourself. The fundamental question is, What do I already know and care about? This does not mean, What can I already give a speech about? Do not try to find a ready-made speech in your head or limit yourself to topics on which you are already an expert. That kind of thinking could lead you to imagine that you can just give a speech "off the top of your head." In fact, giving a good speech takes a lot of work, and part of that work is learning more about your topic. Research is essential to support your personal knowledge, opinions, and experiences; and research can always lead you to change or modify your initial topic.

Conducting a Self-Inventory

By doing a self-inventory—taking a thoughtful look at what you really know and care about—you can come up with a list of potential topics. From the thoughtful consideration of issues that affect you and your community, your intellectual and educational interests, your career goals, and your leisure activities and interests you can begin to generate possible topics that are both meaningful to you and address significant issues for your audience.

Begin by brainstorming—writing down anything that comes to your mind under a particular category without thinking about whether the topic would be interesting to your audience, whether you will be able to get enough material, or anything else. Just put down all the possibilities that come to you. When you have come up with a number of ideas, you can then proceed to evaluating possible topics critically, considering whether the topics address significant issues and would be meaningful to your audience.

Personal Concerns and Community Issues

The best place to begin your search for a topic is with matters that are important to you and important to your community. Here are two major questions to start you thinking of topics in this category:

WHAT IS GOING ON IN MY LIFE THAT BOTHERS OR CONCERNS ME THAT MIGHT HAVE SOCIAL SIGNIFICANCE? All of us know of things that we would like to change. We have all been upset by certain people or events, and we all have values and ideals that we wish others would embrace. Begin a list of things that frustrate or upset you—things that you would like to see changed—and then consider the possible speech topics you might generate from such a list.

One student began her self-inventory of personal concerns by reflecting on the difficulty she and her friends were having completing their degree requirements in four years. That suggested a speech arguing that the college ought to offer more courses during the summer, or perhaps a proposal to change the college's degree requirements. She also considered ways that the university might help students better balance work, study, and classes, leading to a proposal that the university offer workshops or support groups for students. She often worried about proposed cutbacks in student loans, suggesting a speech opposing such cuts or advocating more state support for students. Finally, she recalled that spring break was coming up soon, and she began to wonder if there was a better way to spend that time than lying on a beach. This led her to explore opportunities for getting involved in volunteer work over the break, such as through Habitat for Humanity's Collegiate Challenge.

WHAT IS HAPPENING OUTSIDE MY IMMEDIATE WORLD THAT IS UNFAIR, UNJUST, OR IN NEED OF REFORM? What good things going on in the world deserve more support? As you read newspapers and news magazines, watch television news programs, and search the Internet, write down issues that capture your interest. Ask yourself what kinds of news stories concern you the most, and consider what topics might arise out of those concerns. Perhaps a story about a tragic death on campus will lead you to speak about the dangers of binge drinking. Or maybe a story about consumer spending will lead you to reflect on the record lows in personal savings among Americans or the impact of materialism in our society. As you follow the news about the War on Terrorism, perhaps you will decide to talk about the tension between civil liberties and national security. As you hear news about the development of nuclear weapons in Iran or North Korea, you may reflect on nuclear proliferation treaties and how well they work. The possibilities are limitless. Pay attention to what is happening in your community, your country, and the world and you will generate a long and varied list of possible speech topics.

Intellectual and Educational Interests

Your self-inventory can prod you to consider important topics that you would like to know more about. Ask yourself these questions:

WHAT DO I LIKE TO READ? One student listed the books she had most enjoyed reading in the past year and asked herself what they had in common. Two books that she particularly liked, *Reading Lolita in Tehran* and *The Kite Runner*, dealt with efforts to

Concern for problems, whether in the world, the country, or your community will generate significant topics for speeches. These students from Taylor University, helping to rebuild homes in New Orleans, would have many compelling experiences upon which to build a speech.

impose cultural values through force and intimidation. This led her to consider a speech topic dealing with different cultural values, and then to a possible topic: the differences between Islamic values and traditional Western values. She was still a long way from a specific topic, but she had taken the first step.

WHAT INTERESTING THINGS HAVE I LEARNED FROM TELEVISION OR MOVIES? Another student began by considering the television programs and movies he most enjoyed and came up with a list of sitcoms, dramas, reality shows, and nature films. As he thought about the significant issues that might emerge from the shows he watched, all sorts of possible topics arose. *Will and Grace* suggested that he might talk about sexual stereotyping. Thinking about his favorite TV reality program, *The Apprentice*, led him to consider business ethics. The movie *March of the Penguins* suggested a speech on ocean pollution or the preservation of natural resources. His problem was not to find a topic, but to select and develop one of the many that his brainstorming generated.

WHAT SPECIFIC COURSES, OR ISSUES COVERED IN MY COURSES, HAVE PARTICULARLY INTERESTED ME? Courses in your major field of study can also be a source of topics. Here are some examples of topics generated by students from their majors: a physics major spoke on the benefits of space exploration; an English major chose to talk about the way in which books shape our view of the world and the need to read critically; a psychology major explained how cognitive dissonance is experienced and its consequences in making important decisions; a business major decided to examine the tensions between the profit motive and ethics in large corporations. In each case, the topic grew from something the student had heard about in a course, and all addressed serious issues.

Career Goals

Students will usually have an ultimate career goal in mind; many may already be pursuing a career. The major question to start with here is, What do I hope to do with my life? Follow up on this question by brainstorming possible issues that such a profession might raise. One student who planned to be a lawyer first brainstormed professional issues. He raised such questions as, Do you take any client who can afford to pay? What if you think someone is guilty? Is it right to approach a potential client who has suffered a tragic loss? What do you do if your personal interests conflict with a client's best interests? What can be done about the widespread mistrust of lawyers? As he considered these questions, he soon realized that they all raised important questions about the ethical code that lawyers follow.

Other careers might suggest additional topics. A future teacher might speak about how the success of democracy depends on well-educated citizens. A future engineer might address the dangers of our deteriorating infrastructure. If you plan to be an accountant, perhaps you would speak on the need for tax reform. A future research chemist might speak on generic drugs and how they affect consumers. If you hope to become a marketing analyst, you might choose to address how wise consumers make choices among similar products. A future television producer might speak on how viewers can influence network programming. Giving a speech related to your future career has the added bonus of providing you with information you can use in the future. By thinking about your prospective career, you might not only discover a good speech topic but also learn more about the career you are considering.

Leisure Activities and Interests

Things you do for pleasure or enjoyment may be a source of topics. Yet a word of caution is in order: speeches that some audiences might find useful or interesting may seem ordinary or trivial to others. For example, you may have experience teaching children how to string their own tennis rackets, but your college classmates would not likely respond well to a speech entitled "How to String a Tennis Racket." While playing bridge, dancing, or watching football may be enjoyable for you, they do not suggest topics that will help you craft challenging, significant speeches. They would likely demand little preparation and would give the audience little of importance to take away from the speech.

Nevertheless, a sports enthusiast could come up with some significant topics. Among the sports-related topics that are hotly debated today are the question of whether student-athletes ought to be paid, the obligations of colleges and universities to support women athletes under Title IX of the Educational Amendments of 1972, and whether the United States is becoming a nation of spectators. Similarly, an avid moviegoer might explain how films help to shape the rules of social interaction in our culture, or the ways in which our history is manipulated in films to promote particular political beliefs and values. Someone who sees a lot of movies also might address the topic of censorship or the controversy over how movies and other forms of entertainment are rated.

Conducting a self-inventory that surveys your intellectual and educational interests, career goals, personal and social concerns, and favorite leisure activities and interests will serve as starting points as you search for your own topics. Of course, the broad topics you generate through brainstorming may need to be narrowed and focused. A consideration of the situation and the audience will help you do this.

Brainstorming Topics of Public Concern

Besides conducting a self-inventory, you will also want to read widely as you search for potential speech topics that address issues that affect your community, the nation, and the world. Consider the larger world of which you are a part. Getting or staying connected with the world is absolutely essential if you hope to engage in the public discussion of important issues. To do this you must stay in touch with unfolding events: following local, national, and world news is just as essential to your development as a public speaker as completing assignments and attending class.

Suppose, for example, you read about the controversy surrounding alternative fuel sources. At the outset, you may have given little thought to this controversy, but you begin to see it as an important issue and a good one for a speech. As you read further, you become interested in whether Ethanol might be a good alternative fuel source that we, as a nation, should pursue. You notice contradictory research findings. On the one hand, you read that Ethanol burns cleaner than fossil fuels. At the same time, however, you learn that the *process* of making Ethanol relies on fossil fuels, which results in little if any energy gains (since it takes a lot of energy to produce one gallon of Ethanol). You begin to wonder whether or not we will be able to produce Ethanol more efficiently, as some experts suggest, so that we can reduce our dependence on foreign oil. As your knowledge grows in depth and breadth, you decide that this is an important topic that would likely be of interest to your classroom audience.

However extensive or limited your initial interests, experiences, and knowledge, you should always be willing to consider further diversifying your interests and knowledge by regularly reading *good* newspapers (such as the *New York Times*, the *Wall Street Journal*, and the *Christian Science Monitor*) and exploring other reliable sources such as those available on the Internet. As an example of how one university offers research guides that will help with topic selection, see the *Focus on Civic Engagement* on page 140.

The more you read, the better able you will be to brainstorm speech topics that focus on substantive matters of public concern. These topics may or may not be grounded in your own background and initial interests. As your knowledge base expands, you will develop *new* concerns about substantive issues that you will want to share with listeners.

Narrowing the Topic

Preview. *The potential speech topics that emerge from brainstorming are just that—potential topics. Now you can narrow and refine your choices by understanding how the situation, time constraints, and audience will influence your speech.*

Focus on Civic Engagement

Using Internet Sources to Locate Topics of Public Concern

At Southeast Missouri University, public speaking students are asked to consult the *Kent Library Research Guide*, a guide that suggests resources and research strategies for developing public presentations.

- The *Guide* provides suggestions on where and how to look for journal articles, local and national newspapers, editorials, statistics, Web resources, and other guides.
- It points to valuable resources for selecting current, controversial, or classically debated topics, including:
  - CQ Researcher—provides a print service with comprehensive weekly reports on various topics

- Facts.Com—offers subscription access to Facts on File
- Newseum.org—allows the reader to read the front pages of newspapers from all over the world
- White House News and Policies—offers a policies and initiatives column with topics arranged by group
- World Headlines—allows the reader to follow the links of various news outlets.
- Other resources focus on opinion pieces, Web directories, and video sources

Source: To access this guide, go to http://library.semo.edu/learn/guides/publicspeaking.html. Also, you can ask your own librarian for comparable guides that might be available to you.

Any topic must be appropriate for the audience and the occasion. It must stretch listeners' present understanding or perception of your topic or add to their knowledge. As you refine the purpose of your speech, conduct research, develop arguments and supporting material, and organize your ideas, you will probably find that you need to adjust your topic. The first step is to consider your audience carefully and to decide more precisely what you hope to accomplish. In the previous chapter we discussed audience analysis and adaptation. For now, let us review two guidelines that will help you focus and refine your topic.

Consider the Situation

- Will my audience be familiar with any immediate events or information relevant to my topic?
- Does the topic I am considering relate to recent events that may be of serious concern to my listeners?
- Would I be able to convince my listeners to care as much about my potential topic as I do?
- Do I have sufficient time to cover the topic adequately?

Consider the Audience

- What does my audience already know?
- What common experiences has my audience had?
- What do my listeners and I have in common?
- How diverse is my audience?

Let us consider how to apply the guidelines in specific cases through an example.

Ruiz, a meteorology major, was interested in how weather systems developed. For him, situational factors proved decisive in narrowing his topic. When he asked himself if his audience would be familiar with any immediate events relevant to his topic, he thought of all the recent news stories about the devastation caused by hurricanes. Then he asked himself if this topic would be of serious concern to his audience. Although they had all heard about the recent hurricanes, they did not live in an area that was subject to hurricanes. He wondered how he might encourage his listeners to relate better to weather events, and thus be supportive of investing in improved methods of weather prediction. If his audience could understand how disasters caused by weather have consequences for *everyone*, he reasoned, they would find his speech more interesting and convincing. He also asked himself how much he could say in seven minutes, the time allotted for his speech. This kind of thinking helped him focus on how weather disasters, even in a distant part of the country, could affect his audience. This is how he began his speech:

> Everyone is aware of the devastating effects of the horrific hurricanes this past summer. These terrible storms cost many lives, destroyed people's homes and businesses, and forced their homeless victims to move to all parts of the country. We know that these storms directly affect us because of the huge amounts of money that the government has pledged to help rebuild. We also might have relatives or friends from the areas affected. Schools and universities in our own state took in many students from the affected areas, and many people opened their homes to strangers. From a purely humanitarian point of view, that is probably sufficient for us to support efforts to improve weather forecasting in America.
>
> But there are also other, less dramatic ways that weather-related disasters directly impact us. After you watched scenes of the hurricanes on the Gulf Coast, did you notice that the price of gasoline went up? The same thing happens to the price of bread and breakfast cereals when rivers in the wheat-producing states flood following especially heavy winter snows. It happens all the time: Florida has a deep freeze in December, and in early January your orange juice costs fifty cents more. There's a drought in California, and all of a sudden iceberg lettuce costs twice as much as it used to. As Mark Twain once quipped, "Everybody talks about the weather, but nobody does anything about it." Well, scientific and technological advances in understanding what causes the formation of certain weather patterns have been made, but much more of our energies and resources *must* be devoted to learning still more about how weather affects our lives. Specifically, we need to invest more in weather prediction technologies and early warning systems.

This student had gone from selecting possible topics though a self-inventory to narrowing the possibilities by considering his own interests. He then considered relevant situational and audience factors in order to focus his speech on a topic that mattered to his audience, and that concerned the broader welfare of the community.

Considerations of situation and audience are just as important to speakers outside the classroom. A public health official, for example, might be asked to speak to a community group about avian flu. Just as the student speaker, this speaker needs to consider the situation. Is there a real threat of an epidemic? Has there been a lot of media coverage of the issue? Are flu shots available? He also needs to ask questions about the audience. Do his listeners have much medical knowledge? Is there serious concern among the group that the flu will be widespread? Is the group made up of older persons who are more susceptible to the flu? Does the audience include parents who might be worried about their children? Based on such considerations, it may be that she will decide to narrow the topic to give an explanation of exactly what the bird flu is and how it is transmitted. Or she may wish to explain the symptoms of the flu, how to avoid contracting it, and what to do if one exhibits the symptoms. She may, instead, wish to assure her audience that there is no need to panic and focus on the reasons the flu is *not* likely to affect them. So, from the topic of avian flu, this speaker might narrow the topic in a number of ways to better suit the situation and audience.

Ethical Obligations in Selecting a Topic

Preview. *As you choose a topic, you need to recognize your ethical obligations to the audience. Your topic should be one about which you can become knowledgeable through a careful and extensive consideration of relevant material. Although you will likely pick a topic about which you have strong feelings, you should be sure that your approach to the topic is fair-minded. And you will want to exercise appropriate judgment in considering the audience's standards of good taste.*

Ethics may be described as a set of behavioral standards. Some would argue that ethics are universal and unchanging, but others might argue that they are relative to a particular culture or situation. In either case, such standards represent a code, and a person who lives by that code is considered to be ethical. If an audience senses that a speaker is ethical, they will likely find that speaker more convincing.[1]

As a speaker, you will draw on your own ethical code in choosing a topic, as well as in making decisions about how to approach that topic. Ethical considerations cannot be taken up after you have finished your work, nor can they be dealt with and dismissed early on. A good speaker integrates ethical concerns into the whole process of preparing to speak.

Although we might not always agree on what is ethical, there are some ethical considerations you should take into account as you choose a topic—namely, your responsibility for accuracy, fair-mindedness, taste, and judgment.

Accuracy

When searching for a topic, you would not reject a possibility because you did not know enough to speak about it without any preparation. As we pointed out earlier, you should not expect to have a ready-made speech in your head. A major part of preparing to speak is learning more about your topic. You may not be an established expert in a particular field, but you owe it to your audience to know as much as possible about your topic. What does this have to do with ethics?

First, without careful research, you cannot come to a sound conclusion for yourself. Speaking to influence people carries with it the ethical obligation to know what you are talking about and to believe in what you say. You should not ask someone to give blood to the Red Cross if you are not willing to donate blood yourself. Nor should you seek to convince people to invest their money in a bond fund that you think too risky. When you select a topic, you should choose one that you can both master *and* believe in.

Second, if you are not knowledgeable, you may inadvertently misinform, mislead, or even harm your audience. For example, obesity is a major health problem in America. If you were to give a speech based on just one dieting article that you read, you might suggest practices that would hurt rather then help your listeners. The article may have been outdated, it may not have covered all the potential objections to the diet, it may have asserted as fact matters that are not yet scientifically verified, or it may have come from a biased source. Even if you are not trying to persuade an audience, accuracy will still have an ethical dimension. An informative speech aims to further listeners' understanding; to give information that is misleading or untrue—even if a speaker does so unknowingly—is highly irresponsible.

Just as important as using enough sources is considering source credibility. Would you want to try an amazing marshmallow diet touted by a supermarket tabloid? Or would you feel more comfortable taking advice based on a study reported in the *New England Journal of Medicine*? When you are giving a speech, you are the information resource for your audience. Citing reputable sources will make you a more credible and ethical speaker.

Urging people to take actions or to modify their behavior in ways that could have negative consequences is clearly unethical. The consequences need not be physical, such as endangering one's health. Misinformation or poorly understood and developed ideas can also lead to poor decisions on economic, social, or political matters that affect people's lives.

Objectivity versus Subjectivity

We rarely, if ever, achieve the ideal of perfect objectivity. None of us can be entirely neutral toward topics we know or care about. We cannot help having subjective reactions based on our experiences and the values we have learned and accepted. We have religious feelings, political biases, or expectations for social behavior that are a part of us whether we consciously recognize them or not. As a speaker, you cannot erase your past and approach any topic as if it had no relationship to your life. On the contrary, potential topics grow from such life experiences. Nor does an audience really expect such complete objectivity. What an audience *does* expect, however, is fair-mindedness—a willingness to suspend your own biases and to remain open to competing ideas.

Since you will be selecting topics from your particular areas of interest or expertise, you will likely have preexisting opinions, biases, or strong feelings about those topics. However, an ethical speaker approaches topic selection if not in an absolutely objective manner, at least in a fair-minded way. If you speak on HMOs and the decline of health care in America, you have clearly taken a position critical of HMOs. Such a position is certainly acceptable, but you have the ethical obligation to be open to the possibility that what you learn in your research may lead you to modify your initial point of view. An ethical speaker allows for change as part of the speech preparation process and avoids using the topic as a filter to screen out any information that might enlarge, limit, or redirect it. Once you have gone through such a process and come to a conclusion based on a thoughtful and fair examination of relevant information, you can be more confident in taking a strong, well-reasoned stand on an issue.

Taste and Judgment

Generally, you should avoid topics that audiences might find embarrassing or offensive. Putting listeners in such a position violates ethical norms. An audience-centered perspective is crucial here. *You* might find certain topics appealing, amusing, or of great importance. Thinking of what an audience might feel about a particular topic, however, may cast it in a different light.

Imagine a student in your public speaking class giving a speech that advocated converting to the speaker's religion. Although the student has the right to hold particular beliefs, a classroom audience will likely be made up of people whose beliefs differ and who could well be offended by a speaker trying to convert them. The likelihood of offense increases when the audience is a captive one: listeners in a classroom did not choose to come to hear that particular speech, nor can they simply leave. Attempting to force one's beliefs on an audience will likely be viewed as a tasteless effort showing a lack of judgment on the part of the speaker. Moreover, trying to change a deeply held faith, ingrained skepticism, or even habitual indifference is not a practical goal in a short speech. In a public speaking class, you need to be especially wary of issues on which the audience is deeply divided.

This does not mean that you should avoid controversial topics—being engaged will inevitably lead you to advocate positions that are contested. What is important is that you be sensitive to contrary opinions and aware of the limits imposed by those opinions. It might be that a speech simply explaining the beliefs of a particular religion might be appropriate—as long as you do not try to convert your listeners. In any case, different audiences may view the same topic in different ways. As an ethical speaker, you must consider each audience separately and fully understand its members' particular tastes and dispositions when selecting a topic.[2]

With these steps in topic selection taken, your next task is to hone in on the purpose of your speech.

General Purposes

Preview. *Public speaking is always purposeful—that is, a speaker always aims to get responses from listeners. Sometimes the principal kind of response you want from an audience is understanding, so you give an informative speech. At other times, you want to influence the way* *listeners feel, what they believe, or how they act. In those cases, you give a persuasive speech. Finally, you may give a ceremonial speech when you want to reinforce values and engage in community building.*

Just as speakers contemplate the situation, their own interests, and those of the audience in selecting a topic, they must use those considerations to formulate a specific purpose and a thesis statement. As you refine your topic, you try to translate it into a specific statement of the audience response you anticipate. Everything that can be done to insure successful public communication rests on having a clear purpose. The first step in crafting a purpose is to determine the nature of the response you want from an audience; this is your general purpose. Sometimes you will want to uncover or explain in depth a problem that your listeners are unaware of, while on other occasions, you want to change their understanding of the nature and extent of the problem.

In most classroom situations, you will be assigned a general purpose. It is also true, as we discussed earlier, that you may be asked to speak at work or in a setting related specifically to your interests or expertise. In such cases, you still have to make many other choices based on your general purpose. Let us now consider the three general purposes that will account for most of the speeches you give.

Informative Purposes

When we talk about informing people, we naturally think about giving them new information. But as a speaker, what do *you* want from your audience when you give an informative speech? You want *understanding*; you give an informative speech to gain understanding from listeners.

This is not just playing with words; an important concept is involved. Have you ever been in a class where the instructor gave a lecture with a lot of information that you did not understand? Or have you gotten directions from someone, but then found that you still could not reach your destination? Have you ever gotten instructions on how to do a job, only to find that you still could not complete the task? If anything like this has happened to you, you have experienced the difference between just getting information and gaining understanding. In all of these cases, the person attempting to communicate with you failed to help you understand.

When you give an informative speech, your goal is to help your listeners understand something they did not understand before. After you have finished speaking, listeners will not just have *heard* something new; they will have *learned* something new. We discuss informative speaking in more detail in Chapter 14.

Persuasive Purposes

Persuasion surrounds us; it intrudes on almost every aspect of our lives. We are urged to give our time to worthy causes, to donate money to charity, to vote for particular politicians, or to protest a decision by the local school board. We are asked to embrace new beliefs or values, to accept new ideas, and to defer to the opinions and judgments of others. Like informative messages, persuasive messages aim to get something from us: agreement, empathy, or maybe even some change in our behavior. Persuasive speakers do not just want us to understand their point of view; they want to influence our beliefs, values, and actions.

Persuasion is more than telling listeners what they ought to do or believe. It is more than simply giving an audience facts or statistics. It is more than simply stating your opinion. It is more than asking, recommending, or demanding. We often hear advertisers, politicians, telemarketers, or salespersons give many reasons why we should accept their arguments. But we do not always do what they would like us to do. We are not always persuaded.

Persuasion requires that we give our audience good reasons for accepting our claims. As a speaker, you want listeners to feel more strongly about an issue, to agree with you, or to take some definite action. We discuss the goals of persuasive speaking in more detail in Chapters 15 and 16.

Ceremonial Purposes

Many speaking occasions offer the opportunity for community building. We may be called on to honor someone, celebrate an event of shared significance, or pay tribute to someone we have loved or lost. Ceremonial speaking uplifts us, comforts us, and reinforces our sense of community with others.[3]

When our speaking purpose is ceremonial, we articulate and reinforce shared values. We respond to such questions as, What has brought us together? What defines us as a group? Which of our accomplishments are we most proud of? What are the principles *we* cherish? In some ceremonial contexts, we may also honor heroes, those who personify and illuminate our values. By holding them high, praising their accomplishments, and remembering how they lived their lives, we are reminding ourselves of the values we cherish. There are still other times when those speaking in ceremonial contexts will present awards, deliver commencement speeches, or give motivational speeches. By doing so, they offer encouragement and inspiration to listeners. A life well lived provides a tangible example that shows us that hard work, determination, and the desire to succeed pay off. These examples serve to reinforce shared American values. In other cultures, speakers may hold up different values during ceremonial speeches, such as interdependence and collectivism.[4]

Ceremonial speeches may be given by anyone—political leaders, community leaders, citizens, or by students speaking in a classroom. In their inaugural addresses, for example, U.S. presidents remind us of our common beliefs. John Kennedy did so eloquently when he said, "Let every nation know, whether it wishes us well or ill, that we will pay any price, bear any burden, meet any hardship, support any friend, oppose any foe to assure the survival and the success of liberty."[5] Ronald Reagan reminded us of traits valued by Americans when he eulogized the astronauts killed in the *Challenger* explosion in 1986, referring to them as "seven heroes . . . who were daring and brave and [who] had that special grace."[6] In a speech class, a student giving a speech of tribute said of the retiring director of the local Boys and Girls Club, "I admired her for her wisdom and kindness. She was my anchor when my parents divorced. She comforted me and encouraged me and made me believe that I would survive. She taught me how to strive to be my best, even in

Ceremonial speeches affirm shared values and create a strong sense of community, as did President Kennedy who often spoke eloquently on ceremonial occasions.

tough times." When listeners identify with the personal traits and values celebrated by these speakers, they are affirming their shared values—with the potential for building a stronger bond as a community. We will discuss ceremonial speaking in greater detail in Chapter 17.

A general purpose, then, points you in the direction you want to go. The next step is to refine that general purpose into a specific purpose statement that spells out precisely the response you want from your audience.

Crafting a Specific Purpose

Preview. *Specific purpose statements describe the response you want from your audience. They are shaped by your goals as a speaker, the situation in which you speak, and the potential benefits to the audience.*

Although speakers may hope to accomplish many things in a speech, the specific purpose is the ultimate response that the speaker hopes to achieve. Crafting the specific purpose statement carefully is a vital step in clearly focusing the speech.

Purpose and Response

Successful speakers plan the desired audience response carefully and never allow themselves to be vague or unclear about their purpose. Imagine, for example, a speaker who said, "My purpose is to talk about energy conservation." Such a statement, of course, identifies no specific purpose. It says something very vague about the speaker's topic, but it does not specify an audience response. Furthermore, "energy conservation" is so broad that it says little about the speaker's specific purpose. With the purpose stated in this way, the speaker would have had a difficult time choosing what to include and what to exclude in the speech. If the student planned to give an informative speech, he or she would want to devise a purpose that sought to promote audience understanding and so might devise this specific purpose statement: *I want my audience to understand ways in which each one of them can conserve energy in their daily lives.* What if, on the other hand, the student planned to give a persuasive speech? Does anyone really oppose conserving energy? No, obviously not. But, *how* energy conservation can be achieved through public policy *is* a matter of debate. In a persuasive speech the student could take a position on any number of controversial solutions, such as *I want my audience to agree that the government should impose much stricter gasoline consumption standards on auto manufacturers.* Or, *I want my audience to agree that the production of SUVs should be discouraged through heavy taxation.* Or, *Building more nuclear power plants will significantly reduce the need for reliance on fossil fuel.* All these potential purposes relate to the topic of energy conservation, and each represents a specific statement of what the speaker hopes to accomplish.

Purpose and the Situation

The specific purpose is also shaped by the demands of the situation. Suppose you are to give an informative speech in class and your topic is the problem of crime. You would—after considering the factors influencing the audience, the relationship of crime to the audience, and the amount of time available for the speech— decide that the audience should know more about how crime can affect them directly. In trying to gain understanding, you could devise several possibilities. On a campus in a rural or suburban area, students might not be aware of the extent to which and the ways in which crime could affect them. In that case, you might want a specific purpose, such as *I want my audience to understand the types of crimes and extent of crime that occurs on our campus.* On an urban campus, where students might be more likely to have had direct experience with crime, a better specific purpose might be *I want my audience to understand how they can reduce their chances of being a victim of crime.* Of course, your civic concerns and responsibilities extend beyond your immediate environment, and you will sometimes take on topics of significance to the larger community, formulating such purposes as *I want my audience to understand what "white collar" crimes are and how such crimes affect them,* or *I want my audience to agree that poverty contributes directly to increased crime.*

Purpose and Audience Benefits

In devising a specific purpose, you need to consider how listeners are expected to respond and what they can hope to gain. The benefits to the audience ought to be apparent in the speech. Too often speakers are not aware of this basic principle. A speaker at a large university, for example, addressed a crowd gathered to protest proposed fee hikes for state institutions. The listeners had come because they wanted to know how they could help stop the hikes. The speaker, however, delivered a long, angry speech about student apathy and implied that such ignorant, unresponsive people deserved whatever they got at the hands of an unsympathetic legislature.

Clearly, this speaker should have taken a different approach. He could have talked about the need to become active, or he could have tried to get his audience (already motivated to act) to understand what direct actions they could take to put pressure on lawmakers. He could have suggested a wide range of appropriate responses. Instead he probably decided just to "get up and talk about apathy." The result was that he irritated and alienated an initially friendly audience and injected a depressing note into what should have been an enthusiastic show of unity and determination.

If you were about to go to the grocery store, you would have some clear goal—at least to buy food, at best to buy particular items. Your goal would be to buy something, not just to shop. Shopping is the process, the means to an end. In the same way, "talking about" something is not an end in itself. Instead, you talk with an audience to obtain a desired reaction and to provide some benefit to them. So, instead of "talking about" the graduated income tax, you would develop a specific purpose, such as *I want my audience to agree that a graduated income tax is the fairest way to generate revenues*.

Purposes and Multiple Responses

Beginning speakers sometimes have difficulty understanding the differences between informative and persuasive speeches. Indeed, sometimes speeches must be informative before they can be persuasive. Public service ads, for example, are designed to help people understand the dangers of smoking or how to prevent the spread of AIDS, in the hope that understanding will eventually lead to changes in behavior.

Some speeches promote understanding, reinforce ideas and feelings, seek agreement, and call for action—all within one speech. The specific purpose of such a speech, however, is what the speaker ultimately hopes to accomplish. The more minor purposes are secondary to the main purpose. Consider this example.

A student interested in Native American culture in the Southwest chose to talk about

This public service ad hopes to attract the viewers' attention and make the point that many people who believe that AIDS can't affect them may be more at risk than they believe. Such information may cause those who see the ad to rethink their own behavior.

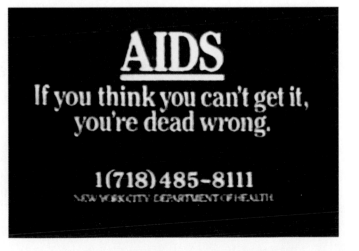

AIDS

If you think you can't get it, you're dead wrong.

1(718) 485-8111

NEW YORK CITY DEPARTMENT OF HEALTH

Indian reservations to fulfill a persuasive speaking assignment. She considered several possible purposes before deciding on this one: *I want my audience to sign up for a work week at an Indian reservation over spring break.* In the speech, the audience was given information that would help them understand the problems on Indian reservations. The speaker then attempted to reinforce the listeners' feelings that it would be good to get a complete break from the routine of school while performing a worthwhile public service. She next presented evidence in an effort to gain agreement that the week would add significantly to their understanding of Native American culture. Finally, she encouraged them to take direct action by signing up to go on the trip. In other words, she aimed at a whole range of responses preceding the ultimate one she desired.

Suppose that listeners, as a result of the speech, learned a good deal about the reservations. Perhaps they agreed that a trip there would be educational and worthwhile. However, if they failed to sign up for the work trip, the speaker would *not* have been satisfied. Her purpose was to get them to take a specific action. To do that, she needed to go *beyond* listeners gaining understanding or agreeing with her. She needed to help the audience see how the trip would directly benefit them and others—and call for action.

Sometimes speakers have to inform before they can hope to persuade. How, for example, could listeners be asked to agree that genetic research is safe and desirable if they did not understand anything about that kind of research? How could listeners be expected to agree that nuclear energy is safe and reliable if they did not understand at least a few fundamental principles about how nuclear reactions work?

The crucial difference among the three speeches is that an informative speech, in aiming to gain understanding, is not directed at resolving a controversy. A persuasive speech, by contrast, offers solutions to problems or suggests actions to take. The ceremonial speech reinforces values that should inspire and motivate us and bind us together as a community. The specific purpose of a speech is the speaker's hoped-for end result. In other words, no matter what else you may accomplish, the speech cannot be considered a complete success if you do not achieve your specific purpose.

Testing Specific Purposes

Preview. *How will you know if your specific purpose is appropriate? You can assess it by making sure that it aims for a specific response from the audience, reflects the realities of the situation, and is clear and ethical.*

Because your specific purpose is the foundation of your speech, we have devoted a great deal of space in this chapter to describing how to develop it. Let us consider some quick ways to test the specific purposes you develop. Basically, there are four questions you can ask yourself to determine whether you have a sound specific purpose statement.

A Good Specific Purpose Asks for an Audience Response

Ask yourself, Does the purpose call for a response from the audience? Here are some ideas that are *not* specific purposes:

- What you should know about your taxes.
- I want to talk about the need for tax reform.
- Tax reform.
- My views of tax reform.

These might be topics or titles, but they do not designate the response you want from the audience. For example, a good specific purpose for an informative speech might be *I want my audience to understand how the alternative minimum tax might affect them.* A good specific purpose for a persuasive speech might be *I want my audience to support the proposal for a flat tax on income.*

A Good Specific Purpose Is Realistic

Ask yourself, Does the purpose reflect the realities of the situation? Among the factors you should consider in crafting a realistic specific purpose are the amount of time you have to give a speech, the probability that your listeners can actually respond the way you want them to, whether the speech's goals have some reasonable expectation of success, and what kind of impact the setting/occasion might have on the outcome of the speech.

Consider the following specific purpose: *I want my audience to understand how Congress works.* This is an absurdly broad topic that could well be the subject of an entire course in political science. What can you accomplish in a short speech? If you are giving an informative speech, you might craft a more focused, achievable purpose in the time available to you, such as *I want my audience to understand how conference committees resolve differences between House and Senate versions of a bill.* If you are giving a persuasive speech its purpose could be *I want my audience to agree that lobbying has too much influence on congressional legislation.* Or, to take another example, suppose you were to offer as a specific purpose, *I want my audience to agree with me that all federal elections should be funded exclusively by the federal government.* This is a correctly stated specific purpose, but you need to consider if such a move is possible in the contemporary political climate. The practicality of your purpose is an important consideration. To take another example, if you are going to ask your audience to give 20 hours a week to volunteering in a good cause, you must ask yourself whether or not full-time students, some of whom have part-time jobs as well, would be at all likely to do this.

Sometimes you may craft purposes that are appropriate in one setting but not in others. *I want my audience to understand how to go about choosing a college that is right for them* might be an acceptable purpose for a speech given at your local high school, but not for one in your college classroom.

A Good Specific Purpose Is Clear

Ask yourself, Is the purpose clear? An audience can often be confused by a strategy that grows out of a vague purpose. Communication is almost invariably unsuccessful when speakers are not clear about what they want to accomplish.

I want my audience to agree with me about health care is not a good purpose. Although it sounds like a purpose statement, it shows that the speaker does not know precisely what he or she wants the audience to believe or do. If you were speaking on this subject, you might want to persuade your audience to share your values about the need for health care and, accordingly, have as your specific purpose *I want my audience to agree with me that everyone in the United States is entitled to adequate health care.* Or, perhaps, you may want to advocate a health-care policy: *I want my audience to support the government-supported universal health-care plan, Medicare for All.*

A Good Specific Purpose Is Ethical

So far, in discussing specific purposes, we have been concerned with issues of response, clarity, and realism. These are all important considerations, but they could all be fulfilled and still the purpose could be unethical.

As we pointed out previously, speakers sometimes pursue goals that are not in the best interests of the listeners or of society at large. The following specific purpose, for example, is clearly not ethical: *I want my audience to understand how they can avoid paying taxes by hiding their cash in offshore accounts.* Cheating on your income tax is not only socially irresponsible, it is clearly illegal. Yet, even if legality is removed as an issue, ethical judgments about speaker purposes can be made.[7] For instance, suppose a speaker wanted to advance this purpose: *I want my audience to understand how to purchase term papers over the Internet.* You will not be sent to jail for doing this, but the action you are advocating is clearly plagiarism. This violates both ethical norms and the specific regulations of every college and university in the country. And surely everyone would agree that it is unethical to promote a fad diet that is seriously questioned by health professionals or to market certain products that might actually cause harm.

Of course, ethical boundaries are often less clear. Conflicts of interest often occur in public debates over controversial issues. Take, for example, the issue of capping medical malpractice awards. Few would disagree with the idea that health-care costs should be kept at reasonable levels. Yet, we know that doctors and insurance companies will benefit financially if malpractice suits are capped, just as lawyers will benefit if they are not. Certainly, physicians have a legitimate concern when their insurance costs are such that they cannot afford to practice medicine. At the same time, patients who have lost all means of livelihood through the act of a careless, ill-prepared, or indifferent health professional have the right to demand compensation. As profit-making organizations, insurance companies have the right to minimize their costs and maximize their profits. Yet, individuals with legitimate grievances must have some means of protection against large and powerful insurance companies. Most of those involved in this controversy may truly believe that their interests and the public interest are the same. The ethical problem arises when one attempts to portray selfish motivations as concern for the public welfare or as upholding cherished principles. We have a right, for example, to be suspicious of politicians who oppose all campaign financing reforms as a violation of their free speech. While some may be sincere, it seems more likely that most are protecting their own sources of campaign financing.

Like other aspects of public speaking, our specific purposes often have ethical implications. As speakers, we need to think about who we are, who our listeners are, and what we have to gain or lose. As speakers, we have an ethical obligation to ask how our audience might benefit or be hurt or misled by the information that we are sharing with them or the actions we are urging them to pursue.

Once you have crafted a specific purpose that meets the tests, you are ready to construct a thesis statement.

Constructing a Thesis Statement

Preview. *The thesis statement grows from your specific purpose. It is a clear declarative statement that embodies the principal idea of your speech. It should be focused without being cluttered with too much detail.*

After you have worked out a specific purpose, you need to formulate a declarative statement that sums up the thesis of your speech, sometimes called the central idea or thesis statement of the speech. You should think of this as your speech in a nutshell. A good thesis statement will help while you are doing research and as you draft the speech. If you are successful in achieving your specific purpose, the thesis statement is what listeners will carry away with them—what they will remember as the heart of your speech.

Guidelines for Constructing a Thesis Statement

There are three basic guidelines to keep in mind when constructing a thesis statement.

The Thesis Statement Is a Single, Complete Declarative Sentence That Embodies the Idea That You Want the Audience to Understand or Accept in Order to Accomplish Your Specific Purpose

It is important to emphasize that the thesis is a *declarative* sentence—an idea you want to convey to your audience—not a question or a phrase that simply announces the topic. *How can we improve our public schools?* and *Improving our public schools* are not thesis statements. A good thesis would answer that question or specify *how* you propose to improve public schools. For example, your thesis might read, *The real key to improving public schools is hiring more qualified teachers.*

The thesis statement grows from your specific purpose. In effect, it answers the question, What do listeners have to understand or feel or believe or do if I am going to get the response I want? Consider the following examples of possible specific purposes and the thesis statements that might grow out of them.

> **Specific purpose:** *I want my audience to understand how one qualifies for unemployment insurance.*
> **Thesis statement:** *Unemployment insurance is available for a limited time period and only for those who meet specific criteria.*
> **Specific purpose:** *I want my audience to agree with me that the North American Free Trade Agreement provides economic benefits for both the United States and its trading partners.*
> **Thesis statement:** *NAFTA stimulates the U.S. economy while providing capital for the improvement of foreign economies as well.*
> **Specific purpose:** *I want my audience to support the Administration's plan for Social Security reform.*
> **Thesis statement:** *The Administration's Social Security reform plan will safeguard the incomes of seniors while providing more profitable investment opportunities for younger workers.*
> **Specific purpose:** *I want my audience to honor the late Dana Reeve's tireless efforts on behalf of individuals suffering from spinal cord injuries.*
> **Thesis statement:** *The late Dana Reeve's work with the Christopher and Dana Reeve Foundation provided an inspirational model for us all.*

The Thesis Statement Should Be Clear and Specific Without Being So Detailed As to Include All Your Main Ideas

The thesis statement is not a summary of all the main points in a speech, but instead it encompasses all those ideas in a single statement. Here is an example of a specific purpose for a persuasive speech: *I want my audience to endorse a living-wage ordinance in our community.*

Compare a poor thesis statement growing from this purpose—one that tries to include all the individual ideas and ends up as a kind of summary of the speech—with a clear and direct one.

The poor statement: *All employees in our community deserve to be paid a living wage because doing so is just and because those who are inadequately compensated are more likely to suffer from stress, less likely to eat properly (leading to health problems), less likely to be able to afford decent housing, and more likely to have strained relationships with others (leading to divorce, neighborhood tensions, and even acts of violence.)*

A much better thesis statement: *Paying employees a living wage is a moral and practical imperative in our community.*

Note also that the thesis is not a presentation of the specific information you will deliver in your speech. Consider this thesis statement: *A recent survey reported in the* New York Times *revealed that when individuals are inadequately compensated for their work, over half of them develop problems with depression and low self-esteem.* This is a poor thesis statement because it neglects the driving idea of the speech—that low wages cause serious psychological damage—in favor of giving specific information that will be used as support in the speech.

The Thesis Statement Should Be Focused and Limited in Scope

You want to be sure that you do not try to accomplish too much or too many different things in one speech. If you have a good specific purpose, this is unlikely to happen. But if you find yourself including more than one idea in your thesis statement—*A school voucher system will improve public education and should be coupled with national standardized tests to measure student achievement and content examinations for teachers*—you are probably taking on too much for a single speech. Such a thesis statement should alert you to potential problems that you can avoid by reworking your specific purpose. Rather than such a comprehensive thesis statement, you might devise more limited, focused statements that stand a better chance of being adequately developed in a single speech. Here are some better examples:

> *School vouchers will give parents the ability to choose the best schools for their children.*
> *Standardized tests lead to greater accountability in public education.*
> *The school board's plan to require periodic content examinations for teachers will improve the quality of classroom instruction.*

Avoiding Common Mistakes

As you put these guidelines into effect when developing your own thesis statement, you should try to avoid the most common mistakes made by students when devising thesis statements. Your thesis statement should

- *not* be written as a question or a topical phrase
- *not* be a preview of the speech
- *not* be too complex and hard to follow
- *not* present excessively detailed information
- *not* present too many ideas for a single speech

The *Highlighting the Process* box reviews and illustrates the process of moving from selecting a topic to devising a thesis statement.

Summary

- Preparing yourself to speak begins with the choice of a topic.
- Doing a self-inventory and/or brainstorming significant public issues when choosing a topic is a helpful first step.
- The next step is to narrow the topic so that it is manageable in the time limit, meets the expectations of the assignment or occasion, and can be made interesting to an audience.
- Since the audience is central to the development of your speech, you will need to pay particular attention to how the topic will reflect the listeners' knowledge and experience.

Highlighting the Process

From Topic to Purpose to Thesis

As a way of reviewing the procedure we have been describing, consider the process step by step.

1. **Select Possible Topics.** Consider the following list of possible topics generated from a self-inventory and through brainstorming public issues.

   - Alcoholism on campus

   - Student financial aid

   - Affordable housing for the working poor

   - Materialism in America

   - Nuclear proliferation

   - United States policy toward Iran

2. **Consider Situational and Audience Factors.** Since there had been so many stories in the media lately about nuclear proliferation and the threat of a nuclear war, you decided that would be a timely topic.

3. **Pick Your Tentative Topic.** Lots of possibilities are open to you as you narrow the topic, such as the nuclear proliferation treaty, the dangers of North Korea or Iran getting the bomb, or the threat of terrorists obtaining nuclear weapons. Perhaps you decide that one very serious problem does not get the attention that it should: the tension between India and Pakistan, two nuclear powers with a history of mutual hostility. So your tentative topic is the threat of nuclear war between India and Pakistan.

4. **Determine the General Purpose.** If your assignment is to give a persuasive speech, you then plan a speech to gain agreement or to support a policy.

5. **Craft a Specific Purpose Statement.** You need to determine exactly what response you want from your audience. After conducting and evaluating an audience survey, you discover that many of your listeners are only mildly aware of the antagonism between India and Pakistan. Because of their lack of awareness, they appear unconcerned about the potential seriousness of the problem. So you develop this specific purpose statement: *I want my audience to agree that the India-Pakistan conflict poses a serious threat to world peace.*

6. **Write a Thesis Statement.** Your purpose will still be somewhat tentative; you can modify it as you gather and organize material for the speech. However, after you have gone through the process from topic selection to specific purpose to thesis statement carefully and thoughtfully and have a well-crafted purpose statement, you are ready to make a thesis statement; in this case it might be *The conflict between India and Pakistan could result in a nuclear war that would ultimately involve the United States.*

- In choosing a topic, you also must remember your ethical obligations to be accurate and fair-minded and to exercise good judgment in accommodating the tastes and standards of the audience.

- Speeches aim at getting responses from audiences. The principal kinds of responses that speakers aim for in most cases—in the classroom, in the community, and in professional settings—are the general purposes: informative, persuasive, and ceremonial.

  - The goal of informative speeches is to gain audience understanding.

  - The goal of persuasive speeches is to reinforce audience feelings, change beliefs, or elicit action.

- The goal of ceremonial speeches is to reinforce shared values as a vehicle of community building.

- Based on the topic that you have chosen, you will be able to create a specific purpose that states precisely the response you want from your audience in a particular situation. A specific purpose is the foundation on which the thesis statement is built.

- The thesis statement—the guiding idea of the speech that you want your listeners to take away from it—should be carefully crafted to be precise and inclusive without being cluttered with too many details.

- As you go through the process of crafting a specific purpose and thesis, you should be mindful of the effects your ideas will have on the audience. You must consider the ethical implications of what you are trying to do.

QUESTIONS FOR REVIEW AND REFLECTION

1. What are the major things to consider when looking for a speech topic? Give a specific example of how each of these categories might relate to you personally.
2. What are some things you will do to make sure that you are exploring significant topics of public concern? Be specific.
3. Why is focusing and narrowing your topic important?
4. What are some of the ethical considerations involved in selecting a topic?
5. What are the general purposes of public speaking? Define each.
6. What is meant by a specific purpose? Why is it important for every public speaker to have a specific purpose? What are the criteria you ought to use to evaluate your specific purpose?
7. Can a single speech have multiple purposes? Why or why not?
8. What is a thesis statement, and why is it important for a speaker to develop one?
9. Suppose someone decides to give a speech with this specific purpose: *I want my audience to vote to repeal the state law that requires motorcyclists to wear safety helmets.* Using the criteria for evaluating purpose statements discussed in this chapter, is this an effective purpose statement? Why or why not?
10. Following are three thesis statements. Which one is the best and why?
    - *Would you like to do something that is both fun and useful this summer?*
    - *Volunteering to work for Habitat for Humanity this summer will be a rewarding personal experience and will provide a very useful public service.*
    - *If you volunteer to work for Habitat for Humanity, you will get good physical exercise, learn new skills, meet interesting people, get to work with kids your own age, provide homes for needy and deserving people, and earn the gratitude and respect of the people you help.*

ENDNOTES

1. See Richard L. Johannesen, *Ethics in Human Communication*, 5th ed. (Prospect Heights, IL: Waveland Press, 2002).

2. See *Communication Quarterly* 38 (Summer 1990) for a special issue on communication ethics.

3. For an account of the functions of ceremonial rhetoric see Celeste Michelle Condit, "The Function of Epideictic: The Boston Massacre Orations as Exemplar," *Communication Quarterly* 33 (1985): 284–98.

4. R. Cohen, *Negotiating across Culture: Communication Obstacles in International Diplomacy* (Washington, DC: Institute of Peace, 1991).

5. John F. Kennedy, "Inaugural Address," in *The Presidents Speak*, ed. David Newton Lott, 313 (New York: Henry Holt, 1994).

6. Ronald Reagan, "Tribute to the Challenger Astronauts," January 28, 1986, www .americanrhetoric.com/speeches/rreaganchallenger.htm (accessed February 15, 2006).

7. See Kenneth R. Andrews, "Ethics in Practice," *Harvard Business Review* 67 (September–October 1989): 99–109.

Responsible and Productive Research

CHAPTER OBJECTIVES

After studying this chapter, you should be able to

1. Understand the importance of establishing a focus to guide your research.

2. Understand how careful, thoughtful note taking helps you develop insight and draft your speech.

3. Appreciate the importance of information literacy.

CHAPTER OBJECTIVES (*CONTINUED*)

4. Better utilize the library for obtaining materials and assistance.

5. Use the World Wide Web more efficiently and productively.

6. Conduct an interview to gather information.

7. Use e-mail more effectively to gather information.

8. Document your sources accurately and know how and when to cite sources in your speech.

After his six-year-old son, Adam, was abducted and brutally murdered, John Walsh made it his mission to help other victims of violent crime.[1] He recalls walking into Cornell University's library one morning and saying, "I'm the father of a little boy who was murdered. I don't go to classes here or anything, and I don't have a card, but I was wondering if I could use the library?"[2] They welcomed him and assisted his research. He discovered that more could be done—and done more quickly—to recover a missing racehorse or an automobile than to track down a missing child. Outraged, he became a man on a mission.[3]

When Walsh landed the opportunity to address legislators on Capitol Hill, he did more than recount his own family's tragic ordeal; he came equipped with facts and figures. Walsh made a compelling case for "a centralized reporting system" and "a nationwide search system for missing children."[4] Well-informed, professional, and articulate, he was someone to be taken seriously.

When the Missing Children Act was finally passed one year later, President Reagan invited Walsh and his wife to the signing ceremony. As he listened to the president commend their work, it dawned on him what they had accomplished—"that a heartbroken couple from Florida with no money and no lobby and no re-sources and nobody behind them except a bunch of caring, passionate people with no real power had actually helped get a federal bill passed."[5]

The Missing Children Act of 1982 was but the beginning of John Walsh's career as one of America's best known crime fighters. For more than 20 years he has hosted television's *America's Most Wanted*—a program that has, to date, helped re-unite hundreds of abducted children with their families and capture more than 920 fugitives.[6]

Not only can we be inspired by Walsh's example, his success underscores the im-portance of informing yourself about your subject if you wish to become an effective advocate. Being knowledgeable allows you to formulate better ideas and have more confidence when you speak. You will also enhance your credibility. As you supply the information that informs your thinking, your audience will find you more believ-able and trustworthy. They will see that you have met your ethical obligation to be knowledgeable about your topic.

This chapter will help you to become better informed. We focus on various possibilities for finding information, including print and electronic media as well as interviewing experts and others who have useful information and experience. First, however, we consider how you can effectively and efficiently conduct your in-vestigation, providing suggestions for taking notes and beginning the construction of your speech. These tips can help make a sometimes overwhelming process more manageable and even satisfying. Finally, this chapter discusses the importance of revealing sources during your presentation and shows you how to do so effectively and properly.

A Productive Start

Preview. *You begin building a speech by identifying your purpose in speaking and narrowing your focus. Once you have established your focus, you can quickly survey material to determine its relevance, and you can better formulate the main ideas of your speech.*

As we pointed out in Chapter 6, you begin the process of crafting a speech by formulating a thesis statement—however tentative—to guide your investigation. The thesis at this stage is a *working thesis*, an attempt to articulate the overall idea you are examining. A thesis, especially at this stage, can foreshadow the main areas you will develop.[7] For example, Eva had long paid attention to the controversy surrounding stem cell research. After learning that researchers at Duke University successfully treated terminally ill babies with the stem cells from the umbilical cords of healthy babies, Eva decided to explore this recent breakthrough for a persuasive speech.[8] She crafted the following basic idea (tentative thesis) to focus her research: *Stem cells taken from the umbilical cords of healthy babies have proven lifesaving while avoiding the moral problems of using stem cells taken from embryos.*

Her thesis mirrored her specific purpose—the response she wanted from her listeners: *I want my audience to understand how stem cells from umbilical cords allow doctors to combat disease while avoiding the moral dilemma associated with using stem cells from embryos.*

You may, like Eva, need some initial investigation to arrive at a purpose and thesis. Some probing may be necessary. For a concise look at how to begin your research, see *Highlighting How to Begin Your Investigation* on page 162.

> Once you have determined the best sources, take notes methodically to save time and maximize productivity.

Finding Relevant Information: A High-Speed Pursuit

Once you have a topic and purpose in mind, you can proceed quickly. Rather than painstakingly reading every article that has a promising title, skim through them, trying to detect which ones contain relevant information and ideas. If an

Highlighting How to Begin Your Investigation

- *Visit the reference section of your library.* A variety of reference materials will acquaint you with what is known about your topic (facts, data, and other information) and how it has been discussed recently as well as in the past. Here are a few noteworthy examples of what is available.
  - *American Decades.* This collection discusses the major issues Americans have grappled with during a particular decade. Since many issues persist (e.g., violence in our public schools), this collection can provide an excellent overview and background information.
  - *Atlas of Contemporary America: Portrait of a Nation.* Maps and text illuminate diversity and other demographics, as well as prevailing attitudes of particular regions in the United States. It also maps/discusses the issues that most affect a region (e.g., water rights).
  - *Contemporary World Issues.* In this series, scholars and nonacademic experts examine international matters of controversy. These book-length works are written for the general public.
  - *Encyclopaedia Britannica.* This award-winning encyclopedia, with peer-reviewed entries by leading authorities, offers excellent background information on historical and contemporary topics and issues. (Your library likely also subscribes to the online version.) In addition to an expert overview, it provides a list of authoritative works for further reading, making it a good place to launch an investigation.
  - *Facts on File: Issues and Controversies.* This collection offers objective, thorough coverage of the hottest issues of our time. Also consult its counterpart, *World Almanac Reference Database*, for background information and data for historical and contemporary issues and events.
  - *Facts on File: World News Digest.* This compilation provides a week-by-week account of major news events, from 1940 to the present day.
- *Discover what reliable news sources have provided.* Newspapers, news magazines, and radio and television news sources often provide background information as well as in-depth reporting. Archives of newspapers, news magazines, and broadcast news sources (often available and searchable on their official websites) transport us back in time, providing a good sense of what happened and how people felt about it. Simply be alert to any bias that might exist, since many news sources have political leanings.[9]

  Finding material in newspapers and news magazines has never been easier. Several databases index and provide access to major U.S. newspapers, and

abstract (a brief summary) is available, use it to determine an article's usefulness. Evaluate a potentially relevant book by scanning its table of contents and index, then skimming pages that seem promising. This quick survey will help you locate the most valuable material.

Keep your mind free to focus on what you are skimming. Rather than trying to keep a mental record of which sources are valuable and where you found what information, make quick notes regarding the usefulness of a source. Once you have identified which sources are valuable, you can read them more closely, carefully extracting information and ideas from them.

The Creative Enterprise of Building a Speech

Preview. *As you compile material for a speech, you can proceed most productively if you establish a method for gathering, recording, and organizing material. The use of index cards for note taking remains a tried and true method for facilitating discovery and organization.*

some also index regional and international newspapers. For example, NewsBank's Access World News provides information and perspectives from more than 600 U.S. and 500 international sources—a mix of newspapers, wire services, and news agencies, with many of the international sources translated into English. Other, similar databases include:

ProQuest Newsstand

LexisNexis Academic

InfoTrac Custom Newspapers

National Newspaper Index

- *Explore government publications*. Federal, state, and local agencies collect and report data on every topic imaginable. For example, *The Statistical Abstract of the United States*, published annually since 1878 by the U.S. Census Bureau (in print and online), provides table after table of information about social, political, and economic conditions. You can learn, for instance, how many households in the United States have one or more computers and whether they have Internet access, and you can compare today's figures with previous years. You can also see the breakdown in terms of age, sex, educational level, and household income, and you can compare your state with other states.

- *See what has been discussed and acted on by policymakers*. Congressional hearings, for example, define the policy issue and bring together expert witnesses and other sources of testimony. The *Congressional Universe* database indexes and provides full text of these discussions and activities as well as relevant documents, such as regulations. It also will keep you apprised of the status of a particular bill. You can obtain similar information from *CQ Researcher*, which provides in-depth reports and commentary on the major issues of the day, allowing various sides to have their say. It is available in print or online. Its publisher, *Congressional Quarterly, Inc*. (cq.com), offers numerous other publications and services that summarize and analyze any bill being considered, and you can even have daily updates e-mailed to you.

- *Consult an opinion series*. Books within these series address contemporary issues. Public and academic libraries likely subscribe to one or more series, such as *Opposing Viewpoints, Current Controversies,* or *At Issue.*

- *Discuss your topic and ideas with others who might offer insights*. You likely have professors, family members, and friends who keep up with news reports and who are otherwise well informed. They may also identify other sources you should consult.

From the moment you begin contemplating your topic, you begin formulating ideas for your speech on the basis of what you already know or believe. You begin envisioning the areas you will discuss, material you will include, your purpose and thesis, and what might provide an intriguing introduction and a moving conclusion. This is not busywork; you have begun the process of preparing the speech and should log these thoughts so that none escape.

As you investigate, you gather information and ideas from a variety of sources and arrive at new insights of your own. Your speech will consist of each of these elements arranged into a coherent form and made more understandable and appealing through good oral style. Your mind will operate on all these levels as you sift through material and record thoughts that ultimately may or may not make it into the final draft of your speech.

While researching your topic, record more than information. You also need to note the idea the information suggests and contemplate where it should appear in your speech. Jot down other thoughts that come to you—possible sources to consult, modifications needed for your thesis, the design of a presentational aid, a possible good analogy, and so forth.

This process of preparation is crucial to being able to present an effective message. Perhaps you have encountered a dynamic, outgoing speaker who seemed to have "a way with words." If that speaker strayed aimlessly or did not support claims he or she made, however, chances are you would think the person did not present an effective message. Encounters such as these remind us that the quality of a speech is directly related to the quality of critical and creative thought that goes into its preparation.

The Creative Process

Critical and creative thought cannot be rushed; an early start is essential. Once you have a topic in mind, you will notice anything that is relevant, and these various stimuli will help you formulate ideas for your speech, including a particular focus.[10] You will also have the necessary time for *reflection*—time to evaluate information, to test ideas, and to begin making sense of all you have found.[11]

If you are like most people, you will have good days when everything seems to make sense and fall into place, and days when you struggle to get anywhere.[12] When your thinking is "stuck," your mind probably needs a "time out."[13] Once you are no longer fixated on the "problem," your mind can operate quietly in the background, making associations and generating new ideas.[14] An early start allows time for these breaks.

A break can be time well spent. When you return to the task you may experience a rush of ideas and a new, improved understanding of the subject and your goals for the speech. You do not have to be "on task" for these ideas to emerge; they may emerge as flashes of insight while you are barely thinking about them. As cognitive psychologists explain, "The classic example of coming up with great ideas while taking a shower may simply reflect the importance of releasing oneself from fixated retrieval processes."[15] When these inspirations appear, jot them down as soon as possible to prevent them from escaping and to free your mind from the burden of trying to keep them in full view. Your energy can then be directed elsewhere, allowing your mind to continue working creatively.[16]

Along with quiet time, you may also benefit from some intensive thinking. For example, you might write down whatever pops into your head without stopping to analyze or critique it. Afterward, you will have something to review and evaluate.[17] You might try a particular brainstorming technique, such as mind mapping or concept mapping.[18] Both of these formalized techniques advocate the use of keywords and phrases and hand-drawn pictures to capture thoughts and discern relationships. Like other brainstorming strategies, these techniques have specific benefits:

- allowing speedy recording for less restricted flow of thought
- promoting free association (rather than any restrictions a sentence might impose)
- stimulating recall of related information, such as previous learning or experiences
- generating new ideas and perspectives
- promoting understanding of relationships

- assisting organization via grouping/classifying
- unleashing creativity, especially for visual learners

You can learn more about these particular techniques by consulting the books we cite in our endnotes or by searching online.[19]

In addition to capturing thoughts on paper, try explaining or working through your thoughts aloud, perhaps with a friend. You may surprise yourself with the ideas that roll off your tongue,[20] and you might also receive potentially valuable feedback from your listener. As with other inspirations, record these as soon as possible.

In addition to allowing time for your creative processes to work, you also need time for incorporation. Incorporation involves deciding if and where specific information and ideas belong in the speech. You will make these evaluations as you search for materials and continue to fine-tune the focus of your speech.

Productive Note Taking: Drafting as You Investigate Your Topic

As you gather information and explore the ideas and opinions of others, you endeavor to determine what is relevant. In doing so, you shift your attention from the particular information and the idea it suggests to the overall idea or purpose of your speech.[21] To keep your information aligned with your theme, take notes methodically.

To maximize efficiency and avoid frustration, devise a format for recording source information and for taking notes, and stick to it. The format should be comprehensive and allow you to find, at a glance, whatever you are looking for—whether it is the page number for a quotation, the title of a source, or the publication date. Use the following coordinated approach and you will save time and maximize productivity.

For source information:

- If you are using a library subscription database, use its built-in citation feature to create a bibliography as you go. Once you know you are going to use an article or other item, take a few seconds to grab the already-formatted bibliographic entry and paste it into a works cited page. Otherwise, you will have to backtrack later.
- For nondatabase sources, record source information correctly, using the style guide (*MLA, APA,* or *The Chicago Manual of Style*) your instructor has approved for your formal bibliography (see sample entries in Figure 7.1). If recording information by hand, use three-by-five index cards so you can easily arrange them into the proper order for later typing your formal bibliography.
- Record source information completely. You will avoid having to retrace your steps to acquire missing information.
- Assign each source a code. The code can be the author's last name (or the last name of the first author listed). Coding each source saves you from having to repeat a full-blown bibliographic entry for each note you make from that source (see Figure 7.1). If you are typing your bibliography as you

Figure 7.1

Sample Source Entry:

Kluger [source code]

Jeffrey, Kluger. "Stem Cells Save Babies." *Time*, May 30, 2005.

Figure 7.2

Sample Note Card [coordinated with the sample source entry]

[Idea] Using stem cells from umbilical cords = less controversial

"The stem cells used at Duke are not the kind that have caused so much anguish and debate in the U.S. . . . These cells are taken not from embryos but from cord or placenta blood. . . . They are also less controversial because no potential human lives are lost if the cells are destroyed." [Quoted material]

(Kluger, p. 59)

go, simply type the code you assign in bold at the front of each entry. You can delete the codes later so they will not appear in your formal bibliography.

For taking notes:

- Four-by-six-inch index cards should work well, since each will have limited content.
- Limit each card to a single idea and the information on which that idea is based (see Figure 7.2). By confining each card to one idea and its basis, you will be able to arrange and rearrange cards and easily organize your speech. Entries with more than one idea and bit of information would defeat the purpose of using cards. You likely will have several cards from some sources and only one or two from others.
- Coordinate your notes with your source entries to save time. As noted above, the codes you have assigned will eliminate what would amount to busywork since they save you from writing comprehensive source information over and over again.
- Format consistently. Record information in the center of the card, and *be sure to place quotation marks around any material you are recording word for word from the source.* Place the code you have assigned the source and the specific page number or numbers (if it is printed material) in parentheses in a bottom corner. Enter the idea suggested by the information as a heading in the upper right (or left) corner.
- Create a meaningful heading. The heading is more than a descriptor; it should relate the information to the goals of your speech. Obviously, you have some sense of why the information is valuable. Force yourself to write it down, even if you believe it will be obvious later. Use a concise phrase to articulate the idea suggested by the information. You might often enter the information before writing the idea because you may not have fully determined the meaning and the best wording. Before moving on, though, articulate the idea, even if it is only an approximation. You can revise it later. The point is that you will want to think about the meaning and relevance of all the information you encounter, especially in terms of how it contributes to your speech.

Think of how inefficient it would be to operate otherwise. Rather than mindlessly taking notes and letting the cards accumulate into a large pile you will have to sort out later, make sense of material as you go. Group the cards into categories, noting the areas that emerge. Contemplate the idea in the heading on each card; the idea may become a subpoint or even a main point in your speech.

As you group and arrange the cards, create a rough sketch of your speech. Watch it grow and evolve as you continue to sort through the cards and arrange them, reflecting on whether the idea and information on a card belongs in the speech, where it belongs, and its implication for your overall idea—the thesis.

Once you have created a rough outline, you will be able to evaluate what you have produced—retaining the good, modifying what needs to be rewritten, and deleting faulty or extraneous material. This activity, called *revision*, is not an "autopsy";[22] it does not merely occur after you have a complete first draft of your speech. Instead it occurs anytime you reassess what you have done, whether it is a word or a sentence or a title. No set formula exists for when and how often revision should occur, but it must occur from time to time throughout the drafting process if you expect to produce a quality message.

The key to good preparation is working through multiple drafts—something even professional speechwriters recognize and do. For example, Peggy Noonan—one of President Reagan's speechwriters—would only begin to get comfortable with her progress "on about the fourth draft."[23] Noonan writes, "I'd see that I'd written three or four sentences I liked, and that would relax me . . . [and I'd think] 'there's something of worth here!' That would get my shoulders down."[24] Other presidential speechwriters report similar experiences. Ray Price, one of President Nixon's speechwriters, recalls that, on average, major presidential addresses went through "14 drafts."[25] Nothing has changed; President George W. Bush's 2006 State of the Union Address reportedly went through about "two dozen drafts."[26]

As you contemplate your speech, there is a constant flow between information and ideas as you check them against each other.[27] Your investigation tests the tentative thesis you have constructed; you will refine your thesis (and points) in light of

Revision is an important part of the writing process and can occur at any time.

what your investigation reveals. You develop and revise your speech as you evaluate content and arrangement, detect and repair weaknesses, recognize the need for more material, and try out the best phrasing for an idea. Preparing the speech, as with any act of composition, involves intense, multidimensional cognitive activity.[28]

Quintilian, an early teacher of speech, emphasized the importance of revision. Quintilian noted that "correction takes the form of addition, excision, and alteration" and that "erasure" is "as important a function of the pen as actual writing."[29] In other words, one has to learn to be critical of her or his own work. Critical thinking is essential for evaluating your own work, and it is also essential as you gather materials, a topic to which we now turn.

Investigating Like a Professional: Utilizing Library Resources

Preview. *Knowing how to find and evaluate relevant information has become increasingly important in our personal, professional, and public lives. At your college or public library, you can get instruction and assistance to acquaint you with the best research tools and to help develop your skills in gathering and evaluating information.*

Information Literacy

Among the most important skills we can learn as citizens in a democracy are those associated with locating and gathering reliable information. The same skills we use to research a speech topic will serve us well throughout college, in our careers, and in our role as informed, active citizens. These skills, termed *information literacy*, involve developing the ability to "recognize when information is needed" and to "locate, evaluate, and use effectively the needed information."[30] Its ability has become increasingly important in the Information Age; we are bombarded with information in "unfiltered formats," making it necessary that we ascertain its "authenticity, validity, and reliability."[31] As the Association of College and Research Libraries has noted, "the uncertain quality and expanding quantity of information pose large challenges for society. The sheer abundance of information will not in itself create a more informed citizenry without a complementary cluster of abilities necessary to use the information effectively."[32]

Let us examine more closely the skills that make up information literacy.

- *Finding information* means knowing where to look for good information.
  - Reference sources with peer-reviewed entries by recognized authorities, such as *Encyclopaedia Brittanica*, are more trusted than *Wikipedia*, which allows anyone to author or alter an entry.[33]
  - Periodicals also vary in type and quality. Cornell University Library provides an excellent overview, distinguishing between scholarly, substantive news, popular, and sensational periodicals.[34]

- *Scholarly*. This type of periodical reports original research or experimentation by a scholar/researcher to the scholarly community. Authors carefully and properly document all sources.
- *Substantive news*. In this type of periodical the author's expertise varies, as does the degree to which sources are cited. Articles are written for an "educated audience" of "concerned citizens."[35]
- *Popular*. Articles in this type of periodical are written by staff members or freelance authors, providing "little depth" and "rarely, if ever" citing sources. Their principal purpose is "to entertain the reader, to sell products . . . and/or to promote a viewpoint."[36]
- *Sensational*. Written with simple language and "flashy headlines," this type of publication is "designed to astonish." Its main purpose "seems to be to arouse curiosity and to cater to popular superstitions," assuming "a certain gullibility in their audience."[37]

As you might surmise, scholarly sources are generally very trustworthy, while substantive news sources vary in quality. Popular sources should be scrutinized especially carefully. As for the sensational, need we even say?

- *Government documents and publications* are highly trusted sources. Topics range from *aquaculture* to *zero tillage*. The publications present census data and other statistical information. States, counties, and some cities also create documents, as do foreign governments and international bodies. These items are now often available online. You'll find the following sites well organized and well maintained.
  - *USA.gov* (www.usa.gov). This site provides links to federal offices and agencies, as well as a number of federally funded entities. It also provides a link to each state or territory's home page.
  - *State and local government on the Net* (statelocalgov.net). As the name suggests, you will find links to each state or territory's official pages, as well as to county and city pages. If a town has a website, you will be able to find it here.
  - *C-SPAN* (c-span.org): You have likely watched the Cable-Satellite Public Affairs Network at some point and know of its mission to provide unfiltered access to legislative activity and various civic meetings and events. Its website provides links to governmental and nongovernmental sites, including blogs.
- *Evaluating information* entails assessing the credibility of a source and the information it offers so you will not be misled or mislead others. Penn State's Libraries provide a good inventory of essential factors to consider, including the following (which we have adapted).[38]
  - *Currency*. Does the date of publication meet your needs? Examine a book's copyright page, a periodical's publication date, or the date a Web page was created and/or updated.
  - *Authority*. Is the author an expert? Printed works, especially journals and books, provide an author's note that reveals the author's expertise and also commonly lists other works the author has written. Also consult biographical

reference sources, such as *Contemporary Authors*. For websites, determine who has posted the pages and what the person or group's motivation may be. Also check to see whether it lists experts or professional organizations that endorse the site.

- *Validity/accuracy.* Is evidence provided for claims? Are sources cited? Is the information consistent with that provided by other sources? If the information is dated, is it still accurate?
- *Audience.* Who is the intended audience? Experts? The general public? Is the level of the content and wording appropriate for you and your needs?
- *Point of view (bias).* In light of what you know and have acquired from other sources, is the information complete or one-sided? Does it promote a particular viewpoint or seem to have an agenda? Does it acknowledge other viewpoints and represent them fairly? If any sponsor or sponsors are indicated, would they favor a particular view?

- *Properly using information.* Information literacy also requires one to use information responsibly. Guidelines for proper use include:
  - Integrate information from a variety of sources.
  - Acknowledge any biases or agenda a source may have.
  - Cite sources properly and accurately within a speech and in a bibliography.
  - Quote or paraphrase accurately.
  - Respect others' intellectual property and adhere to all guidelines pertaining to copyrighted material and fair use.

Developing and exercising these abilities for finding, evaluating, and properly using information will serve you well. The same skills that employers find attractive will set you up for lifelong learning and productive citizenship. You can begin developing these skills immediately and reaping the rewards.

Virtual and Actual Visits to the Library

The college environment provides ample opportunities for developing information literacy. In addition to instruction in classes, other professional support exists, namely from librarians. Skilled librarians can also be found in many of our public libraries and may offer training in information literacy for the general public.

Once we understand who librarians are, we can begin to understand their value to us—individually and as a nation. Professional librarians are schooled in the latest information and communication technologies, and they use this knowledge and skill daily. They are adept at locating and retrieving information and also work cooperatively with other librarians in the academic, public, and private sectors to classify and organize information so that it is well managed and easily retrieved. Citizens, government officials, manufacturers, researchers, and others rely on librarians and their work.[39]

You, too, can benefit from a librarian's expertise. A library's staff of professionals can help you locate and retrieve current, reliable information about your topic. They offer this assistance in person, of course, but they also provide much help online. You will be well served by the combination.

We disadvantage ourselves when we ignore the assistance librarians can provide. Given the abundance of information available on the Web, many people may think searching via Google or another popular search engine is the best way to locate and gather information for a speech or other assignment. In fact, *Newsweek* reports that "71% of middle and high school students use the Internet as their number one research venue."[40] According to the Online Computer Library Center (OCLC) this trend continues into college.[41] Certainly, a Web search can prove fruitful (as we will discuss momentarily), but a library's online resources can produce superior and even quicker results. The power of the library and personal assistance from a librarian are as close as a computer with Internet access. Once you have an account and a password to log on to the campus system, you can use your access in many productive ways.

Each library, of course, will vary in terms of its resources and services. Spend a few minutes perusing your library's home page to see what is available. Even though libraries differ, certain features will be pretty much constant.

- *Subscription databases*. Your school's library likely subscribes to several databases (e.g., ProQuest; LexisNexis; EBSCOhost)—immense, searchable collections of indexes, abstracts, and full-text materials. Your status as a student allows you access, and you will certainly want to harness their power. As the American Library Association notes, "database searching has become a central tool in modern research."[42] The popularity of databases is understandable in light of the advantages they offer in terms of variety, timeliness, and efficiency.
  - *Variety*. Databases index and include a variety of materials, allowing you to cast a wide net. Some index articles from newspapers and news magazines as well as scholarly journals, government documents, chapters in books, and broadcast news and commentary.
  - *Timeliness*. Databases are updated frequently, indexing and providing access to materials very recently produced. For example, *EBSCOhost* and *LexisNexis* (two popular databases) are updated continually, as are many other databases that index and/or provide full-text articles from newspapers and other news sources. Others, like *CQ Researcher* (a weekly review of contemporary issues, also available in print) is updated weekly. The profile of any given database should reveal how often it is updated.
  - *Efficiency*. Databases are an efficient way to find relevant articles and other materials. An electronic database allows you to search a span of 10 years or more, simultaneously, in multiple indexes, and you often can combine two or more keywords to focus the search. Each database will differ in its search procedures, especially if you are using more than one keyword. Be sure to take a minute to consult its tips for searching so you can obtain the best results.

    Efficiency varies from database to database. Some list only titles, whereas others provide an abstract or even the full text of the item.

So far we have provided a quick overview of what a library offers online. Now let us examine what is available when you actually visit a library.

Highlighting Databases as a Research Tool

Most academic and public libraries feature subscription databases—often your best and most efficient means of obtaining quality information. These tips and a sample search will assist you in your use of library databases.

TIPS

1. *Determine the best search term(s)*. Finding the right search terms made quite a difference when researching television's effects on the cognitive development of very young children. While searching *EBSCOhost's Academic Search Premier,* we entered "television" and "children," which yielded more than 6,200 entries, with most not on target. When we conducted the search using "television" and "toddlers," we got 59 entries, with nearly every one containing precisely the information we were seeking.

   Trickier searches include those where the search terms may not be as obvious. For example, if you wished to research the social benefits of youth involvement in team sports, you would probably have to experiment with various keywords. Once a promising title appears, launch the search again using the search terms under which the item was indexed, or—if available—choose the option to "find other, similar items."

2. *Determine the best database*. Read the database description to see what material it indexes and search the ones most relevant (e.g., EBSCOhost's *Health Source Plus: Consumer Edition*, if researching the issue of vaccines for the human papillomavirus). If the results are lacking in one database, search another. You can search multiple databases at the same time, though doing so may or may not prove productive. One risk is that you will have too many entries to wade through. It may prove more effective to launch one database at a time, until you find one or two that produce the best results.

3. *Ask an expert*. If you experience problems, visit the library in person and ask a librarian to assist you. Librarians are usually found at the reference desk during regular business hours.

4. *Select the best full-text option*. If you wish to print out an article and can choose between HTML and PDF formats, choose PDF. It will provide the most comprehensive printing—including all tables and charts. HTML may also contain typographical errors and other mistakes. In addition, PDF will preserve the original pagination, allowing you to cite your sources more easily.

- *Catalogs*. A library offers a wide variety of resources, including periodicals, books, films, and so on. The library's online catalog simplifies finding materials, allowing users to search by subject, author, title, or keyword. The catalog will also indicate whether an item is available or on loan. Once you discover a relevant item, the catalog likely will allow you to search for similar items. For instance, you may be able to find books on the same subject by clicking on its call number. The catalog may also feature integrated shelving, allowing you to locate relevant items across mediums—books, films, government documents, reference books, and other holdings.

- *Access to other libraries' collections*. If your library has little available for a particular topic, it will still be able to help. Your library provides a gateway to other libraries' catalogs, allowing you to search their collections and easily request an interlibrary loan (especially since many libraries now belong to a consortium of libraries with regular courier service among the members). Your library is also most likely a member of the OCLC, a group of more than 53,000 libraries from around the world that cooperatively produce and maintain *WorldCat*, a supercatalog available online. *WorldCat* will help you discover what relevant items exist, sometimes providing an abstract or full text.

- *Assistance searching the World Wide Web*. A library may also provide links to trusted sites on the Web, such as the Librarian's Internet Index (www.lii.org), a well-organized, well-maintained directory that indexes thousands of popular and important issues (Figure 7.3). At the Librarian's Internet Index, experts evaluate Web content and provide links only to sites they deem reliable and trustworthy, saving you from having to wade through lots of questionable sites while searching for information.[43]

In addition to the Librarian's Internet Index, librarians also recommend libraryspot.com, which provides links to expert-approved reference and library sites on a variety of subjects. The University of Michigan hosts another trustworthy site, the Internet Public Library (www.ipl.com). It features links to various reference materials, governmental agencies, and domestic and international newspapers.

- *Assistance evaluating Web resources.* Libraries often provide pointers for evaluating sources and content found on the World Wide Web (akin to what we provide later in this chapter). For example, the Cornell University library provides excellent primers on evaluating Web content and effectively searching the Web.

- *Reference materials.* The library's site likely provides online access to reference materials, such as almanacs, encyclopedias, yearbooks, and dictionaries.

- *Customized assistance.* Libraries often provide online research guides (also called subject guides), customized for certain disciplines or classes. These, such as the one featured in Figure 7.4 (for public speaking), can greatly assist your research.

- *Personal assistance.* Many libraries allow patrons to e-mail a question to a librarian or to instant message or chat with a librarian. They may also post the phone number for the reference desk—the area of the library staffed by librarians.

Figure 7.3 At lii.org, experts provide links to Web sources they have evaluated as credible.

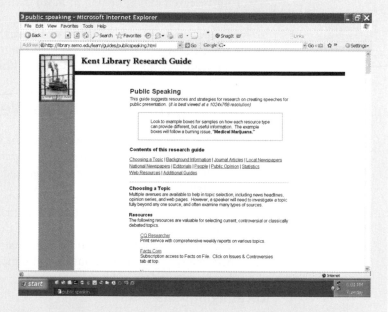

Figure 7.4 Research guides, such as this one at Southeast Missouri State University, can help you investigate your topic.

Face-to-Face Contact

Visiting your library in person can prove profitable. You can more quickly develop your proficiency at locating and gathering quality information, and you will have access to some materials not available online.

Get to know your library's layout and resources. Take a guided tour if one is offered. Knowing what is available and where it is located will allow you to be more efficient and productive. You will spend less time asking questions and more time on research.

When you do have questions, though, librarians can help. They can help you select and use the appropriate index or database for your search for articles, editorials, and other publications or transcripts. Once they understand the type of information you need, they can recommend appropriate resources and help you learn how to use them.

Being at the library also allows you to search its collections thoroughly. Once you have found an item in the catalog that seems relevant, scout the stacks. For example, if you discover a book, scan the spines of neighboring books for titles that seem promising. Even if the book is on loan, you may wish to visit its location on the shelves to scout the area. You might also try a traditional method for locating relevant books—searching by Library of Congress (LC) subject headings. These foot searches can often turn up books that otherwise might be overlooked. A librarian can teach you this method in a matter of minutes.

Your research may take you to more than one library. Some campuses, especially large universities, have specialized libraries for particular disciplines (e.g., journalism) or special collections (e.g., the papers of a particular political figure). Remember your local public library, too. It likely has many of the same databases and reference materials that academic libraries offer, as well as librarians to assist you.

Searching the World Wide Web

Preview. *Computer applications have simplified the storage and exchange of information. The World Wide Web has become replete with information and easy to navigate. Experts help lead us to the best information online and offer guidance for determining the quality of information encountered.*

Most of us take "the Web" for granted, but it is quite a phenomenon when you stop and think about it. Since it came on the scene in 1992, the World Wide Web has grown exponentially and beyond textual form to images, sound, and video.[44] It increasingly influences the way we conduct business and make decisions—personal and political.[45]

Locating Information

Easy-to-use browsing software (such as Netscape and Internet Explorer) and highly refined search technologies allow users to find information on the Web with relative ease. Continued innovations will make searches even simpler.[46]

To locate information, you can proceed in various ways:

- *Keyword search*. Choose any popular search engine (e.g., Lycos) and search by keyword(s), much like you do with a database. (Consult each engine's directions for specific guidance.) Vary the keywords, proceeding through trial and error to determine which word or words yield the best results. For example, launching Google with "smoking and children" will produce results that are too broad if you want to find out how exposure to tobacco smoke affects children differently from adults. "Smoking and children and health" will yield better results; the returns will be more precise and more manageable in number.

Table 7.1		
POPULAR SEARCH ENGINES		
altavista.com	ask.com	msn.com
excite.com	google.com	looksmart.com
lycos.com	yahoo.com	alltheweb.com
POPULAR METASEARCH ENGINES		
dogpile.com	metacrawler.com	search.com

Be aware that each search engine uses different criteria for a search and will, as a result, generate a unique list. If you do not find what you want with one engine, try another one. Or try a metasearch engine—such as Dogpile—which launches several engines for the search (see Table 7.1).

- *Subject directory.* In some instances you might find it more effective to explore by subject heading. Most search engine sites offer this alternative, providing shortcuts to information sites for various common subjects. For example, if you wanted coverage about a particular news item, Yahoo!'s "News" would provide direct links to major media outlets. The "News" option is searchable, and it is also subdivided into categories such as science, technology, health, and politics. A subject directory can also help you establish a focus. If you are interested in alternative energy but are not sure what alternatives exist, a subject directory will provide an inventory and general information about each. You will also discover the key terms to use for a productive search.

- *Traveling direct.* If you know of a promising site you can simply go there. Fortunately, most Web addresses (Uniform Resource Locators, or URLs) are kept simple so users can remember the address or be able to guess what it might be. The Environmental Protection Agency's site, for example, is at epa.gov. The website of the Sierra Club, an environmental group, is at sierraclub.org. To guess more accurately, be aware that the last three letters designate the organization's kind of Internet membership. The most common extensions are:

  - .com (commercial companies)
  - .edu (educational institutions)
  - .gov (government agencies)
  - .org (nonprofit organizations)

Regardless of how you get there, when you find a good site, make note of its URL so you can return directly to it and have the information you need to cite it in your formal bibliography. To determine whether the site *is* a good one requires careful scrutiny, a matter we will now take up.

Evaluating Internet Resources

The Internet can be described as a seemingly endless expanse of "unorganized fragments" that are added to daily by "a myriad of cranks, sages, and persons with time on their hands who launch their unfiltered messages into cyberspace."[47] Anyone who has spent any time on the Web recognizes the truth in these words and knows not to take everything found on the Web at face value. Five critical questions can help us evaluate information on the Web.

1. *What is the source of this information?* You would certainly dismiss a story from a supermarket tabloid that told you aliens had landed in Arizona. Although we may readily spot a tabloid as a sensational source, the Web presents a challenge because we do not have as clear an understanding of the source. Extensions offer some idea. Sites ending in .edu indicate an educational institution as sponsor, and .gov is government sponsored. Sites ending in .org are usually sponsored by nonprofit organizations, many of them advocacy groups. Sites with .com usually are trying to market goods or services.

   For many sites we have to look beneath the surface to determine authorship. If a group sponsors the page, what do you know about it? Do not be fooled by the name. For example, in the summer of 2000 a group calling itself Citizens for Better Medicare posted "information" on the Web. Their name suggested an admirable goal, but the Web page did not disclose that the group had been formed by the drug industry to lobby against the Clinton administration's proposal to provide drug coverage for the elderly.[48] Conducting an online search of the name of the group might help you determine who they are, or the browser's View menu may have an option to identify an opened page's sponsor.

2. *What is the purpose of the page?* Some Web pages are designed to give information, while others advocate certain policies or ideologies. It is not always easy to tell the difference, since advocacy groups frequently try to give the impression that they are just giving you the facts. The purpose of the page is sometimes given as a mission statement or a Who We Are or About Us link. When considering information provided by an advocacy group, remain aware of the source's agenda and use that information accordingly—checking other sources to verify accuracy. Information on sites sponsored by companies should also be investigated. If advertisements appear on the site, you can suspect that the content may be influenced.

3. *How balanced and accurate is the content?* Careful study of a Web page can illuminate bias. Are a variety of viewpoints acknowledged? Are the claims supported by good arguments and credible evidence? Are credible sources cited? What about the links to other pages—does this page send you to other sites that are credible? Is there any information presented that you know to be inaccurate or misleading? How do the information or claims hold up when considered against what you have learned from reputable sources?

   In short, judge a website the same way you would judge any attempt to persuade you to do or believe anything. In the chapters that follow, we will be very specific about what makes a sound argument, how to detect fallacies, and what kind of evidence is both effective and ethical. You will want to apply all these tests to material you find on the Web. But for now, at least ask yourself if the content that is presented seems fair, if it is convincing to you, and why you find it so.

4. *How current is the site?* Check to see how recently the site was updated. Regular updating indicates that the site is still active. A page that has been left unchanged for a long time should be viewed with suspicion. If a site *is* main-

tained regularly, the information is more likely to be up-to-date, though one can never be certain what, specifically, has been updated.

5. *When was the site created?* The creation date lets you know the site has been around a while as opposed to having been newly erected. A longer history may suggest some integrity.

If it turns out that you cannot answer most of these questions after close inspection of the site, that in itself should raise doubts in your mind about the site's credibility. Be skeptical of a source that does not identify itself or its purpose, that makes unsubstantiated claims, or that is out-of-date. The thing to remember is that the Internet is not a one-stop research source. Information should be cross-checked with other sources. By all means, use the Internet in your research, but do not use it thoughtlessly and do not use it exclusively. Purdue University's Online Writing Lab provides a good summary of the attitude you should take toward Internet research: "Internet sources can be very timely and very useful, but they should not be your sole source of information."[49]

Gathering Information through Interviews

Preview. *Interviewing can provide valuable information for your speech. Determine if persons with expert knowledge or direct experience are available to help you. Prepare carefully by gathering the background information you need and generating good questions. Conduct the interview professionally and efficiently, and follow up appropriately.*

Interviewing for information can yield numerous benefits. Interviews can furnish information and a perspective that otherwise could be lacking—especially for local concerns. In addition to providing valuable information, an interview can lead you to additional resources. The person you interview may provide or suggest other sources of information, perhaps handing you a pamphlet or published report or referring you to an article or website. The interviewee may also be able to critique your ideas or your working bibliography, commenting on the quality or credibility of the sources you have consulted and identifying essential sources that are missing. The person may also help you establish a focus for the speech—discussing, for example, an angle you had not considered.

A variety of people can provide valuable information and insights. Once you determine what you need to know, you can determine whom to consult. If you need to know about the history, latest developments, or technical issues related to your topic, you might want to interview an expert. Also consider laypersons who have direct experience with your topic and can recount real-life experiences. They help put a human face on a problem or illustrate the connection to the local community. For many topics you would benefit from interviewing experts *and* laypersons.

Megan knew her speech would benefit from both expert and lay opinions. After reading a *Newsweek* cover story, "The Meth Epidemic," she decided to investigate the problem in her community and propose some solutions. *Newsweek* reported methamphetamine to be a "highly addictive stimulant" that often went undetected until users were hooked.[50] The report rang true for Megan; she had witnessed this firsthand. The husband of one of her best friends had become unpredictable and undependable. The once self-assured young professional grew nervous and made less and less sense when he talked. He lost weight, had no appetite, and paid scant attention to his wife or their two daughters. He refused his wife's pleas to see a physician. It was only after his business folded and he defaulted on their home loan that she learned he had been using methamphetamine.

Megan wondered how we might detect meth use and what sort of intervention might be best. Her focus suggested assistance from experts, particularly a counselor who helped people overcome addictions and a professor from the Criminal Justice program on her campus (part of a local drug task force) who could explain clues that signaled use of methamphetamine. She could also talk with her girlfriend again, as well as a person she knew who had served jail time for using meth and was now undergoing rehabilitation. Interviewing this combination of people would give her speech greater meaning and authenticity than relying on media reports alone.

Interviews can prove beneficial. To derive the greatest benefit, you will want to prepare for an interview carefully, conduct it efficiently, and report it accurately. A few simple tips will yield good results. These include what to do before, during, and after the interview.

Preparing the Interview

- Determine what you need to know or confirm. What is missing from existing reports/coverage? What needs further confirmation? Generate a set of specific questions that get at your curiosities.
- Determine who might supply the answers—experts? laypersons? a combination?
- Contact the person (or the person's secretary/assistant) to schedule some time together. Briefly explain who you are, what you are doing, and how you believe he or she may be able to help you. If the person feels unable to provide the assistance you need, she or he might refer you to someone who can.
- Once you have scheduled a time to meet, you might request a fax number or e-mail address so you can provide a brief set of questions in advance. The person would then have time to consider her or his responses before talking with you.
- Fine-tune your questions as follows:
  - Keep questions simple and to the point, as well as few in number.
  - Ask a combination of closed and open questions. Closed questions ask for a simple yes or no response, whereas open questions ask the interviewee to express and explain a belief or opinion.
  - Let the person you are interviewing see that you have done your homework and are sincere and thoughtful in your approach to the topic.
  - Feel free to ask tough questions, but do so respectfully and diplomatically.

Megan followed these guidelines when devising the following questions for the person she knew on the drug task force. (She would alter or change questions for other persons she would interview.)

1. According to *Newsweek*, meth users often go undetected by friends and family. Is this true? Why?

2. What are some signs that someone is using meth?
3. Why do users find meth so attractive?
4. What should we do if we suspect a friend or family member is using meth?
5. What sort of intervention has proven most successful?
6. What sorts of intervention have had less positive results?
7. What explains the high rate of recidivism for meth offenders reported in local news?
8. What measures might make a relapse less likely?

Megan did well crafting her questions. She encouraged elaboration by employing mostly open questions. She was also diplomatic. She did not ask the law enforcement official, "What explains your failure to rehabilitate meth users?" Instead, she posed the question more tactfully, using the term "recidivism"—a concept that law enforcement officials regularly discuss. The questions also revealed that Megan had done her homework. She did not ask basic, factual questions that she could have answered with other sources. Instead, she asked questions that showed she had prepared and that called for the expertise of the person she interviewed.

When discussing the matter with a former user, Megan might alter her questions slightly. Inquiring about intervention measures that work, she might ask, "What have your family or friends done that has been helpful?" She could also ask, "What have they done that wasn't helpful?" or "What would you suggest to someone who's trying to help a friend quit meth?"

Interviewing experts and laypersons can provide invaluable information and insights for your speech.

Conducting the Interview

No matter how well you prepare in terms of initial research and formulating questions, the actual act of conducting the interview will be a crucial point in the information-gathering process. A few simple pointers will help produce good results.

- *Be professional.* If you hope to be taken seriously, you need to act professionally. Dressing appropriately and arriving on time, for example, create a positive impression, as does beginning the interview by thanking the person and establishing a cordial and respectful tone.
- *Quickly get down to business.* After the brief thank-you, remind the person of the purpose of your project and how you believe she or he can help you. Once you clarify your goals as an interviewer, the person can understand how to assist. (e.g., "I'm trying to discover why meth is so attractive to its users and how we might better address a problem *Newsweek* calls an epidemic.")
- *Let the person see what you know and don't know.* Mention some of the sources you have consulted and what they suggest. Megan might have asked the professor, who was part of the task force, this question: "Assistant U.S. Attorney Christopher Casey told *Newsweek* that meth has 'seduced whole families and turned them into 'zombies.'[51] Does this seem accurate?"
- *Be genuinely involved.* Focus on their responses, providing nonverbal feedback such as nods or smiles, whatever is appropriate, to show you are listening and processing the person's remarks. Quick comments, too, such as "hmm . . . interesting," or "really?" can convey how you are processing the message or when you would like elaboration. Taking notes, too, signals you find the remarks valuable or noteworthy.
- *Employ a good system for taking notes.* Enter your questions on one side of a page, reserving the other side for the interviewee's responses and for your reflections about those responses. Also leave plenty of space between questions in case the person pursues an angle you had not considered. Be sure to obtain permission before using an electronic recording device.
- *Be courteous.* Sometimes an interviewee relates anecdote after anecdote and goes off on tangents. If this happens, politely steer the person back on topic when you get the opportunity to speak. Let the interviewee know that what she or he said was interesting, then redirect attention to what you want to explore further or another item you would like to address. Your courtesy and respect will help sustain the person's enthusiasm and keep him or her talking, but you may need to nudge the interviewee back on track from time to time.

    Another tactic for keeping the interviewee on track and to conduct the interview more efficiently is to make open questions less open. For example, instead of asking "What are the chief motivators that prompt people to try meth?" you might ask, "What is one of the biggest reasons that people decide to try meth?"
- *Be respectful.* Allow the person to have his or her say, even when you disagree with what is being said. You can question specific statements, but do so with diplomacy and tact.

- *Be accurate.* Accurately record statements made during the interview. Repeat key phrases you wish to quote, for verification, and likewise repeat paraphrased material to check your accuracy. The interviewee will welcome follow-up questions that begin, "If I understand correctly, what you're saying is . . ." These questions can also prompt helpful elaboration.

  Also make sure you have the person's name and any title entered correctly—perhaps request a business card. You will need the information for your bibliography.
- *Conclude on schedule.* If the interviewee wants to keep going, that is another matter.
- *Display your gratitude.* Smile and thank the person for her or his time.

Rather than a face-to-face meeting, you may have to interview the person using some other means, such as telephone or e-mail (which we will discuss below). When interviewing by phone, follow the same general guidelines discussed above, with these additional pointers.

- *Use a three-part introduction.* Supply the following information to the person taking your call.
  - Indicate the person you are calling.
  - Identify yourself and your affiliation.
  - Briefly explain why you are calling.
  - For example, you might say, "May I speak with Officer Dunleavy? This is Megan Juarez, a student at Oklahoma State, and I'm seeking information about the methamphetamine problem in our region."
  - This three-part introduction tells the person taking your call what they need to know so they can respond immediately and not have to ask for additional information.
- *Be considerate.* When the person with whom you wish to speak appears on the line, quickly thank the person by name and repeat your purpose for calling. As a courtesy, ask whether the person has time to answer a few questions or if there is a better time to call.
- *Be brief.* People do not expect to be interviewed for an hour on the phone. Keep the number of questions reasonable so that the interview can be concluded within about 15 minutes.
- *Be well-prepared.* Follow a set of questions as you would during a face-to-face interview. The questions will keep you on track and will ensure you cover all you wish to cover.
- *Convey a positive impression with your voice.* Pay attention to volume—speaking neither so softly that the interviewee has trouble hearing you nor so loudly that you blow them away. Either extreme can be irritating. Enunciate clearly. If you mumble or slur your words, the person may have trouble understanding you or taking you seriously. Speak fluently, avoiding vocalized pauses and verbal fillers. Also, be as attentive to your facial expressions as you would be if you were face-to-face; your manner will affect the tone of your voice.

- *Bring the conversation to a close.* It is your responsibility to end the call. Begin signaling the end when you are nearly done asking questions, noting something like, "I only have two more quick questions." When you are ready to end the conversation, express your gratitude with closing language such as "I certainly appreciate your time and have enjoyed talking with you. The information you have provided has been very helpful for my speech. Thank you."
- *If you must leave a recorded message . . .* If voicemail picks up, use the same three-part introduction you would with a secretary. Request that the person return your call. Provide your number, stating it very clearly. As a courtesy, repeat your number. You may also indicate when you are available, saying something such as "I have class until two o'clock but will be available after then." Be sure your voice creates a positive impression. Thank the person.

After the Interview

As soon as possible after the interview, review your notes to make sure you accurately recorded the person's statements and his or her position on an issue. With the interview fresh in your mind, you will be in a better position to fill in the details for anything that appears sketchy.

Sometime soon after the interview, send a quick thank-you to the person interviewed as well as to his or her secretary/assistant, if appropriate.

Gathering Information through E-mail

Preview. *E-mail can be an effective and efficient means to gather information, offering several noteworthy advantages. A few pointers increase the likelihood of getting good results.*

E-mail can assist your investigation in several ways. For one thing, you can send source citations and full-text materials to your e-mail account for safe storage and later use, taking full advantage of material already in electronic form. After e-mailing citations from an online database, for example, your formal bibliography can likely be assembled through some simple reformatting. E-mail can also be a good way to request information from a relevant person or agency. Often experts on your subject may be too busy to meet you in person but would be happy to answer questions via e-mail. E-mail can also make long-distance inquiries feasible.

E-mail proved essential to Mia while she investigated her topic. Mia learned from a news report about a city that had implemented new regulations for barking dogs that addressed the problem 24 hours a day. Owners faced fines that increased incrementally with each disturbance. Mia's own town, a larger municipality, only addressed the problem between the hours of 11:00 PM and 7 AM, and then it only sent law enforcement to ask the owner to hush the animal. Mia thought her city's policy was too lax, *and* it ignored the rights of persons like her aunt, who had to work at night and should be able to sleep, undisturbed, during the day. When discussing the matter with a friend, the friend provided another instance of dogs being a nuisance. An elderly man who had hospice care in his home had a neighbor whose dogs barked continuously throughout the day, only a few yards from the bedroom where he tried to rest. The man's wife asked the neighbor to do something so the man could rest, but the dogs continued to bark.

Mia and her friend felt that something had to be done for citizens in their community. They went online and found the city's website, which had an e-mail address that allowed questions. Mia sent an e-mail requesting more details about their new regulations for addressing the barking nuisance. Within 24 hours they e-mailed her a copy of the actual ordinance. Mia was now ready to attend a city council meeting and request that they adopt a similar policy.

E-mailing for information can pay off. Be mindful, though, that not all sites that allow inquiries are as prompt or as helpful as the city Mia had contacted. Continue your search for information elsewhere while awaiting a reply. Also, before making any request for information, be sure it is not information you can find with relative ease on that agency's Web pages or elsewhere.

E-mail can also assist in the interview process. An electronic mailing may be appropriate for requesting and arranging an interview by phone or in person. In addition, it can allow you to acquaint the person with the questions you wish to ask. You may even find that an e-mail exchange will suffice if it yields all the information you had hoped to gather in an interview, eliminating the need to meet face-to-face.

E-mail presents another advantage as well. As noted above, the material already exists in electronic form, allowing for easy storage, transferal, and use. For example, Mia was able to provide copies of the nearby city's regulations for the city council members, appended to her written argument for a revised disturbance ordinance.

In order to obtain the best results from e-mail inquiries or other e-mail communications, it pays to follow certain guidelines. For the best results:

- *Keep inquiries short, simple, and to the point.* Since e-mail is used for its quickness, receivers do not want to be burdened by lengthy messages or inquiries that require elaborate responses.
- *Format for a quick read and quick response.* Keep paragraphs short, and leave a blank line between them. Keep sentences short and easy to process—and conversational yet professional. Use a bulleted or numbered list when you are making a series of points or asking a series of questions.
- *Be careful with the subject line.* Craft a subject line that clearly identifies you and your purpose and also reduces the risk of the message being deleted before it is opened (e.g., "citizen re: ordinance for dogs").
- *Disclose your objective in the first line of the message.* Receivers do not want to guess what a message is about. Let them know immediately (e.g., "After seeing a report about your new ordinance for barking dogs, I hope to have my city adopt a similar policy.").
- *Keep the look simple and professional.* Leave out fancy fonts, colors, and avoid emoticons (such as smiley faces).
- *Remember that what you see may not be what they get.* Be mindful that formatting (e.g., italics, indentations) may appear differently on the recipient's monitor.
- *Critique and proofread before sending.* Check clarity, grammar, spelling, and punctuation. Mistakes can harm your credibility and have a negative impact on the response you will receive.

■ *Never say anything in e-mail that you would not want shared in public.* E-mail is not private communication; it can be easily forwarded and shared (intentionally or otherwise) with others.

Citing Sources of Quoted and Paraphrased Material

Preview. *Once you have gathered information from a variety of sources and integrated it into your speech, you will want to be sure to reveal those sources to your audience. You may also need to assemble a comprehensive bibliography for your formal outline, formatting it correctly.*

Although you probably have a great interest in your speech topic, you likely are not an expert. Even if you can be regarded as an expert, you still need to seek additional information and opinions, just as most experts do.

Guidelines for Incorporating Material

When you incorporate material into your speech, you might quote the source verbatim, or you might choose to paraphrase. In either instance, you will need to reveal the source *during* your presentation. As we discussed in Chapter 2, plagiarism is a serious matter. Be sure that material taken from another source is properly acknowledged and that the audience understands when you are quoting or paraphrasing material from an outside source.

Deciding whether to quote or paraphrase can be determined in light of a few simple guidelines. Quote information when

■ you wish to bolster your own ethos by associating your ideas with that of a recognized authority
■ the information you are presenting is so startling or unusual that the audience will doubt its accuracy unless a respected source is cited
■ you support an unpopular position and wish to blunt its unpopularity by citing the opinion of a source whom the audience will respect
■ the material is expressed so eloquently that you could not say it more clearly or in a more memorable fashion

Revealing sources during your presentation does more than safeguard against plagiarism; it fulfills one of your most important ethical obligations as a speaker. As duty would have it, ethical speakers openly recognize what others have contributed to their knowledge and thinking.

Revealing sources is not only right, it is smart. As we will see in Chapter 15, speakers who cite quality sources during a presentation will bolster their ethos, and their audience will more likely accept their message.[52] Suppose, for example, that two speakers asserted that "violent crime has dropped dramatically over the past few years." How would you perceive the speaker who cited no outside sources to back up such a claim? Would you be more likely to trust a speaker who drew on a reputable source versus one who cited a questionable source? As Professor William

Norwood Brigance observed more than a half century ago, "One is known by the company he [or she] keeps; and when listeners find that you have been keeping company with eminent people of ideas and with expert collectors of information, they are impelled to accept you and your ideas."[53]

In short, by citing reputable sources you will meet your ethical responsibility and you will impress your audience with how well you did your homework. The audience will see that you were well prepared to speak.

Guidelines for Citing Sources during Your Presentation

When you cite sources during your presentation, you do not need to provide complete bibliographic information. Simply provide enough information to convince the audience of the credibility of the source and—if necessary—the currency of the information. For example, you could say, "*Time* magazine reported last month that . . ." or "In a recent interview on ABC's *20/20*, former secretary of state Colin Powell stated . . ." or "Dr. George Edwards, professor of political science here at Texas A&M, told me in a recent interview that . . ." Notice how Dr. Edwards's expertise is revealed. Not only is the audience provided with his title, but they are also informed of his area of expertise so they will know why he should be considered credible.

Although citations in the speech can be abbreviated, your instructor will likely require complete bibliographic information in a list of sources at the end of your formal outline. You should also provide full citations on PowerPoint slides or other visual aids you might use when the content is taken from a source. Finally, you should always be ready to provide complete information about a source to anyone who might ask about it after your presentation.

To ensure that you cite your sources orally during your presentation, cite them parenthetically in your speaking outline. If, for instance, you were making reference to Colin Powell in the manner described earlier, you might place (Powell, *20/20*) in your speaking outline. For the formal outline you submit to your instructor, format sources according to whatever style guide your instructor has approved. For example, Powell's appearance on *20/20* would be cited as follows, using the *Chicago Manual of Style*:

Colin Powell, interview by Barbara Walters, *20/20*, ABC, August 7, 2005.

Note: For additional examples of *Chicago Manual* style, see the endnotes after each chapter in this text.

Summary

Learning how to conduct productive and responsible research will allow you to do well in your speeches, and it will also be vital in your career and in your role as a citizen. The skills discussed in this chapter will allow you to

- formulate well-founded ideas
- provide quality support for your ideas

- have confidence when you speak
- enhance your credibility
- meet your ethical responsibility

Specifically, this chapter teaches you how to

- launch your investigation in terms of how and where to obtain background information, particularly by using reference sources, news sources, government publications, and other credible sources

- craft a working thesis to focus your investigation, allowing you to discern whether information is relevant and which sources will likely prove most valuable

- record information thoughtfully and systematically, contemplating how the information ultimately will function in your speech

- maximize your creative potential and productivity during the speechwriting process

- use information responsibly, understanding that information literacy is not only a set of skills but a set of responsibilities: it is not enough to find information; you must also be able to evaluate it and use it properly

- utilize your library's resources—what is available electronically and in print and in other forms, as well as consult professional librarians for assistance

- use the World Wide Web judiciously, careful to evaluate postings and compare information with that gathered from sources already known to be trustworthy

- interview experts and others who have helpful information and relevant experiences, exercising professionalism and efficiency as you initiate contact, conduct the interview, and respond to their assistance

- use e-mail to gather information, having it substitute (when appropriate) for a face-to-face interview or using it to manage information found in an electronic form

- avoid plagiarism by using information from outside sources properly and responsibly

- reveal your sources during your presentation in a manner that allows your audience to evaluate their integrity

- provide complete documentation in a written list of references at the end of your outline, so that information is available to your instructor and any listener who might inquire about it after your speech

John Walsh and other successful advocates have learned the importance of having good information to back up their opinions. Using what you learn in this chapter, you, too, can develop the research skills necessary to effectively inform or influence others. Like John Walsh, you can help change our world for the better.

QUESTIONS FOR REVIEW AND REFLECTION

1. How will a working thesis statement help you to formulate ideas and find relevant material?
2. Identify the various creative processes that are involved in crafting a speech.

3. What are the important do's and don'ts in recording information?

4. Why is revision so important in speech preparation?

5. What is information literacy? Why is it especially important today?

6. Describe at least three important library resources and explain how they could be helpful to you in preparing a speech.

7. How would you go about finding information using the World Wide Web?

8. How would you evaluate the integrity of a website?

9. What is the role of interviewing in speech preparation?

    a. How would you prepare for an interview?

    b. What are the guidelines for conducting an interview?

    c. How would you follow up an interview?

10. How can e-mail be useful to you when preparing a speech?

11. Under what circumstances should you quote material in your speech?

12. How should you cite sources as you deliver a speech, and why is it important to do so?

ENDNOTES

1. John Walsh and Susan Schindehette: *Tears of Rage: From Grieving Father to Crusader for Justice: The Untold Story of the Adam Walsh Case* (New York: Pocket Star Books, 1997), 53–143.

2. Ibid., 158.

3. Ibid., 158–60.

4. Ibid., 169.

5. Ibid., 191.

6. America's Most Wanted, "About John Walsh," www.amw.com/captures/ (accessed March 8, 2007).

7. Richard A. Katula and Celest A. Martin, "Teaching Critical Thinking in the Speech Communication Classroom," *Communication Education* 33 (1984): 160–68.

8. Jeffrey Kluger, "Stem Cells Save Babies," *Time*, May 30, 2005, 59.

9. For example, major newspapers often endorse a particular candidate. For a listing of papers and whom they endorse, go to http://wheretodoresearch.com/Political.htm.

10. Stephen K. Reed, *Cognition, Theory and Application*, 3rd ed. (Pacific Grove, CA: Brooks/Cole, 1992), 223.

11. Ilan Yaniv and David E. Meyer, "Activation and Metacognition of Inaccessible Stored Information: Potential Bases for Incubation Effects in Problem Solving," *Journal of Experimental Psychology: Learning, Memory, and Cognition* 13 (1987): 187–205. Also see Peggy Milam, "The Power of Reflection in the Research Process," *School Library Media Activities Monthly* 21 (February 2005): 26–29.

12. Renate Nummela Caine et al., *12 Brain/Mind Learning Principles in Action: The Fieldbook for Making Connections, Teaching, and the Human Brain* (Thousand Oaks, CA: Corwin Press, 2005).

13. Ronald A. Finke et al., *Creative Cognition: Theory, Research, and Applications* (Cambridge, MA: MIT Press, 1992), 149–50.

14. John B. Best, *Cognitive Psychology*, 5th ed. (Belmont, CA: Brooks/Cole Wadsworth, 1999), 420–23.

15. Finke et al., *Creative Cognition*, 166.

16. Steven Pressfield, *The War of Art: Break through the Block and Win Your Inner Creative Battles* (New York: Warner Books, 2002).

17. Peter Elbow, *Writing with Power: Techniques for Mastering the Writing Process* (New York: Oxford University Press, 1981).

18. See Tony Buzan and Barry Buzan, *The Mind Map Book: How to Use Radiant Thinking to Maximize Your Brain's Untapped Potential* (New York: Penguin Books, 1993). For concept mapping, see Joseph D. Novak and D. Bob Gowin, *Learning How to Learn* (New York: Cambridge University Press, 2002).

19. Ibid. For free mind-mapping software, go to www.jcu.edu.au/studying/services/studyskills/mindmap/index.html or simply search "mind mapping" using Google or your favorite search engine.

20. R. Keith Sawyer, *Explaining Creativity: The Science of Human Innovation* (New York: Oxford University Press, 2006). Sawyer also emphasizes the importance of an early start and the other strategies we have discussed.

21. Linda Flower and John R. Hayes, "A Cognitive Process Theory of Writing," *College Composition and Communication* 32 (1981): 380–81.

22. Jean Wyrick, *Steps to Writing Well: A Concise Guide to Composition*, 6th ed. (New York: Harcourt Brace, 1996), 103.

23. Peggy Noonan, *What I Saw at the Revolution: A Political Life in the Reagan Era* (New York: Ivy Books, 1990), 77. To learn more about how a president's speeches are written, go to www.americanpresident.org/action/orgchart/administration_units/officeofspeechwriting/a_index.shtml.

24. Ibid.

25. Public Broadcasting Service, "Forum Featuring Presidential Speechwriters," www.pbs.org/newshour/inauguration/speech3.html (accessed February 10, 2006).

26. David Greene, "Bush Prepares to Deliver State of Union Address," National Public Radio, 2006, www.npr.org/templates/story/story.php?storyId=5179164&ft=1&f=1001 (accessed 10 February 2006).

27. Sondra Perl, "Understanding Composing," *College Composition and Communication* 31 (1980): 363–69.

28. Flower and Hayes, "Cognitive Process," 365–87.

29. Quintilian, *The Institutio Oratoria of Quintilian*, trans. H. E. Butler (New York: Putnam, 1992), 109–111.

30. American Library Association. *Information Literacy Competency Standards for Higher Education* (Chicago: Association of College and Research Libraries, 2000), 2–3.

31. Ibid.

32. Ibid.

33. Jon Udell, "Wikipedia's Future," *InfoWorld* 28 (January 9, 2006): 30.

34. Cornell University Library, "Distinguishing Scholarly from Non-Scholarly Periodicals: A Checklist of Criteria" www.library.cornell.edu/t/help/res_strategy/evaluating/scholar.htm (accessed January 14, 2006).

35. Ibid.

36. Ibid.

37. Ibid.

38. Penn State University Libraries, "How to Evaluate the Information" www.libraries.psu.edu/instruction/infolit/andyou/mod7/eval_i.htm (accessed January 15, 2006).

39. Sandy Whitely, ed., *The American Library Association Guide to Information Access: A Complete Research Handbook and Directory* (New York: Random House, 1994), xvii.

40. Steven Levy, "All Eyes on Google," *Newsweek*, March 29, 2004, 54.

41. A study by the OCLC found that less than 35 percent of college students reported that they had used online databases, whereas 82 percent responded that they had used search engines (13). See Online Library Computer Center, "Libraries and Information Sources— Use, Familiarity, Favorability," in *Perceptions of Libraries and Information Resources* (Part I), www.oclc.org/reports/pdfs/Percept_pt1.pdf (accessed July 21, 2006).

42. Whitely, *Guide to Information Access*, 34.

43. Brad Stone, "Little Engines That Can," *Newsweek*, March 29, 2004, 59.

44. Lee Rainie, "Internet Librarians Own the Future," *Information Today* 22 (January 2005): 42.

45. Patricia Hayes Andrews and Richard T. Herschel, *Organizational Communication: Empowerment in a Technological Society* (Boston: Houghton Mifflin, 1996): A1.

46. Levy, "All Eyes on Google," 54.

47. Michael Gorman, "The Corruption of Cataloging," *Library Journal* 120 (September 15, 1995): 34.

48. *New York Times*, June 28, 2000, 1.

49. Purdue University Online Writing Lab, "Evaluating Internet Sources," http://owl.english.purdue.edu/handouts/print/research/r_evalsource4.html (accessed June 10, 2005).

50. David J. Jefferson, "America's Most Dangerous Drug," *Newsweek*, August 8, 2005, 42.

51. Ibid, 47.

52. John C. Reinard, "The Empirical Study of the Persuasive Effects of Evidence: The Status after Fifty Years of Research," *Human Communication Research* 15 (1988): 3–59.

53. William Norwood Brigance, *Speech: Its Techniques and Disciplines in a Free Society*, 2nd ed. (New York: Appleton-Century-Crofts, 1952), 211.

CHAPTER 8

Supporting Your Ideas with Evidence

CHAPTER SURVEY

Supporting Ideas with Evidence

Testing Evidence

CHAPTER OBJECTIVES

After studying this chapter, you should be able to

1. Understand the importance of making ideas understandable and believable.

2. Identify the principal types of evidence used to support ideas: facts, definitions, examples, statistics, testimony, and comparison and contrast.

3. Apply tests to determine the quality of different kinds of evidence.

4. Choose evidence carefully to support your ideas.

In daily conversations, most of us assert our views without necessarily substantiating them with a great deal of support. We may refer to an article we have read or a website we have visited. We may cite an occasional statistic. But we rarely feel the pressure to support our assertions or opinions with extensive evidence. By contrast, when we prepare to make some *public* statement about a matter of public importance, the expectations and norms shift considerably. As speakers we should anticipate having to establish our knowledge and credibility by showing what we have learned from specific reputable sources. And as discerning listeners we hope to encounter speakers who substantiate their opinions with excellent supporting material.

The need to use evidence to support ideas varies with the situation, the audience, our relationship to the listeners, and the complexity of the idea. If you and your listeners agree on a topic, for example, you will not need to use such extensive supporting material to make your ideas understandable and believable. Let us suppose that you are asking a group of listeners to vote for a political candidate who is running on a platform that features a number of educational reforms. If the listeners are in favor of the kind of reforms your candidate supports, then you may not need to use a great deal of supporting material to sway them. However, if you are asking for the support of a different group of listeners—a group that is worried about the cost and effectiveness of your candidate's reform platform, then you will have to come armed with *extensive* statistics, comparisons, and other forms of evidence. In short, the nature and amount of proof you need to make an idea believable for some audiences may not be sufficient for others.

Of course, not all supporting material is of equal quality. One speaker might point out, "Police report that the problem of theft is growing on our campus—with over 20 robberies reported this year so far. That is nearly *twice* as many as last year— and the school year is far from over!" Another, who is talking about the problem of domestic violence, might share this statistic: "According to the Middle Way House website, one woman is beaten every 15 seconds in this country."[1] Still another speaker might attempt to make his statistics meaningful to listeners by saying, "According to Dr. Richard A. DeVaul at Texas A&M University's College of Medicine, 100,000 people die annually in the United States from adverse drug reactions. This is the same as if a 727 airliner crashed every day, killing all aboard—approximately 274 individuals per day."[2] Yet another might use a powerful comparison by arguing that "most people seldom set out with the deliberate intent of breaking the law. They are drawn into it, almost as a boa constrictor defeats its prey."[3]

As listeners, what should we make of the supporting material used by these speakers? Does it serve to strengthen or undermine the speakers' arguments? Does it enhance or hinder each one's credibility? What critical standards should we use to assess the quality of supporting material used by speakers in classroom and community settings?

In this chapter we are concerned with *both* issues. First, we discuss how speakers should incorporate supporting material into their speeches in ways that enhance their ability to enlighten and move their listeners. Second, we want *also* to consider critical criteria for examining evidence—whether you are thinking of using it to craft your own speech, or listening to someone who has presented it to you for your consideration and acceptance. Developing a critical view of supporting material is essential for all speakers and listeners who want to participate in the democratic process as constructive, ethical communicators and discerning citizens.

In Chapter 7, we discussed the process of gathering relevant information for speeches. We pointed out that your task, as a speaker, is to search for information that will help you achieve your desired audience response. We want to begin, then, by turning to the kinds of information that will most likely benefit you as you develop your speech.

Supporting Ideas with Evidence

Preview. *Good evidence can make ideas and arguments more understandable and convincing. Good speakers use varied evidence, including facts, definitions, examples, statistics, testimony, and comparison and contrast.*

Suppose you were speaking in your public speaking class. You might assert, "We need to revitalize our minority recruitment program here at the university." On the basis of that assertion alone, the audience would be unable to determine whether your idea was sound. You have not described the existing program, compared it to other programs, or offered information about its decline. To strengthen your assertion, you would need to support it with evidence. Evidence is the body of fact and opinion pertaining to a subject.

In most of your speeches, you should use several different kinds of evidence. Some kinds of speeches, such as technical reports, rely heavily on statistical evidence, often reinforced with presentational aids. But even a technical speech can be enhanced by the use of examples, comparison and contrast, and the opinions of experts. In almost every public speaking situation, you will communicate more effectively if you use good and varied kinds of evidence. And, as we have pointed out, you should substantiate that evidence by citing its source. You will find comprehensive guidelines for citing sources in Chapter 7.

Facts

Nearly every speaker will commonly use facts as evidence. Some facts take the form of statistical support, but many do not. Facts are data that can be verified by observation. The more consistently facts are verified by observers and experts, the more they become viewed as established. We generally judge factual information in terms of its truth, correctness, or verifiability. A speaker might share facts such as these:

- More local families applied for federally subsidized housing in 2007 than ever before.
- In the state of Indiana, voter registration closes 30 days before the day of the election.
- The U.S. Constitution was ratified in 1788.

Speakers often take facts and interpret them by adding qualifiers that color their meaning. One student speaker, for example, had unsuccessfully tried to register to vote a week before a national election in the state of Indiana. In giving her speech on unfair voting rules, she said, "Without valid justification, voter registration in Indiana closes *30 days* before the election!" So, she presents the voting rule as a fact, but also labels it as "unfair" and "invalid." Using this kind of interpretive language is not a problem so long as the speaker remembers that she will need to explain her claim of unfairness by offering examples, testimony, comparisons, and statistics. For example, how do voting rules in Indiana compare with those in other states? Are some people more likely to be disadvantaged by this rule than others? How might a change in rules affect voter turnout? What do voting experts say about the rule's fairness?

Sometimes, the language used to describe facts is interpretive, but we do not easily recognize it as such. The Gulf War of 1990 was precipitated when Iraqi troops crossed its border with Kuwait and occupied land. Now the Iraqis maintained that they had "reclaimed" the territory, suggesting that they were taking back what was theirs—a legal action. The United States and its allies described the action as the "invasion" of Kuwait, implying the illegal occupation of territory belonging to a sovereign state. So, the troops crossing into Kuwait was a fact, but whether that was an act of reclaiming or invading was an interpretation. After the War in Iraq began in 2002, there was no question that American troops were stationed in Iraq—that was a fact. Whether the Iraqi people saw them as invaders or as liberators was a matter of interpretation.

To make sure your facts are sound, validate them by consulting multiple, credible sources. If you find inconsistencies, keep reading. Pay particular attention to the credibility of your sources. You should be able to trust the reported observations of those who are genuinely trustworthy. With contemporary topics, make sure your sources are up-to-date. What looks like a factual discrepancy at first glance may simply reflect differences when the data were collected or reported.

Definitions

Sometimes speakers need to define a word or concept addressed in their speeches. It is important to insure a common understanding of key concepts, especially if a word or term can be understood in diverse ways. You and your listeners need to be on the same page. In general, you should provide definitions for any technical terms that are unfamiliar to your audience the first time you use them. Similarly, define acronyms with which listeners may be unfamiliar. A speaker talking to a group of new nonprofit leaders about funding opportunities might say, "Many of you will want to consider applying for CBDG monies. These are Community Block Development Grants—and they are intended to assist nonprofits with ensuring decent, affordable housing, providing services to the most vulnerable in our communities, and creating new jobs."[4]

Definitions can be persuasive, as well as informative. A persuasive definition reflects your way of looking at a controversial subject. Others may define the same term or concept quite differently, but *yours* is the definition you want the audience to reflect on, and hopefully find engaging and appealing. Pulitzer Prize–winning author David Shipler uses this approach in defining poverty. He writes, "'Poverty' is an unsatisfying term, for poverty is not a category that can be delineated by the government's dollar limits or annual income. In real life, it is an unmarked area along a continuum, a broader region of hardship than society usually recognizes. More people than those officially designated as "poor" are, in fact, weighed down with the troubles associated with poverty. Therefore, I use "poor" not as a statistician would. I use it imprecisely as it should be used, to suggest the lowest stratum of economic attainment, with all of its accompanying problems."[5]

Definitions, then, can be straightforward—meant only to clarify and provide uncontroversial information—or they can challenge the audience to think in different and creative ways. When new definitions are embraced, listeners may see problems in a new light or be called on to think or act in different ways. See the following *Focus on Civic Engagement* for an extended illustration of how one author defines leadership.

Examples

One of the most difficult challenges public speakers face is trying to make general principles or abstract notions interesting and meaningful to the audience. One of the best ways of doing this is through examples. Examples provide concrete frames of reference and interject life and meaning into the ideas you are communicating.

The case of Anne Frank offers a concrete and moving example of horrors of the Holocaust by translating numbers into the story of a real human being.

Focus on Civic Engagement

Defining Leadership in a New Way

Getting people to travel from one fixed point to another is what the work of leadership is about. It takes no leadership to get teachers to support higher teacher salaries or Sierra Club members to oppose the destruction of forests or national parks. They don't have to traverse any distance to arrive at such positions, because these are the positions they're starting from in the first place. But it does take leadership to convert conservative business leaders into supporters of federally funded school lunch programs and breakfast programs, or to persuade financially stretched taxpayers to support funding for the arts.

If you accept the above definition of leadership as true, several other truths are inherent in it.

One of these sample truths follows:

. . . The most effective leaders do not concentrate all their energies on addressing and organizing those who agree with them, but rather on building bridges to those who disagree and winning them over to their point of view. Advocacy is not advocacy when aimed at those who share your views. This is redundancy. The key to solving most problems is in building a larger consensus than previously existed for a solution.

The definition concludes with a discussion of how leaders use persuasion:

Leaders employ a variety of tactics to move their followers. They give speeches, tell stories, make reasoned arguments, serve as examples, and conduct symbolic acts. All of these tactics are designed to do one thing: persuade. Persuasion is most successful when it shows how the recommended course of action is in one's self-interest. The intersection of self-interest and a larger public interest is where leaders stake their claim.

In the larger context of the book, Shore suggests that leadership is as much about consensus building as winning arguments. He also believes that leadership potential resides within many citizens, who can truly make a difference in their communities.

Source: Bill Shore, *The Cathedral Within: Transforming Your Life by Giving Something Back* (New York: Random House, 2001), 182–84.

When judiciously selected, examples can function as compelling forms of evidence. We could talk about the atrocities committed during the Holocaust by indicating the numbers of people killed or imprisoned. The enormity of the crime, however, becomes more apparent through the experience of reading such powerful books as Elie Wiesel's *Night*, or watching film versions of real and fictional accounts, such as *Playing for Time, Sophie's Choice, The Diary of Anne Frank, Schindler's List*, and *Life Is Beautiful*. Characters are seen as people. Anne Frank is not a number but a person who hid for years from Nazi persecutors, only to be discovered at last and sent to die in a prison camp. In this case, a real little girl—a concrete example—makes the abstraction of numbers both more terrible and more real.

There are two principal kinds of examples that a speaker can use to support ideas: actual examples and hypothetical examples. Each kind may be brief or developed as a more extended narrative.

Actual Examples

An actual example deals with a real case; it is something that actually happened. Even a very brief example, if well chosen, can make a main point vivid and memorable. In a speech delivered at Yale, J. Edward Hill, president of the American Medical Association, discussed the dangers of being overweight. He noted that "at any one time, six in ten Americans are overweight and about one in three are considered obese." After sharing this and related statistics, he offered this specific example:

> Perhaps more telling [than statistics] is a newspaper item I read last week, about the Batesville Casket Company, which last year launched its "Dimensions" line of super-sized coffins. Think about that for a second.[6]

Later in the speech, Edwards discussed obesity as one of the "eight scourges" that are destroying our health. He also noted that one of the AMA's priorities for the year 2005 was reducing risky behavior "by promoting healthy lifestyles."

Actual examples also allow the audience to see or imagine a problem or solution—perhaps grasping, for the first time, the actual form that an abstract concept might take. For instance, in a speech delivered to the National Education Summit on High Schools, Bill Gates argued that there *is* hope for public education in the United States. To support his point, Gates offered specific examples of U.S. high schools that had become models of effectiveness. The following is one of them:

> At the Met School in Providence, Rhode Island, 70 percent of the students are black or Hispanic. More than 60 percent live below the poverty line. Nearly 40 percent come from families where English is a second language. As part of its special mission, the Met enrolls only students who have dropped out in the past or were in danger of dropping out. Yet, even with this student body, the Met now has the lowest dropout rate and the highest college placement rate of any high school in the state. These are the kind of results you get when you prepare *every* [italics added] student for college.[7]

After sharing this and other real examples, Gates went on to discuss the characteristics that distinguish these schools from less successful schools, and to provide a specific set of guidelines that might influence initiatives aimed at reforming public education.

Narratives as Actual Examples

More extended examples may come from literature, from compelling stories the speaker has discovered through careful research, or from the speaker's own personal experiences. The following excerpt from a student speech illustrates the use of a narrative example based on the student's personal experience.

> Did your parents go to college? How about your brothers and sisters, or your cousins? Did you just assume that you would attend college from the time you were a child? I didn't. No one in my family had attended college—not even for a year or two. No one in my family even *talked* to me about the possibility of attending college. I think they just thought that I'd work on the farm like everyone else in the family. But when I was in high school, I had a wonderful English teacher who took an interest in my writing. She told me she thought I had some real ability. No one had ever talked to me like that before. She encouraged me

to enter a writing contest during my junior year. When I actually *won* the contest, she started giving me college brochures and urging me to check out some websites. Before I knew it, I had applied to three colleges and been accepted by all of them with financial aid packages. Without the kindness, support, and encouragement of this *one* teacher, I might never have even *applied* to any college. It is even less likely that I would be about to graduate from one of the best colleges in the state this coming May.

The student went on in her speech to talk about the vital role that adults can play in mentoring, encouraging, and serving as role models for youth. She invited her fellow classmates (nearly all graduating seniors) to go out into their communities and function as such role models.

Vivid, engaging examples are usually well received by listeners, and those that grow from the speaker's life experiences can be especially moving. At the 1992 Democratic National Convention, for example, Elizabeth Glaser used her own experience as an example to urge her audience to support AIDS research. Glaser began her speech by telling her own story:

A vivid, personal example, such as that given by AIDS victim Elizabeth Glaser, serves as a powerful form of supporting material.

> I'm Elizabeth Glaser. Eleven years ago, while giving birth to my first child, I hemorrhaged and was transfused with seven pints of blood. Four years later I found out that I had been infected with the AIDS virus and had unknowingly passed it to my daughter, Ariel, through my breast milk and to my son, Jake, in utero.
>
> Twenty years ago, I wanted to be at the Democratic Convention because it was a way to participate in my country. Today I am here because it is a matter of life and death. Exactly four years ago my daughter died of AIDS. She did not survive the Reagan administration. I am here because my son and I may not survive four more years of leaders who say they care but do nothing.
>
> I am in a race with the clock.[8]

Glaser's use of her own tragic experience demonstrates how narratives taken from real life can function as a powerful form of supporting material. When speakers do not have actual examples to share, they may, on some occasions, choose to use hypothetical examples to illustrate and support their ideas.

Hypothetical Examples

A hypothetical example is one that represents an action or an event that could plausibly take place in the way it is described. It is not, however, an actual account of a particular incident or event. Although it is in a sense a "made-up" example, it must not be exaggerated or distorted, and it must be based on accurate information if it is to be effective.

Throughout history, speakers have used hypothetical examples effectively. For instance, Angelina Grimké, a nineteenth-century crusader for the abolition of slavery and for women's rights, sought to characterize the experiences of Northerners who refused to condemn slavery based on their contact with Southern slaveholders. She did not single out any particular persons; rather she pictured a hypothetical group who exemplified their reactions. "Many persons go to the South for a season," she said, "and are hospitably entertained in the parlor and at the table of the slave-holder. They never enter the huts of the slaves; they know nothing of the dark side of the picture, and they return home with praise on their lips of the generous character of those with whom they have tarried."[9]

Narratives as Hypothetical Examples

Some speakers may choose to use proverbs, stories, or folktales to illustrate an idea or make a compelling point. When used in this way, narratives use imagination and symbolism to convey a moral, instead of describing events that might actually take place. For instance, in her speech delivered to the 96th Annual Convention of the NAACP, national board member Roslyn Brock shared an African folktale about a band of elephants who were crossing a river.

> As they were traveling across the terrain, they came upon a river. The big elephants did not have a problem stepping into the rough . . . waters. However, there were some very small elephants in the group who were afraid to step in the water. Somebody in the middle of the river shouted to the front of the line to those who had crossed over and said, "Brother leaders, we have some folks still standing on the banks of the river who haven't made it into the water to cross over."
>
> Viewing the situation, the larger elephants turned around, got back in the water and stood shoulder to shoulder, allowing their bodies to create a dam that parted the waters to allow those little elephants to cross over on dry ground.
>
> The moral of the story is: once YOU MAKE IT and get to the other side, don't forget . . . to turn around . . . and get back in the water and help someone else cross over.[10]

After sharing the moral of her narrative, Brock concluded with a powerful call to action, defining the NAACP as the "conscience of the nation," and asking her listeners to persevere in addressing such pressing concerns as HIV education, declining urban schools, and prison reform.

Because examples are easy to identify with, they can be a powerful tool for supporting your ideas. Even so, they must be used with care. In addition, listeners will want to exercise a great deal of caution in evaluating ideas and arguments supported by examples.

Thinking Critically about Examples

Several criteria should be used in assessing the quality of examples.

Perhaps the best test of an example is its typicality. If a speaker is trying to support a specific claim by the use of examples, listeners must ask themselves whether these examples really represent the normal course of events. If a speaker were to describe, as a specific example, a newspaper article in which a homeless person was arrested for shoplifting and then argued from that example that homeless people cannot be trusted, the listener should be very skeptical. This isolated example clearly does not support such a sweeping generalization. It would be as if someone argued that because one professor was arrested for hit-and-run driving, all professors are reckless drivers who would flee the scene of an accident. These kinds of distortions in the use of specific examples produce stereotyping. As we explained in detail in Chapters 4 and 5, stereotyping occurs when one group member's behavior is generalized to an entire group. It is up to both the speaker and the listener to look very carefully at the relationship between an example and the conclusion to which that example leads.

The listener also should evaluate the importance of an example. Occasionally an example will show that certain actions or results *could* occur, but not necessarily that they *frequently* occur. One speaker, for instance, argued that listeners should beware of buying prewashed bags of spinach from the grocery store. She supported her argument with one specific example of a boy who had died from *E. coli*–related illnesses after consuming some of this spinach in 2006 (citing studies reported on the national news and in major U.S. newspapers). In this case, whether that actual example was typical would probably be a secondary consideration. Even if thousands of people had consumed this spinach with no ill effects, the seriousness of the matter would be more crucial than the number of actual cases. In this particular speech, the student was able to further strengthen her argument by also pointing to well over 100 people who had become ill after eating the bagged spinach.[11]

While examples often function as a "human interest" form of support, they are perhaps most compelling when used in tandem with other forms of evidence, such as statistics.

Statistics

Speakers commonly use statistics as one kind of supporting material. As they attempt to show that a policy or program has had a real impact, for example, speakers will offer statistics to demonstrate how many people signed up for the program or were affected by the policy. They will also use statistics to make predictions about the future. When the executive director of a soup kitchen tells listeners, "We served more than 60,000 meals last year—an increase of 16 percent over the year before," he means to impress them with the growing need for funds. Statistics provide a numerical method of handling large numbers of cases. When used appropriately, they provide some of the most precise information available to public speakers.

Understanding Statistical Support

Statistics offer a way of showing how some things are related to others. They may tell us about the typicality of an occurrence and thus validate the examples used. In a speech addressing the problem of jail reform, for instance, a speaker gave an extended example dealing with the experience of a young man who had been in and out of jail 63 times over the course of his life! This actual example was coupled with statistical information demonstrating the general problem of repeated offenses and imprisonment (known as recidivism), highlighting the extent to which individuals return to jail again and again, often for relatively minor offenses.[12]

Statistics also might be used to show cause-and-effect relationships, or at least correlations between certain phenomena. One student, in a speech addressing the problem of ozone depletion, used statistical information to argue that the thinning of the ozone layer has led to increased incidents of skin cancer and cataracts.

Statistical information can be helpful in pointing out trends over time. For example, we can better appreciate how quickly and significantly the price of gasoline has increased if we can see the year-by-year costs. If we contend that crime is becoming a more serious problem in suburban and rural areas, we must show the crime rate over a period of time, along with specific data on the number of crimes committed.

Finally, statistics can highlight or reinforce an important point the speaker is making. This might be done by using a presentational aid to visually depict the most important figures. But when delivered effectively by the speaker, excellent statistics can have considerable impact on their own. In a speech delivered at Georgetown University, Laura Bush used compelling statistics to dramatize the problem of educating America's youth:

Laura Bush's use of statistics in her speech on education dramatized problems youth face in our contemporary culture.

> Earlier this month, President Bush announced a nationwide effort called Helping America's Youth. We're reaching out to young people in our country, with a particular emphasis on boys—because the statistics on boys are alarming. Boys begin to fall behind girls in elementary school. In fact, nearly 70 percent of children in special education classes are boys. . . . More girls than boys go on to college in the United States and earn degrees. Boys are more likely than girls to commit crimes or to be the victim of violent crime. The U.S. Department of Justice estimates that more than 90 percent of gang members in the U.S. are boys. And by age 18, boys are 17 times more likely than girls to be in jail or prison."[13]

Statistics, then, are one important way of making ideas more understandable and believable. They should, however, be used responsibly by the speaker and viewed critically by the listener. One should not assume that a statistic always "proves" something conclusively. It is part of the total structure of evidence and should be considered in light of other supporting material.

Using Averages Reliably

The speaker and the listener both must recognize that statistics can sometimes be misleading. *Average*, for example, is a notoriously vague measure, even though it seems to give an air of statistical weight when it is used. Many people just assume that the words *mean* and *average* are synonymous, but they are not.

Averages can be computed in different ways, such as by adding up a list of figures and dividing by the number of figures (the mean), by choosing the figure that occurs most often (the mode), or by choosing the figure that is the midpoint between the two extreme figures (the median). These three methods of computing an average may lead to quite different conclusions. The mean is the arithmetic average, but it is not necessarily the best or the preferred average to quote. If there are extreme scores in the distribution of numbers, the mean will reflect a greatly distorted version of the real central tendency.

Consider the following array of numbers: 17, 18, 19, 20, 21, 22, 23, 24, 25, 26, 26, 29. Here the mean is 22.5, a sensible indication of that distribution's central tendency, or true average. But suppose the numbers being examined were salaries, as follows: $180,000, $127,000, $70,000, $68,000, $65,000, $60,000, $57,000, $52,000, $50,000, $48,000, $45,000. Here the mean is nearly $75,000. If you were going to work for a department with that salary distribution, however, you would not expect to make $75,000, because 9 out of the 11 employees earn only $70,000 or considerably less. You can see that the two high salaries in the distribution distort the mean, causing it to be much higher than the true average.

If you have reason to believe that the mean would not fairly represent the true average of the distribution you are discussing, it would be better for you to use the mode or the median. (In the example above, the median, $60,000, would be a much more accurate indication of the "average" salary.) Both the mode and the median are unaffected by extreme scores. When large numbers of scores are involved, the mode and the median are often quite similar.

Descriptive versus Inferential Statistics

Still other issues should be considered when using statistics or listening to speakers using statistics. First, most statistics quoted in speeches are inferential rather than descriptive; that is, they deal with probabilities rather than with observable facts. In inferential statistics, one generalizes from the small group to the larger population. For example, political polls taken during a campaign are inferential—they make inferences about what voters will do based on what the pollster hopes is a representative sample. When the votes actually come in and are counted on Election Day, the fact that one candidate got 51 percent of the vote and the other got 49 percent is a descriptive statistic—it describes how the entire population actually voted.

Many times, speakers will turn to inferential statistics because it is inconvenient or impossible to obtain descriptive data. Using inferential statistics is quite acceptable, so long as you recognize that whenever you generalize from a sample to a larger population, there is always some margin of error. That margin may be quite small, perhaps 1 in 1,000, but it does exist. Whether or not an inferential statistic is sound depends on the size and representativeness of the sample on which the statistic is based.

If you want to know how students at your college feel about a particular issue, you need to gather the opinions of a cross section of the entire college, including first-year students through seniors, women and men, different ethnic and racial groups, and students proportionately representing different majors in the arts, business, the sciences, and other fields. In addition, if there are 10,000 students in your school, your sample size ought to number in the 100s, not 25 or 30. Inferential statistics *can* function as excellent pieces of evidence. Since, however, they are based on large and representative samples, it is almost impossible for you to gather such information yourself. Rather, you must rely on reputable sources.

If you wanted to generalize about your own class, of course, you could more easily get a representative sample from which you can draw a confident inference. In Chapter 5, we explained how you can survey your audience to adapt your message to them. If *everyone* in your class responded to your audience survey, you would obtain a descriptive statistic.

Thinking Critically about Statistics

Sometimes speakers use statistics in ways that are confusing to listeners. The figures used may be accurate, but the interpretations can differ radically.

Statistics by themselves don't necessarily "prove" anything. Take, for example, tax legislation passed in May 2006. The Democratic National Committee called the $70 billion in cuts a "tax break for the wealthy and Wall Street," and used this statistic to support its claim that benefits to middle-class families would be meager: "Middle-income households would receive an average tax cut of $20 from the agreement."[14] While this may be a valid statistic, it is not at all clear what "average" means in this case. And the label, "tax break for the wealthy" is not "proven" by the statistic. For their part, The Republican National Committee announced that "House and Senate Republican negotiators reached a final agreement yesterday on a five-year, nearly $70 billion tax package that would extend President Bush's deep cuts to tax rates on dividends and capital gains, while sparing about 15 million middle-income Americans from the alternative minimum tax [AMT]."[15] The GOP statistic emphasizes the number of citizens who would be "spared" the minimum tax without mentioning what the "minimum" is. Issues, such as who benefits from the tax cuts or their long-range implications, are not addressed by a simple statistic. Even if the statistic is accurate, what that statistic *means* is not always as evident as the source would have you believe. That is why we all should learn how to evaluate statistics.

Like other forms of evidence, statistics should be used only when they provide needed support. No speech should be "padded" with statistics simply because they seem impressive. Moreover, too many statistics can overwhelm listeners. When you need to use many statistics, you might want to present some visual representation or summary of the statistics to help the audience follow you.

Also, every attempt should be made to present the statistics clearly and meaningfully. One student speaker, for example, dramatized the need for improved sanitation at a global level when he said, "In human costs internationally, one child dies every 8 seconds from waterborne disease! . . . [T]he human and economic costs are staggering."[16]

It is often helpful to translate a statistic into audience-specific terms. Instead of saying that a new school will cost $7 million, you might point out that each tax-payer should expect a property tax increase of about $100 per year over a 10-year period. In this way, the audience can understand what the proposal would mean to them personally.

Finally, statistics change rapidly. Although all evidence should be as recent as possible, nothing is more useless than outdated statistics. Always gather statistical information from current sources and cite those sources in your speech.

In short, statistics must be approached cautiously. Both the speaker and the listener should carefully evaluate the place of statistics in the total pattern of evidence.

Testimony

Another way to support your ideas is to offer supporting evidence based on opinions or testimony. Whereas statistical evidence seems more "factual" or "objective," testimonial evidence tries to illuminate information by offering interpretation and judgment. There are three kinds of testimonial evidence: personal testimony, lay testimony, and expert testimony.

Personal Testimony

Regardless of the kind of speech you are making, you are likely to offer your own personal testimony from time to time. For many topics and in many speaking situations, this is entirely appropriate. We have pointed out in previous chapters that a speaker's ethos or personal appeal can have a significant impact on listeners. However, you should avoid overreliance on your own testimony to the exclusion of other kinds of support. Equally important, you need to ask yourself a fundamental question: To what extent am I perceived by my audience as being a credible source of information on this subject?

If you have high credibility with your listeners, then your personal views may be an extremely convincing source of support. If, for example, you are a campus police officer addressing campus safety, a nonprofit leader speaking about funding sources for new programs, or a college student discussing how students benefit from participating in student organizations, your personal experiences and views will likely be considered quite credible. In the *Focus on Civic Engagement* that follows, a student uses her personal experiences to emphasize the need for a renewal of citizens' commitment to rebuild the ravaged Gulf Coast.

In other speaking contexts, using personal testimony to support ideas may be less effective. This can be a particular challenge for you as a college student. You may choose to speak about something of great interest to you, but you may have no direct experience or expertise with the topic. For instance, you may be very concerned about the problem of identifying alternative energy sources, how to formulate and administer a fair and manageable immigration policy, or how the United States can play a constructive role in bringing about peace in the Middle

Focus on Civic Engagement

A Student Speaks from Personal Experience

This past January, I had the opportunity to travel to New Orleans, along with a group of other students from around the Midwest, to help rebuild homes and buildings that were destroyed or badly damaged by Hurricane Katrina. I'm sure you're familiar with our school's "Learning through Service" program, which takes place at the end of the holiday break. For two weeks, I worked together with about two dozen students to help rebuild homes, schools, and hospitals. We lived in those famous FEMA trailers and spent a lot of time getting to know the New Orleans residents who had been displaced by the hurricane. Many worked side by side with us—whether on their own homes, the homes of strangers or neighbors, or on public buildings that would benefit the common good.

Although I've taken a lot of great courses during my three years of college, this was, by far, my most meaningful learning experience. I learned some basic skills—how to rebuild foundations, how to install siding, and even how to put on a roof that is unlikely to easily blow away. But far beyond that, I learned about community and caring and the wonderful resilience of the human spirit.

Source: Anonymous student speaker, delivered to a public speaking class in 2006.

East. However interesting these subjects might be to you and your audience, neither of you would assume that you are an expert in these matters. In this case, you need to go beyond your personal views and gather other kinds of supporting evidence.

Lay Testimony

Another kind of opinion evidence is lay testimony. Like personal testimony, lay testimony is based on firsthand experience—except in this instance, the experience is not your own. Nor is it the experience of an expert. Rather, lay testimony comes from ordinary women and men whose direct experiences make their testimony compelling.

Let us say, for example, that you wanted to encourage your classmates to become involved in the kind of "Learning through Service" program described in the last *Focus on Civic Engagement*. But suppose you have not actually participated in the program yourself. While conducting your research, you may have discovered excellent statistics on the popularity of these kinds of programs. You may have learned that students who participate in these programs tend to be better students and, upon graduation, more likely to function as engaged citizens in their communities. But, beyond sharing statistics and factual outcomes, you want also to *humanize* the program. You want to convey to your listeners the sorts of concrete experiences they might expect to have and how those experiences might impact their thoughts and feelings, and perhaps even influence their future behavior. Because you cannot testify from your own personal experience with the topic, you may choose to quote a credible lay person who *has* had such direct experience.

How effective is lay testimony? Like other forms of evidence, it depends on how carefully and judiciously you choose the testimony. Standing alone, lay testimony is probably insufficient as evidence. But, when used in tandem with other strong supporting material, it can be quite effective. For instance, in addressing the economy, you might quote the chairman of the Federal Reserve, as well as a family struggling to pay their bills. In quoting lay testimony, you will still want to look for the qualifications of those you are quoting, but qualifications rooted in the nature and extent of their firsthand experience rather than in their training, education, or expertise.

Expert Testimony

Perhaps one of the most effective ways of being persuasive is, in a sense, to borrow the ethos of someone to whom the audience will respond positively. In public speaking, expert testimony is one of the most frequently used forms of support when one is addressing important and complicated issues. In such cases, we rely on those whom we regard as experts or on those whom we have some particular reason to trust. For example, after three years of fighting and with U.S. casualties mounting, controversy over the war in Iraq accelerated. Advocates argued that the United States should "stay the course," while critics demanded a specific timetable for U.S. troops withdrawal. In the spring of 2006, a number of recently retired generals with direct knowledge of war preparation supported the critics and called for the resignation of Secretary of Defense Donald Rumsfeld.[17] This expert testimony—coming from those who had played key leadership roles in planning and executing the war—was designed to influence public opposition to the war.

In using expert testimony, you will need to decide whether you want to quote the exact words the expert used, or whether you want simply to paraphrase his or her ideas. If you plan to use the expert's *exact* words, you may want to insure accuracy by writing them out on a note card that you will refer to while delivering your speech. You will also want to quote precise words when those words are especially compelling, eloquent, or memorable. If you are encouraging listeners to go out and make a difference in their community, you might quote Margaret Mead, who said, "Never doubt that a small group of thoughtful, committed people can change the world. Indeed, it is the only thing that ever has."

On other occasions, you may prefer to quote the basic sense of an expert's argument or capture his or her idea in your own words. In this case, you will name the expert, and perhaps the title of his or her work, before *paraphrasing* the main idea conveyed. If you were addressing the issue of generational poverty, for example, you might paraphrase the words of an education expert by saying, "Long-time educator Ruby Payne has written two books that address the issue of generational poverty. In *Bridges Out of Poverty*, she argues that the poor lack access to basic resources that range from financial resources to emotional and spiritual resources to basic support systems. She points out that most of us focus only on the financial aspect, but it is much more complicated than that." You would then go on to offer concrete examples of these resources and how, when missing, they function to keep individuals entangled in poverty. In paraphrasing, it is important to fairly and accurately represent the expert's views—never exaggerating or distorting.

As a student, using excellent expert testimony is often one of the best ways to demonstrate that you are well read while at the same time advancing your arguments. However, like other forms of evidence, not all expert testimony is of equal value, so critically examining it is essential.

Testimony by those whose experience and credentials qualify them as experts can be especially effective in addressing important and complicated issues.

Thinking Critically about Expert Testimony

Both the ethical speaker who wants to present accurate and relevant information and the critical and discerning listener need to evaluate expert testimony carefully. By raising questions about the nature of the testimony, we seek to determine whether it is or is not enlightening or persuasive.

It is, of course, essential that any authority we quote be considered an authority by the audience. So we need to begin by asking, Is the authority I am quoting known to my listeners? If there is any doubt in your mind, identify the authority during your speech. You might say, for instance, "Professor Martin Wilson, distinguished Harvard economist, has argued that Social Security is one generation away from complete failure." Specifying the authority's position clarifies his expertise and enhances the credibility of your argument.

Sometimes speakers provide only vague references to their sources, perhaps by saying, "Political analysts have noted that . . ." or "One member of the New York City police department said that . . ." In such cases, listeners are uncertain about whom you are quoting. "Political analysts" could mean political science professors, media consultants, or political spin doctors. The police officer could be a rookie cop or the chief of police. Audience members who are also good critical listeners are unlikely to be impressed or persuaded by such ambiguous references to authorities.

Another important question that might be asked of testimony is, How timely is it? Experts' views may change as a situation changes. At one time, for example, the generals mentioned above may have supported the Iraq war. Over time, however, with elections held, Iraqi soldiers trained, war-related costs skyrocketing, international support waning, and U.S. soldiers continuing to die, the generals' opposition to the war solidified. It is important, therefore, to understand the timing and circumstances in which testimony is given. When using testimony, one must also be sure to use it in context. In an OP-ED piece in *The New York Times*, Jerry Falwell, explaining his invitation to Senator John McCain to give a commencement speech at Liberty University, wrote, "The next election for president is two years away. Mr. McCain is the front-runner for the nomination and is the kind of conservative candidate whom I would have little trouble supporting." This statement might be used to support the contention that Senator McCain was Jerry Falwell's candidate for the presidency. But this comment is taken out of a context in which Falwell explicitly denies such an implication. "The senator's speech," Falwell wrote, "does not symbolize an endorsement of an unannounced candidacy on my part, and it does not mark the quest for such an endorsement on his part. Mr. McCain had never sought such an endorsement, and I have not offered one."[18] The quotation, taken out of context, clearly misrepresents Falwell's views.

Whenever possible, quote those individuals who have nothing to gain from the position they are taking. One would expect the president of General Motors to oppose policies that would hurt the auto industry's profits. Similarly, NASA officials could be expected to support added government expenditures for space exploration. Although these people may be authorities in their fields, quoting them may not further your cause, because they may be seen as biased.

Perhaps the *most critical factor* in evaluating testimony is the nature of the authority. Ask yourself if the person being quoted is a *relevant* authority. One of the most common misuses of expert testimony in public communication occurs in advertising. Often someone who is an authority in one field is used to give testimony in a field in which he or she has no particular expertise or experience. A famous tennis player may know a great deal about the best kind of equipment to use for tennis, but he or she does not necessarily know more about politics or social welfare policies. This sort of shift of authority occurs frequently in the political arena when celebrities speak out on issues and candidates. While entertainers or sports figures have every right to express their opinions, we would do well not to base our own behavior and actions on their urging alone. Because someone is a good musician, a fine actor, or a star quarterback does not mean that he or she qualifies as an expert on social, political, or economic issues.

Should Prestige Testimony Be Used as Evidence?

There may be speaking situations where it is acceptable, and even desirable, for a person with high credibility and/or visibility to speak on behalf of an important cause. This kind of prestige testimony would be appropriate when the speaker is lending his or her good will, fame, popularity, or high regard to a worthy cause but is making no claim to expertise. Angelina Jolie, for example, serves as Goodwill Ambassador to the United Nations Commissioner for Refugees. With her high public profile, Jolie has focused attention, through her extensive travels and financial contributions, on the plight of refugees throughout the world. The Church World Service, in presenting her with a humanitarian award, cited her as one whose "work on behalf of refugees has made her a role model of individual humanitarian action, an inspiration to people around the world, especially the young. She gives a voice to the often forgotten refugees and displaced persons whose lives have been torn by persecution and war. Her active concern brings the promise of hope."[19]

In all these areas of concern, it might not always be possible for the listener to make an informed judgment about testimony. The listener might not always be able to tell when the testimony was given, what the total context was, or even how expert or objective the authority might be. However, the listener should maintain a critical mindset and be prepared to raise any concerns during the question-and-answer period. As for the ethical speaker, he or she will make every effort to be sure that the testimony used is recent, consistent with its meaning in context, and relevant.

Comparison and Contrast

One of the principal ways we learn is by comparison and contrast. We compare the unknown to the known. We look for similarities and differences between a new experience and an old one. We try to see ways in which new problems that need to be solved are similar to or different from old ones that have been solved. Comparison and contrast are not evidence in the strict sense of the word, but they are a form of support for ideas, and they often work in combination with the kinds of evidence we have been discussing to enhance clarity or persuasiveness.

Techniques of Comparison and Contrast

One of the most frequently used ways to make ideas more understandable or believable is by comparing the known with the unknown, the more familiar with the less familiar. New legislation, programs, and ideas are compared with old ones. Thus, a good way to help an audience understand what you are talking about is to compare your idea with something the audience is familiar with or has experienced. You might compare the challenge of entering politics with the challenge of working with groups in one's community. You might discuss the architectural design you had in mind for a new municipal complex by comparing it to one in a neighboring town with which the audience is familiar. By using these comparisons, you hope to enlighten, to make the unknown more familiar, perhaps to make your audience less afraid, more comfortable, or more at ease with something you are advocating.

Comparisons are often used by speakers who want to make a difficult or abstract concept more concrete and understandable to listeners. Speaking to an assembled group of lawyers in New York, the president of Columbia University, Lee Bollinger, quoted Judge Learned Hand's explanation of how democracy works:

> Learned Hand offered a simple parable about the kind of intellectual capacities required in a democracy, and why democracies fail when these capacities are absent. He compared a democracy to a group of children at play, confused about how to organize their games and deferring to an older, more experienced peer for direction. But that solution satisfies no one, as each child is unhappy to be bossed about by another, and eventually, confusion reigns again—until, Hand wrote, "in the end, slowly and with infinite disappointment, they do learn a little; they learn to forbear, to reckon with one another, [to] accept a little where they wanted much, to live and let live, to yield when they must yield; perhaps,

we may hope, not to take all they can. But the condition is that they shall be willing at least to listen to one another, to get the habit of pooling their wishes. Somehow or other, they must do this, if the play is to go on."[20]

By using this comparison, the speaker hoped to translate the task of making democracy work into common and understandable terms. At the same time, by quoting Judge Hand, he also incorporated impressive expert testimony.

On occasion, you may want to inform an audience about a concept or principle by showing them its opposite. By using contrast rather than comparison, you are highlighting differences. This can be a compelling form of support when your goal is to stress the value of some approach or plan that you advocate by contrasting it to the proposals of others. Such efforts to stress differences are common in political speeches. When George H. W. Bush accepted the Republican nomination for the presidency in 1988, he contrasted his own and his party's positions with those of his Democratic rival.

The stakes are high this year and the choice is crucial, for the differences between the two candidates are as deep and wide as they have ever been in our long history. Not only two very different men, but two very different ideas of the future will be voted on this Election Day.

What it all comes down to is this:

My opponent's view of the world sees a long slow decline for our country, an inevitable fall mandated by impersonal historical forces. But America is not in decline. America is a rising nation.

He sees America as another pleasant country on the UN roll call, somewhere between Albania and Zimbabwe. I see America as the leader—a unique nation with a special role in the world. . . . There are those who say there isn't much of a difference this year. But America, don't let 'em fool ya. Two parties this year ask for your support. Both will speak of growth and peace. But only one has proved it can deliver. Two parties this year ask for your trust, but only one has earned it.[21]

Democrats would certainly take issue with these contrasts, but Mr. Bush sought to use them to distinguish himself from his opponent and establish himself as the stronger, more visionary leader that the United States needed.

Thinking Critically about Comparison and Contrast

Although listeners may find comparison and contrast helpful and persuasive, the basis of comparison should be carefully considered.

Speakers and listeners should ask the same question: Are the persons, events, places, or objects being compared really comparable in essential ways? Some may be similar in obvious or superficial ways, but comparison on such bases could be misleading. Those who urge an American-style democracy for Iraq are accused of setting up a false comparison, since the histories, cultures, and values of the two countries are so different. On the other hand, proponents of the war in Iraq reject comparisons to the "quagmire" of the Vietnam war because the geopolitical contexts of the two wars are not at all comparable. So care must be exercised in using comparisons. Speakers and listeners should try to satisfy themselves that the things being compared are really similar in ways that are essential to the argument.

Sometimes speakers will use a colorful analogy as a way of dramatizing a comparison or contrast they hope to emphasize. In addressing health-care reform, the CEO of AARP, William Novelli, advanced the following bold comparison:

> We might compare fixing our health-care system to wrestling an octopus: Two arms are hugging you, two arms are trying to strangle you, and God knows what the other four arms are doing. Every time you think you're making headway, another arm reaches out and grabs you and pulls you back.
>
> This octopus that is the American health-care system seems at times to have us by the arms, legs, and throat . . . and the pocketbook. One reason that it seems to be an octopus rather than a Clydesdale, steadily pulling the wagon along, is that the system is not really a system at all, as many of you know so well.
>
> As we try to grapple with one part of the octopus—say the affordability of prescription drugs—we find another tentacle threatening us, then another and another. . . . The lack of health insurance, the need for more geriatric training in medical schools, the problems with long-term care. This octopus has more than eight arms."[22]

The critical listener would likely conclude that this comparison works well, so long as the octopus analogy does not unfairly exaggerate the seriousness of the challenge. If judged as fair and reasonable, the listener would also probably see Novelli's comparison as reinforcing the complexity of the challenge Americans face—making it memorable and compelling.

Testing Evidence

Preview. *Now that we have examined several different kinds of evidence, let us look carefully at how to determine its quality. There are several criteria to use when testing evidence: accuracy, recency, completeness, source reliability, audience appropriateness, and ethical considerations. All evidence, regardless of type, should be carefully scrutinized.*

Not all evidence is of equal quality. Simply collecting a great deal of information on a subject is not enough. As you read, talk with individuals, and ponder the information you have unearthed, you have the intellectual and ethical responsibility to make judicious decisions about what should be included in your speech and what should be omitted.

Accuracy

Naturally, you want to determine the accuracy of your evidence. Accurate information is redundant and verifiable. You should, for example, be able to examine several independent sources and discover essentially the same factual or statistical information. For instance, experts are likely to agree on the facts underlying the cause of rising oil prices (even if they dispute the best ways to solve the problem).

Statistics describing the number of teenage pregnancies, the cost of constructing a new highway, or the number of crimes committed in major U.S. cities should be relatively consistent in different sources. When serious inconsistencies occur, you should question the accuracy of your sources, as illustrated by the *Highlighting Source Accuracy* that follows.

Recency

You should also strive to obtain the most recent information possible. Of course, the significance of recency as a criterion for evaluating information depends on the subject being discussed. If, for example, you are addressing economic trends, consumer demands, the unemployment rate, or the financial stability of a particular nonprofit organization, you need to be armed with the most recent information you can obtain. Advances in technology have made recent information far more accessible. Because so many audience members are computer literate and have access to 24-hour news on the Internet and on television, the burden on the speaker to be up-to-date is even more pressing.

Completeness

You should also test information for completeness. Although you cannot know all there is to know on a subject, the more thorough, complete, and well rounded your knowledge is on a topic, the better your speech will be.

Completeness and accuracy are clearly related. As you check for accuracy, you will consult numerous sources, making your evidence more and more complete. Having complete information will also help you during the question-and-answer period.

Highlighting Source Accuracy

Beware of Wikipedia

Wikipedia is a free online encyclopedia that started in 2001. Its content is written collaboratively by users around the globe.

- The site is called "wiki," meaning that anyone with Web access can add to, correct, or amend it by clicking on an edit function.
- The site had 25.6 million visitors in a single month in 2006, making it the 18th most popular site on the Internet.
- Due to the nature of the site, a sobering possibility for misinformation and vandalism exists.
- Already, political operatives have covertly rewritten— or defaced—candidates' biographical entries to make

their boss look good, or to make the opponent look ridiculous. Altering senators' ages, entering highly personal information, and posting damaging "jokes" are just a few of the problematic practices that have surfaced.

- Experts in communication technology believe that the sheer size of Wikipedia and the huge number of entries make it impossible to monitor or police it in any effective way.

Source: "Wikipedia: An Online Encyclopedia Being Used for Political Tricks," *Bloomington Herald-Times* (April 30, 2006), D3.

Source Reliability

It is also important to assess the reliability of your sources of information. We have already addressed this concern, but we want to stress here that if you find an impressive piece of testimony or a compelling statistic, you must ask yourself about the credibility of the magazine, newspaper, website, or other source in which the information appears.

The same considerations apply to the people you interview. Ask yourself, Are they promoting a position out of self-interest? Are they known to possess some bias on the subject I'm discussing? In general, whenever you doubt a source's objectivity, trustworthiness, or competence, it is best to disregard the information and look elsewhere.

Audience Appropriateness

Regardless of the quality of the evidence you find, it should not be used if its appropriateness to the audience and the situation is in question. Rarely should a human interest story or personal narrative find its way into a technical report. Yet the same kind of evidence is almost a necessity in sermons, political speeches, and after-dinner speeches. Humorous anecdotes can provide excellent support for many topics, but with really serious subjects, such as addressing the problem of poverty, AIDS, or child abuse, humor would be considered tasteless. The kind of speech you are giving, the topic you have selected, and your perceptions of the audience's needs and values should guide you in your selection of appropriate evidence.

Ethical Considerations

In a sense, ethical considerations in using evidence are related to all the other tests of evidence we have discussed. If a speaker uses evidence that he or she knows to be inaccurate, incomplete, biased, or tasteless, that speaker does not have the audience's best interests at heart. Sometimes speakers lose track of their responsibility to the audience. They want, more than anything, to get the audience to respond, vote, contribute, or commit. They want these things so badly that they use evidence in ways that they know to be unethical—perhaps by quoting expert testimony out of context, visually distorting statistics, or portraying unusual examples as typical.

Although anyone can unwittingly make mistakes in using evidence, a speaker's ethical obligation is to scrutinize his or her own intentions carefully, guarding against the temptation to "get the job done" even if the audience is somehow misled in the process. Civic responsibility demands a commitment to ethical public speaking.

Summary

- Even if your ideas have merit, they need to be developed and supported if they are to be understandable and believable to your listeners. Using good evidence is critical.

- For most speech topics, several different kinds of communicative evidence might be used effectively:
  - Facts that are accurate and verifiable
  - Definitions that are either informative (straightforward) or persuasive (interpretative)
  - Actual or hypothetical examples that are typical and important
  - Statistics that accurately show how things are related and what trends have occurred over time
  - Testimony that is authoritative, timely, and in context
  - Comparisons that simplify difficult concepts and compare things that are essentially similar, and contrasts that focus on essential differences
- Regardless of the specific kind of supporting material used, you will want to carefully examine its
  - accuracy and completeness
  - recency
  - source reliability
  - appropriateness to the audience and the situation
  - ethics

QUESTIONS FOR REVIEW AND REFLECTION

1. Why should public speakers use supporting material?
2. What are the major kinds of evidence that speakers might use? Briefly define each.
3. How will you determine whether factual information is of high quality?
4. Explain the difference between offering an informative definition and a persuasive one. Offer an example of each.
5. Compare and contrast the actual example with the hypothetical example. Which do you think is generally better to use in speechmaking? Why?
6. Describe how narratives can be especially effective as examples. Think of one narrative you might use with a speech topic of interest to you.
7. Contrast the three different kinds of averages—mean, median, and mode. Under what circumstances might the mode or median be preferable to the mean as a measure of the true average?
8. Whenever you use statistical support in a speech, what criteria will you use to assess its effectiveness?
9. Under what circumstances might you choose to use personal testimony or lay testimony? How will you make sure you do so effectively?
10. If you were going to use expert testimony in a speech, what criteria would you use in choosing this kind of evidence?
11. How might comparisons or contrasts be compelling as supporting material?
12. What are some basic tests for evidence? Why are they important?

ENDNOTES

1. "General Information on Domestic Violence and Sexual Assault," www.midlewayhouse .org (accessed May 1, 2006).

2. Taken from *Healthwise*, Richard A. DeVaul's weekly radio program, broadcast on Texas A&M's National Public Radio affiliate, KAMU, 90.9 FM, September 12, 1996.

3. A. Thomas Young, "Ethics in Business," *Vital Speeches of the Day 58* (1992): 726–27.

4. For more information about the CBDG program, visit www.hud.gov. The CBDGs are de- scribed under "Community Development Programs" (accessed September 11, 2006).

5. David K. Shipler, *The Working Poor: Invisible in America"* (New York: Alfred A. Knopf, 2004), x–xi.

6. J. Edward Hill, "Priorities in Prevention," *Vital Speeches of the Day 72* (1995): 88.

7. Bill Gates, "Teaching Kids What They Need to Know," *Vital Speeches of the Day 71* (2005): 397.

8. Elizabeth Glaser, "AIDS: A Personal Story," in *Public Speaking*, 3rd ed., ed. Michael Osborn and Susan Osborn, B17 (Boston: Houghton Mifflin, 1994).

9. Angelina Grimké, "Address at Pennsylvania Hall," in *Man Cannot Speak for Her: A Critical Study of Early Feminist Rhetoric*, vol. 2: *Key Texts of the Early Feminists*, ed. Karyl Kohrs Campbell, 27–28 (New York: Praeger, 1989).

10. Roslyn Brock, "A Refueling Stop on the Road to Freedom," *Vital Speeches of the Day 71* (2005): 654.

11. See, for example, "The Source of Sickness Proves Elusive," *The New York Times*, September 17, 2006, sec. 4, 2.

12. For a detailed description of this and related problems, visit www.therapeuticjustice.com, where you will find a description of the "Community Model," based on the writings of Morgan Moss.

13. Laura Bush, "Making Education a Reality for All the World's People," *Vital Speeches of the Day 71* (2005): 322.

14. "GOP Plan Leaves Middle Class behind," May 10, 2006, http://dnc.org/a/p/ gop_tax_plan_leaves_the_middle_class_behind.html (accessed May 15, 2006).

15. "Republicans Put Forth $70 Billion Tax Relief Measure," May 10, 2006, www.gop.com/News/Read.aspx?ID=6308 (accessed May 15, 2006).

16. Steve Loranger, "How Do We Begin to Solve the Problems?" *Vital Speeches of the Day 71* (2005): 364.

17. For example, Paul D. Eaton, a retired U.S. Army major general, was in charge of training the Iraqi military from 2003–2004; retired major general John Batiste led the First Infantry Division in Iraq.

18. Jerry Falwell, "An Invitation, Not an Endorsement," *The New York Times* (Sunday, May 7, 2006): Section 4, p. 13.

19. "UNHCR Goodwill Ambassador Angelina Jolie Receives CWS Humanitarian Award," August 23, 2002, www.churchworldservice.org/Immigration/archives/2002/08/11.html (accessed May 9, 2006).

20. Lee C. Bollinger, "Reaffirming Our Principles That Have Guided Us for the Past Hundred Years," *Vital Speeches of the Day 71* (2005): 465.

21. George H. W. Bush, "Nomination Acceptance Address," www.presidentialrhetoric.com/ historicspeeches/bush/nominationacceptance.html (accessed April 20, 2006).

22. William D. Norvelli, "Transforming the Healthcare System," *Vital Speeches of the Day 71* (2005): 745.

Barbara Boxer, Democratic Senator from California, served for ten years in the House of Representatives before being elected to the Senate in 1993. She was elected for a third term in 2004. A member of the Foreign Relations Committee, Senator Boxer is a long-time critic of President Bush's policy in Iraq. She called for the resignation of the Secretary of Defense, Donald Rumsfeld, and urged the White House to implement the recommendations of the Iraq study group. In this speech, given on December 20, 2005, Senator Boxer begins with an allusion to the disastrous Vietnam War in her attack on Administration policy.

In 1968, Martin Luther King told us: "If we do not act, we shall surely be dragged down the long, dark, and shameful corridors of time reserved for those who possess ... strength without sight."

Dr. King was talking about ending the Vietnam War. But 40 years later, his warning is increasingly relevant to the Iraq war.

Strength without sight has now led us into a war based on mistaken intelligence, and down a thorny path of pain for too long.

And none of us can afford to be silent, because as Martin Luther King also said: "Our lives begin to end the day we become silent about things that matter."

So we must have the courage to speak out about things that matter.

It matters that 2,158 servicemen and women have given their lives in Iraq, leaving their families grieving.

It matters that 16,155 have been wounded, many with scars that will last a lifetime.

It matters that the majority of the American people are demanding a new strategy so that we don't have a war without end.

We saw seventy-nine Senators recently back an amendment saying that the Iraqis should take the lead in providing their own security next year. That matters too.

We heard Congressman Jack Murtha's brave statement against the war, calling it a "flawed policy wrapped in illusion." He is a decorated Marine, a war hero who bled on the battlefield, the military's best friend.

And he now advocates redeploying U.S. forces at the earliest possible date, while maintaining a quick-reaction U.S. force in the region to be called upon if necessary.

So how did the Administration and its supporters respond to his thoughtful proposal? Congressman Murtha, with his two Purple Hearts and Bronze Star, was insulted by the White House Press Secretary and branded a coward by the newest Republican in the House. People who never bled on the battlefield tried to demean a war hero.

And that is what we see again and again. Instead of thoughtful dialogue about the life and death issues in Iraq, the Administration lashes out at those who dare to disagree with them.

Recently, the Republican National Committee issued a video news release attacking Democrats, including me. I'm used to being attacked, and I normally just ignore them. But this one was so incendiary that I have to respond.

The ad said Democrats were waving a white flag of surrender. And their evidence? My statement that we should start reducing our troop strength in Iraq after the Iraqi election.

Well, guess who else said that last weekend? The U.S. Ambassador to Iraq, Zalmay Khalizad, appointed by President Bush. His words were, "we can begin to draw down our forces in the aftermath of the elections." Are they going to run an ad against him now?

SENATOR BOXER BEGINS HER SPEECH BY QUOTING DR. MARTIN LUTHER KING, JR., WHO WARNS OF THE DANGERS OF REMAINING SILENT "ABOUT THINGS THAT MATTER."

BOXER CITES STATISTICS ON SOLDIERS KILLED OR WOUNDED IN IRAQ—DEMONSTRATING THE SERIOUSNESS OF THE SITUATION.

BOXER QUOTES CONGRESSMAN JACK MURTHA AND ESTABLISHES HIS CREDIBILITY BY IDENTIFYING HIM AS A WAR HERO, WHO "BLED ON THE BATTLEFIELD." SHE FOLLOWS THIS WITH THE TESTIMONY OF THE U.S. AMBASSADOR TO IRAQ, ZALMAY KHALIZAD (A BUSH APPOINTEE) WHO AGREES WITH HER.

Democrats aren't waving any white flags. We are doing the jobs we were elected to do. We have a right—and a responsibility—to tell the truth, whether the topic is Iraq or any other policy. We have a right—and a responsibility—to wave a warning flag about a war that is making our nation less secure.

And so, regardless of how many times they attack me, I will continue to speak out, just as I am doing today. I have four points.

First: We must restore our credibility.

If we want the American people to be optimistic and if we want the nations of the world to consider us a leader to be trusted, our motives must be clear, our justifications must be sound, and our policies must reflect our ideals.

During the Cuban missile crisis, Secretary of State Dean Acheson offered to show Charles de Gaulle satellite images of Soviet missiles in Cuba as proof of their existence.

President de Gaulle responded by saying, "the word of the President of the United States is good enough for me."

Today, the word of this President and his administration has been called into question. Frankly, it is hard to believe those words any longer on Iraq.

Remember all of the false expectations that the Bush Administration peddled?

Remember when Secretary Rumsfeld said that the war "could last six days, six weeks. I doubt six months?"...Or that we knew exactly where to find the Weapons of Mass Destruction?

Remember when Vice President Cheney predicted, "...my belief is we will, in fact, be greeted as liberators?"

Remember when White House Budget Director, Mitch Daniels said that Iraq will be "an affordable endeavor" and reported that it "will not require sustained aid?"

Remember when the case for Weapons of Mass Destruction was called a slam dunk?

Remember Vice President Cheney's now-famous assessment that the insurgency was in its "last throes"?

Remember when the President told us about the yellow cake from Niger?

Remember when we were told "mission accomplished" and that Iraqi oil would pay for the war?

Remember when Secretary Rice said she didn't want the smoking gun to be a mushroom cloud?

Remember Secretary Colin Powell's forceful presentation before the United Nations Security Council...that he now calls a blot on his record?

That is 0 for 10.

Yet, even in light of all this history, the Bush Administration refuses to do more than a perfunctory mea culpa.

In his last speech, the President took responsibility for going to war on false intelligence. The President is only two years behind the American people, who figured this one out long ago, but I'll take it. But he keeps repeating the false statement that Congress saw the same intelligence that he did even though a congressional report recently found that the Administration had access to more than they shared with us.

And he still doesn't answer the central question: Was the intelligence cherry picked or manipulated to make the case for war?

Democrats are insisting that we complete the Senate investigation into this matter. And it's not about politics. It's because if the intelligence was cherry picked or manipulated, the American people deserve to know and the Congress will need to act.

TO SUPPORT HER BELIEF THAT OUR CREDIBILITY HAS BEEN ERODED, BOXER CONTRASTS THE CREDIBILITY OF PRESIDENT KENNEDY WITH PRESIDENT BUSH. SHE THEN OFFERS TEN SPECIFIC EXAMPLES OF MISLEADING INFORMATION, FALSE PROMISES, AND FAULTY VIEWS ADVANCED BY LEADING MEMBERS OF THE BUSH TEAM.

And it's because the next time we need to convince the world of an imminent threat, it will be far more difficult unless we clear the air and restore our credibility.

You know, America is more than an economic and military power. Our ideals have made us a shining light for those around the world seeking freedom, democracy and human rights.

Now that moral standing is at risk.

We all saw the horrific photos of Abu Ghraib, which were at odds with everything this country stands for. We all know that torture does not produce accurate intelligence or make us safer. Instead, as Senator McCain says, "It's killing us." But, amazingly, banning torture was extremely controversial for this Administration. Dick Cheney even worked non-stop to exempt the CIA from the torture ban passed by the Congress.

Fortunately we won this one, but we still don't know everything about the secret prisons or secret spying on Americans, all of which chips away at our reputation as a great beacon of freedom and gives an eerie sense of a secret government. And now we face the issue of our government spying on Americans without a warrant. This is serious and must be investigated to restore our credibility.

Second and third, we must reverse the strain on our military and get our budget priorities straight.

This Administration says dissent hurts our military. But what really hurts our military is sending men and women to war without a plan and without the necessary armor and equipment. What really hurts our military is stretching it to the breaking point and deploying our soldiers for third and fourth tours of duty. What really hurts our military is a lack of candor.

Our men and women in the military serve bravely and skillfully in Iraq. They have sacrificed so much since the war began. We need to honor their sacrifices not just with words, but also with actions. That means treating their caskets and families with the respect they deserve. And that means opening our eyes to their injuries, and getting them the help they need.

Medical studies reveal that 17 percent of soldiers returning from Iraq are suffering from mental health problems including depression, anxiety and PTSD.

The VA says that 17,000 Iraq and Afghanistan vets have been diagnosed with mental disorders through February.

Despite this huge problem, the American Legion says that mental health programs are being under funded by $500 million a year. I offered an amendment to provide these critical resources by canceling future tax cuts for millionaires. Sounds reasonable, right? Well, it failed. The President says he loves our military, but he loves tax cuts for millionaires as much or more.

Let's be clear: To finance a war that has already cost $251 billion, this Administration did not ask the wealthiest in our own country to sacrifice.

Under the Bush tax cuts, millionaires got $242 billion dollars back over the past five years. In the first two years of the Iraq war, the average millionaire received $112,000 in tax cuts.

And the President did not secure enough real financial commitments from other countries.

Instead, our needs are being sacrificed and our children and senior citizens are paying the price.

Talk about waving a white flag of surrender? The Republican Congress and this administration are waving a white flag over our children, cutting their after school programs by 1.3 billion from what this President and Congress authorized. No Child Left Behind was funded at 13.1 billion less than what their own legislation asked for.

They are waving a white flag of surrender over our seniors, causing them anxiety and threatening their Social Security and Medicare by using those trust funds to finance the war and the tax cuts.

They are waving a white flag over fiscal responsibility by creating a debt which is more than $8 trillion. Of the total debt held by the public, 45% is in foreign hands. That means that approximately $92 billion is leaving this country every year to pay off the interest to foreign entities.

And, they are waving a white flag over our homeland security, instead of making it a top priority. The Administration says all the right things in public, and then shortchanges homeland security at every turn

It's been four years since 9/11. Why are we still dangerously unprepared for another terrorist attack?

Why haven't we provided the additional $555 million needed this year to better secure our ports?

And, why in the world, haven't we provided the $14.3 billion still needed to make sure that our firefighters, police officers, and health care providers can communicate with each other in a time of crisis, whether it is a terrorist attack, a hurricane, or an earthquake?

On December 5, the 9/11 Commission released a report card on the status of the recommendations it made a year and a half ago. It was full of Ds and Fs, and showed us that we are falling short, far short. This is unacceptable.

So we must help our military and get our priorities right.

Fourth and finally, it is time to change course in Iraq.

The President continues to present a false choice between leaving immediately and staying indefinitely.

He continues to just say "stay the course," despite evidence that the war is making us less, not more, safe from terrorism.

And he continues to begin almost every speech about Iraq with a reference to 9/11 even though the 9/11 Commission and his own Administration's documents have been clear: There was no link between Iraq and 9/11 and no collaboration between Saddam Hussein and al Qaeda.

In fact, the war in Iraq was a diversion from the war against al Qaeda.

Like the Soviet invasion of Afghanistan in the 1980s, the war in Iraq is helping al Qaeda recruit, radicalize, and train a new generation of terrorists.

According to National Memorial Institute for the Prevention of Terrorism, worldwide terror attacks increased by more than 1,200 in the last year alone.

Even the President's own Director of Central Intelligence, Porter Goss, says: "Those jihadists who survive will leave Iraq experienced in and focused on acts of urban terrorism."

I agree with the President about the importance of spreading democracy across the globe. But as Robert Pape of the University of Chicago has written, "...spreading democracy at the barrel of a gun in the Persian Gulf is not likely to lead to a lasting solution against suicide terrorism."

Last week's election in Iraq was an important step forward. I view each election as a landmark and I hope and pray that this one will result in a government that is able to unite the Sunni, Shiite, and Kurdish people.

Early next year, Iraqis will have a choice to amend the Constitution to protect the interests of the Sunni minority and this will be another defining moment.

I also view each election in Iraq as a chance to turn Iraq over to its own people, who must ultimately chart their own destiny. Reducing our presence would be a sign of success, not failure.

The fact is, as long as our presence is perceived as open-ended, there is little incentive for the Iraqis to make the necessary political compromises.

Indeed, if we want the Iraqis to move toward a political solution we must lessen their dependence on a U.S. military solution which almost everyone agrees is not the answer.

Too many Iraqis believe that the United States has no intention of leaving Iraq. And with good reason. The Bush Administration continues to answer all reasonable requests for timeframes or benchmarks with the same "as long as it takes" mantra.

This, despite the fact that General Casey made it clear to me earlier this year that our long term presence would be counter-productive. And this despite the fact that two-thirds of Iraqis oppose the presence of U.S. troops in their country.

We must dispel the common and dangerous perception that we are occupiers and instead articulate a clear mission for this Iraq war, with an exit strategy based on real political, military, economic benchmarks.

How?

We need to accelerate efforts to train Iraqi troops and reduce our military footprint.

Second, the President must immediately declare that the United States has no desire to maintain permanent U.S. military bases in Iraq.

Third, the President must work more with Iraq's neighbors and reduce our visibility in rebuilding Iraq's institutions. In fact, we should have been doing this from the beginning.

Last week, the Egyptian Ambassador lamented the fact that so few troops had been trained in his country, saying: "We have the capacity to train about 3,000 Iraqi troops in Egypt each month." How in the world can we fail to take advantage of offers like this?

It doesn't matter if you were for the war, against the war, or undecided. None of us can remain silent or on the sidelines now.

As a Senator, I feel obligated to tell the people of my state how I feel. It's time for a new policy. It's time for a new strategy that makes us more safe and secure. It's time to put to rest the notion that to speak out for a new strategy in Iraq is unpatriotic.

It's time to realize that turning Iraq over to the Iraqis is what they expect and what we should do.

It's time for a real strategy to stop the spread of terrorism and prevent the proliferation of WMDs—not preemptive wars that isolate America from the rest of the world.

It's time to remember that a strong America begins at home, and that we cannot have real security if we abandon our children and families, our fiscal responsibility or if we cannot prepare for a terrorist strike or an emergency like Katrina.

It's time for America to once again be a shining example for the rest of the world.

We can do it.

Again, let's be honest about the past and restore our credibility. Let the Administration support Congressional inquiries and not fight them—on the past use of intelligence; on the secret prisons in Europe; on the secret surveillance of Americans.

Two, let's truly honor our military by articulating a real plan for success in Iraq and taking care of our soldiers.

Three, let's get our priorities straight and get back on a solid fiscal footing.

Fourth, let's get Iraq right by working in a bipartisan way—not running ugly 30-second commercials while our soldiers die and get wounded.

We can do it. We can do better and with the wisdom of the American people, we will.

HERE SHE ARGUES THAT THE IRAQIS ARE OVERLY DEPENDENT ON THE U.S. MILITARY AND QUOTES THE EXPERT TESTIMONY OF GENERAL CASEY.

BOXER CALLS ON THE PRESIDENT TO WORK MORE WITH IRAQ'S NEIGHBORS TO ASSIST WITH THE TROOP TRAINING AND REBUILDING. BOXER REITERATES HER CALL FOR IMMEDIATE ACTION, NOTING "IT IS TIME" TO FIND A NEW STRATEGY, TO TURN IRAQ OVER TO IRAQIS, TO DEVELOP A REAL STRATEGY TO STOP THE SPREAD OF TERRORISM, TO REORDER OUR DOMESTIC BUDGETARY PRIORITIES, AND TO ONCE AGAIN MAKE AMERICA "A SHINING EXAMPLE FOR THE REST OF THE WORLD." SHE CONCLUDES WITH AN EXPRESSION OF CONVICTION AND OPTIMISM.

Organizing Your Speech

CHAPTER OBJECTIVES

*After studying this chapter, you
should be able to*

1. Discern the importance of
   sound organization.

2. Evaluate the quality of ideas.

3. Select and apply appropriate
   organizational patterns and
   sequences.

4. Recognize basic principles of
   good organization.

5. Understand how to construct
   and use good transitions.

6. Construct effective introductions and conclusions.

Many speakers carefully select and focus their topics, judiciously choose a specific purpose and thesis, seek out good supporting materials, and still never experience success in their public speaking endeavors. Part of their failure may relate to how they have organized their materials. This chapter is devoted to helping you understand how good ideas for a speech are crafted and how they are organized in a structure that will help you achieve your purpose.

The Importance of Good Organization

Preview. *Nearly everyone recognizes that a speech must have strong content and be delivered effectively. Yet, some may wonder what impact, if any, the organization of those ideas and supporting material might have on the listeners' response. Research and experience have shown that sound organization influences practical outcomes, including the audience's willingness and ability to listen and their impressions of the speaker's credibility.*

Recently, two of the authors of this book attended a meeting during which the executive directors of fourteen local nonprofit agencies delivered brief persuasive presentations to the Community Advisory Council, a group empowered to award them up to $25,000 in grant money to fund local projects. Each of the speakers had submitted a written proposal before the presentations. During the meeting, each was allotted only four minutes to speak and a few more minutes to respond to questions. Although all of the speakers were competent advocates for their agencies, some were clearly more convincing than others. What made the difference? Far more than content (they were addressing real needs with sound proposals) or delivery (most appeared to have practiced), the most effective speakers were *clearly better organized* than were their less-effective competitors. They knew what to leave out and what to include. They did not introduce irrelevant or redundant information. The best speakers seemed to understand how much background to cover, which pressing concerns to address, and how to balance the limited time available between articulating the problem and advancing a compelling solution. Interestingly, the best, most organized speakers *were* awarded the largest grants.

Good organization is important for many reasons. Speakers who are well organized appear to be more competent, focused, and knowledgeable. They seem to better grasp the problem and are better able to explain it to listeners in a coherently organized manner. As a result, they appear more credible.[1] In addition, it is easier for listeners to attend to a clearly organized presentation, so they are more likely to learn, retain, and be influenced by the information and ideas presented.[2] Delivering a well-organized presentation is one of the *best* ways for speakers to show respect for their listeners. When speakers take the time and effort to organize their comments clearly and coherently, they show that they care about making themselves understood. Even though the engaged listener should be willing to work hard at listening, no audience member should have to struggle to listen to a presentation that is disorganized or incoherent.[3]

Of course, the quality of organization will also depend on the clarity and soundness of the ideas the speaker is advancing. The main ideas, then, are the building blocks that the speaker will use to develop an organizational strategy.

Determining When an Idea Is a Good One

Preview. *When deciding whether an idea is a good one, a speaker should consider how well it is designed to help the speaker get the desired audience response. A good idea is clear, simple without being oversimplified, appropriate to the demands of the situation, and sensible.*

All of us have probably been guilty at one time of saying something like, "Well, I know the answer to that, but I just cannot put it into words." This sort of comment is often a way of fooling ourselves. The reality is that if we cannot say it, we probably do not know it, and if we cannot explain it, we probably do not truly understand it. If we are to be confident that we *do* understand the ideas we are advancing, we will want to begin by expressing those ideas in language that is accurate, correct, and clear.

Clarity of Ideas

To be clear, an idea must first of all be complete. Consider, for example, Curtis, who wants to speak as an advocate for tax reform. His first outline draft read like this:

> **Specific purpose:** *I want my audience to endorse a national sales tax as a way of improving the present tax system.*
> **Thesis statement:** *Adopting a national sales tax would solve problems in the current system as well as produce a number of added benefits.*
> **Main Ideas**
> I. Present system—time and money
> II. Retail sales affected
> III. Complicated tax code
> IV. Individual benefits
> V. Creating more jobs

Although Curtis's thesis and specific purpose are clearly articulated, his main points are not. None is a complete sentence. As a result, each is underdeveloped and unclear. In addition, in the first three main points, he seems to be pointing to problems with the present system. In all likelihood, these could be more clearly and coherently presented as one main idea. To do this, the speaker's first main idea might read like this:

> I. Our current tax system is riddled with problems.

If this were main the idea, he might then go on to list and explore the problems, including the excessive time taken to complete one's own income tax forms, the expense involved in hiring a professional to complete them, the errors often made (even by experts), and the impact on retail prices.

Now that Curtis has clearly explored the problem, he is ready to move on to explain what he believes to be the solution. The solution phase of his speech might be logically divided into these two main ideas (based on points IV and V in the previous draft outline):

   II. A national sales tax would benefit individual citizens and families.
   III. A national sales tax would benefit our country as a whole.

As he developed his second main idea, Curtis would explain that the *only* tax individuals would pay would be the sales tax. All other taxes would be eliminated (including income, Social Security, and Medicare taxes). He might then further explain how this approach could benefit all citizens and argue that the poor and elderly would especially benefit from a national sales tax.

For his third and final main idea, Curtis might address benefits to society in general by arguing that, with more money in their pockets, individuals would pump more money back into the economy. In addition, businesses that have left the United States would return, and the economy in general would flourish, by 10 percent or more in the first year. He would likely use expert testimony and statistics to bolster his case.[4]

This speech plan is clear, with straightforward main ideas stated in complete sentences. Developing subordinate ideas and information to elaborate on each main point will create a coherent and understandable whole.

Simplicity of Ideas

Audiences must understand ideas if they are to respond to them. In addition to clarity, each idea must be directly and simply stated, without distortion. Your objective is to establish *balance*—to communicate ideas intelligently and accurately, yet simply.

With that specific purpose in mind, you should ask yourself whether the idea is as basic as it can be. If your idea cannot be simplified in order to be understood, then you may wish to reexamine the specific purpose to see if it is appropriate to the audience. You might be trying to do too much in the time allotted and need to focus more sharply.

Furthermore, speakers often try to include too much information or even a whole series of ideas within one idea. For example, Barbara had as her specific purpose, *I want my audience to become actively involved in politics.* Her thesis was, *Political involvement leads to positive results.* Her first main idea read like this:

   I. People who take an interest in politics can restore idealism to the process as well as learn valuable skills themselves and make a practical impact.

This idea tries to incorporate too much. It is not a single idea. Instead, it is really two interrelated ideas. Barbara needed to sort out the idea from the material necessary to develop the idea. A revised form of this might be the following:

   I. There are direct benefits to society when citizens participate in politics.
   II. There are direct benefits to individuals who participate in the political process.

If Barbara can induce her audience to agree that there are important benefits to be gained from participating in the political process, and if she can inspire them to become actively involved, she will have achieved her purpose. To accomplish this, of course, she will have to take the next step of developing the ideas. She will want to enumerate the benefits that come from participation, show that they are indeed beneficial, and make them real and motivating for an audience.

Simplicity, then, goes hand in hand with clarity as a basic characteristic of a well-stated idea. Of course, clarity and simplicity are relative concepts. Since ideas grow out of and are adapted to particular speaking situations, simplicity and clarity will be defined, in part, by the context.

Situational Considerations

We have already considered in Chapter 6 the notion that a speech is designed for a specific audience. A speech is also influenced by the occasion that prompts it and the setting in which it occurs. Thus, the ideas must be appropriate for the listener and the context.

The level of complexity of any idea will be significantly influenced by the audience's relationship to the topic. If, for example, you wanted to address the threat posed by the growing federal deficit, you might choose to introduce ideas that are highly technical, sophisticated, and complex if you were addressing a group of business majors at a university conference. If, however, you were speaking on the same topic to your classmates (likely a more mixed audience), you would probably want to offer more background and definitions and a more basic treatment of your topic. The degree to which you should offer a technical or complex treatment of any topic, then, will depend in part on what the audience brings to the speaking occasion by way of background, experience, and expectations.

Ideas That Make Sense

You also need to ask yourself whether your ideas are sensible, and then consider how an audience might view them. Speakers sometimes propose main ideas that are perceived by listeners as unreasonable or unrealistic. As a result, they tend to dismiss them.

A speaker's ideas will not seem sensible to listeners if they appear to be overly romantic, sentimental, or idealized. Suppose a speaker at a large university proposed that the university should require *and* fund a junior-year-abroad for every undergraduate. Listeners are likely to reject such a proposal. For one thing, they might view it as economically unfeasible for the university. They might also feel that such an opportunity should be an option, but not a requirement. In other words, the speaker is seen as being impractical and too idealistic.

At the other extreme, listeners may also reject ideas that seem too cynical or pessimistic. For many decades, for example, politicians have predicted the imminent demise of Social Security. Listeners who have heard this prediction many times may reject the speaker's arguments as overly pessimistic. Similarly, the religious speaker who argues that the end of the world is near may also face rejection. Of course, how listeners react will depend on their own values and beliefs related to these issues.

How Patterns of Organization Connect Ideas

Preview. *To make a set of ideas reasonable and coherent for your audience, you need to put the ideas together so that they accomplish the specific purpose of the speech. To do this, you will use such basic patterns of organization as chronological or sequential, spatial, categorical, climactic, cause-and-effect, problem-solution, and narrative.*

When you have developed a good idea or series of ideas, you then face the job of arranging them in some order. It is important to recognize that most topics can be approached from a variety of organizational perspectives. *Your* task is to make a judicious decision in choosing the most appropriate one for the particular topic and situation in which you are speaking.

There are many organizational patterns from which to choose, some of which we will develop more fully in later chapters. Here, however, we introduce several of the most commonly used organizational patterns.

Chronological or Sequential Order

One commonly used pattern of arrangement is chronological order. You begin with a specific point in time and then move forward or backward, depending on the nature of the subject. Chronological order may be useful with a variety of topics, most notably those that deal with a process or a historical event. Thus, the development of the labor movement in the United States, the events that led up to the dissolution of the Soviet Union, or the evolution of the Christian Coalition as a national political force might all be appropriate subjects for chronological arrangement.

Here is how one student, giving a speech that was basically a historical account, arranged his ideas in a chronological pattern:

> **Specific purpose:** *I want my audience to understand how the Nazis came to power in Germany.*
> **Thesis statement:** *Nazism grew because of social and political unrest.*
>   I. In 1919, the Treaty of Versailles created several serious problems for Germany.
> II. Financial crises encouraged the National Socialists to attempt an unsuccessful coup in Bavaria in 1923.
> III. By 1930, the National Socialist Party had emerged as a major political party.
> IV. The violent election campaign of 1933 brought the Nazi Party to power.

Similar to the chronological pattern is the *sequential pattern*, which you would use if you wanted your audience to understand some step-by-step procedure or process. For instance, if you wanted listeners to understand the process involved in applying for government-subsidized housing, you could begin with the first step that the applicant takes and follow the process in order, step by step. You could similarly use a sequential pattern to help listeners understand how they can file their tax returns on the Internet, how terrorists make dirty bombs, or the steps involved in applying for graduate school.

Spatial Order

A second common pattern is spatial arrangement. With this pattern, you use space as your ordering principle. A speech explaining the architectural plans for a new library, a presentation describing major tourist attractions of a big city (as one travels from north to south), or a speech describing the most progressive, reform-oriented prisons in the United States might all be appropriate candidates for spatial organization.

The following is an example of how one student arranged ideas in a spatial pattern determined by geography. He is addressing the need for universal emergency preparedness in the United States.

> **Specific purpose:** *I want my audience to recognize the serious natural disasters that increasingly threaten all of our geographical regions.*
> **Thesis statement:** *The threat of natural disasters is a growing reality throughout the United States.*
>   I. Hurricanes threaten our coasts.
> II. Wildfires threaten our woodlands.
> III. Tornadoes threaten our midwestern regions.
> IV. Floods threaten low-lying areas along streams and lakes.
>   V. Earthquakes affect not only the West Coast (along the San Andreas Fault), but also potentially could affect a large portion of the Midwest and the South.

The student then went on to offer specific examples of each of these natural disasters, as well as illustrating how each has increased in frequency.

Categorical Order

Ideas can also be arranged in a pattern that emphasizes distinct topics—a categorical pattern. When you arrange your ideas categorically, you address types, forms, qualities, or aspects of the speech subject. For example, if you were giving a speech on the benefits of higher education, you could develop ideas related to the intellectual, social, or economic advantages of education. Similarly, you might discuss teen pregnancy in terms of those most at risk, prison reform in terms of different models that have been tried, or the types of behaviors and attitudes that doctors associate with good mental health in the later years of life.

The following example shows how one student arranged her ideas categorically:

> **Specific purpose:** *I want my audience to gain an understanding of the types of drugs most commonly abused in the United States.*

Thesis statement: *Many different types of drugs are widely abused in the United States.*

   I. Marijuana has been widely abused for many generations.

   II. Crack cocaine is one of the most dangerous drugs abused by people from all walks of life.

   III. Meth abuse is perhaps the most recent and rapidly spreading form of drug abuse.

   IV. While many abused drugs are illegal, prescription drugs are the most widely abused type of drug.

Under each category, the speaker then develops her speech by briefly describing each drug, offering user statistics, demonstrating growth in abuse, and describing the drug's impact on the user's behavior and health.

Climactic Order

Another way of arranging ideas is to use a sequence that goes from simple to difficult, from least important to most important, or from emotionally neutral to emotionally intense. When the climactic order reflects audience needs and priorities, it can be an especially effective way to arrange ideas if the goal is to gain audience agreement or action. As you assess your ideas or arguments, you would then arrange them to build up to your strongest argument or most compelling idea.

Like a playwright, a speaker may wish to build on the listeners' interests and concerns until a climactic moment is reached. If, for example, you were addressing an audience with a strong sense of concern for ethics, you might talk about the solution to a community problem in terms of its affordability and its benefits to the community, concluding with the moral imperative to act. The following is an example of ideas patterned climactically, from least to most important, with rising emotional intensity:

Specific purpose: *I want my audience to agree that action to stop environmental pollution must begin now.*

Thesis statement: *Stopping environmental pollution should be a top priority for our community.*

   I. Pollution of air and water in this community has direct consequences for your health.

   II. Pollution effects can drastically alter the standard of living in this country.

   III. Pollution can ultimately lead to the destruction of human life on this planet.

You can also use this pattern in reverse, so that you begin with your strongest information or argument, follow through with other important ideas or arguments, and then return briefly to review the best one again.

Cause-and-Effect Order

Ideas can be arranged in an order that leads from cause to effect or from effect to cause. This causal pattern is a useful one for speakers who want an audience to

This speaker, at a rally protesting a proposed Alaska pipeline, is appealing to the concerns of those who believe that drilling will cause serious harm to the environment.

understand how an idea or event has unfolded, or for speakers who want to suggest changes in a chain of relationships that will bring more desirable outcomes. If, for example, you wanted your audience to understand why urban violence occurs, you could arrange ideas so that they would show the relationship of an event or circumstance (unemployment, poverty, broken homes) to another event or circumstance (young people with nothing to do, desire for material goods, lack of family support), thus forming a chain of events that has violent behavior as its final link. You could also use cause-and-effect order to discuss such topics as the causes of ozone layer depletion, the effects of gang activities on communities, or economic factors that typically lead to a recession.

The following is an example of ideas arranged in a causal pattern by a neighborhood association president who argued that the lack of traffic lights and signs produced harmful results and urged the city council to take action.

> **Specific purpose:** *I want council members to agree that a better system of traffic lights and signs is needed in this community.*
> **Thesis statement:** *The present system of traffic control is inconvenient and dangerous.*
> I. *Effect:* Pedestrians, young and old alike, have been struck and killed at unguarded crossings.
> II. *Effect:* At the main mall entrance, several accidents have resulted when oncoming traffic has failed to stop for the red light.

III. *Effect:* Traffic jams causing long delays occur every weekday during rush hours.

IV. *Cause:* The real culprit contributing to this safety hazard is poor traffic control procedures.

When using causal arrangement, keep in mind that a chronological relationship does *not* necessarily equal a causal relationship. One event following another may represent chance as easily as cause. In addition, whenever you look at a given effect to seek its causes, you must guard against oversimplification. The quest for the single cause is usually unrealistic. Finally, sometimes cause-and-effect order is incorporated into an overall problem-solution pattern. Within the structure of a problem-solution speech, you will analyze the problem (effect) in terms of contributing causes, and then go on to propose solutions.

Problem-Solution Patterns

The problem-solution pattern is one of the most common in political speeches. Typically, we associate this kind of pattern with persuasive speaking, although it is possible to discuss a problem and inform the audience of proposed solutions without taking a stand on the best solution. Most of the time, however, when you choose a problem-solution pattern of organization, you will take a position on your preferred solution, the one you hope the audience will adopt. You might propose solutions to such problems as credit card fraud, the rise in eating disorders among college students, or regulating drugs obtained through the Internet.

Reflective Thinking Sequence

The traditional problem-solution pattern is based on educational philosopher John Dewey's Reflective Thinking Sequence[5] and typically addresses these questions:

1. How shall we define and limit the problem?
2. What are the causes and extent of the problem?
3. What are the effects of the problem? Who has been hurt?
4. What are the criteria by which solutions should be judged?
5. What are the possible solutions and the relative strengths and weaknesses of each?
6. What is the best solution?
7. How can we put it into effect?

Depending on the problem and your assumptions about the audience's prior knowledge, you might spend more or less time discussing the nature of the problem and its contributing causes. In situations where the audience is well versed on the problem, you might only briefly describe it and spend most of your speaking time exploring viable solutions.

The following is an example of ideas from a student speech that employs a problem-solution pattern:

Specific purpose: *I want my audience to take the actions needed to end deforestation.*

Thesis statement: *Deforestation must be stopped before its adverse effects make the world unfit for future generations.*

  I. *Problem (causes):* Deforestation has accelerated in recent years for a variety of reasons.
  - A. One cause of deforestation is agriculture (massive tree cutting to make fields for farming crops).
  - B. Another cause is cattle ranching, which needs land for grazing.
  - C. Still another cause is related to developing Third World countries—cutting trees for shelter and firewood.
  - D. Perhaps the greatest contributor is overpopulation.

  II. *Problem (effects):* The effects of deforestation are often devastating.
  - A. With over 50 percent of the world's plants and animals living in 7 percent of the world's forests, the majority of them are headed for extinction—thus significantly decreasing biodiversity.
  - B. Deforestation also leads to serious flooding (since tree roots no longer gather and store rainwater).
  - C. Some experts argue that perhaps the most serious effect of deforestation is global warming.

  III. *Criteria for solution:* The solutions might be weighed against such criteria as feasibility, affordability, and fairness.

  IV. *Possible solutions:* There are a number of actions that we can take to help end deforestation.
  - A. We can support "reforestation" legislation, wherein designated areas of land are left alone (as in clear-cutting), so that trees can grow back naturally.
  - B. We can tackle population control—by educating Third World countries concerning birth control and acting responsibly in building our own families.
  - C. We can inform others about the problem while making a good example of ourselves (by recycling, using laptop computers, monitoring our use of paper products, etc.).

  V. *Best course of action:* In this case, all three solutions are interrelated, and all should be pursued. Some actions are personal and immediate; others are more long-range and deal with developing new policies and educational outreach.

The Motivated Sequence as a Special Problem-Solution Pattern

One specific approach to organizing a problem-solution speech is the *motivated sequence*.[6] This pattern is organized around five steps:

1. *Arouse:* capture the audience's attention and focus on the problem.
2. *Dissatisfy:* make listeners understand that this is a serious problem that needs their attention and action.
3. *Gratify:* tell listeners that it is within *their* power to remedy the situation.
4. *Visualize:* show them *exactly* how much they can improve the situation.
5. *Move:* appeal to the audience to take a specific action.

The motivated sequence is best suited to those topics that combine emotional with logical appeals. So, if you were addressing the community's need for safe housing for domestic abuse victims, creating a program to drastically reduce the practice of euthanizing shelter animals, or building after-school programs for at-risk teens, the motivated sequence might work quite well. The motivated sequence allows you to engage the audience's emotions and urge them to act. It provides a balanced treatment of the problem *and* the solution (although you can choose to shorten the problem component if you think the audience is already aware of it). Above all, you must be able to convince the audience that they *do* possess the power to act, and to help them visualize *how* their actions can address the problem in very specific ways. Your own passion and commitment, an awareness of the audience's needs and values, and a thorough understanding of the details of the solution you are advancing are central to the effective use of this problem-solution pattern.

Narrative Patterns of Organization

In addition to the traditional organizational patterns examined above, other options exist. Due to cultural backgrounds or personal preference, some speakers may prefer to use less direct and more organic patterns of organization.[7] For instance, a speech may be organized around telling one or more stories, using a narrative pattern. Rhetorical scholar Walter Fisher points out that the most compelling narratives are coherent, rather than scattered or fragmented.[8] The speaker may begin by introducing a theme, such as the idea that the best government leaders are highly ethical. Then, various stories would be shared to illustrate and reinforce the speaker's thesis. Or, a speaker might pay tribute to a single person by sharing an extended narrative of the person's life. The speech is a continuous narrative with various internal stories drawn out and emphasized. Each would relate to an overarching theme, perhaps by demonstrating how the person being honored lived a courageous life. Narratives should also possess what Fisher calls *fidelity*—so that they ring true with the stories that listeners know to be true in their own lives.[9] In this example, the speaker would want to share examples of courageous acts that, while admirable and unusual, will still be seen as plausible.

If the speaker wants to build in a sense of drama or climax within a narrative pattern, he or she may choose to use a *spiraling* narrative. For

Narrative patterns of organization can be especially compelling for listeners. Garrison Keillor is a particularly adept storyteller whose amusing narratives enthrall audiences.

Highlighting a Narrative Approach to Organization

The Exemplum

For hundreds of years, communication educators have used a narrative pattern of organization called the exemplum. Five elements are included:

- State a quotation or a proverb.
- Identify and explain the author or source of the proverb or quotation.
- Rephrase the proverb in your own words.
- Share a story that illustrates the quotation.

- Apply the quotation or proverb to the audience.

In short, the speaker using this pattern builds the speech around a quotation that is developed through a narrative. This pattern can be especially useful for inspirational or motivational speeches that elaborate on a shared value such as integrity.

Source: J. R. McNally, "Opening Assignments: A Symposium," *Speech Teacher* 18 (1969): 18–20.

instance, the speaker might give the speech of tribute described by sharing stories that build in intensity. The person's simple acts of courage might be shared first, moving to more unusual acts, and perhaps culminating with uncommon acts of valor. Again, each would be united by the general theme. When delivered effectively, narrative patterns can contribute to a powerful, engaging presentation. See *Highlighting a Narrative Approach to Organization* for an extended illustration of another common narrative pattern.

This list of organizational patterns is not exhaustive, but it does include the principal ways in which you can arrange your ideas. Although we tend to associate problem-solution and cause-and-effect patterns with persuasive speaking, both can be used with informative speeches as well. For example, a speaker could discuss a problem, articulate its causes, and then go on to help the audience understand three different solutions that have been proposed by different experts, without advocating any one of them.

In addition, there are many variations on persuasive organizational patterns, depending on whether the topics addressed are related to issues of fact, cause, value, or policy.

Guidelines for Organizing Your Speech

Preview. *Regardless of the particular pattern of organization you select, you will want to keep in mind some basic guidelines. It is important to view the choice of an organizational pattern as a strategic decision. At the same time, you will want to consider issues of balance (as you develop your ideas), the number of main ideas to include in your speech, and where to place your strongest, most compelling ideas and information.*

Given the wide variety of organizational patterns from which you can choose, a few general principles should be kept in mind. First, select your organizational pattern carefully. The way you present your ideas and information should be *strategic*, designed to enhance the chance that you will elicit the audience response you are seeking. If you are talking to an audience about a problem that is quite complicated or one with which they have little knowledge or experience, you will want to devote a good portion of your speech to educating your listeners. A good organizational strategy in this case might be a traditional problem-solution pattern (as previously outlined)—one in which you devote substantial time to defining and exploring the problem and its causes and effects *before* moving forward to propose possible solutions.

Second, give some thought to symmetry or balance. If you decide that each of your main ideas is worthy of equal emphasis, then you will want to organize your remarks so that each one is equally well developed. But, if you decide that one idea is clearly more controversial, complex, or important than the others, you may consciously decide to devote more time to that idea. In some cases, then, a balanced presentation would be precisely what is needed, while in other cases, an imbalanced treatment might be more effective.

Sometimes, speakers have questions about how many main ideas they can convey in a single speech. To some extent, the time allowed for the speech will influence how many main ideas can be fully developed. If you are giving a 6–8 minute speech, you might be hard-pressed to cover more than two or three main points adequately. A 20-minute presentation might allow you to advance a larger number of main ideas (usually no more than five). But there are two constraints to keep in mind. First, many listeners cannot attend to or absorb a large number of main ideas during a single presentation (refer to Chapter 4 on listening challenges). In addition, a well-formulated specific purpose statement should serve to limit and focus the speech. You can test each idea you are considering by asking if it serves to advance your speech's specific purpose. If it does not, you will want to eliminate it.

Finally, be aware of primacy and recency effects. Although researchers have not been able to agree on whether arguments are more memorable and persuasive if they are placed first (primacy) or last (recency), they *do* agree that those two positions are the most powerful—and that information or arguments embedded in the middle of a message are less likely to be as memorable or have as much impact on listeners.[10] In most instances, then, you will want to lead with and conclude with information and ideas that are especially crucial to the case you are making.

Using Transitions and Transitional Devices

Preview. *Transitions and transitional devices can add clarity and smoothness to a speech. Without strong transitions, even a well-organized speech may strike listeners as confusing or disorganized. When crafted well, transitions can contribute significantly to the impact of the speaker's overall message.*

As a responsible speaker, you need to help the audience see the relationships among your ideas. Once you have drafted your speech, you must consider how you will progress from one idea to another so that listeners can see the connections.

A transition is a bridge from one idea to another. Listeners cannot be expected to pay complete attention to the speaker, nor can they be expected to understand the sequence of ideas and information as clearly as the speaker does. You must alert your listeners to a new idea about to be introduced and help them see how it relates to your overall message.

In addition to alerting listeners to the progression and relevance of the main ideas in your speech, you also need to assist them as you develop those ideas. To do so, you can rely on transitional devices. Let us examine transitions and transitional devices, when to use them, and how to craft them.

Transitions

These structural elements are small but mighty. They are, perhaps, the most unappreciated and underutilized components of effective speechmaking. A transition links one major idea with another in a speech, showing their relationship to each other. However, a transition does more than show how an idea fits into a speech. It also reinforces an idea that a speaker wishes to share.

Let us examine the transitions that one student provided in a persuasive speech in which he wanted his audience to agree that steel-framed homes are better for you *and* the environment than wood-framed homes.

> **Thesis statement:** Steel-framed homes are a better choice than wood-framed structures.
> **The first main idea read:**
>   I. Steel-framed homes are more durable than wood-framed homes.

Following the development of this idea, the student used the following transition:

As you can see, then, steel-framed homes are better than wood-framed homes because they're stronger and provide superior protection against natural disaster. The benefits do not end there, though; steel-framed homes are also better for the planet.

This transition led to the second main idea:

>   II. Steel-framed homes are environmentally friendly.

This example illustrates that transitions not only connect ideas to one another, but they also reinforce and reiterate those ideas. A transition is a quick glance back at the idea just discussed and then a quick look forward to the next main idea. The transition helps the speaker achieve his or her specific purpose while advancing the speech's thesis. In a sense, it functions as a miniature review and preview of ideas.

Sometimes, in lengthy speeches, this reviewing and previewing should be done more extensively. When this is the case, the speaker can rely on an internal preview or an internal summary, both of which are extended transitions.

Internal Previews

When moving from one idea to the next, you can give your audience a very brief internal preview of the point you are about to make. For example, suppose a speaker has just discussed this point: "Pollution of air and water in this community has direct consequences for your health and your pocketbook." The next main idea he plans to take up is: "Pollution effects can drastically alter the standard of living in this country." To transition into this second point, he might combine a simple re-statement of the first idea with an internal preview in this way:

> Pollution, then, can cost you both your health and your money. But its effects are even more far-reaching. If pollution isn't controlled now, drastic steps will have to be taken that could curtail your ability to travel, determine at what level you heat or cool your home, or restrict the foods available to you. Let us consider now the ways in which our standard of living is at risk because of pollution.

Internal Summaries

Sometimes, getting from one idea to another has to be more elaborate because the material is complex. In these cases, you may use an internal summary, briefly going over the information covered so far before moving on to the next point. A speaker explaining the background of the American Revolution, for example, used an internal summary in her transition:

> We've seen how the Stamp Act in 1765 aroused the first successful organized resistance on the part of the colonists to the British government. Then, British attempts to deal with the problems of taxation and defense, coupled with a growing spirit of independence in the colonies, caused an ever-widening breach between North America and Great Britain. Now let us see how the events in the months preceding the Declaration of Independence led the young colonies to a final break with the mother country.

That kind of transition—a short summary of what has been said—helps keep the audience mentally on track. It also reinforces key ideas.

Sometimes internal summaries can be brief phrases embedded in new ideas. This is how one speaker used transitions to develop her first main idea in a speech on poverty and dental health:

> I. Poor people with impaired dental health confront a variety of problems.
>   A. Their general health can be at risk (including heart disease).
>   B. Not only can poor dental health lead to other serious health consequences *[transition]*, it adversely influences the individual's ability to get a job.
>   C. In addition to basic health and employment problems, *[transition]*, those with poor dental health often find it challenging to establish meaningful relationships with others in their daily lives.

These sample transitions illustrate how words and phrases can help listeners process information and ideas as they are advanced by the speaker.

Transitional Devices

Transitional devices help listeners understand and follow developing ideas through the use of linguistic markers. Transitional devices consist of words and phrases such as "for instance" and "on the other hand."

In some instances, you may merely want to provide verbal markers to alert your audience to the fact that you are moving from one idea to another by enumerating each point or by signaling the next point to be made. If so, you can rely on transitional devices known as *signposts*. You might, for example, tell your listeners that you have three good reasons for asking them to sign up for the Big Brothers/Big Sisters program. Your transitional devices might be as simple as this: "*The second reason* for you to sign up now is that the need is so urgent in our community." As you move into the third reason, you might say: "*A final reason* for volunteering is that you will derive great satisfaction from knowing you have really made a difference in a child's life."

Other signposts include words such as *next, another*, and *finally*. Here are some examples:

"*The next* good reason is . . ."
"*Another* reason you should sign up is . . ."
"*Finally*, you should join now because . . ."

Taken together, transitions and transitional devices help listeners make the right connections and follow the progression of ideas in your speech. In any speech, you will use a variety of these devices.

So far, we have discussed organizational principles and approaches that largely apply to the way you will arrange the main ideas in the body of your speech. Now we turn our attention to how you will begin your speech. The effectiveness of your speech's introduction will likely influence the audience's frame of mind as you move into the presentation of your main ideas.

Introducing Your Speech

Preview. *Although speech introductions may be structured in different ways, the most effective introductions will capture and hold the listeners' attention, stress the relevance of your topic, establish your credibility as a speaker, clarify your purpose, and provide a preview of your ideas.*

No matter which organizational pattern you follow, you will need to introduce your speech in an effective way. It is not enough to say, "Today I am going to talk with you about why the community needs a free health clinic." Hardly any listener will be riveted by that. Instead, the introduction needs to be structured so that audience members *want* to listen to your speech, view you as a credible source, and have some idea of your speech's purpose and main ideas.

Capturing and Maintaining the Listeners' Attention

When you first get up to speak, listeners will usually give you their full attention. But that attention may prove to be fleeting. Let us consider several approaches to maintaining the audience's attention and how some speakers have used them.

Establish Common Ground

Audiences tend to listen to speakers with whom they share common experiences, problems, or goals. Karen, giving a speech on student loans in a class with several other working students, began her speech this way:

> When I get to this class at 8:00 AM, I have had four hours' sleep. I work full-time as a waitress at Nick's and do not get home until about 2 AM. Like many of you, I need to work to support myself while going to school. Some of you have full-time jobs and some are part-timers. Some of you also have families to care for as well as working and going to school. And I know that at least one of you is also a single parent. For us, getting an education and making ends meet is not easy.

In other speaking contexts outside the classroom, the speaker may not be part of the group of listeners. Perhaps the speaker holds a position of high status or influence, or has had life experiences that are quite different from those of the audience. In this case, establishing common ground with listeners creates a sense of "we-ness" that will invite the audience to listen. President George W. Bush opened his speech at the Naval Air Station in San Diego, California, in August 2005 by alluding to his father's experience in the navy. He said:

> Thank you all. Thanks for the warm welcome. It is good to be back in California. Good to be here at North Island. This is the birthplace of naval aviation, and I want to thank you for making this son of a naval aviator feel right at home.[11]

By introducing his remarks in this way, the president sought to demonstrate a common bond he shared with many members of the audience.

Tell a Story

An interesting story—whether it is emotional, humorous, puzzling, or intriguing—commands attention. The story can be real or hypothetical. It can be a personal story that reveals something of your own experience, or it can be something you have read. Speaking to a group of teachers, Carmen Mariano, an assistant superintendent in the Massachusetts public school system, began with this narrative:

> Ernest Hemingway tells the story of a Spanish man who has a bitter argument one morning with his young son, Paco. When he arrived home later that day, the man discovered that Paco's room was empty—he had run away from home.
>
> Overcome with remorse, the man realized that his son was more important to him than anything else. He went to a well-known grocery store in the center of town and posted a large sign that read, "Paco, come home. I love you. Meet me here tomorrow morning." Signed, your father.
>
> The next morning, the man went to the store. There, he found his son and seven other young boys who had also run away from home. They were all answering the call for love, hoping it was their dad inviting them home.[12]

Mariano used this opening to lead into the point that teaching children who come from tension-filled homes where they do not feel loved or wanted is a great challenge for teachers in the public school system.

Use Rhetorical Questions

Rhetorical questions do not seek immediate responses. Rather, they are intended to get listeners thinking about an issue or idea. Lin began his speech by raising questions that challenged listeners to consider how they might deal with ethical dilemmas:

> This is an honors public speaking class, and, as honors students, we're all used to getting good grades. Grades are very important to us and we can be very competitive. Well, you might not kill for an A—but, what *would* you do for an A? Would you consider taking a peek at the answers to someone's exam if you had the chance to do so and were sure you wouldn't get caught? Would you tell a professor that he or she made a mistake in grading an exam if it meant that your grade was lowered? Would you let a friend write a short paper for you and turn it in as your own? Can you think of any time when you've done something that you wouldn't like anyone else to know about to get a good grade? If we're perfectly honest with ourselves, we know that these questions are not so easy to answer in a "socially approved" way. Maybe you've never cheated or plagiarized or lied to a friend—but, have you never been tempted?

Lin's audience will likely find their thinking stimulated by these rhetorical questions that relate directly to their lives as students.

Begin with a Memorable Quotation

No doubt someone has said or written something that captures the thesis of your speech. The idea has been expressed so well, perhaps by a person whom the audience respects and admires, that you know it will get the listeners' interest and attention right away. An esteemed scholar, scientist, or political figure can be quoted. Or you can use the words of a popular entertainer, author, athlete, or singer or other well-known and highly respected figures.

A student speaker, Micah, wanted his listeners to realize that trying to understand how the universe came about was very important, and so he began with this quotation from a famous physicist:

> Stephen Hawking said, "If we do discover a complete theory of the universe it should in time be understood in broad principle by everyone, not just a few scientists. Then we shall, philosophers, scientists and just ordinary people, be able to take part in the discussion of the question of why it is that we and the universe exist. If we find the answer to that, it would be the ultimate triumph of human reason—for then we should know the mind of God."[13]

Use Humor

Some speakers like to begin a speech with a humorous story, but you need to approach humor with caution. No matter how funny a story might be, it must be relevant to the point you want to make. Just telling a few jokes is not a good way to begin a speech, and a joke that falls flat is embarrassing. Humor should never be disrespectful or aimed at ridiculing someone or something, so you need to be careful. In the following introduction, Richard Lamm, representing the University of

Denver's Center for Public Policy and Contemporary Issues, begins his speech to the World Future Society with this humorous anecdote:

> A priest was riding in a subway when a man staggered toward him, smelling like a brewery, with lipstick on his collar. He sat in the seat right next to the priest and started reading the newspaper.
>
> After a few minutes, the man turned to the priest and asked. "Excuse me, Father, what causes arthritis?"
>
> The priest, tired of smelling the liquor and saddened by the lifestyle, said roughly, "Loose living, drink, dissipation, contempt for your fellow man and being with cheap and wicked women!"
>
> "That's amazing," said the drunk and returned to his newspaper. A while later, the priest, feeling a bit guilty, turned to the man and asked nicely, "How long have you had arthritis?"
>
> "Oh," said the man, "I don't have arthritis. I was just reading that the Pope did."

The story, of course, is a lesson on assumptions.[14]

Of course, these techniques are not mutually exclusive—you can use several at once. You might, for example, tell an interesting story that also establishes common ground and arouses curiosity. And you will want to deliver the introduction effectively. For example, pausing after telling a compelling story, posing an engaging rhetorical question, or sharing a memorable quotation may help listeners ponder what you are about to say. The key factor is capturing and holding the audience's attention and interest.

Stressing Relevance

Either consciously or unconsciously, your listeners will soon ask themselves why they should care about your topic. Even when we find something very interesting, we soon begin to wonder whether it has any relevance to us. In the introduction, you should take the time to establish the significance of your topic, answering for your audience the question, "Does this have anything to do with me?"

Kelly knew that many students were not particularly interested in politics and did not care much about who was elected in the upcoming congressional elections. Her purpose was to get her audience to understand the major policy decisions that faced the next Congress and what difference these decisions could make to them. She began her speech this way:

> Some of you who are on scholarships might find that you are paying more taxes on their value next year than you are this year. Your grandparents might be able to get home health care and not be forced into

Ann Richards, the late Governor of Texas, was known for her ability to employ humor to hold listeners' interest and attention while reinforcing the point she wished to make.

nursing homes in a couple of years. The city streets may be safer or more dangerous. The job you want when you finish college might be a lot harder to get in a couple of years. What Congress decides to do about a whole host of policy questions can affect you directly in your everyday lives. Who runs Congress is a lot more than "just politics"—your money, your future, your life is at stake here, and you can do something about it.

No one listening to these introductory remarks could fail to see how the speaker's topic might affect their lives, as well as those of their loved ones and other, vulnerable members of the community.

Establishing Credibility

The audience should know of any special relationship you have with the topic that would enhance your ethos. Of course, credibility is an ongoing issue throughout any speech, but the introduction represents an especially critical time for establishing your credentials. For seasoned professionals, this process may be less daunting. We expect doctors to know about medicine, attorneys to know about law, and accountants to be able to answer questions about our taxes. For student speakers, however, establishing ethos can be more challenging.

Yet student speakers can establish their ethos in compelling ways. Let us look at how one student did it. In her speech urging students to volunteer for a summer work project, Kristin began by relating her own experience:

> Last year I took a different kind of summer vacation. I did not go to the beach to try to get a fabulous tan. I did not go to a lake and learn to water ski. I did not go to a big city to visit museums and see shows. I went to a hot, dry desert. There was no air conditioning anywhere. After a night spent sleeping in a sleeping bag on a bare floor, I got up, had breakfast, got into an old truck with about a dozen other kids and took off over a dusty road to a house that badly needed repair. In the hot sun I helped plug cracks in the wall, learned how to mix and apply plaster, and stripped and painted peeling boards.
>
> I did this for nothing. Well, that isn't right. I did not get paid money, but I did get something a lot more valuable. Working as a volunteer in a remote town in an Indian reservation, I learned so many things about a different culture. I made close friends among the people I worked with. I helped to make a real difference in real people's lives. I came back from this experience a different—and richer—person than I was when I went. I am going to tell you today how you can enrich your life, too.

Having established her credibility, this speaker is well positioned to use her personal experience to convince her listeners that they should get involved as well.

Clarifying Your Purpose/Advancing Your Thesis

A key function of the introduction is to advance your speech's thesis—stating, in a single declarative statement, the central idea of your speech. By articulating your thesis as part of the introduction, you help the audience discern your central theme, overarching point, or principal argument. No speaker wants to move into the body of the speech with the audience still wondering, What's the point? Where is this going?

Sometimes you might discuss a subject of such interest or significance that the most appropriate introduction is to go directly to the speech's thesis. This is especially fitting if the audience is aware of your subject in advance, already wants to learn about it, and views the subject as serious. Under these conditions, listeners are likely to take a "Let's get on with it" attitude.

Usually, such a situation occurs when a speaker is considered an expert on a topic or holds an important position in an organization. When John C. Nelson, immediate past president of the American Medical Association, was invited to address the crisis in health care with a group of concerned citizens in Eugene, Oregon, he began his speech by directly addressing the serious nature of the problem. His audience knew his thesis to be: *The inability of ordinary people to have any sort of health coverage constitutes the most fundamental kind of crisis in health care.*

> It is an honor and privilege to be here on behalf of the nation's physicians at a time of growing crisis in health care. I'm not speaking about an epidemic, though our world is painfully fragile in the face of threats of pandemics. . . . I'm really speaking about the most fundamental kind of crisis in health care—the inability of ordinary people to have any sort of health care coverage at all.
>
> Strange as it sounds, in a land of unprecedented economic growth, in a land of compassion and concern . . . 45 million people have no health care coverage. And 15 million more are classified as "under-insured." . . . What does this mean? How can we get our arms around [these] huge numbers?[15]

Had the speaker chosen a more circuitous approach to addressing this compelling topic, waiting to reveal his thesis, the audience might have become restless, wondering when the speaker would get to the point.

Providing a Preview

Before moving into the body of your speech, you should give a preview. The preview introduces your main ideas, offering a road map so that listeners can more easily follow your speech. In previewing, you are also signaling what you feel is most important—those things you want the audience to remember and reflect on long after you have finished speaking. If, after giving your preview, you follow through with your plan, you will have further enhanced your credibility by demonstrating your careful organization and preparation.

Consider, for example, the speech given by the student whose purpose was to get her audience to register to vote in time for the next election. After relating her topic to the audience and clarifying her purpose in her introduction, she went on to preview the ideas she would develop:

> Today I'm going to show you how your life will be directly affected by the different policies advocated by different political candidates. First, I'll explain how the results of the election could influence the amount of taxes that you and your parents pay. Second, I'll show you how aid to higher education could be

affected by the outcome of the election. Finally, I'll give you some quick examples of a whole range of other issues related to your everyday life that could be settled by this election.

Having forecast what she plans to do in the speech, the speaker's challenge is to deliver on the promise by developing each point she has mentioned in the preview.

Final Tips about Introductions

Remember the power of first impressions. Part of your first impression as a speaker will be based on the way you introduce your speech. Craft your introduction with care. Most speakers wait until after they have outlined the body of the speech to develop the introduction. For instance, they may experiment with several different attention-getting devices before they settle on the one they feel is most compelling.

The length of the introduction varies with the needs of the speaking situation. Some very formal events require the speaker to offer an introduction that refers to the events at hand and acknowledges or thanks several significant persons related to the event. Usually, however, introductions should be reasonably brief, and especially so in the classroom context. We have all heard speakers who ramble on for some time, then say, after ten minutes or so, "What I'd like to talk about today is . . . " This can be a signal for the audience to tune out. So, in most speaking situations, you should keep your introduction brief.

Although we have discussed the main components that are typically present in good speech introductions, it is important to remember that each introduction should be tailored to the situation. For example, if the person introducing you fully establishes your credibility, you may have little need of augmenting what has already been said. If the audience is already keenly aware of the significance of the problem you are addressing, you will not need to offer an elaborate justification. Instead, you may simply say, "We are all aware of the urgency of the problem that has brought us here tonight." In short, each introduction should be crafted not according to a formula but based on the demands of the topic, the listeners, and the situation.

If you develop your introduction carefully and deliver it effectively, you will set the stage for the audience to attend to the main ideas that you will go on to develop throughout the rest of your speech. A strong introduction makes the audience want to hear more.

Bringing your speech to an effective conclusion is also important. Sometimes speakers primarily think about how to arrange and present their main ideas, without paying attention to what they will say at the end of their speech. Yet, the conclusion is the last thing the audience hears. If it is memorable and compelling, the conclusion can truly enhance the overall impact of the speech.

Concluding Your Speech

Preview. *Carefully planning your speech's conclusion is an essential part of preparing to speak. By summarizing your main ideas, challenging your audience, appealing to your audience, visualizing the future, using good quotations, or referring to the introduction—or by using a combination of these techniques—you can craft an effective ending for your speech.*

Many speakers do not really conclude their speeches—they simply stop talking. Others may stumble through their concluding remarks, reducing the effectiveness of the presentation. Sometimes speakers say something like, "Well, I guess that's about it. Any questions?" The conclusion is very important. If you construct it properly, you will bring your speech to a strategic close and create a final positive impact.

As you approach the speech's conclusion, you will want to signal to the audience that you are, in fact, concluding. One of the major vehicles for transitioning into the conclusion is to offer a summary.

Summarizing Your Ideas

One of the most common techniques used to conclude a speech is to present a summary. Summaries are especially important when the speech is complex or rather long. The summary reinforces your ideas and reminds the audience of your most important points. When combined with the preview in your introduction and the development of each main idea in the body of your speech, the summary provides a final chance to reiterate key ideas and help the audience remember them.

Summaries are often used in conjunction with another concluding device. Jon used the following summary, followed by a rhetorical question, to conclude his speech on the Community Service and Leadership Program, a new interdisciplinary curriculum at the university:

> In short, the Community Service and Leadership Program (CSLP) is an excellent alternative to a traditional college degree. Your volunteerism—combined with a strong education in the arts and sciences—will give you an excellent education, both inside and outside the classroom. And, you will have a lot of contact with your professors because CSLP is small, with several courses team-taught by faculty, together with community and government leaders. If you are interested in using your education to contribute to your community, why not look into this exciting new program?

Challenging Your Audience

Most of the time, summaries do not stand alone. Often they are—or should be—accompanied by some other interesting concluding device. One such device that can be very effective is a challenge to the audience to act on what you have said. This was the strategy that U.S. Congresswoman Jane Harman chose when she spoke at a town hall meeting in Los Angeles:

> We must use all the tools of our so-called toolbox: our economic power, our diplomacy, and the power of our example to defend America's interests in an era of terror. In the Internet Age, we are all interconnected as never before. From L.A. to London, from Mosul to Marrakesh, from Baghdad to Beirut to Jerusalem and Ramallah—we share a common fate. We must build a future of hope, prosperity, and security together, or we who have known these things will surely lose them.
>
> I often say that I'm an optimist or I would never stay in politics. The challenges we face are, in my view, an opportunity for the world's only superpower which harbors no wish to aggrandize territory, to instead shape a world free of tyranny, free of hopelessness, and free of inequality. Will we do it? You bet.[16]

Speakers who feel strongly about their topic will make every effort to challenge their listeners to act.

Appealing to Your Audience

In your conclusion, you can make a final attempt to move your audience to act or believe more strongly about your proposition. Speaking to an audience of company representatives who had been honored as Parent Magazine's Best Companies for Working Families, Richard Lamm concluded his speech with this appeal:

> I close with a metaphor on the need for cooperation and community . . . . The metaphor is an Amazon legend which tells of a priest who was speaking with God about heaven and hell.
>
> "I will show you hell," said God.
>
> They went into a room that had a delicious beef stew on the table, around which sat people chained to their benches and who looked desperately famished. They held spoons with long handles that reached into the pot, but were too long to put the stew back into their mouths. Their suffering was terrible.
>
> "Now, I will show you heaven," said God.
>
> They then went into an identical room with the savory stew on the table, around which sat people with identical spoons and handles, but they were well nourished and joyous.
>
> The priest was baffled until God said, "Quite simply, you see, these people have learned to feed each other."[17]

Lamm's appeal is for the audience to recognize their responsibility for taking care of *everyone* who is part of the organizational family.

Visualizing the Future

In a speech in which you advocate some important changes, visualizing the results of those changes is an especially appropriate and powerful way to conclude. This device (which is built into the motivated sequence) allows you to picture concretely the projected results of your ideas in an appealing way. One of the most famous examples of visualization occurs in Martin Luther King Jr.'s "I Have a Dream" speech. In his conclusion, he offered this picture of the future:

> And when this happens, and when we allow freedom to ring, when we let it ring from every village and hamlet, from every state and city, we will be able to speed up that day when all of God's children—black men and white men, Jews and Gentiles, Catholics and Protestants—will be able to join hands and to sing in the words of the old Negro spiritual, "Free at last, free at last; thank God Almighty, we are free at last."[18]

Ending with a Quotation

Ending your speech with a good quotation can help reinforce your thesis and restate the major points you made. Poetry, plays, songs, speeches, and literary works can all supply effective quotations. In the early 1990s, Lowell Weicker, Republican senator from Connecticut, spoke from the pulpit of the United Church on the Green in New Haven on the issue of a constitutional amendment to allow school prayer. Senator Weicker, who opposed the amendment, used biblical passages to sum up his viewpoint:

> The Apostle Paul wrote that "faith without works is dead." And in the Old Testament text read this morning, Isaiah seems to be saying that . . . the people's piousness is an abomination to God until they first act on His social agenda. Isaiah writes: "Is not this the fast that I have chosen? To loose the bands of wickedness, to undo the heavy burdens, to let the oppressed go free? Is it not to deal thy bread to the hungry, and that thou bring the poor that are cast out to thy house?"
>
> This, I believe, should be the agenda of each of us as individuals, and indeed for me as a Senator. It pains me to see the Congress diverted into these moral crusades when there is so much real suffering in our land, when so many people are losing their livelihoods and so many going without the necessities of life. And when there are so many people denied the justice which should be accorded them by law.
>
> Let us rededicate ourselves to taking up this agenda. Let us get involved in our public and private lives to shape a fairer society. Then, and only then, does God promise to hear our prayers. "Then shalt thou call, and the Lord shall answer," writes Isaiah. "Thou shalt cry and He shall say, Here I am."[19]

Referring to the Introduction

You can achieve a sense of symmetry and reinforce your major theme by coming back to the introduction in the conclusion of your speech. This commonly happens when a speaker uses both a preview and a summary, but you can find more interesting ways to do this, often by using one of the techniques we have already discussed. For example, you might return to a story, quotation, or rhetorical question that you used in the opening.

Consider the following example from a speech given by Robert C. Purcell, executive director of General Motors Advanced Technology Vehicles, at the 1998 MBA Recognition Ceremony at the Kelly School of Business, Indiana University. He had introduced his speech with a riveting story from May 1961, in which a group of black and white students, riding on a bus together, were attacked by an angry white mob. One young black seminary student, John Lewis, was nearly killed. His life was saved only because a white Alabama public safety officer, Floyd Mann, chased off the crowd by firing shots into the air. Purcell concludes his speech like this:

> There's a postscript to the story I shared with you when I began today. Not long ago, John Lewis, the young seminary student, returned to Alabama, to the site of that historic attack 37 years ago, for the dedication of a civil rights memorial. . . . By that time, Lewis had a long and distinguished career.
>
> As we waited for the ceremony to begin, an older gentleman, who seemed vaguely familiar, came over to him.
>
> "You're John Lewis, aren't you?" the man said. "I remember you from the Freedom Rides."
>
> It was Floyd Mann—the same Floyd Mann who had waded into that mob with his revolver, more than 35 years before.
>
> Lewis was overcome with emotion. "You saved my life," he said. And then he embraced Floyd Mann. Not sure as he did so, if even then, black men and white men hugged each other in contemporary Alabama.
>
> But Mann hugged him back, and John Lewis began to cry.
>
> And as the two men released each other, Floyd Mann looked at Lewis and said, "You know . . . I'm right proud of your career."
>
> And if there is one hope that I hold for each of you today—it is that 10 or 20 or 30 years from now, when you look back on your careers, you'll be just as proud.[20]

Most speakers use a combination of techniques. Jon combined a summary with a rhetorical question. Congresswoman Harman also used a rhetorical question, as well as offering an extended challenge. Reverend King quoted from an old spiritual while visualizing the future. Senator Weicker quoted extensively from the Bible while also challenging his audience to create a fairer society. Robert Purcell brought closure to his speech through an extended story that referred to his introduction. These combined approaches are fairly typical and often work more effectively than any one technique used alone.

Final Tips about Conclusions

Just as the introduction of your speech contributes to the audience's first impression of you, the conclusion represents your last chance to reach out to listeners and reinforce your speech's purpose. The conclusion should be brief; this is no place to introduce new information or to tack on something you forgot to say earlier.

Speakers sometimes have trouble ending their speeches. A speaker may say, "Let me leave you with this thought," then ramble on for several more minutes. Or the speaker may pepper his or her remarks with signposts such as "finally" or "in conclusion"—but not stop talking. When a speaker uses these verbal markers, listeners take him or her seriously. If the speaker uses them and continues to speak, listeners may become frustrated or bored, and they will probably stop listening. Even a good speech (and a good speaker) can lose considerable ground if the conclusion is poorly crafted and delivered.

You can signal to the audience that you are concluding by your content and your delivery. Offering a summary clearly communicates that you are approaching the end of your speech, as do signposts such as "finally," or "in closing." You may also move physically closer to the audience and connect with them directly through eye contact and vocal expressiveness as you offer a concluding quotation, help them visualize the future, or call them to action. Your conclusion is your last opportunity to connect with your audience, and it should never be lost.

Summary

- Effective speakers strive to organize their ideas carefully and strategically.
  - Well-organized speakers are usually viewed as competent and knowledgeable—greatly contributing to their perceived credibility.
  - They are also viewed as being invested in their topic and respectful of the audience.
  - The better organized the speaker, the more likely the audience will learn from the speech and be influenced by it.
- The foundation of a well-organized speech is a set of main ideas that are well thought out and clearly formulated.
  - You design ideas with a specific purpose in mind, making sure that they are clear, simple without being oversimplified, appropriate to the situation, and sensible.
- Ideas have to be organized in a coherent and reasonable fashion. The principal patterns of organization discussed in this chapter are:
  - chronological or sequential (arranged in a time or step-by-step order)
  - categorical (a pattern that emphasizes distinct topics)
  - climactic (arranged according to importance, size, or degree of simplicity)
  - causal (moving from causes to effects or from effects to causes)
  - problem-solution (a logical progression that moves from perceived difficulties to an examination of alternatives to a best solution)
  - narrative (based on a storytelling model).

- Speakers will also want to consider issues of balance, the number of main ideas to include, and idea placement as they move forward in finalizing their choice of an organizational pattern.

- Once you have chosen the basic organizational pattern and worked on good transitions, you are ready to think about how to begin and conclude your comments.

- In general, the speech's introduction should help you do the following:
  - capture and hold the audience's attention
  - show them why your topic is relevant to them
  - establish your credibility
  - advance the speech's purpose
  - preview your main ideas

- Crafting an effective conclusion also is important. Conclusions allow you to:
  - summarize your main ideas
  - challenge your audience
  - appeal to listeners
  - visualize the future
  - offer a memorable quotation
  - create balance and closure by referring to the introduction

- The conclusion is your last opportunity to connect with your audience and realize your specific purpose.

QUESTIONS FOR REVIEW AND REFLECTION

1. Why is good organization important?
2. In what ways does the purpose of your speech influence the main ideas?
3. What makes an idea a good one? Examine the main ideas you advanced in your last speech. How do they measure up in light of these criteria?
4. What are the principal patterns of organization? Why would you choose one pattern over another?
5. How might each of these concepts be important to you as you go about organizing your next speech?
   a. strategic organization
   b. balance/symmetry
   c. the number of main ideas to include
   d. primacy and recency effects
6. What is the function of transitions? What are the different kinds of transitions and transitional devices that you might use? Briefly define each.
7. What are the major components of the speech introduction? Why is each important?
8. Give some examples of how you might capture the listeners' attention in your introduction.
9. What should you accomplish in the conclusion to your speech? What are some techniques that will help you do this?

ENDNOTES

1. James C. McCroskey and R. Samuel Mehrley, "The Effects of Disorganization and Nonfluency on Attitude Change and Source Credibility," *Communication Monographs* 36 (1969): 13–21.

2. Studies generally show that organized speeches are better understood than those that are less well organized. See, for example, Ernest C. Thompson, "An Experimental Investigation of the Relative Effectiveness of Organizational Structure in Oral Communication," *Southern Speech Communication Journal* 26 (1960): 59–69.

3. When listeners are forced to listen to a disorganized presentation, they are unlikely to respond in a way that is consistent with the speaker's specific purpose. See Raymond G. Smith, "An Experimental Study of the Effects of Speech Organization upon Attitudes of College Students," *Communication Monographs* 18 (1951): 292–301.

4. Curtis might consult, for example, Neal Boortz and John Linder's book, *The Fair Tax Book* (New York: HarperCollins, 2005).

5. John Dewey, *How We Think* (Boston: Heath, 1910).

6. This pattern was originally introduced by Alan H. Monroe in *Principles and Types of Speech* (New York: Scott, Foresman, 1935) and has been refined in later editions. See, for example, Alan H. Monroe, Bruce E. Gronbeck, and Douglas Ehninger, *Principles and Types of Speech Communication*, 14th ed. (Boston: Addison Wesley, 2002).

7. See Karen Zediker, "Rediscovering the Tradition: Women's History with a Relational Approach to the Basic Public Speaking Course" (paper, Western States Communication Association, Albuquerque, New Mexico, 1993). This paper reviews the work of Christine Jorgensen-Earp, who argues that these patterns are often used by women and ethnic speakers.

8. Walter R. Fisher, "Narration as a Human Communication Paradigm: The Case of Public Moral Argument," *Communication Monographs* 51 (1984): 1–22.

9. Fisher, 8.

10. See James C. McCroskey, *An Introduction to Rhetorical Communication*, 7th ed. (Boston: Allyn and Bacon, 1997), 205–22; and Howard Gilkinson, Stanely F. Paulson, and Donald E. Sikkink, "Effects of Order and Authority in an Argumentative Speech," *Quarterly Journal of Speech* 40 (1954): 183–92.

11. George W. Bush, "Men and Women Like You Keep Us Free," *Vital Speeches of the Day* 71 (September 1, 2005): 642.

12. Carmen Mariano, "You as Teachers Are Saving the World," *Vital Speeches of the Day* 71 (October 1, 2005): 760.

13. Stephen William Hawking, *A Brief History of Time* (New York: Bantam Books, 1988), 189.

14. Richard Lamm, "Unexamined Assumptions: Destiny, Political Institutions, Democracy and Population," *Vital Speeches of the Day* 64 (September 15, 1998): 712.

15. John C. Nelson, "Uninsured Americans: A Growing Epidemic," *Vital Speeches of the Day* 71 (October 1, 2005): 749.

16. Jane Harman, "Building a Future of Hope and Prosperity," *Vital Speeches of the Day* 72 (November 1, 2005): 62.

17. Richard Lamm, "Family Friendly Institutions," *Vital Speeches of the Day* 72 (October 15, 2005): 30.

18. Martin Luther King Jr., "I Have a Dream," in *Contemporary American Speeches*, 8th ed., ed. Richard L. Johannesen, Ron R. Allen, Wilmer A. Linkugel, and J. Bryan Ferald, 369 (Dubuque, IA.: Kendall/Hunt Publishing, 1997).

19. Lowell Weicker, "Prayer in the Public Schools," in *Contemporary American Voices*, ed. James R. Andrews and David Zarefsky, 325–26 (New York: Longman, 1992).

20. Robert C. Purcell, "Values for Value: Integrity and Stewardship," *Vital Speeches of the Day* 64 (October 1, 1998): 766.

CHAPTER 10

Outlining Your Speech

CHAPTER SURVEY

Types of Outlines

Basic Principles of Outlining

CHAPTER OBJECTIVES

After studying this chapter, you should be able to:

1. Describe the different types of outlines and the purposes served by each.

2. Explain the basic principles of outlining.

3. Develop outlines as you work on a forthcoming speech.

It is easy to view outlining as an academic exercise—something that is required by the instructor, but that serves no useful purpose. Yet, by outlining, many mistakes in organizational strategy and the use of supporting material can be corrected *before* the speech is delivered. Outlines can help you sort through ideas to determine which ones work well together. Outlines can also assist you in determining whether you need to conduct additional research before you are ready to advance a persuasive argument. And outlines can enhance the effectiveness of your delivery.

Although we have chosen to discuss outlining at this point in the book, the outline is, in fact, something that develops over time as you prepare your speech. Most speakers construct a rough outline early, representing their initial thinking and ideas they would like to explore. Later, as they read widely and begin to choose some strategy of organization, the outline will grow, change, and be refined. The outline, then, *evolves* as your ideas emerge and you gather new information. Sometimes it is rearranged; often it is expanded to include more detail or support. The final formal outline will reflect your total speech preparation process.

Types of Outlines

Preview. *An outline emerges from careful preparation. Working outlines include your first thoughts; formal, full-sentence outlines contain fully developed ideas and support; and keyword outlines serve as notes for speakers.*

Although we have spoken of "the" outline, the reality is that you will use several different kinds of outlines as you prepare to speak. While no one prepares a speech in exactly the same way, outlining is a valuable tool. Through outlining, you can record your early thoughts, experiment with varied organizational strategies, consider whether evidence "fits" by visualizing the relationship between ideas and supporting material, and endeavor to improve the delivery of your speech.

Working Outlines

First, there is the working outline. This is the outline that you develop as you brainstorm and reflect on what you already know, as you investigate your topic through research, and as you continue to reflect on your emerging views. You will change the working outline many times, inserting new information and revising and rearranging main ideas and supporting points. By examining your working outline, you can see if you have given each main idea the emphasis you had intended. You can also note whether you have developed your arguments with sufficient supporting material. In short, this outline is a kind of *diagnostic tool* that helps you see where you've been and where you are going. You may choose to jot down your working outline(s) in longhand, or, if you prefer, type out your thoughts on your computer. Working outlines are for you to use as you see fit.

Formal Outlines

When you have completed your research and are moving toward the delivery of your speech, your instructor will ask you to prepare a formal outline. Usually, you will develop your outline in full sentences, and you will include a bibliography of the sources you consulted while preparing your speech. When you read through your formal outline, you will see your ideas and arguments as they are fully developed, complete with supporting material. This formal outline is a blueprint of the speech you will give.

When your instructor examines your formal outline, he or she will be able to see what you have planned and can assess whether you have

- chosen an effective organizational strategy
- achieved proper structure with coordinated thesis, main points, and transitions
- consulted sufficient sources
- developed your main ideas well

Whenever the formal outline is prepared sufficiently far in advance and submitted to critical scrutiny (either by you, a classmate, or your instructor), it can be altered and strengthened until the time you must submit it and deliver the speech. When you learn to use the outline to diagnose your own work, you will see your writing improve.

The sample outline in the *Focus on Civic Engagement* on pages 254–255 illustrates the kind of formal outline you will develop. This sort of outline serves as a tangible symbol of the time, effort, and thought you have put into your speech.

Keyword Outlines

Finally, you will typically use a keyword outline when you deliver your speech (which is recommended by most instructors). In doing so, you will transfer your outline onto note cards, using as few words as possible to represent your ideas and remind you of the main ideas you want to convey. You may want to write out a few specific things, such as transitions, statistics, and quotations—to make sure you quote them accurately. When well constructed, the keyword outline can enable you to present your speech using effective extemporaneous delivery.

Some speakers make the mistake of working painstakingly on the formal outline and then throw the keyword outline together at the last minute, without allowing sufficient time for practice. Practicing with your keyword outline will help you relax and will contribute to a smooth, conversational style of delivery. Also, if your speaking notes are not working well for you, you can revise and refine them as you practice. A specific example of a keyword outline appears in the *Focus on Civic Engagement* on page 261. You can also find another illustration of a keyword outline for a speech on Habitat for Humanity on page 307 in Chapter 12.

A speaker using carefully prepared note cards can stay in direct contact with her audience.

Job Training for the Poor: A Speech of Advocacy

CULINARY ARTS FOR SHALOM: BASED ON A PRESENTATION PREPARED FOR A COMPETITIVE GRANT

Note: The Shalom Community Center is a daytime shelter and resource center for people who are experiencing poverty and homelessness in Bloomington, Indiana. The Shalom Center also operates a hunger relief program—serving breakfast and lunch five days each week. In a typical month, Shalom provides more than 4,000 meals.

SPECIFIC PURPOSE: I want my audience to award Shalom the funding needed to establish a Culinary Arts Job Training Program.

THESIS: Creating a program that offers certification in the Culinary Arts will lead to job opportunities for many.

INTRODUCTION
ATTENTION-GETTING DEVICE

I recently met a man named Sam who was homeless for five years. He slept in his car until it was towed away. After that, he slept under a bridge. Sam's life turned around when a friend took him in and helped him find a job cooking at a small café. Sam had always liked to cook, and he soon became famous for his excellent cakes and pies. After working in the café for a couple of years, Sam went back to school and studied the culinary arts. Now, he has a job as head chef in an upscale restaurant.

You may wonder if Sam's situation is unusual. Will training in the culinary arts actually lead to good jobs?

CREDIBILITY

I believe so, and I speak from experience. I am a member of the Shalom board, where I chair the Operations Committee. For four years, I have also worked as a volunteer in the Shalom kitchen and as a job counselor in the Job Links employment program.

JUSTIFICATION

One of our greatest challenges is helping our guests find decent jobs—jobs that pay a living wage (see Ehrenreich's *Nickel and Dimed*). Oftentimes, our guests lack education, training, or certification—and this poses a huge barrier to employment. If we could provide training in an industry in which jobs are *growing*, we believe that we could make many of our guests employable. Because the restaurant industry is growing all over the country—and our community is no exception—we think it wise to begin there.

THESIS

We are convinced that creating a culinary arts job training program at Shalom will lead to job opportunities for many.

ENUMERATED PREVIEW

I'd like to begin by telling you why I think a culinary arts job-training program is right for Shalom. Then I'll describe the model we will use to develop our program and explain how we will use the grant money.

BODY

I. The restaurant industry is growing—with abundant job opportunities.
   A. Food service jobs are among the most commonly advertised in our community—in restaurants, hospitals, hotels, and schools.
      1. This past week alone, over 20 food-service ads appeared in the *Bloomington Herald Times*.
      2. Nearly 60 percent of these jobs were in traditional restaurants (i.e., *not* fast-food).
   B. In 2006, the National Restaurant Association and the Bureau of Labor Statistics predicted that employment opportunities in the restaurant industry will increase by more than two million job openings over the next seven years.

TRANSITION: Clearly restaurants need a trained workforce, and at Shalom we can help meet that need.

II. The Shalom Center is a logical place to offer training in the culinary arts.
   A. Our state-of-the-art commercial kitchen is sufficiently large and versatile to provide an effective training arena.
   B. We have partners who are interested in helping us develop and offer this kind of program.
      1. We already have an ongoing alliance with Ivy Tech Community College.
      2. The Bloomington Cooking School has agreed to offer classes.
      3. A number of local chefs have also signed on to serve as instructors and mentors.
   C. Many Shalom guests have had diverse experiences working in restaurants—as line and prep cooks, servers, and dishwashers.

TRANSITION: The training we provide will infuse our community with a high-quality workforce.

III. Our program will be available to anyone who qualifies.
    A. Candidates must be unemployed or underemployed.
    B. They must be in good physical condition.
    C. They must be drug-/substance- free.

TRANSITION: The training they receive will be first-rate.

IV. Our program will build on a successful job-training model while creating several *new* components of our own.
    A. A foundational portion of our program will be modeled after the *Second Helpings* job-training program in Indianapolis.
        1. *Second Helpings* has placed 70 percent of their graduates, and 72 percent of those remain employed six months later.
        2. Like *Second Helpings*, we will offer a food handler course that will meet the new Indiana law requirements for manager certification in the food service industry.
            a. The law requires that each establishment will employ at least one individual who is trained and certified in food safety.
            b. Our Basic Food Handler's course will be co-taught by our own culinary instructor and personnel from Ivy Tech.
    B. In addition to the Food Handler's Certification, we anticipate that the Shalom Culinary Arts Certification Program will contain a number of *new* components.
        1. A Cooking Fundamentals Component will feature special workshops led by local chefs and the Bloomington Cooking School.
        2. A Workforce Readiness Component will be offered by personnel from Work One and our own Job Links program.
        3. An Apprenticeship Component will enable those who are recently certified to receive further training in local restaurants.
        4. A Service Component will require everyone in the program to plan, prepare, and serve at least five meals to those experiencing hunger, poverty, and homelessness.
    C. The handouts we distributed show you our proposed budget and tentative timetable for developing the program.
        1. As you can see, we have already begun collaborating with our partners.

2. With the funds we receive from your foundation, we hope to establish a new administrative culinary arts position.
    a. We will hire someone who will work with our partners to develop and refine the new program.
    b. He or she will also be responsible for administering all aspects of the program, such as advertising, admissions, and testing.
3. The first students will enter the program in the summer, move through the requirements, be tested, and receive certification by the early fall.
4. After completing brief apprenticeships, graduates will be placed in area restaurants.
5. All graduates will be eligible to receive three credits toward Ivy Tech's Culinary Arts Career Development Certificate program—thus encouraging them to pursue additional education.

CONCLUSION

SUMMARY

The program we are proposing is easily within our grasp. We have the partners, the facility, and the basic program model in place. With this program, we will be able to offer valuable job training that will surely lead to employment opportunities and better lives for a number of the guests we serve.

APPEAL

Remember the story of Sam that I shared in the beginning? No longer homeless, Sam glows with pride when he talks about his job and home. He is filled with hope and optimism! It is our dream that Sam's story will become a story shared by many others here in our community. With your foundation's support, we can make it so.

BIBLIOGRAPHY

"Cooking Classes: Culinary Arts Career Development Certificate." *Ivy Tech Workforce and Economic Development Course Catalog.* (Spring 2006): 3–4.

Ehrenreich, Barbara. *Nickel and Dimed.* New York: Holt, 2001.

Kilty, K., and E. Segal. *Rediscovering the Other America: The Continuing Crisis of Poverty in the United States.* Binghamton, NY: Haworth Press, 2003.

Leonhardt, David. "U.S. Poverty Rate Was Up Last Year." *New York Times,* August 8, 2005, A1 and A14.

Second Helpings, www.secondhelpings.org (Accessed October 10, 2006).

Shalom Community Center, www.shalomcommunitycenter.org (Accessed October 23, 2006).

Basic Principles of Outlining

Preview. *A basic system of rules governs outlining. These principles identify the key components to be included in each formal outline and the use of consistent labeling through a system of universal symbols. They mandate focusing on a single idea at a time in the speech's body and coherently developing ideas with supporting material. The keyword outline has guidelines of its own, such as using words sparingly, writing out key portions, and producing legible notes.*

Although nearly all of us have drafted an outline at some point in our lives, many remain unclear about the proper way to develop a formal, full-sentence outline. Following a few simple principles will help.

Guidelines for Developing the Formal Outline

The principles that follow are not intended as petty rules. Rather, each one is aimed at getting us to think clearly about how our ideas are related, to examine the nature and extent of our supporting material, and to make sure that our ideas are coherently developed.

Include the Key Elements

The sample formal outline on pages 254–255 offers an illustration of an outline broken into clear parts. Most formal outlines should include the following components, with each clearly labeled:

- *Speech title*. If you are preparing a classroom speech, your instructor may or may not be interested in having you list a title at the top of your outline. In most other speaking situations outside the classroom, speakers are typically asked to give the program planner a speech title. This title would be placed at the top of your formal outline.
- *Specific purpose and thesis statement*. Both the specific purpose and the thesis statement should be listed at the top of the outline. Articulating your central idea and specific purpose at the very beginning allows anyone who reads your outline to discern whether your thesis is supported and your specific purpose advanced by the *way* you have organized and developed your speech. You will also want to include and label your thesis statement as part of your introduction, perhaps highlighting it with italics or bold print.
- *Introduction, body, and conclusion*. These major elements should be labeled and included in the outline. As we noted in Chapter 9, sometimes introductions and conclusions are not carefully thought out in advance. By clearly labeling them on the outline, you will be sure that they are present and well developed. It is also helpful to label the specific components of each, such as the attention-getting device, credibility step, and so forth. (Your instructor may insist that you do so.)
- *Transitions and transitional devices*. Transitions and transitional devices provide the connectives that hold the speech together and show the progression

of ideas, as well as their relationship to one another. Strong transitions help listeners follow the speech and see how the ideas advanced form a coherent whole. Writing out and labeling transitions on your formal outline will ensure that you *have* included them and given them the attention they deserve. You may also want to italicize them, so that they stand out from the rest of the text.

■ *Bibliography*. Normally a list of sources or works consulted is required at the end of a formal outline. Various forms of bibliographic citations are available for you to use. Your instructor may suggest that you use a specific guide, such as the *Chicago Manual of Style*, or the style manuals of the Modern Language Association (MLA) or the American Psychological Association (APA). For assistance with locating different bibliographic formats, visit the Web, where you will find links to the most current formats available.

Use a Consistent System

Use a consistent system of symbols and indentations. Learning a system will help you fix in your mind the relationships between ideas and supporting material that the outline represents and is important in organizing your speech into a coherent structure. These symbols also designate for your instructor the various components of your speech, facilitating diagnosis and enabling precise feedback. Figure 10.1 illustrates how the system looks when outlining the body of the speech. As with most speeches, some ideas are more fully developed than others—depending on the speaker's assumptions about the relative importance of each idea and the extent to which each needs to be explained or illustrated.

Figure 10.1

Outline Form for the Body of the Speech

I. MAIN IDEA
  A. First main subpoint
    1. Support for this subpoint
      a. First piece of specific information
      b. Second piece of specific information
    2. Additional support for this subpoint
  B. Second main subpoint
    1. First supporting statement
    2. Second supporting statement
      a. Specific information
      b. More specific information
        (1) Very detailed support
        (2) More detailed support
      c. More specific information

  C. Third main subpoint
    1. First supporting statement
    2. Second supporting statement
II. SECOND MAIN IDEA
  A. First main subpoint
    1. First supporting statement
    2. Second supporting statement
  B. Second main subpoint
    1. Support for this subpoint
      a. First piece of specific information
      b. Second piece of specific information
    2. Second supporting statement
III. THIRD MAIN IDEA
And so forth . . .

Focus on a Single Idea

Each main point in the body of your outline should contain only one idea. Here is a poor example:

I. Becoming media literate is important since so much information is communicated through the news; yet, we have many excuses for avoiding watching the news.

This example is poor because it contains several different ideas in a single statement. Following is an improved example that conforms to the first principle:

I. Most of us avoid watching the news.
   A. Viewership of TV news has declined dramatically.
   B. Young people, in particular, have "tuned out."
II. People give a number of reasons for avoiding the news.
   A. Many people feel that the news is too negative.
   B. Others argue that there's simply too much information to take in—and they feel overwhelmed by it.
   C. Still others are cynical—believing that much of the news has been "managed" or "manipulated" in some way.

Notice the clarity and simplicity that results as we focus on a single idea per statement. This simplification will assist you as a writer, and it will also assist your listeners, helping them process your message better and retain it.

Coherently Develop Ideas and Supporting Material

Your outline should accurately reflect relationships between ideas and supporting material. The main ideas are listed with roman numerals, the subpoints that support those ideas with capital letters, the material that develops the subpoints with arabic numbers, the support for these with lowercase letters, and a final level with numbers in parentheses. See Figure 10.1 for a skeletal illustration of proper outlining form.

The outline thus becomes a *visual representation* of the supporting relationships between ideas and evidence. By examining your outline carefully, you should be able to discern whether the supporting material actually works to develop, support, or elaborate on your main ideas. Consider the following poor example:

I. Negativity and cynicism stand in our way of becoming media literate.
   A. There is a difference between an "informed" citizen and an "informational" citizen.
   B. Media gatekeepers make it challenging for anyone to become media literate.
   C. Much of the information we must process from the media is cognitive, based on facts.
   D. There are several steps we can take to improve our media literacy.

Any one of these ideas could be explored on its own. But they clearly do not fit together, nor do they advance the main point (that negativity and skepticism stand in the way of media literacy). Subpoint A offers a definition of an informed citizen while B explores one of the media literacy challenges. Subpoint C introduces a model of media literacy development, and the final subpoint addresses actions to be taken to improve media literacy.

Here is a better approach to this outline:

I. Becoming media literate requires us to develop our ability to think discerningly in several areas.
   A. According to scholar James Potter, we must be able to evaluate facts—separating false information from that which is valid and reliable—using our *cognitive* ability.
   B. Potter argues that we must also understand the *emotional impact* that visual images and moving language can have on our ability to think critically.
   C. Finally, Potter insists that we must strive to separate "art from artificiality"—becoming more capable of dealing with the *aesthetic dimension* of information.[1]
II. Media scholar Carla Johnson outlines several specific steps we can take to enhance our media literacy.
   A. First, we can develop an *awareness* of how media may be influencing us.
   B. Next, we must exercise our "critical reading/viewing" skills.
   C. We must also reflect on the political, social, economic, and cultural *context* in which information is presented.
   D. Finally, we can exercise media advocacy by calling or writing to those who control the media to express our concerns.[2]

As you can see, these subordinate points serve to illuminate the main ideas they support. Thus, each of the main ideas is coherently developed. Of course, in a completed formal outline, each of these subpoints would also include more specific development through concise explanations, examples, and so forth.

The *Focus on Civic Engagement* presents a fully developed outline that illustrates these principles of formal outlining.

When the speaker delivered his speech of advocacy, he did not use the formal outline as his speaking notes. It is far too detailed and would have distracted him from the audience. Instead, he prepared the keyword outline shown in the *Focus on Civic Engagement* on page 261, which he used to make sure that he did not forget any major points but which did not restrict his ability to stay in contact with the audience.

The Keyword Outline: Some Special Considerations

Many speakers make the mistake of trying to deliver their speech from their formal outline. But these outlines are too cumbersome. Using them will likely tempt the speaker to read each sentence instead of speaking more directly with the audience.

However, there is nothing magic about transferring one's formal outline onto note cards. We have seen speakers who demonstrate their expertise for putting an entire formal outline onto small note cards, using cramped writing, and sometimes using both sides of the cards. Using note cards, then, may or may not generate a useful set of speaking notes. Following some simple guidelines will help.

Use Words Sparingly

When you create the notes from which you will speak, you should try to write out as *little* as possible so that you will not be tempted to read your notes and risk losing contact with your listeners. Certainly it makes sense to write out and read direct quotations and specific statistical information, but you will stay focused on the audience if you have practiced enough so that you do not need to rely on your notes too much.

Write Out Key Portions of the Speech

Even though you do not want to use excessive speaking notes, you may want to write out transitions and other key portions of your speech to ensure accuracy. When we are delivering a speech, we are most likely to forget what comes next when we finish discussing one idea and are ready to move on to the next one. Writing out transitions serves as a memory prompt and will help you emphasize *how* your ideas are connected in the minds of your listeners. You may also wish to write out *parts* of your introduction and conclusion, such as a preview and summary, as well as statistics and quotations appearing anywhere in the speech. In fact, when a speaker reads statistics or directly quoted material from a note card, he or she is demonstrating to the audience a concern for accuracy and precision.

Notes that are used correctly allow the speaker to feel confident that he will keep on track with his speech while still staying in touch with the listeners.

Strive for Legible Notes

You will want to make sure that you can easily read your notes, so print or write neatly and boldly. If you prepare your notes on a computer, use large font (14 point or larger) and emphasize important words in bold. Leave adequate space between points. Follow the basic format of your formal outline.

Avoid cramming too much onto any one card. You may want to use four-by-six rather than three-by-five note cards, so that you can put more notes on each card and reduce the total number needed. Write on only one side of the card, to avoid card turning and possible confusion. Number your cards and, of course, practice several times until you are comfortable with your speaking notes. Refer to Chapter 12 for more specific guidelines on how to practice and use speaking notes.

Give Yourself Delivery Hints

When presenting your speech, it is easy to get caught up in following your notes and end up forgetting to deliver your remarks as effectively as possible. During practice, you will probably realize that you have to guard against certain tendencies, such as speaking too rapidly, forgetting to move, or failing to look around the room to include all your listeners. In the margins of your notes, then, you may want to jot down delivery reminders, such as "Pause Here," or "Slow Down!!"

Consider Your Options

Some speakers prefer to use a sheet of paper instead of note cards for their keyword outline. When using note cards, you can easily carry them with you as you speak, gesturing and moving with ease. However, you *do* have to coordinate moving from card to card. If you use a sheet of paper, you can see the entire outline at a glance, but you will probably need to rest the outline on a table or podium because carrying it around while you speak may look awkward and restrict your gestures. Practice with each method to see which you prefer, and seek guidance from your instructor.

Use Speaking Notes Openly

Unless you have been asked to deliver your speech from memory (which is a rare occurrence), feel free to consult your keyword outline openly as you speak. Hold your cards comfortably or place your full sheet of notes on the podium. Look at your notes as needed, and read from them whenever you are trying to quote precisely. Avoid staring at your notes, however, out of nervousness or to avoid looking at the audience. The purpose in having a keyword outline is to encourage as much connection between you and your listeners as possible.

The *Focus on Civic Engagement* presents a keyword outline, based on the formal outline presented below.

Focus on Civic Engagement

A Keyword Outline for a Speech of Advocacy

INTRODUCTION

SHARE STORY OF SAM—leads to question, "Will training in the culinary arts actually lead to good job?"

SHARE PERSONAL BACKGROUND at   `Eye contact!`
Shalom, working with Job Links

JUSTIFY TOPIC—need to find jobs that pay a living wage in a growing industry (refer to Ehrenreich's *Nickel and Dimed*).

THESIS
We are convinced that creating a culinary arts job-training program at Shalom will lead to job opportunities for many.

PREVIEW

- I'll explain that this job-training program is right for Shalom
- Describe what the model will look like   `Slow down here!`
- Explain how we will use the grant money

BODY

I. Restaurant industry is growing—with lots of job opportunities.
- 20 food service job ads in *HT* during past week
- 60% in traditional restaurants, schools, hospitals, etc.—not fast-food
- National Restaurant Assoc. and Bureau of Labor stats—2 million jobs predicted over 7 years

(continues)

Focus on Civic Engagement *(continued)*

TRANSITION: Clearly, restaurants need a trained workforce, and at Shalom, we can help meet that need. `Might move here`

II. Shalom Center—logical place to meet the need.
 • Has state-of-the-art commercial kitchen
 • Partnerships already formed—Ivy Tech, Cooking School, local chefs
 • Shalom guests—cooking backgrounds common

TRANSITION: The training we provide will infuse our community with a high-quality workforce.

III. Program available to anyone who qualifies:
 • Unemployed or underemployed
 • Good physical condition
 • Drug/substance free

TRANSITION: The training they receive will be first-rate.

IV. Our program built on successful *Second Helpings* model in Indy
 • Program places 70% of grads, with high retention rate (72%)
 • Like *SH*, we will offer a food handler course `Watch speed!`
  • New Indiana requirement
  • Course co-taught by Ivy Tech faculty, plus our own instructor

• New components in our program!
 • Cooking Fundamentals `Show enthusiasm!!`
 • Workforce Readiness
 • Apprenticeship
 • Service
• See handouts for budget and timetable for program development
 • Collaboration with partners ongoing
 • With grant money, will hire new administrator/teacher
 • Early summer through late fall, then apprenticeships and placement
 • Grads receive 3 credits toward Ivy Tech program

CONCLUSION

SUMMARY
• Program within our grasp—have partners, facility, and model in place
• Can offer valuable job training—enriching lives of guests and benefiting the greater community `Eye contact!`

APPEAL
• Refer to Sam's story—no longer homeless, filled with hope!
• Others can share this story—with your foundation's support!

Taken together, these outlining tools assist speakers throughout the speech preparation and delivery process. The working outline helps as the speaker begins to brainstorm, conduct research, and think through how best to approach the subject. The full-sentence outline reveals the final product—showing how well each main idea is articulated, developed, and supported, as well as how ideas are arranged and balanced. Finally, the keyword outline provides an aid to delivery, serving as a confidence booster while keeping the speaker on track.

Summary

■ As you prepare yourself to speak, an outline will begin to emerge.

■ Outlining is important as a diagnostic tool, as well as a visual representation of your speech.

- You will use different types of outlines:
  - Working outlines incorporate preliminary thoughts.
  - Full-sentence outlines contain fully developed ideas and support.
  - Keyword outlines typically serve as speaking notes.
- As you craft your formal outline, you should:
  - include and label key elements (such as the introduction, body, and conclusion, transitions, and bibliography)
  - use a consistent set of symbols and indentations
  - make sure that each point contains only one idea
  - coherently develop ideas and supporting material
- A keyword outline is used in delivering your speech. It should:
  - usually, be written on note cards (with other options possible)
  - use words sparingly
  - include a few extended quotations and statistics
  - be written legibly
  - include delivery prompts
  - be used openly
- When the audience perceives your speech as well planned and structured, they will be more likely to view you, the speaker, as a credible source of information and a person whose ideas and proposed initiatives are worthy of their consideration.

QUESTIONS FOR REVIEW AND REFLECTION

1. What are the different kinds of outlines, and what purposes does each serve?
2. What are the main components that need to be labeled and included in a formal outline? Why is each important?
3. Why is it important to restrict each point in the outline to a single idea?
4. How does the outline reflect relationships between ideas and supporting material?
5. How does the use of a consistent system of outlining symbols and indentation help make these relationships clear?
6. What are the most important guidelines to remember when preparing speaking notes?

ENDNOTES

1. See W. James Potter, *Media Literacy*, 3rd ed. (Thousand Oaks, CA: Sage Publications, 2005).
2. See Carla Johnson, *Screened Out: How the Media Control Us and What We Can Do about It* (Armonk, NY: M. E. Sharpe, 2000).

Using Language Effectively

CHAPTER OBJECTIVES

After studying this chapter, you should be able to:

1. Discuss the symbolic nature of language.

2. Make more effective language choices.

3. Use language that is interesting and engaging for listeners.

4. Choose language that is ethical and appropriate to the situation.

5. Explain how "style" can influence listeners' responses.

Style is a difficult term to define, partly because we use it in so many different ways. If we say a person has style, we may mean that the person dresses well, sings in a unique voice, or plays basketball with a special flair. In that situation, the context of our remark will clarify what we mean when we say that a person has style. When we talk about a speaker's style, however, we mean something different. We still might mean that, in a general sense, they have a pleasing style of speaking—that is, they project a good image, use language, movement, and gestures well, or relate to the audience effectively. But in the ancient tradition of rhetorical theory, style has a more specific meaning: *style is the use of language in oral presentations.*

This chapter focuses on this more specific meaning of style: how you choose the language for your speech and the effects of those choices on your overall success as a speaker. We will begin by discussing the connections between language and meaning, keeping in mind that the speaker who wants to use clear language must begin with clear thinking. If you first develop a clear grasp of the ideas you hope to communicate, it will be much easier for you to find the right language to get your message across. Then we will discuss how to choose language that is clear, interesting, effective, and appropriate to the particular situation. By the end of the chapter, you should have a better sense of the importance of style and what you can do to improve your style as a public speaker.

Language and Meaning

Preview. *Speaking style is fundamentally concerned with how the speaker chooses to use language. When crafting a speech, it is critical to use what you know about your audience to choose appropriate language. The language you choose has the potential to influence listeners through its symbolic power and explicit and implicit meanings. Your choices can help you connect with listeners or can create barriers and misunderstandings.*

One thing that is often difficult for speakers to appreciate is that they and their listeners do not always speak exactly the same language. All of us may speak English, but we do not choose and use language in the same ways. We may come from different backgrounds that provide us with different words or different meanings for words. Regional uses of English, ethnic uses of language, and generational variations in language can be confusing to those outside a particular linguistic group. When your grandmother talks about going out to purchase a CD, for example, she is probably planning to go to the bank to get a certificate of deposit, not to the local music shop to purchase a compact disc. Of course, such "different languages" can cause problems in many areas. As we pointed out earlier in our chapter on audience analysis, the demographics of an audience will influence how listeners respond. As you prepare to speak, it is also important to recognize that language is a symbol system that allows for a variety of meanings.

The Symbolic Nature of Language

Words are symbols. They are abstractions that allow us to talk about persons, places, things, actions, and ideas without providing every detail. The more abstract our words, the more details we omit. Abstractness makes it possible to communicate more easily; it allows us to manipulate great chunks of the world verbally without getting bogged down in details. It permits us to talk about the past and the future, and things that are absent. It allows us to conceptualize ideas—such as love, honor, and beauty—that may lie beyond concrete experience. Yet using too many abstract words can also cause problems in communication.

As we speak more abstractly, ideas can become more and more difficult to grasp, and the chances of misunderstandings or varied interpretations increase. When we talk about significant issues, abstraction can cause us to assume meanings that are not necessarily shared by our audience. If a speaker describes a course of action as the "patriotic thing to do," how we respond will depend on what "patriotism" means to us. Some, for example, believed that they were being patriotic by supporting the War in Iraq; others believed that it was their patriotic duty to protest against a war that they consider wrongheaded and dangerous. Similarly, some might assume that "supporting our troops" means sending them care packages or letters of encouragement, while for others the best way to support our troops is to bring them home to their friends and families.

Abstractions are a powerful source of personal identity. We live in a diverse country, made up of people of many different cultural and social backgrounds. The word *American*, for example, can apply to all of us, but it is also an abstraction that can be variously interpreted. Consider how listeners might have responded differently when former secretary of state Colin Powell used the word *American* in a speech to the National Volunteer Summit. Urging his listeners to work toward the day when everyone would live the "American Dream," Powell appealed to the widespread belief that America was especially blessed by a "Divine Providence." He also invoked the principle that we must all be "good stewards of each other":

> Let us make sure that no child in America is left behind, no child in America has their dream deferred or denied. We can do it. We can do it because we are Americans. We are Americans who draw our strength from this place. We are Americans who believe to the depth of our hearts that this is not a land that was placed here by historic accident, it is a land that was put here by Divine Providence who told us to be good stewards of our land, but especially to be good stewards of each other. Divine Providence gave us this land, blessed it and told us always to be proud to call it America. And so we go forward. Let us go save our children.[1]

Powell's use of abstractions was broad enough so that many people with different specific convictions could agree with his statement. Yet people with different backgrounds may have had different views of what it meant to be an "American," and people of differing religious beliefs may have reacted differently to his reference to "Divine Providence."

Sometimes speakers exploit abstract terms to encourage listeners to endorse their ideas without seriously considering what lies beneath their abstractions. Most of us favor "family values," for example, but Republicans and Democrats often disagree over which policies best promote those values. Similarly, we may all agree that accountability in government is good, or that we should all be responsible citizens.

But what it means to be accountable or responsible may vary from person to person. When a speaker uses such abstract words, details are lost and differences may be glossed over.

Perhaps, for example, you have heard a political candidate claim that we need a "safety net" to protect the poorest and most disadvantaged among us. Does that mean that we need more government spending on social services? Or should we encourage private charities to close the gap as we reduce government spending? The vigilant listener will ask questions of the speaker to clarify the meaning of vague or abstract terms and will search for clues as to how abstractions might translate into concrete policies. Being aware of the symbolic nature of language and its potential pitfalls is important for both speakers and listeners if they are to engage in a meaningful and mutually beneficial dialogue.

Denotative and Connotative Meaning

While meaning may vary according to the understanding we bring to specific words, many common meanings are generally held; if this were not so, we could hardly communicate at all. The meanings of words can generally be divided into two groups: denotative and connotative meaning. Denotative meaning refers to the literal, objective meaning of words stripped of any emotional baggage they may carry. These meanings tend to be more objective and less susceptible to a wide variety of interpretations. Often denotative meanings describe the relationship between a word and some object to which it refers. For example, the denotative meaning of pencil is "a writing implement consisting of a thin rod of graphite or similar substance encased in wood or held in a plastic or metal mechanical device." Its meaning is relatively objective; there are likely no personal interpretations and feelings involved. When we hear the word *pencil*, few of us feel fear, joy, or anger.

Connotative meanings, by contrast, derive from the emotional implications of words and suggest a range of subjective and personal interpretations, depending on the listener. Many words have both denotative and connotative meanings. Many words in our culture carry strong connotations because of their association with events or political controversies. For many U.S. citizens, words like *terrorist, traitor,* or *un-American* carry strong connotations because they automatically provoke feelings of fear, hostility, or even hatred.

Connotative meaning is infused into language by the context in which words appear and by the perceptions of the listener. Nonetheless, in our society, some words seem to be more emotionally charged than others: *mother, honor, free enterprise, racist,* and *neo-Nazi* are just a few examples. All of these words are liable to conjure up a wide variety of intense personal responses.

During a congressional campaign, pollsters for a political action group conducted focus groups to determine connotative responses to certain words. They issued a pamphlet suggesting "good" words for candidates they supported to use in their campaigns, and "bad" words to use when discussing their opponents. Figure 11.1 lists some of the words candidates were urged to use in letters, speeches, and ads, labeled "Optimistic." The "bad" words, labeled "Contrasting," were to be used when referring to an opponent's "record, proposals and party."[2] If you examine

Figure 11.1

Optimistic		Contrasting	
common sense	passionate	anti-child	greed
courage	pioneer	anti-flag	hypocrisy
dream	pride	betray	incompetent
duty	principle(d)	cheat	lie
empowerment	pro-environment	collapse	radical
fair	prosperity	corruption	self-serving
family	reform	crisis	shallow
freedom	rights	decay	steal
hard work	strength	destroy	taxes
liberty	truth	devour	traitors
moral	"workfare"	failure	welfare

Source: "Language: A Key Mechanism of Control," from, *Power Persuasion: Moving An Ancient Art into the Media*, by Cooper and Williams. © 1992 by Educational Video Group. Used by permission.

these words closely, you'll see that the "optimistic" words all evoke positive feelings and associations, while the "contrasting" words are meant to raise fears, anxieties, disapproval, or discomfort. Thoughtful speakers and listeners will understand the evocative power of such words and will look beyond immediate, surface reactions to their connotative meanings.

As speakers, we all should heighten our sensitivity to language. Not only must you understand the symbolic nature of language, you should also realize that your language choices will not automatically suggest the same meanings to every listener. Nor will your language necessarily be understood by listeners unless you strive to make yourself clear. Clarity of language must be considered along with the symbolic power of language if you hope to communicate effectively.

Using Language That Is Clear and Accurate

Preview. *The most profound idea, clever remark, or astute observation will have little impact if your listeners cannot grasp it. Clear speakers use language familiar to their audience. They also speak with specificity, concreteness, precision, and clarity. Finally, they avoid the use of clichés, empty words, and distracting language, and they construct their sentences with a concern for good oral style.*

As you consider the ways in which language choices help you connect with your audience, keep in mind that oral style and written style are not the same. In most situations, you will use less formal, more conversational language in speeches than you do in written manuscripts. A good oral style is more informal, simpler, and more repetitious than a written style. Also—and this is very important—oral style is more spontaneous. It allows you the flexibility to adapt your language as you speak. In this chapter, we encourage you to make careful and effective language choices. But if you plan to deliver your speech extemporaneously, you probably will not write out every single word of your speech in advance. Rather, you will need to choose appropriate language as you speak.

Also keep in mind that a speech delivered orally is received very differently from a written presentation. If you are reading a page and come across difficult or unfamiliar words, you can always stop, reread the passage, and try to figure out the meaning of the word from the context. Or you can put down the book altogether and consult a dictionary. Indeed, a good book often challenges readers to learn new words and expand their knowledge of the language. But a speech is a different matter.

When you are giving a speech, your listeners cannot stop you and ask you to repeat an unfamiliar word. Nor can they whip out the dictionary and look up a word that they did not understand. As speakers, we need to be sensitive to the differences between oral and written communication and do all we can to achieve clarity and understanding. If our speaking is to be meaningful, we must make sure that what we say is *instantly* intelligible.

Familiar Language

One of the most important things you can do is to use words familiar to the audience. Most of the great speakers in our history did not use big, pompous, important-sounding words. Rather, they used simple, direct language that listeners could easily grasp. In one of Abraham Lincoln's greatest speeches, given when he was nominated for the United States Senate in 1858, for example, he put his suspicions of the power of the slaveholders and their allies into clear, unequivocal words. He began with a simple and familiar biblical phrase:

> 'A house divided against itself can not stand.' I believe this government can not endure permanently half slave and half free. I do not expect the Union to be dissolved—I do not expect the house to fall—but I do expect it will cease to be divided. It will become all one thing or all the other. Either the opponents of slavery will arrest the further spread of it, and place it where the public mind shall rest in the belief that it is in the course of ultimate extinction; or its advocates will push it forward till it shall become alike lawful in all the states, old as well as new—North as well as South.[3]

Nothing in the language of this passage would have been puzzling to listeners. Every single word was familiar to Lincoln's audience. The same is true of the next example. In a speech a senior student gave to incoming freshman at her university, she described the many opportunities to become involved in significant projects and activities outside the classroom. In her introduction, she used familiar language to get her audience to look at an ordinary phrase in a different way, and to lead into her suggestions for how to get the most out of their college experience:

> "Multitasking" is something that all of us know a lot about. If you were like me when I was in high school, you could listen to music and do your homework at

the same time. You could listen to your Mom or Dad while text messaging a friend—even though your parent kept asking you, "Are you listening to me?'—and not miss a beat. Well, you can keep on multitasking now that you're in college, but if you're going to get the most out of your four years here, you're going to have to think about what "tasking" means. If it means playing computer games far into the night while blasting your favorite tunes into your headset and then sleeping through your morning class, or if it means setting off with your fake ID on Thursday night to begin a long party weekend, your stay here might be one year and not four. This kind of "tasking" is not a very good choice if you have any intention of living in the real world when you graduate. Today, I want to talk about a different kind of "multitasking" that you can do at this university by exploring how you can better prepare yourself to be a productive, useful contributor to your community and—and this is a very important "and"—and a happy, satisfied person.

Since the familiarity of the words you use is important to the clarity of your speech, it is important that you learn as much as you can about your audience's education and vocabulary. Then you will be able to better choose the language most suitable to them.

Technical Language

You need to remember that listeners may not know the meaning of technical words. It is perfectly appropriate to use technical language in a speech to a specialized audience who will understand it. But, in a speech addressed to a general audience, you should never use language that excludes people who lack technical expertise. If you do employ technical terms, it is your job to define them for listeners who may not have the knowledge or training to understand their precise meaning. In a ceremony dedicating the Earth and Planetary Sciences Building at Washington University in St. Louis, for example, John McDonnell, former CEO of the aerospace company McDonnell Douglas, defined "paleo-environmental reconstruction" for an audience unfamiliar with the term:

> And there is a third group in the department interested in what is called "paleo-environmental reconstruction." They are looking at major environmental changes that occurred long ago in different parts of the earth. Rather than desert, Egypt, for instance, was once a wet environment. What caused it to change, and what can we do better today to enhance the sustainability of a wet and fertile environment? The same set of questions applies to changes in climate, viewed from both a geologic and a present-day perspective.[4]

If you use terms that are not readily understandable to your listeners, you have a responsibility to define and explain them in ways that your audience can comprehend.

Abbreviations and Acronyms

The same is true, of course, of technical or specialized abbreviations or substitutions for longer words or titles. The best example of this is the acronym, which is a series of letters that stand for some longer name or title. Few may know that "RFID" stands for "radio frequency identification," a technology used in tracking drugs to insure they are not tampered with. But even more common acronyms may need a quick explanation. Anyone who is interested in broadcasting will know that the FCC stands for the Federal Communications Commission, but others in your audience may not be familiar with this acronym. College students all know what a GPA is, but persons not associated with the university may not know this shorthand for grade-point average. As speakers, we need to be conscious of the fact that our language grows out of our experience and knowledge and sometimes needs to be translated for listeners.

Concreteness and Specificity

Words chosen for their concreteness and specificity increase clarity. Compare the two brief passages below from students' speeches given on related topics.

Student #1: The tragedy of civil war falls heavily on women and children. They are displaced from their homes and suffer so many hardships from disease and injuries. They have the most primitive medical care in the large refugee camps and are attacked by lawless militias. It is hard to imagine the hardships they must endure.

Student #2: Women and children are the innocent victims of civil wars raging in Africa. Life in the refugee camps is a constant struggle to get enough food to survive. Lack of clean water and proper sanitation means that diseases like cholera spread rapidly, and diarrhea is rampant. Those who stray just a few feet outside the camp may be attacked by militiamen wielding machetes. It is not uncommon to see children lying, glassy-eyed, on makeshift beds, with missing limbs and flies swarming over the wounds.

The second passage is clearly more moving. "Hardships" are specified; the results of the "attacks" are made real through the choice of concrete language that helps listeners visualize the enormity of the situation.

Precise Language

Mark Twain once observed that there is no such thing as a synonym; he admonished writers to seek the right word, not its "second cousin." Twain's advice is also good for public speakers. Precise words are important because they allow us to communicate our meaning as accurately as possible.

If you wanted to describe someone walking down the street, how would you do it? Specifically, what verbs would you choose? This would depend entirely on the kind of image you wanted to create. If you wanted to portray the person as being in a hurry, you might use verbs such as *raced, hustled,* or *hurried.* But each of these is different. Which is faster? Which is more informal? To take a different example, suppose you wanted to describe a negative feeling about something. You might say you *disliked* it, but if you felt more strongly, you might choose a verb such as *hated, detested,* or *loathed.* Which conveys the most accurate description of your feeling? In general, you will be more effective with your language if you choose words precisely.

Consider these sentences from student speeches as originally given and as revised to convey more precisely the point the speaker wishes to make:

Original: Many troops have been hurt by these homemade bombs.
Revised: Young American men and women serving in Iraq have been killed or maimed by roadside bombs.

Original: Homeless persons increasingly run the risk of random violence.
Revised: People who live in the street have been subjected to beatings with baseball bats; they've been kicked, stabbed, punched, and even killed for no reason other than they're easy targets, and their assailants like to beat up "bums."

Not only do carefully chosen words enhance meaning and promote clarity, they also contribute to the kind of specificity we discussed above, thus heightening the impact of your message.

Avoiding Clichés, Empty Words, and Distracting Language

Effective public speakers avoid using clichés—trite, overused expressions. At one time, these expressions were probably fresh and interesting. "The bottom line" conveys a clear enough meaning, but the phrase has been used so much that it does not show any originality and may have lost its precise meaning: the total cost of something. Because of overuse, clichés are tired and lifeless, and they are less likely to engage listeners' thoughts and hold their interest.

It is also important to avoid empty words—those that add nothing but length to your sentences. For instance, why say "a number of," when you can say "several" or "many"? You might say "because" instead of "due to the fact that," "after" instead of "subsequent to," "about" rather than "in connection with," and "I must" instead of "it will be necessary for me to."

Even though we might think of a speaking situation as an enlarged conversation, there *are* stylistic differences between the two. A conversation is more interactive. We don't always finish sentences, we may be interrupted from time to time, or others in the conversation may verbalize reactions. Casual conversations are often littered with unnecessary language that may be acceptable in that setting but not in a public speaking situation. You might say to a friend that "he was, like, very tall and, you know, well built." But "like" and "you know" only clutters a public speech and should be avoided.

If you can avoid empty words, clichés, and distracting language in your speaking, you will say more, say it more efficiently, and speak more clearly. And your audience will benefit through greater knowledge and understanding.

Constructing Sentences to Promote Clarity

Individual words must be clear, and so should sentences. Construct sentences with well-chosen words, but arrange those words so that the sentences they form are direct and easy to follow.

For good oral style, craft sentences so that the subject and the verb are close together. This makes the sentence easier to understand, and it sounds more natural. Consider the following sentence, in which the subject and verb have been separated: "This new program, which has been tried at other colleges similar to our own and has been enormously popular, is worthy of your support." Surely the sentence would be more understandable if it were reworked to say: "This program is worthy of your support. Other colleges like our own have tried it, and it has been enormously popular."

Repetition and Restatement

Speakers may have to repeat certain words, phrases, or ideas to make them stick in listeners' minds. Repetition is especially effective when the speaker wants the audience to remember specific, vivid, or especially meaningful words or phrases. You may wish to use restatement if you want to emphasize or clarify an idea by discussing it in several different ways. Of course, speakers should not overuse these devices. When used carefully, however, they can help you reinforce main ideas and make important expressions memorable.

Perhaps one of the most famous uses of repetition was in a speech given by Winston Churchill in the early days of World War II. In refusing to consider negotiating with the enemy, Churchill told the House of Commons, "We shall defend our island, whatever the cost may be. We shall fight on the beaches. We shall fight on the landing grounds. We shall fight in the fields and in the streets, and we shall fight in the hills. We shall never surrender."[5]

Through the simple device of repeating a phrase at the end of each example, one student speaker reinforced his contention that all of us are contributing money to large corporations for foolish or wasteful projects:

> Let's take a look at someone like Lockheed Martin, a defense manufacturer. They received only a paltry twenty-five thousand dollars in a tax write-off in 1996. But what did the tax write-off come for? Entertainment expenses that were grounded in twenty thousand dollars' worth of golf balls. That's your tax money at work! Then we have the Walt Disney Corporation, a company whose profits are over one billion dollars per year. They received a $300,000 federal subsidy in order to research bigger and better fireworks for their theme parks. That's your tax money at work! But probably the biggest and most insulting federal subsidy of all that I came across happened between 1990 and 1994, when General Motors received $110.6 million in federal technological subsidies under the auspices of a jobs program. During that time period, their profits skyrocketed. And what happened? They laid off 104,000 of their workers—twenty-five percent of their U.S. workforce. That's your tax money at work!

Short, Concise Sentences

In an oral style, you also should keep sentences relatively short. Shorter sentences are easier for listeners to follow. Also avoid needless repetition, unnecessary modifiers, and circumlocutions, such as, "The reason why I think this plan will work is because . . ." Instead, say "This plan will work because . . ." One way to eliminate unnecessary words is to use the active voice. Consider the following examples:

> "Great frustration with the lack of progress in the war has been expressed by the Administration's critics." (*passive voice, too wordy*)

"Administration critics have expressed frustration with the lack of progress in the war." (*active voice*)

"It has been argued by those who are advocates of free speech that the Patriot Act has had a chilling effect on dissident groups who oppose government policies." (*passive voice, too wordy*)

"Free speech activists argue that the Patriot Act discourages dissident groups from opposing government policy." (*active voice*)

Modifiers

It is best to use only necessary modifiers. There are two kinds of modifiers: those that comment and those that define. Commenting modifiers include *very, most*, and *definitely*. These modifiers tell us nothing new; instead they try to boost the meaning of the word they modify. Yet, if you select your words precisely, they should be able to stand alone without the assistance of such modifiers. Saying that the president is "very, very seriously worried" about the Iraq situation adds little to the statement that the president is "seriously worried." Raising the question, Are you better off now than you were four years ago? is not improved at all by asking, Are you definitely better off now than you were four years ago?

By contrast, defining modifiers provide information that the noun standing alone cannot convey. They tell us something we need to know. It is informative to know that a policy is supported by a *narrow majority* of voters, or that the govern-

In urging passage of the Voting Rights Act of 1965, President Johnson used simple, direct, and forceful language to demand justice for African Americans.

ment has a *contingency* plan to deal with the Avian Flu. Modifiers also are used to color audience perceptions; depending on whether an idea is described as innovative, brilliant, outdated, or preposterous, listeners will respond to it quite differently.

Simplicity

Simple and precise words and sentences help contribute to active speech. Consider, for example, the way President Lyndon Johnson urged members of Congress to support him in passing the Voting Rights Act of 1965. When Johnson delivered this speech at a joint session of Congress, the United States was engulfed in great racial turmoil. In Alabama, bloody confrontations between police and civil rights protesters (both black and white) were regularly televised. In the United States, the rhetorical climate was one of great tension and urgency. In the following passage, there are no exceptional or unusual words and there are no particularly striking sentence constructions, but the clarity and forcefulness of the language suggest action.

> The bill I am presenting to you will be known as a civil rights bill.
>
> But in a larger sense, most of the program I am recommending is a civil rights program. Its object is to open the city of hope to all people of all races, because all Americans just must have the right to vote, and we are going to give them that right.
>
> All Americans must have the privileges of citizenship, regardless of race, and they are going to have those privileges of citizenship regardless of race.
>
> But I would like to caution you and remind you that to exercise these privileges takes much more than just legal right. It requires a trained mind and a healthy body. It requires a decent home and the chance to find a job and the opportunity to escape from the clutches of poverty.
>
> Of course people cannot contribute to the nation if they are never taught to read or write; if their bodies are stunted from hunger; if their sickness goes untended; if their life is spent in hopeless poverty, just drawing a welfare check.
>
> So we want to open the gates to opportunity. But we're also going to give all our people, black and white, the help that they need to walk through those gates."[5]

Apart from the ideas that are discussed, language can have a force of its own. When used to promote interest, it can help make a speech more persuasive and effective.

Using Language That Is Interesting

Preview. *As speakers, we can keep listeners interested by using active language—language that is lively and vivid—and figures of speech. We can also use rhetorical questions and parallelism to promote audience interest and identification with the topic.*

Even if a speaker's language is clear—so that listeners understand the main ideas or arguments—that language may fail to move them unless it is also compelling. Gaining and maintaining listeners' interest is essential if the speaker is to achieve the desired response. When speakers use language that stimulates the listeners' imagination, offers memorable images, and is pleasing to the ear, they will have a better chance of also engaging their minds and hearts.

Using Active, Vivid Language

Action holds interest and commands attention. The way we choose language and the way we put it together can create a type of action for our listeners. We can create the illusion of action and help listeners understand more precisely what we have in mind in several ways.

Language promotes a feeling of action when it is lively. Language that gives a realistic and specific description of events, people, and ideas is the liveliest. Further, listeners' emotions are often engaged through the use of vivid descriptions of pleasant or unpleasant situations. In Chapter 8, we noted that telling a story about real people tends to promote identification between the audience and the subject. The simple narrative can make us feel ashamed or angry or experience a host of other emotions.

Montel, a public speaking student, began a speech by describing an automobile accident in vivid detail. He explained how the victims of the accident were rushed to the nearest hospital and how one of the victims was examined very quickly, put on a stretcher, and left in a hallway unattended. He described the patient's deteriorating condition as the hours passed, and how doctors and nurses hurried by, some occasionally stopping for a quick look and then going on. As he told the story, the sense of frustration, surprise, and anger in the audience was apparent. Everyone wondered why on earth something wasn't being done for that patient. Montel concluded his story by explaining that the accident, which took place several years ago, involved a black woman who had been taken to a hospital in a predominantly white neighborhood. The example was so vivid and the emotions so real that the speaker had little more to do to finish his speech on the evils of racism.

In using vivid language, speakers often try to appeal to listeners' senses. Through sensory appeals, audience members are encouraged to see, hear, smell, taste, or feel something. Notice how the following speaker helps the audience visualize the violence he associates with animal rights protesters:

> Here are a few protest activities conducted in the name of animal rights. A few months ago PETA's vegetarian campaign coordinator from the Washington headquarters was in Denver attempting to unload a truckful of manure in front of the Colorado Convention Center. She was protesting against the World Meat Congress that was meeting there. Signage on the side of the truck said, "Meat Stinks." Police arrested her before she completed the job. At a dog show, PETA protesters opened the cages of several of the show dogs and turned them loose; they also put antifreeze in the water bowls of some cages. One of the protesters said, "A dead dog is better than a caged dog." Add to this such incidents as PETA protesters throwing paint or blood onto fur coats worn by women walking down the street. . . .
>
> There's another animal rights group, the Animal Liberation Front, which has been blamed for the firebombing of an animal-research lab at Michigan

State University. Police reported an estimate of $200,000 in damages and the destroying of 30 years' worth of primary research data. . . . Last year, the Animal Liberation Front planted incendiary devices in four downtown Chicago department stores.

Another dimension of the fight for animal rights was provided by vegetarians who broke into the shop of a German butcher. They smashed equipment worth $21,000 and painted the message "Meat is murder, animal killer," on the shop windows. Subsequently, they slashed the butcher's tires and left a phone message, "Yesterday your store, tomorrow you.[6]

Listeners exposed to such a vivid and detailed narrative have a strong likelihood of identifying with it. With the bulk of the appeal resting on visual images, the result is a more persuasive presentation.

Lively, vivid language is important, but much still depends on the speaker's ability to marshal excellent arguments and on the listener's ability to be open to new and alternative viewpoints. In this situation, as in so many others, speaker and listener depend on each other for a mutually satisfying outcome.

Using Figures of Speech

Language that is striking or impressive can create interest and contribute to understanding. For centuries, students of rhetoric have studied what are called figures of speech; these are special ways of using language to heighten the beauty of expression, or the clarity of ideas, or the emotional impact of speeches. It is not important for the beginning student of public speaking to understand and identify all the technical names for the different figures of speech. But both listeners and speakers should be aware of some common ways of using language effectively.

Simile

Language can be used to compare things. A direct comparison can be made between things that an audience might not see as being similar. This kind of comparison, a simile, is typically introduced by the word *like* or *as*. When President Bush appointed Tony Snow as his new his press secretary in May of 2006, one reporter used similes to describe the situation Mr. Snow faced: "Any press secretary taking over the podium for the first time comes off as a substitute teacher trying to take control of a restless high school class. With the president's standing in the opinion polls this low, *Mr. Snow was more like a stepfather meeting his wife's children for the first time.*"[7]

Indira Gandhi, the Prime Minister of India, presented the Jawaharlal Nehru Award for International Understanding to Coretta Scott King in New Delhi on January 24, 1969. In her speech, Mrs. Gandhi used a simile to describe Martin Luther King's vision of racial equality:

While there is bondage anywhere, we ourselves cannot be fully free. While there is oppression anywhere, we ourselves cannot soar high. Martin Luther King was convinced that one day the misguided people who believed in racial superiority would realize the error of their ways. *His dream was that white and black, brown and yellow would live and grow together as flowers in a garden with their faces turned towards the sun.*[8]

Metaphor

Another common kind of comparison is the metaphor, which compares two objects that the audience might think of as being quite dissimilar. (A metaphor, unlike a simile, does not employ the word *like* or *as*). One freshman college student, about to join a group heading to the Gulf region to help with cleanup after the Katrina disaster, described her feelings through a metaphor: "I think I understand the principles of swimming, but I'm about to find out by jumping into the deep end of the pool; I just hope I can swim to the other end." And, in a moving tribute to the murdered Mahatma Gandhi, Indian prime minister Jawaharlal Nehru expressed the sadness felt by his fellow Indians: "A glory has departed and the sun that warmed and brightened our lives has set and we shiver in the dark."[9]

These images create a certain feeling or mood in the audience. In this way, they make an important contribution to the audience's total appreciation of a speech.

Antithesis

Language can be used to make contrasts between words or ideas. The special device known as antithesis is a way of putting together two things that have sharply different meanings. Through antithesis, ideas can be reinforced and compelling contrasts in thought can be suggested. A definition of *classics*, for example, is that they "are examples of *how* to think, not *what* to think."[10] One student speaker argued, "Right on this campus we're engaged in an important struggle. We must not support the forces of death and personal profit, but, instead, we must choose the forces of life and personal sacrifice." This speech attacked those who would risk the effects of pollution in order to make money. The antithesis pitted life against death, sacrifice against profit, effectively associating those who would put money first with death.

Irony

Other stylistic devices can be used to make ideas more believable or understandable. Through irony, a speaker can strongly imply a meaning that is opposite that which is stated. Mary Church Terrell was a graduate of Oberlin College, a teacher, the first president of the National Association of Colored Women, and a professional lecturer who spoke out against racism at the beginning of the twentieth century. In a speech given in Washington in 1906 she used irony skillfully to point out the contradictions of racial discrimination evident in the trip from Washington, D.C., to George Washington's tomb at Mount Vernon. In a speech before the United Women's Club she said:

> As a colored woman I cannot visit the tomb of the Father of this country, which owes its very existence to the love of freedom in the human heart and which stands for equal opportunity for all, without being forced to sit in the Jim Crow section of an electric car which starts from the very heart of the city—midway between the Capitol and the White House. If I refuse thus to be humiliated, I

am cast into jail and forced to pay a fine for violating the Virginia laws.[11]

Alliteration

A speaker who uses a repetitive pattern of initial sounds that can hold the audience's attention and reinforce the idea is using alliteration. One returning student, proud of her new U.S. citizenship, said that becoming an American was "more than just a passport to plenty," it was "a doorway to democracy." In his 1989 inaugural address, George H. W. Bush used alliteration when he said, "The President is neither prince nor pope."[12]

Poets commonly use alliteration and other figures of speech. Edgar Allan Poe wrote of the "silken, sad, uncertain rustling of each purple curtain"[13] to capture the sound of curtains being blown about by an open window. Whether used in a poem or a speech, alliteration, if not forced or overdone, is memorable and pleasing to the ear.

Personification

The speaker who uses personification gives the characteristics of human beings to nonhuman forms or things: "This city can be a very hostile place. It can ignore you, it can frighten you, and it can punish you very severely if you ignore its unwritten rules." This student speaker then went on to talk about such urban problems as loneliness, homelessness, and crime. One very common form of personification is a phrase we hear almost every day; it is a variation of the phrase "The White House says . . ." or "The White House reacted to the Congressional Action. . . ."

Oxymoron

Through an oxymoron, a speaker can combine seemingly contradictory expressions, such as "thunderous silence" or "cheerful pessimist," using such contradictions to emphasize the contrast between two things. Oxymorons give an unexpected twist of meaning that can be amusing—such as "found missing," or "negative increase"—while others are arresting and thought-provoking and can reinforce opinion in a memorable way. Those, for example, who are frustrated by official bureaucracy and red tape will find "government organization" an oxymoron. Popular films have been given oxymoronic titles such as *Back to the Future* and *Eyes Wide Shut*. Bob Dole, commenting on his political opponent Bill Clinton in the 1996 presidential race, said that "he talks right and runs left."

While some terms we use, like *virtual reality*, have become such a part of our language that we no longer even recognize their contradictory quality, oxymorons are often memorable and usually capture listeners' interest and attention.[14]

Mary Church Terrell actively attacked racism in America in the early twentieth century. She pointed to the irony of an American of color being forced to sit in a segregated section of a trolley car when traveling from the nation's capital to George Washington's tomb at Mount Vernon.

Memorizing the definitions of these figures of speech is not nearly as important as recognizing this basic principle: choosing language that is effective in promoting your meaning and conveying your feelings helps better connect you with your audience.

Using Rhetorical Questions

Speakers sometimes ask listeners questions. When they do so, they are usually not actually looking for an answer or expecting real dialogue with the audience. Instead, by using rhetorical questions, they are trying to pique the audience's curiosity and stimulate thinking. As we noted in Chapter 9, rhetorical questions may be used to gain the audience's attention during the speech's introduction. But they can also be used in other places in the speech.

Rhetorical questions are effective because when someone asks us a question, we start to think. In most communication contexts, when we are asked questions, we are being invited to participate. Questions trigger guesses, speculation, and other forms of thought. In short, questions activate our brains.

Rhetorical questions can also be used as transitions, as noted in Chapter 9. As with other devices of language, they must be chosen carefully. Imagine how interested you would be if a speaker asked you such an unimaginative question as, "Now, what are some reasons we should all wear seat belts?" or "Why is smoking really bad for you?"

The effectiveness of any rhetorical question depends on its wording, its timing, and the way the speaker develops the response to the question. Having posed the question, the speaker is, of course, obliged to answer it. For example, one speaker, who wanted audience members to understand the urgency of supporting a local day shelter and hunger relief program, posed this question: "What does the face of hunger look like in our community?" After pausing to let the audience contemplate the question, she then offered these examples:

A young couple living in their car with their two young children. Unable to afford child care, the mother stays with the children while the father goes to work.

A Vietnam Veteran, who lives in a tent in a wooded area west of town. War injuries have made it impossible for him to maintain steady employment.

A young mother, on work release from jail, struggles to rebuild her life while doing volunteer work for a church and working part-time for a local cleaning company.

A 60-year-old woman—a former nurse's aid, working most of her life in nearby hospitals and nursing homes—is diagnosed with leukemia. Too weak to work, she stays at a local emergency shelter.

Is this how *you* pictured poverty and hunger in our community?

These are only a few of the *real* women, men, and children who take their meals at the Shalom Community Center each day.

Using Parallelism

Some speakers use parallelism to suggest equality among their ideas. When used effectively, parallelism can bring force, clarity, rhythm, and interest to a speech. Using either parallel construction or phrases of about equal length also emphasizes the similarity of ideas. Franklin Roosevelt spoke forcefully about the plight of many Americans; in using parallel structure, he emphasized that the problems were many and widespread. The following example shows how several features of good oral style can work together. As well as the parallelism in its overall structure, this quotation from Roosevelt contains repetition (at the beginning of each line and in the last line).

> I see millions of families trying to live on incomes so meager that the pall of family disaster hangs over them day by day.
> I see millions whose daily lives in city and on farm continue under conditions labeled indecent by a so-called polite society half a century ago.
> I see millions denied education, recreation and the opportunity to better their lot and the lot of their children.
> I see millions lacking the means to buy the products of farm and factory and by their poverty denying work and productiveness to many other millions.
> I see one-third of a nation ill-housed, ill-clad, ill-nourished.[15]

In short, the language you choose can make a difference in the way your audience responds. Becoming conscious of language and learning to use it effectively are critical parts of your growth as a speaker and listener. Another important aspect in using language effectively is making stylistic choices that are appropriate to your speaking situation.

Using Language That Is Appropriate to the Situation

Preview. *Except in the most formal speaking situations, a conversational style is appropriate. The setting, the context, and the occasion all may call for language to be used in different ways. Audience expectations are also critical in deciding what sort of oral style is appropriate.*

Speakers must be prepared to modify the way they use language, depending on the situation in which they are speaking. Although each speaker must be authentic, the best speakers are those who are sensitive to audience expectations and respectful of the purpose and formality of the speaking situation. Nevertheless, across speaking contexts, speakers must strive to use language that is tasteful, gender-inclusive, and ethical.

Appropriateness and Context

One of the most dramatic examples of contrasting uses of language was demonstrated by the release of the famous Watergate tapes. These recorded conversations illustrated the startling differences between the public and private language of President Richard Nixon and many of his advisers.[16] One of the things that shocked people was not so much the use of vulgar words, but the fact that those words were used by the President of the United States in the Oval Office of the White House. To many people who had surely heard such words before and perhaps even used some of them themselves, the use of those words in the White House did not seem appropriate.

Contextual Factors Affecting Audience Perceptions

Language choices should be influenced by the context in which your speech occurs. In general, you will probably think about language choices and choose your language more carefully in a public speech than you would in a private setting. The language you choose to introduce your city's mayor at a public forum, for example, might be more formal than the language you use when giving a book report in class.

At the same time, a good speaker never "fakes" language to sound like someone else. For example, it would be inappropriate for a well-educated speaker to use poor grammar or coarse language intentionally because he or she is addressing an uneducated audience. This would not only be unethical, but it also might be interpreted as condescending and insulting. It would also be unwise for a speaker to use the slang or the technical language of a particular audience if that language did not come naturally to that speaker.

Certain aspects of a situation—the audience, the topic of the speech, and the occasion or setting in which the speech takes place—also have an impact on language choice. Martin Luther King Jr.'s "I Have a Dream" speech in 1963 is probably the best example of language adapted to the situation. His first words were, "Five score years ago a great American in whose symbolic shadow we stand today signed the Emancipa-

The opening of Martin Luther King Jr.'s famous "Dream" speech was made even more dramatic by the fact that it was delivered from the steps of the memorial dedicated to "the great emancipator," Abraham Lincoln.

tion Proclamation."[17] King said this standing on the steps of the Lincoln Memorial. It was well calculated to remind the audience of Lincoln, his Gettysburg Address, and, by extension, the long and bloody struggle over slavery and racial prejudice.

The *Focus on Civic Engagement* shows how one speaker adapted his presentation to the demands of a special context. Following the 1992 Los Angeles riots,

Focus on Civic Engagement

"I Had a Dream," by David Owen

When I first saw the fires in Los Angeles I remembered a much earlier dream—another dream of America, her cities and her people—a dream of faith and hope rather than desolation and fear. . . .

I also glimpsed that dream in my grade school where I was helped to understand that America is a country composed of many different kinds of people. In other countries, I was told, opportunities were often restricted to an elite few. But here in our American democracy all people were free, all people were considered equal, the rules for pursuing happiness were fair, and liberty and justice were offered to all. It was such a beautiful dream:

Give me your tired, your poor,
Your huddled masses
yearning to breathe free,
The wretched refuse of your teeming shore.
Send these, the homeless,
tempest-tossed, to me . . .

I rightly sensed that only a brave and confident country could dream such a dream.

As I grew older, I began to see that the dream was not yet fulfilled for all. During my sixteenth summer I worked for a bottling company in Milwaukee and spent some days delivering cases of soft drinks to the poorest—mostly black—neighborhoods of our city. In early morning deliveries we regularly woke homeless men who had spent the night on storeroom floors of neighborhood bars. In the basements of restaurants and grocery stores we often groped for empty cases in darkness, shaking the cases before picking them up so as to scare the rats away. . . . The stench in my nostrils from certain stores and restaurants stayed for days. I didn't understand all that I was experiencing, but I knew that it was a different America than I had previously seen.

After a few years I began attending meetings of CORE—the Congress of Racial Equality. We met on Sunday evenings in a storefront church within the black community. It was a small group. Typically fifteen blacks and a few whites attended. As we arrived and when we left plainclothes policemen photographed us from an unmarked car across the street. On other occasions they stood on the sidewalk photographing us more openly. The police were beginning to treat us as subversives. I did not understand why. I did not see myself as subversive. I had a dream.

One summer night marching with a group of black youths who were seeking a Fair Housing law for the city, we crossed the long 16th Street Viaduct to Milwaukee's south side. No blacks lived there. Crowds of whites were waiting. First they hurled obscenities—then rocks and bottles. The police added tear gas. Despite such opposition, the youths marched for 200 straight nights. With hundreds of other people I walked such gauntlets with them many times. It seemed important. I had a dream. . . .

The dream went on for more than ten years, carrying me to Montgomery, Alabama, with Dr. Martin Luther King…to Senators' offices and the basements of black churches in Washington, D.C.; to midnight strategy sessions with friends, and secret meetings in hotel rooms with officials of the Justice Department, and marches and demonstrations of many kinds. . . . It all seemed quite natural. I believed what my parents and church had taught me. . . . I believed in America. I believed in that day spoken of by Martin Luther King "when all God's children would be able to join hands and sing." I had a dream. From Maine to Mississippi, let freedom ring!

Source: David Owen, "I Had a Dream" (excerpt from speech delivered at St. Mark's United Methodist Church, Bloomington, IN., May 31, 1992). Reprinted by permission.

which erupted after the acquittal of four white police officers in the beating of black motorist Rodney King, Reverend David Owen delivered a powerful sermon that both grappled with the tragic state of race relations in the U.S. and honored the memory of Martin Luther King Jr. After describing his dream, Reverend Owen went on to explain how, for a while, he lost faith in King's dream for America. After considerable inner struggle, he was eventually able to regain his faith. His effective oral style, the power of his language, and his ability to relate his sermon to this tension-filled context resulted in a moving and memorable speech.

Gender-Inclusive Language

As we have pointed out, language is a powerful force in shaping our perceptions and beliefs. Research has shown that gendered language, typically language that excludes women, has negative effects on those excluded.[18] The statement "If a student expects to get into medical school, he will have to work hard to get excellent grades" implies that those who expect to become doctors will be male. Speakers often use gendered language thoughtlessly, unaware that there are accepted, gender-neutral alternatives.

The list in Figure 11.2, adapted from a website on gender-sensitive language, offers some common examples of gendered language, as well as some possible alternatives. Also, there are several guides to nongendered language that you can consult, such as the International Association of Business Communication's *Without Bias: A Guidebook for Nondiscriminatory Communication* (Wiley, 1982) or *The Dictionary of Bias-Free Usage: A Guide to Nondiscriminatory Language* (Oryx, 1991). A good website to consult is Carolyn Jacobson's "Some Notes on Gender-Neutral Language."

The important point to keep in mind is that your audience will be made up of both men and women, and the use of gender-inclusive or gender-neutral language is most appropriate.

Figure 11.2

Gendered	Gender-neutral
man	person, individual
mankind	people, human beings, humanity
man-made	machine-made, synthetic
the common man	the average (or ordinary) person
to man	to operate, to cover, to staff
mailman	mail carrier, letter carrier, postal worker
policeman	police officer
congressman	congressperson, legislator, representative

Source: "Gender Sensitive Language," The Writing Center at the University of North Carolina at Chapel Hill. www.unc.edu/depts/wcweb/handouts/gender.html.

Audience Expectations

Most of us do not speak in settings quite so dramatic as the March on Washington in 1963, where Martin Luther King Jr. delivered his famous speech. No matter where you are, however, you need to ask what the audience knows and thinks about the topic. Also, you should consider the audience's level of linguistic sophistication, how formal or casual the setting might be, and the physical characteristics of the setting for your speech.

In a public speaking class, one speaker began this way: "I'm planning to say something today that is very important. It's of great interest and significance—not only to us here in this room, but to people everywhere. I just hope I can say it in a way that is fitting and proper." Conveying much the same idea, a minister in a church preceded his sermon with the old prayer, "May the words of my mouth and the meditations of our hearts be always acceptable in thy sight, O Lord our strength and our redeemer."[19] Each of these speakers opened with remarks appropriate to the particular situation in which they were speaking; each expressed essentially the same idea. Yet if the student had opened with the minister's words, it would have seemed inappropriate to the situation.

The wise speaker thinks carefully about audience expectations and makes reasonable, ethical, and appropriate adjustments to the situation. This does not mean that you simply tell the audience what you think they want to hear. Rather you develop your speech with an understanding of what your audience might consider appropriate in a specific context, taking their expectations into account and respecting, but not pandering to, those expectations.

Appropriate Language as Ethical Language

When we think of speaking appropriately, we may be thinking only about what seems to "fit" the speech situation. But another dimension of appropriateness involves the ethics of our language choices with regard to promoting mutual respect and avoiding offensive language. Using language the audience considers offensive or tasteless is not just ineffective; it communicates a lack of respect for the audience. As in any communication situation, mutual respect is the hallmark of ethical public speaking.[20] You have an *ethical* obligation to choose language that communicates this respect.

Most speakers have certain expectations for how they will be treated by their audiences. They expect to be made to feel welcome, they expect not to be interrupted while they speak, and they assume that any audience member who wishes to challenge them will do so only after they finish their speech, during the question-and-answer period. More important, speakers have a right to expect that listeners who have questions or object to their speech will raise those issues respectfully and without resorting to personal attacks.

These expectations go both ways, of course. If you, as a speaker, do not show respect for your listeners, you should not be surprised if they respond in kind. As partners in the communication process, both speakers and listeners have an obligation to display mutual respect, civility, good taste, and sensitivity to the feelings of others. This obligation extends even to the specific words you choose to use in your speech.

Ethical speakers must also guard against the use of language that demeans a particular gender, race, religion, or culture. We are not just talking about being "politically correct." We are talking about showing respect for your listeners and others in society. Most of us know that grown women do not want to be referred to as "girls" or "chicks." Hispanics do not tolerate the label "spic," and homosexuals rightly take offense at being called "fags" or "dykes." There are, of course, dozens of other slurs that one might use to insult or demean people of particular groups. It should go without saying that the use of such slurs is unethical, particularly when they substitute for substantive argument or are intentionally designed to silence or intimidate members of minority groups.

Critical listeners are not moved by style alone but also listen thoughtfully to the substance of a speech, carefully attending to arguments and evidence.

Of course, offensive language is not only unethical; it is highly impractical, as well. Listeners who are offended by a speaker are much less likely to be persuaded and may well be distracted from the content of an informative message.

Responding Critically to a Speaker's Style

Preview. *When a speaker has good style, listeners are likely to be moved. Critical listeners will be aware that style in language can have an impact. They will look for sound arguments, good evidence, and substance of thought—regardless of the speaker's style. They will avoid overreacting to style in either a positive or a negative sense.*

It should be apparent by now that style can have a strong impact on listeners—almost apart from the ideas being expressed. That is, the *way* in which ideas are expressed can be as important as the ideas themselves in influencing the listeners' reactions. A clear and appropriate speaking style can enhance a speaker's ethos, while an otherwise good speech can be undermined by poor stylistic choices.

Using Emotional Language Ethically

The ethical public speaker will never use language to whip the audience into an emotional frenzy. As we have made clear, emotional appeals are quite appropriate and often necessary to move an audience to action. Most people do not respond to reasoned arguments alone if they do not feel emotionally engaged as well. Ethical emotional appeals, however, are backed up with strong evidence and sound reasoning. The ethical speaker *wants* the audience to think critically and constructively, and he or she will do nothing to get around their inclination to do so.

Style Substituted for Argument

Speakers have been known to dismiss an idea not by dissecting it, analyzing it, or examining its weaknesses or strengths, but simply by labeling it. For example, a speaker might simply declare that an idea is too "simplistic," too "radical," or perhaps too "reactionary." Such a speaker is substituting style for argument. Here's one example: instead of pointing to the shortcomings of a plan, one speaker simply said, "This is another one of those ultra-conservative ideas; it's just what you would expect from right-wingers, and it hardly merits our consideration." What is the listener to do when confronted with this kind of so-called argument? Good critical listeners will ask, On what basis will I respond? What does the speaker mean by "ultra-conservative" idea? What are the implications of that label? In this example, is there evidence that this *is* an ultra-conservative idea? And, if so, does that necessarily mean it's a bad idea? Asking these kinds of questions will help a listener avoid falling prey to a stylistic substitution for argument.

In Chapter 8, we discussed the need for supporting ideas with evidence. Listeners should keep the same principle in mind when they are faced with persuasive uses of language. Here, too, listeners must be wary of accepting the speaker's words alone, even if those words are aptly chosen and emotionally compelling. It is always reasonable for listeners to ask for evidence. Good speakers anticipate being asked to provide support for their ideas.

Summary

- To make a prepared speech truly effective you must also use language that is appropriate for the topic and the audience.
- The purpose of having a good speaking style is to promote the audience's understanding and acceptance through the use of effective language.
  - At the foundation of good language use is clarity. In general, using language that is familiar to listeners, as well as concrete, specific, and precise, will help you achieve a good speaking style.
  - It is also important to avoid crowding sentences with clichés and empty words or constructing sentences so that they are tediously long, overly complex, and hard for listeners to follow.
- Language should be interesting to the audience.
  - Listeners find active language more engaging than passive language.
  - Use figurative language such as metaphors, antithesis, alliteration, and other language devices.

- Language should be appropriate to the situation—well adapted to the speech setting, the listeners' expectations and levels of understanding, and the constraints of the occasion—and ethical.

- Using language ethically entails showing respect for the audience, striving not to offend them, using good judgment and good taste, and encouraging listeners to respond thoughtfully rather than impulsively.

- Both speakers and listeners must beware of the possibility of substituting style for argument.
  - A speaker may use emotionally charged words, and the listeners may respond without carefully examining the substructure of evidence and reasoning underlying the speaker's powerful style.
  - It is the speaker's and the listeners' responsibility to be careful in using and responding to language.

QUESTIONS FOR REVIEW AND REFLECTION

1. What is meant by "style" in public speaking? How does it differ from other notions of style?
2. Can you identify denotative and connotative language in messages you hear or read? How might charged language affect your response?
3. What are some ways that a speaker can strive to make his or her language clearer?
4. What is wrong with using expressions such as "it goes without saying," "last but not least," and "due to the fact that" when you speak?
5. Why is active language more interesting to listeners than passive language?
6. Provide a good example of each of the following and explain how it makes an idea more effective:
   a. simile
   b. metaphor
   c. antithesis
   d. irony
   e. alliteration
   f. personification
   g. oxymoron
   h. parallelism
   i. rhetorical question
7. To be effective, a speaker must speak appropriately. What are three key guidelines for using language appropriately in a public speech?
8. What is the relationship between using language appropriately and using it ethically?
9. What language do you find offensive and how would you react to a speaker who uses such language?

ENDNOTES

1. Colin Powell, "Sharing the American Dream," *Vital Speeches of the Day* 62 (June 1, 1997): 485–86.

2. "Language: A Key Mechanism of Control," excerpted in Pamela Cooper and William Nothstine, *Power and Persuasion: Moving an Ancient Art into the Media Age* (Greenwood, IN: Educational Video Group, 1992): 163.

3. Abraham Lincoln, "A House Divided," in *A Treasury of the World's Great Speeches*, ed. Houston Peterson, 491 (New York: Simon and Schuster, 1965).

4. John F. McDonnell, "Pushing the Envelope of Knowledge in Geologic Time and Space," *Vital Speeches of the Day* 71 (July 1, 2005): 560.

5. Lyndon B. Johnson, "The Voting Rights Act of 1965," in *Great Speeches for Criticism and Analysis*, ed. Lloyd Rohler and Roger Cook, 231–32 (Greenwood, IN: Alistair Press, 1988).

6. Lee W. Baker, "The Ethics of Protest: Is It Right to Do Wrong?" *Vital Speeches of the Day* 62, (February 1, 1996): 255.

7. Alessandra Stanley, "At White House Briefing, Polish Replaces Testiness," *New York Times*, May 17, 2006, A19.

8. Indira Gandhi, "Martin Luther King," http://gos.sbc.edu/g/gandhi2.html (Accessed October 1, 2006).

9. Qtd. in Jane Blankenship, *A Sense of Style: An Introduction to Style for the Public Speaker* (Belmont, CA: Dickenson Publishing, 1968), 70.

10. Eugene E. Brussell, ed., *Webster's New World Dictionary of Quotable Definitions* (New York: Prentice Hall, 1988): 91.

11. Mary Church Terrell, "What It Means to Be Colored in the Capital of the United States," *Man Cannot Speak for Her: A Critical Study of Early Feminist Rhetoric*, 2 vols., ed. Karlyn Kohrs Campbell (New York: Praeger, 1989), 2:422.

12. Qtd. in Davis Newton Lott, ed., *The Presidents Speak* (New York: Henry Holt, 1994), 362.

13. Edgar Allan Poe, "The Raven," in *The Viking Book of Poetry of the English Speaking World*, vol. 2, 866 (New York: Viking, 1959).

14. Many of these examples, plus several others, can be found on the Web. One site, for example, is www.oxymorons.info/reference/oxymorons/oxymoron-quotes.asp.

15. Blankenship, *Sense of Style*, 101.

16. See Dennis S. Gouran, "Communicative Influences on Decisions Related to the Watergate Coverup: The Failure of Collective Judgment," *Central States Speech Journal* 34 (1984): 260–68.

17. Martin Luther King Jr., "I Had a Dream," in Rohler and Cook, *Great Speeches for Criticism and Analysis*, 325.

18. See, for example, Julia Wood, *Gendered Lives: Communication, Gender, and Culture*, 4th ed. (Belmont, CA: Wadsworth, 2001).

19. Psalms 19:14.

20. See Richard L. Johannesen, "The Emerging Concept of Communication as Dialogue," *Quarterly Journal of Speech* 57 (December 1971): 373–82; and Maurice S. Friedman, *Dialogue and the Human Image: Beyond Humanistic Psychology* (Newbury Park, CA: Sage, 1992).

The 1960s were a time of turbulence and change. John Kennedy was assassinated in November of 1963 and Lyndon Johnson became president. The new president announced ambitious domestic reforms—"the Great Society"—and signed two civil rights bills in the summer of 1964. In 1963, Betty Friedan wrote The Feminine Mystique, *in which she urged women to break free of traditional prescribed roles, setting the stage for the establishment of the National Organization of Women, which she founded in 1965. Between those two events, in 1964, Lady Bird Johnson gave this speech. The first lady, in addressing this audience of home economists—teachers and county agents—all of whom were women, stressed the need for women to become involved at a time when they were beginning to strive for the fulfillment of their rights as citizens.*

Address to the National Convention of American Home Economics Association in Detroit, Michigan, on June 24, 1964

While we meet here on an evening in June, the horizons of women all over the world are widening from home to humanity—from our private families to the family of man.

A quiet revolution of emancipation has been taking place in the lives of women everywhere—from Detroit to Delhi. Millions of women have achieved the right to vote, to own property, to be educated. Technological marvels now can free women from the total bondage of home chores. You, as home economists, have helped to make it so. You have taught American women to master the intricacies of push-button washer-dryers, automatic ranges, and convenience foods. More and more, you will be exporting this know-how to other parts of the world.

With these newly won rights and with a rising standard of living, women can move beyond the struggle for equal status and for material goods to the challenges and opportunities of citizenship. Increasingly, we are going to be concerned with what my husband calls "the Great Society"—the quality of goals and the achievement of goals which will mean a better life for all.

As American women, we hold a tremendous potential of strength for good. I do not refer to the sense of power that comes from flicking a switch or turning an ignition key. But to the force we exert when we mark a ballot, teach our children, or work for a better community.

The question is: How can we best mobilize this potential? How can the individual woman practice citizenship to the fullest extent, both at home and abroad?

Ernest Hemingway once said, "Talk and write about what you know." One sees change in terms of one's own experiences.

As a girl, my home was in East Texas. It was a place where Spanish moss was draped from age-old cypresses, where alligators slithered down muddy banks into dark, enchanted bayous. While we fished through the long summer days, we enjoyed the illusion that time was standing still. But time never stands still. I grew up, went to college and married a tall Texan. My horizons have been broadening and my involvement getting deeper ever since.

In the past few years, my own participation has included travel with my husband to all corners of our own land, to Thailand and India, to Senegal and Iceland, and a score of other countries.

This spring, I have been traveling some myself. I have been to areas of serious unemployment and limited opportunities, such as Wilkes-Barre, Pennsylvania, and Breathitt County, Kentucky. For me, it helps me see in human terms the objectives of the war on poverty.

AS SHE BEGINS HER SPEECH, JOHNSON CHOOSES FIGURATIVE LANGUAGE THAT ANNOUNCES HER THEME. IN USING THE PHRASES "FROM HOME TO HUMANITY," AND "FROM OUR PRIVATE FAMILIES TO THE FAMILY OF MAN," SHE SUGGESTS THAT HER MESSAGE TO WOMEN IS TO MOVE FROM PERSONAL PREOCCUPATIONS TO INVOLVEMENT IN LARGER ISSUES.

NOTE THE MANY WORDS THE SPEAKER CHOOSES THROUGHOUT THE SPEECH THAT HAVE POSITIVE CONNOTATIONS, SUCH AS "CHALLENGES," OPPORTUNITIES," "POTENTIAL," "STRENGTH," "COMMUNITY." ALL OF THESE SUGGEST BOLD, POSITIVE ACTION.

Once in a while I ask myself, "What am I doing here?" Perhaps when I visit, it helps draw the curtain open a little more. Perhaps it gives national attention to a local problem. Perhaps it exposes us to ourselves and says, "This is the other side of America. Look! And Act!"

I am only one of 65 million American women. Almost all of us are involved, one way or another, in being the best citizens we know how to be. Actually, none of us just sat down and said, "I'm going to get involved." It happens gradually, inspired by husband and family, sometimes triggered by crisis, always influenced by circumstances and opportunity.

For example, let me tell you about one woman who has made a mark on her community and on the lives of many people around her. I went to college with her at the University of Texas. She was—and is—a beautiful girl, gay, filled with character and grace. Then, after she married, she was hit by one of life's hardest blows: her second child was born with cerebral palsy.

After two or three years of fighting this fact, and carrying her child to many, many doctors, she accepted it. She discovered that there were different degrees of this illness, and that in many cases, the victims could be helped. So she went to work.

Largely through her untiring persuasion, she brought together local organizations and city fathers. We now have a clinic in Austin where hundreds of children come from hundreds of miles around for treatment and training. Behind every achievement or success is one dauntless person who keeps gathering together the strength that makes the web of success.

Tonight we met a high school home economics teacher with four children who, I understand, has a daughter born with a physical handicap and a sister-in-law who suffered loss of an arm recently.

Far from restricting her activities because of these family problems, this home economist has gone beyond the call of duty to organize a place of worship for her religious denomination in the community, to initiate and lead a 4-H group, to introduce the National Honor Society in her high school and to serve as the faculty adviser for the student council and the yearbook. And, she is volunteering as bookkeeper for her husband who has just opened his own business! These are just two examples among thousands.

All of us are acquainted with many women working at citizenship. You, yourselves are doing it each day of your lives—bringing home economics know-how to girls and women who have or will have a home of their own.

That has been your role since your Association was founded 55 years ago. I like what your founder, Ellen Richards, the first woman graduate from Massachusetts Institute of Technology, said. It is as applicable today as it was in 1909; to apply principles of science to the home so we may have—and these are her words—"Freedom of the home from the dominance of things."

What better formula with which to develop the full potential of the home as a springboard to citizenship!

For, as someone once said, "When you teach a man, you teach an individual; when you teach a woman, you teach a family." And in this age, I would add to that—You also teach a nation and a world."

For me, your work has a very personal meaning. In Texas, our county home demonstration agents have helped homemakers to live better, to make wiser choices, to tackle problems more intelligently within the family and the community. At the ranch, we have always been delighted to see her coming. We know that when she leaves, we shall have learned much in a few hours.

THROUGHOUT THE SPEECH JOHNSON USES SIMPLE BUT APPROPRIATE LANGUAGE. IN RELATING SPECIFIC EXAMPLES, SHE DESCRIBES THE EXPERIENCES OF WOMEN WITH LANGUAGE CHOSEN TO BE BOTH CLEAR AND INTERESTING.

Over the past 15 years, as Americans moved to town, the home economist has followed them.

I do not need to tell you that the cities reach out for you—to help people in the public housing units and the crowded slum areas who do not know how to cope with the new and unaccustomed conditions of city life.

Indeed, as I consider your profession, there are so many ways in which the nation needs your help in the unfinished business of America.

You have long been alert to the fact that poverty's roots are deepest in the family structure. Now I am delighted you are stepping up your activities for the low-income family.

An education program geared to the family without modern equipment, the family that can read, perhaps not well or, not in English, may offer these people the lifeline they need.

Your president, Florence Lowe, tells me of the El Paso Project in which a bilingual set of instructions about Food for Fitness was mailed out to Mexican-American families. It brought tremendous results.

One reason was that the mail got top attention because these families received so little mail.

The all-out war on poverty needs home economists in the front brigade. And, I commend all you are doing to be a full participant in this force.

New thinking and teaching is needed if we are to communicate fully to the low-income family. We must reexamine the college curriculum which produces the home economists. As in other professions, this curriculum may be geared too much to the values of the middle-income family.

Our state departments of welfare are realizing, more and more, how important it is to have the home economist to reinforce the case worker. Family problems often stem from a lack of knowledge of wise buying habits. Seventeen states now have full-time home economists on their staffs.

One of the most exciting new horizons for the home economist is helping solve the problems that daily face ten million homemakers in this country who are permanently or temporarily disabled.

The blind woman with the baby needs advice on how to care for it in her own home.

The woman with only one arm needs a little extra attention to learn how to manage her home and bathe the baby.

A mother paralyzed by polio was asked several months ago what she wished she had known when she returned home from the hospital.

"I wish someone had told me to buy a different type of carpet, one that would be right for my wheelchair," she said.

Help from an expert can make life more comfortable and productive.

I trust your professional efforts on behalf of women and families in the developing countries will receive a big push in the coming years. The fact that over 300 home economists are in the Peace Corps—some of them women who came out of retirement to volunteer for service in Sierra Leone and Peru—is an indication of your concern for your fellow man around the world.

One of the great joys of your work is that you can see the results. My husband has often told me that the years which gave him the most intense personal satisfaction were those in which he served under President Roosevelt as a state director of the National Youth Administration. Boys were taken from boxcars and given back their self-respect along with part-time jobs which enabled them to stay in school. To watch this happening, to have a part in its happening, was an experience we shall never forget.

For me, it was the beginning of seeing how politics can bring tangible results. I always hope that the very best of our people will go into politics, and I am sure that some of our best are

THE WAR ON POVERTY WAS ONE ASPECT OF PRESIDENT JOHNSON'S GREAT SOCIETY. JOHNSON EMPLOYS THIS METAPHOR TO DIRECTLY INVOLVE HER AUDIENCE, DESCRIBING THEM AS THE "FRONT BRIGADE."

women. It was for this reason that the President began his effort last winter to bring more women into government.

You home economists are examples of women who manage several lives successfully. Most of you have both a home and a professional career. Many of you, like several of the award-winners tonight, also have children. You have much to share.

So, I say: "Don't hold back. Don't be shy. Step forward in every way you can to plan boldly, to speak clearly, to offer the leadership which the world needs."

For me, and probably for most women, the attempt to become an involved, practicing citizen has been a matter of evolution rather than choice. Actually, if given a choice between lying in a hammock under an apple tree with a book of poetry and watching the blossoms float down or standing on a platform before thousands of people, I don't have to tell you what I would have chosen 25 years ago. But 25 years and the invention of the nuclear bomb have left us no choice. The hammocks and apple trees are happy memories except for a few short, cherished moments.

Edmund Burke said, almost 200 years ago, "The only thing necessary for the triumph of evil is for good men to do nothing." I hope he would forgive me if I modernize and amend his statement to say, "The only thing necessary for the triumph of evil is for good men *and good women to do nothing*."

I am sure that will not be.

Source: "New Horizons by Women," by Mrs. Lyndon Johnson, 1964.

HERE, JOHNSON USES SIMPLE, DIRECT LAN- GUAGE TO CHALLENGE HER AUDIENCE—HER IM- MEDIATE AUDIENCE OF HOME ECONOMISTS AS WELL AS THE MILLIONS OF AMERICAN WOMEN SHE HOPES TO ENCOUR- AGE TO PLAY AN ACTIVE ROLE IN CIVIC AFFAIRS.

SHE ENDS HER SPEECH BY TAKING A FAMOUS QUOTATION AND ADDING TO IT THE WORDS "AND GOOD WOMEN," REIN- FORCING HER PLEA FOR WOMEN TO GET INVOLVED IN CIVIC AFFAIRS. HER SIMPLE FINAL SENTENCE IS BOTH AN AFFIRMATION OF HER OWN CONVICTION AND A CALL TO ACTION.

CHAPTER 12

Delivering Your Speech Effectively

CHAPTER SURVEY

Sounding Good versus Being Sound

Principles of Good Delivery

Speaking Extemporaneously

Alternative Styles of Delivery

Responding to Audience Questions

CHAPTER OBJECTIVES

After studying this chapter, you should be able to

1. Distinguish ethically sound from ethically questionable delivery.

2. Describe and apply the basic characteristics of good delivery.

3. Deliver an effective extemporaneous speech using a keyword outline.

4. Compare and contrast different styles of delivery, describing the strengths and weaknesses of each.

5. Anticipate audience questions and various ways of responding to them.

In 1847 a young woman graduated from Oberlin College and began a career as a reformer, lecturing throughout the country first in support of the abolition of slavery and then, by 1850, on behalf of women's suffrage. In a time when the few women who dared to speak in public were subjected to ridicule and abuse, it took conviction, courage, and a commanding presence to appear before often hostile audiences. She was frequently praised for her logic and her command of the facts. According to one listener, her message was "wholly irresistible to every person who cares for reason or justice." It would, however, have been difficult to hold a skeptical audience without powerful delivery—and that Lucy Stone had. She was, one observer wrote, "small in stature but large of soul . . . her bearing modest and dignified, her face radiant with feeling, and speaking all over, as it were, in eloquent accord with her earnest voice."[1]

You are not likely to confront the kind of challenges faced by Lucy Stone, and most of us would have a hard time meeting them as well as she did. But in all cases of public speaking—from the classroom, to the meeting hall, to the public platform, delivery will play a significant part in any speaker's success or failure. Delivery is one of the most obvious aspects of public speaking, and one that draws the initial focus of both speakers and listeners. Yet, an engaging delivery cannot compensate for a speech that is poorly structured or lacking in substance. We might begin, then, by considering the impact that substantive and ethical concerns may have on the way we respond to delivery—our own and other speakers' as well.

Sounding Good versus Being Sound

Preview. *One of the speaker's ethical obligations is to try to present a message of substance. Good delivery, while important and desirable, is no substitute for sound ideas. Having ethical and effective delivery means remaining audience centered, avoiding behaviors that distract from the message, and promoting the listeners' understanding.*

Sometimes we find ourselves thinking that a speaker sounded good but did not have anything important to say. On other occasions, we might feel that a speaker's delivery is so striking that it actually distracts from the content of his or her speech. This may be a purposeful act on the part of the speaker, or it may be an accident. In either case, it is not good delivery.

Beyond Delivery: Listening to the Message

The immediacy of a public speaking situation—in which the speaker and the listener actually encounter each other and the audience witnesses the speech's presentation—sometimes gives unwarranted influence to delivery. A speaker who is poised and articulate, has a good voice, and appears confident and friendly may impress us. Sometimes, however, such a speaker is merely facile—he or she can speak easily but might not be saying very much. It is important to distinguish between a speaker who *is* sound and a speaker who just *sounds* good.

A sound speaker's ideas pass the rigorous tests that grow out of the principles embodied throughout this book. As much as we might admire the ease and grace with which a particular speaker addresses an audience, we need to be on our guard against the slick, superficial speaker who tries to manipulate or deceive us rather than engage us in a discussion of important ideas.

The Foundation of Ethical Delivery

Ethical delivery grows out of a collaborative, audience-centered model of communication (as described in Chapter 3). The speaker communicates with the utmost respect for listeners—never seeking to manipulate them, but aiming instead for mutually beneficial outcomes. The ethical speaker then is not putting on an "act," but is speaking authentically—always concerned with the greater good and ever mindful of the needs, values, and priorities of those assembled to listen.

Ethical delivery does not subvert the content or meaning of the speech. It is appropriate to the situation, including the size and character of the audience. An ethical speaker avoids intentionally using dramatic gestures, striking movement, or exaggerated vocal patterns to distract the audience from the speech's content. Not only is this kind of delivery ethically questionable, it also can backfire. Effective and ethical delivery should *reinforce* rather than compete with the speaker's ideas.

Finally, ethical delivery promotes the listeners' trust and comprehension. When you make a speech, your body, voice, and gestures must be in tune with the mood and nature of your message. Never forget that your audience will form impressions of you and your ideas based, in some measure, on how you deliver your speech. A speaker may have some compelling reasons for urging an audience to take an action, but if the speaker, through a dull and lifeless delivery, does not seem to care, the message may be lost. And if the message is important to the welfare of the community, then everybody loses.

Keeping these fundamental principles in mind will guide the way you approach the delivery of your own speeches. In addition, experience and research suggest a number of practical strategies that are generally associated with effective, engaging delivery. Even though delivery is only one aspect of the speaking process, it remains quite noticeable and influential.

Principles of Good Delivery

Preview. *Certain basic principles of effective delivery are applicable across a wide variety of public speaking situations. You will want to adapt your delivery to the specific situation and to audience expectations. In general, effective delivery is associated with proper attire; good eye contact; appropriate gestures, movement, and facial expressions; and a dynamic yet conversational speaking voice.*

Most of us recognize the importance of delivery, and sometimes we may become apprehensive at the thought of "standing and delivering" a speech.[2] You will confront many questions related to delivery. Should I use a podium? Should I move around during my speech? How quickly should I speak? Will everybody be able to hear me?

There are no absolute answers to any of these questions. You will need to adjust your style of delivery to the demands of each speaking situation.

The person who invited you to speak should be able to offer you some guidance concerning the formality of the occasion and the expectations of audience members. It is wise to find out as much as you can about the situation before moving forward with plans for delivering your speech. Above all, you will want to use a delivery style that allows you to connect with the audience.

Understand the Situation and Audience Expectations

What is appropriate in one speaking situation may be inappropriate in another. The more you learn about audience members' needs, norms, and preferences, the more likely you are to deliver your speech effectively. Do these listeners expect a formal presentation, or do they like to sit in a circle and have the speaker "chat" with them? Is this an after-dinner speech, to be delivered in a hotel conference room equipped with a podium and technological support? If so, will the listeners expect you to speak from behind the podium and make use of technology?

One woman embarrassed herself when she arrived to give her manuscript speech and discovered that there was no podium anywhere in the building. Since she did not want to hold the manuscript in front of her and read from it, she asked the president of the organization what could be done. The best he could do was to produce a large cardboard box, which he turned upside down and placed on top of a table to create a makeshift podium. Unfortunately, the box detracted from the seriousness of the speaker's remarks about suicide among college students: it boldly advertised Red Dog Beer!

Dress for the Occasion

How should you dress when you deliver a speech? Your appearance can influence audience perceptions of your ethos. Although there are no fixed rules for attire, listeners generally expect speakers to look well groomed and to be nicely dressed.[3] How listeners themselves are dressed provides one clue. You would not want to be wearing jeans and a polo shirt if audience members were wearing suits and ties. In your public speaking class, casual attire is probably appropriate. Check with your speech instructor for further guidance.

When you go to the trouble of looking good and dressing well, you are conveying to the audience that you respect them and that you take the occasion seriously. You want to feel confident about the way you look and to feel comfortable as well. Dress comfortably by avoiding shoes that are too tight or clothes that are too snug. Also avoid any attire that detracts from your speech, such as a flamboyant blouse or a baseball cap.

Establish Eye Contact

Have you ever talked with someone who did not look you in the eye? Did you feel that the person was uncomfortable? Nervous? Ashamed? Preoccupied? Dishonest?

In U.S. culture, when a communicator cannot or does not look us in the eye, we often respond negatively.[4] Our response is no different in public speaking situations. As listeners, we respond more positively to speakers who make eye contact with us.

Of course, there are cultural variations in practices and reactions to eye contact. For instance, Puerto Ricans consider it disrespectful to make prolonged eye contact with superiors.[5] In Japan, meeting participants often look down or close their eyes while others are talking. By doing so, they show their attentiveness to and even agreement with the speaker.[6]

Regardless of cultural differences, our eyes can be very expressive. As we squint, smile, laugh, frown, or scowl, we communicate many emotions: concern, commitment, joy, or anger. When we fail to establish eye contact, we must rely solely on our words, voice, gestures, and facial expressions to convey emotions. In U.S. culture, we clearly place ourselves at a disadvantage if we do not use our eyes to communicate.[7]

Another reason for establishing eye contact is to convey sincerity. In general, we are more likely to believe a speaker who looks us in the eye while defending his or her point of view.[8] When we establish eye contact with our listeners, we come across as truthful, candid, open, and trustworthy.

Finally, looking at the members of the audience gives us a chance to observe their reactions to our speech. How can we clarify what we are saying if we have not noticed that our listeners seem confused? How can we benefit from appreciative smiles and nods of encouragement if we are not looking? Almost all audience feedback will be nonverbal until after the speech is over. So if we "close our eyes," we miss out on an important chance to make our speech more of a dialogue and less of a monologue. When we *do* respond appropriately to audience reactions, we are behaving with sensitivity and respect.

As you establish eye contact with your audience, remember to share your attention with everyone. Avoid focusing on only a few friendly faces or your speech instructor. Try to include all sections of the room, and avoid staring at particular audience members as if in a trance. Also avoid darting your eyes or glancing up and down from the outline as if bobbing for apples. Table 12.1 highlights several pat-

Table 12.1

INEFFECTIVE EYE PATTERNS

The Bobber:	Bobs up from notes, like that little dog folks used to display in the back glass of their cars.
The Stargazer:	Looks above and beyond the audience at a spot on the back wall.
The Obsessor:	Limits eye contact to one, two, or a few individuals. The intensity of the gaze can become uncomfortable for the victim(s), while the rest of the audience feels left out.
The Excluder:	Limits eye contact to one side of the room—obliterating everyone on the other side.

terns of eye contact to be avoided. Of all the principles of effective delivery, maintaining good eye contact with your listeners may be the most important.

Reinforce Ideas through Gestures, Movement, and Facial Expressions

Most of us use a number of gestures in ordinary conversation. We wave our hands, point, or pound on the table to emphasize a point. Our movement can also communicate to others, intentionally or unintentionally.[9] We pace, slouch in our chairs, move closer to someone to express liking or intimacy, or move farther away to create distance or convey aloofness. We communicate a great deal with our faces, too.[10] Through facial expressions, we smile broadly, scowl, raise an eyebrow, or clench our teeth to communicate our determination, anger, or stubbornness.

Our words and actions should be mutually reinforcing.[11] If you were talking to a friend about something that mattered to you, you might say, "I *really* want you to consider doing this!" At the same time, you might lean forward, look into her or his eyes, and nod your head. Some public speakers might use very similar words in speaking to an audience but deliver them with a deadpan face, little eye contact, and limited movement or gestures. No audience is likely to be moved by such a bland and contradictory appeal. If what we say and how we say it contradict each other, listeners will place more faith in our nonverbal behavior.[12]

Lively delivery is often sparked by the speaker's passion for his or her subject. Speakers who are animated and in contact with an audience are more interesting to listen to.

Perhaps you are uncertain about whether your movement, gestures, and facial expressions are appropriate. If so, you need to watch yourself speak in front of a mirror or on videotape, or ask someone to watch you practice your speech and give you feedback. Here are some questions you might want to consider to guide your thinking:

- Do I gesture enough? Too much?
- Does my movement seem to reinforce the flow of the speech?
- Are my gestures distracting in any way?
- Do I rely too much on any one gesture?
- Does my face seem to convey the meaning or feeling I am trying to communicate?
- Are there different gestures, movements, or facial expressions that might convey my intended meaning more effectively?
- Does my nonverbal communication consistently convey a respectful attitude toward the audience?[13]

Although a few basic gestures and movements can be planned in advance, *most* should occur spontaneously as you interact with your audience. Your movements will vary as you give your speech at different times, in different rooms, and to different audiences. For instance, the same gestures that you use in ordinary conversation might work well if you are speaking to an audience of 25 or fewer. But if you are speaking to 150 people assembled in an auditorium, you might need to enlarge your gestures so that they can be seen by everyone.

Finally, make sure that your movements are not perceived as nervous or distracting. Some speakers pace nervously. They play with their earrings, stroke their hair, chew gum, hang onto the podium, or tap with a pencil. Still others use such exaggerated gestures that they look foolish or melodramatic. Whenever a gesture calls attention to itself, you should eliminate it.

Strive for an Effective Speaking Voice

One of the most obvious aspects of any speaker's delivery is, of course, his or her voice. Have you ever listened to a speaker whose voice really bothered you? Perhaps she or he spoke in a monotone, stumbled over words, or inserted "you know" between every sentence. Or maybe the speaker's pitch was too high and squeaky or too low and unvarying. Clearly, our voices can get us into trouble as public speakers. But they can also be used compellingly to convey our passion about an issue. When we use our voices effectively, we can emphasize key ideas, display a wide variety of emotions, establish our commitment, and enhance our credibility.

You will want to consider seriously how you can best use your voice. You might try speaking into an audio recorder and playing it back to see what your voice sounds like to others. Obtaining feedback from friends also can be helpful, since they are likely to notice peculiarities that might sound "normal" to you. You can modify some features of your voice by recognizing their importance, paying attention to them in oral practice, and monitoring them as you speak. These features are volume, rate, pitch, and clarity.

Volume

If listeners cannot hear your message, they obviously cannot learn from or be per-suaded by it. Nor will they be able to concentrate on your message if you speak so loudly that they feel uncomfortable.

The volume of your delivery should be determined by the setting in which you speak. Naturally, a small room calls for a quieter voice than does a large lecture hall or an outdoor setting. If you are concerned that you are not being heard when you begin to speak, you may show your respect for your listeners by asking them. They will appreciate your asking and will be glad to give you feedback.

Rate

It is not uncommon for a beginning speaker to sit down after giving a speech, look at the clock, and be amazed to find that the planned 10-minute speech took only 5 minutes. Several miscalculations could account for this, but often the problem is simply that the speaker rushed through the speech. Keep in mind that your audience needs time to absorb and process your speech—especially if you are addressing a complex or thought-provoking issue.

The needs of the listeners are paramount. Just as they cannot keep up with a speaker who is talking too quickly, they will lose interest in one who speaks too slowly. Rate and fluency can be interrelated. Often, speakers who have not practiced will drag through a speech, stumbling along with "ums" and "ahs," pausing too fre-quently, or filling in gaps with the ubiquitous and irritating "you know." In fact, some research suggests that listeners may perceive speakers who speak quickly (though not breathtakingly fast) as quite knowledgeable, thus potentially enhancing their ethos.[14]

Your rate should be determined by your audience's ability to process the infor-mation. If you are offering a brief historical perspective on a problem that is widely acknowledged by the audience, such as the high cost of fuel, you can speak fairly briskly. But if you are advancing some innovative solutions to the problem of U.S. dependence on foreign oil suppliers, you would likely need to speak more slowly. To increase the potential for achieving your desired response, strive to speak at a rate that is appropriate to the audience's knowledge level and the complexity and novelty of the ideas you are presenting.

Finally, your speaking rate can be used to emphasize key ideas. Pausing gives the audience the opportunity to absorb information and ideas. At the same time, by using silence to reinforce a compelling statistic, quotation, or narrative, you are saying to the audience, "Let's stop to contemplate this for a minute. This is important." Similarly, you may slow down or use restatement to emphasize an idea. When you vary your rate—by pausing, slowing down, or using restatement or repetition at critical and strategic moments—you enhance your chances of delivering a memorable speech.

Pitch

Sometimes a speaker's voice is simply unpleasant to listen to. It may be squeaky or raspy, or it may be pitched so low that you can hardly distinguish one word from the next. Pitch refers to the highness or lowness of your voice on a musical scale. It is the voice's upward or downward inflection. A speaker's vocal pitch can be too high, too low, or too unvarying. When the pitch is too high, listeners tend to cringe. When the pitch is too low, listeners may be unable to hear what the speaker is saying. An unvarying pitch is called a *monotone*—a vocal quality guaranteed to put your audience to sleep.

Rightly or wrongly, listeners often draw conclusions about speakers whose pitch seems inappropriate. A high pitch may be associated with immaturity, inexperience, tension, or excitability. A low pitch or a monotone may cause listeners to view the speaker as being bored or unengaged. By contrast, a richer pitch, one with depth and variety, can communicate a sense of authority and competence.[15]

What can you do about pitch? Start by audio-recording your voice and listening to what you hear. If you are not satisfied, you may want to use some vocal exercises to improve your pitch. In extreme cases, you may want to seek assistance from someone trained in voice therapy. Here are a few pointers to keep in mind:

- Your pitch will vary throughout your life. It will be higher when you are younger and lower later in life. Working with it is an ongoing process.
- If you are tense, your pitch tends to rise. Use the relaxation techniques outlined in Chapter 3 to help you manage communication apprehension.
- Strive for variety in your pitch. You want your voice to be interesting, and you want to use all aspects of your voice to emphasize the things you most value.

Clarity

To be effective in informing or persuading, you must be understood. While speaking at an appropriate speed can certainly help you communicate more clearly, other vocal considerations are also important. Your achievement of vocal clarity depends on your speaking in ways that reflect the following qualities.

First, strive for distinctness in articulation. Dropping the endings of words, slurring sounds, and running words together can interfere with the meaning of a message. For example, the speaker whose use of "locked out" is mistaken by listeners for "lucked out" is probably suffering from poor articulation. Articulation is especially likely to suffer when a speaker rushes through the speech, so monitoring speed is quite important.

Second, strive for correct pronunciation of the words you use. This may mean using a dictionary to determine the correct way to pronounce unusual or unfamiliar words. Practice aloud so that you are comfortable saying the words you are using, and especially check the pronunciation of words used in quoted material.

Finally, try to avoid disruptive vocal mannerisms. It is pointless and distracting to keep saying "you know." One speaker obscured the clarity of his message by concluding almost every statement with the unnecessary question, "Right?" Also, there are regional mannerisms that clutter speech and thus reduce clarity, such as the question "Hear?" at the end of a sentence, or the unnecessary "at" tacked on to statements such as "He didn't know where I was *at*." Such mannerisms are distracting to listeners.[16]

Remain Flexible

No matter how carefully you plan and practice in advance, some speaking situations will surprise you. Flexibility is the key to responding successfully to these situations. You might find the podium is missing or the microphone not working. You might be told at the last minute that you have less time to speak than originally planned, and that you will have to cut your speech short. Or, imagine that you expected to deliver a formal speech to a large audience, but when you arrived, there were only five or six people present. Rather than standing behind a podium and speaking formally, you might want to adapt to the situation by sitting on the edge of a table and informally "chatting" with the group.

The foundation of flexibility is spontaneity and open-mindedness—a willingness to recognize that there are many different ways to deliver a good speech and an ability to discover a "better" way whenever a situation seems to demand it. Speakers need not always stand or use a podium, and they *can* engage the audience in dialogue if doing so seems fitting and consistent with the audience's norms and expectations. The *Highlighting Flexibility* that follows offers a highly dramatic example.

Highlighting Flexibility

A Dramatic Example

Perhaps the most extraordinary—and certainly unique—example of flexibility came during a presidential election. Former president Theodore Roosevelt, who had failed to secure his party's nomination in 1912, was running for president as a candidate of a third party, the Progressive or "Bull Moose" Party. With scarcely three weeks to go before the election, Roosevelt's campaign pulled into Milwaukee, where he was scheduled to speak before a huge rally of supporters. As Roosevelt left his hotel, a man stepped up to him and fired a gun at point-blank range. The bullet passed through the copy of Roosevelt's speech, which was 50 pages, folded over—long speeches were typical in pre-TV days—and his glasses case before lodging in the candidate's chest muscle. Feeling as if he had been "kicked by a mule," but determined to continue, TR refused to go immediately to a hospital, insisting instead that he go on and give his speech. Usually a dynamic speaker with a robust, energetic style, Roosevelt quieted the cheering crowd that greeted him. Raising his arm, he said quietly, "I shall ask you to be as quiet as possible. I don't know whether you fully understand that I have just been shot; but it takes more than that to kill a bull moose." Opening his coat, revealing the blood-stained shirt, Roosevelt showed the crowd the speech text with the bullet hole. Since "the bullet is in me now," Roosevelt explained, he would not give a very long speech. "But," he said, "I will try my best." Speaking without the bullet-torn manuscript, Roosevelt spoke extemporaneously for a very painful hour and a half before his anxious aides were able to get him off the platform and to a hospital.

This example is, of course, very dramatic and makes the loss of a note card or facing a larger audience than you anticipated seem like a very small thing. But while you will not experience such an extreme situation, you will find times when circumstances are not what you expected them to be, and you will need to be prepared to be flexible.

Sources: See H. W. Brands, *TR: The Last Romantic* (New York: Basic Books, 1997): 720–22; Nathan Miller, *Theodore Roosevelt: A Life* (New York: William Morrow, 1992): 530–31.

Practice Your Speech

Sometimes speakers think that once they have carefully researched their topic, organized their thoughts, and prepared their outline, all they need to do is read through the outline silently a few times—and they will be ready to go. Nothing could be further from the truth. If you have not practiced your speech aloud several times, chances are you are not prepared to speak.[17]

The following are a few guidelines for practicing your speech:

- Practice delivering your speech aloud with your keyword outline. But first read through your notes silently several times until you feel ready to begin.
- Practice your speech all the way through—noting sections that are rough, rereading and revising your notes, and then practicing again.
- Break the speech into parts and practice major sections, such as the introduction, several times in a row.
- Always take breaks. Avoid practicing so much at one time that you begin to lose your energy, voice, or concentration.
- Record (either audio or video) your speech and play it back. Avoid focusing on minor aspects of your delivery, and focus on major issues.
- Practice in front of a small audience and ask for their constructive feedback.
- Over a period of time, practice your speech again several times, all the way through, but do not try to memorize your speech.
- Be sure to incorporate your visual aids into your practice sessions. If possible, visit the room where you will speak and practice using the equipment there.
- Be sure to time yourself several times. If your speech is too long, make appropriate cuts. For instance, you might cut a section that is less important, use fewer examples, or edit long quotations. It is important to remember that practicing your speech is something you do *before* the beginning of class or *before* you are seated in front of the audience in a community or professional setting. Sometimes speakers read through their notes while others are speaking. Do not fall into this trap. Practice sufficiently beforehand, so that you will be able to listen to other speakers. Not only do they deserve your respectful attention, but you even might learn something that you can refer to in your own speech.

Seek Out Opportunities to Speak

As you gain experience and confidence as a public speaker, you will tend to deliver your speeches more effectively. This is especially true if you ask for listener feedback and strive to improve by addressing whatever weaknesses they identify. In addition, if you are speaking about an issue of importance that deeply concerns you, you are more likely to speak with confidence and passion. When you deliver your remarks with personal commitment, you are more likely to speak with force, clarity, directness, and spontaneity—all hallmarks of effective delivery.

Depending on the occasion, listener expectations, and other demands of the speaking situation, speakers may choose to use varying styles of delivery, ranging from those that are more informal and flexible to those that are more formal and scripted. In *most* speaking situations, however, the preferred delivery style is extemporaneous.

In 2003, Proposition 54 on the California ballot, which sought to amend the Constitution to prohibit using race as a factor in education and employment, was vigorously opposed by civil rights groups. At this anti-Prop 54 rally, the speaker's delivery was appropriately extemporaneous and enlivened by the passion she felt about this issue.

Speaking Extemporaneously

Preview. *Extemporaneous speaking requires careful preparation. Using this delivery style and speaking from a keyword outline allows you to be completely involved in your speech. At the same time, you can maintain the flexibility you need to be adaptable and dynamic.*

Sometimes people confuse extemporaneous speaking, which requires careful preparation, with impromptu or spur-of the moment speaking. This leads them to believe that they do not have to do very much to prepare for an extemporaneous speech. In fact, to give an extemporaneous speech, you must engage in thoughtful, thorough research, organize, develop, and outline your ideas carefully, practice your speech several times without memorizing it word for word, and deliver it using limited notes.

When delivering a speech extemporaneously, you may commit some key ideas to memory, but words, phrases, and examples typically vary during practice sessions as well as during the actual presentation of the speech. Thus, you have the advantage of being well prepared, yet you also have the ability to adapt to the situation when changes seem prudent.

Preparing and Using a Keyword Outline

When you deliver a speech extemporaneously, you will typically use speaking notes in the form of a keyword outline, discussed in Chapter 10. This outline keeps you on track and reminds you of your main ideas, but it does not provide so much information that you are tempted to use it as a crutch. You will stick to your main ideas, but you will be encouraged to speak directly with your audience, to watch for their responses, to move as you speak, and to make changes that seem justified by the situation.

On many occasions, you will not be the only speaker. For example, in class you will typically speak on a day when several other people are also speaking. Should someone refer to a piece of evidence or an event that is relevant to your topic, you may decide, during your speech, that you will make some reference to what that speaker has said. For example, you might say: "Joan has already made us keenly aware of how poorly our campus is equipped to serve disabled students. Well, our campus has another problem that affects all of us: it is not a very safe place to go to school." Or, you might be speaking as part of a community forum during which several speakers will be addressing the same basic topic, such as affordable housing. In these situations, it is essential that you listen closely to your fellow panelists and refer to their comments and perspectives. Doing so demonstrates respect for your fellow citizens and helps you to avoid repeating what others already have said. You can then make the most of your time to present fresh, relevant, and useful information and ideas.

Whenever you are able to do some last-minute fine-tuning, you show others in your audience that you have been paying attention to what others have said. Doing so helps you to connect with your audience, establish a sense of community among your fellow speakers, and enhance your own ethos. The *Focus on Civic Engagement* provides an example of a keyword outline for a persuasive speech. (See Chapter 10 for another example.)

Keep in mind that there are no absolute rules for constructing your keyword outline. That is, you may choose to record only a few words to jog your memory and guide your delivery. Or, you may elect to write out those things that you especially want to emphasize, such as statistics, a compelling quotation, or particular language that you have worked hard to craft as part of your assignment. In any case, practicing with your notes (as well as revising and refining them as you practice) is essential.

Reasons for Using Extemporaneous Delivery

With extemporaneous speaking, you have the ability to adapt to the audience and the situation. You can make changes, clarify or elaborate with examples or illustrations, omit a minor point if time is running short, and more effectively involve the audience in your speech. You can choose to spend more time responding to questions if the audience seems eager to talk with you.

Extemporaneous speaking demands total involvement from you. You cannot just read from a manuscript or rely on an overly detailed outline. Nor can you "zone out" or speak from a hastily prepared outline. Speaking extemporaneously demands a carefully constructed set of notes, encourages you to remain audience centered, and makes it possible for your speech to react creatively.

Using an extemporaneous style of speaking also encourages you to show your passion for your topic. As you speak extemporaneously, you are able to interject spontaneous comments that allow you to really connect with the audience. Because

Focus on Civic Engagement

A Keyword Outline for a Speech Advocating Involvement with Habitat for Humanity

INTRODUCTION

I. Story of single-parent domestic abuse survivor
II. Personal participation in Habitat builds
III. Show relevance—helping others—college is a good time to start
IV. Thesis: Becoming actively involved with Habitat is an excellent way of making a difference in others' lives.
V. Preview—define Habitat, look at where it operates, explain how the system works, and describe how to get involved.

BODY

I. Habitat is a terrific organization, with many distinguished accomplishments.
  A. Nonprofit Christian housing ministry (according to the Habitat website)
  B. Started in the U.S. in 1976 by Millard Fuller
  C. Eliminating substandard housing worldwide
  D. Makes adequate housing a matter of conscience and action
II. HH has gained a large following in its 30 years.
  A. All 50 states in the U.S. (*Habitat World*, January 2006)
  B. Nearly 100 other countries
  C. Over 2,200 total affiliates
  D. Local Habitat building 64th house (*Habitat News*, March 2006)
III. Habitat has developed a model system that is both fair and efficient.

A. Selection criteria for homeowners (local Habitat director, Thomson)
  1. Need
  2. Ability to repay no-interest mortgage
  3. Willingness to put in "sweat equity" hours
B. Builds modest homes
  1. About 1,100 square feet
  2. Low mortgage payments—under $300 per month
C. Money reverts to a "Fund for Humanity"—supports future projects
IV. Getting involved in HH is easily done.
  A. Find local affiliate
  B. Gifts from the heart (financial and food donations)
  C. Global village—Habitat volunteer vacation
  D. Women's Build
  E. Campus chapters and programs
  F. Jimmy Carter's Work Project (distribute handouts)

CONCLUSION

I. Revisit personal story—working with great people, community building.
II. Summarize—we've looked closely at Habitat—what it is, how it works, and how you can get involved.
III. Appeal for action—offer immediate opportunity to join local chapter and end with moving quote from homeowner: "This is the first time my three children have had a real home. Without HH, this never would have been possible."

you are intellectually engaged, you are able to speak in the moment and communicate with the conviction and passion that you feel. When well done, an extemporaneous style of speaking contributes to your ethos as a committed and effective advocate.[18] Former president Bill Clinton excels in delivering speeches extemporaneously but sometimes struggles with other delivery styles, as is illustrated in the by the observations of a *New York Times* reporter in the following *Highlighting Connecting with the Audience*.

Occasionally speakers will want to consider using a style of delivery that is not extemporaneous but that is well suited to the demands of a particular event or situation. Every speaker should be aware of existing options, and the contexts in which they would be most appropriate.

President Clinton's Delivery

Remember how Bill Clinton electrified a joint session of Congress in 1993 by brandishing a prototype of a national health care card and calling for "health care that can never be taken away, health care that is always there"?

That speech still stands as one of the most impressive formal addresses of his Presidency. And perhaps it was no accident that Mr. Clinton could hold that Congress in his sway even though he was winging it for seven minutes as the wrong text scrolled across the teleprompter. But he might not be as dramatic Tuesday when he delivers his State of the Union Address.

For Mr. Clinton has a curious split personality when it comes to oratory. Speaking extemporaneously, he can be arresting, eloquent, and amusing. . . . His turns of phrase twang with a delicious backwoodsiness. During the campaign, he said of the Republican budget proposal: "It is their dog. And it was a mangy old dog, and that's why I vetoed that dog." And at the pulpit of a church, Mr. Clinton can burn with a preacher's passion that rivals the Reverend Jesse Jackson's.

But put this president in the most stately settings of government with a written text and a teleprompter and his eloquence sometimes fades. Connectedness is the key to his best oratory, his aides say. Mr. Clinton needs the synergy of the crowd; he needs to feel people's enthusiasm or their pain.

Source: From "State of the Speech: Reading between the Lines," by Alison Mitchell, *The New York Times*, February 2, 1997, p. E5. Used by permission of The New York Times.

Alternative Styles of Delivery

Preview. *Besides the extemporaneous style of delivery, speakers can choose from several other presentation styles that range from very informal to quite formal. The style you choose will depend on your preference, the demands of the speaking situation, and audience expectations.*

When it comes time to give your speech, you need to choose the type of delivery you want to use. Most speakers need to develop the ability to use different styles of delivery, since different topics or occasions call for different approaches. You would not want to speak to a large, formal meeting with a casual, off-the-cuff style; nor would you want to speak to your classmates about the need to become involved in student government by writing out and then reading a speech word for word. It is important to fit the delivery style to the situation.

In addition to the extemporaneous style, there are three other styles of delivery: impromptu, manuscript, and memorized speaking. Although the extemporaneous style is appropriate in most public speaking situations, each of the others deserves some attention.

The Impromptu Speech

Impromptu speaking is off-the-cuff and casual, delivered with little or no preparation. In general, you should never choose to make an impromptu speech if you are given time to prepare in advance. There may be occasions, however, when you find yourself in a situation where impromptu speaking is the only option.

As a member of the audience at a forum on health-care reform, for example, you may feel compelled to respond to what other speakers have said. Perhaps you want to share a hair-raising experience you once had in the local hospital's emergency room, or maybe you want to argue for a new health-care facility for low-income citizens. On other occasions, you may be called on to articulate your point of view, make a brief report, or explain a procedure. Requests for these "speeches" often arise during business or professional meetings when someone needs information. In some of your classes, instructors may occasionally hold unannounced discussions or debates, and you may be asked to make brief, spontaneous comments or to defend your point of view. It is important to recognize all of these as serious speaking opportunities, even if there is little time to prepare for them.

Your speech instructor also may choose to hold occasional rounds of impromptu speeches. These speeches are usually designed to help you get accustomed to standing up and speaking in front of your classmates without having to worry about formal evaluation. They also give you a chance to "think on your feet." Impromptu speeches can be creative and enjoyable in this context.

Guidelines for Giving Impromptu Speeches

When giving an impromptu speech, you have limited time to organize your thoughts. Even so, here are a few things you can do to succeed:

- *Anticipate the possibility that you might be called on to speak, and make some preparations.* If you are taking a class and the instructor knows that you have had a specific experience relevant to a topic being discussed, you might be asked to share your experience. What might you share? Jot down a few notes and take them to class with you. Similarly, when you are going to a meeting or community forum, examine the agenda or the speakers' topics to get some sense of the topics that might be discussed. Even if no one has asked you to speak, you might find yourself wanting to share your views. If so, prepare in advance.
- *Practice active listening.* In a meeting, it is critical that you follow the flow of the conversation. If you are daydreaming and you suddenly hear someone say, "Kevin, does this plan make sense to you?" you will be hard-pressed to say anything, much less offer a coherent opinion. Of course, when you are listening to others who are presenting formal speeches, you will want to follow all of the guidelines for engaged and active listening discussed in Chapter 4.
- *Increase your feelings of confidence by reminding yourself that no one expects you to be perfect when you offer impromptu remarks.* Listener expectations are always higher when the speaker is delivering a planned presentation. In impromptu speaking, however, listeners expect some small mistakes in fluency, more repetition, or perhaps more pauses as you gather your thoughts or think of more examples.

- *Use even limited preparation time to your advantage.* At community forums or in professional conferences, you can take notes while listening to a panel or symposium. These notes will help you recall more accurately what others have said, and can also serve as the foundation for your impromptu remarks.
- *Use basic principles of speech organization.* Even an impromptu speech should have an introduction, a body, and a conclusion. Within the body, you will want to follow some basic structure, such as chronological or categorical order. Your organizational pattern can be simple yet easy to follow. You may want to offer a preview and summary, depending on time constraints. It is also a good idea to sketch out a rough outline, in whatever limited preparation time is available to you.
- *Speak briefly and concisely.* Regardless of the situation, impromptu speeches should not consume too much time. When people gather together—for a class, a conference, a business meeting, or a community forum—there is usually a planned agenda. When someone is asked (or volunteers) to make impromptu comments, he or she is adding to what might be an already full agenda. Keep your impromptu comments brief, allowing time for others to participate.
- *Think of impromptu speaking as an opportunity to practice and develop your delivery.* When you speak without notes or with very limited notes, you have an opportunity to focus even more on your vocal and physical delivery and how listeners react to your style of speaking.

The Manuscript Speech

At the other end of the delivery continuum is the manuscript speech. Although you may or may not deliver speeches from manuscript in your public speaking class, some occasions invite the use of a prepared manuscript. For instance, you may be representing an organization and addressing an important, controversial topic. Perhaps the press will be covering your comments, and you want to be careful to use just the right words. Or perhaps you are delivering a ceremonial address, and you have carefully chosen language that you think is eloquent or even poetic. In these situations, the manuscript not only allows you to say precisely what you planned to say, but also provides a written record of your remarks.

Some settings may call for manuscript speeches because of their formal nature. When delivering a commencement address, for example, you would probably want to write out the speech. Or you could be called on to make some formal remarks at the installation of officers of an organization to which you belong. The president of the United States delivers many important speeches from manuscript, such as the State of the Union address.

Using a manuscript allows you to exercise considerable control. You can time your speech accurately, choose your words carefully, and decide precisely how to state your most important ideas. The underlying principles of good public speaking also apply to the manuscript speech: you should be well prepared, practice your speech, and make sure that you prepare a manuscript copy that you can read easily while speaking.[19]

Guidelines for Giving Manuscript Speeches

Delivering a manuscript speech presents special challenges related to eye contact, movement, the use of your voice, and flexibility. Here are some guidelines to follow:

- *Use a manuscript for the right reasons.* Use a manuscript when it is important to choose your words carefully and say exactly what you mean. Do not use it as a crutch to hide behind or as a way to manage your anxieties.
- *Use good oral style.* Even though you are speaking from a manuscript, you should still use language that is more characteristic of oral than written style. This means that you will choose words and construct your sentences in ways that are still easily understood by listeners.
- *Practice extensively.* You must know the material well enough to look at the audience and get back to the manuscript without losing your place. You need a clean, double-spaced copy printed in an easily readable font. The more important the speaking event, the more pressing the need for practice. In the following *Highlighting the Significance of Practice*, a *New York Times* reporter described President George W. Bush's painstaking practice as he prepared to deliver his

Highlighting the Significance of Practice

President George W. Bush Prepares to Address Congress

The president had to rehearse. It was the first thing he'd thought of after deciding to do the speech. The more he practices, the better his speeches come off. The downward furl of his mouth relaxes. His tendency to end every sentence with an upward cadence diminishes. The first teleprompter rehearsal was at 6:30 Wednesday night [the night before he would deliver the speech]. The president came out in his blue track suit with his baseball cap on . . . The president weighed the sounds in his mouth. He came to lines about the administration's domestic agenda . . .—the energy plan, the faith-based initiative, the patients' bill of rights. "This isn't the time," he said and cut them. Hughes [one of his advisers who often worked with the president on his speeches], agreed. This was the time for Bush to assert his credentials on foreign policy and not retreat into the domestic sphere.

The president made more cuts. When he saw how many billions of bailout dollars the speech promised for the airline industry, he insisted the line be deleted.

"We're still negotiating that," he said. He put in little things for sound. After "The United States respects the people of Afghanistan," he inserted the phrase "After all" to begin the next sentence, "we are currently its largest source of humanitarian aid." It would give him a chance to breathe.

Thursday morning, the day of the speech, Bush rehearsed again. He didn't like the clunky paragraph that contained the list of our allies: the Organization of American States and the European Union, among others. It was too much of a mouthful. They would no longer hear their names spoken.

The president took a nap at 4:30, was awakened by an aide and rehearsed one more time.

[He] walked into the Capitol, a president in wartime. . . .

During the course of his speech, he was interrupted for applause over 30 times.

Source: D. T. Max, "The Making of the Speech," *New York Times Magazine*, October 7, 2001, 37. Used by permission of D. T. Max.

speech to a joint session of Congress, one week following the terrorist attacks of 9/11.

■ *Look for opportunities to move and gesture.* When you speak from a manuscript, you may feel compelled to stand in one place—behind the podium and close to your script. You may even feel tempted to lean on the podium or to grasp it as if you were trying to anchor yourself in a strong wind. Do not succumb to these temptations. With planning and practice, you can speak from a manuscript and still move around, use appropriate gestures, and engage your audience with eye contact and facial expressions. The more comfortable you are with your manuscript, the freer you will feel to move and gesture in natural and content-reinforcing ways.

■ *Use your voice effectively.* Some speakers sound artificial or flat when delivering a manuscript speech. Their inflection may be less animated than in normal speaking, or they may sound singsong, as if they were doing a poor job of reading some bad poetry. To avoid falling into this trap, commit yourself to using your voice in ways that add variety, color, and emphasis—just as you do when speaking extemporaneously. You may want to write self-directives on your manuscript, such as

Formal speeches, such as the president's State of the Union speech, call for using a manuscript.

"slow down," "pause here for emphasis," or "project this/maybe repeat." You can also underline or otherwise highlight keywords and important phrases.

■ *Maintain flexibility*. Rather than adapting to the moment or reacting to audience feedback, speakers often feel compelled to read from their manuscript, word for word, with no deviations, no matter what. Yet, your manuscript is not intended to be a straitjacket. It can be changed. You *can* add different examples. You can (and often should) include spontaneous comments. When you use your manuscript with flexibility, you can remain connected with the audience and monitor their feedback.

The Memorized Speech

There are few situations where giving a memorized speech is a preferred option. Some students who enter speaking contests, such as the American Legion Oratorical Contest, are required to memorize their speeches. Similarly, more formal or ceremonial occasions might call for a short memorized speech: you might not want to use notes or a manuscript when you are proposing a toast at a wedding or paying tribute to a close friend or relative. Also, when giving an extemporaneous speech, you might want to memorize the introduction, the conclusion, or a striking piece of poetry for use during the course of the speech.

Guidelines for Giving Memorized Speeches

When you find yourself in a speaking situation in which you plan to speak from memory, keep these pointers in mind:

■ *Stay focused on your specific purpose and the key ideas you want to convey.* When you memorize, you may be tempted to focus on the specific words you plan to use. You may try to memorize, literally, word for word. But do not forget that the response you are trying to get from your audience depends more on the basic ideas you are conveying than on the exact phrasing. So, concentrating on your main ideas as you address them is critical.

■ *Speak in the moment.* Sometimes when speakers deliver a speech from memory, they go on "automatic pilot." They appear to forget the immediate situation and simply recite the words that they have drummed into their head. Under these conditions, their mind may wander or even go blank. The speech has become a performance rather than a communicative exchange with an audience.

   If you stay focused on your listeners and remember your specific purpose—and if you remain centered on ideas rather than on exact words—you will more likely stay tuned in to the moment and maintain your poise, focus, and flexibility.

■ *Practice, practice, practice.* To be effective, all speakers must practice, regardless of the style of delivery they plan to use. But the memorized speech may require even more practice—especially if the memorization is part of a speaking contest and the speaker must memorize a fairly long text.

When faced with such a situation, you should read through the text several times, then practice it in sections before trying to memorize the entire speech.

Practice sessions should be distributed over time rather than crammed into a few hours.

We can acknowledge benefits and potential liabilities associated with each style of delivering a speech. Even so, it is also important to remember that you will develop your own distinct style and preferences for delivering speeches. If your instructor will permit it, experiment with different styles of delivery. Find the one with that makes you most comfortable and that allows you to speak with conviction while connecting with your listeners.

Many public speeches are followed by opportunities to interact with the audience. During these question-and-answer sessions, speakers have the chance to listen to audience members, clarify and build on remarks made during the formal presentation, and continue to establish rapport with listeners.

Responding to Audience Questions

Preview. *After you make a speech, you will often be asked to entertain questions. The question-and-answer period is particularly important because it allows you to interact informally with the audience, to provide additional information, to enhance your credibility, and to initiate a respectful and mutually beneficial dialogue.*

Some speakers give little thought to the question-and-answer period. Instead they focus all their attention on the preparation and delivery of the formal speech. Yet many speakers damage their credibility when attempting to respond to audience questions. They reveal their ignorance, defensiveness, or prejudice through thoughtless or insensitive answers.

The question-and-answer period (sometimes referred to as a forum period) is a potentially crucial aspect of the public communication event. It is a time when the speaker and the listener exchange roles—when the listener does the speaking and the speaker does the listening. It is a dynamic time when the speaker genuinely engages the audience in dialogue.

Preparing for the Question-and-Answer Period

Although you cannot anticipate everything listeners might ask, you can make some good guesses. You should expect questions about controversial ideas you bring up in your speech. Try to anticipate arguments that listeners might use to challenge your ideas and how you would answer them. Be absolutely sure of your sources. Consider which parts of your speech might be most difficult to understand because of their technical nature or because they are outside the realm of listeners' experience. Try to think of additional examples or analogies or different ways to restate your explanations.

The more you know about your topic, the better prepared you will be to deal with questions. If all you know about a topic can be contained in a short speech, you are not thoroughly prepared. Gather and assimilate a lot more information than can fit into your speech. This will be very helpful to you in answering audience questions.

Fostering a Respectful Attitude toward Listeners

In addition to anticipating content-related issues, spend some time thinking about the attitude you will convey as you interact with your listeners. Even if you have had extensive experience with your topic, you should still approach the forum period with an open mind. You should display your interest in learning from your listeners and a genuine willingness to engage in a respectful dialogue with them. At times, listeners may challenge or disagree with you. Occasionally, they may even do so in ways that you consider abrasive or rude. Although being challenged in this way can be unpleasant, you can still respond with dignity and civility. As the speaker, *you* can establish the tone for the exchange and serve as a role model for the audience members. If you model respectful dialogue yourself, most audience members will appreciate your efforts and follow your lead.

Conducting the Question-and-Answer Period

Decide where you will stand as you receive audience questions. One option is to remain behind the podium. This conveys a sense of formality, maintaining some distance between you and the audience. Another option is to stand at the side or in front of the podium, where you can interact more directly with the audience. Finally, in informal settings, you might sit on a table and move into a "chatting" mode. Any of these options might work well, depending on the situation in which you are speaking, the audience's expectations, and your own preferences.

The following general guidelines may help you conduct the question-and-answer period. If you handle audience questions well, you can make your message more compelling.

The question-and-answer period following a speech is a time for respectful and mutually influential dialogue.

- *Listen carefully to each question posed.* If you can't hear the questioner very well, ask her or him to stand and repeat the question. Or move away from the podium and stand closer to the audience. As you listen, provide a few nonverbal cues, such as nodding your head, to let the questioner know that you are following the point being raised.
- *If appropriate, repeat each question so that everyone can hear it and keep track of what is happening.* In repeating the question, you may need to rephrase it, since audience members sometimes phrase their questions in awkward or rambling ways.
- *Do not allow one person to dominate the forum period.* If many people raise their hands at once, make sure you call on ones who have

not spoken previously. If someone who has already posed a question raises his or her hand again, you might ask, "Is there anyone else who has a question?" Occasionally a persistent questioner may try to engage you for an extended period of time. If that happens, you might invite that person to stay after the meeting to talk with you, and then move on to the next question.

- *Do not try to fake your way through a response.* If you do not know the answer to a question or are not familiar with some topic raised by a questioner, admit it. Perhaps a questioner will ask if you have read a particular book that relates to your presentation. Admitting that you do not know something is not always bad. Listeners respect speakers who admit that they do not know it all.

    If a listener poses a challenging or important question that you cannot answer, you can always offer to investigate the answer and get back to him or her. It is easy to get a listener's e-mail address following your talk—then, do your research and follow through with a thoughtful response. When you do this, you are behaving responsibly and respectfully toward the listener. At the same time, you are learning more about your topic—which may prove useful when you deliver similar speeches in the future.

- *Respect time limits.* Question-and-answer periods cannot go on forever. Like speeches, they have time constraints. Sometimes you will be asked to speak briefly and leave plenty of time for audience questions. Other times you will have only a little time left for interaction with the audience. Ask in advance what the audience expects or desires, and then follow through, cooperating with listener norms and expectations.

- *If appropriate, actively encourage listeners to participate.* Sometimes you may deliver a speech that generates a strong audience response. Or perhaps you have presented a lot of new information and you want to find out whether listeners have followed you. In these cases, you may want to solicit audience participation. You may begin in a very general way with: "What questions do you have?" Though useful in some situations, this approach does not provide any clues as to the kind of questions or comments that might be appropriate. In addition, some listeners are reluctant to speak up in front of others, so you may have to encourage them in various ways. One way to encourage audience participation might be to ask a more specific question, such as: "What do you think of the idea of making condoms widely available in public schools?" That kind of question signals an area of controversy and might inspire more reaction. Finally, you might encourage listeners to talk by moving from behind the podium or desk and standing closer to the audience or sitting on a table or desk. This action removes potential barriers and establishes the context for an informal exchange of ideas. As you continue to encourage listeners to interact with you, they will see that you are interested in engaging them in a respectful dialogue.[20]

Summary

- Ethical delivery grows from a collaborative, audience-centered approach to public speaking.
    - Good speakers try never to distract the audience through their delivery style.

- They do all they can to promote audience comprehension and understanding.
- They know that good, ethical delivery not only sounds good, it grows from a solid foundation—a carefully constructed, thoughtfully reasoned, and well-supported speech.
- There are many different ways to deliver a speech, ranging from the formal manuscript presentation to the very informal impromptu speech.
- For most public speaking situations, you will likely want to use the extemporaneous style, which involves meticulous preparation and is delivered from a keyword outline.
  - When you speak extemporaneously, you are encouraged to speak with flexibility, adapting to audience expectations and to the speaking context.
  - As you speak, you are able to establish eye contact with audience members, to use appropriate gestures, and to use your voice effectively.
  - Using extemporaneous delivery also encourages you to speak with passion and conviction.
  - Practicing your speech aloud and seeking out opportunities to speak can help you to develop an effective extemporaneous style of delivery.
- Other styles of delivery can also be appropriate, but each presents some special challenges.
  - Even impromptu speaking requires some preparation and organization.
  - Manuscript speaking demands a special focus on using good oral style, incorporating gestures and movement, using your voice effectively, and dedicated practice.
  - Memorized speaking also requires extensive practice; it challenges you to speak "in the moment," and to stay focused on the ideas you are conveying.
- The question-and-answer period is an important part of nearly any public speech.
  - As you respond to audience questions, you have the chance to show listeners how well informed you are and how quickly you can think on your feet.
  - You can also demonstrate how carefully you listen, how open you are to others' ideas, and how honest you are in responding to difficult questions.
- Anticipate and prepare for possible questions from your audience, and do all you can to establish the climate for respectful and mutually beneficial dialogue.

QUESTIONS FOR REVIEW AND REFLECTION

1. Describe the difference between "sounding good" and "being sound."
2. Your friend has to make an important presentation at a fund-raising event for the local Boys and Girls Club. He comes to you and asks you for advice on how to deliver his speech. What three things would you stress? Why are they important?
3. To what extent might cultural differences influence the way listeners respond to a speaker's delivery?
4. You have heard many people give speeches (classroom speeches, lectures, political speeches, after-dinner speeches, speeches at memorial services). Given your experience as

an audience member, what are the things that most annoy you about some speakers' delivery habits or styles? What are some delivery characteristics you especially admire?

5. Define each of the following styles of delivering a speech:
   a. extemporaneous
   b. impromptu
   c. manuscript
   d. memorized

   Compare and contrast the advantages and disadvantages of each delivery style.

6. Why is a keyword outline useful in delivering a speech? Can you think of any potential disadvantages to using such an outline?

7. You have given a speech, and now it is time for audience questions. How would you deal with each of these situations?
   a. An audience member is hostile.
   b. An audience member asks three questions in a row.
   c. Someone asks you a question you do not know the answer to.
   d. No one asks you a question.

ENDNOTES

1. Doris G. Yoakam, "Women's Introduction to the American Platform," *History and Criticism of American Public Address*, ed. William Norwood Brigance (New York: McGraw-Hill, 1943), 1:74–76.

2. See, as examples, Joe Ayres, "Speech Preparation Processes and Speech Apprehension," *Communication Education* 45 (July 1996): 228–35; Joe Ayres and Tim Hopf, *Coping with Speech Anxiety* (Norwood, NJ: Ablex, 1993); Ralph R. Behnke and Chris R. Sawyer, "Anticipatory Anxiety Patterns for Male and Female Speakers," *Communication Education* 49 (April 2000): 187–95; and Thomas Robinson II, "Communication Apprehension and the Basic Public Speaking Course: A National Survey of In-Class Treatment Techniques," *Communication Education* 46 (1997): 188–97.

3. See John T. Molloy, *Dress for Success* (New York: Warner, 1975), one of the first books to address the importance of appearance in the professional world. For a more recent work, see Molloy's *New Women's Dress for Success* (New York: Warner, 1996).

4. For a classic work on nonverbal communication, see Edward T. Hall, *The Silent Language* (Garden City, NY: Doubleday, 1959). More recent works include Edward T. Hall, *The Dance of Life* (New York: Doubleday, 1983), and Mark Knapp and J. Hall, *Nonverbal Communication in Human Interaction* (Philadelphia: Harcourt Brace Jovanovich, 1997).

5. See, for example, Edward T. Hall and M. R. Hall, *Understanding Cultural Differences* (Yarmouth, ME: Intercultural Press, 1990); and Richard D. Lewis, *When Cultures Collide*, rev. ed. (London: Nicholas Brealey, 2000).

6. Carolyn Calloway-Thomas, Pamela J. Cooper, and Cecil Blake, *Intercultural Communication: Roots and Routes* (Boston: Allyn and Bacon, 1999); Virginia P. Richmond et al., *Nonverbal Communication: The Unspoken Dialogue* (New York: Harper and Row, 1989); and Michelle Le Baron, *Bridging Cultural Conflicts: A New Approach for a Changing World* (San Francisco: Jossey-Bass, 2003).

7. Enrolling in a course in intercultural communication will provide an extensive treatment of this and related topics.

8. Virginia P. Richmond and James C. McCroskey, *Nonverbal Behavior in Interpersonal Relations*, 3rd ed. (Boston: Allyn and Bacon, 1995).

9. Nathan Bierma, "Hand Gestures May Expand, Express Unspoken Thoughts," *Chicago Tribune*, August 5, 2004, sec. 5, 2.

10. Paul Ekman, *Emotions Revealed: Recognizing Faces and Feelings to Improve Communications and Emotional Life* (New York: Henry Holt, 2004), 84–112.

11. Mark L. Knapp and Judith A. Hall, *Nonverbal Communication in Human Interaction* (Fort Worth, TX: Harcourt Brace, 1996).

12. Albert Mehrabian, *Silent Messages: Implicit Communication of Emotions and Attitudes*, 2nd ed. (Belmont, CA.: Wadsworth, 1982); Paul Ekman and Erika Rosenberg, *What the Face Reveals* (New York: Oxford University Press, 1998).

13. For an excellent collection of readings on all aspects of nonverbal communication, see Laura K. Guerrero, Joseph A. DeVito, and Michael L. Hecht, eds., *The Nonverbal Communication Reader: Classic and Contemporary Readings*, 2nd ed. (Prospect Heights, IL: Waveland Press, 1999).

14. Richmond and McCroskey, *Nonverbal Behavior*, 68–70.

15. "A Powerful Tool: Your Voice," *Costa Connection* (June 2004): 9.

16. For an extensive guide on vocal communication, see Jeffrey C. Hahner, Martin A. Sokoloff, and Sandra L. Salisch, *Speaking Clearly: Improving Voice and Diction*, 5th ed. (New York: McGraw-Hill, 1996).

17. John O. Greene, Marianne S. Sassi, Terri L. Malek-Madani, and Christopher N. Edwards, "Adult Acquisition of Message-Production Skills," *Communication Monographs* 64 (1997): 181–200. This article emphasizes the importance of practicing speech delivery.

18. See Herbert W. Hildebrandt and Walter W. Stevens, "Manuscript and Extemporaneous Modes of Delivery in Communicating Information," *Communication Monographs* 30 (1963): 369–72.

19. For one of the best guides on the techniques of manuscript speaking, see James C. Humes, *Talk Your Way to the Top* (New York: McGraw-Hill, 1980), 125–35.

20. For additional advice on managing question-and-answer sessions, see Thomas K. Mira, *Speak Smart* (New York: Random House, 1997), 115–23.

CHAPTER 13

Supporting Your Ideas Visually

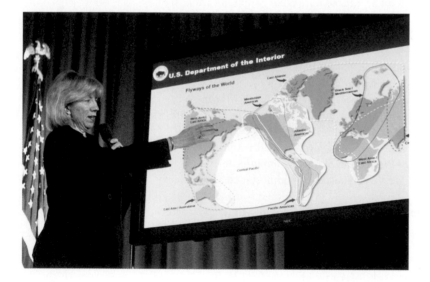

CHAPTER SURVEY

Functions of Presentational Aids

Options for Presentational Aids

Guidelines for Preparing
Presentational Aids

Guidelines for Using
Presentational Aids

CHAPTER OBJECTIVES

*After studying this chapter, you
should be able to*

1. Understand the diverse ways
   that presentational aids can
   help you as a speaker.

2. Describe the types of
   presentational aids commonly
   available to speakers.

3. Follow basic guidelines for
   creating presentational aids.

4. Follow basic guidelines for
   using presentational aids.

Visual material has a powerful impact on how we react to information. Everyone had heard of police brutality, but when people saw the video of Los Angeles police beating Rodney King in 1991, there was intense national indignation resulting in substantial reform.[1] Similarly, photographs from inside the Abu Ghraib prison, capturing the mistreatment of detainees by American military personnel, generated outrage in the United States and abroad and fueled the insurgency in Iraq.[2] More recently, live shots of the tsunami coming ashore in Indonesia and Thailand in 2004—sweeping away all in its path—shocked television viewers around the world, as did media coverage of Hurricane Katrina's fury. These shots, and the diagrams and charts experts created, reminded us of how destructive natural disasters can be and prompted calls for improved early-warning systems and better-coordinated evacuation and relief.[3]

These, of course, are very dramatic examples. But visual images can generate quite an impact in less spectacular situations—such as in a public speaking classroom or a civic meeting. Presentational aids are an important communication tool, especially in our increasingly visually oriented society.

Presentational aids must be used carefully, however. Using visual and audio aids effectively calls for careful thinking, strategic planning, and rehearsal. There is nothing magical about presentational aids. They assist us only if they function as intended and if we are able to present them effectively.

Functions of Presentational Aids

Preview. *Presentational aids can help a speaker be perceived as credible and well prepared. They can also help audience members follow, retain, and be moved by the speaker's ideas. Given these possible benefits, a speaker will do well to learn to develop and use presentational aids skillfully.*

Both speakers and listeners can benefit from the effective use of presentational aids. Presentational aids engage the senses (e.g., sight, hearing) and can strengthen the speech. From the speaker's perspective, presentational aids can

- help support and highlight key ideas
- facilitate understanding
- encourage emotional involvement
- assist with delivery
- enhance the speaker's credibility

Listeners also benefit from the effective use of presentational aids. From the listeners' perspective, presentational aids can

- help separate important from less important information
- assist comprehension and retention
- add interest and color

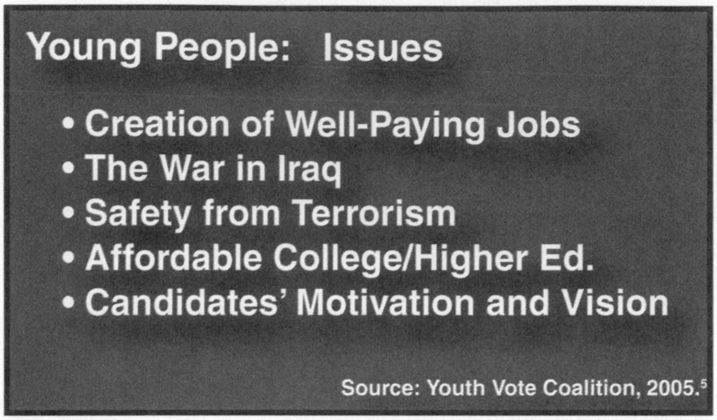

Young People: Issues

- Creation of Well-Paying Jobs
- The War in Iraq
- Safety from Terrorism
- Affordable College/Higher Ed.
- Candidates' Motivation and Vision

Source: Youth Vote Coalition, 2005.[5]

Figure 13.1
What Issues Concern Young People?

Let us examine some specific ways presentational aids will be important to you as a speaker and a listener.

Providing Emphasis

One challenge for every public speaker is to find ways to help the audience distinguish what is most important from what is less important. Research has shown that even a simple list can visually reinforce key ideas, as shown in Figure 13.1.[4] By using this presentational aid, a student speaker highlighted issues of importance to her classroom audience, before examining how the students could influence these issues simply by voting.

A list, of course, is not a particularly impressive presentational aid; and other, more sophisticated, aids may be required by the speech (or your instructor). Nevertheless, a list can help your audience follow your speech and remember its main ideas. If you are using a list, consider using graphical icons—such as a dollar sign to designate "wasteful spending." Graphical icons can be even more memorable than a list of keywords.[6] Let the material dictate the format best suited to achieving the desired emphasis. For example, a speaker might argue that hurricane readiness should be a top priority for key coastal regions of the United States. By displaying a map that illustrates the number of direct hits by hurricanes throughout the country, the speaker allows listeners to see for themselves the areas at greatest risk.[7] Rather than have listeners attempt to detect the pattern, the speaker shows them. Doing so promotes accuracy and helps maintain listeners' attention as the speaker moves forward with the presentation. Showing the map also emphasizes the widespread extent of the threat, as can be seen in Figure 13.2.

Providing Support

Presentational aids can also function as a form of evidence, helping support your ideas. Suppose you have asserted that nationally televised debates have an impact on the outcome of presidential elections. You might argue, for example, that those candidates who look more relaxed, engaged, and energetic stand the best chance of winning. You could support your assertion by offering the testimony of expert analysts who have examined the debates, assessed the communication style of the candidates, and then related their observations to polling data. But you would not want to deliver this speech without also showing the audience short video clips to demonstrate your argument and make it more compelling. For instance, you might show a clip from the Kennedy-Nixon debate in which Kennedy (who was actually suffering from back pain) *appeared* vigorous and energetic while Nixon appeared tired and drawn.

Visual aids also can lend another type of support. When you present a graph, chart, drawing, or photograph that comes from a reputable source, you

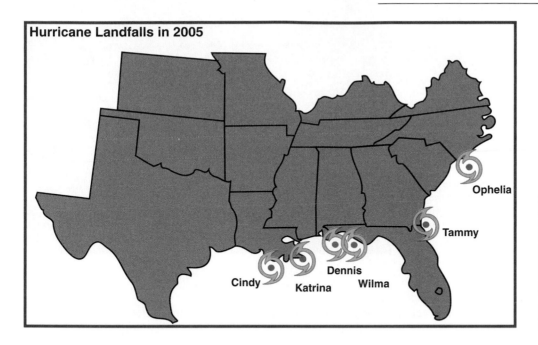

Hurricane Landfalls in 2005

Figure 13.2
Direct Hits by Hurricanes on the Continental United States
Source: National Oceanic and Atmospheric Administration, 2006.

will, in effect, add credibility to your ideas. You will show your listeners how a problem has grown, what poverty looks like on the face of a child, or the beauty of protected wilderness areas, such as the Selway-Bitterroot Wilderness in Montana. They will not have to take your word for it; they can see for themselves.

Promoting Clarity

Effective presentational aids also promote clarity. Researchers have found that "human brains extract valuable information from audiovisuals more quickly and more easily than from purely verbal information" and do so with "a more error-free grasp of information."[8] For this reason, as explained in *Highlighting Visual Perception and Thinking*, a speaker will do well to utilize the visual medium. For example, photographs of urban areas in decay provide a clearer understanding of problems confronting American cities than words alone. A visual outline of a budget should provide more clarity than merely describing it in words. And listeners who see a statistical trend via a graph are more likely to understand it—and to do so more immediately—than if they are left to chart it mentally on their own.[9]

It is easy to understand the popularity of graphs and charts and why speakers who fail to use them appear remiss. When you use statistical support, some sort of visual reinforcement will help the audience comprehend and remember your figures. One of the reasons graphs are so pervasive is that they make quantitative information easy to understand.[10]

Speakers often use graphs to make statistical information more vivid and to show relationships. No graph format is necessarily any better overall than any

The look and manner of these two presidential candidates greatly impacted public perceptions.

other; rather, each kind of graph is well suited to portraying different types of information.[11] The most familiar and useful kinds of graphs are line graphs, bar graphs, pictographs, and pie graphs.

- *Line graphs*. Line graphs are especially well suited to showing comparative relationships through time. Many business and professional presentations focus on information relating to time-based trends. For example, a hospital administrator might use a line graph to show how emergency room visits increase over time among populations who lack access to primary health care.

  It is possible to place more than one line on a single graph, but it may be at the expense of clarity. If you plan to use multiple lines or curves, try to use strikingly different colors and restrict yourself to two or three lines. It is also impor-

Highlighting Visual Perception and Thinking

Today, people get most of their day-to-day information through graphic images. In fact, some 99 percent of all the information we receive comes through the eyes from *objects* we see.

We are a visual species. Television, graphic novels, picture magazines, and multimedia are just some examples of the visual media that we're exposed to. Icons abound—no-smoking signs, computer menus, traffic signs, the men's room, restaurant menus. . . . Are we reinventing communication with pictographs? Perhaps.

The point is that we do most of our thinking in terms of graphic images—visuals such as pictures, icons, and facsimiles. . . . We don't think much in words per se. Vision is the primary medium of thought. Simply, visual perception is visual thinking. Graphic images are the most powerful way of enhancing our perceptual thinking. And without such visual stimuli, productive thinking is impossible.

Source: S. M. (Marty) Shelton, "Special Issue: Visual Communication: Introduction," *Technical Communication, Fourth Quarter* (1993): 617–18.

tant to guard against distorting a trend by compressing or elongating the space allotted to time periods while keeping the other dimension of the graph constant. Whenever you do selectively focus on a particular segment of data, be sure to label the graph so that your audience can fully understand what you have elected to show them.[12]

Figure 13.3 provides an example of a line graph. By using this graph, the speaker sought to emphasize the rising number of individuals testing HIV-positive in his community. The graph could help underscore the upward trend.[13]

■ *Bar graphs.* A bar graph can be used to show comparisons and contrasts between two or more items or groups. Even if listeners have little background in reading graphs, the bar graph is easy to understand. In addition, these graphs have a dramatic visual impact. As with line graphs, whenever you focus on a particular segment of data, be sure to label the graph so that your audience can fully understand what you have elected to show them.[14]

Figure 13.4 compares the estimated percentage of overweight boys and girls from several countries in 2006. The speaker using this bar graph quoted Dr. Philip James, chairman of the International Obesity Task Force, in arguing that we have "a truly global epidemic" and detailing its impact on healthcare systems around the world.[15]

■ *Pictographs.* Listeners often find pictographs particularly interesting. In a pictograph a graphical icon is used to form lines or patterns to convey information in the same way other graphs do. Figure 13.5 shows how a pictograph can communicate information in an interesting, meaningful way. A student speaker used this pictograph to support his argument that students who drink excessively suffer from impaired academic performance in college. Pictographs are more

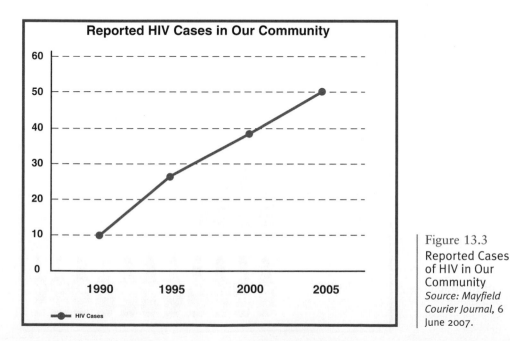

Figure 13.3
Reported Cases of HIV in Our Community
Source: Mayfield Courier Journal, 6 June 2007.

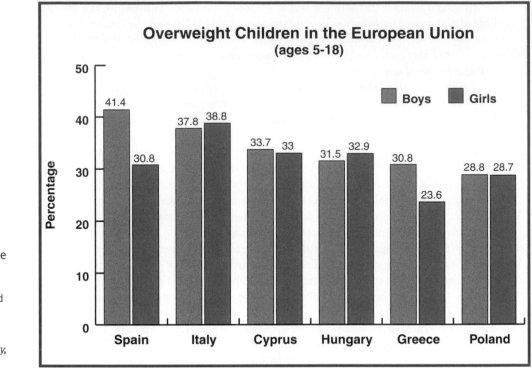

Figure 13.4
Overweight
Children in the
European
Union
Source: Adapted
from the
*International
Journal of
Pediatric Obesity,*
2006.

challenging to construct than traditional graphs. They require more creativity and original labor.

- *Pie graph.* The final type of graph is the pie graph, most often used to show numerical distribution patterns. When you need to show how a total figure breaks down into different parts, you will probably want to use a pie graph. Suppose, for example, you are addressing ethnic and racial diversity on your campus—perhaps making the point that your campus lacks such diversity. A pie graph,

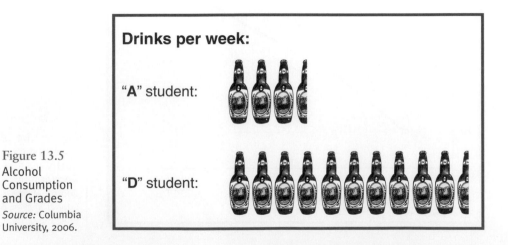

Figure 13.5
Alcohol
Consumption
and Grades
Source: Columbia
University, 2006.

like the one depicted in Figure 13.6, could reinforce your point. Because of their simplicity, pie graphs are easily processed by an audience. Additional examples of pie graphs appear in Figures 13.8 and 13.9.

When constructing a pie graph, observe two central guidelines. First, create a two-dimensional, rather than a three-dimensional, pie. As Joel Best, author of *Damned Lies and Statistics*, explains, "Showing the edge of a tilted pie chart to the viewer (so that it seems to be a three-dimensional disk) . . . exaggerates the visual importance of those slices that can be viewed edge-on."[16] In addition, be mindful that the most important sector should be featured on the right. For added emphasis, it can be pulled out slightly from the rest of the pie.[17]

You might use several different kinds of graphs in a single presentation. When carefully constructed and used strategically, they can help you depict statistical information in ways that listeners will likely find understandable, interesting, and clarifying.

Creating graphs has become increasingly easy because of software like PowerPoint and Keynote. Some of the design options that are available, though, can allow a speaker to easily distort data—intentionally or unwittingly. The author of *How to Lie with Charts*, Gerald Everett Jones, provides some basic pointers for communicating accurately and ethically when presenting data in graphs. See *Highlighting Using Graphs to Communicate Data*, on page 328.

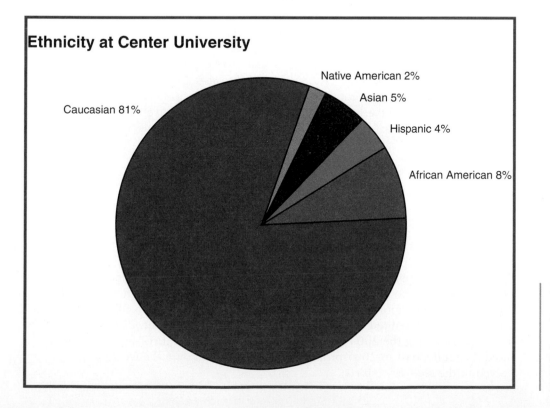

Ethnicity at Center University

Caucasian 81%
Native American 2%
Asian 5%
Hispanic 4%
African American 8%

Figure 13.6
Ethnic Diversity at Center University
Source: Office of Student Affairs & Diversity at Center University, 2007

Highlighting Using Graphs to Communicate Data

Some Practical and Ethical Guidelines

- *Label every element.* Numbers alone will not suffice. Explain their meaning via a simple label. For instance, each sector of a pie graph should be labeled in terms of its category and percentage, as should the meaning of the whole pie.
- *Avoid overwhelming the audience.* Pies should be confined to five or six slices—never more than eight. Line graphs should have no more than two or three lines—each easily distinguished. Bar graphs should feature six or fewer bars (though each bar can be clustered into two or three sectors).
- *Use each type of graph properly.* Pie graphs depict relationships in terms of percentages or ratios. Line graphs emphasize trends, whereas bar graphs emphasize results at each division of a particular point in time. Pictographs compare basic amounts.
- *Adhere to traditional formats.* Line graphs and bar graphs consist of a *y* axis and an *x* axis. As Jones explains, "Quantity goes up and down on the vertical axis—the *y axis*. Time progresses from left to right along the horizontal axis—the *x axis*."[18] Departing from this conventional arrangement (as many software packages may allow one to do) will impede understanding and/or distort the data. For example, a program may allow you to turn a conventional vertical bar graph on its side, but Jones advises against it. Pictographs, on the other hand, can show increasing magnitude along either axis; each depicted unit of measure can be stacked or can build from left to right, as modeled in Figure 13.5.

- *Be sensitive to the implications of range.* Graphs should always begin with zero on the *y* axis. Notice, too, that expanding or compressing the range of either axis (*y* or *x*) can distort the data and suggest different interpretations of the data. It may make sense to violate the rule of beginning with zero, so that differences can be better detected when one zooms in to a particular segment. When doing so, just be sure all is labeled clearly, as well as noted aloud for your audience.
- *Avoid "stacked" bars.* They are harder to read and can obscure relationships.
- *Make labels easily readable.* Employ a simple, easy-to-read style for fonts, and a large size.
- *Proofread.* Be careful with spelling, usage, correctness, and so on.
- *Choose colors carefully.* Use colors that yield good contrast so each element depicted is easily distinguished. Make sure, too, that the color scheme can be seen in the lighting conditions under which you will be making your presentation. Be mindful that what appears on your monitor will likely be much more vivid than what is projected on a screen.
- *Reveal your sources.* Cite the source(s) of all information at the bottom of the chart or graph. Also include the date (e.g., Bureau of Labor Statistics, June 2007).

Source: Gerald Everett Jones, *How to Lie with Charts* (San Jose, CA: Authors Choice Press, 2000).

Encouraging Emotional Involvement

A speaker can use pictures that will elicit greater emotional involvement than if the audience were left to conjure up their own images.[19] During the war in Vietnam, a widely published photograph of Vietnamese children fleeing their village after a napalm attack was credited with igniting strong antiwar sentiment. Pictures of human suffering following the 2004 tsunami in Indonesia and the hurricanes that devastated the Gulf Coast in 2005 prompted people from all over the world to get involved in the recovery efforts.

This photo of 9-year-old Kim Phuc, badly burned and fleeing her village during a napalm attack, ignited strong antiwar sentiment during the Vietnam war. The journalist, Nick Ut, helped the children to safety, and his photo won a Pulitzer Prize.

If a speaker wanted to move the audience to become actively involved in community programs that feed the poor, she might want to help the listeners visualize those who are hungry. She might, for example, share some of the paintings of Tammy Grubbs, an artist whose paintings poignantly portray the faces of hunger in America (see Figure 13.7).

Figure 13.7
The paintings of Tammy Grubbs portray the faces of hunger in America.

Source: National Coalition for the Homeless. www.nationalhomeless.org.

Assisting Retention and Recall

Presentational aids can make information and ideas more understandable and memorable. A 1989 University of Minnesota study concluded that people remember 43 percent more information when visuals are used than when they are not.[20] Subsequent research has supported these findings and suggests that effective presentational aids can make recall easier, faster, and more accurate than "memories of purely verbal messages."[21] If you want to leave a lasting impression on your audience, consider using good presentational aids.[22]

Helping with Extemporaneous Delivery

Presentational aids can assist delivery by serving as speaking notes. For example, speakers who give workshop presentations often project bulleted lists of keywords onto a screen to orient the audience and bolster their comprehension. As each item appears on the screen, it functions as a speaking outline, reminding the speaker of what he or she wishes to address next. Some speakers also find that these prompts alleviate speaking anxiety.[23]

Of course, you should be aware of the risks of using bulleted lists. For one, a speaker can use too many lists. Constantly displaying and quickly removing list after list can confuse the audience, just as leaving one up long after it is useful can bore or otherwise distract them. A speaker also should avoid visuals that feature too many words, or that simply duplicate his or her oral presentation. If you put your whole outline on a transparency, listeners will concentrate on the display instead of on you.[24] At the other extreme, simply posting key words and failing to supply a needed graph, chart, or other aid may diminish your effectiveness and tarnish your image. For this reason, your instructor may insist that you devise something other than a bulleted list as a visual aid.

Enhancing Your Credibility

Using good presentational aids can enhance your credibility. When you use well-constructed aids, you show the audience that you care enough about your presentation to prepare carefully. A well-constructed graph, for example, shows listeners that you took pains with your preparation, and it also shows your concern for their understanding. A speaker who does not use presentational aids may be seen as less organized and less interested in audience understanding.[25]

You also demonstrate your trustworthiness when you use presentational aids. Rather than ask your listeners to rely exclusively on your judgment, you let them "see for themselves" when you share a photo or chart the numbers.[26] As a result, listeners may see you as more open to scrutiny and more willing to let them share in determining the true nature of the problem or the meaning of data. Being seen as trustworthy and fair-minded boosts your credibility—a matter we will explore further in Chapter 15.

Engaging Multiple Senses to Promote Interest

As we have noted, presentational aids can make a speech easier to follow and understand. They also stimulate interest. When you think of the problems with listening we discussed in Chapter 4, you will quickly recognize the value of presentational aids. By engaging multiple senses, presentational aids can help keep listeners from feeling bored, distracted, or passive. Research indicates that visual aids bolster interest and involvement.[27]

Color

Researchers have reported that color adds interest.[28] Colorful poster boards, well-chosen video clips, and vivid graphs all attract attention. Most people prefer color to black-and-white—or at least most would like some color to break up black-and-white handouts, lists, and transparencies.[29] Vivid colors are usually more striking than lighter shades, with blue, red, and green among those preferred.[30] Note how color enhances the graph shown in Figure 13.9 (in contrast to the colorless image presented in Figure 13.8). In addressing the local chamber of commerce, an executive director of a homeless shelter used the pie graph shown in Figure 13.9 to support his argument that local businesses should be doing more to assist the poor.

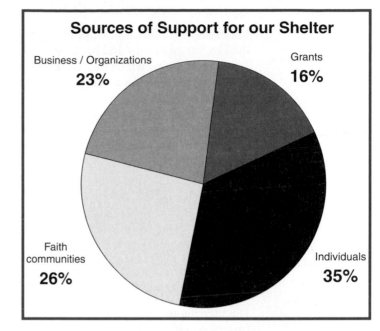

Figure 13.8
Sources of Support for a Nonprofit Organization Serving the Poor

Source: The Shalom Community Center, Bloomington, IN, 2006.

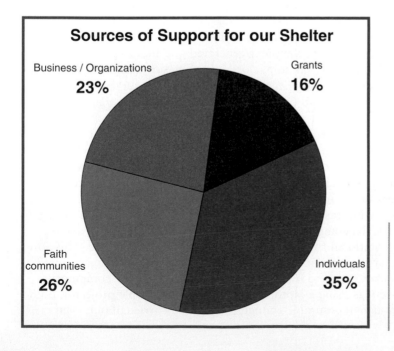

Figure 13.9
Sources of Support for a Nonprofit Organization Serving the Poor

Source: The Shalom Community Center, Bloomington, IN, 2006.

Variety

Variety is one of the best ways to maintain audience interest. A presentation accompanied by varied graphs and perhaps a few illustrative pictures will likely be more interesting than one in which the speaker presents list after list on an overhead projector.

Not every presentation (particularly short ones) will lend itself to such a variety of visual support. However, speakers should consider the presentational options available and, if suitable, use some variety. As speakers, we must always ask ourselves, "How can I make information more interesting to my audience?"

Options for Presentational Aids

Preview. *Presentational support can range from the low-tech chalkboard to sophisticated computer-generated graphics. A variety of options can reinforce your speech visually or through sound.*

What kind of presentational aids should you use? The answer to this question depends on many factors—from listeners' expectations to available equipment to whether the room lends itself to the kind of support you have in mind. If a room cannot be effectively darkened, for instance, you would be hard-pressed to use slides effectively. In short, consider what options will work best in the setting, for the particular audience and occasion, and for the content of the speech.

Computer-Generated Slideshows

Computers allow us to generate very sophisticated and professional-looking multimedia slideshows, complete with movement and sound. One of the best illustrations of this power appears in the classic movie *Star Wars*. Near the end of the film, Luke Skywalker and his fellow warriors receive instructions on how to destroy the Death Star. The military strategist projects computer-generated graphics to provide an overview of the enemy's massive battleship, close-ups of its surface, and diagrams of its infrastructure. Without the visual display—complete with movement—the speaker would not have been able to provide this information to Luke and the rest of the force with such clarity, impact, and efficiency.

The visual displays that Luke and others seem to take for granted are no longer confined to science fiction but have become commonplace for us as well. On television we regularly view full-motion weather maps, graphical depictions of what has happened on Wall Street, and computer-generated models of what likely occurred during a tragic accident or natural disaster.

Similar technology is increasingly available for our own use because of the enhanced capacity of personal computers, the portability of the required hardware, and user-friendly presentational software, such as PowerPoint or Keynote. This software allows for the easy creation of slides and the integrated use of images, sound, and video clips. Businesspeople and other professionals often display computer-generated slides at meetings using a laptop computer and a portable projector, both of which are small enough and durable enough to be easily carried about, even taken along on trips. On campus, professors and students commonly deliver computer-assisted presentations, often in specially outfitted, high-tech classrooms where they simply insert their flash drive or disk into the computer on-site.

Computers have simplified the creation of visual aids. Presentational software allows us to enter the information and select the type of graph, chart, or other device that is best suited for conveying the information. With creativity, we can even design our own graphics, such as the pictograph in Figure 13.5, as described in *Highlighting Computer-Generated Visual Aids*. In addition, a presentational aid created via computer can easily be modified or updated by simply editing or adding data, even during a live presentation.

One can also easily add images downloaded from the Internet, copied using a scanner, or loaded from a digital camera. For example, in a speech discussing visual pollution, one of our students inserted pictures he had taken from a community that restricted billboards and other signage and placed them alongside shots he had taken in a community with no restrictions and abundant signs. Another student, advocating that her university follow the lead of Texas A&M University and participate in The Big Event—a day of widespread, intensive volunteer work in the local community—also supplied illustrative pictures. Within minutes, she located pictures that A&M and other schools had posted on the Internet, documenting their good deeds. With a few clicks, she imported a few of the images into the slides for her presentation.[31] (Note: "Fair Use" often applies to the use of pictures in unpublished speeches, such as a speech to a classroom or community gathering. In some instances, though, one may need to obtain permission prior to use. For more information regarding copyright and fair use, go to copyright.gov.)

Even though this technology has become increasingly attractive, it cannot always be used. Obviously, you must have access to the hardware and software needed to create such aids. Your school must also provide the proper equipment to present the aids you create. Many campuses lack the funding necessary to purchase the equipment, set aside appropriate classroom space, and maintain an adequate staff to service the hardware and software.

Given these constraints, not every student will be able to deliver a computer-assisted presentation. Nonetheless, even if you cannot use computer technology

Highlighting Computer-Generated Visual Aids

How We Generated the Pictograph in Figure 13.5

To design this graph, we downloaded the image of a longneck bottle found on the Web, removed the brand name (using the program Photoshop), and then imported the altered image into a PowerPoint slide. We also used Photoshop to cut the bottle in half. We simply copied the bottle in a new file and saved the new version once we had cut it in half.

Note the power of this visual aid to emphasize the content; it is much more powerful than merely reciting the statistics for an audience. How would you evaluate the power of this pictograph compared with the same information conveyed in a bar graph? (No pun intended!)

directly during your speech, you can use it indirectly. Using PowerPoint, or even a basic word processing program, you can construct a graph, table, or other visual display that you print out and use as a transparency with an overhead projector. A copy shop, such as Kinkos, can transfer from paper to transparency. (We discuss transparencies and overhead projectors later in this chapter.)

In any case, it will benefit you to recognize the strengths of this technology and learn to use it competently and comfortably. Ultimately you will need to experiment with it, following the guidelines we provide later in this chapter, in the sections Guidelines for Preparing Presentational Aids and Guidelines for Using Presentational Aids. Also review the lighthearted cautionary notes we provide in *Highlighting How Not to Use PowerPoint*. Since so many people use presentational software poorly (prompting many detractors), you will want to study the guidelines very carefully.[32]

Chalkboard or Whiteboard

The chalkboard (now commonly replaced by a whiteboard) remains a useful device for speakers who have no other option for displays or who wish to compile a list while working cooperatively with an audience. The chalkboard allows the speaker to highlight information visually and put terms, diagrams, or sketches on the board as an explanation unfolds or a list develops. In addition, moving to and from the board allows the speaker to be active in communicating his or her ideas and can also help the speaker channel nervous energy.

A flipchart is ideal for recording ideas and assisting brainstorming during discussion.

Highlighting How *Not* to Use PowerPoint

We have synthesized various authors' advice—some empirically based—to offer these surefire ways to irritate, insult, and otherwise alienate an audience when using PowerPoint (or any other slideware). We hope you enjoy this tongue-in-cheek look at some of the more common infractions.

1. Use a lot of slides. The more the better! Always have something posted onscreen.

2. Read your slides to your audience (and preferably with your back to them, facing the screen).

3. Give them a handout, before your speech, that duplicates the same slides you will read to them.

4. Write out what you intend to say, completely, with full sentences, filling up each slide as much as possible.

5. If you use bullets, post them all at once, rather than bring them up individually.

6. For textual content, use a font that is itsy-bitsy or otherwise difficult to read.

7. Avoid charts, graphs, and graphical icons. Stick to text-based content.

8. If you must use charts, graphs, or graphical icons, do not fret over their substance, such as whether they actually convey or clarify information central to the meaning of your speech.

9. Do not fret over explaining any chart, graph, or depiction. Let the audience figure it out on their own, while you are plodding ahead.

10. When using any graph, chart, or other visual content, simply flash it onto the screen, giving the audience only a millisecond or two to process it.

11. Use auto-timing features to advance your slides—never mind that you may have to speed up or slow down or even stop from time to time to keep pace with your slide show.

12. Present multiple ideas on a single slide, and do not bother explaining their connection or lack thereof.

13. Do not obsess over spelling, grammatical correctness, and the like.

14. Use lots of special effects. Always have something spinning or pulsating on screen. Accompany visual effects with sound effects—squealing and rat-a-tat-tats and the like!

15. Do not worry about a backup plan in case the slideshow cannot be used. Simply insist on rescheduling your speech.

16. Remember: The screen is king! Serve the screen!

SELECTED SOURCES:

Jean-Luc Doumont, "The Cognitive Style of PowerPoint: Slides Are Not All Evil," *Technical Communication* 52 (February 2005): 64–70.

Keith Barker et al., "To Read or Not to Read PowerPoint Slides," *The Teaching Professor* 18 (November 2004): 4.

T. Trent Gegax, "Not Another PowerPoint Presentation!" *Newsweek*, May 9, 2005, E29.

Peter Norvig, "PowerPoint: Shot with Its Own Bullets," *Lancet* 362 (August 2, 2003): 343–44.

Geoffrey Nunberg, "The Trouble with PowerPoint," *Fortune*, December 20, 1999, 330–31.

Thomas A. Stewart, "Ban It Now! Friends Don't Let Friends Use PowerPoint," *Fortune,* February 5, 2001, 4.

Of course, the chalkboard has its limitations. Because it is so familiar to most audiences, it may seem less interesting or original than other types of visuals. Poor handwriting and a tendency to look at the board rather than at the audience can also detract from effective communication. In most cases, it is wise to choose a different vehicle for visually enhancing your presentation.

Flipcharts

A flipchart is essentially an oversized writing tablet, offering the same advantages and disadvantages of chalkboards. Flipcharts are commonly used in business, conference, and workshop settings. In these settings, speakers often use flipcharts to record ideas generated during discussions or brainstorming sessions. If you use a flipchart, remember that you will need a tripod for displaying it.

Poster-Board Drawings and Displays

In settings where no other option is available, poster-board drawings and displays can work well. These presentational aids can be constructed well in advance and can be either simple or sophisticated. They also can be colorful and engaging. The advantages end there, however. Aside from the time, effort, and artistic ability necessary to construct content for posters, they are clumsy to transport and handle. You must also make sure that you will be able to display them. For example, will a tripod be available? Will tape or thumbtacks be necessary? If you decide to use poster boards, make sure to investigate the speech setting and prepare adequately.

Handouts

Handouts are helpful when listeners need to be able to recall information accurately for use at a later time, but they can distract when made available during a speech. Consider selecting another means of visual assistance *during* your presentation. For example, you might present a budget on an overhead transparency or PowerPoint slide and tell listeners you will be distributing a handout containing the budget at the end of your speech. If you distribute multiple handouts, you may want to use a different color, per handout, so listeners can easily find the information of interest to them.

Handouts can also be useful in encouraging listeners to act. If you urge them to send an e-mail or phone a specific person or agency about a particular issue, for example, you can provide a handout with this information. By simplifying the task for listeners, you will increase the chances that they will follow through.[33]

Objects

Occasionally, a speech may involve the discussion of an object. If the object is large enough to be seen but small enough to carry, you may want to use it as a presentational aid. For example, when raising awareness about methamphetamine, law-enforcement officers often display some of the common items used to manufacture the drug. Presenting the actual items makes the information more concrete, vivid, and memorable.

Avoid small items that need to be passed around. Circulating something while you are talking can present problems. First, only one person will have the object while you are describing it; other listeners will be in the dark. Moreover, the act of passing something around will distract your listeners, taking their attention away from your speech.

Be vigilant if you are considering using a living creature as an aid. For example, some cities have adopted ordinances that ban specific breeds of dogs. If your community is contemplating such a policy and you are speaking against it at a community meeting, you need not bring in a pit bull to show how gentle the breed can be. You might consider, instead, showing pictures of the dogs interacting and cuddling with people in loving, affectionate ways.

Be mindful, too, of objects and items that would certainly be prohibited in a classroom speech setting, such as firearms and illegal substances or materials. When in doubt, always consult your instructor.

Models

Some speeches call for a model as a visual aid. When informing classmates about "green" architectural design, one student brought in a simple model she had constructed to illustrate how a wide overhang, positioned to work with the angle of the sun in winter versus summer months, can reduce energy consumption. Holding a flashlight at different angles, representative of the different seasons, she was able to show how the overhang allowed direct light in the windows during the winter months but shaded the windows in the summer, allowing only indirect light to enter.

Obviously, constructing a three-dimensional model requires skill and effort. Many times our students have been able to borrow models, thus simplifying the task.

Transparencies and Overhead Projectors

Overhead projectors, particularly those used to display transparencies, are very common in classrooms and in community and business meeting rooms. They allow a speaker to project lists, figures, charts, graphs, and other information onto a large screen in supersize form.

Overhead projectors offer other advantages as well. First, transparencies can look professional and can be easily created by computer. If your printer will not accept transparency stock, you likely can e-mail the file to a copy shop or take it in on a disk or flash drive or on a paper printout to be transferred to a transparency. Transparencies are also easy to transport, allowing a speaker to use several in a single presentation.

Slides and Slide Projectors

Speakers sometimes use slides to accompany their presentations. For example, in a presentation acquainting citizens with a mobile health unit that will be serving their area, a speaker used slides depicting some of the unit's basic services, such as blood-pressure checks, nutrition education, fluoride treatments, immunizations, and HIV testing.

This option is rapidly becoming obsolete. Slides made from photographs or pictures must be professionally prepared and require a slide projector, screen, and dimly lit room. Computers, presentational software, and digital cameras are rapidly replacing this older technology—providing similar quality, greater efficiency, and images with the ability to serve double duty on a website.

Audio and Video Materials

Some topics cannot be explained by using only words and still images. One student, for example, wanted to show her listeners how the 1963 March on Washington, where Martin Luther King Jr. delivered his "I Have a Dream" speech, brought black and white Americans together in a powerful spirit of reconciliation. Still another wanted to illustrate the behaviors and speaking skills that caused President Reagan to be dubbed "the Great Communicator." These speakers would have been hard-pressed to speak clearly and compellingly about their topics without using brief, highly selective video clips for support.

The force, speed, and destruction of a tsunami, as it rushes onshore, cannot be captured adequately with a single picture. A short video clip is necessary.

In an increasingly media-oriented society, many listeners are attracted to presentations that use audio and video support. These sensory experiences, as we have noted earlier, help generate interest and involvement. Using them successfully, though, requires careful planning and preparation. In general, the more heavily your presentation depends on any form of technology, the more time and effort you must devote to creating what you will use and to making sure the appropriate equipment will be available and in working order. Also, the room in which you will be speaking must lend itself to using these aids effectively.

A speech that uses audio or video technology well can be extremely interesting and powerful. But if things go wrong—if pertinent clips cannot be located or the equipment malfunctions—the speaker may find it difficult to recover and achieve his or her purpose. Fortunately, most presentational software allows insertion of a clip, making for a more seamless and trouble-free multimedia presentation.

Be mindful that clips should be short, since they are used to illustrate an idea. Showing a clip that takes up most of your speaking time is not using a presentational aid; it is substituting an audiovisual presentation for a major portion of your speech. Your instructor will likely have particular guidelines for your speaking assignments, and you will want to consult her or him if you contemplate using a clip.

In short, whenever you choose presentational aids, do so with the audience, setting, and occasion in mind. Find out which presentational options are available and expected in a particular setting—including your classroom. Once you know your options, you can select which one(s) will best serve your needs. Whatever the option, you will want to prepare each one for maximum impact, a matter we will now take up.

Guidelines for Preparing Presentational Aids

Preview. *Presentational aids must be carefully planned and prepared for maximum impact. In this section, we offer some basic guidelines for constructing presentational materials, ranging from practical tips to ethical considerations.*

Through the years we have seen speakers, in the classroom and in the community, use a variety of presentational aids. We have seen aids that were thoughtfully devised, those that made no real contribution to the speech, and several that actually detracted from the speech. In these latter instances, what was *supposed* to be an aid became a hindrance. A few guidelines can help ensure that you will use your presentational aids successfully.

- *Make sure it is truly an aid.* As you contemplate your speech, note places where a presentational aid would help. Keep in mind that an aid does one or more of the following:
  - adds clarity/promotes understanding
  - adds emphasis
  - encourages interest or emotional involvement
  - helps the audience remember what you have said

If a presentational aid does not fulfill one of these functions, it will not contribute to your speech, and it may serve only to distract the audience.

There are exceptions, of course. A prop can sometimes add a healthy element to a speech. A prop is any visual or audio material that enlivens a presentation but is not integral to its success. For example, a student who advocated closer ties with Mexico wore a shirt, pants, and sandals made in Mexico, simply to set the mood. A prop may be appropriate if it does not distract listeners' attention from the content of the speech.

■ *Design your aid for quick processing.* Your listeners should be able to grasp the meaning of the aid with minimal effort.

■ Visual aids
  • *Make them large enough to be seen.* Your audience should never have to strain to see.
  • *Be smart with fonts.*
    • Choose a font that is easy to read. Sans serif fonts, such as Arial and Helvetica, are excellent standard choices.
    • Be sure the font style you select is supported by the computer you will use during your presentation. Otherwise, the text will be garbled.
    • Size the characters so that they can be read. In most font styles you will need to use at least an 18-point size, but you may need a 40- or 44-point font, depending on the size of the room.
    • Experiment with bold versus plain characters to see which provides the most clarity.
  • *Employ good contrast.* Contrast promotes clarity.[34] Start with a fairly light or fairly dark background color and choose an opposite (dark or light) color for the text (see Figure 13.10).[35] For computer-generated color slides, a dark blue background with white content works best.[36] Use the opposite scheme for black and white transparencies: dark content on a white/clear background. The contrast between dark and light helps prevent problems with washout of a projector's beam so you can leave the lights up a bit. When using colors, be mindful that they are less vivid when projected than they appear on a computer monitor or printout.

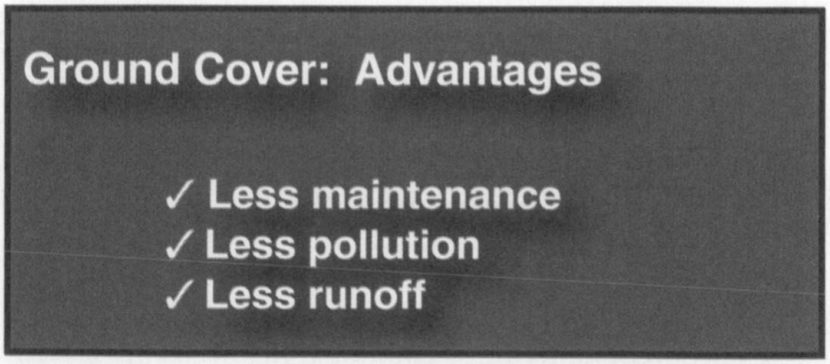

Ground Cover: Advantages

✓ **Less maintenance**
✓ **Less pollution**
✓ **Less runoff**

Figure 13.10
Ground Cover
versus Lawn

- *Consider using fill patterns (for example, dots or stripes) for sectors of a pie graph or bar graph.* Doing so will assist anyone who has trouble distinguishing colors.
- *Keep everything simple.* Use as few words as possible for labels and listings. Your audience should be able to process what is on the screen with a glance. Feature only those terms or expressions that categorize or highlight what you want to emphasize and discuss. Ignore rules, such as "limit each bullet point to six words, with no more than five bullets per slide,"[37] and concentrate, instead, on using as few words as possible, rarely if ever exceeding one line per bulleted entry.[38] For other visuals, avoid complicated details; show only the essentials and illustrate only one idea in each chart, graph, or diagram.[39] The idea suggested by the content should be stated at the top.
- *Handwriting (as in the case of using a flip chart) should be large, legible, neat, and—if appropriate—color coded for clarity.*

- ■ Audiovisual aids
  - *Sound and video recordings should offer sufficient quality for easy viewing or listening.*
  - *Limit sound and video recordings to a brief clip that illustrates a single idea.*
  - *Inquire about the feasibility of using audiovisual material.* Find out whether using this kind of aid is possible in the classroom or community setting in which you will speak.
  - *Avoid razzle-dazzle.* Presentational aids are there to support, emphasize, and clarify key points and information. They are not a show unto themselves. They should not compete with (or merely duplicate) what you are saying. They should support your presentation, not *become* your presentation. Avoid too much distracting detail or too many effects. For example, if you are using presentational software, you may be tempted to have a new element come flying and spinning in, accompanied by a dramatic sound. During a presentation, though, effects can be distracting, as well as annoying. Likewise, use moderation when selecting or creating a background or border for your slide. Your visual displays should not upstage you as the speaker.[40]

- ■ *Strive for professional quality.* The best results can be achieved by one of many computer programs that can generate graphs and crisp, legible letters and symbols as well as easily resize photographs and other images. If you must rely on a poster, take great pains to make it of superior quality. If you must use a chalkboard, whiteboard, or flipchart, observe the guidelines provided below for using them.
- ■ *Employ "silence."* Avoid using too many visual displays or sounds. For example, when using presentational software, display blank slides when you want listeners focused on your spoken words rather than on something on the screen. These can be your most important slides, even helping to accentuate subsequent slides containing visual content; when a new slide with content appears, the audience will be even more attracted to it.

■ *Anticipate problems.* Much can go wrong, especially when technology and electricity are involved. When relying on presentational software, make sure you have a backup file of your slideshow saved on another disk or available by some other means. You might, for example, also have slides printed for use with an overhead projector. In this way, you can safeguard against potential disaster if the computer malfunctions or you encounter software incompatibility.

Guidelines for Using Presentational Aids

Preview. *Presentational aids must be used properly for maximum impact. In this section, we offer some basic guidelines for using presentational materials, ranging from practical tips to ethical considerations.*

Even when presentational aids are well designed, they must be used effectively. We have endless examples we could provide, ranging from presenters unintentionally blocking a projector's beam to others who placed transparencies upside down on a projector and did not know how to correct the problem. No doubt you have witnessed similar mishaps. We offer the following guidelines to help you avoid similar embarrassment.

■ *Practice!* Many speakers practice their speeches aloud several times, yet fail to practice using their presentational aids. Perhaps it never occurs to them, or they think it is not necessary. Maybe they just do not want to take the trouble. Practicing with those aids, though, allows one to present more smoothly and

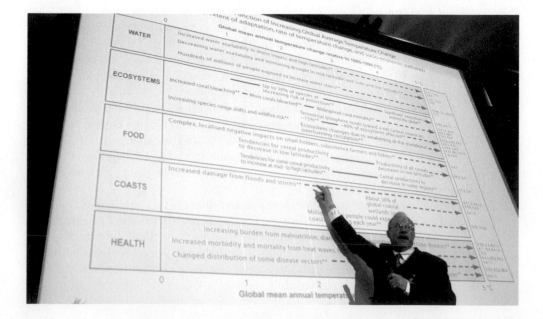

Many speakers do not use visual aids effectively.

confidently. It also safeguards against unwelcome surprises (such as transparencies sticking together, which—by the way—can be eliminated by placing a sheet of paper between each one in the stack).

■ *Preview in the venue.* Check out the actual setting ahead of time, if possible, to become familiar with any equipment you will use. Test for sight and sound— from different areas of the room. Audience members who must squint to see the print on a transparency or strain to hear the words on a recording can easily become frustrated and simply tune out the speaker. Too loud a volume, of course, can be annoying and disruptive. If you are using a projector on a rolling stand, you may need to move it farther away from or closer to the screen for an appropriately sized image. Also note where you should stand to avoid blocking the audience's view or interfering with the beam. It is easy to unwittingly cast a large shadow on the screen. Determine, too, how well you will be able to see your speaking notes under the specific lighting conditions.

■ *Have everything set to go.* For example, have presentational software positioned on the first slide (a blank slide, so not to interfere with your introduction) and audiovisuals cued to the proper spot with the proper volume and/or focus. Have transparencies stacked in the proper order. If using a marker, make sure it has ink. With all ready to go, you can relax and get off to a good start.

■ *Use only when needed.* Any visual aid must be displayed long enough for the audience to process the information and make sense of it, then put away when it is no longer relevant to the point being made. Visual images attract attention and can easily upstage a speaker. Keep them out of sight until you are ready to refer to them. Remove/cover them when they are no longer needed. Doing so will help you maintain control of the audience's attention. (*Note:* If you are using presentational software, accomplish this by inserting blank slides between content slides, and at the beginning and end of the slide show.)

■ *Help listeners focus.* The effective public speaker uses presentational aids so that the audience knows what to focus on, and the speaker helps them process the aids. If, for example, your visual aid has more than one part, direct the audience's attention to the part being discussed by pointing to it with your finger, a pencil, or a laser pointer. Rather than project an entire bar graph, you might display and discuss it one bar at a time to help the audience process the information. Presentational software (like PowerPoint) may allow you to bring up one element at a time. Otherwise, you can duplicate a slide several times and then work backward, deleting one element at a time so that during your presentation a click forward results in an added element. If you are using transparencies, you can either produce ones that become progressively more complete and layer one on top of the other as you proceed, or you can create one complete transparency and use a cover sheet to expose its elements one at a time.

■ *Stay connected with your listeners.* As you direct the audience's attention to your visual aid, monitor your bodily movement. Talk to your audience, not to the aid. Avoid turning away from them and facing the screen, for example. Be mindful, too, that even though a room may be darkened, the audience will be able to see you, especially after their eyes have adjusted to the dim lighting. It is important to maintain eye contact with the audience and to gesture and speak with them directly.

■ *Use presentational aids ethically.* Speakers often create their own visuals. You might create, for instance, a simple graph to illustrate a statistical trend. Remember that you will need to reveal the source of the data—orally and with a written acknowledgment on the visual aid for the audience to see. Reveal the source on the bottom of the display, simply by noting, for instance, "*Source: Newsweek*, March 20, 2006." (Notice how the sample presentational aids presented throughout this chapter consistently cite their sources.)

Sometimes a speaker will discover an existing visual, such as a graph in the *Washington Post*, or some other publication. In most settings, it is permissible to use this material (blown up and transferred onto a transparency, for example), but you must acknowledge the source orally and on the visual. Before using existing visual material, be sure to ask your instructor whether it is permissible to use it in the classroom; she or he may want you to design your own.

Highlighting Presentational Aids and Ethics

- *Recognize and respect the power of visual symbols.* Media scholars such as James Potter have pointed out that visual symbols function as powerful means of influencing our ideas and behavior. Visuals can attract and sustain attention, enhance emotional appeals, and even function as proof. Using them judiciously, fairly, and along with other substantiating evidence, then, becomes paramount.

- *Use presentational aids to promote understanding—never seeking to distract or mislead the audience.* Listeners can be overwhelmed by too many handouts, too many or too fast-moving images, or by "aids" that cannot be easily viewed or heard with clarity.

- *Select visuals that fairly represent the data you are presenting.* Avoid using graphs that exaggerate trends, for example.

- *Make sure that presentational aids are in good taste.* Showing pictures of traumatized and abandoned dogs following the 2006 war between Israel and Lebanon to evoke sympathy (and perhaps to solicit donations), for instance, would probably be considered moving and legitimate. However, using an image of a plane flying into the Twin Towers to sell

insurance would be in very poor taste, and would likely repel listeners.

- *Recognize that presentational aids function as a form of evidence, and follow the criteria for using evidence presented in Chapter 8.* Openly reveal information sources, and always strive to present accurate, recent, and complete information.

- *Openly acknowledge visual manipulation.* If, for example, you "enhance" a picture to dramatize an effect or encourage an emotional reaction, you should alert listeners to whatever changes you have made. Changing colors, for example, can change the tone and feeling of an image, as when *Time* magazine electronically manipulated a cover photograph of O.J. Simpson to "achieve a brooding, menacing quality."[41]

- *Make sure your speech can stand on its own—never substituting visual representations for sound argument.* While presentational aids can greatly enhance your speech, the substance of your speech should remain strong, even if technology were to fail you.

Sources: W. James Potter, *Media Literacy*, 3rd ed. (Thousand Oaks, CA: Sage Publications, 2005); and Kathleen Hall Jamieson, *Eloquence in an Electronic Age: The Transformation of Political Speechmaking* (New York: Oxford University Press, 1988).

In any case, remember that citing the sources you have drawn upon for creating presentational materials is part of being an ethical public speaker. See *Highlighting Presentational Aids and Ethics* for a review of ethical considerations in preparing and presenting visual and audiovisual aids.

Summary

- Most public speakers use presentational aids. In an increasingly visual society, using aids helps engage listeners' senses.
- From the speaker's perspective, using carefully prepared presentational aids is an excellent way to enhance a speech. By using presentational aids, the speaker can
  - highlight and support main ideas
  - facilitate understanding
  - engage listener emotions
  - deliver the speech effectively
  - enhance his or her credibility
- From the listeners' perspective, presentational aids can help them to
  - focus their attention on what is especially important in the presentation
  - find the presentation more interesting and engaging
  - aid in comprehension and retention
- Almost any speech can benefit from the use of presentational aids. Diverse options abound, ranging from the chalkboard to computer-generated slideshows.
- Each aid should be carefully chosen and/or constructed, with the audience, the speech, and the setting in mind. In many speaking contexts, ranging from the community to the classroom, listeners *expect* speakers to use presentational aids.
- In developing effective presentational aids, keep these guidelines in mind:
  - Make sure that each aid truly assists the presentation.
  - Design all aids for quick processing by listeners.
  - Strive for professional quality.
  - Learn to employ "silence" (i.e., avoid using too many visuals or sound displays).
  - Anticipate potential problems by always having backups.
- As you use presentational aids, follow these guidelines:
  - Practice your speech *with* the aids.
  - Preview the speaking venue, if possible.
  - Have everything set up, tested, and ready to go before listeners arrive.
  - Reveal presentational aids for as long as needed, but only for as long as needed.
  - Direct the audience's attention to the part of the aid you are discussing and explain/clarify as you move through the presentation.

- Remain connected with the audience—avoid talking to the aid.
- Use all presentational aids with a concern for accuracy and integrity.

QUESTIONS FOR REVIEW AND REFLECTION

1. What are some of the ways that using presentational aids can help speakers?
2. How do presentational aids assist audience members as they try to listen attentively to a speech?
3. Can you think of any topic for which no presentational support would be needed? Explain.
4. What are some ways that graphs can be used to clarify and illuminate ideas and information?
5. What are the major presentational options available to most public speakers? What are the potential advantages and disadvantages of each?
6. How might audience expectations influence your choice of presentational aids?
7. How will you go about developing your presentational aids to maximize the chances that they will enhance the effectiveness of your presentation?
8. What are the key principles you will want to remember as you are setting up and using your presentational aids?
9. In what ways might the motto "less is more" be advisable for the speaker planning to frame her or his presentation with bulleted lists?

ENDNOTES

1. See, for example, Laurie Goodstein, "New 'Philosophy' of Policing: Departments Seek to Join Forces with Public," *Washington Post*, December 23, 1991, A1.
2. See, for example, Stephen Kinzer and Jim Rutenberg, "Grim Images Seem to Deepen Nation's Polarization on Iraq," *New York Times*, May 13, 2004, A11; "Abu Ghraib— An Indelible Stain on U.S.," *Christian Science Monitor*, May 7, 2004, 9; Charles Krauthammer, "Abu Ghraib as Symbol," *Washington Post*, May 7, 2004, A33; Michael M. Phillips, "The Abu Ghraib Fallout: Marines in Iraq See Prison Photos Creating Enemies," *Wall Street Journal*, May 10, 2004, A10.
3. See *Newsweek's* special report: "After the Tsunami," *Newsweek*, January 10, 2005, 22–45. See *Time* magazine's special report on Hurricane Katrina: "An American Tragedy," *Time*, September 12, 2005, 28–85.
4. Michael P. Verdi and Janet T. Johnson, "Organized Spatial Displays and Texts: Effects of Presentational Order and Display Type on Learning Outcomes," *Journal of Experimental Education* 65 (Summer 1997): 303–17.
5. For additional information on youth and voting, go to www.youthvote.org. Also see Mark Lopez, *Facts about Young Voters* (College Park, MD: School of Public Affairs, University of Maryland, 2005).
6. Verdi and Johnson, "Organized Spatial Displays and Texts," 303–05.
7. Maria L. Berg and James G. May, "Parallel Processing in Visual Perception and Memory: What Goes Where and When?" *Current Psychology* 16 (Winter 1998): 247–83. Also see Lih-Juan Chanlin, "Visual Treatment for Different Prior Knowledge," *International Journal of Instructional Media* 26 (1999): 213–19.
8. Doris A. Graber, "Say It with Pictures," *Annals of the American Academy of Political and Social Science* 546 (July 1996): 85–96.

9. Shu-Ling Lai, "Influence of Audio-Visual Presentations on Learning Abstract Concepts," *International Journal of Instructional Media* 27 (2000): 199–207.

10. Priti Shah and James Hoeffner, "Review of Graph Comprehension Research: Implications for Instruction," *Educational Psychology Review* 14 (2002): 47–51.

11. Ibid., pp. 53–54.

12. Joel Best, *More Damned Lies and Statistics: How Numbers Confuse Public Issues* (Berkeley and Los Angeles: University of California Press, 2004), 45–46.

13. Berg and May, 254–62.

14. Best, 45–46.

15. "Study Predicts Number of Fat Children Will Rise," *Bloomington Herald-Times*, March 6, 2006, C7.

16. Best, 49. Also see Gerald Everett Jones, *How to Lie with Charts* (San Jose, CA: Authors Choice Press, 2000), 30.

17. Jones, *How to Lie with Charts*, 28–29.

18. Ibid., 48.

19. Graber, "Say It with Pictures," 90–93.

20. Claire Morrison and William Jimmerson, "Business Presentations for the 1990s," *Video Manager* (July 1989), 18.

21. Graber, 86. Also see Carol L. Hodes, "Processing Visual Information: Implications of the Dual Code Theory," *Journal of Instructional Psychology* 21 (March 1994): 36–43.

22. Lih-Juan Chanlin, "The Effects of Verbal Elaboration and Visual Elaboration on Student Learning," *International Journal of Instructional Media* 24 (1997): 333–39.

23. Joe Ayres, "Using Visual Aids to Reduce Speech Anxiety," *Communication Research Reports* (June–December 1991): 73–79.

24. Chanlin, "Effects of Verbal Elaboration," 333–39.

25. A study conducted at Indiana University found that an instructor received much better course evaluations when she projected keywords to outline her lecture's main points than when she gave the identical lecture without using visuals.

26. It is important to recognize that speakers *do* exercise judgment in choosing photographs, deciding how to display data, and so forth. The ethical speaker will choose never to knowingly distort information. Likewise, the ethical speaker will be mindful of the *potential* for bias when using visual images to present information and will offer support for arguments.

27. Hodes, "Processing Visual Information," 36–40.

28. Elizabeth Keyes, "Typography, Color, and Information Structure," *Technical Communication, Fourth Quarter* (1993): 638–54.

29. It is important to remember that some listeners may be unable to distinguish among colors. In addition to the correctives we offer, there are other ways of dealing with this issue. See William Horton, *Illustrating Computer Documentation* (New York: John Wiley and Sons, 1991), 219–44.

30. There is considerable research on effective color combinations that consider hue, value, and saturation. See Edward Tufte, *Envisioning Information* (Cheshire, CT: Graphics Press, 1990).

31. Student Government Association, Texas A&M University, "The Big Event," March 21, 2006, http://bigevent.tamu.edu (accessed March 13, 2007).

32. Cornelius B. Pratt, "The Misuse of PowerPoint," *Public Relations Quarterly* 48 (2003): 20–26.

33. James Price Dillard, ed., *Seeking Compliance: The Production of Interpersonal Influence Messages* (Scottsdale, AZ: Gorsuch-Scarisbrick, 1990).

34. Tufte, *Envisioning Information*, 26–64.

35. Amy C. Bradshaw, "Effects of Presentation Interference in Learning with Visuals," *Journal of Visual Literacy* 23 (2003): 41–68.

36. We have found this color scheme to be the best—even in rooms with minimal dimming, and it's also recommended by Jones, *How to Lie with Charts*, 215.

37. Jeremy Caplan, "Tips on Talks," *Time,* November 15, 2005): 93.

38. Jean-Luc Doumont, "The Cognitive Style of PowerPoint: Slides Are Not All Evil," *Technical Communication* 52 (February 2005): 64–70.

39. Chanlin, "Visual Treatment for Different Prior Knowledge," 213–19.

40. See, for example, L. Rieber, "Animation as a Distractor to Learning," *International Journal of Instructional Media* 23 (1996): 53–57.

41. Arthur Goldsmith, "Digitally Altered Photography: The New Image Makers," *Britannica Book of the Year: 1995* (Chicago, IL: Encyclopedia Britannica, 1995), 135.

Speaking to Inform

CHAPTER OBJECTIVES

*After studying this chapter, you
should be able to*

1. Understand the different
   functions of informative
   presentations.

2. Compare and contrast the
   different types of informative
   speeches.

3. Describe the different ways
   that speakers can make
   information interesting and
   memorable to an audience.

4. Organize and deliver an
   informative speech, following
   the guidelines for effective
   preparation and presentation.

5. Understand the ethical issues
   surrounding informative
   speaking.

As a professional and as a citizen, you frequently will be called on to deliver informative speeches. In informative speeches, you aim to educate or enlighten rather than persuade. You act as a teacher, not an advocate, providing facts and other information but not taking a stand on controversial issues. Thus, for example, an attorney might enlighten a group of concerned citizens about new laws governing the release of convicted child molesters. The leader of a task force might explain how his organization will generate and administer aid to newly arrived citizens displaced by a natural disaster. A security expert might brief the Parent Teacher Association on new security measures for their school. A senior student might explain to a group of first-semester students different ways of becoming involved with student government. You, too, will inevitably be called on to give informative presentations throughout your life—in professional, classroom, and community settings. You may speak in workshops, orientation and training sessions, business meetings, board meetings, and community forums.

Some informative speeches may be preliminary to persuasion. You may transmit information to build a common ground of understanding before urging the audience to support a given point of view or to act in a certain way. In these cases, providing information *might* become the foundation for persuasion. Nevertheless, when we speak of informative speaking in this chapter, we are thinking of a speech whose ultimate purpose is to help the audience gain some understanding of a theory, concept, process, program, procedure, or other phenomenon. Informative speakers do not advocate for any particular position in a public controversy, but rather seek to educate, enlighten, or inform audiences about matters they will find interesting or useful.

Listeners should be especially cautious about speakers who attempt to disguise their persuasive efforts as informative. Speakers who claim to be "objective" about an issue of public controversy should be viewed with skepticism. A political candidate who just wants to "explain" her plan for improving Social Security really wants to *convince* you that her plan should be accepted. A builder who says he only wants to "inform" you of how a tract of land could be best developed probably seeks to persuade you to accept his scheme for using the land. Speakers who try to disguise a persuasive message as informative are clearly acting in an unethical manner. Furthermore, if an audience sees through the speaker's deception, the speaker's ethos is damaged and his or her effectiveness diminished.

Functions of Informative Speeches

Preview. *All informative speeches seek to gain audience understanding. Yet, they may function in different ways. Some speakers inform by offering audiences ideas and information. Others strive to shape perceptions. Still others articulate alternatives. Different types of informative speeches may describe, demonstrate, explain, or report on some process or phenomenon of interest.*

Many of you will be called on to give informative presentations, not only in your speech class but also later in life. When you give an informative speech, you often will be imparting new information—helping the listeners understand something for the first time. On other occasions, you will take a familiar topic and present a different perspective or a new interpretation.

Although informative speeches function in a variety of ways, they all impart ideas and information. Audiences gain understanding by listening to, understanding, and contemplating what the speaker has to say.

Sharing Ideas and Information

Perhaps the most common function of an informative speech is to provide information or to share ideas. The speaker may decide that the audience needs to be briefed, taught, or informed about some data, program, issue, or problem. He or she aims to stimulate learning and understanding.

For instance, one student decided to give an informative speech about biometric scanners. He was not trying to get everyone in the class to purchase one of these scanners. Rather, he wanted to make them aware of what a biometric scanner is, how the technology works, and the purposes it serves.[1] He described its history as an outgrowth of fingerprinting—a tool used in law enforcement since the early 1900s. In the final section of his speech, he discussed the ways in which this new technology has been adapted for use by civilians and businesses (such as allowing employees to clock in and out of work efficiently and accurately monitoring access to high-security areas).

Raising Awareness

We are surrounded by a dazzling array of information—from the Internet, television, newspapers, and lectures. It is impossible to take it all in. We have our own interests and information sources, and we tend to limit ourselves as we strive to become well versed on a manageable number of subjects. Inevitably, we will overlook many important issues.

Sometimes a public speaker will call our attention to something that, in the speaker's view, is worthy of our consideration. When she does this, she is saying, "Here is something worth knowing. This could prove helpful, enriching, or worthy of further exploration." One speaker might talk about twenty-first century careers in health care made possible by advances in technology. Another might discuss the history of New Harmony, Indiana—the site of two of America's nineteenth-century utopian communities—known for its innovative and influential reforms in education.[2] Still another could describe the principles of feng shui (the Chinese science and art of creating harmony between inhabitants and their environment).[3] In these situations, the speaker's purpose is to raise your awareness, to arouse your interest and curiosity, and to enlighten you. With this heightened awareness, you may decide to pursue the topic further.

Articulating Alternatives

Most complex issues can be addressed in a variety of ways. Often we are not aware of our options, or we may know of only a few possibilities when in fact many others exist. Sometimes a speaker will give a presentation aimed at helping listeners grasp the number, variety, and quality of alternatives available to them. A pharmacist might speak to a group of soon-to-be senior citizens about the alternatives among the new Medicare prescription drug benefit plans. An academic adviser might speak to a group of college students about the latest alternatives for completing a semester abroad while simultaneously completing the university's requirements for a service learning certificate.

In articulating alternatives in an informative speech, the speaker must be certain that he or she presents the information in a fair and unbiased manner. The speaker who secretly favors one program or plan but feigns objectivity with listeners commits a serious ethical breach. Trustworthy speakers should be able to set aside their own interests in articulating alternatives in the interest of empowering listeners to make free choices among alternatives that they truly understand.

For instance, a real estate agent was recently hired by a city council to investigate possible properties that might work well as a recreation center for the young people of the community. The agent's job was to study the options and present them, fully and accurately, to the members of the council. His specific purpose was: "I want my audience to understand the array of properties available for creating a community youth recreation center." Preparing this kind of informative presentation required a great deal of careful research, a thorough consideration of all possible alternatives, and a willingness to present the information with accuracy and open-mindedness. This speaker might have been tempted to promote one building that happened to be among his own company's listings. Instead, he wisely chose to acknowledge the various firms with which the different properties were listed and go forward with an accurate account of each. In doing this, he used the criteria the council had given him—and weighed each alternative accordingly. Using this approach, the realtor looked at each property in relationship to these criteria:

- number of square feet
- existing features that might adapt well to the recreation center concept (for instance, an existing usable gymnasium)
- accessibility to youth (traveling from schools, for example)
- accessibility to those with disabilities (need for structural alternations, such as ramps or elevators)
- special renovation challenges (for instance, a property with a historic designation)
- space for future expansions (adequate surrounding land that might be purchased for future use, for example)

By faithfully adhering to these criteria, the speaker was able to present each property alternative, together with pros and cons, and leave the audience to weigh the options and make a decision—or keep seeking new alternatives.

It is especially difficult to explain alternatives fairly and objectively when issues of public controversy are involved. In choosing topics for informative speeches, then, such controversies are best avoided in favor of topics that aim to educate or enlighten the audience.

Types of Informative Speeches

Preview. *Speakers may be called on to present several different types of informative speeches. They may prepare and deliver informative speeches that describe, demonstrate, explain, or report on some process or phenomenon of interest.*

As noted earlier, the major purpose of any informative speech is to share knowledge and ideas with the hope of promoting the audience's understanding or competence. Even so, several different types of informative speeches exist. Understanding their differences can help you prepare and deliver each type more effectively.

The Speech of Description

Sometimes speakers want to describe a place, an event, or a person. By giving a speech of description, they hope to help the audience get a clear picture of their subject. Topics that might work well for this kind of speech include green spaces in urban planning, life on an Indian reservation, public transportation options in major metropolitan areas, the wetlands of North America, or experiences while serving in the army in Afghanistan.

If you decide to give a descriptive speech, you will want to take great pains with your language. Precision, color, and clarity are essential. Usually you will want to use presentational aids. A computer-generated slide show, for example, might be very useful in showing the beauty of nearly extinct birds in North America, the grandeur of old homes on the historic preservation list in your community, or the ravages of war, disease, or poverty in nearly any part of the world. However, avoid being overreliant on visuals. Do the best you can to describe fully the subject of your speech without them, and then add the visuals as a final clarifying touch, or use them to present images too complex or difficult to capture in words alone.

Many speeches with purposes other than informing listeners may use description. For instance, a speech of tribute or a eulogy will usually include highly descriptive passages that celebrate someone's accomplishments or personal attributes. But unlike the informative speech, the primary purpose of these speeches is to move the audience, remind them of their values, and get them to honor the person who is the focus of the speech.

The Speech of Demonstration

If you aim to teach an audience how something works or how to do something, you are giving a speech of demonstration. A lawn care expert, for example, might demonstrate how listeners can care for their lawns and gardens in environmentally friendly ways, such as opting for ground cover instead of grass. An exercise science major might review how fitness programs in our schools can reduce the stress on our health care system and curb our costs. A Habitat for Humanity crew leader might demonstrate to a group of volunteers how to build storage sheds that accompany most Habitat homes. In each case, the speaker is demonstrating some sort of process.

This speaker is describing the complicated process by which uncontrollable wildfires develop. Understanding the process is necessary before changes in policy can be effected.

The speech of demonstration may focus on application along with understanding. In some cases, the speaker wants the audience to apply certain principles or steps—to learn how to do something during the course of the speech. The exercise science major would want her audience to understand how fitness programs in our schools can directly affect the cost and availability of health care. The Habitat crew leader would expect that the volunteers who had listened to her presentation would actually be able to help build storage sheds, using the procedures and specifications she had described. On other occasions, the speaker may be describing a more complicated process, simply hoping that the audience will grasp that process and not necessarily perform it. For instance, a nurse in a hospital's cardiovascular unit uses a dummy to teach a group of heart patients the procedures that are involved in their surgery preparation, the surgery itself, and their subsequent recuperation. She wants her listeners to understand what to expect, not to undertake the procedures themselves.

Most speeches of demonstration involve the use of visuals to show, clarify, and make the information more memorable. Many use a sequential pattern of organization (discussing consecutive steps in a process). To make sure the audience clearly understood what was demonstrated, the speaker should allow ample time for questions.

The Speech of Explanation

A speaker who wants to help the audience understand concepts that are complicated, abstract, or unfamiliar will give a speech of explanation. One of the more challenging types of informative speeches, the explanatory speech, demands that the speaker be extremely knowledgeable about the topic and be able to explain it clearly to the audience.

A professor's lecture, for instance, is a speech aimed at explaining abstract or difficult concepts to students. Skilled teachers carefully define concepts being introduced, explain their importance or relevance, offer good clarifying examples, and give students the chance to show what they have learned through some kind of application exercise.

If you are giving a speech of explanation, you must be able to define the concept's main features or parts, explain its significance, and offer compelling examples that illustrate it. One student speaker gave a speech whose purpose was to help his classroom audience understand the meaning of LD *(learning-disabled)*.[4] As part of his speech, he offered the legal definition of LD, gave examples of some of the most common kinds of learning disabilities, explained the extent to which LD students have been placed in special education classes in the past, and concluded by examining how each type of disability might influence the student's ability to learn in different kinds of classroom environments.

When a speaker is able to illuminate a concept that listeners previously did not understand, he or she makes a real contribution to their learning. Because explanations of unfamiliar or difficult concepts can be challenging, speakers will want to allow plenty of time for audience questions.

The Informative Oral Report

In professional and community settings, people are often called on to present an informative oral report. In some cases, these reports are given informally (perhaps even to one or two listeners) and may be quite brief. On other occasions, the speaker may be asked to prepare a more formal presentation, often technical in nature, to inform others in the organization of recent events, discoveries, or other vital information.

The need to give an informative oral report can arise in diverse professional contexts, but informative reports are not limited to professional contexts.[5] For instance, one of the authors of this book volunteers with a homeless shelter's employment program and recently attended a conference on "supported employment."[6] Upon her return, she was asked to present an oral report to the shelter's employment task force concerning the various forms of supported employment that were being used successfully by similar agencies around the state. Or, in a different context, a student was elected to the Student Senate and was later asked to represent the Senate at an important meeting of the university's board of trustees. At this particular meeting, the trustees were considering several different plans for substantially increasing student tuition—a possibility that had attracted the concern of students and parents alike. The next time the Senate met, the student was asked to present an oral report detailing the main features of each option the trustees were considering. To clarify the options, she prepared some handouts to accompany her presentation.

Informative reports often provide background that a group will use in making decisions or solving problems. For example, as a result of the report on supported employment, the shelter's task force decided to hire a new case worker who would also be an employment specialist, to further strengthen their program. Following a report (or even a series of reports), a group may go ahead with other business.

Although the primary purpose of a speech might be to report, explain, demonstrate, or describe, any speech can include a combination of these goals. For example, a speaker reporting on an innovative product would almost certainly devote part of his or her speech to describing the product and perhaps even take a few minutes to demonstrate how it works. Thus, the various types of informative speeches are not always distinct, but they always have the ultimate goal of gaining audience understanding.

Organizing the Informative Speech

Preview. *Several different strategies exist for organizing informative speeches. Although most of the organizational patterns described here can be used to arrange other types of speeches, they lend themselves particularly well to informative speeches. These patterns include chronological, sequential, spatial, categorical, and causal.*

The basic principles of organization that we discussed in Chapter 9 should guide your efforts as you begin to organize your informative presentation. You will want to pay attention to issues of balance, developing each of your main points fully and sufficiently. You will want to think about which ideas you want to emphasize most—and consider placing them first or last, rather than embedding them in the middle of your speech.[7] You will also recognize that your speech can be organized in a variety of ways, and you may want to experiment with different approaches until you find the one that seems best suited to your specific purpose.

Chronological or Sequential Patterns

One way you might organize your informative speech is by using a chronological or sequential pattern. If you wanted your audience to understand a particular step-by-step process or procedure (such as the process of voter registration), you would choose a sequential organizational pattern. If, however, you were interested in describing how an important trend, program, or phenomenon evolved over time, you would choose a chronological pattern.

For example, suppose you wanted to inform fellow classmates about the history of your own community's award-winning program, "Middle Way House," which combats domestic violence and sexual assaults. You would likely proceed chronologically, beginning with the creation of the original programs and continuing, decade by decade, until you discuss current programs and future plans. After sharing Middle Way's mission—"To end violence in the lives of women and children by implementing or sponsoring activities and programs aimed at achieving individual and social change"[8]—you would proceed by describing the program's roots. You might devise the thesis, *Middle Way House has served the particular needs of this community for over 35 years, evolving into the nationally acclaimed program that it is today.*

I. Over 35 years ago, Middle Way House had a different mission and served a different population than it serves today.
   A. Beginning in 1971, Middle Way provided rehabilitative services to Indiana University students who had experimented with drugs but could not find support within the university system (*Indiana Daily Student* article, March 2006).
   B. Throughout that decade, the agency operated as a volunteer organization, responding to diverse needs that arose in the community.
      1. Middle Way provided peer counseling to people abusing drugs and alcohol.
      2. It operated a venereal disease clinic, headed by a local volunteer physician.
      3. Volunteers also answered the phone 24 hours a day, to provide a listening ear for people who were anxious, lonely, or in need of information or referral services.

Transition: By the end of the decade, however, Middle Way refined its focus.

II. Early in the 1980s, agency leaders selected abused women and children as Middle Way's target population (according to their website).
   A. In 1981, Middle Way first opened a domestic violence shelter.
      1. The shelter provided safe housing and offered case management.
      2. It also facilitated in-house peer support groups for women and children from a six-county area in south central Indiana.
   B. In 1984, a new program offered support groups for local women *not* living in the shelter but who needed help coping with the aftermath of intimate-partner violence.
   C. For the first time, in 1987, Middle Way began to provide children's programming in the shelter setting.
   D. One year later, at the request of the city, the agency opened a Rape Crisis Center and established a Legal Advocacy Program.

Transition: As you can see, Middle Way successfully advanced its mission in many ways during the 1980s, but there was still much to accomplish in the next decade.

III. The 1990s were a time of continued growth as well as creative new business ventures for Middle Way.
   A. In the early 1990s, the agency expanded its services to open offices and support group programming in several surrounding counties, as well as expanding selected local services (according to Charlotte Zietlow, director of economic development for Middle Way).
      1. Surrounding counties' programs focused on crisis intervention and legal advocacy for victims of domestic violence and sexual assault.

       2. Middle Way also began providing *on-the-scene* services in Bloomington, immediately following a police investigation in cases of domestic violence and sexual assault.

  B. The late 1990s also saw the creation of new Middle Way initiatives aimed at helping women with employment.

      1. According to Toby Strout, executive director of Middle Way, the agency spearheaded the creation of the Bloomington Area Micro-enterprise Initiative, which provides training, access to loans, and technical assistance to women interested in starting small businesses.

      2. In 1997, Middle Way began its own first business, Confidential Document Destruction.

          a. This business provided training and marketable skills for women who were entering the job market after leaving abusive relationships.

          b. It also paid them a living wage and offered benefits and appropriate supports.

      3. By the end of the 1990s, Middle Way had begun construction of transitional housing known as "The Rise!" for battered women and their children.

          a. The Rise! symbolized Middle Way's commitment to providing a continuum of low-cost housing for the population it serves.

          b. In 1998, The Rise! began receiving families into its 28-unit complex with supportive case management and children's programming.

Transition: Now that we've reviewed the amazing accomplishments of Middle Way House over three decades, you have to wonder what other accomplishments are possible, and what the future might hold.

IV. Fortunately, Middle Way House continues to thrive in the twenty-first century.

  A. In 2006, Middle Way celebrated its thirty-fifth anniversary!

  B. The winner of numerous awards, Middle Way was one of only six domestic violence programs in the country to be highlighted in a PBS documentary called "Best Practices in Domestic Violence Programs." See Middle Way's website for more details.

  C. In 2002, the agency created Food Works, a program that provides a needed community service, while offering women good jobs and good training in transferable skills (according to a 2006 article in the *Bloomington Alternative*).

      1. Operating out of a commercial kitchen in the First United Methodist Church, Food Works provides nutritious meals for such agencies as the Area 10 Agency on Aging and the area's Head Start program.

      2. In addition to providing over 1,400 meals and snacks each day, Food Works also operates its own highly successful catering business.

      3. Food Works also caters Middle Way's own fund-raising events, such as the annual art fair that celebrates Women's History Month.

  D. In 2007, Middle Way will begin work on its new home, called New Wing—a larger facility that will provide space for Food Works and badly needed additional space for an emergency shelter.

By using the chronological pattern to organize this speech, you are able to emphasize how this organization has flourished over several decades and to illustrate its increasingly ambitious and progressive programs. In a time when non-profit agencies come and go, this agency's status in the community is enhanced by its ability to withstand the test of time, a fact the chronological pattern helps underscore.

Spatial Pattern

You can also use space as your organizing principle. For example, the volunteer coordinator for the Shalom Community Center in Bloomington, Indiana (a safe daytime shelter and resource center for those experiencing homelessness and poverty),[9] often introduces prospective volunteers to the center by taking them on a tour of the two buildings that house the Shalom programs. Each program is described in relationship to its spatial location. This kind of presentation is typically made as the coordinator walks the volunteers from place to place. Operating with the thesis *The Shalom Community Center addresses the immediate and long-term needs of its guests*, she might organize her remarks in the following way.

I. The centerpiece of the Shalom Center is the hunger relief program—located here, in the church basement.
   A. Most volunteers work in the hunger relief program—preparing, cooking, and serving over 200 meals each day.
      1. In 2006, Shalom served over 60,000, an increase of 16 percent over the previous year (according to our executive director, Joel Rekas).
      2. You can volunteer for the breakfast or lunch shifts.
   B. In the kitchen, you may have several different assignments (moving around the room).
      1. You may work at the food prep island in the middle of the room, to chop vegetables, assemble salads and casseroles, and prepare desserts.
      2. You may also be asked to cook, using the large commercial stove—and placing hot dishes in a heated retainer bin until mealtime arrives.
      3. You may be asked to wash dishes—using the heavy-duty, fast-paced, industrial dishwasher, located at one end of the kitchen.
   C. You may also be asked to work in the dining hall, where there are several options for involvement.
      1. You may help serve food during one of the meals—as you stand behind the heated food server and put food onto plates, according to requests.
      2. You may stand in the dining hall and monitor food and drink supplies.
      3. You may go through the line and sit at one of the dining tables—eating and chatting with the guests.
         a. Volunteers who dine with guests help break down barriers that might exist between the two groups.
         b. You may also find that you learn a great deal about the individuals with whom you interact—giving you insights into poverty issues.

Transition: The Shalom Center not only offers nutritious meals, it also offers a safe daytime space for guests and assistance in connecting them with other agencies and programs.

II. Across the street from the church's hunger relief program is another invaluable resource, Shalom's expanded day shelter and resource center (see October 2005 article by former board president Shirley St. John in *Safety-Net*).

A. One option for working in this wing of the center is to sign up for the Job Links program—a program that is administered in the computer room.

1. You would do job in-takes, finding out about the guests' backgrounds and employment needs.

2. You would also help guests identify potential jobs in the area by conducting online searches.

3. You might also help guests fill out job application forms, draft letters of application, and create résumés.

4. You can also facilitate guests' registering with Work One by going online at www.workone.org.

5. To work with the Job Links program, you will need to go through further training and supervision (according to Norm Horrar, head of the Job Links program).

B. You might also choose to work in the Gathering Place, located in the center of the building.

1. Here, we need volunteers to serve as receptionists.

a. In this role, you will greet guests—making them welcome and helping them connect with those they need to see.

b. You will take and convey phone messages—with the utmost concern for confidentiality.

c. You may also be asked to sort and "deliver" mail to guests' mail slots.

d. You will also sign guests in and out of the shower room and monitor the towel supply.

2. You may also want to work with the Shalom literacy program—situated at one end of the Gathering Place.

a. In this role, you might tutor guests in math or reading.

b. You might help maintain the library.

c. You could organize and lead reading groups.

C. Finally, you may want to work with the children and family programs, located at the bottom of the stairway—in a section that is separate from the general Gathering Place.

1. You can work in this program with diaper and resource distribution.

2. You may interact with children—playing games with them and reading to them.

3. You may interact with parents, offering a comforting, supportive ear, and referring them to agency and staff resources, as requested.

The speaker would also refer briefly to parts of the facility where staff members and visiting agency personnel (such as the local Housing Authority, Ivy Tech

Community College of Indiana, and the local branch of St. Vincent DePaul) have office space to meet with guests. A volunteer would occasionally direct guests to these offices but would be unlikely to work there as part of his or her volunteer efforts.

If the volunteer coordinator were to give this type of presentation away from the Shalom facilities, to a group of volunteers who were *not* on-site, she would most likely organize her remarks differently—perhaps by discussing volunteer options in terms of types/categories of volunteer opportunities. She would still need, though, to emphasize the location of each program (so that volunteers would understand where to go to volunteer), so she might use a floor plan as a presentational aid to point to the location of each.

Spatial organizational patterns are often used by speakers in community settings—by docents who offer tours of museums or historical properties, by architects who use models to help listeners understand key design features of proposed new buildings, and by health-care professionals who use models of the human body to show the audience the impact of alcohol or drug abuse on various parts of the body. As a student, you might use a spatial pattern to show listeners what a new campus bus route would look like, to explain the proposed additions to the student recreation center, or to explore three alternative spring break destinations.

Categorical Pattern

Another potential organizational pattern for an informative presentation is categorical. When you arrange your ideas categorically, you address types, forms, qualities, or aspects of the speech subject. This was the organizational strategy chosen by the executive director of Second Helpings, a nonprofit organization based in Indianapolis, Indiana. She had been invited to speak with the citizens of a neighboring community about their interest in establishing a similar program in their town. To better inform her listeners about the values and mission of Second Helpings, she discussed the organization's three major commitments: food rescue, job training, and hunger relief. Offering as her thesis, *Second Helpings operates with the principle of coordinated relief and adopts a holistic approach to assistance*, she proceeded to develop her discussion of each of the organization's commitments (food rescue, job training, and hunger relief) by exploring each category in the following way.

I. We help address the problem of wasted food.
    A. Americans throw away about 27 percent of all available food in the United States.
    B. To address this waste, we developed a program to "rescue" food from local food-service businesses and organizations and deliver it to qualified nonprofits that assist those experiencing poverty.
        1. During the first month, 37 volunteers rescued 7,099 pounds of food and prepared 3,074 meals.
        2. Today, we rescue over 100,000 pounds of prepared and perishable food products each month and serve over 45,000 meals.
        3. Over the years, we have had hundreds of partners who want to see their overprepared or overpurchased food be put to good use (e.g., O'Malia's

Food Market, Outback Steakhouse, St. Vincent's Hospital, and Smilin' Babe Produce).

C. In rescuing food, the first issue we must address is safety.
   1. To guarantee safety, we use only refrigerated trucks and vans.
   2. To pick up the food, we now hire drivers (paid staff—not volunteers), who are trained in food safety and sanitation.
   3. These drivers will not collect food that they deem to be unsafe or inedible.

D. The other issue of importance is efficiency.
   1. We pick up food in a timely manner from donors, who can donate food whenever it is available, either on a one-time basis or on an ongoing, regular schedule.
   2. We also deliver the food promptly to about 50 participating nonprofit organizations.
      a. We serve nonprofits directly, not individuals.
      b. Qualified nonprofits must have adequate kitchen facilities.
      c. Those handling the food must attend a Safe Food Handling class.

Transition: In addition to rescuing food that ultimately will rescue those in need, we take other measures to help them, as well.

II. We help people develop skills that will allow them to work and earn a living wage.
A. Because so many jobs fail to pay a living wage, many individuals and their families live at or below the poverty line.
B. At the same time, the food-service industry often struggles for lack of skilled employees.
C. We developed a 10-week culinary job-training program to provide the skills necessary to start a career in the food-service industry.
   1. We have our own full-time culinary instructor/professional chef who teaches our classes.
      a. Guest chefs provide diverse role models and incorporate hands-on kitchen work.
      b. Students learn in varied ways—through field trips, videotapes, lectures, and classroom activities.
      c. Students come from diverse backgrounds—often at the recommendation of a case worker or job counselor.
      d. All instructional materials are available in both English and Spanish.
      e. Our program offers an excellent opportunity for adults who are motivated but lack job skills.
      f. Visit our website at www.secondhelpings.org for a complete list of admissions requirements for our job-training program.
   2. Our program has been highly successful.
      a. We have placed over 70 percent of our graduates in restaurant positions.

    b.   The average starting salary for a Second Helpings graduate is $8.75 an hour.

    c.   Over 72 percent of our programs' graduates remain employed after six months on the job.

    d.   Our graduates possess the skills and professionalism that are so much in demand in the food-service industry.

Transition: As you can see, we take a holistic approach to addressing the immediate and ongoing needs of people in need. We also work cooperatively with other organizations and agencies who share our mission.

III. We work hard to support others whose mission is to provide hunger relief.

    A. A 2001 study by the Department of Agriculture estimated that 33 million people are hungry or food insecure in the United States (1 in 10).

    B. Many nonprofit organizations represent the front lines in the fight against hunger.

       1. These agencies include homeless shelters, after-school programs, and soup kitchens.

       2. Unfortunately, these programs are chronically underfunded and operate on extremely tight budgets.

       3. Such agencies struggle to balance the need to provide both nutritious meals and quality services.

    C. Using rescued food, Second Helpings provides high-quality nutritious meals at no cost to programs serving our neighbors in need.

       1. The meals are usually delivered directly to the participating program, hot and ready to eat.

       2. We are regularly serving well over 2,500 meals each day, six days a week.

       3. We have served over 2 million meals since our inception in 1998 to men, women, and children living in the Indianapolis area.

    D. Because of the food that we are able to provide, the recipient agencies are able to utilize their own resources more effectively to provide rehabilitative, educational, and other program services.

After providing her listeners with this helpful information about the mission, structure, and effectiveness of the Second Helpings program, the speaker then responded to questions about special challenges she had faced. She also sought to compare and contrast the two communities to illuminate which programs might work best.

    The categorical pattern was well suited to this speech and is commonly used by all kinds of speakers. A financial-aid specialist might speak to a group of students about several different kinds of financial-aid packages. A reading specialist might explain to a group of volunteer trainees two or three different approaches to teaching adult literacy, depending on the learner's type of problem and motivation level. As a student, you might use the categorical pattern to explore some novel curricular options that most students are unfamiliar with (such as certificate programs, the interdisciplinary major, and the individualized major).

This student describes his group's project at the 18th Service Learning Annual Conference at the Albuquerque Convention Center March 28, 2007.

Causal Pattern

Some informative speeches might follow the causal pattern, focusing on causes only, effects only, or moving either from cause to effect or from effect to cause. For instance, you may want your audience to understand the causes or effects of a specific event, problem, or program. Suppose, for example, you are a student at a university where there is no service-learning requirement. You have considered taking a service-learning course, but you are uncertain if you have the time, or even if you would find taking it to be all that valuable. You decide to do some research on the topic and share your findings with your public speaking class. Based on your research, you develop this thesis: *For the most part, students who take service-learning courses benefit from the experience.* After defining *service learning* and explaining your reasons for investigating it, you would then proceed, in the speech's body, to explore the benefits of taking service-learning classes, as well as offering a few caveats.

I. Students benefit in a variety of ways from taking service-learning (SL) courses.
   A. An extensive study of over 22,000 students by the Higher Education Research Institute at UCLA reported an impressive array of positive student outcomes.
      1. Students' academic performance was enhanced (measured in terms of GPA, writing skills, and critical-thinking skills).
      2. Positive values were also promoted, including commitment to activism and to promoting social justice and racial understanding.
      3. Students who successfully completed SL courses also assessed themselves higher on such measures as leadership ability and interpersonal skills.
   B. Other studies have reported that SL students actually learn more of the course content than those who take standard versions of the same class.
      1. These studies examined all kinds of courses, including political science, criminal justice, communication, environmental studies, business, anthropology, and sociology. See the *Michigan Journal of Community Service Learning, 1996 to the present.*
      2. This learning is further enhanced if students are asked to process their experience with fellow students and reflect on their service experience through papers and journaling.
   C. SL students also report that they intend to participate in service or volunteer activities after college.

1. A 2005 study of hundreds of alumni suggests that these student intentions are lived out after graduation: as the majority of SL alums reported a high degree of involvement with service in their communities (see Wang and Rodgers).[10]
2. This post-graduation involvement seems to depend somewhat on the extent to which the SL course taken directly encouraged civic engagement or advocacy.

D. Finally, SL students are more likely than others to choose a career in service—in some cases switching majors in order to do so.

Transition: Although all these SL outcomes are really positive, a couple of caveats are in order.

II. Students benefit *most* from SL courses under certain circumstances.
   A. First, they must have realistic expectations.
      1. The typical SL class requires students to volunteer for two or three hours each week (at a minimum)—and these are in addition to the regular class meeting times.
      2. Students may assume that they will be allowed to work with whatever agency they choose, but the instructor may have preselected an agency for the class to volunteer with (Marty Long, personal experience, 2007).
      3. SL classes typically have a few extra requirements, including reflection papers and journaling—in addition to the standard exams and papers.
   B. It is also important to anticipate logistical challenges.
      1. SL students may have to coordinate their schedules with other students if the class is organized around group work (a fairly common practice).
      2. Some students may experience transportation challenges, since some nonprofit agencies are off bus routes or far from campus.
      3. Sometimes agencies only need volunteers at specific times—such as over the lunch hour, or during the daytime, late afternoon, or early evening.
         a. This issue is likely to surface with agencies that operate after-school programs, such as Boys and Girls Clubs, or those who operate feeding programs.
         b. SL students need to make sure that they *are* available at the hours and times when they are needed by their agencies.
   C. Finally, approaching SL classes with genuine discipline and commitment is a must.
      1. Distribute service-learning hours throughout the semester.
         a. If students have limited experience with the agency during the early part of the semester, they will find it much harder to complete many class assignments.
         b. It is tough to catch up, once you fall behind (example of student who had to volunteer 25 hours during the last two weeks to fulfill her requirements).
      2. Recognize, too, that the hours your instructor requires you to volunteer are actually a *minimum* (according to a professor who has taught SL classes for more than a dozen years).

    a.   The more time you spend working with your agency, the more you will learn and the better you will perform in the class.

    b.   Genuinely giving something back to the agency may require you to go the extra mile.

You would then conclude your speech by pointing out that when students approach service-learning courses with a real sense of commitment to learning *and* to service, then both they and their agencies reap many benefits. Moreover, many students choose to continue volunteering with their agencies after the semester is over. Students who cannot make this kind of commitment may not want to take a service-learning course.

In choosing your organizational pattern, you should let your specific purpose be your guide. What pattern is most likely to produce the response you hope to get from your audience? What strategy is most likely to assist their awareness and understanding? Table 14.1 includes some guidelines, along with sample topics.

Table 14.1

GUIDELINES FOR CHOOSING AN ORGANIZATIONAL PATTERN

Pattern	Use When . . .	Possible Topics
Chronological/ Sequential	You want to discuss an event, phenomenon, or concept over time *or* you want to show a step-by-step progression	■ Trends in public schooling from the twentieth century to the present ■ The changing demographics of the United States ■ How our voting procedures have evolved from paper-and-pencil to machine voting ■ How to organize a successful town hall meeting
Spatial	You want to help the audience visualize something you are describing *and/or* you want to describe something by moving from point to point through space	■ The spread of AIDS in Africa ■ Introducing the new, affordable health-care clinic ■ Homeland security expenditures: regional differences ■ Options for bike trails in our community
Categorical	You want to emphasize the significance of the categories or divisions in some way *or* you are interested in a flexible approach to organization	■ Bringing education to prison: innovative programs ■ Health-care options for low-income families ■ Environmentally friendly vehicles ■ New drugs for treating HIV ■ The best service-learning programs in higher education
Causal	You want your audience to understand those factors (causes) that have contributed to some outcome (effects) *or* you want your audience to understand the impact (effects) of some problem or phenomenon	■ Factors that influence civic engagement ■ Media influences on women's body image ■ The decline of math scores in the United States. ■ Academic misconduct on our campus

How Audiences Learn from Informative Speeches

Preview. *Listeners who are motivated to learn make the speaker's job much easier. Often, however, listeners are not as motivated as the speaker might hope, challenging the speaker to find ways to capture and maintain their interest and attention.*

Speakers need to understand the strategies available for heightening listener interest and helping them learn and retain information.[11] A good place to start is by thinking about the extent to which listeners are motivated to listen.

The Role of Listener Motivation

Perhaps you have heard the old saying: "You can lead a horse to water, but you can't make it drink." Any teacher will tell you that the learning process works like that: you can give people information, but you cannot make them learn. In informative speaking, much depends on the listeners and the understanding, beliefs, and attitudes they bring to the speaking situation. The ideal listener, as we discussed in Chapter 4, is the motivated listener, who is intrinsically interested in the topic, willing to work at listening, and eager to gain some new understanding. When listeners are motivated to listen and learn, the speaker's job is much easier.

Unfortunately, listening sometimes takes place under less than ideal circumstances. Sometimes audience members do not have the background they need to be truly prepared to listen. Sometimes they resent having to listen to a presentation. At other times, they are simply bored. Under these circumstances, trying to impart information can be very challenging.

Usually when we are called on to make informative presentations, audience members are a mixed bag. Some are eager, some knowledgeable, and others less than motivated. Fortunately, there are things you can do to heighten listeners' interest and overcome, or at least reduce, initial inertia and apathy.

Capturing and Maintaining the Audience's Attention

A good place to begin is with thinking about how to interest listeners in what you are saying. Interest motivates learning.[12] In general, audience members will respond with interest to ideas and information that are relevant, novel, important and varied.[13]

Relevance

In Chapter 6, we discussed the importance of choosing a topic that the audience will perceive as relevant. You will want to address the matter of relevance right away, during the introduction of your speech. Why should your listeners want to hear about hybrid cars or the proposed community public transit system? One student speaker established her topic's relevance by pointing this out:

> Sometimes, as students, we get so busy that we don't pay attention to what experts are saying that might directly affect our lives. I know this happens to me sometimes. Do you ever imagine yourself being the victim of some kind of natural disaster—such as an earthquake, flood, wildfire, or tsunami? How about being the victim of a terrorist attack? After the September 11 attacks, many of

us *did* harbor such fears, but over time, we tend to become less concerned. Recently, however, leaders of FEMA and the American Red Cross have argued that every household *should* have an emergency supplies kit. And this is especially so if we live in an area that is particularly vulnerable to disasters—natural or otherwise. As you know, our college is located in an area where wildfires are quite common. So, knowing what items to collect for this kind of emergency kit ought to be a real priority for us.

Of course, the issue of relevance needs to be addressed throughout the speech, not just during the introduction. If your listeners begin to think: "Wait a minute! What does this have to do with me?" they are probably not learning very much.

Novelty

Listeners are often interested in things they find startling, unusual, or new. Novelty gains attention. By contrast, overly familiar or trite topics are often perceived as boring or unimaginative. Of course, topics that lack novelty for some audiences might be fine for others. For example, a speaker who explains how to organize a town hall meeting to an audience of seasoned community leaders would likely find her listeners unengaged by what for them is an overly familiar subject. However, the same topic might be seen as novel and engaging by an audience of listeners who want to organize such a meeting but have had no experience doing so.

Whether information is seen as novel, then, will depend on the audience and what they already know. If listeners know little about urban sprawl, how to protect themselves from identity theft, or recognizing Internet scams, such topics might generate interest. With any topic, some initial audience interest must exist—a readiness to learn or at least openness to becoming interested. If a topic is seen as bizarre or irrelevant, the fact that it is also seen as new or unusual may not help very much.

Sometimes a speaker can approach a familiar topic in a novel or unusual manner and immediately gain the audience's interest. In general, when a speaker has personal, direct experience with a topic—due to personal experience, years of work experience, or achievements in the area—he or she will bring a fresh perspective that audience members may find interesting. For instance, at the time of the Olympic Games, a student named Julie spoke about competitive gymnastics for young women. During that same semester, other students had chosen to speak on the same topic. Having participated in competitive gymnastics herself, however, she was able to transport her listeners behind the scenes, exposing the dark side of a sport, as well as illuminating its appeal. Because of her personal involvement and the depth of her knowledge, she was able to provide a unique perspective on a widely discussed topic.

Importance

No one wants to waste a lot of time listening to someone talk about trivia. Even an amusing speech can lose an audience if no insights or bits of wisdom emerge. Not everyone agrees on what is worth knowing. However, speeches that deal with substantive topics that affect the welfare of the community are likely to be seen as worthy of the listening time invested.

As you select topics for informative speeches, make sure the subjects are significant and engaging. One speaker might examine factors influencing U.S. efforts to ensure that cargo shipments arriving at our ports are safe. Another might address the qualifications for becoming a naturalized citizen. Still another might discuss the proliferation of chat rooms and blogs and the nature of their content. In each case, the speaker has chosen a topic that demands a good mind and thorough research, and a topic of substance that requires real interest and commitment.

Variety

Most of us have had the experience of being bored during others' presentations. Speakers can be very predictable, overly repetitive, or dull. Longer presentations entail special challenges in this regard, since listener attention spans are often far too short.[14]

Speakers can help sustain the audience's interest by introducing some variety into their presentations. Variety is not so much about the topic chosen for a speech as it is about the way the speaker presents it. Variety can come in many forms. Speakers may mix humor with more serious speech segments. They may use presentational aids in imaginative ways to create visual variety. Speakers may deliver a speech with varied movement, voice, and facial expressions. In almost all cases, they will want to use a variety of supporting material, such as testimony, statistics, comparison, and narrative. These are just a few of the options available to help sustain listener attention. With variety comes unpredictability—a certain level of suspense, and increased interest.

An effective speaker will use the attention-capturing factors just discussed in combination and in varying ways throughout his or her speech. For instance, a substantive topic may be of little interest to the audience unless the speaker is able to show its relevance. A novel topic may capture limited attention unless the speaker can show its importance. And no matter how effectively the speaker presents a topic, if its relevance has not been established, the speech will likely fall on deaf ears. Remaining mindful of the need to establish and maintain the audience's attention is an ongoing concern for every speaker.

Helping Listeners Learn

In Chapter 4, we discussed the audience's listening challenges, including ways to help them better attend to messages. If you are to give a successful informative speech, you have to present information that is, among other things, new to your listeners. However, new information can also be overwhelming if it is not presented effectively. You will want to pace yourself carefully, provide clarifying visual reinforcement as needed, and use language that is well adapted to the audience's knowledge level and background. Let us consider a few other things you might do to promote listener learning in your informative speech.

Limit the Number of Details.

No listener can absorb list after list of facts and figures. Instead you can use statistical and other detailed information to support major ideas you want listeners to remember. When you use statistical and other detailed support, translate it into audience-specific terms. One speaker, for example, noted that, on average, three teens attempt suicide every 100 minutes, and compared it to two 50-minute class periods.

Remember, too, not all topics are equally suited to a short presentation; choose wisely. Look at your specific purpose statement. Have you selected a purpose that is realistic, or is it too ambitious, given the time allotted for your talk? Decide what listeners really need to know to gain the kind of understanding you are hoping for. Ask yourself, "What is essential for my audience to understand, recall, and perhaps use?" As discussed in Chapter 10, use your outline to make sure you stick to the main ideas you planned to cover.

Use Restatement and Repetition.

One of the main ways that all of us learn is by being exposed repeatedly to information. When information is restated or repeated, we tend to learn it better. As discussed in Chapter 11, restatement and repetition can be effective stylistic devices, and they are often used by great speakers. By providing emphasis, restatement and repetition help you make ideas and information stick in the minds of your audience.

Take Time to Respond to Questions.

Whenever people grapple with new ideas and information, they are bound to have questions. It is important, therefore, to build time for questions into your speaking schedule if it is possible for you to do so. The question period gives the audience a

Speakers can learn about audience concerns and clear up confusion or misunderstanding if they listen carefully and thoughtfully during the question-and-answer period.

chance to clarify their confusion, seek further information, and share ideas of their own. Not all speaking situations can accommodate time for questions (perhaps not even your public speaking classroom can do so), but whenever they can, they should.

Look for Ways to Involve Listeners Actively.

Learning experts agree that people learn far more when they are actively involved in the learning process than when they remain passive.[15] Do all you can to engage your audience. Choose a topic that allows you to share relevant, important, or novel information that you hope the audience will find intrinsically interesting. Beyond that, you may pose provocative questions, test listeners with a short quiz, ask them to write down questions or objectives, or engage them in dialogue along the way.

With a longer presentation, such as a workshop, you may build in all sorts of activities, such as small discussion groups or exercises. You may present a concept, illustrate it with a brief video example, and then follow up with an audience discussion. You may provide breaks, which build in time for informal chitchat. Be creative in thinking of ways to get the audience involved. A student speaker recently gave an informative presentation on the barriers faced by disabled students at the university. As part of her presentation, she asked listeners to try to exit the room in a wheelchair, to climb a stairway with a leg brace, and to brush their teeth using only one arm.

In *Highlighting Getting Listeners Involved* that follows, HIV educator Mike Bryson describes his strategy for engaging the audience during his presentation. As you can see, Bryson's audience has a chance to get involved and to set the agenda for the speech.

Assess Learning, if Possible.

Sometimes, when you are giving an informative presentation in a professional setting, you can take the time to check and see whether the audience is picking up on what you are "teaching" them. You may want to stop occasionally to ask them questions, as your college professors often do. You may give them an example and ask them if it is good or bad. If you do this kind of checking along the way, you can adjust your remarks as you go. If there is confusion, you may want to repeat, offer

---

Highlighting Getting Listeners Involved

From an Interview with Mike Bryson, HIV Educator

Whenever I make a presentation, I like to interact a lot with the audience. I tell them from the beginning that I hope they will ask me questions—and I stop a lot and ask them what questions they have on their minds. Since I am talking about HIV-related issues, sometimes people are uncomfortable. They may find it hard to ask questions—to be singled out in any way. But I am patient and I keep on encouraging them to ask. I want them to set the agenda for my presentation because I have no way of knowing what their concerns are unless they tell me. I want to talk about what they want to hear. If they help me by guiding me, I can do that. I tell them this and eventually most audiences come through. When they do, then we really start to communicate.

new examples, or encourage listeners to ask questions so that you can better understand why they are confused.

Not every informative occasion presents assessment opportunities. You may have only 10 minutes to talk. Or the speaking situation may be such that checking on audience comprehension and retention would be considered rude or inappropriate (if, for instance, you were a young employee called on to brief the top management team). When the situation permits, however, take every chance to touch base with your listeners as the process unfolds.

Ethical Considerations

Of primary importance is the point we made earlier in the chapter: it is inherently unethical to camouflage a persuasive purpose by portraying it as informative.

When you give an informative speech, be certain of the accuracy of the information you present. Invite the audience to investigate on their own, encourage them to listen to you critically and constructively, and give them sufficient time to raise questions and clear up misunderstandings. When they do ask questions, respond honestly, indicating when you are uncertain or when you need to do further research.

To reinforce the value of ethical communication, you might want to think of yourself as a teacher. Ask yourself, "What have I learned from good teachers?" You know that good teachers have your best interests at heart. They go to great pains to make sure that you understand. They strive to be clear as they make abstract concepts concrete through excellent examples. They watch for your confusion and respond to it. They ask you questions to make sure you are following. They encourage you to apply what you are learning, and they give you plenty of chances to ask them questions. Striving for this degree of integrity lies at the heart of effective and ethical informative speaking.

Summary

- Informative speeches are commonly made in diverse professional, classroom, and community settings. The informative speaker aims to help listeners gain understanding.
  - Some speakers do this by sharing ideas and information, others through shaping listeners' perceptions, and still others by articulating alternatives.
  - Informative speeches may describe, demonstrate, explain, or report on some process, problem, or phenomenon of interest.
  - Informative speeches should *not* be given when the speaker's aim is really persuasive, as is the case with most issues of public controversy.
- Various organizational strategies are available for arranging informative speeches. Among the organizational patterns commonly used for informative speaking are:
  - chronological/sequential
  - spatial

- categorical
- causal

- Like other speeches, informative speeches can be approached in a variety of ways, depending on the speaker's specific purpose.
- Every informative speaker must concern himself or herself with listener learning.
  - Unfortunately, not all listeners are intrinsically motivated to learn.
  - If listeners are resentful, bored, or simply not convinced that they need to know what is being discussed, they can present real challenges for the speaker.
- Most listeners' attitudes can change, and many will improve if the speaker is able to show how ideas and information are relevant, useful, novel, and important, and if he or she uses presentational, stylistic, and content variety while delivering the speech.
- The informative speaker should think about the learning process and strive to help listeners acquire information. Learning is more likely to take place if the speaker:
  - limits the number of details
  - uses restatement and repetition
  - takes time to respond to questions
  - actively engages the audience
  - assesses how much listeners have learned
- Finally, the ethical informative speaker will speak with accuracy and honesty. He or she will:
  - avoid giving a persuasive speech under the guise of an informative one
  - use reliable, accurate sources
  - openly acknowledge any existing bias
  - present alternatives in a fair-minded manner
  - encourage listeners to ask questions if they have doubts or confusion
- Informative speakers may want to use excellent teachers they have known as role models.

QUESTIONS FOR REVIEW AND REFLECTION

1. What is the overarching purpose of an informative speech? What are the three functions of informative speeches discussed in this chapter? Describe special issues and challenges associated with each.
2. What are some topics that might be appropriate for a speech of description? How important are visual aids to this kind of speech?
3. What are some of the key points you will probably want to address in giving a speech of explanation?
4. Think of one context in which a student might be called on to give an informative oral report. What would be the keys to effectiveness in this situation?

5. In what ways are the patterns discussed in this chapter (chronological/sequential, spatial, categorical, and causal) particularly well suited to informative speaking?

6. Describe the role of listener motivation in the context of informative speaking.

7. What are some ways that speakers can make their ideas and information interesting to listeners? Which are the most important and why? Can you think of other ways of capturing the audience's attention?

8. The informative speaker's challenge is to help listeners learn. Think of your most effective teachers. What do they do to facilitate your learning in the classroom? How can you apply what they do to your own informative presentations?

9. When you listen to someone make an informative presentation, how do you determine whether he or she is communicating ethically? How will you ensure that *you* communicate ethically?

ENDNOTES

1. Paul Korzeniowski, "Fingerprinting Plays a Key Role in Biometrics Boom," *TechNewsWorld*, January, 18, 2005, www.technewsworld.com. (Accessed April 25, 2006).

2. See, for example, William E. Wilson, *The Angel and the Serpent: The Story of New Harmony Indiana* (Bloomington: Indiana University Press, 1984).

3. See, for example, Simon Brown, *Practical Feng Shui* (London: Ward Lock, 1997).

4. Lois Burke et al., *A Cornucopia of Strategies for Working with LD and ADD Students* (Columbus: Ohio State University Office for Disability Services, 1999).

5. Laura J. Gurak, *Oral Presentations for Technical Communication* (Boston: Allyn and Bacon, 2000).

6. For information about supported employment, visit the Web site of the Association for Persons in Supported Employment (APSE) at www.aspe.org. They define supported employment as follows: "Supported employment enables people with disabilities who have not been successfully employed to work and contribute to society."

7. H. RaoUnnaba, Robert E. Burnkrant, and Sunil Erevelles, "Effects of Presentation Order and Communication Modality on Recall and Attitude," *Journal of Consumer Research* 21 (1994): 481–95.

8. Information about the mission of Middle Way House is available at www.bloomington .in.us/~mwhouse/aboutus.htm (Accessed May 17, 2006).

9. For more information about Shalom's mission, values, and programs, visit the Shalom website at www.shalomcommunitycenter.org (Accessed March 9, 2007).

10. See, for example, Yan Wang and Robert Rodgers, "Impact of Service-Learning and Social Justice Education on College Students' Cognitive Development," *NASPA Journal* 43, no. 2 (2006): article 7; and various articles in the *Michigan Journal of Community Service-Learning*, www.umich.edu/~mjcsl/.

11. For a discussion of retention, see Robert L. Greene, *Human Memory: Paradigms and Paradoxes* (Hillsdale, NJ: Erlbaum, 1992).

12. Abraham Maslow, *Motivation and Personality* (New York: Harper and Row, 1954).

13. See Jane Blankenship, *A Sense of Style: An Introduction to Style for the Public Speaker* (Belmont, CA: Dickenson Publishing, 1968); Pamela J. Cooper, *Communication for the Classroom Teacher*, 5th ed. (Scottsdale, AZ: Gorsuch Scarisbrick, 1995); and James C.

McCroskey, *An Introduction to Rhetorical Communication*, 7th ed. (Boston: Allyn and Bacon, 1997).

14. See, for example, Joan Middendorf and Alan Kalish, "The 'Change-up' Lectures," *National Teaching and Learning Forum* 5 (1996): 1–4.

15. See William J. McKeachie, *Teaching Tips: Strategies, Research, and Theory for College and University Teachers* (Boston: Houghton Mifflin, 1999), 209–15; and Martha Petrone, "Teaching and Learning as a Transactional Process," in *Teaching and Learning in College: A Resource for Educators*, 4th ed., ed. Gary S. Wheeler, 143–76 (Elyria, OH: Info-Tec, 2002).

CHAPTER 15

Persuasive Speaking in a Democratic Society

CHAPTER OBJECTIVES

*After reading this chapter, you
should be able to*

1. Define *public controversy*.

2. Discuss what it means to
   deliberate "in good faith."

3. Distinguish among the
   different types of persuasive
   issues.

4. Define *ethos* and discuss what
   contributes to strong
   credibility.

5. Discuss the techniques and
   ethics of appealing to an
   audience's emotions.

A student urges his fellow students to boycott a speech by a controversial public figure. A public health nurse urges the distribution of condoms in the local high schools. A lawyer argues against imposing limits on the amount of money juries can award in medical malpractice cases. The president of the United States goes before a national television audience to urge public support for the war in Iraq.

Every day all sorts of people—from ordinary citizens to world leaders—try to persuade other people. That is, they seek to influence the beliefs, values, or actions of others or "make the case" for a new policy or program. Sometimes we seek to persuade others about trivial or purely personal matters. We might persuade a friend to go to a movie, for example, or to eat more vegetables. In a democracy, however, persuasion takes on greater significance. Persuasion is the chief mechanism through which we select our leaders, determine our civic priorities, resolve controversies and disputes, and choose among various policies. Indeed, the reliance on persuasion rather than coercion or force is what distinguishes a democracy from a dictatorship.

Perhaps you have studied persuasion before in another public speaking class. You may even have studied persuasion in psychology, sociology, or public relations and advertising. In all of these fields, persuasion is important, because to understand persuasion is to understand human behavior. In this chapter, however, we are concerned with the role of persuasion in our democratic society. We will consider, first, how public controversies invite persuasion and the sorts of issues we debate as citizens in a democracy. Then we will reflect on some of the means of persuasion and the ethical constraints on persuasive speaking in a democracy.

The Anatomy of Public Controversy

Preview. *Persuasion is rooted in controversy. We deal with personal controversies every day, yet not all controversies involve matters of public importance. When you speak about a public controversy, you have an obligation to do more than simply express your opinion. As a citizen, you have an obligation to back up your opinions with arguments and evidence and to "test" those opinions in the give-and-take of public debate.*

Prayer in the schools. The future of Social Security. The Patriot Act. Illegal immigration. Affirmative action. Medical malpractice. Gay marriage. All of these issues spark controversy because people have strong yet conflicting opinions. They are *public* controversies because they affect large numbers of people—and because they require that we make decisions about new laws, how to spend our tax dollars, or what programs and policies to adopt. Not every difference of opinion leads to a public controversy, of course. You may have disagreed with your parents over which college you should attend, or perhaps you have debated with your friends over where to go on spring break. These issues may be important to you personally, but they are not *public* controversies. Public controversies involve the choices we must make as *citizens*; they affect the whole community, perhaps even the nation or the world.

Some public controversies literally involve matters of life and death. When we debate whether the government should restrict stem cell research, for example, our decision could affect tens of thousands who potentially might benefit from such research. So, too, do people's lives hang in the balance when we debate whether to send more troops to Iraq or to intervene to stop the genocide in Darfur, Sudan. Obviously, not all public controversies have such grave implications. Sometimes we may address little known controversies or try to call attention to problems that we believe have been ignored or neglected. We have only recently begun to hear speakers warn of the environmental hazards posed by "e-waste,"[1] for example, and we're now hearing predictions of an "acute shortage" of nurses in America.[2] Every day new controversies arise over our nation's economic, social, and political problems and policies. As a citizen in a democracy, we need to participate in public discussions of these important issues. Indeed, that's what it *means* to be a citizen in democracy: participating in the processes of governing ourselves.

Let us begin by reflecting on one recent controversy and what that controversy can teach us about the anatomy—that is, the shape, structure, and parts—of a public controversy. During George W. Bush's second term as president, news reports revealed that he had issued a secret Executive Order authorizing the National Security Agency (NSA) to monitor the phone calls and other electronic communications of suspected terrorists. According to the administration, the monitoring targeted only people with links to al-Qaeda, and the president claimed that he had the legal authority to keep potential terrorists under surveillance. Moreover, the White House claimed that Congress had implicitly endorsed such efforts when it authorized the president to use "all necessary and appropriate force" in response to the 9/11 attacks. According to the administration's critics, on the other hand, the NSA's "domestic spying" was not only illegal but posed a threat to the civil liberties of all Americans. By eavesdropping on domestic phone calls without warrants, the critics argued, the administration not only violated the law but exceeded the executive powers of the presidency.[3]

Like most complex public controversies, the debate over the NSA's "domestic spying" raised a number of factual questions: How many people's phone calls were wiretapped? How did the intelligence agencies choose the targets of their surveillance, and what sorts of information did they collect? And how, if at all, was this information used in the war against terrorism? Was the White House justified in claiming that such programs helped to prevent more terrorist attacks after 9/11? Beyond these questions, the debate over domestic spying raised larger, more difficult questions about the powers of the presidency and the proper balance between civil liberties and national security. Did the president have the legal authority to "spy" on citizens within the United States? In time of war, must we inevitably sacrifice some of our civil liberties to protect our national security? If so, who should have the power to decide when national security must take precedence over our personal freedoms or our constitutional protections? These are just a few of the larger questions raised by the debate over domestic spying.

In today's political climate, some people inevitably try to exploit such controversies for personal or political gain. On talk radio and TV "debate" shows, politicians and representatives of various special interests have put their own spin on the domestic spying story, eager to score points. For most Americans, however, the whole debate over domestic spying was not about who might gain the political advantage. Rather, it was about finding the right balance between two equally worthy goals—protecting our national security and preserving our civil liberties. Unfortunately, answers to the legal and political questions raised by the controversy were neither simple nor obvious. Like most complex public controversies, the debate over domestic spying produced no clear "winner." Americans will continue to debate whether the Bush administration acted properly in authorizing such intelligence programs and how best to preserve the proper balance between civil liberties and national security.

As citizens in a democracy, we have a right to our opinions on controversial issues. If we express those opinions in public, however, we assume a greater responsibility—the responsibility to back up our opinions with *arguments*. By speaking out in public, we also invite those who disagree to speak out as well. As citizens in a democracy, we have an ethical obligation to treat with civility and respect those who accept the invitation to debate. The success of our democracy depends on our willingness to subject our ideas to the scrutiny of public debate—and to be tolerant and respectful toward those who disagree with our opinions.

Deliberating in Good Faith

Perhaps you have heard the phrase *deliberating in good faith*. What does that mean? What does deliberating in good faith mean in terms of your responsibilities as a speaker? First, it means telling the truth, at least as you see it. Your beliefs and opinions may not always turn out to be right. Yet speakers who *deliberately* misrepresent the facts, or speakers who publicly advocate ideas that they do not *sincerely* believe, are not merely mistaken; they are irresponsible and unethical. They deserve to be condemned by all who value free and open debate.

Second, deliberating in good faith means backing up your personal opinions. In public debate, you not only have an obligation to be honest but also to *prove* your claims. Proving one's claim does *not* mean presenting conclusive or irrefutable evidence; it does *not* mean settling an issue once and for all. It *does* mean presenting a *reasonable* argument—one at least worthy of serious consideration and further debate.

Third, deliberating in good faith means accepting your burden of proof, or your responsibility to meet a certain standard of proof in a particular context. Perhaps you have heard the phrase "burden of proof" in a legal case. In a courtroom, the burden of proof refers to the level of proof necessary for the prosecution to prevail. Depending on the type of case, that burden of proof may range from a "preponderance of the evidence" to the much higher standard employed in criminal cases: "beyond a reasonable doubt." In public debate, the burden of proof is not so clearly defined, yet we do expect some advocates to meet a higher standard of proof than others. As in the courtroom, those who accuse others of wrongdoing carry a heavier burden of proof than those who speak in self-defense. Likewise, those who advocate new policies carry a heavier burden of proof than those who defend the status quo. In public debate, of course, there will be no judge to instruct you on your burden of proof or to enforce the rules of debate. Nevertheless, it is important that you understand the expectations and standards of proof in public debate.

We will return to the practical implications of meeting your burden of proof in Chapter 16. For now, it is enough to understand that public deliberations, like

The "rules" of democratic deliberation often break down on TV talk shows designed to make headlines and attract ratings. Here, panelists on "The McLaughlin Group" engage in a combative debate, apparently more intent on scoring political points than finding common ground.

courtroom debates, are governed by *rules*, and that you have an obligation to live up to those rules—however irresponsible or unrestrained other speakers might seem. No doubt you have seen speakers on television or at political rallies attack their political opponents, cite dubious evidence, or stir up ugly emotions. That does not mean that you should resort to the same tactics. To the contrary, the fact that other speakers may be irresponsible is all the more reason for you to uphold higher standards. By following the rules yourself, you can set a good example for other speakers and contribute to a more constructive tone in our public discussions.

Questions of Fact, Value, and Policy

Preview. *Persuasive issues revolve around questions of fact (what is true), value (what is good or bad), and policy (what should be done in the future). As you prepare to speak about a particular topic, you need to identify the types of issues surrounding that topic and focus your efforts on unresolved controversies.*

Is That the Truth?

Normally we use the word *fact* to describe something that is already established as true. We think of a fact as something that we can just look up in a reference book, or that we can establish by utilizing the appropriate measurement device. Thus, we might say that it is a fact that Peru is in Latin America, or that the thermometer shows that it is currently 80 degrees. These are not the sorts of facts that are disputed or debated. In ordinary usage, a "fact" is something that we all agree is true.

On many occasions, however, we disagree over the facts relating to a particular subject, and we discuss and debate what may or may not be "true." Does the Loch Ness Monster really exist? How many people are currently unemployed in this country? Do artificial sweeteners cause cancer or other health problems? What might account for the rash of hurricanes in recent years? These are the sorts of issues where the "facts" themselves are in dispute. Many public controversies, ranging from the debate over Social Security to the debate over the causes of global warming, rest largely on unresolved questions of fact.

Issues of fact typically involve questions of existence, scope, or causality. We would address a question of *existence* if, for example, we tried to persuade our audience that the ivory-billed woodpecker, a bird once thought extinct, still survives in remote forests of the American Southeast. Issues of *scope* might emerge in debates over the extent of the AIDS or the bird flu epidemics, while debates over *causality* can be heard when the topic is the prevalence of cancer or child obesity in America. In addition to involving different sorts of questions, some factual controversies may revolve around questions about the past (How many people have died from breast cancer in the past decade?), while others might involve predictions about the future. During recent debates over Social Security, for example, advocates of privatization predicted that giving retirees more control over their own investments would lead to higher returns for beneficiaries.

Whatever the specific focus, issues of fact invite empirical proof: real examples, statistics, and testimony from experts. In addition, we typically try to resolve questions of fact *before* we debate questions of value or policy. If, for example, we cannot agree about the existence or causes of global warming, it makes little sense to discuss possible solutions. Similarly, before we debate how best to control illegal immigration, we should first answer some factual questions: How many immigrants enter America illegally each year? Where and how do they enter the country? And what motivates them to enter our country illegally? Again, an analogy to courtroom debates might help clarify how controversies evolve. In a criminal trial, lawyers must first establish the "facts of the case." Only then do they debate which laws may have been violated. And only after the court has decided which laws have been broken do the lawyers debate the appropriate sentence. In public controversies, the rules are less clearly defined but the process is essentially the same: only after we have resolved major factual controversies does it make sense to debate how to *evaluate* those facts or how to *act* in response.

Is This Good or Bad?

Issues of value focus on what we consider good or bad, right or wrong, just or unjust, and moral or immoral. Questions of value focus not just on what we believe to be true but what we consider appropriate, legal, ethical, or moral. Advocates of animal rights try to persuade us that medical experiments on animals are morally wrong, for example, while their opponents deem them necessary to save human lives. Opponents of affirmative action contend that racial preferences violate our commitment to equal treatment under the law, while those who favor such preferences deem them necessary to "level the playing field." In both of these debates, it is not so much the facts that are in dispute as the differing *values* applied to those facts by the advocates involved. That is what debates over questions of value are all about: determining how we should *evaluate* specific facts, ideas, or actions.

In the courtroom, the law itself provides the general principles we use to evaluate facts. Yet it is not always clear which laws ought to apply in a particular case, and the meaning of the law itself is sometimes disputed. Once they have determined the facts of the case, for example, lawyers in a murder trial still might debate whether the facts warrant a verdict of first-degree murder or "justifiable homicide." Outside the courtroom, the general principles or criteria that we use to evaluate ideas and actions are even more diverse and unsettled—and hence more "debatable." During the civil rights debates of the 1960s, for example, some people condemned civil rights protestors for deliberately breaking local laws that segregated the races in the South, while the activists themselves invoked "higher laws"—the Constitution's guarantee of equal rights under the law, for example, or even "God's law" that all people are created equal.

How do we choose and define the general principles that we employ in value-level argument? In some cases, we might find such principles written down, in a law book or in a professional code of ethics. In other cases, we might rely on reputable authorities to suggest the appropriate principles or criteria of judgment. If we wish to judge the constitutionality of a particular action, for example, we might consult with experts in constitutional law. If we wish to render a moral judgment, we should consult whoever our audience might consider a credible moral authority—a religious leader, perhaps, or maybe a well-known philosopher or ethicist. In many cases, the best source of the standards or criteria we employ in value-level arguments will be the audience itself, for such arguments work best when they are grounded in our listeners' own value system. Only after we have convinced our audience that a problem exists or that some wrong has been done does it make sense to move on to the highest level of argument: debate over issues of policy.

What Are We Going to Do?

Issues of policy have to do with our actions in the future: there is something wrong in our world, and we need to correct it; we have a problem that needs to be solved. Yet even when we agree that we have a problem, we still may not agree about how best to solve it. In our complex society, we inevitably have a variety of options for addressing various problems. And in considering each option, we must weigh not only its effectiveness in solving the problem, but also its costs, its feasibility, and any advantages or disadvantages that it might have.

We may all agree that health care for the poor and the elderly in the United States is a serious problem. Yet still we debate how best to respond to that challenge, with some arguing for universal health-care coverage and others emphasizing "market solutions." Likewise, everybody seems to agree that our current income-tax system should be reformed. Still, we continue to debate a wide variety of policy alternatives, ranging from minor changes in the existing tax code to a "flat tax," to a national sales tax that would eliminate income taxes altogether.

Even when we all agree on a particular approach to some problem, we may find ourselves debating the details of implementation, financing, or administration. We may agree that wealthy nations should do more to fight the spread of AIDS in developing nations. But exactly how much should the United States contribute to that effort? And where should our aid go? People worried about the effects of television on children likewise seem to agree that the government should do more to regulate children's programming. But what should those regulations say? How are they to be enforced? And how, if at all, do we balance the protection of children with the rights of those who produce and advertise on children's television?

Whatever issues you address in your speeches, it is important that those choices be grounded in thorough research and analysis of both your topic and your audience. Controversies evolve, and what were once hotly contested issues may no longer be seriously debated. At one time, for example, there was a vigorous debate over the health hazards posed by cigarette smoking—a question of fact. That debate has largely been settled now, of course, and the debate over smoking now revolves around questions of policy: Should smoking be banned in public places? Should tobacco companies be held liable for the health costs of smoking? In some persuasive speeches, your sole purpose may be to establish a disputed fact, while in other speeches your audience may already agree that there is a serious problem. In that case you can focus on policy issues. Whatever your purpose, it should reflect *the current status of the public controversy surrounding your topic* and the *existing beliefs and opinions of your audience.*

It is important that you make your persuasive purpose clear when you speak. Given the nature of the issue and the existing attitudes of your audience, do you hope merely to stimulate their thinking—perhaps to put your issue on the agenda of a previously apathetic or indifferent audience? Or do you aspire to change minds, convincing listeners to reconsider their opinions? Do you hope to inspire your audience to *act* in some way, perhaps by sending money to some organization or

---

Highlighting the Challenge of Persuading Others

Will You Give Blood?

In a study of people's willingness to donate blood, a group of people reluctant to donate were asked to listen to a powerfully emotional speech, delivered by a young hemophiliac. Immediately following the speech, a questionnaire revealed an impressive reversal in attitudes. More than 70 percent of those who previously had refused to give blood now indicated that they *would* donate blood if given the opportunity! Yet when presented with official Red Cross blood donation sign-up cards, nearly 80 percent of those with "changed" attitudes *still* declined to commit themselves to the *action* of donating blood. The authors concluded from this study that while it may be difficult to change minds, inspiring people to *act* is an even greater challenge.

Source: Patricia Hayes Andrews and John E. Baird Jr., *Communication for Business and the Professions*, 6th ed. (Madison, WI: Brown & Benchmark, 1995), 359–60.

volunteering their time? As you might imagine, getting people to *do* something is harder than getting them merely to *think* about it.

Ethical Proof in Persuasive Speaking

Preview. *Since ancient times, theorists of persuasion have recognized three broad categories or "modes" of proof: ethos, pathos, and logos. We begin our examination of the modes of proof with ethos, or ethical proof, which refers to the audience's perception of the credibility of the speaker and his or her sources. The constituents of strong ethos are trustworthiness, competence, open-mindedness, and dynamism. Your ethos as a speaker is shaped by the content, structure, and clarity of your speech, how you deliver it, and the ways in which you relate to your audience.*

Have you ever responded negatively to a speech, only to realize later that it was not the content of the speech that bothered you so much as the person delivering it? Perhaps the speaker's voice irritated you. Or maybe the speaker belonged to a group or political organization that you have always distrusted. On the other hand, you also may have followed someone's advice not so much because he or she gave you good reasons, but because that person seemed knowledgeable and trustworthy. For good or ill, we all react to messages on the basis not only of what is said but of who says it. The perception we have of a speaker—whether that perception is positive or negative—constitutes that person's ethos.

Students of public speaking have long recognized the importance of ethos. More than 2,000 years ago, the Greek rhetorician and philosopher Aristotle identified the speaker's character, intelligence, and good will as the most important dimensions of ethos.[4] Later theorists have refined and modified Aristotle's original concept. Modern researchers have stressed that ethos depends on what an audience *thinks* about the speaker, and they have noted that people sometimes have very different *perceptions* of the same speaker. In other words, ethos refers to *how the audience sees a speaker*, not to the *actual* intelligence or character of that person.

Ethos is not the same thing as *ethics*, but the two concepts are closely related. A person who is perceived as ethical has a good reputation—a positive ethos—even before he or she speaks. If, on the other hand, a speaker is perceived as unethical, we may find his or her arguments less convincing. Whatever the speaker's true ethical commitments, what is important, again, is our *perception* of the speaker.

Scholars have identified a number of specific qualities that influence our perceptions of a speaker.[5] From their research, we can identify four major qualities that contribute to a positive ethos:

- trustworthiness
- competence
- open-mindedness
- dynamism

Trustworthiness

Not surprisingly, we are more likely to listen to and act on the advice of people who we think are honest and concerned about our best interests. Integrity and sincerity are qualities that inspire trust. Suppose, for example, you were trying to decide what to do after you graduate from college. An older friend whom you trust—a teacher, a counselor, or a family friend—suggests that you join Teach for America, a program in which college graduates spend two years teaching in public schools in economically depressed areas. You are more likely to take this advice if you believe this person is not only knowledgeable about the program but also has your best interests at heart.

Public figures often rely on perceptions of their trustworthiness when trying to persuade listeners. In 1986, for example, President Ronald Reagan, who enjoyed high public approval ratings, tried to capitalize on that trust during the biggest scandal of his career. Accused of secretly trading weapons for American hostages held in Iran, Reagan never denied the charges. Instead, he asked the American people to trust that his intentions were good and that, overall, his record of achievement outweighed any mistake he might have made. In his 1987 State of the Union address, Reagan adopted a personal tone as he explained his role in the arms-for-hostages scandal. In the passage that follows, he admitted that he had made a mistake, but he asked the American people to trust that he had *tried* to do the right thing:

> But though we've made much progress, I have one major regret. I took a risk with regard to our action in Iran. It did not work, and for that I assume full responsibility. The goals were worthy. I do not believe it was wrong to try to establish contacts with a country of strategic importance or try to save lives. And certainly it was not wrong to try to secure freedom for our citizens held in barbaric captivity. But we did not achieve what we wished and serious mistakes were made trying to do so. We will get to the bottom of this and I will take whatever action is called for.[6]

Because of his strong personal ethos, Reagan convinced many Americans that his *intentions* had been good.

Competence

Listeners tend to be persuaded more easily by speakers they view as intelligent, well-informed, or personally competent. Whether it comes from native intelligence, education and training, or firsthand experience, the perceived competence of the speaker is a crucial part of his or her ethos. Consider, for example, how Janice Payan, a vice president of U.S. West Communications, established her ethos in her keynote address to a conference of Hispanic-American women in Denver. Payan's message was simple: if women believe in themselves and work hard, they can overcome any discrimination that they might face and achieve their goals. Payan, of course, was a high-ranking executive at a major company, which proved she had certain business abilities. But if her message was to be believed, she also had to convince her audience that she understood the cultural obstacles many of them faced. She did that by talking about her own life and the obstacles she herself had overcome:

> I am more like you and you are more like me than you would guess. I'm a third-generation Mexican-American . . . born into a lower middle-class family right here in Denver. My parents married young; she was pregnant. My father worked only about half the time during my growing-up years. He was short on education, skills, and confidence. There were drug and alcohol problems in the family. . . .

For all my suffering in high school, I finished near the top of my graduating class. I dreamed of attending the University of Colorado at Boulder. You want to know what my counselor said? You already know. That I should go to a business college for secretaries, at most. But I went to the University of Colorado anyway. I arranged my own financial aid: a small grant, a low-paying job, and a *big* loan. I just thank God that was an era when jeans and sweatshirts were getting popular. That was all I had!

. . . During my freshman year, I received a call that my mother had been seriously injured in a traffic accident. Both of her legs were broken. So was her pelvis. My younger brother and sister were still at home. My father was unemployed at the time, and I was off at college. . . . So I drove home from Boulder every weekend; shopped, cleaned, cooked, froze meals for the next week, did the laundry, you know the list. And the truth is, it did not occur to me until some time later that my father could have done some of that. I had a problem, but I was part of the problem. I *did* resist when my parents suggested I should quit school. It seemed better to try doing everything than to give up my dream. And it was the better choice. But it was also very difficult.[7]

By talking about her personal experiences, Janice Payan convinced her audience that she was competent to speak about the challenges they faced.

Open-Mindedness

A speaker's ethos is also influenced by the impressions listeners have of his or her open-mindedness. Nobody is perfectly objective. But audiences value speakers who seem willing to enter into a dialogue with them, consider various points of view, and search for common ground. Of course, open-mindedness is not the same thing as empty-headedness; a speaker has the right to take sides in a controversy. Yet that does not mean you should distort, exaggerate, or otherwise misrepresent the facts in order to "win" the debate. Nor does it give you the right to dismiss the arguments, feelings, or values of those who disagree with you. To say that you are open-minded is not to say that you are wishy-washy. Rather, it means that you are willing to listen to others, treat their ideas fairly, and remain open to changing your own mind.

In many situations, a speaker's objectivity may be in doubt because of his or her position or reputation or because of the setting in which the speech takes place. In 1976, for example, an African American congresswoman from Texas, Barbara Jordan, was invited to deliver the keynote address to the Democratic National Convention. Jordan had become famous for speaking out against President Richard Nixon during the Watergate scandal, and she was addressing fellow Democrats in a setting where partisanship was expected. Nevertheless, Jordan rose above partisanship and displayed her broader vision of America's promise, which helps to account for why the speech is still remembered today as one of the great keynote addresses in American history:

I could easily spend this time praising the accomplishments of this party and attacking the Republicans but I don't choose to do that.

I could list the many problems Americans have. I could list the problems which cause people to feel cynical, angry, frustrated; . . . I could recite these problems and then I could sit down and offer no solutions. But I don't choose to do that either.

The citizens of America expect more. They deserve and they want more than a recital of problems.

We are a people in a quandary about the present. We are a people in search of our future. We are a people in search of a national community.

We are a people trying to solve the problems of the present . . . but we are attempting on a larger scale to fulfill the promise of America. We are attempting to fulfill our national purpose; to create and sustain a society in which all of us are equal.[8]

Again, Jordan was hardly an objective observer. She believed in her party and what it could do for America. But by rising above partisanship and emphasizing our common dreams, she delivered a memorable speech and earned a positive ethos.

Barbara Jordan's keynote address at the 1976 Democratic Convention is remembered as one of the great keynote addresses in U.S. history because she rose above partisanship and emphasized the values and aspirations of all Americans, regardless of political party.

Dynamism

Finally, audiences look positively on those speakers who are energetic and enthusiastic—in other words, speakers who are dynamic. Dynamism does *not* mean ranting and raving; it means achieving the right balance of enthusiasm and self-control. It means setting the right tone for the occasion. On the one hand, we want to avoid appearing as if we're just "going through the motions," talking in a colorless monotone or focusing more on our notes than our listeners. On the other hand, we do not want to scream at our audience, engage in distracting physical gyrations, or appear so intense that our audience thinks we're crazy! A dynamic speaker takes the middle ground, enthusiastically engaging the audience but not getting "in their face." Dynamic speakers talk *with* us rather than *at* us, communicating their personal enthusiasm but remaining "tuned in" to our reactions.

Perhaps the best way to summarize ethos is to consider the constituents of ethos as a kind of filter: everything you say is filtered through the *perception* your audience has of your trustworthiness, competence, open-mindedness, and dynamism. What an audience thinks of a speaker—a speaker's ethos—may sometimes be determined by his or her past reputation. Still, every speech you give should be viewed as an opportunity to improve your ethos by demonstrating that *you* have the qualities we admire in a speaker.

Contextual Factors Influencing Ethos

Although ethos is always important, the characteristics that we admire in speakers may vary from situation to situation. If we attend a public briefing on a new sewage treatment plant, we might not care if the engineers explaining the system are dynamic or open-minded. We are more concerned with whether they can explain technical aspects of the plant clearly—whether they have the *competence* to answer our questions about how the plant would work. Conversely, we do not expect everybody at a town hall meeting to be an "expert" on every issue. Not everybody understands the tax laws or the best way to build a bridge. In that situation, we might be more concerned with the speaker's sincerity and open-mindedness, or we might be impressed by how passionately a speaker feels about some issue.

The context in which we speak thus determines what characteristics—or combination of characteristics—will affect our ethos. As speakers, we should reflect on which of the constituents of ethos might be most important to our audience in particular situations. As citizens, we should ask whether other speakers have *earned* the right to be trusted. Do they have the experience or knowledge necessary to speak convincingly about that issue?

In today's society, we are often tempted to judge the credibility of speakers by standards that have little to do with their background or training. Many advertisers, for example, pay celebrities to endorse their products. Perhaps it makes sense for a basketball player to endorse Nike shoes or a nutritional supplement. But should we believe Tiger Woods when he says he drives a Buick? Is stock car driver Mark Martin a good source of information about the prescription drug Viagra? Should we believe Jessica Simpson when she tells us that Proactiv cured her acne? Does anybody really believe that Paris Hilton eats at Hardee's? Perhaps these celebrities have, in fact, *tried* some of these products. But it would be naïve to think that their opinions do not have *something* to do with the millions of dollars they are paid for their endorsements.

Sometimes factors beyond our control influence our ethos. When Barbara Bush was invited to deliver a commencement address at Wellesley College in 1990, some students objected that she had done nothing to earn that honor—besides marrying the president of the United States! To her credit, Bush won over her audience at the women's college by establishing her *own* ethos during the course of the speech. Reflecting on the challenges of balancing life as a mother with her role as First Lady, Bush concluded on a humorous note: "And who knows? Somewhere out in this audience may even be someone who will one day follow in my footsteps, and preside over the While House as the President's spouse. And I wish *him* well!" Disarming her critics with humor, Mrs. Bush thus communicated that she shared their feminist values.

Depending on the context, the same individual might have both a highly negative and a highly positive personal ethos. A good case in point is Texas Tech and former Indiana University basketball coach Bob Knight. To many Americans, Knight is known for losing his temper, for screaming at players and officials, and—on one famous occasion—for throwing a chair across the basketball court. For others, however, Knight is an inspiration, an old-school teacher and disciplinarian, and a generous philanthropist who has helped raise millions of dollars for university libraries. In the eyes of these supporters, Knight has nothing to apologize for. To the contrary, he deserves praise for his blunt honesty, his loyalty to his players, and his unheralded philanthropy.

At this point in your life, you probably do not have to worry about how press coverage might affect your ethos. Each time you speak, however, people *will* form impressions of you, so it is important to keep the constituents of ethos in mind. Even in your speech class, your listeners will draw conclusions about your trustworthiness, competence, open-mindedness, and dynamism. It is never too early to begin building a positive ethos—a reputation that will help you succeed as a public speaker.

So what can you do to enhance your ethos? There is no simple answer, since everything you do affects how listeners perceive you: the content of your speech, how you organize and deliver it, and how you come across in general. But here are some specific things you can do to strengthen your ethos:

Show your Audience That You Share their Experiences and Concerns.

Showing your audience that you have something in common with them can strengthen your ethos. We feel a natural attraction to people we perceive to be like ourselves; we assume they face the same challenges and understand our values and priorities. In a speech advocating tougher penalties for academic cheating, for example, one student recalled the pressures he faced from his parents and others to get into a top college. At one point, he even admitted that he had been tempted to cheat in order to get better grades. The students listening to the speech not only appreciated the fact that he had chosen a topic relevant to their lives, but also that he shared their aspirations and understood the pressures they faced. He was honest enough to admit that he had been tempted to cheat, yet in the end he realized he would only be cheating himself.

Highlighting Credibility

Credibility is an essential quality in a candidate for public office. Following are excerpts from George W. Bush's speech accepting the Republican nomination for president in July 2000. Notice how Bush emphasized his trustworthiness by contrasting the fundamental American values he learned growing up in a small town with the "polish" of Washington. Also note how he established his competence by referring to his accomplishments as governor of Texas. Open-mindedness is suggested by his reference to how he got things done by reaching across party lines.

> In Midland, Texas, where I grew up . . . there was a restless energy, a basic conviction that, with hard work, anybody could succeed, and everybody deserved a chance. . . . This leaves me with more than an accent, it leaves an outlook. Optimistic, impatient with pretense. Confident that people can chart their own course. That background may lack the polish of Washington. Then again, I don't have a lot of things that come with Washington.
>
> The largest lesson I learned in Midland still guides me as Governor. Everyone . . . has an equal claim on this country's promise. So we improved our schools . . . moved people from welfare to work . . . budgets have been balanced . . . we cut taxes. . . . We accomplished a lot.
>
> I don't deserve all the credit, and I don't attempt to take it. I worked with Republicans and Democrats to get things done.

Source: George W. Bush, "Acceptance Speech," *New York Times*, Friday, August 4, 2000, A20.

Bolster your own Ethos with the Ethos of Reputable Experts.

Sometimes you will give speeches on highly complex or technical issues that require information from experts. Your own lack of expertise on such topics need not undermine your ethos. In these circumstances, support from acknowledged experts helps the audience to have confidence in what you say. In Chapter 8, we explored the use of expert testimony in greater detail, but it is worth repeating here that you can bolster your own ethos by using testimony from highly reputable sources.

Suppose, for example, that you wish to speak about the effects of global warming on weather patterns or our forest ecosystems. You may have read many newspaper articles on the subject, and perhaps you have seen several reports on TV about global warming. But does that make you an expert? Of course not. You are a concerned citizen, and perhaps you know more about the topic than the average citizen. Yet if you hope to be persuasive, you will still need testimony from reputable experts who have studied the problem, such as meteorologists, climatologists, and ecologists.

If you are genuinely open-minded, you might modify your own opinion as you read what the leading experts on your topic have to say. But once you have settled on a firm opinion, the challenge is to communicate not only your conclusions but also the impression that credible experts back up your opinion. Remember, a speech is not like a term paper, where you can just footnote your sources. Rather, you need to identify and establish the credibility of your expert sources *in the speech itself*. That means both naming your sources and saying something about their credentials. By offering support from a variety of highly qualified experts, you can improve your own ethos and make a more convincing argument.

Strengthen your Ethos with Personal Experiences.

You are more likely to be seen as trustworthy and competent when you have had some personal experiences related to your topic. A student aiming to help her audience understand the plight of Native Americans, for example, established her special qualifications to speak on this topic by recalling how she had spent three weeks on an Indian reservation, helping to repair homes and paint schools. Of course, you will not always have firsthand experience with the issues you speak about. But when you do, you can strengthen your ethos by talking about those experiences during your speech.

Strive To Be Clear and Interesting.

Listeners appreciate speakers who make their ideas understandable and who make an effort to keep the audience interested. Unfortunately, some speakers try to impress their audiences with "big words," or they fail to make the effort to organize their speeches in ways that make them easy to follow. Other speakers may come across as not genuinely interested in their topic. We have all sat through dull and uninteresting speeches—speeches that hardly provide any "news" at all. Typically, it is not the topic itself that is the problem, but the failure of the speaker to consider ways to make the speech relevant and interesting to his or her audience.

You should try to gain the audience's attention and interest from the very outset of the speech—in your introduction. Doing so will create a positive first impression and improve your ethos throughout the speech. You also can maintain interest throughout the speech by citing examples that are familiar and relevant to the audience and by speaking directly *to* your listeners rather than staring down at your notes or reading the speech from a manuscript. Sometimes little things make all the difference in whether your audience develops a positive view of your ethos. For example, some speakers hurt their ethos simply by talking too long. By showing respect for your audience's comfort and expectations, you can enhance your ethos as a speaker.

Show your Audience That You Have Considered Different Points of View.

If you can show that you have considered other people's opinions, you will demonstrate that you are both well informed and open-minded. For example, when the Indiana Department of Natural Resources proposed to allow a two-day hunt to thin the deer population in Brown County State Park, both experts and ordinary citizens disagreed passionately over the idea. A student who wished to argue in favor of the hunt began by showing that she initially shared some of the emotions felt by its opponents. She then explained how she changed her mind after carefully researching the topic and discovering all the problems caused by overpopulation, including disease and starvation in the deer herd. Recalling her interviews with both activists opposed to the hunt and DNR officials who favored it, she showed that she was open-minded and had considered both sides of the controversy.

Develop a Dynamic, Audience-centered Delivery.

How you deliver your speech can dramatically affect your ethos. One student with a very well-prepared speech about crime and personal safety on campus failed to persuade her audience simply because listeners had trouble hearing her. Sitting in the back of the room and straining to hear what she said, some listeners became irritated and concluded that the speaker did not care about her topic or her audience. Likewise, speakers who use lots of vocalized pauses—"um," "you

Jesse Jackson's dynamic delivery contributes to his *ethos* as a sincere, committed, and passionate advocate for the poor and dispossessed. Jackson is shown here eulogizing the late singer Lou Rawls during a funeral service in Los Angeles in 2006.

know," and "like," for example—often irritate listeners and come across as inarticulate or even unintelligent. Finally, speakers who read rapidly through written manuscripts, without looking up or otherwise engaging listeners, may hurt their own ethos.

Dynamic speakers remain continuously in touch with their audiences. Speakers who seem bored or detached themselves cannot expect their audiences to respond any differently, and they may even be perceived as less knowledgeable, competent, or sincere. As we suggested in Chapter 12, there are many things you can do to improve your presentational skills. Vocal variation, gestures, facial expressions, and eye contract can all have a significant effect on your ethos. Delivery may not be the only thing affecting your ethos, but it *can* make a difference.

Your audience's perceptions of your intelligence, character, and sincerity can affect the success of your speech. You can bolster your ethos by establishing common ground with your audience, by showing that you share common concerns, by citing reputable experts, and by mentioning personal experiences that qualify you to speak on your topic. Making an effort to be clear and interesting also can help your ethos, as can showing your audience that you have considered other points of view. Finally,

Focus on Civic Engagement

Former Presidents Bury the Political Hatchet

Former presidents George H. W. Bush and Bill Clinton were bitter political rivals. During the 1992 presidential campaign, Bush attacked the challenger Clinton as a "tax-and-spend liberal" and, in an especially enthusiastic moment, even called him a "bozo." For his part, Clinton portrayed Bush as an agent of "privileged private interests" who had betrayed his promise of a "kindler, gentler" America. In his speech accepting the Democratic nomination in 1992, Clinton accused Bush of talking a "good game" but having "no game plan to rebuild America."[9]

Imagine people's surprise, then, when the two former presidents joined hands to lead the U.S. relief effort following the devastating tsunami in the Indian Ocean in 2004. Traveling to the region and raising millions of dollars to help rebuild homes and lives ravaged by the disaster, they exploited their ethos as former presidents and political rivals to make an important point: that even in an era of deep partisan divisions, people can work together for the common good. Following Hurricane Katrina, the two again joined forces

to raise more than $120 million for rebuilding colleges and churches devastated by the storm. Since they joined forces, the pair have raised more than $1 billion for disaster relief. The "Odd Couple," as Barbara Bush has characterized them, not only did a lot of good but became close personal friends. Perhaps most important, they took advantage of their return to the public spotlight—and their unique ethos as former presidential rivals—to call for more civility and cooperation in American politics. "Politics doesn't have to be uncivil and nasty," Clinton said when asked about his relationship with Bush. "Where we can find common ground and do something for the future of the country and for the future of our children and grandchildren, I think we ought to do it."

Sources: Michael Duffy, "Bill Clinton and George H.W. Bush," *Time*, April 30, 2006, www.time.com/time/magazine/printout/ 0,8816,1187350,00.html (accessed June 23, 2006); ABC News, "People of the Year: Bill Clinton and George H.W. Bush," *World News Tonight*, December 27, 2005, http://abcnews.go.com/ WNT/print?id=1446477 (accessed June 23, 2006).

you can enhance your ethos by delivering your speech effectively. By engaging your audience and delivering your speech with enthusiasm, you can show your listeners that you care about them and your topic.

Appealing to Audience Emotions

Preview. *For persuasion to take place, you need to engage your listeners' emotions. You can engage your audience's emotions by using strong, affective language, appealing to shared social values, providing specific, vivid details, helping listeners to visualize what you are talking about, or comparing the unfamiliar to the familiar. Emotional appeals, however, can be deceptive and manipulative and should never replace reasoned arguments.*

Listeners who have little or no emotional involvement in a speech are unlikely to be persuaded. Appealing to an audience's emotions is fundamental to motivating them to act. You may even need to engage their emotions to get them to listen in the first place. If people are not emotionally involved in a topic, they just do not care, which means they are not likely to be persuaded.

Fear, pride, anger, reverence, hatred, compassion, and love—all are strong emotions and can be powerful motivators. Successful speakers know that listeners can be motivated by appeals to such emotions. Notice how, former president Ronald Reagan, the "Great Communicator," used emotional appeals to build support for dramatic increases in military spending. Instead of reviewing the "long list of numbers" in his proposed defense budget, Reagan tapped into some of his audience's most basic emotions: their fear of nuclear war, their sense of "duty" as citizens, and their concern for protecting their children and their "free way of life":

> The subject I want to discuss with you, peace and national security, is both timely and important. . . . This subject involves the

Former president Ronald Reagan, the "Great Communicator," used emotional appeals to build support for dramatic increases in military spending.

most basic duty that any president and any people share, the duty to protect and strengthen the peace.

At the beginning of this year, I submitted to the Congress a defense budget which reflects my best judgment of the best understanding of the experts and specialists who advise me about what we and our allies must do to protect our people in the years ahead. That budget is much more than a long list of numbers, for behind all the numbers lies America's ability to prevent the greatest of human tragedies and preserve our free way of life in a sometimes dangerous world.[10]

Appeals to your audience's emotions should never substitute for logical arguments backed by the best available evidence. Yet neither can we ignore the role of emotions in human behavior, especially if we hope to motivate our audience to act. A speech that fails to engage the audience's emotions is dull, boring, and lifeless—and, in the end, probably ineffective. There are techniques that you might use to engage your audience emotionally: using affective language, identifying shared values, using vivid detail, using visualization, and comparing the familiar with the unfamiliar.

Using Affective Language

Affective language is strong language that plays on emotions or feelings. Consider the emotional impact of this series of statements:

"I see things differently from Bob."
"I think Bob's statement is not quite accurate."
"What Bob is saying seems misleading."
"Bob is a liar."

To call Bob a "liar" is to use strong, affective language. As a persuader, you must choose your language carefully, taking into account both the ideas you hope to convey and the emotional connotations of the words you choose.

Eugene Debs, a four-time Socialist candidate for president of the United States, passionately opposed American involvement in World War I. Yet in the prowar climate of the time, Congress passed laws that limited the right to criticize the government's war policies. Along with other antiwar speakers, Debs was arrested, tried, and convicted under one of these laws, the Sedition Act of 1917. At his sentencing, however, Debs refused to tone down his rhetoric. Instead, he spoke out against social injustice in emotionally powerful language:

Your Honor, years ago I recognized my kinship with all living beings, and I made up my mind that I was not one bit better than the meanest on earth. I said then, and I say now, that while there is a lower class, I am in it, while there is a criminal element, I am of it, and while there is a soul in prison, I am not free. . . .

I am thinking this morning of the men in the mills and the factories; of the men in the mines and on the railroads. I am thinking of the women who for a paltry wage are compelled to work out their barren lives; of the little children who in this system are robbed of their childhood . . . and forced into the industrial dungeons, there to feed the monster machines while they themselves are being starved and stunted, body and soul. I see them dwarfed and diseased and their little lives broken and blasted because . . . money is still so much more important than the flesh and blood of childhood. . . .

Your Honor, I ask no mercy and I plead for no immunity. . . . I never so clearly comprehended as now the great struggle between the powers of greed and exploitation on one hand and upon the other the rising hosts of industrial freedom and social justice.

I can see the dawn of a better day for humanity. The people are awakening. In due time they will and must come to their own.[11]

By today's standards, Debs' language may seem excessive, with its references to children "robbed" of their childhood, "dwarfed and diseased," their "little lives broken and blasted." But nearly 70 years later, César Chavez used equally powerful language to describe the plight of migrant farm workers in America. In a speech before the Commonwealth Club of California on November 9, 1984, Chavez began by describing what motivated him to fight for the rights of migrant workers:

Today, thousands of farm workers live under savage conditions, beneath trees and amid garbage and human excrement near tomato fields in San Diego County. . . . Vicious rats gnaw at them as they sleep. They walk miles to buy food at inflated prices and they carry in water from irrigation ditches.

Child labor is still common in many farm areas. As much as 30 percent of Northern California's garlic harvesters are underaged children. . . . Some 800,000 underaged children work with their families harvesting crops across America. Babies born to migrant workers suffer 25 percent higher infant mortality rates than the rest of the population. Malnutrition among migrant workers' children is 10 times higher than the national rate. Farm workers' average life expectancy is still 49 years, compared to 73 years for the average American.

All my life, I have been driven by one dream, one goal, one vision: to overthrow a farm labor system in this nation that treats farm workers as if they were not important human beings. Farm workers are not agricultural implements; they are not beasts of burden to be used and discarded.[12]

Chavez, of course, had statistics to back up his argument, but it was his affective language—his references to "savage conditions," living amid "garbage and human excrement," sleeping among "vicious rats," and so on—that gave his speech its emotional power.

Identifying Shared Values

Listeners are more likely to be emotionally engaged when their own values are involved. You should aim to identify values that you and your audience hold in common and show how your ideas or proposals relate to those values.

When Geraldine Ferraro became the first woman nominated for vice president of the United States on a major party ticket, she used her acceptance speech to identify the values she shared in common with her running mate, Walter "Fritz"

Speaking as the first woman ever nominated for the vice presidency by a major political party, Geraldine Ferraro moved her audience emotionally by emphasizing their shared values: love of family, love of country, and faith in the American dream.

Mondale. According to Ferraro, those values were not merely shared by the two candidates, they defined the American dream for *all* Americans:

> We are going to win, because Americans across this country believe in the same basic dream.
>
> Last week, I visited Elmore, Minnesota, the small town where Fritz Mondale was raised. And soon Fritz and Joan will visit our family in Queens. Nine hundred people live in Elmore. In Queens, there are 2,000 people in one block. You would think we would be different, but we're not. Children walk to school in Elmore past grain elevators; in Queens, they pass by subway stops. But, no matter where they live, their future depends on education—and their parents are willing to do their part to make those schools as good as they can be. In Elmore, there are family farms; in Queens, small businesses. But the men and women who run them all take pride in supporting their families through hard work and initiative. On the Fourth of July in Elmore, they hang flags out on Main Street; in Queens, they fly them over Grand Avenue. But all of us love our country, and stand ready to defend the freedom that it represents.[13]

Using Vivid Detail

Using vivid detail can help your audience relate to your topic emotionally. Listeners respond more positively to concrete examples and stories than they do to abstractions. Charities that raise money to help sick children, for example, often choose a "poster child" who represents thousands of other children afflicted with disease. The "poster child" gives potential donors somebody they can relate to emotionally—a real person whose suffering they can help to allay.

Persuasive speakers engage audiences' feelings by reinforcing their ideas with vivid details. In 1996, Senator Robert Dole, the Republican candidate for president, urged leaders of the entertainment industry to reduce the violence and sexual content in popular films, television, and music. In one of his speeches, Dole provided a series of vivid examples to illustrate his concern:

> A line has been crossed—not just of taste, but of human dignity and decency. It is crossed every time sexual violence is given a catchy tune. When teen suicide is set to an appealing beat. When Hollywood's dream factories turn out nightmares of depravity.
>
> You know what I mean. I mean "Natural Born Killers." "True Romance." Films that revel in mindless violence and loveless sex. I'm talking about groups like Cannibal Corpse, Geto Boys, and 2 Live Crew. About a culture business that makes money from "music" extolling the pleasures of raping, torturing, and mutilating women, from "songs" about killing policemen and rejecting law. The mainstreaming of deviancy must come to an end, but it will only stop when the leaders of the entertainment industry recognize and shoulder their responsibility.[14]

The details in this passage are concrete and specific, calling up vivid images that shocked and troubled many of Dole's listeners, especially parents of young children.

Using Visualization

In an effort to make messages more concrete, speakers often employ *visualization*, or techniques that allow their audience to "see" what they are talking about. By helping your listeners to visualize some problem or crisis, you can stir their emotions, get them thinking more deeply about your topic, and clarify information that otherwise might be vague or unclear.

The most obvious way to help your audience visualize a problem is, of course, to show them a picture. Perhaps you have heard the old saying "Pictures don't lie." In an age of digitally altered photos, pictures *can* lie. But used responsibly, they can communicate information that may be difficult to communicate in words. Pictures also can have a strong emotional impact on your audience. "A picture is worth a thousand words," goes another old saying, and that is especially true for pictures that surprise, shock, scare, or otherwise engage our emotions.

Sometimes pictures can provide powerful, irrefutable evidence for a speaker's claims. During the Cuban Missile Crisis in 1962, for example, the American ambassador to the United Nations, Adlai Stevenson, confronted the Russian ambassador with high-altitude reconnaissance photos that dramatically disproved Russia's denial that nuclear missiles had been stationed in Cuba. On other occasions, photos might be used simply to increase the emotional impact of an argument. Mothers Against Drunk Driving, for example, personalize their statistics with photos of young victims of alcohol-related crashes. Similarly, supporters of the War on Terror frequently replay footage of those two hijacked planes crashing into the Twin Towers of the World Trade Center. By rekindling the feelings of horror and anger many Americans felt on that day, they hope to sustain support for the War on Terrorism.

Visualization is not just something you do by showing pictures to your audience. By painting "word pictures," you can use language to help your audience visualize a problem, "see" an abstract idea, or grasp an otherwise incomprehensible statistic. During the building of the Panama Canal, for example, reporters helped their readers back home visualize the magnitude of the project with a variety of mind-boggling comparisons. One wrote of how the dirt removed from the canal route would build 63 pyramids the size of the great pyramids of Egypt. Others compared the canal to digging a tunnel 14 feet in diameter "through the very heart of the earth," or building a longer version of the Great Wall of China—"from San Francisco to New York." One account even reported that the soil excavated for the canal would fill a train long enough to encircle the earth four times—a train that could be pulled only by a string of locomotives reaching from "New York to Honolulu."[15]

Visualization also can be used to contrast a troubling present with a brighter future. In his famous "I Have a Dream" speech, for example, Martin Luther King Jr. imagined a racially integrated America, where "little black boys and black girls" would "join hands with little white boys and white girls as sisters and brothers."[16] Similarly, former New York governor Mario Cuomo asked his audience at the 1992 Democratic National Convention to visualize a parade like those used to honor military heroes. This time, however, the parade would celebrate safe communities, affordable housing, adequate health care, and economic security:

> A year ago, we had a great parade in New York City to celebrate the return of our armed forces from the Persian Gulf. . . . But as joyous as those parades were, I'd like to march with you in a different kind of celebration—one, regrettably, we cannot yet hold.
>
> I'd like to march with you through cities and rural villages where all the people have safe streets, affordable housing, and health care when they need it.
>
> I want to clap my hands and throw my fists in the air, cheering neighborhoods where children can be children, where they can grow up and have the chance to go to college and one day own their own home.
>
> I want to sing—proud songs, happy songs—arm in arm with workers who have a real stake in their company's success, who once again have the assurance that a lifetime of hard work will make life better for their children than it's been for them.
>
> I want to be part of a victory parade that sends up fireworks, celebrating the triumph of our technology centers and factories, outproducing and outselling our overseas competitors.[17]

Cuomo's language helped his listeners to "see" this parade, at least in their mind's eye.

Comparing the Unfamiliar to the Familiar

Speakers often relate new ideas, plans, or proposals to familiar things, not so much to prove their value, but to help listeners *feel* more comfortable with something new.

By this means, complicated and even controversial ideas can be made to seem more familiar and "everyday"—and hence more acceptable. Before America entered World War II, for example, Franklin Delano Roosevelt defended his controversial plan to supply ships and other war materials to the British—his "lend-lease" plan— by comparing it to how you might help a neighbor whose house was on fire. Logically, perhaps, the two situations were not really comparable. Yet FDR's illustration helped many Americans *feel* that his lend-lease plan was a good idea—the "neighborly" thing to do:

> Well, let me give you an illustration: Suppose my neighbor's home catches fire, and I have got a length of garden hose four or five hundred feet away; but, by Heaven, if he can take my garden hose and connect it up with his hydrant, I may help him to put out his fire. Now what do I do? I don't say to him before the operation, "Neighbor, my garden hose cost me $15; you have got to pay me $15 for it.". . . I don't want $15—I want my garden hose back after the fire is over. All right. If it goes through the fire all right, intact, without any damage to it, he gives it back to me and thanks me very much for the use of it. But suppose it gets smashed up—holes in it—during the fire. . . . I say to him, "I was glad to lend you that hose; I see I can't use it anymore, it's all smashed up." He says, "How many feet of it were there?" I tell him, "There were 150 feet of it." He says, "All right, I will replace it." Now, if I get a nice garden hose back, I am in pretty good shape. In other words, if you lend certain munitions and get the munitions back at the end of the war, if they are intact—haven't been hurt—you are all right; if they have been damaged or deteriorated or lost completely, . . . you have them replaced by the fellow that you have lent them to.[18]

Ethical Considerations in Emotional Appeals

In advertising, we are constantly bombarded with emotional appeals. Yogurt commercials feature an elderly man and his even older mother, implying that if we eat yogurt we too can live to a ripe old age. Ads for athletic shoes exploit the dreams and ambitions of young people, suggesting that if they wear the same shoes as their heroes, they, too, can be superstars. Political ads show candidates sympathizing with the sick or the elderly, or they try to frighten us into thinking that the other candidate might take away our social security or blow up the world. Advertisers know that successful marketing often depends on an audience's emotional reactions. Thus, they persuade us by associating their products with personal success, physical or economic security, or love and "family values."

Emotional appeals, however, can be deceptive and manipulative. More than 2,000 years ago, the rhetorician Aristotle warned that emotional appeals could warp an audience's judgment, producing hasty, ill-considered decisions.[19] When feelings such as fear, anger, love, rage, and guilt are stirred, the results can be powerful and unpredictable. Ethical public speakers recognize and respect the power of emotions. They never use emotional appeals to distract, disorient, or manipulate their listeners.

In speaking persuasively, you should never short-circuit the reasoning process or provoke an overreaction on the part of your listeners. Vivid stories about brutal crimes, the suffering of victims of natural disaster, or the horrors of war may sometimes be appropriate, depending on the situation and the audience. However, we all have heard speakers who go too far. In striving to stir audience emotions, some speakers use crude or tasteless language and images, justifying such tactics as necessary to get people "fired up." Apart from the possibility that such tactics may backfire, the ethical speaker avoids overwhelming listeners with emotions so strong that they can hardly think. Appeals to emotion should supplement and complement well-reasoned arguments, not undermine calm deliberation or provoke hasty, violent actions.

When in doubt, ask yourself this question: Underneath the emotional appeal, do I have a sound argument—a substructure of evidence and reasoning—that can withstand critical scrutiny? You do not want your audience members to respond unthinkingly. Rather, you want to appeal to their minds while recognizing that emotions inevitably play a role in human behavior.

Summary

- Persuasion is rooted in public controversy, or disagreements over matters of political and social significance.
- As citizens in a democracy, we have an obligation to deliberate "in good faith," respecting our fellow citizens and backing up our opinions with good reasons and evidence.
- Public controversies typically revolve around questions of fact, value, or policy.
  - Questions of fact involve controversies over existence, scope, or causality.
  - Questions of value revolve around how ideas and actions should be evaluated or judged.
  - Questions of policy involve choices among future courses of action.
- Ethical proof, or *ethos*, refers to the audience's perceptions of the credibility of the speaker and his or her sources.
  - The constituents of ethos are trustworthiness, competence, open-mindedness, and dynamism.
  - Your ethos will be influenced by the context or situation in which you speak.
  - You can enhance your ethos by showing your audience that you share their concerns, citing reputable sources, relating personal experiences, striving to be clear, considering different points of view, and delivering your speech effectively.
- Emotional appeals can be powerful motivators.
  - You can engage the emotions of your audience by using affective language, appealing to shared values, providing vivid details, helping your audience to visualize your topic, or comparing the unfamiliar to the familiar.
  - Emotional appeals should never be used to deceive or manipulate, or to *replace* well-reasoned arguments.

QUESTIONS FOR REVIEW AND REFLECTION

1. Define *public controversy* and identify two or three public controversies that you think are important today. Do you believe that public debate over those controversies has helped to clarify the issues involved or the options for resolving those controversies?

2. What does it mean to deliberate "in good faith"? Do you think most politicians today deliberate in good faith? What about the political commentators and representatives of interest groups and "think tanks" that you hear on radio or TV talk shows? Do they deliberate in good faith?

3. What are the differences between questions of fact, value, and policy? Can you think of a major public controversy today that revolves mostly around questions of fact? Can you identify other controversies that focus more on questions of value or policy?

4. Below is a list of well-known public figures. How would you describe the ethos of each, and what do you think have been the most important influences shaping their ethos?
   - George W. Bush
   - Hillary Clinton
   - Bono
   - Michael Moore
   - Rush Limbaugh
   - Britney Spears
   - Katie Couric

5. What, in your opinion, determines whether appeals to emotion are ethical? Are there certain types of emotional appeals—or appeals to certain emotions, like fear or hatred—that are inherently unethical? Does a speaker's purposes influence your assessment of whether their emotional appeals are ethical?

ENDNOTES

1. Brad Stone, "Tech Trash, E-Waste: By Any Name, It's an Issue," *Newsweek*, December 12, 2005, 11.
2. Anne Underwood, "Diagnosis: Not Enough Nurses," *Newsweek*, December 12, 2005, 80.
3. Richard Lacayo, "Has the President Gone Too Far?" *Time*, January 9, 2006.
4. *The Rhetoric of Aristotle*, trans. George Kennedy (New York: Oxford University Press, 1991).
5. Gary Cronkhite and Jo Liska, "A Critique of Factor Analytic Approaches to the Study of Credibility," *Communication Monographs* 43 (1976): 91–107; J. C. McCroskey and T. J. Young, "Ethos and Credibility: The Construct and Its Measurement after Three Decades," *Central States Speech Journal* 32 (1981): 24–34; Jack L. Whitehead, "Factors of Source Credibility," *Quarterly Journal of Speech* 54 (1968): 59–63.
6. Ronald Reagan, "State of the Union Address," in *Three Centuries of American Rhetorical Discourse*, ed. Ronald F. Reid, 743 (Prospect Heights, IL: Waveland Press, 1988).
7. Janice Payan, "Opportunities for Hispanic Women," *Vital Speeches of the Day* (September 1, 1990): 698–99.
8. Barbara Jordan, "Keynote Address to the Democratic Convention," *Vital Speeches of the Day* 39 (1976): 654.

9. William Jefferson Clinton, "1992 Democratic National Convention Acceptance Address," *American Rhetoric*, www.americanrhetoric.com/speeches/billclinton1992dnc .htm (Accessed June 26, 2006).

10. Ronald Reagan, "National Security," in *Contemporary American Voices*, ed. James R. Andrews and David Zarefsky, 349 (New York: Longman, 1992).

11. Eugene Debs, "Statement to the Court," in *American Voices: Significant Speeches in American History, 1640–1945*, ed. James R. Andrews and David Zarefsky, 415–16 (New York: Longman, 1989).

12. Cesar Chavez, "Commonwealth Club Address," November 9, 1984, www .americanrhetoric.com/speeches/cesarchavezcommonwealthclubaddress.htm (accessed May 26, 2006).

13. Geraldine Ferraro, "Acceptance of the Democratic Nomination for Vice President," in Andrews and Zarefsky, *Contemporary American Voices*, 365–66.

14. Robert Dole, "Sex and Violence in the Entertainment Industry," in *Contemporary American Speeches*, 8th ed., ed. Richard L. Johannesen, Ron R. Allen, Wilmer A. Linkugel and J. Bryan Ferald, 245–46 (Dubuque, IA: Kendall/Hunt, 1997).

15. J. Michael Hogan, *The Panama Canal in American Politics* (Carbondale: Southern Illinois University Press, 1986), 49.

16. Martin Luther King, Jr., "I Have a Dream," in *Great Speeches for Criticism and Analysis*, 4th ed., ed. Lloyd Rohler and Roger Cook, 352 (Greenwood, IN: Alistair Press, 2001).

17. Mario M. Cuomo, "Nominating Address," *Vital Speeches of the Day* 58 (August 18, 1992): 619.

18. Franklin D. Roosevelt, *Selected Speeches, Messages, Press Conferences and Letters*, ed. Basil Rauch (New York: Holt, Rinehart and Winston, 1960), 271.

19. *Rhetoric of Aristotle*, 235.

On September 13, 2007, President George W. Bush delivered a televised address to the nation, reporting on the success of a troop "surge" in Iraq that he had ordered eight months earlier. Building on testimony before Congress by his chief civilian and military advisers in Iraq, Ambassador Ryan Crocker and General David Petraeus, Bush conceded that the challenges in Iraq remained "formidable," but he focused on evidence that the "troop surge is working." Announcing a plan to gradually reduce U.S. troop levels in that troubled nation, Bush called on Americans of all political persuasions to "come together" at this crucial moment and to support his efforts to bring peace to the region. The speech failed to silence debate over the issue, however. Responding for the Democrats only moments after the speech, Democratic Senator Jack Reed (D-R.I.) complained that the president had still "failed to provide either a plan to successfully end the war or a convincing rationale to continue it." For another opposing view on the war in Iraq, see the speech by Barbara Boxer at the end of Chapter 8.

THE PRESIDENT: Good evening. In the life of all free nations, there come moments that decide the direction of a country and reveal the character of its people. We are now at such a moment.

In Iraq, an ally of the United States is fighting for its survival. Terrorists and extremists who are at war with us around the world are seeking to topple Iraq's government, dominate the region, and attack us here at home. If Iraq's young democracy can turn back these enemies, it will mean a more hopeful Middle East and a more secure America. This ally has placed its trust in the United States. And tonight, our moral and strategic imperatives are one: We must help Iraq defeat those who threaten its future and also threaten ours.

Eight months ago, we adopted a new strategy to meet that objective, including a surge in U.S. forces that reached full strength in June. This week, General David Petraeus and Ambassador Ryan Crocker testified before Congress about how that strategy is progressing. In their testimony, these men made clear that our challenge in Iraq is formidable. Yet they concluded that conditions in Iraq are improving, that we are seizing the initiative from the enemy, and that the troop surge is working.

The premise of our strategy is that securing the Iraqi population is the foundation for all other progress. For Iraqis to bridge sectarian divides, they need to feel safe in their homes and neighborhoods. For lasting reconciliation to take root, Iraqis must feel confident that they do not need sectarian gangs for security. The goal of the surge is to provide that security and to help prepare Iraqi forces to maintain it. As I will explain tonight, our success in meeting these objectives now allows us to begin bringing some of our troops home.

Since the surge was announced in January, it has moved through several phases. First was the flow of additional troops into Iraq, especially Baghdad and Anbar province. Once these forces were in place, our commanders launched a series of offensive operations to drive terrorists and militias out of their strongholds. And finally, in areas that have been cleared, we are surging diplomatic and civilian resources to ensure that military progress is quickly followed up with real improvements in daily life.

Anbar province is a good example of how our strategy is working. Last year, an intelligence report concluded that Anbar had been lost to al Qaeda. Some cited this report as evidence that we had failed in Iraq and should cut our losses and pull out. Instead, we kept the pressure on the terrorists. The local people were suffering under the Taliban-like rule of al Qaeda, and they were sick of it. So they asked us for help.

BUSH OPENS BY ANNOUNCING THAT THE NATION FACES A CHOICE THAT WILL CHANGE THE COURSE OF HISTORY AND REVEAL THE "CHARACTER" OF THE AMERICAN PEOPLE.

HERE BUSH INTRODUCES THE INSPIRATION FOR HIS SPEECH, A REPORT BY HIS MILITARY AND CIVILIAN LEADERS ON THE GROUND IN IRAQ. GENERAL DAVID PATRAEUS AND AMBASSADOR RYAN CROCKER HAD JUST FINISHED TESTIFYING BEFORE CONGRESS ON THE SUCCESS OF THE "SURGE" IN U.S. FORCES.

AFTER SUMMARIZING THE GOALS AND STRATEGY BEHIND THE "SURGE," BUSH DEVELOPS AN EXTENDED EXAMPLE OF HOW IT HAS WORKED IN JUST ONE

To take advantage of this opportunity, I sent an additional 4,000 Marines to Anbar as part of the surge. Together, local sheiks, Iraqi forces, and coalition troops drove the terrorists from the capital of Ramadi and other population centers. Today, a city where al Qaeda once planted its flag is beginning to return to normal. Anbar citizens who once feared beheading for talking to an American or Iraqi soldier now come forward to tell us where the terrorists are hiding. Young Sunnis who once joined the insurgency are now joining the army and police. And with the help of our provincial reconstruction teams, new jobs are being created and local governments are meeting again.

These developments do not often make the headlines, but they do make a difference. During my visit to Anbar on Labor Day, local Sunni leaders thanked me for America's support. They pledged they would never allow al Qaeda to return. And they told me they now see a place for their people in a democratic Iraq. The Sunni governor of Anbar province put it this way: "Our tomorrow starts today."

The changes in Anbar show all Iraqis what becomes possible when extremists are driven out. They show al Qaeda that it cannot count on popular support, even in a province its leaders once declared their home base. And they show the world that ordinary people in the Middle East want the same things for their children that we want for ours—a decent life and a peaceful future.

In Anbar, the enemy remains active and deadly. Earlier today, one of the brave tribal sheikhs who helped lead the revolt against al Qaeda was murdered. In response, a fellow Sunni leader declared: "We are determined to strike back and continue our work." And as they do, they can count on the continued support of the United States.

Throughout Iraq, too many citizens are being killed by terrorists and death squads. And for most Iraqis, the quality of life is far from where it should be. Yet General Petraeus and Ambassador Crocker report that the success in Anbar is beginning to be replicated in other parts of the country.

One year ago, much of Baghdad was under siege. Schools were closed, markets were shuttered, and sectarian violence was spiraling out of control. Today, most of Baghdad's neighborhoods are being patrolled by coalition and Iraqi forces who live among the people they protect. Many schools and markets are reopening. Citizens are coming forward with vital intelligence. Sectarian killings are down. And ordinary life is beginning to return.

One year ago, much of Diyala province was a sanctuary for al Qaeda and other extremist groups, and its capital of Baqubah was emerging as an al Qaeda stronghold. Today, Baqubah is cleared. Diyala province is the site of a growing popular uprising against the extremists. And some local tribes are working alongside coalition and Iraqi forces to clear out the enemy and reclaim their communities.

One year ago, Shia extremists and Iranian-backed militants were gaining strength and targeting Sunnis for assassination. Today, these groups are being broken up, and many of their leaders are being captured or killed.

These gains are a tribute to our military, they are a tribute to the courage of the Iraqi security forces, and they are the tribute to an Iraqi government that has decided to take on the extremists.

Now the Iraqi government must bring the same determination to achieving reconciliation. This is an enormous undertaking after more than three decades of tyranny and division. The government has not met its own legislative benchmarks—and in my meetings with Iraqi leaders, I have made it clear that they must.

Yet Iraq's national leaders are getting some things done. For example, they have passed a budget. They're sharing oil revenues with the provinces. They're allowing former Baathists to rejoin Iraq's military or receive government pensions. Local reconciliation is taking place. The key now is

AREA, ANBAR PROVINCE. THE EXAMPLE RELIES ON THE TESTIMONY OF PATRAEUS AND CROKER, BUT BUSH ALSO CITES TESTIMONY FROM LOCAL SUNNI LEADERS HE MET DURING A RECENT VISIT.

BUSH CITES TWO MORE EXAMPLES OF AREAS WHERE THE SURGE APPEARED TO BE WORKING, INCLUDING THE CAPITAL CITY OF BAGHDAD, WHICH HAD BEEN THE SITE OF MOST OF THE VIOLENCE AMERICANS HAD WITNESSED OR READ ABOUT IN THE NEWS.

BUSH RESPONDS TO WIDESPREAD CRITICISMS OF THE IRAQI GOVERNMENT, REMINDING LISTENERS OF THE MAGNITUDE OF THE CHALLENGES THEY FACE AND POINTING TO SIGNS OF PROGRESS.

to link this progress in the provinces to progress in Baghdad. As local politics change, so will national politics.

Our troops in Iraq are performing brilliantly. Along with Iraqi forces, they have captured or killed an average of more than 1,500 enemy fighters per month since January. Yet ultimately, the way forward depends on the ability of Iraqis to maintain security gains. According to General Petraeus and a panel chaired by retired General Jim Jones, the Iraqi army is becoming more capable—although there is still a great deal of work to be done to improve the national police. Iraqi forces are receiving increased cooperation from local populations. And this is improving their ability to hold areas that have been cleared.

Because of this success, General Petraeus believes we have now reached the point where we can maintain our security gains with fewer American forces. He has recommended that we not replace about 2,200 Marines scheduled to leave Anbar province later this month. In addition, he says it will soon be possible to bring home an Army combat brigade, for a total force reduction of 5,700 troops by Christmas. And he expects that by July, we will be able to reduce our troop levels in Iraq from 20 combat brigades to 15.

General Petraeus also recommends that in December we begin transitioning to the next phase of our strategy in Iraq. As terrorists are defeated, civil society takes root, and the Iraqis assume more control over their own security, our mission in Iraq will evolve. Over time, our troops will shift from leading operations, to partnering with Iraqi forces, and eventually to overwatching those forces. As this transition in our mission takes place, our troops will focus on a more limited set of tasks, including counterterrorism operations and training, equipping, and supporting Iraqi forces.

EMBRACING THE RECOMMENDATIONS OF GENERAL PETRAEUS, BUSH ANNOUNCES THAT ENOUGH PROGRESS HAS BEEN MADE TO START WITHDRAWING AMERICAN TROOPS. HE ALSO ANNOUNCES THAT PETRAEUS AND CROCKER WILL REPORT AGAIN IN MARCH OF 2008, AND HE DEFINES THE PRINCIPLE THAT WILL BE USED TO DETERMINE FUTURE TROOP WITHDRAWALS: "RETURN ON SUCCESS."

I have consulted with the Joint Chiefs of Staff, other members of my national security team, Iraqi officials, and leaders of both parties in Congress. I have benefited from their advice, and I have accepted General Petraeus's recommendations. I have directed General Petraeus and Ambassador Crocker to update their joint campaign plan for Iraq, so we can adjust our military and civilian resources accordingly. I have also directed them to deliver another report to Congress in March. At that time, they will provide a fresh assessment of the situation in Iraq and of the troop levels and resources we need to meet our national security objectives.

The principle guiding my decisions on troop levels in Iraq is "return on success." The more successful we are, the more American troops can return home. And in all we do, I will ensure that our commanders on the ground have the troops and flexibility they need to defeat the enemy.

Americans want our country to be safe and our troops to begin coming home from Iraq. Yet those of us who believe success in Iraq is essential to our security, and those who believe we should begin bringing our troops home, have been at odds. Now, because of the measure of success we are seeing in Iraq, we can begin seeing troops come home. The way forward I have described tonight makes it possible, for the first time in years, for people who have been on opposite sides of this difficult debate to come together.

BUSH GIVES VOICE TO WHAT HE SEES AS THE SHARED GOALS OF ALL AMERICANS AND CALLS FOR PEOPLE ON ALL SIDES OF "THIS DIFFICULT DEBATE" TO "COME TOGETHER."

This vision for a reduced American presence also has the support of Iraqi leaders from all communities. At the same time, they understand that their success will require U.S. political, economic, and security engagement that extends beyond my presidency. These Iraqi leaders have asked for an enduring relationship with America. And we are ready to begin building that relationship—in a way that protects our interests in the region and requires many fewer American troops.

The success of a free Iraq is critical to the security of the United States. A free Iraq will deny al Qaeda a safe haven. A free Iraq will counter the destructive ambitions of Iran. A free Iraq will marginalize extremists, unleash the talent of its people, and be an anchor of stability in the region. A free Iraq will set an example for people across the Middle East. A free Iraq will be our partner in the fight against terror—and that will make us safer here at home.

Realizing this vision will be difficult, but it is achievable. Our military commanders believe we can succeed. Our diplomats believe we can succeed. And for the safety of future generations of Americans, we must succeed.

If we were to be driven out of Iraq, extremists of all strains would be emboldened. Al Qaeda could gain new recruits and new sanctuaries. Iran would benefit from the chaos and would be encouraged in its efforts to gain nuclear weapons and dominate the region. Extremists could control a key part of the global energy supply. Iraq could face a humanitarian nightmare. Democracy movements would be violently reversed. We would leave our children to face a far more dangerous world. And as we saw on September the 11th, 2001, those dangers can reach our cities and kill our people.

Whatever political party you belong to, whatever your position on Iraq, we should be able to agree that America has a vital interest in preventing chaos and providing hope in the Middle East. We should be able to agree that we must defeat al Qaeda, counter Iran, help the Afghan government, work for peace in the Holy Land, and strengthen our military so we can prevail in the struggle against terrorists and extremists.

HERE BUSH EMPHASIZES POINTS OF AGREEMENT IN ANOTHER APPEAL FOR UNITY.

So tonight I want to speak to members of the United States Congress: Let us come together on a policy of strength in the Middle East. I thank you for providing crucial funds and resources for our military. And I ask you to join me in supporting the recommendations General Petraeus has made and the troop levels he has asked for.

To the Iraqi people: You have voted for freedom, and now you are liberating your country from terrorists and death squads. You must demand that your leaders make the tough choices needed to achieve reconciliation. As you do, have confidence that America does not abandon our friends, and we will not abandon you.

To Iraq's neighbors who seek peace: The violent extremists who target Iraq are also targeting you. The best way to secure your interests and protect your own people is to stand with the people of Iraq. That means using your economic and diplomatic leverage to strengthen the government in Baghdad. And it means the efforts by Iran and Syria to undermine that government must end.

To the international community: The success of a free Iraq matters to every civilized nation. We thank the 36 nations who have troops on the ground in Iraq and the many others who are helping that young democracy. We encourage all nations to help, by implementing the International Compact to revitalize Iraq's economy, by participating in the Neighbors Conferences to boost cooperation and overcome differences in the region, and by supporting the new and expanded mission of the United Nations in Iraq.

To our military personnel, intelligence officers, diplomats, and civilians on the front lines in Iraq: You have done everything America has asked of you. And the progress I have reported tonight is in large part because of your courage and hard effort. You are serving far from home. Our nation is grateful for your sacrifices, and the sacrifices of your families.

HERE BUSH SPEAKS TO THE VARIOUS STAKE-HOLDERS IN THE DEBATE: THE CONGRESS, THE IRAQI PEOPLE, IRAQI'S NEIGHBORS, THE INTERNATIONAL COMMUNITY, AND AMERICA'S MILITARY AND CIVILIAN PERSONNEL "ON THE FRONT LINES" IN IRAQ. HE ADDRESSES EACH AUDIENCE DIRECTLY, ASKING FOR THEIR HELP AND REMINDING THEM OF THEIR OBLIGATIONS.

Earlier this year, I received an email from the family of Army Specialist Brandon Stout of Michigan. Brandon volunteered for the National Guard and was killed while serving in Baghdad. His family has suffered greatly. Yet in their sorrow, they see larger purpose. His wife, Audrey, says that Brandon felt called to serve and knew what he was fighting for. And his parents, Tracy and Jeff,

BUSH BEGINS HIS CONCLUSION WITH TESTIMONY FROM THE FAMILY OF A SOLDIER KILLED IN IRAQ, ILLUSTRATING HOW EVEN THOSE WHO HAVE wrote me this: "We believe this is a war of good and evil and we must win even if it cost the life of our own son. Freedom is not free."

This country is blessed to have Americans like Brandon Stout, who make extraordinary sacrifices to keep us safe from harm. They are doing so in a fight that is just, and right, and necessary. And now it falls to us to finish the work they have begun.

Some say the gains we are making in Iraq come too late. They are mistaken. It is never too late to deal a blow to al Qaeda. It is never too late to advance freedom. And it is never too late to support our troops in a fight they can win.

Good night, and God bless America.

Arguing Persuasively

CHAPTER OBJECTIVES

*After studying this chapter, you
should be able to*

1. Distinguish between
   persuasion and
   demagoguery.

2. Define *argument* and
   identify the components of a
   complete argument.

3. Understand what it means
   to make a "reasonable"
   argument.

4. Identify and critique
   different *types* of reasoning.

5. Recognize and describe
   some common fallacies of
   reasoning and evidence.

Democracies are fragile things. They require committed, honest leaders, and they depend on ordinary citizens to assume the responsibilities of citizenship. That means that citizens must participate in public deliberations and learn to distinguish between good and bad arguments. They must be committed to deliberating in good faith, and they must be willing to put the common good ahead of their own selfish interests. In a diverse democratic society, it is sometimes difficult to reconcile all the competing interests in major public controversies. That is all the more reason that we must learn to deliberate responsibly. If our democracy is to thrive, we must discuss and debate public issues with intelligence, civility, and respect for our fellow citizens.

Historically, America has not always lived up to this democratic ideal. In the 1950s, for example, a reckless demagogue named Joseph McCarthy rose to power by exploiting the fears and uncertainty of the cold war era. Claiming that "card-carrying" communists had infiltrated the government, McCarthy inspired anticommunist "witch hunts" across the nation, throwing our political system into chaos and destroying innocent lives. At another time, McCarthy's outrageous accusations might have been ignored. In an era of doubt and political complacency, however, he caused a national sensation and became the most feared man in America.[1]

Today we live in another era of complacency and political uncertainty. Pointing to low voter turnout and declining involvement in civic affairs, some worry that another great demagogue might throw the nation into political chaos. Could a modern-day Joseph McCarthy exploit today's economic uncertainties or our fears of terrorism to advance a narrow and selfish political agenda? Are we so ill-informed and complacent that we would fall for such tactics again? Or have we learned the lesson of the McCarthy Era: that as citizens in a democracy, we have a responsibility to guard against the deceptions and manipulations of the demagogue?

In this chapter, we pick up where we left off in the previous chapter, exploring in greater depth the role of persuasion in our democratic society. More specifically, we will distinguish between persuasion and demagoguery, defining persuasion as "reason-giving argument" and contrasting it with demagoguery. Then we will reflect more practically on what it means to construct a *reasonable* argument, examining the components of a complete argument and identifying some of the most common fallacies or errors in reasoning and evidence. Contrary to what one might conclude from watching political talk shows, arguing about civic affairs does *not* have to mean attacking your political enemies or stirring up public passions. To the contrary, it *should* mean *engaging* your fellow citizens in a constructive dialogue about issues of mutual concern.

Persuasion and Demagoguery in a Free Society

Preview. *Persuasion is an essential tool of democratic governance. Indeed, the reliance on persuasion to resolve conflicts and induce social cooperation is the main difference between a democracy and a totalitarian or authoritarian state. Yet precisely because they depend so much on persuasion, democracies are especially vulnerable to demagoguery, or deceptive and manipulative speech. With advances in technology, demagoguery has become an even greater threat. If* *we hope to sustain our democratic way of life, we must understand the differences between per-suasion and demagoguery and demand high standards from all who speak in public.*

Persuasion, as we have emphasized throughout this book, is an essential tool of democratic citizenship. The earliest treatises on persuasion, such as Aristotle's *Rhetoric*,[2] prepared citizens to participate in the judicial and legislative assemblies of the Greek city-state. Passed down over centuries, this classical tradition evolved in response to changing social and political conditions, but its essential purpose re-mained the same: to educate people for citizenship. As part of that education, citi-zens were taught to distinguish between good and bad arguments, between the legitimate techniques of democratic persuasion and the tricks of the sophist or the demagogue.

America's founders were well schooled in this classical rhetorical tradition. Taught to view demagoguery as "the peculiar vice to which democracies were sus-ceptible," they designed our constitutional system to guard against what Alexander Hamilton described as the "temporary delusions" of a public misled by those who might "flatter their prejudices to betray their interests." As James Madison ob-served, there would be times in any democracy when the public might be "misled by the artful misrepresentations of interested men." In those "critical moments," Madison looked to the Senate—the legislative branch more insulated from public opinion—to moderate public passions until the people regained their "cool and de-liberate" judgment.[3]

More than a hundred years later, a young scholar named Woodrow Wilson echoed the founders' concerns. As a student of oratory and politics, Wilson wrote at length about how America might protect itself against demagoguery by properly ed-ucating both its leaders and its citizens. Like the ancient rhetoricians, Wilson drew a clear, *ethical* distinction between responsible, civic-minded orators—those he called "orator-statesmen"—and those "artful dialecticians" who manipulated public opin-ion through "subtle word-play," "dialectic dexterity," or "passionate declamation." As an educator, Wilson taught that "high and noble thoughts" and emotional self-restraint were the hallmarks of the responsible "orator-statesman," and he professed his faith in the ability of ordinary citizens to "exercise intelligent discretion."[4] As Wilson wrote early in his career, "A charlatan cannot long play the statesman suc-cessfully while the whole country is looking critically on."[5]

Today, some doubt the public's ability to "exercise intelligent discretion." Many Americans lack even the most basic understanding of our nation's democratic insti-tutions and traditions,[6] and advances in communication technologies have created new possibilities for propaganda and demagoguery. So how, in the modern world, might we distinguish persuasion from demagoguery? In an age of global propaganda and the politics of spin, does the ancient distinction between persuasion and dema-goguery still have meaning?

We believe that it does, for regardless of the political context or the technologies of communication, we can still distinguish between good and bad *arguments*. The ancient Greeks lived in very different times, but their basic lesson remains relevant: if democracy is to thrive, every citizen must learn to distinguish between sound and deceptive or misleading arguments. Today, as in ancient times, *reasoned* arguments are the substance of democratic deliberation, while demagoguery relies on personal and emotional appeals. Claiming a monopoly on truth, demagogues cultivate a *charismatic* ethos, setting themselves apart from ordinary citizens and demanding deference to their supposedly "supernatural, superhuman, or at least specifically exceptional powers or qualities."[7] Appealing to "dark" emotions, demagogues use *pathos* as a distraction, *substituting* emotion for argument and concocting various scapegoats and "enemies." Demagogues do *not* appeal to what Abraham Lincoln called the "better angels of our nature."[8] To the contrary, they exploit the envy, resentment, hatred, or fears of their audiences.[9]

Focus on Civic Engagement

The Politics of Outrageousness

In her 2006 book *Godless: The Church of Liberalism*, political commentator Ann Coulter took her reputation for making outrageous statements a step further by accusing four women who had lost their husbands in the September 11 terrorist attacks—the so-called "Jersey Girls"—of exploiting their personal loss for political purposes. "These broads are millionaires, lionized on TV and in articles about them, reveling in their status as celebrities and stalked by grief-arrazies," Coulter wrote. "I've never seen people enjoying their husbands' deaths so much." And just for good measure, Coulter added: "And by the way, how do we know their husbands weren't planning to divorce these harpies?"

Broads? Harpies? Had Coulter "gone off the deep end?" as some observers suggested? Or were her remarks simply a marketing ploy, an effort to "rise above the din" of the 24-hour news cycle and to stand out in the "blogosphere," where such rhetorical excess has become common?

At one level, perhaps, Coulter made a "reasonable" argument: that simply because they lost loved ones in the 9/11 attacks, the "Jersey Girls" should not be given a "free pass" to criticize the Bush administration or to make partisan speeches without backing up their claims. At another level, however, Coulter was obviously trying to provoke people, as she deliberately used offensive language. Whatever her point, Coulter crossed the line of propriety and civility. Not only did Senator Hillary Clinton protest the remarks as "vicious" and "mean-spirited," but New York's Republican Governor George Pataki and even Fox News commentator Bill O'Reilly criticized her as well.

Of course, Coulter is not the only practitioner of the politics of outrageousness. Radio talk-show host Rush Limbaugh perfected the form, and Howard Stern, Al Franken, and Michael Moore are just a few of the public figures who have become well-known for offensive or outrageous remarks. In our media-saturated culture, the politics of outrageousness may be one way to rise above the din and attract attention to one's self. But does such rhetoric contribute anything constructive to the public dialogue? Do these commentators help us to understand or resolve important public controversies? Does such talk encourage citizens to participate in politics and civic affairs? In short, does the politics of outrageousness serve the public good?

Ann Coulter and the other practitioners of the politics of outrageousness have a right to their opinions—and even to their confrontational and polarizing ways of expressing those opinions. But they do *not* have a right to be heard, much less to be taken seriously. Calling Coulter a "hater," at least one newspaper editor, Bob Unger of the *Centre Daily Times* in State College, Pennsylvania, canceled her syndicated column, provoking cries of censorship from her admirers. But does refusing to publish hateful rhetoric constitute censorship? Do media "gatekeepers" like Unger have a right to silence people like Coulter? Should newspapers also banish columnists on the left who some consider hateful? In principle, Unger has a point: Coulter and others like her poison the public dialogue. Yet who is to decide who should be censored or silenced? Who do *you* trust to make that call? Ultimately, it is up to the citizenry to decide who has crossed the line of acceptable public debate. Coulter and others like her may have a right to talk, but we have no obligation to listen.

Source: Jocelyn Noveck, "Outrageousness an Art Form for Top Practitioners," *Centre Daily Times*, June 14, 2006, A2.

As rhetorical scholar James Darsey has reminded us, the agitator, the political *provocateur*, even the zealot has a role to play in our democratic system. Occasionally, we *need* speakers to "shake things up," shattering our complacency and motivating us to act. Radical speakers *can* be a source of democratic inspiration and renewal, reminding us of our revolutionary heritage and demanding that we live up to our ideals.[10] But in the day-to-day business of democratic governance, we still must guard against rhetorical excess and extremism. The hard work of self-governance cannot be done by speakers who divide and polarize the citizenry.

As we discuss what it means to "argue persuasively," our emphasis will be on the constituents of a "reasonable" argument. We will first examine the various components of an argument and the major types of reasoning. Then we will discuss some of the most common errors or "fallacies" of reasoning and evidence. As we shall see, arguing persuasively is not about getting your own way or manipulating an audience. Rather, it is about coming together with your fellow citizens to discuss and debate the issues of the day.

Constructing a Reasonable Argument

Preview. *A good argument is not one that echoes our own views, nor is a good argument simply one that "works." To the contrary, a good argument is one that adheres to certain rules of evidence and reasoning. A good argument may not always win the day. Indeed, the best argument may be one that forces us to reconsider our own opinions. Good arguments engage our emotions and draw strength from our ethos. But, in the final analysis, a good argument is one that meets certain tests of reasoning and evidence and fulfills its "burden of proof."*

We all know that there are good and bad arguments. But what do we mean when we make that judgment? Unfortunately, many of us seem to think that a good argument is one that confirms what we already believe—an argument that has us shaking our head up and down in agreement. Others take a more pragmatic view: a "good" argument is one that "works"—one that persuades other people. That too seems a bit shortsighted. As we have noted, a demagogue's arguments may "work," but they have *ethical* shortcomings—they twist the truth, or they appeal to ugly emotions. Obviously, we do not want to praise a speaker for being an effective liar.

Like any artistic creation, an argument can be judged not only in terms of how it is received, but also by certain theoretical and ethical principles. We already have suggested some of those principles: truth, for example, and a commitment to deliberating in good faith. But what does it mean to say that an argument is *theoretically* sound? What, in theory, defines a "good" argument, and how do we go about evaluating an argument?

Unfortunately, there is no simple list of rules defining a "good" argument. The whole tradition of rhetorical studies, dating back more than 2,000 years, might be seen as a search for such rules. Today, some even reject the need for rules altogether, arguing that any such rules reflect cultural biases or "silence" some voices.[11] Yet most who study speech would still agree on a couple of points. First, a "good" argument must be complete; that is, it must have all the basic components of the so-called Toulmin model of argument (Figure 16.1): a claim, evidence to back it up, and a "warrant" (or general principle) that links the evidence to the claim.[12] Second, a "good" argument must be *reasonable*—that is, it must be worthy of serious consideration by a hypothetical listener who is reasonably intelligent, well-informed, and fair-minded. Perhaps you have heard of the "reasonable person" test in a court of law.[13] Something *like* that test can help us to distinguish between reasonable and unreasonable arguments in public debate.

Claims

Claims are the debatable assertions put forward by a speaker. They are the contested positions you want your audience to accept, like the *claim* that illegal immigration poses a threat to our national security, or the *claim* that capital punishment deters crime. When you make a claim, you do not expect your listeners to automatically nod their heads in agreement. By definition, a claim takes sides on a controversial matter and invites *debate*. If you hope to prevail in that debate, you still need to *prove* your claims.

Claims take many different forms, mostly arising out of the types of persuasive issues or controversies discussed in Chapter 15. If you are debating whether something does or does not exist, what *caused* something to happen, or the *scope* or *magnitude* of some phenomenon, you are debating *claims of fact*. If you are debating whether something is good or bad, you are making *claims of value*. Value claims assume a variety of forms, including claims about what's effective or ineffective, just or unjust, moral or immoral, legal or illegal, and beneficial or harmful. In debates

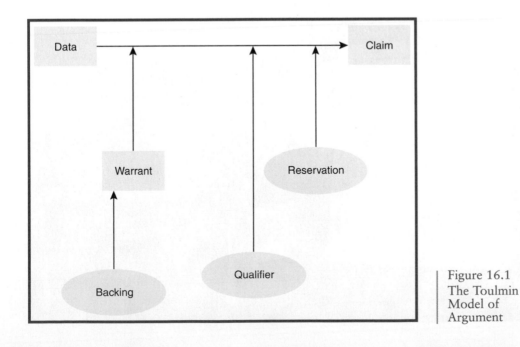

Figure 16.1
The Toulmin
Model of
Argument

over what we should do—debates over future courses of action—we make *claims of policy*. These are, by their very nature, the hardest to prove, since they involve, in effect, predicting the future.

Precisely because they are the hardest to prove, policy claims tend to come more heavily qualified than other sorts of claims. *Qualifiers* are simply those words that indicate our level of confidence in our claims—words like "possibly," "probably," or "beyond any doubt." So, for example, we might qualify a factual claim if our evidence is not conclusive: "The major cause of increased levels of mercury in fish is *probably* emissions from coal-fired power plants." If we overqualify our claims, of course, we sound unsure or wishy-washy, but if we do not qualify our claim at all, we may overstate our case. A "reasonable" argument is one that is qualified at a level appropriate to the strength of the reasoning and evidence behind it.

Reservations are exceptions to our claim, or stipulated conditions under which we no longer hold to our claim. Thus, for example, the chairman of the Federal Reserve might argue that a proposed increase in interest rates will be sufficient to control inflation—*unless* energy prices continue to escalate. As with qualifiers, reservations can be overdone, leaving virtually no conditions under which you still hold to your claim ("I predict inflation will remain low *unless* prices for food, shelter, clothing, and energy go up!"). By identifying one or two major reservations, however, you can assert your claim more confidently ("Inflation will *almost certainly* remain low, *unless* energy prices go up.") and still make a reasonable argument.

Whatever sorts of claims you make, you will be expected to back them up with evidence. Evidence, as we discussed in Chapter 8, might include statistics, testimony,

Even well-known, credible speakers are expected to back up their claims with evidence. Here U.S. Congressman Duncan Hunter (R-CA) speaks to the press alongside a chart illustrating the decline in U.S. manufacturing trade with China. Hunter is a co-sponsor of new legislation aimed at protecting U.S. manufacturers against unfair currency exchange rates.

examples, or comparison/contrast. But whatever types of evidence you choose, you need to use it properly and make sure that it meets certain tests of quantitative and qualitative sufficiency.

Evidence

When attempting to persuade an audience to accept a factual claim, you might use statistics, specific examples, testimony by experts, and other sorts of evidence. When long-distance telephone companies sought approval from the public utilities commission for a reduction in the fees they paid to local phone companies, for example, one student used a variety of evidence to convince his audience that consumers would save little, if any, under the plan. The factual claim and supporting material he used looked like this:

The proposed reduction in fees will not result in lower costs for consumers.

A. According to the *New York Times*, documents filed by AT&T indicate that basic rates on One Rate plans would increase by 66 percent. *(statistic)*
B. According to the Consumers Union, new per-minute fees would go up every day except Sunday, resulting in higher bills for low-volume callers. *(testimony)*
C. A customer who made 45 minutes of long-distance calls on Saturday would pay $4.95 under the old plan and $13.05 under the new plan. *(example/statistics)*
D. Even if the companies changed to a flat 19-cents-per-minute rate, the cost would still go up to $8.55. *(example/statistics)*

In proving claims of value—claims about good and bad, right and wrong—you need more than just factual evidence. Not only must you cite examples, statistics, and other empirical evidence, but you also must consider the *criteria* or *standards* that support your *evaluations* of those facts. In a murder case, for example, it is one thing to prove that that the accused pulled the trigger, resulting in the death of the victim. It is quite another to convince a jury that the defendant committed premeditated, first-degree murder. Depending on the circumstances, the same action—shooting another person dead—*might* be considered first-degree murder, or it might be reckless homicide or even justifiable homicide. In this sort of case, the facts alone do not determine the verdict. The facts must be considered *in light of the law*.

In public policy debates, the standards of judgment are rarely as clear as they are in a court of law. Still, it is important that we reflect on the rules, principles, or standards we employ in making our judgments. In a speech on medical malpractice, for example, one student cited the example of her uncle, who had undergone what was supposed to be a routine operation but ended up seriously disabled. She also cited other examples of people hurt by medical errors. Yet in order to convince her listeners that medical malpractice was a "very serious problem" in America, she needed some broader basis for her judgment. She was able to establish that basis with statistics on the leading causes of death and through comparisons to other, more familiar health threats like car accidents and AIDS. With this evidence she was able to show that medical malpractice was as "serious" a threat as these other, more familiar threats.

Policy arguments pose the greatest challenge because they involve choices about what we *should* do in the future. Since we cannot present *direct* evidence of a proposed policy's feasibility, costs, or effects, we typically must rely on comparisons to similar policies, or we might use testimony from experts in the field. If we wished to propose a new program for recycling high-tech waste, for example, we might look for evidence of how similar programs have worked in other communities. Or we might turn to experts in waste management for testimony on the value, cost, feasibility, or additional benefits of such programs. In the final analysis, however, we really cannot say for sure how a policy that has worked well in the past will work under different circumstances in the future.

Whatever sort of evidence you use, it needs to be sufficient, both quantitatively and qualitatively, to convince a "reasonable person" that your claims are worthy of serious consideration. There are three basic tests of the adequacy of your evidence.

First, the quality of the evidence should justify the audience's acceptance. As we discussed in Chapter 8, there are certain questions that should always be asked about particular types of evidence, such as:

- Are the examples representative?
- Are the statistics reliable?
- Is the testimony authoritative?
- Are the comparisons sound—that is, are the objects or ideas being compared really comparable?

Beyond these questions, there are some general "tests" of evidence that we should always apply: Is the evidence accurate, recent, and complete? Is the source of the evidence credible?

Second, the evidence must be relevant to the claim. Evidence can be accurate and truthful and still not prove the claim. Consider, for example, Meagan's argument in favor of voting for Josh as student government president:

What we need most in a president is strong leadership. Josh has been my friend since we arrived here at the university. He has always been there for me, often putting aside his own problems or needs to help me when I needed help.

Everyone likes Josh. He has a great sense of humor. When things got tense in our study group, Josh always found something funny to say to break the tension.

Everything that Meagan said about her friend may be true; Josh is no doubt a nice guy. But is that relevant to Meagan's claim? Does the fact that Josh has been a good friend to Megan, or the fact that he makes people laugh, support the claim that he would be a strong leader?

Third, the amount of evidence used must be sufficient to support the claim. Your evidence must not only be true and relevant, but also quantitatively sufficient. Of course, what constitutes a sufficient *amount* of evidence depends on your topic and your audience. If you are addressing a highly controversial issue or an especially skeptical audience, you will need to present more evidence. If your topic is relatively uncontroversial and your audience open-minded, less evidence may be required.

Consider, for example, what would be "sufficient" evidence to refute claims made by former player Jose Canseco that steroid use is widespread in Major

League Baseball. To fans of sluggers Barry Bonds and Sammy Sosa, the players' denials that they used performance-enhancing drugs might be sufficient. When the scandal reached Congress in March of 2005, however, members of the House Government Reform Committee demanded more proof. Sosa, Rafael Palmeiro, and Mark McGwire all denied—or at least refused to admit—that they had used illegal substances. Yet when executives from Major League Baseball (MLB) appeared before the committee, the legislators "all but scorned" their denials that baseball had a drug problem. Despite more than eleven hours of testimony, the committee remained unconvinced. "I have not been reassured one bit," Representative Steven Lynch of Massachusetts concluded.[14] Obviously, the baseball executives failed to provide *sufficient* evidence to overcome the committee's doubts.

There are, of course, no set rules to determine what constitutes sufficient evidence. In the final analysis, that depends on your audience—their existing knowledge and beliefs, their attitude toward the topic and the speaker, and their willingness to take the evidence you present at face value. That is one more reason to always analyze your audience carefully.

Major League Baseball (MLB) players Sammy Sosa (sitting next to his translator, Patricia Rosell), Mark McGwire, Rafael Palmeiro, and Curt Schilling appear before a House Committee investigating efforts to eradicate steroid use in baseball. The committee appeared unconvinced by later testimony from MLB executives that they were doing all they could to prevent drug abuse in the sport.

Warrants

Warrants are the general assumptions, principles, or rules that connect our evidence to our claims. Suppose, for example, that a politician claims that his opponent in the next election is "unfit for office." And suppose further that he bases that claim on the fact that his opponent never served in the military. In this debate, the evidence may not be in dispute; the candidate's service record is a matter of public record. But does fitness for office *require* military service? Is the claim that the candidate is unfit for office *warranted* by the fact that she did not serve in the military? In this case, the argument turns not on the evidence but on a general principle: that politicians who have not served in the military are unfit for office. For most Americans, of course, that would be a dubious assumption. Military service might *contribute* to one's fitness for office, but few Americans would agree that military service is a *necessary* qualification.

Some warrants may already be accepted by your audience and may go unstated in your argument. In the United States, for instance, most listeners would agree that, under our Constitution, everyone is entitled to fair and equal treatment under the law. Thus, we might use that warrant to link evidence about a particular policy— say, racial profiling by police—to the claim that the policy is unconstitutional. In that argument, there would be little need to back up or even state the warrant; most

Americans agree that our Constitution entitles us to fair and equal treatment. Our main burden, then, would be to prove that racial profiling does, in fact, exist, and that it violates the principle of "fair and equal treatment" under the law.

When we invoke general rules or principles that are themselves controversial, we may need to provide *backing* for those warrants. Returning to our earlier example, suppose that our hypothetical candidate claimed that his opponent was unfit for office because she was divorced or because she was gay. Does either of these characteristics warrant the argument that she is unfit for office? Fifty or sixty years ago, many people *did* view divorce as a moral failing that disqualified people from high political office. Today, some people still think one's sexual preference is a relevant political credential. Yet in an age of greater social tolerance, divorced candidates are now routinely elected to political office, and in many communities homosexuality is no longer seen as a political liability. The point, of course, is that warrants themselves are sometimes controversial, and that you may need to back them up with additional support.

The Burden of Proof

There is no such thing as an argument that is "reasonable" under any and all circumstances. What qualifies as a reasonable argument in one situation may not seem so reasonable in another, depending on the audience and the situation. One way to anticipate what *might* be considered a reasonable argument is to reflect on your burden of proof. Although meeting your burden of proof does not guarantee that you will "win" a debate, it does mean that you have made an argument that is at least reasonable enough to warrant further debate.

As we noted in the previous chapter, the theory of "presumption" and "burden of proof" is most familiar in the legal context. We have all heard how, in a court of law, we are *presumed* innocent until *proven* guilty. That means that a defendant has the *presumption* of innocence; the prosecution has the burden of proof. In civil cases, that burden of proof means that the prosecution must prove the defendant guilty by a "preponderance of evidence," while in criminal cases the burden of proof is greater: "beyond a reasonable doubt." Because more is at stake in a criminal trial, it makes sense that our system demands a higher burden of proof.

In public debates, the burden of proof is not so clearly defined, but there are certain expectations about what constitutes a *reasonable* case. In debates over public policy, for example, advocates of change have the burden of proof because change involves risk—because it means abandoning the known for the unknown. Advocates of new policies are therefore expected to establish, first, that there is some *need* for change. Then we expect them to present a specific *plan*, not only describing their proposed policy or program, but also explaining how it is to be implemented, funded, and enforced or administered. Finally, we expect policy advocates to prove that their plan is *workable*—that is, that is it feasible, will solve the problem, and perhaps even have some benefits or advantages over other possible solutions. In sum, a "reasonable" argument for a policy change answers these questions: Why do we need a new policy? What would that new policy entail? How would the plan be implemented and funded? Would it be workable and solve the problem? And why should we prefer that plan over other alternatives?

A reasonable argument does not end but begins the discussion. If you make an argument that is, on its first face, "reasonable" (in Latin, a *prima facie* case), you have a right to expect that your listeners will take it seriously. At the same time, you should be willing to defend your position in debate, perhaps responding to questions or even offering additional arguments and evidence. Part of making a reasonable argument is remaining open to further discussion. Democratic deliberation is an ongoing conversation, and you should never expect to have the "final word."

The Forms of Reasoning

Preview. *The process of reaching a sound conclusion involves reasoning, or the process of drawing inferences from known facts. Reasoning always involves some mental leap from the known to the unknown. There are four common types of reasoning: inductive, deductive, causal, and analogical. Understanding these types of reasoning and how they work can help you to build solid, well-reasoned persuasive speeches.*

Rarely do the facts speak for themselves. More commonly, we must *reason* from facts to conclusions, asking our audience to accept certain *inferences* we make. Thus, for example, we may know that 1,200 respondents to a poll said they planned to vote for the incumbent in an upcoming election—say, by a margin of 55 to 45 percent. But to predict the outcome of the election based on that evidence involves several assumptions and inferential leaps. First, of course, we assume that the respondents did not lie to the pollster. More important, we trust that those 1,200 respondents are *representative* of the larger population. Finally, we assume that no major events will change voters' minds between the time the survey was taken and election day. In short, we assume *a lot* when we reason from a poll to a prediction of how an election will turn out. All that we *really* know is how 1,200 people said they *planned* to vote. To predict the outcome of the election from that evidence requires an inferential leap.

The process of making inferential leaps is called *reasoning*, and it commonly assumes one of four forms: (1) *inductive reasoning*, where we reason from specific instances to a more general conclusion; (2) *deductive reasoning*, where we reason from an accepted generalization to a conclusion about a particular case; (3) *causal reasoning*, where we reason from cause to effect or effect to cause; and (4) *analogical reasoning*, where we reason that what is true of one case will be true of a similar case. Each of these types of reasoning involves inferences; none leads to conclusions that are absolute or certain. All lead to *probable* conclusions, with the strength of those conclusions dependent on the quality of our evidence and reasoning.

Inductive Reasoning

Inductive reasoning involves reasoning from a set of specific examples or a series of observations to a general conclusion. So, for example, we might investigate 10 medical malpractice cases in order to draw a more general conclusion about the typical case—and whether such cases tend to be justified or frivolous. Polls and surveys also rely on inductive reasoning, of course, when they generalize from a small but representative sample to some larger population. So, too, do many other kinds of scientific research: the forester reasons inductively about the threat posed by pine beetles based on an examination of a sample of trees; the sociologist interviews a sample of juvenile delinquents before drawing conclusions about what, in general, motivates bad behavior; and the communication researcher tests reactions to violent images on a small group of experimental subjects before drawing larger conclusions about the effects of media violence.

The strength of inductive reasoning rests on (a) the number of cases examined, and (b) the representativeness of those cases. The first questions one should ask about inductive reasoning are thus obvious: How many examples support the generalization? And is that a sufficient number to warrant the generalization? Representativeness is a trickier matter, since it requires us to make assumptions about the characteristics that might be most relevant to the generalization. When designing election surveys, for example, pollsters go to great lengths to design samples that reflect all the characteristics that might affect voting: age, gender, race, education, income, occupation, party affiliation, and so on. Similarly, it would be crucial to ask, when generalizing about the problem of medical malpractice, whether the cases examined were *typical* of malpractice suits. Did the cases involve errors *commonly* made by doctors? Or were they the sort of "freak accidents" that make headlines but do not commonly occur?

When reasoning inductively, you should *qualify* your claims carefully, avoiding sweeping generalizations based on just one or two examples. You also might attach reservations to your claim, identifying conditions under which your generalization might not hold true. Thus, for example, a pollster might conclude that the incumbent president will win reelection—*unless* there is a major crisis or a downturn in the economy before election day.

Finally, inductive reasoning can be strengthened by testimony and/or statistics that establish the reliability or representativeness of your examples. Are there experts willing to testify that your examples are typical of those they have encountered in their research? Do statistics show that the kind of examples you cite are common or widespread? In inductive reasoning, it is important that you not only have *enough* examples, but also that your examples are both true and typical.

Deductive Reasoning

Deductive reasoning is the process of drawing conclusions about specific cases based on inferences from a generally accepted premise or principle. A classic example of deductive reasoning, called a *syllogism*, looks like this:

A. All ministers are pious. *(major premise)*
B. Reverend Smith is a minister. *(minor premise)*
C. Therefore, we may conclude that Reverend Smith is pious. *(conclusion)*

Most of us do not think or talk this formally, of course, and it is rare in the world of practical affairs to reason from universal premises like "All ministers are pious." In the real world, we more commonly reason from *qualified* premises

("Most ministers are pious") to *probable* conclusions ("Reverend Smith is probably pious.").

Suppose, for example, that you were trying to persuade an audience that we cannot win the War in Iraq because we are fighting an indigenous, or "homegrown," religious insurgency. Your claim is that we cannot win; perhaps you have evidence that the insurgency is indigenous and motivated by religious beliefs. What's missing, of course, is what we earlier called the "warrant": the assumption that, in general, indigenous religious insurgencies are difficult to defeat. Of course, history may show that it is not *always* true that indigenous religious insurgencies prevail militarily, and you also may discover evidence that some of the Iraqi insurgents are neither "homegrown" nor religiously motivated. Thus, you would want to *qualify* your argument: "It will be *difficult* to win the war in Iraq because *many* of the insurgents are indigenous and motivated by strong religious beliefs."

Often speakers do not even state their premises because they are already accepted by their audience. That is, they assume that the audience will supply the missing premise from their own store of beliefs and values. Thus, for example, we might assume that our audience already believes that "politicians who have lied in the past will lie in the future." If we can prove that a particular politician has lied in the past, our audience will probably accept the conclusion that he or she is likely to lie again. This sort of reasoning is called a "rhetorical syllogism," or *enthymeme*. It reflects how we typically construct deductive arguments in everyday talk. If our audience does, in fact, already accept our general premises, these arguments can be persuasive.

If your audience is likely to be skeptical of your premises, you should not only state them but provide evidence to back them up. Suppose, for example, that you wanted to argue for a ban on selling carbonated soft drinks in school vending machines. Your deductive reasoning might look something like this:

Major premise: Sugary carbonated sodas are a major cause of the epidemic of obesity and related health problems in America.
Minor premise: School vending machines are the chief source of carbonated sodas for millions of young people.
Conclusion: Therefore, banning the sale of carbonated sodas in school vending machines will help combat obesity and related health problems among young people.

As with all deductive reasoning, the persuasiveness of this argument depends, in part, on whether you can prove that school vending machines are "the chief source" of carbonated sodas consumed by young people. But it also depends on whether your audience is willing to accept the major premise: "Sugary carbonated sodas are a major cause of the epidemic of obesity and related health problems in America." Thus, just to be sure, you might provide *backing* for that generalization, quoting something like the following statement from the Center for Science in the Public Interest:

The empty calories of soft drinks are likely contributing to health problems, particularly . . . obesity. Those conditions have become far more prevalent during the period in which soft drink consumption has soared. Several scientific studies have provided experimental evidence that soft drinks are directly related to weight gain. That weight gain, in turn, is a prime risk factor for type 2 diabetes, which, for the first time, is becoming a problem for teens as well as adults. As people get older, excess weight also contributes to heart attacks, strokes, and cancer.[15]

Causal Reasoning

Another everyday form of inference is causal reasoning—reasoning from effect to cause, or from cause to effect. Suppose, for example, that we notice a significant increase in crime or a decrease in the number of traffic deaths across the nation. We naturally want to know about the *causes* of these trends. By the same token, we often want to know what *effects* might result from some change in policy. What impact will a proposed welfare reform policy have on the number of people on welfare? Would allowing social security recipients to invest in private accounts help solve the system's financial crisis or provide more secure retirements for the elderly? These sorts of questions invite causal reasoning.

Causal reasoning is at the heart of all scientific investigation. In trying to solve the mysteries of the world, researchers routinely reason from cause to effect and effect to cause. What causes some volcanoes to violently explode, while others lay dormant for centuries? What caused the great chestnut forests of the Eastern United States to disappear? What are the causes of a recent increase in the number of high-school dropouts?[16] Why do some men become violent sexual predators, preying on innocent children? These are just a few of the questions scientists and social scientists are trying to answer through causal reasoning.

Scientists know just how difficult it can be to establish causation. In the natural world, causation is often complex, involving multiple causes or chains of causation. What is *the* cause of declining songbird populations? The answer is that there *is* no *single* cause. Some ornithologists point to climatic change, acid rain, or disappearing habitat as the primary culprits. Others emphasize the destruction of nesting habitats resulting from the planting of nonnative shrubs, competition or parasitism among different species of birds, or the proliferation of such predators as domestic cats, gray squirrels, and raptors. No doubt still more causes will be discovered as the research continues. The decline in songbird populations is a complex problem with multiple and dynamic causes. It is impossible to point the finger at any single cause.

Imagine how much more difficult it can be to prove what causes humans to do some of the things they do! What causes the anorexic literally to starve herself to death, or the bulimic to binge and purge? What leads people to a life of crime, or to a life of violence against others? Why do some people become obsessive about their work, neglecting their families and all of the pleasures of life just to "get ahead"? Again, these are complex questions with no simple answers. Even more than the natural world, human behavior involves systems of multiple and interrelated causes that even the best experts have difficulty sorting out.

In short, establishing causation is rarely simple. The responsible public advocate recognizes the difficulty of proving causation and seeks out the best information and evidence available from reputable sources. The responsible advocate also *qualifies* his or her causal claims, acknowledging that we can rarely assert causal claims with absolute certainty or talk about any single factor as *the* cause of a complex problem.

Analogical Reasoning

Consider the following two arguments, both of which you have probably heard before in one form or another:

1. "The War in Iraq is 'another Vietnam.' We should withdraw our troops before we get bogged down in another 'quagmire' that damages our reputation around the world and results in another humiliating defeat for the U.S. military."
2. "Politics is like a horserace. It doesn't matter who's first out of the gate, and even the best horses occasionally stumble. True champions have stamina, perseverance, and the courage to let others take the early lead. But as the race heats up, true champions emerge out of the pack, charging to the front with the race on the line. They have a nose for the finish line."

Both of these arguments are based on comparisons. Both illustrate *analogical reasoning*, in which we conclude that what is true of one case will also be true of the other. Yet, are the two arguments equally "reasonable"? Of course not. In the first example we are comparing one war to another war. This is what we call a *literal* analogy, comparing two similar examples. In the second, we are comparing electoral politics to a horserace. That is a *figurative* analogy, like the metaphors discussed in Chapter 11. Figurative analogies might be useful for illustrating a point or giving a speech stylistic color. But they rarely *prove* anything. If we hope to make serious, logically compelling analogical arguments, we should use only *literal* analogies.

The explanation for this is simple: the logical strength of analogical reasoning rests on the degree of similarity between the cases being compared. So, for example, if we really hoped to convince people that the War in Iraq is "another Vietnam," it would be important to establish as many similarities as possible between the two wars. Similarly, if we advocated a new recycling program for our city, it would be important to establish that such a program has worked well in a similar city—a city with the same population, perhaps, or one that has similar waste management problems. In short, the more

Bill Clinton was an effective advocate for welfare reform, persuading state leaders to try a number of new initiatives to "end welfare as we know it."

similar the cases, the stronger the analogical argument. That is why figurative analogies carry little persuasive weight.

Analogical reasoning is most frequently used in policy arguments. When proposing a new policy, you should investigate whether similar policies have been tried elsewhere. Then you might draw your evidence from places where the policy has already been tried. During the late 1990s, for example, welfare reform swept the nation, with state after state setting tougher eligibility requirements and adopting a variety of new policies to encourage aid recipients to find work. Overall, these reforms reduced the welfare rolls nationwide by more than half. Yet what worked in one state did not necessarily work in another, even though all the policies reflected the Clinton administration's goal of "ending welfare as we know it."[17]

Like all forms of reasoning, analogical reasoning involves a leap from the known to the unknown. In policy arguments, we may know that a particular program has, in fact, worked in the past. But we never know for certain what the future will bring, nor can we identify all the circumstances that might affect how well a particular policy might work. Thus, analogical arguments, like all arguments, should be *qualified* at the appropriate level of certainty. Based on the fact that a policy has worked in the past, we can conclude that it *probably* will work in the future. But we can never say that with certainty; the future is always, to some extent, unknown.

Fallacies of Reasoning and Evidence

Preview. *Arguments are unsound when they have flaws of reasoning or evidence, called "fallacies." Common fallacies occur when speakers draw irrelevant conclusions, employ faulty reasoning, provide insufficient evidence, or indulge in personal attacks.*

As we have pointed out, any claim is only as good as the reasoning and evidence that support it. Many things can go wrong during the reasoning process, leading one to draw a faulty conclusion. Following are some common *fallacies* of reasoning and evidence that ought to be avoided by speakers—and rejected by listeners. Also sometimes known by the Latin names given to them centuries ago, the fallacies may be categorized as:

- fallacies of relevance
- fallacies of faulty reasoning
- fallacies of inadequate evidence
- fallacies of personal attack

Fallacies of Relevance

Fallacies of relevance occur when a speaker, in effect, changes the subject, talking about matters that are simply not relevant to the issue at hand. Fallacies of relevance are sometimes deliberately employed to distract audiences and divert attention away from the real issues.

Appeal to Ignorance (Ad Ignorantium)

Speakers will sometimes try to convince audiences that because a certain proposition has not been proven wrong, it must be right! If a friend told you that it has never been proven that aliens from other planets have *not* visited earth, would you conclude that we have, in fact, been visited by aliens? Of course not! Yet we hear similar arguments every day from people who do not really have any evidence to prove their claims. A legislator, for example, might offer the following argument:

> I am convinced that my bill to require teachers to lead children in reciting the pledge of allegiance each day in school will instill stronger feelings of patriotism and loyalty to our country. So far, no one has been able to prove that I'm wrong about this. Why would anyone oppose teaching our kids to be more patriotic?

True, nobody can prove that reciting the pledge will *not* make children more patriotic. Yet neither does this legislator have any evidence that it *would* increase patriotic feelings.

The *ad ignorantium* fallacy may assume the opposite form as well: just because something has not been proven to be true does not mean that it is false. In the following example, a student committed the *ad ignorantium* fallacy in an argument about television's effects on children:

> So we've seen that, while there are instances which seem to suggest that some children act violently after watching television and some studies indicate that television violence can desensitize children to violent acts, no one has been able to establish a direct link between TV and violence. We can only conclude that television is not to blame for violent behavior among children.

This student may be right that nobody has established a "direct link" between TV and violence. But his own evidence suggests the *possibility* of such a link, and the fact that nobody has proven that connection conclusively does not mean that there is *no* link between TV and violence.

Appeal to Popular Beliefs (Ad Populum)

Sometimes known as a *bandwagon appeal*, this fallacy occurs when a speaker urges listeners to accept something simply because so many others accept it. Many of us are tempted to "follow the crowd," and public speakers sometimes take advantage of this by urging us to do something because "everybody is doing it." Knowing that other people support an idea or a policy is certainly one piece of information that you might want to take into account. But that fact alone should not be persuasive.

In a democracy, the majority rules, of course, so the fact that 63 percent of Americans support some plan may be *one* reason for adopting it. But majority support does not prove that it is a *good* policy—that it will solve some problem or serve the national interest. In American history, the majority has proven wrong on more than one occasion, and over time minority views sometimes *become* the majority view. In the following excerpt, for example, we hear a line of argument commonly used to silence debate over controversial wars. It was an argument heard during the Vietnam War, which most Americans initially supported but *later* came to oppose:

> The polls are clear, the people have spoken: the vast majority of Americans supports this war. The time for dissent has passed, and now is the time to support our men and women in uniform, no matter how we feel about the war.

There may well be good reasons for supporting our troops regardless of how we feel about a war. And in a democracy, majority opinion must be respected. Yet in a free society, we should never allow an appeal to popular beliefs to silence debate.

The Disconnected Conclusion *(Non Sequitur)*

Non sequitur is Latin for "it does not follow." In other words, this fallacy occurs when a conclusion simply does not follow logically from the arguments and evidence that precede it. In a sense, all logical fallacies are more specific types of non sequiturs. But when the problem with an argument is that, in general, the evidence simply is not relevant to the claim, we say that the speaker has committed a *non sequitur*.

To continue with our previous example, suppose now that our prowar speaker began the same way: "The polls are clear, . . . the vast majority of Americans supports this war." Instead of concluding that we should stop criticizing the war because a majority supports it, however, now imagine that our speaker said the following: "So, as we can see, the president's decision to go to war was constitutional under his powers as commander in chief." Here the problem is not that the speaker is asking us to jump on the bandwagon, but rather that public support for the war simply has nothing to do with the constitutionality of the president's actions. That is a question for experts in constitutional law, not a matter to be resolved by public opinion.

Appeal to Tradition *(Ad Verecundiam)*

You have probably heard this fallacy expressed this way: "We've never done it that way before." Or perhaps you have heard it expressed another way: "This is the way we've always done it." People get set in their ways, and speakers sometimes exploit this fact to argue against change. An advocate of change *does* have the burden of proof in a policy debate, but that does not mean that those who oppose change can simply respond, "We've always done it this way." Tradition is *not*, in itself, a good reason for sticking with the status quo.

Appeals to tradition are often heard in contexts where the ideas or policies being challenged have a long history. So, for example, the Virginia Military Institute appealed to tradition for many years to justify excluding women from its programs. In 1996, however, the Supreme Court, in *United States v. Virginia et al.*, ruled that women had a right to attend VMI under the equal protection clause of the Constitution.[18] Similarly, students at Texas A&M University resisted for many years efforts to end a 90-year tradition of building "the world's largest bonfire" on the eve of their annual football rivalry with the University of Texas. Yet after the 59-foot-high structure collapsed in 1999, killing 12 students and injuring 27 others, arguments about safety and liability finally prevailed over appeals to tradition.[19]

At Texas A&M University, it took a terrible tragedy to overcome appeals to tradition, as a log structure built for the "world's largest bonfire" collapsed, killing 12 students. Rescue workers are shown here at the scene of the tragedy.

Tradition can be a good thing, of course, but it is unreasonable to use it as a shield against compelling arguments for change. Change involves risk, and advocates of change must meet their burden of proof. But if they meet that burden, they have a right to a real debate, not a deflection of their arguments by appeals to tradition.

The Red Herring

The term *red herring* comes from an old practice of using the strong odor of smoked herring to throw hunting dogs off the track of a fox, either as a training exercise or to keep them out of farmers' fields. In argumentation theory, a red herring is an attempt to throw an audience off track by raising an irrelevant, often highly emotional issue that prevents critical examination of an argument. In a debate over whether prayer ought to be allowed in the public schools, for example, an advocate might divert attention from the real issues involved by declaring, "The issue here is whether we are going to allow atheists to determine what happens in our schools." Many who oppose prayer in schools, of course, are not atheists at all, but are simply concerned about the separation of church and state. The real issue is not the threat posed by atheists, but whether school prayer violates the Constitution.

Consider another example of how a red herring might distract attention from the real issue at stake. Imagine a defense lawyer saying the following:

> My client is a fine, upstanding citizen who has spent his life in community service. He was a Boy Scout leader, sang in his church choir, and coached Little League. This man has lived in this town all his life and never has been charged with a crime. Would such a man embezzle money from his employer?

Perhaps it is hard to imagine such a man embezzling money, but his attorney has avoided the real issue here. The man's guilt or innocence must be established by the evidence, not by a recitation of his personal virtues. The introduction of his exemplary life is a red herring, designed to distract attention from the real issue at hand.

The Straw Man

In the straw man fallacy, a speaker attributes a flimsy, easy-to-refute argument to his opponent, then proceeds to demolish it. In the process, of course, the speaker misrepresents the opponent's real position. In some cases, the speaker may even try to make the opponent look silly for making such a ridiculous argument. So, for example, an environmentalist might portray a so-called wise use advocate—one who supports *some* logging and mining on public lands—as favoring "the sale of our national forests to the highest bidder." That exaggerates the position of the wise use advocate, creating a straw man that is easy to attack.

Straw men have been prominent in debates over welfare reform in the United States. The following example is hypothetical, but it sounds like some of the arguments we actually heard during the welfare debates of the late 1990s:

> We need to find ways to reform the welfare system so that our tax dollars are not wasted on those who just want a free handout. Opponents of reform believe that anyone who doesn't want to work shouldn't have to. They argue that if a woman wants to have children out of wedlock, well, that's her right, and the state should take care of those children. I, for one, disagree with those who think that taxpayers' money ought to be used to encourage people not to work, not to get married, or to have more children out of wedlock. My opponents want to continue this culture of welfare dependency that has cost taxpayers billions of dollars. I say the time has come for a new approach.

Opponents of welfare reform never made such arguments, of course. Almost everybody agreed about the need for reform. The real debate was over what *sorts* of policies might get people off welfare and end the "culture of dependency." The welfare advocate who *favored* "free handouts" and *wanted* to see more children born out of wedlock was what is referred to as a straw man.

These fallacies—appeal to ignorance, appeal to popular beliefs, the disconnected conclusion, appeal to tradition, the red herring, and the straw man—all produce conclusions that do not follow logically from the evidence. They are all ways to distract attention from the real issues at stake. They all violate the spirit of deliberating in good faith.

Fallacies of Faulty Reasoning

Fallacies of reasoning are errors in analogical or causal arguments, or they may involve "arguing in circles" or creating false choices. Like fallacies of relevance, fallacies of faulty reasoning may be unintentional, reflecting only fuzzy thinking on the part of an advocate. Or they may be used deliberately as propaganda techniques.

False Dilemma

This fallacy occurs when a speaker suggests that we have only two alternatives, when in fact more than two alternatives exist. Typically this takes the form of an either-or proposition: "Either we fight to win in Iraq, or we 'cut and run' like we did in Vietnam." This reasoning is faulty, of course, because there are a number of policy options between the extremes of all-out escalation and total retreat.

The false dilemma is routinely evident in budget debates. Consider, for example, the following passage:

> The budget deficit has once again become a serious threat to our economy and to the future welfare of our children. The only way to make sure that the budget deficit doesn't continue to grow out of hand is to cut social programs. Some people may be hurt by this, but we have no choice—either we cut these programs, or we run the risk of huge budget deficits that will stop our economic growth and create a huge burden for the next generation of American taxpayers.

The problem here, of course, is that there are other choices possible. One choice is to do nothing and see if an improving economy takes care of the budget deficit. Another is to raise taxes to bring down the deficit. Still another is to combine cuts in social programs with tax increases. Perhaps radical cuts in social programs really are needed, but that remains to be proven. To say that we must *either* make drastic cuts *or* suffer huge budget deficits is to create a false dilemma.

The false dilemma may assume more complex forms, of course, proposing three or more false alternatives. Thus, for example, an advocate might say that we *must* do one of three or four things—or face horrible consequences. Again, what determines whether such reasoning is fallacious is not the number of alternatives per se, but whether the advocate has, in fact, listed *all* the alternatives. In dealing with complex issues, we typically have many options, so we should always be suspicious of those who say that we have only one or two choices.

Begging the Question

Begging the question occurs when a speaker makes a claim that *assumes* the very thing he or she hopes to prove. This typically takes the form of circular reasoning, where rather than offer support for a claim, the speaker simply restates the claim itself in different words. Thus, for example, a speaker might claim that "illegal immigrants are a drain on our nation's economy." When asked for evidence of that, the response might be: "Well, we all know that illegal immigrants utilize expensive social services yet pay no taxes." Here the speaker has not offered any evidence at all for the original assertion, but has simply restated the original claim in different, more specific terms. In effect, the speaker is offering one unsupported assertion as support for the other.

Speakers often attempt to disguise efforts to beg the question with words such as "obviously," "of course," or "as we all know." So, for example, a speaker might say the following:

> As we all know, capital punishment deters crime. Obviously, potential criminals will think twice before committing a crime if they know they will be executed if they are caught. With capital punishment reinstated in every state, we would, of course, see a dramatic reduction in the murder rate.

This speaker here claims that capital punishment deters crime. But what is her evidence? When forced to support her contention, she simply restated the same claim in another way, speculating that criminals "obviously" would "think twice" if they faced execution.

The Faulty Analogy

As we noted earlier, the strength of analogical reasoning depends on the similarity of the two things being compared. When speakers compare things that are not, in fact, similar, they commit the fallacy of "faulty analogy." There are no clear rules for when an analogy becomes "faulty," but *figurative* analogies—almost by definition— are logically faulty. Literal analogies *may* provide support for an argument, but the legitimacy of such comparisons is always open to debate. Suppose, for example, that an opponent of gun control made the following argument:

> Gun control is not a new idea. In Nazi Germany, guns were confiscated to prevent any groups from taking actions that might have undermined Hitler. In Cuba, Castro made sure that no one but his own Communist followers had guns. Whenever dictators want to stifle opposition, they take away people's guns. Now we have men and women in Washington who want to pass gun control legislation and take away your guns.

Is the speaker's comparison of gun control advocates in America to Hitler and Castro legitimate? Are the similarities between the United States and Nazi Germany—or between the United States and Cuba—sufficient to warrant such comparisons? The analogies used by this speaker may add *pathos* to the argument, but scaring listeners is not the same as arguing logically. From a logical point of view, this is a faulty analogy, ignoring the very different political cultures of the nations being compared. In addition, the analogy wrongly equates all gun control measures with the *confiscation* of guns. Not only is this argument based on a faulty analogy, but it also creates something of a "straw man."

The Slippery Slope

The fallacy of the slippery slope occurs when a speaker claims that some cause will *inevitably* lead to undesirable effects, ultimately resulting in some worst-case scenario. If you take the first step down the slippery slope, or so the reasoning goes, you will quickly slide all the way to the bottom. Again, opponents of gun control are probably guilty of this fallacy when they insist that any gun control legislation inevitably will lead to the confiscation of all guns. The slippery slope also can be heard in debates over rising tuition costs, as in this passage from a student speech:

> The Board of Trustees is once again considering raising tuition next year. This is a very dangerous action and threatens to undermine the very foundation of public education. A state university is supposed to serve the interests of the citizens of the state; if this tuition increase is implemented, it will be the first step in an ever-increasing spiral of rising costs for students. Eventually, only the rich will be able to attend our state universities and have the opportunity to get a college education.

Of course, it is not necessarily fallacious to argue that some action will lead to bad consequences down the road. We reason like that everyday—for example, in arguing that bad eating habits will lead to health problems. The slippery slope, however, treats *probable* or *possible* causal links as certain and inevitable, and it preys on fears of the worst-case scenario.

These fallacies—false alternatives, begging the question, the faulty analogy, and the slippery slope—are all perversions of otherwise legitimate forms of reasoning. It is not the form of reasoning per se that leads to fallacious arguments, but rather faulty assumptions and unwarranted inferential leaps in otherwise legitimate forms of reasoning.

Fallacies of Inadequate Evidence

Fallacies of inadequate evidence occur when a speaker simply does not have sufficient evidence to back up his or her claim. Generally, speakers who commit these errors have some but not enough evidence to prove their claims.

False Cause (*Post Hoc*)

This very common fallacy occurs when a speaker confuses a chronological relationship with a causal one. It is often known by its Latin name, *post hoc, ergo propter hoc*—"after this, therefore because of this." Simply because one event precedes another, of course, does not mean that it *caused* it. Crime might decline after a new gun control law is passed, but that does not prove that the legislation *caused* the decline. The economy might improve in the wake of tax cuts, but that does not mean that tax cuts *caused* the improvement. As we noted earlier, most political, economic, and social trends have complex, often multiple causes that may be difficult to sort out. In their effort to simplify explanations, advocates sometimes *oversimplify* causation, and that often takes the form of the *post hoc* fallacy.

The Hasty Generalization

This fallacy occurs when a speaker generalizes from too few examples. Perhaps the speaker observed but a handful of students at one university before concluding that all college students are binge drinkers. Or maybe she talked to just three senior citizens before generalizing that all seniors suffer from depression. In either case, the speaker committed a hasty generalization. He or she drew a sweeping generalization based on too few examples.

Highlighting the Post Hoc Fallacy

The Gun Control Debate

As is often the case in long-running, highly emotional public debates, *both* sides in the gun control debate have been guilty of logical fallacies. Indeed, one can often find the same logical fallacies committed by advocates both for and against gun control. Consider, for example, the following two arguments:

1. "The only policy that effectively reduces public shootings is right-to-carry laws. Allowing citizens to carry concealed handguns reduces violent crime. In the 31 states that have passed right-to-carry laws since the mid-1980s, the number of multiple-victim public shootings and other violent crimes has dropped dramatically. Murders fell by 7.65%, rapes by 5.2%, aggravated assaults by 7%, and robberies by 3%."

   Source: "The Media Campaign against Gun Ownership," *Phyllis Schlafly Report* 33, no. 11 (June 2000).

2. "[E]vidence shows that even state and local handgun control laws work. For example, in 1974 Massachusetts passed the Bartley-Fox Law, which requires a special license to carry a handgun outside the home or business. The law is supported by a mandatory prison sentence. Studies by Glenn Pierce and William Bowers of Northeastern University documented that after the law was passed handgun homicides in Massachusetts fell 50% and the number of armed robberies dropped 35%.

   Source: "Fact Card," Handgun Control, Inc.

Both of these examples commit the *post hoc* fallacy, reasoning that because a drop in crime occurred *after* new legislation was passed, the legislation must have *caused* the drop. In the first example, Phyllis Schlafly claims that "right-to-carry" laws "effectively reduce[d]" public shootings and violent crime. This claim is supported by statistics on falling crime rates since the mid-1980s in states that have passed such laws. In the second example, Handgun Control, Inc., claims that state and local gun control laws "work" to lower handgun crime—another causal claim. Again, the claim is supported by statistics on falling crime rates.

Violent crime fell generally in the United States in the late 1980s and 1990s, and a number of factors may have contributed to that trend. Moreover, neither Schlafly nor Handgun Control, Inc., provides us with the *comparative* data necessary to prove that declining crime rates can be attributed to the passage of new legislation. Schlafly provides no data from states that did *not* pass "right to carry" laws, so we have no way of knowing if crime declined any faster in states that passed such laws than in those that did not. Likewise, the pro-gun-control argument provides no basis for comparison to other states. In addition, it doesn't even make clear *when* Massachusetts' drop in crime occurred, except that it occurred "after"—"post hoc"—passage of the new handgun control law. Gary N. Curtis, author of *The Fallacy Files*, concludes, "The very fact that comparative information is *not* supplied in each argument is suspicious, since it suggests that it would have weakened the case."

Source: "Post Hoc," *The Fallacy Files*, www.fallacyfiles.org/posthocf.html (accessed June 23, 2006).

Consider the following argument from a student speech about funding for public schools in poor neighborhoods. Drawing on his own personal experience, the student made the following argument:

Last spring I spent three weeks as an observer in one of these poor schools. What I saw was lazy teachers and lazy students. Everyone seemed to be going through the motions. Students weren't motivated to learn and teachers were just too tired and frustrated to try to get anything out of these kids. I don't believe that pouring money into these poor schools will help them much. People just won't do things they don't want to do.

In this case, of course, the student probably did not actually observe "everyone" in the school. Moreover, all of the teachers and students he observed were from just this one school. To generalize about *all* "poor schools" based on this limited experience would be to commit a hasty generalization. Most reasonable people would agree that generalizing from just one school is unwarranted and fallacious.

These two fallacies—the false cause *(post hoc)* and the hasty generalization—occur when conclusions are drawn without sufficient evidence to support them. Evidence that one thing occurred after another does not prove causation, and sound inductive reasoning requires more than just one or two examples.

Fallacies of Personal Attack

Personal attacks are perhaps the most troubling fallacies, because they contribute to a negative tone in our public discourse and "turn off" many citizens. Fallacies of personal attack are sometimes used deliberately to shift attention away from the real issues at hand. They substitute name-calling and character assassination for engagement of other people's arguments.

Attack against the Person *(Ad Hominem)*

Unfortunately, this fallacy has become increasingly familiar in our political campaigns. While the character, integrity, or even the intelligence of a political candidate may be a legitimate "issue" in some elections, too often attacks on the person are substituted for arguments about a candidate's ideas or proposals. That constitutes an *ad hominem* fallacy.

Here is an example of an *ad hominem* fallacy that may sound vaguely familiar:

> The congressman's attack on the president's behavior is hypocrisy of the worst sort. The congressman has, for many years, had an extramarital affair. Who is he to attack the president for moral indiscretions? The congressman himself has behaved immorally on more than one occasion, showing his utter lack of sincerity when he preaches about "family values."

Now it might be true that the congressman is a hypocrite. If he attacked the president for his personal misconduct, perhaps it is only fair that he be subjected to the same sort of criticism. Still, this argument commits the *ad hominem* fallacy because it sidesteps the accusations against the president. The response does not deny the charges against the president, nor does it defend the president's actions. Instead, it attacks the person who raised the issue, in effect changing the subject.

Guilt by Association

This fallacy arises when we judge an idea, person, or programs solely on the basis of their association with other ideas, persons, or programs. If you view yourself as politically liberal, for example, you might be tempted to dismiss any idea or proposal that comes from the likes of Newt Gingrich or Rush Limbaugh. If you consider yourself conservative, you might be equally likely to dismiss—without serious thought or analysis—the ideas of a liberal like Howard Dean or Al Franken. Research shows that many people rate an idea, an essay, a speech, or even a painting higher if they are told that it came from a person they respect.[20] This, of course, illustrates the power of ethos. Put in more negative terms, however, it also suggests how we might discredit an otherwise good idea simply by associating it with an unpopular source.

Guilt by association refers to attacking the worth of people or their ideas solely on the basis of their associations. Rather than assessing the quality of an idea or argument, guilt by association dismisses it by connecting it to something already discredited in the minds of the audience. Consider, for example, the following hypothetical argument:

> How can we believe that this proposal is made with our best interests in mind? Mr. Morgan says it will save us a lot of money. But Mr. Morgan belonged to an investment club in which the investors lost almost everything. One member of that club was actually indicted for fraud, while others pulled out just in time to make a lot of money at the expense of their fellow members.

Mr. Morgan was not the one indicted for fraud, nor was he likely one of the members who pulled out "just in time." If he had been guilty of either of those things, his critic probably would have mentioned it. Indeed, Mr. Morgan may have been one of the victims himself. But bent on discrediting Morgan's proposal, the speaker suggests that his plan is suspect simply because of his former associations. This is fallacious because it diverts attention from the real issue at hand—whether the proposal is a good idea—by discrediting the source.

Arguments that are based on personal attacks—the *ad hominem* attack and guilt by association—are flawed because they sidestep the real issues. More than that, they debase the quality of our public discourse, undermining the politics of ideas with what former president Bill Clinton once called "the politics of personal destruction."

The fallacies we have discussed are not the only forms of faulty reasoning. Scholars of argumentation have identified hundreds of fallacies and propaganda devices, all of which can detract from the quality of our public deliberations. As responsible citizens, we should avoid committing fallacies in our own speeches, and we should learn to recognize and speak out against the fallacious arguments of others. Fallacies are among the techniques that demagogues and propagandists use to deceive and mislead the public. As citizens in a democracy, we need to recognize and resist such techniques and speak out against those who deliberately use them.

Summary

- Persuasion is a legitimate, essential tool of democratic deliberation, while demagoguery subverts reasoned deliberation with personal and emotional appeals.
- A "good" argument is not one that confirms our existing beliefs or "works" to persuade an audience, but one that is complete, reasonable, and meets certain tests of reasoning and evidence.

- *Claims* are the debatable assertions about fact, value, or policy that we put forward in a persuasive speech.
- *Evidence* provides support for our claims and should meet certain tests of quantitative and qualitative sufficiency.
- *Warrants* are the general assumptions, principles, or rules that connect our evidence to our claims.
- The burden of proof is the level of proof necessary in particular situations to warrant serious consideration of an argument.
- The process of drawing inferences from known facts is called *reasoning*.
- There are four common types of reasoning: inductive, deductive, causal, and analogical.
  - Inductive reasoning draws a general conclusion from a set of specific examples.
  - Deductive reasoning draws conclusions about specific cases from a generally accepted premise or principle.
  - Causal reasoning makes inferences from cause to effect or effect to cause.
  - Analogical reasoning infers that what is true of some known case is or will be true of a similar case.
- Fallacies are errors or flaws of reasoning and evidence.
- There are four major categories of fallacies: fallacies of relevance, fallacies of reasoning, fallacies of inadequate evidence, and fallacies of personal attack.
  - Fallacies of relevance include the Appeal to Ignorance, the Appeal to Popular Beliefs, the Disconnected Conclusion (or Non Sequitur), the Appeal to Tradition, the Red Herring, and the Straw Man.
  - Fallacies of faulty reasoning include the False Dilemma, Begging the Question, the Faulty Analogy, and the Slippery Slope.
  - Fallacies of inadequate evidence include the False Cause (Post Hoc) and the Hasty Generalization.
  - Fallacies of personal attack include the Attack against the Person (Ad Hominem) and Guilt by Association.

QUESTIONS FOR REVIEW AND REFLECTION

1. How would you distinguish between persuasion and demagoguery? Can you identify one or two public figures today who you would consider demagogues? *Why* do you think they deserve that label?
2. What makes for a good argument? Is a good argument always *persuasive*? Is there such a thing as a *reasonable* argument that people do not find *persuasive*? What, exactly, does it mean to say that an argument is *reasonable*, and what sorts of standards or tests might we use in judging arguments?
3. Distinguish among the different types of *claims* discussed in this chapter, and think of one example of each type of claim. Can you think of a major public controversy that still revolves around claims of fact? What about claims of value and policy?

4. What is meant by "burden of proof," and who would have the burden of proof in debates over (a) an allegation of wrongdoing by a public official, and (b) a proposal for a new tax policy? If you meet your burden of proof, what does that mean? Does that mean you "win" the debate?

5. Distinguish among the four types of reasoning discussed in this chapter and discuss what makes for strong inductive, deductive, causal, and analogical reasoning. Besides the examples given in the book, can you think of one more example of each type of reasoning that you have heard in a speech or public debate?

6. Which of the *fallacies of relevance* discussed in this chapter do you think are most common in today's political environment? In other words, do we hear more red herrings than straw man fallacies? More appeals to popular belief than appeals to tradition?

7. Are the fallacies discussed in this book *always* errors in reasoning? Are they *always* "illogical"? Is there ever a time, for example, when an appeal to popular beliefs is reasonable? Is an appeal to tradition ever legitimate? Is it ever reasonable to attack the person or to discredit the source of an argument because of the people or groups they associate with ("guilt by association")?

ENDNOTES

1. See Albert Fried, *McCarthyism: The Great American Read Scare: A Documentary History* (New York: Oxford University Press, 1997).

2. Aristotle, *Rhetoric*, trans. W. Rhys Roberts (Chicago: University of Chicago Press, 1952).

3. See Jeffrey K. Tulis, *The Rhetorical Presidency* (Princeton, NJ: Princeton University Press, 1987), 27–39.

4. For a detailed discussion of Wilson's rhetorical philosophy and his ideal of the "orator-statesman," see J. Michael Hogan, *Woodrow Wilson's Western Tour: Rhetoric, Public Opinion, and the League of Nations* (College Station: Texas A&M University Press, 2006), esp. 27–41.

5. Woodrow Wilson, "Congressional Government," *The Papers of Woodrow Wilson*, ed. Arthur S. Link et al., 69 vols. (Princeton, NJ: Princeton University Press, 1966–1994), 1:565–66.

6. In a recent survey sponsored by the McCormick Tribune Freedom Museum, for example, it was found that only about one in a thousand Americans could identify all five rights protected by the First Amendment: freedom of speech, freedom of religion, freedom of the press, freedom of assembly, and the right to petition the government for redress of grievances. About two-thirds of the sample were able to name freedom of speech as a First Amendment right, but fewer than a quarter (23 percent) named freedom of religion and only 10 percent identified freedom of the press as First Amendment rights. Interestingly, a number of respondents attributed other rights to the First Amendment that are not guaranteed by the Constitution at all, including the right to drive a car (17 percent) and the right to own pets (21 percent). Also, the study revealed that the characters in the television show *The Simpsons* were more familiar to most Americans than their First Amendment rights. See "Characters from 'The Simpsons' More Well Known to Americans Than Their First Amendment Freedoms, Survey Finds," McCormick Tribune Freedom Museum, news release, March 1, 2006, www.mccormicktribune.org/mtf/pressroom/2006/pr030106.htm (Accessed June 28, 2006).

7. Max Weber, *The Theory of Social and Economic Organization*, trans. A. M. Henderson and Talcott Parsons (New York: Oxford University Press, 1947), 358.

8. Abraham Lincoln, "First Inaugural Address (1861)," in *American Voices: Significant Speeches in American History, 1640–1945*, ed. James R. Andrews and David Zarefsky, 290 (New York: Longman, 1989).

9. For more on the rhetorical techniques typically employed by demagogues, see J. Justin Gustainis, "Demagoguery and Political Rhetoric: A Review of the Literature," *Rhetoric Society Quarterly* 20 (1990): 155–61.

10. James Darsey, *The Prophetic Tradition and Radical Rhetoric in America* (New York: New York University Press, 1997).

11. For a recent debate over the "rules" of public discourse, see Patricia Roberts-Miller, "Democracy, Demagoguery, and Critical Rhetoric," *Rhetoric and Public Affairs* 8 (Fall 2005), 459–76; and J. Michael Hogan and Dave Tell, "Demagoguery and Democratic Deliberation: The Search for Rules of Discursive Engagement," *Rhetoric and Public Affairs* 9 (Fall 2006), 479–87.

12. See Stephen E. Toulmin, *The Uses of Argument* (Cambridge: Cambridge University Press, 1958). Also see Wayne Brockriede and Douglas Ehninger, "Toulmin on Argument: An Interpretation and Application," *Quarterly Journal of Speech* 46 (1960): 44–53.

13. In law, the "reasonable person" is a "legal fiction" used primarily in negligence and contract law cases. Under this test, the court imagines how a "reasonable person"—a hypothetical person who is intelligent, informed, aware of the law, and fair-minded—might react to arguments before the court. So, for example, a negligence case might raise the question of whether a defendant took the necessary precautions to avoid an accident—with those "necessary precautions" defined, of course, by the "reasonable person" test. Would the reasonable person have anticipated the circumstances that led to the accident? What kinds of precautions would the "reasonable person" have taken? What would the "reasonable person" have recognized as his or her legal rights and obligations in the aftermath of the accident?

14. Sean Gregory, "Hall of Shame: Hearings Leave a Legend Stained, a Commissioner under Fire and a Game Still under Suspicion," *Time*, March 20, 2005, www.time.com/time/archive/preview/0,10987,1039703,00.html (Accessed June 10, 2006).

15. Center for Science in the Public Interest, "Liquid Candy: How Soft Drinks Are Harming America's Health," www.cspinet.org/liquidcandy/ (Accessed June 28, 2006).

16. See Nathan Thornburgh, "Dropout Nation," *Time*, April 17, 2006, 31–40.

17. See Thomas Gais and R. Kent Weaver, "State Policy Choices under Welfare Reform," Policy Brief 21, Bookings Institution, www.brookings.edu/es/research/projects/wrb/publications/pb/pb21.htm (Accessed June 22, 2006).

18. See *United States v. Virginia et al.*, www.law.cornell.edu/supct/html/94-1941.ZO.html (Accessed June 23, 2006).

19. See "Texas A&M University Bonfire Memorial," http://bonfirememorial.tamu.edu (Accessed June 23, 2006).

20. Jack L. Whitehead, "Factors of Source Credibility," *Quarterly Journal of Speech* 54 (1968): 59–63.

Speaking on Special Occasions

CHAPTER OBJECTIVES

After studying this chapter, you should be able to

1. Discuss the role of ceremonial speaking in a free society.

2. Explain how ceremonial speeches define and reinforce social values.

3. Identify and describe different types of ceremonial speeches.

4. Define *eloquence* and discuss the importance of style and delivery in ceremonial speaking.

At some point in your life, you will be called on to deliver a ceremonial speech—the type of speech that the ancient Greeks called *epideictic*. This is the sort of speech you deliver when you pay tribute to someone, present or accept an award, or mark some special occasion or event. Ceremonial speeches are often associated with culturally significant occasions: weddings, funerals, graduation ceremonies, awards banquets, conferences and conventions, or major political events. We also deliver ceremonial speeches to mark important dates in our history, such as Memorial Day or the Fourth of July.

Traditionally, ceremonial speeches were considered less "serious" than informative or persuasive speeches. In Aristotle's *Rhetoric*, for example, epideictic speeches were treated as mere "display," a sort of "poetic" speech in which speakers showed off their speaking skills but did not say anything of great political or social significance. According to Aristotle, epideictic speeches engaged in "praise and blame," and they focused on the present rather than the past or the future. Some have interpreted this to mean that the audiences for such speeches are mere "observers," judging the "skill of the orator" but not rendering judgments or collective decisions. In this view of epideictic speech, the speaker aims not to elicit action but only to influence "the general attitude of the audience toward a particular person or behavior."[1]

Today, we recognize that ceremonial speaking plays a crucial role in defining and sustaining our civic culture. More than a mere display of the speaker's skill, ceremonial speeches shape our collective identity, remind us of our history and traditions, and imagine the world "as it ought to be rather than as it is."[2] Epideictic speeches bring us together as members of a community, and they remind us of our responsibilities as citizens. Honoring our heroes and commemorating important events, ceremonial speeches articulate and reinforce important social values and strengthen the bonds that unite us. In short, ceremonial speeches help to sustain our civic culture.

We begin this chapter by reflecting further on the role of ceremonial speaking in a free society. Identifying four important functions of ceremonial speaking, we examine how epideictic speeches remind us of our heritage, celebrate our heroes, identify important social values, and give us inspiration and encouragement. Then we will reflect in more detail on the role of ceremonial speeches in articulating and reinforcing social values. In the third section of the chapter, we will review the wide variety of epideictic speeches we encounter in everyday life, ranging from brief speeches of introduction to historic inaugural and keynote addresses. Finally, we will discuss the importance of language and delivery in ceremonial speaking, reflecting on what it means to be "eloquent" and offering some tips for writing and delivering ceremonial speeches.

Ceremonial Speaking in a Free Society

Preview. *Ceremonial speeches are often presented on formal occasions and may be associated with important cultural rituals. Through ceremonial speeches, we remember the past, honor our heroes, celebrate shared beliefs and values, and offer inspiration and encouragement.*

New York Mayor Rudy Giuliani addressing the Republican National Convention in Madison Square Garden on August 30, 2004. Giuliani was an obvious choice to speak about his memories of 9/11 when the Republicans met in New York three years after the worst terrorist attack in American history.

Speeches given on ceremonial occasions are rich in symbolic content. They help to define who we are as a people and bind us together as members of a group, community, or nation. As we honor our heroes, pay tribute to those we love or have lost, or celebrate our accomplishments, we remind ourselves of our shared history and traditions. We articulate and reinforce our shared beliefs and values and find inspiration and encouragement to take on new challenges. Ceremonial speeches comfort us, inspire us, and reinforce our faith in ourselves and in one another. Ceremonial speeches may be ritualistic and symbolic, but in some ways that makes them even more important than other types of speeches.

Remembering the Past

In 1863, Abraham Lincoln pledged in his Gettysburg Address that the world would "never forget" the soldiers who "gave the last full measure of devotion" to assure that "government of the people, by the people, for the people" would not "perish from the earth." A century and a half later, New York mayor Rudy Giuliani, in an address to the 2004 Republican National Convention in New York, recalled that sunny September morning when he looked up and saw smoke pouring out of the World Trade Center—and realized that the world had changed forever:

> On September 11, this city and our nation faced the worst attack in our history. On that day, we had to confront reality. For me, when I arrived there and I stood below the North Tower, and I looked up, and seeing the flames of hell emanating from those buildings, and realizing that what I was actually seeing was a human being on the 101st, 102nd floor that was jumping out of the building, I stood there—it probably took 5 or 6 seconds; it seemed to me that it took 20 or 30 minutes—and I was stunned and I realized, in that moment, in that instant, I realized we were facing something that we had never, ever faced before. We had never been confronted by anything like this before.[3]

Remembering historic events is more than "mere ritual." When we remember the past, we come to a clearer understanding of ourselves and the challenges we face. We also look to the past for "lessons of history." In a variety of settings, ceremonial speakers recall past events to help define who we are, what we stand for, and where we are headed in the future.

Consider how just one historical event, the American Revolution, has supplied inspiration and guidance for generations of Americans. For the first generation of Americans, of course, the Revolution was a live memory, and for more than a decade large crowds gathered in Boston to commemorate an incident that took place on March 5, 1770: the so-called Boston Massacre. According to scholars, the Boston "massacre" was little more than a "barroom brawl" between "wharf-side rabble" and a few "surly" British soldiers. Yet between 1771 and 1783, some of the most famous orators in America came to Boston every year to reflect on the "massacre" and its "lessons."[4] Speaking on the fourth anniversary of the incident, for example, John Hancock, one of the signers of the Declaration of Independence, spoke about the threat posed by standing armies in a free society and declared: "[L]et our misfortunes teach posterity to guard against such evils for the future."[5]

During the Civil War, Abraham Lincoln also drew inspiration from the Revolution. Lincoln began his famous "Gettysburg Address" by referring to the founding and reminding his audience of the principles that more than 360,000 union soldiers died for during that bloody conflict: "Fourscore and seven years ago our fathers brought forth on this continent a new nation, conceived in liberty, and dedicated to the proposition that all men are created equal." After the war, a progressive Southerner, Henry Grady, also recalled the Revolution but for a different purpose: to urge Northerners to forget the "Old South" and embrace the "New South" of "union and freedom." As Grady reminded his audience, both Northerners and Southerners "were lost in the storm of the first Revolution," and out of that storm was born the "American citizen," who taught the whole world about the blessings of democracy.[6]

Today, we still invoke the Revolution as the source of our ideals and inspiration. Yet so, too, do we remember a long list of other historical events that have shaped our character and purposes as a nation: the Civil War, the abolition of slavery, the Great Depression, two World Wars, the Cuban Missile Crisis, and the assassinations of John F. Kennedy and Martin Luther King Jr., to name just a few. Many of those memories are painful, but they serve as important reminders. When speakers urge us to "Remember the Alamo" or the sacrifices of D-Day, they hope to inspire respect for our men and women in uniform. When they recall building the Panama Canal or landing a man on the moon, they hope to rekindle our "can do" spirit and inspire us to take on new challenges.

For today's generation, of course, the terrorist attacks of September 11, 2001, represent an important public memory. Already that day has been commemorated in countless ceremonial speeches, ranging from eulogies and dedications to keynote and commencement addresses. Whatever the occasion, the events of 9/11 have become a fertile source of "lessons"—both positive and negative—about the principles and ideals that define us as a nation. In the years to come, 9/11 will continue to both sadden and inspire, as speakers invoke memories of that fateful day in a variety of ceremonial settings.

Honoring Heroes

Part of remembering the past is celebrating our heroes. In honoring our heroes, we emphasize themes of *character* and *personal virtue*, hoping to inspire others by holding up role models worth emulating. In praising our heroes, we remind ourselves of the ideals that define the life well lived.

Some of our heroes are "larger than life," while others are ordinary people—our parents, teachers, neighbors, or friends. But whoever we count as a hero, we honor their achievements, invite them to share their wisdom with us, and mourn them when they die. Honoring our heroes allows us to speak about those personal characteristics we admire and to reflect on the social values we share as a community. Like remembering the past, honoring our heroes is an educational act, illuminating the "lessons" to be learned from their lives.

Some of the most famous speeches in our history have been eulogies to our national heroes. Campaigning for the Democratic presidential nomination in 1968, for example, Robert F. Kennedy delivered an impromptu eulogy to Dr. Martin Luther King Jr. just moments after learning that King had been assassinated in Memphis, Tennessee. After sharing the news with his predominantly African American audience, Kennedy summarized, in but a single sentence, the essence of King's "dream": "Martin Luther King dedicated his life to love and to justice between fellow human beings." Next, he elaborated on the "lesson" to be learned from King's life: "What we need in the United States is not division; what we need in the United States is not hatred; what we need in the United States is not violence and lawlessness, but . . . love and wisdom, and compassion toward one another, and a feeling of justice toward those who still suffer within our country, whether they be white or whether they be black." Finally, Kennedy urged his audience to rededicate themselves to the ancient ideals King championed: "Let us dedicate ourselves to what the Greeks wrote so many years ago: to tame the savageness of man and make gentle the life of this world. Let us dedicate ourselves to that, and say a prayer for our country and for our people."[7]

Over the course of American history, epideictic speakers have celebrated a remarkable array of heroes, ranging from presidents and explorers to military heroes, movie stars, great writers, and popular musicians. We still honor the founders of our nation, of course—George Washington, Thomas Jefferson, and Benjamin Franklin, among others. We also honor some of the presidents who came later: Lincoln, Roosevelt, and Kennedy, to name just a few. Yet ceremonial speakers have also paid tribute to philanthropists like Andrew Carnegie, great thinkers and writers like Einstein and Harriet Beecher Stowe, and successful entrepreneurs from Henry Ford to Bill Gates. Mother Teresa has been honored for her charitable work, and aviation pioneer Amelia Earhart for her courage and determination. Even controversial figures have sometimes found redemption in ceremonial speeches. While widely criticized in her own day, for example, we now honor Susan B. Anthony for her tireless efforts to secure the vote for women.

Occasionally, we even elevate ordinary citizens to the status of heroes. In his 1982 State of the Union Address, for example, President Ronald Reagan introduced the nation to a government worker named Lenny Skutnik, who had helped rescue people from a jetliner that had crashed into the Potomac River. "We don't have to turn to our history books for heroes," Reagan began. "They're all around us." Reagan then introduced Skutnik, who was sitting in the audience:

> Just two weeks ago, in the midst of a terrible tragedy, we saw again the spirit of American heroism at its finest—the heroism of dedicated rescue workers saving crash victims from icy waters. And we saw the heroism of one of our young Government employees, Lenny Skutnik, who, when he saw a woman lose her grip on the helicopter line, dived into the water and dragged her to safety.[8]

Since Reagan's speech, other presidents have honored "everyday heroes" in their State of the Union addresses, making the practice something of a tradition.

Honoring our heroes is not just a meaningless ritual. In doing so, we define the personal virtues and social values that we admire as a culture, and we create role models for others, especially our young people. Occasionally, of course, we also recall notorious or infamous figures in history, like Adolph Hitler or Saddam Hussein. In doing so, however, our mission remains essentially the same: to teach important lessons about personal character and civic virtue.

Celebrating Shared Beliefs and Values

Ceremonial speeches articulate and reinforce common beliefs and values. As you think about delivering an epideictic speech, you should ask: What is the occasion for this speech? What defines the audience as a group? Which of the group's victories or accomplishments inspire the most pride? What do they believe most deeply, and what principles do they cherish? These questions might lead you to an inventory of beliefs and values shared by your audience and, then, to the major themes of your speech. The shared beliefs and values you identify might be philosophical or practical, religious or political, social or economic. But whatever their nature, they reflect the audience's collective understanding of themselves.

In their inaugural addresses, U.S. presidents typically emphasize those beliefs and values that unite *all* Americans, regardless of party. In his celebrated inaugural address, for example, John F. Kennedy identified "freedom" as just such a value and embraced the responsibility of "defending freedom in its hour of maximum danger."[9] Similarly, Dwight D. Eisenhower concluded his second inaugural address by reemphasizing the themes of freedom and peace. Like Kennedy, Eisenhower articulated the ideals that he believed were shared by all Americans: "May the light of freedom, coming to all darkened lands, flame brightly—until at last the darkness is no more. May the turbulence of our age yield to a true time of peace, when men and nations shall share a life that honors the dignity of each, the brotherhood of all."[10]

Other ceremonial speeches revolve around the beliefs and values of smaller groups or subcultures, or they emphasize values associated with a specific occasion. In delivering the keynote address to a conference of newspaper editors, for example, a speaker might celebrate our constitutional guarantee of a free press, while commencement addresses invariably stress the value of education. Similarly, it might be appropriate for a minister to praise Jesus in a sermon before an audience of believers. In addressing a religiously diverse audience of civic leaders, however, the same preacher might celebrate the constitutional separation of church and state.

It is important to recognize that the shared beliefs and values of one group may be controversial or rejected altogether within another community. In a keynote address to the National Organization for Women, for example, one might expect to hear a celebration of feminist values, while speakers before a more conservative group might praise traditional family values. By the same token, the beliefs and values celebrated in some types of ceremonial speeches might be wholly inappropriate in others. In a humorous after-dinner speech, for example, one might "roast" the honoree by recalling some embarrassing flub or failure. At that same person's funeral, however, it would be the height of bad taste to recall such an incident.

Offering Inspiration and Encouragement

When speakers present awards, pay tribute to individuals, speak at commencements, or deliver "keynote" addresses, they offer encouragement and inspiration to their listeners. In effect, they deliver motivational speeches. A life well lived provides an example for all of us. Thus, the speaker accepting an award might suggest to the audience: "You can do this, too! I have every confidence." Similarly, the commencement speaker does not simply congratulate the graduates, but encourages them to continue striving—to "reach for the stars." Even a eulogy can be inspirational, reminding us that life is short and inspiring us to live life to the fullest. Whatever the specific type of speech, the goal remains the same: to inspire and encourage people to be good citizens, do good work, and "give back" to their communities.

Occasionally, speakers are called on to sustain people's morale through difficult times. That is precisely what British prime minister Winston Churchill did in one of his best-known speeches during World War II, an address to the House of Commons on June 4, 1940. In this famous speech, Churchill reported on a "colossal military disaster"—the evacuation of Dunkirk, in which French and British forces were driven off the European continent by the advancing German army. Churchill also mourned the loss of 30,000 men and warned of an impending invasion of the British homeland. Yet pledging to "defend to the death" his "native soil," Churchill reassured his fellow citizens that their cause would prevail:

> Even though large tracts of Europe and many old and famous States have fallen . . . into the grip . . . of Nazi rule, we shall not flag or fail. We shall go on to the end, we shall fight in France, we shall fight on the seas and oceans, we shall fight with growing confidence and growing strength in the air, . . . we shall defend our Island, whatever the cost may be; we shall fight on the beaches, we shall fight on the landing grounds, we shall fight in the fields and in the streets, we shall fight in the hills; we shall never surrender. . . .[11]

Churchill's pledge to "never surrender" illustrates the power of words to sustain public morale through even the most trying of times.

Social Values in Ceremonial Speaking

Preview. *Ceremonial speeches do not merely entertain us but perform important educational and cultural functions. Most important, they reinforce the shared social values that define us as a community. Sometimes ceremonial speeches affirm traditional values and work to preserve things as they are. Yet ceremonial speeches can also be powerful agents of change when they challenge prevailing values or point to contradictions between our ideals and our actions.*

In an informative speech, you hope to teach your audience something new. In a persuasive speech, you aim to change your audience's beliefs or opinions. In a ceremonial speech, however, your purpose typically is to articulate and reinforce *existing* social values. As the speaker on a ceremonial occasion, you aim to give eloquent expression to the beliefs and values *already* held by the audience.

Consider, for example, how a eulogy neither informs nor persuades, but rather reinforces existing beliefs and values. In delivering a eulogy, we may safely assume that we need not inform the audience about the person who has passed away. After all, people generally do not attend the funerals of strangers. Nor does the eulogist typically persuade, trying to convince us that the dearly departed was not such a bad fellow after all. Instead, the eulogist typically gives voice to the shared feelings of love and loss among family and friends. Put another way, the eulogist tries to "put into words" the feelings already held by the audience.

Ceremonial speeches supply the "glue" that holds our communities together. Even in ancient times, when ceremonial speeches were viewed as a kind of artistic performance, it was recognized that they also served important educational and cultural functions. In Greek funeral orations, for example, listeners were called on to imitate the virtues of the deceased,[12] while the Roman rhetorician Quintilian viewed education itself as a form of epideictic rhetoric.[13] Today, we recognize even more clearly the political, social, and cultural importance of ceremonial speaking. In a wide variety of contexts, ceremonial speakers not only help us celebrate special occasions, but also remind us of the values, traditions, and aspirations we share as a people. They also work to define our social identities, and they make implicit political arguments by honoring people associated with particular ideas and policies.

Some argue that because they articulate and reinforce *existing* social values, ceremonial speeches are inherently conservative.[14] Historically, however, ceremonial speeches have been powerful agents of change, invoking "shared values as a basis for promoting a vision of what could be."[15] That certainly was true of the most famous ceremonial speech in U.S. history: Martin Luther King Jr.'s "I Have a Dream" speech. It is also true of many other ceremonial speeches, ranging from abolitionist and suffrage speeches in the nineteenth century to contemporary speeches marking Earth Day or Gay Pride Week.

One of the most famous ceremonial speeches in our history was a Fourth of July speech in 1852 by a former slave named Frederick Douglass. Calling slavery "the great sin and shame of America," Douglas chose to mark Independence Day with an ironic speech highlighting the contradictions between our revolutionary ideals and the institution of slavery. Posing a famous question, Douglass called attention to the hypocrisy of a nation founded on the principle of liberty yet built on the labor of slaves:

> What to the American slave is your Fourth of July? I answer, a day that reveals to him . . . the gross injustice and cruelty to which he is the constant victim. To him, your celebration is a sham; your boasted liberty, an unholy license; your national greatness, swelling vanity; your sounds of rejoicing are empty and heartless; your denunciations of tyrants, brass-fronted impudence; your shouts of liberty and equality, hollow mockery; your prayers and hymns, . . . are to him mere bombast, fraud, deception, impiety, and hypocrisy—a thin veil to cover up crimes which would disgrace a nation of savages. There is not a nation on the earth guilty of practices more shocking and bloody than are the people of these United States, at this very hour.[16]

Calling on the nation to live up to its professed ideals, Douglas's speech illustrates how ceremonial speeches can be powerful agents of social change.

Actor Bill Cosby is a popular yet sometimes controversial speaker at commencement and awards ceremonies. He has become well-known for challenging African Americans to take resopnsibility for solving the problems in their own communities.

On occasion, ceremonial speeches even provide an opportunity for groups or communities to reassess their *own* traditions, beliefs, or social values. In a speech to civil rights activists in 2004, for example, actor Bill Cosby asked African Americans to honor the pioneers of the civil rights movement by facing up to the problems in their own communities. The speech, featured in *Focus on Civic Engagement* on page 447 shows how ceremonial speeches can challenge an audience to reassess their own values even as they celebrate common heroes and a shared history.

The Forms of Ceremonial Speech

Preview. *There are many different kinds of ceremonial speeches: introductions, presentation and acceptance speeches, welcome and farewell speeches, commemoration and commencement speeches, tributes and eulogies, inaugural and keynote addresses, after-dinner speeches, and even some sermons. Each type of ceremonial speech is unique, but all share the same basic mission: to reflect on the significance of a special occasion and to give voice to the shared beliefs and values of the audience.*

What does a commencement address have in common with a eulogy? A keynote address with an after-dinner speech? The answer, as we have already suggested, is that they are all ceremonial speeches, or what the ancient Greeks called *epideictic*. They are all speeches delivered on special occasions, when people gather to honor other people or to celebrate some special anniversary or event. Those special occasions

Bill Cosby's "Pound Cake" Speech

On May 17, 2004, actor Bill Cosby accepted an award from the National Association for the Advancement of Colored People (NAACP) for his generous support of historically black colleges and universities. The occasion was a gala celebration commemorating the 50th anniversary of *Brown v. Board of Education*, the landmark Supreme Court decision desegregating America's public schools. The occasion called for a celebration of the civil rights movement and the progress of African Americans since that landmark decision. For Cosby, however, it also was an occasion for serious reflection on the problems facing the black community in America, particularly in parenting, education, and popular culture.

Proud of both his acting career and his doctorate degree in education, Cosby thanked the gathered dignitaries for the award and paid tribute to those who had fought for equal educational access 50 years earlier. But that is where the resemblance to a typical ceremonial speech ended. Cosby devoted most of the address to lamenting the high dropout rate among black students, the large number of young black males in jail, and the problem of black women "having children by five, six different men." Blacks could not "blame white people" for these problems, Cosby insisted, nor could they just keep "asking Jesus" for help. The problem was a lack of parenting, along with a materialistic culture that devalued education. As Cosby put it: "They're buying things for the kid—$500 sneakers—for what? They won't buy or spend $250 on *Hooked on Phonics*."

Cosby criticized those who blamed all their problems on the police or the criminal justice system. "Looking at the incarcerated," he said, "these are not political criminals. These are people going around stealing Coca Cola. People are getting shot in the back of the head over a piece of pound cake! Then we all run out and are outraged: 'The cops shouldn't have shot him.' What the hell was he doing with the pound cake in his hand?" Cosby

also criticized those who put their "clothes on backwards," pants "down around the crack," and took African names like Shaniqua, Shaligua, or Mohammed. "Those people are not Africans," Cosby observed; "they don't know a damned thing about Africa." Pointing to fashion trends as a "sign of something . . . wrong," Cosby concluded by making his point directly: "What's the point of giving them strong names if there is not parenting and values backing it up?"

Recalling those who had sacrificed in the fight for school desegregation, Cosby observed that the early civil rights activists must be "wondering what the hell happened." All these people "marched and were hit in the face with rocks and punched in the face to get an education," and now we have "these knuckleheads" walking around "who don't want to learn" proper English. These people are not "funny anymore," Cosby concluded. They were "faking" and forcing others to "pick up the tab" because they did not "want to accept that they have to study to get an education."

Not surprisingly, Cosby's speech provoked controversy. The audience reacted with a mixture of "astonishment, laughter, and applause," and none of the speakers who followed, including NAACP president Kweisi Mfume, seemed "amused in the slightest."[17] Later, cultural critic Michael Eric Dyson accused Cosby of blaming poor people rather than white racism or failed policies for problems in the black community.[18] Cosby, however, refused to apologize. Speaking several weeks later in Chicago, he accused his critics of trying to hide the black community's "dirty laundry" and dismissed concerns that white racists might use his comments "against our people." "Let them talk," he said.[19]

Source: Bill Cosby, "Pound Cake Speech," *American Rhetoric*, www.americanrhetoric.com/speeches/billcosbypoundcakespeech.htm (Accessed July 21, 2006.)

vary widely, of course, so there are important differences between, say, an inaugural address and a eulogy. Yet all ceremonial speeches have the same basic mission: to reflect on the larger meaning of the occasion and to "put into words" the shared beliefs and values of the audience.

The Speech of Introduction

The speech of introduction sometimes sounds like an informative speech, introducing us to an unknown speaker. More commonly, it celebrates the achievements of a well-known speaker who has been invited to speak on a special occasion.

Many people who introduce other speakers underestimate the importance of their role. They prepare very little, hastily scratching down a few notes about the speaker or quickly underlining a few points on the speaker's résumé. Some cop out completely, saying, "I'm delighted to welcome our speaker tonight, a person who needs no introduction." Others go to the opposite extreme, giving a lengthy introduction to a person who is already quite familiar to the audience. When introducing other speakers, keep in mind your purpose: to *introduce* another speaker, not to steal the spotlight yourself. You should never take away from the principal speaker's time or try to upstage his or her message.

The effective speech of introduction should do three things. First, it should extend a genuinely warm welcome to the speaker. Second, it should reinforce the speaker's ethos by emphasizing key educational or professional accomplishments. Finally, it should provide listeners with any information they might need to understand or process the speech. At the very least, the person introducing the main speaker should mention the topic or title of the speech, and the introductory speaker also might indicate whether the speaker will take questions following the address.

Although most introductory speeches are short, you still should prepare carefully. Here are just a few tips for preparing a good speech of introduction:

- *Do your homework.* As any speech, the speech of introduction should be well researched. Study any materials the speaker has provided, such as a biographical sketch or résumé. Call and chat with the speaker if you lack information, and make sure to ask about the topic or title of the speech.
- *Look for connections between the speaker and the audience.* Most speakers have accomplished many things. You cannot cover them all. You will want to highlight information that would be important for your group to know. What does the speaker have in common with this particular audience? What values do they share? If you are able to make these connections, you will assist the speaker in establishing common ground with the audience.
- *Stay focused on the speaker.* The purpose of the speech of introduction is to introduce the speaker, not focus attention on yourself. Some people end up sharing stories about how they met the speaker or talk about their common experiences. It may be fine to share a brief anecdote, but do not get carried away.

Welcome and Farewell Addresses

Comings and goings do not, under ordinary circumstances, inspire speech making. When you come back from your vacation, you do not expect your neighbor to deliver a speech. When the president of the United States visits another country, however, we *do* expect speeches, both upon his arrival and as he prepares to depart.

In addition, politicians and other prominent people often give "farewell addresses" at the end of their careers, reflecting on their years of service or giving advice to their successors.

Welcome addresses are not just for world leaders. They are also common at conventions, festivals, trade shows, and other large public gatherings. When a college or university hosts an academic conference, for example, it is common for a dean or even the president of the university to offer a few words of welcome. Similarly, when a city attracts a major business conference or trade show, the mayor or some other local official typically welcomes the group. Generally, the task of the speaker in such situations is simple: on behalf of the hosts, convey a sincere welcome. When welcoming a group, you also might offer tips for making the most out of their visit. The mayor's welcome might mention some local attractions, for example, while a conference organizer might preview some highlights of the upcoming meeting.

Farewell addresses are sometimes short, simple expressions of gratitude. Yet even short farewells can be powerfully moving. On July 4, 1939, for example, one of the greatest players in the history of baseball, Lou Gehrig, delivered a farewell address that was barely 250 words long, but it said everything that needed to be said to the 62,000 fans at Yankee Stadium. Struck down in the prime of his career by amyotrophic lateral sclerosis (ALS), a rare degenerative disease later named Lou Gehrig's disease, the all-star player began by mentioning his "bad break"—a reference to the terrible disease that would take his life just 2 years later. Then proclaiming himself "the luckiest man on the face of the earth," Gehrig shifted the focus to his positive experiences over 17 years of professional baseball. "Sure I'm lucky," Gehrig repeated as he recalled the "kindness and encouragement" of the fans, all the great players he had known, and even the support of his mother-in-law. Fighting back tears, Gehrig concluded, "So, I close in saying that I might have been given a bad break, but I've got an awful lot to live for." When Gehrig finished, there was "not a dry eye in Yankee Stadium," and the speech remains "one of the most poignant and emotional moments in the history of American sports."[20]

Not nearly so sentimental was Dwight D. Eisenhower's famous "farewell address" on January 17, 1961. Stepping down after two terms as president, Eisenhower took to the airwaves "with a message of leave-taking and farewell," including just a "few final thoughts" about matters of politics and national security. Those "few thoughts" turned into a somber and famous warning about "the acquisition of unwarranted influence" by what he labeled the "military-industrial complex." Urging his fellow citizens to avoid becoming "captive" to the "scientific-technological elite," Eisenhower worried out loud about how the technology of war was outpacing human understanding. He then closed with a hope and a prayer: that "in the goodness of time, all peoples will come to live together in a peace guaranteed by the binding force of mutual respect and love."[21]

Not all welcome and farewell addresses are so historic or philosophical, of course. Many consist of little more than a few brief remarks, thanking a visitor for coming or bidding a fond farewell. Like all ceremonial speeches, however, welcome and farewell addresses should be carefully prepared and adapted to the particular audience and situation in which they are given.

Presentation and Acceptance Speeches

Award ceremonies may or may not be occasions for formal speeches. Nowadays, most presentation and acceptance speeches consist of a few brief remarks, with presenters announcing the winner of the award and the winner simply thanking the presenter and perhaps a few other people. On a few occasions, however, an award ceremony calls for a longer, more substantive speech. If you someday win the Nobel Peace Prize, for example, you will be asked to deliver a formal speech before a distinguished audience of royalty and Nobel laureates in Oslo, Norway. With the King and Queen of Norway and several hundred guests in attendance, you will express your gratitude and reflect on the larger significance of the Nobel Prize.

That is precisely what His Holiness the Dalai Lama did in his Nobel Prize acceptance speech in 1989. Like most acceptance speeches, the Dalai Lama's address began with an expression of gratitude and humility: "I am very happy to be here with you today to receive the Nobel Prize for Peace. I feel honored, humbled and deeply moved that you should give this important prize to a simple monk from Tibet." Then, he offered his interpretation of the award itself as "recognition of the true value of altruism, love, compassion and non-violence." Accepting the award "on behalf of the oppressed everywhere," the Dalai Lama spoke of the injustices against his own Tibetan people and his determination, despite their suffering, to see that their "long struggle" remain "non-violent and free of hatred." Transcending that immediate conflict, he then articulated the broader, more universal principles that motivated his efforts to build a more peaceful world:

> I believe all suffering is caused by ignorance. People inflict pain on others in the selfish pursuit of their happiness or satisfaction. Yet true happiness comes from

His Holiness the Dalai Lama, winner of the 1989 Nobel Prize for Peace, speaking on a less formal occasion.

a sense of brotherhood and sisterhood. We need to cultivate a universal responsibility for one another and the planet we share. Although I have found my own Buddhist religion helpful in generating love and compassion, . . . I am convinced that everyone can develop a good heart and a sense of universal responsibility with or without religion.[22]

Generally, the formula for *presenting* an award is simple: introduce yourself and your purpose in speaking, say a few words about the purpose and history of the award itself, then extol the virtues of the recipient. Sometimes the winner will be known in advance; on other occasions, you might reveal the recipient in your speech. In either case, your goal is to deliver a speech that clearly expresses the purpose of the award and honors the recipient.

When *accepting* an award, you want to convey a sincere sense of gratitude, as well as acknowledge the support of others who may have contributed to your success. This does not mean that you should read a long list of names, including everyone who has ever done you a favor. But you do want to thank those most responsible for your moment in the limelight—a teacher or a coach who prepared you for a competition, perhaps, or a partner or spouse who supported you. Finally, you might acknowledge the deeper meaning of the award, using language that fits the dignity of the occasion. Of course, you also want to show that you genuinely appreciate the honor.

Whether presenting or accepting an award, it is important that you do the following:

- *Learn as much as you can about the award.* Knowing about the award—its history and meaning—can help you prepare your speech. If you are the first person to present or receive the award, you may want to note that fact. If other people have received the award previously, you might want to acknowledge one or two of those previous winners.
- *Plan and practice your speech in advance.* A person asked to *present* an award typically prepares a speech in advance, but some people think it is wrong or even "bad luck" to prepare to *accept* an award. That may explain why we hear so many bad speeches at the Academy Awards! Generally, however, you will be told in advance if you have won some award and whether you are expected to speak at the awards ceremony. In that case, you definitely should prepare the speech ahead of time. Even if you will not know whether you have won an award before the ceremony itself, you can still sketch out some brief remarks— just in case you *do* win. Then, if you win, you can deliver those remarks extemporaneously, without pulling notes or a manuscript out of your pocket. After all, you do not want to look *too* prepared, as if you fully *expected* to win!
- *Make your tone and language fit the occasion.* Presentation and acceptance speeches are usually delivered in formal settings, and your language should reflect a sense of dignity. Your tone should be sincere. This is a time to speak formally yet "from the heart."
- *Make your speech brief.* Most presentation and acceptance speeches should be very brief, probably no longer than a minute or two. In many settings where

awards are presented, there is other business to conduct, perhaps even a keynote speaker. So a brief yet carefully crafted speech is usually expected and appreciated.

Commemoration and Commencement Speeches

A commemoration is a ceremonial speech that marks an important date or event, while a commencement address celebrates one specific type of event: a graduation ceremony. Commemorative speeches are heard on a wide variety of occasions, ranging from national holidays to dates with special significance for particular groups to personally significant occasions like birthdays or wedding anniversaries. We may hear a commemorative speech on the Fourth of July, or we might hear one marking Black History Month. We still hear speeches commemorating the bombing of Pearl Harbor on December 7, 1941—a "date which will live in infamy," as FDR correctly predicted. We also hear speeches commemorating more positive events, such as the Wright Brothers' first flight at Kitty Hawk or Astronaut Neil Armstrong's first step on the moon. Some people reserve formal commemorative speeches for public holidays, while others may view their own birthday or retirement party as an occasion for speech making. People still toast the bride and groom at wedding receptions, although toasts often consist of a few impromptu remarks rather than prepared speeches.

The commencement address, of course, is a special kind of commemorative speech. Delivered at graduation ceremonies, commencement speeches have acquired an unfortunate reputation for being dull, predictable, and lacking in substance. Indeed, graduation speakers often joke about the insignificance of commencement speeches and promise to keep their remarks brief. Speaking to the graduates of Howard University in 1994, for example, former secretary of state Colin Powell cited a make-believe poll on student attitudes toward commencement addresses, then joked about how most people forget their commencement speaker:

> The real challenge . . . of being a commencement speaker . . . is trying to figure out how long you're gonna talk. If you ask the students, the answer is very, very simple. Talk for about four minutes and then sit down. Polls have been taken that show that ten years after the event, 80 percent of all graduating students don't have a clue who their commencement speaker was. Well, you ain't gonna do that to me. The name is Powell, P-o-w-e-l-l.[23]

Despite their bad reputation, commencement addresses have played an important role in American history. Indeed, some of the most famous and memorable speeches in our history have been delivered at graduation ceremonies. With Hitler's armies overrunning Europe in 1940, for example, Franklin Delano Roosevelt used a commencement address at the University of Virginia to condemn the invasion of France by Mussolini's Italian fascists. "On this tenth day of June 1940," the president solemnly intoned, "the hand that held the dagger has stuck it into the back of its neighbor."[24] President John F. Kennedy delivered another historic commencement address at American University on June 10, 1963. Speaking at the height of the cold war, Kennedy used the occasion to reflect on the horrors of modern war. Kennedy's address had a remarkable effect on world opinion and is still considered one of the greatest speeches in American history. Far from a series of platitudes about the "challenges of life," Kennedy's speech thoughtfully reflected on the insanity of war in the atomic age:

> I speak of peace because of the new face of war. Total war makes no sense in an age where great powers can maintain large and relatively invulnerable nuclear forces and refuse to surrender without resort to those forces. It makes no sense in an age where a single nuclear weapon contains almost ten times the explosive force delivered by all the allied air forces in the Second World War. It makes no sense in an age when the deadly poisons produced by a nuclear exchange would be carried by wind and water and soil and seed to the far corners of the globe and to generations yet unborn.
>
> Today the expenditure of billions of dollars every year on weapons acquired for the purpose of making sure we never need them is essential to the keeping of peace. But surely the acquisition of such idle stockpiles—which can only destroy and never create—is not the only, much less the most efficient, means of assuring peace. . . . I realize the pursuit of peace is not as dramatic as the pursuit of war, and frequently the words of the pursuers fall on deaf ears. But we have no more urgent task.[25]

Not all commencement speeches address such weighty and serious topics, of course. Most focus on the immediate event—the graduation ceremony—and offer advice on how to find success and happiness in life. Like all commemorative speeches, commencement addresses should reflect on the larger significance of the day and offer inspiration and guidance. But they are also part of a celebration and should, as a rule, be positive and upbeat in tone.

Tributes and Eulogies

We commemorate events, but we pay tribute to *people*. And, of course, there are no more important speeches than those with which we celebrate our heroes and honor our dead. In paying tribute to people—living or dead—we both reinforce our shared social values and define the meaning of *virtue* and *character*. By recognizing the special talents, unique accomplishments, and extraordinary contributions of people we admire, we define the life well lived and create role models for the next generation.

Tributes to living people are delivered on many occasions, such as award ceremonies, birthdays, anniversaries, and retirement celebrations. Whatever the occasion, the purpose remains the same: to highlight the person's unique contributions or talents and to praise them as individuals. In a speech honoring composer John Williams at the Kennedy Center for the Performing Arts, for example, filmmaker Steven Spielberg called Williams a "national treasure," as "American as apple pie."[26] At a White House ceremony, Secretary of Defense Donald Rumsfeld praised a very different man in similar terms, calling economist Milton S. Friedman "a rare talent—indeed, a talent to be treasured." Praising Friedman for "unleashing the power of human freedom," Rumsfeld marked the ninetieth birthday of this champion of free markets by crediting him with changing "the course of history."[27]

Television star Oprah Winfrey speaking at a memorial service for Rosa Parks in Washington, D.C., on October 31, 2005.

Funerals are typically private affairs, with eulogists mourning the loss and giving voice to the pain and grief of loved ones. When famous people die, however, eulogists typically say more, proclaiming the deceased an inspiration, perhaps even a national "hero." Speaking at the funeral of civil rights pioneer Rosa Parks, for example, Oprah Winfrey recalled how her father had told her about "this colored woman who had refused to give up her seat," and she imagined that Parks must have been "really big"—"at least a hundred feet tall." When she had the honor of meeting Parks, of course, she was in for a surprise. "Here was this petite, almost delicate lady who was the personification of grace and goodness." Winfrey thanked Parks at that meeting for all she had done for African Americans, and she thanked her again at her funeral, crediting Parks with all that she had achieved in life: "That day that you refused to give up your seat on the bus, you, Sister Rosa, changed the trajectory of my life and the lives of so many other people in the world."[28]

The death of a president or other political leader likewise tends to inspire eulogies that go beyond simply mourning. Typically, eulogies for political leaders urge us to honor their legacy by continuing their work. In a speech to Congress two weeks after the assassination of President Kennedy, for example, Lyndon Johnson mourned Kennedy's death, reminding the nation that the "greatest leader of our time" had been "struck down by the foulest deed of our time." Voicing the sentiments of millions, Johnson added: "No words are sad enough to express our sense of loss." Yet then repeating "let us continue," Johnson declared it the "duty" of all Americans to carry on Kennedy's crusade for civil rights and world peace, thereby assuring that "John F. Kennedy did not live or die in vain."[29]

Inaugural and Keynote Addresses

Inaugural addresses are speeches we give upon assuming a new office or position. Inaugural addresses may be delivered by newly appointed corporate CEOs, incoming officers of private clubs or fraternal associations, or newly elected politicians. The best-known inaugural addresses, of course, are delivered every four years by the newly elected president of the United States. Indeed, a handful of presidential inaugurals—those of Thomas Jefferson, Abraham Lincoln, Franklin Delano Roosevelt, and John F. Kennedy—are counted among the greatest speeches in U.S. history.[30] Like all inaugural addresses, presidential inaugurals perform certain rituals of office taking, such as articulating one's "vision" of the future. Yet presidential inaugurals also perform other political functions, such as reunifying the nation after a divisive campaign or laying the groundwork for a specific legislative agenda.

The power of an inaugural address to build unity after a divisive election is perhaps best illustrated by Thomas Jefferson's celebrated inaugural address in 1801. During the election of 1800, sharp partisan divisions emerged for the first time in U.S. history. The Federalists, led by John Adams and Alexander Hamilton, favored a strong central government. The Republicans, led by Jefferson, wanted government to play a more limited role. Both parties claimed to be the true heirs to the American Revolution, and both suspected the other of conspiratorial designs, even disloyalty. The campaign was one of the most bitter in all of American history; some even doubted that the Federalists would relinquish power peacefully. When he delivered his inaugural address, few expected Jefferson to reach out to the Federalists in a spirit of reconciliation. Yet he did just that, calling the election a mere "contest of opinion" and declaring that, *of course*, all would now "unite in common efforts for the common good." Urging his "fellow citizens" to "unite with one heart and one mind," Jefferson declared that "every difference of opinion is not a difference of principle," then delivered the most famous lines of the address: "We are all Republicans; we are all Federalists. If there be any among us who would wish to dissolve this Union or change its republican form, let them stand undisturbed as monuments of the safety with which error of opinion may be tolerated where reason is left free to combat it."[31]

John F. Kennedy delivering his inaugural address in Washington, D.C., on January 20, 1961. Kennedy's speech, along with those of Jefferson, Lincoln, and Franklin Delano Roosevelt, is counted among the greatest inaugural addresses in American history.

Other inaugural addresses have been more like policy addresses, sketching at least the broad outlines of the new president's agenda. In his first inaugural, for example, Franklin D. Roosevelt proposed no detailed plan for combating the Great Depression, but he did promise "action, and action now" before sketching the major aims of his New Deal policies: "put people to work," make better use of natural resources, support agriculture, stop foreclosures on homes and small farms, "drastically reduce" the costs of government, unify relief activities, and establish "national planning" and "supervision of all forms of transportation and of communications . . . that have a definitely public character."[32] Similarly, John F. Kennedy's inaugural address foreshadowed his administration's aggressive cold war policies by sounding a metaphorical trumpet and calling his fellow Americans to "a long twilight struggle." Speaking as the voice of a "new generation" of Americans—"born in this century, tempered by war, disciplined by a hard and bitter peace, [and] proud of our ancient heritage"— Kennedy made clear his determination to defend freedom around the world: "Let every nation know, whether it wishes us well or ill, that we shall pay any price, bear any burden, meet any hardship, support any friend, oppose any foe to assure the survival and the success of liberty."[33]

Keynote addresses are featured speeches at meetings, conferences, or other formal gatherings. Keynote addresses typically give expression to the purposes and significance of the group and its gathering. The best-known keynote addresses, of course, are those delivered every four years at the presidential nominating conventions of the two major political parties. Although these keynotes have become increasingly partisan in recent years, they still include some of the most memorable speeches in U.S. history.

Among those celebrated keynote addresses is Texas congresswoman Barbara Jordan's speech to the 1976 Democratic National Convention in New York City. As an African American woman, Jordan began by noting that, in the past, it would have been "most unusual for any national political party to ask a Barbara Jordan to deliver a keynote address." Thus, her very presence on the podium became, for Jordan, "evidence that the American Dream need not forever be deferred." The rest of the speech was a classic keynote address, articulating the ideals of the Democratic Party and celebrating the values shared by all Americans. In the wake of the Watergate scandal, Jordan also spoke to people's skepticism toward government. "We as public servants must set an example for the rest of the nation," she declared at a time of widespread political cynicism. "More is required . . . of public officials than slogans and handshakes and press releases. . . . We must hold ourselves strictly accountable. We must provide the people with a vision of the future."[34]

You may never be elected president of the United States or address a national political convention, but you can emulate the spirit of the great inaugural and keynote addresses. Whether speaking as the new president of a local civic club or as the keynote speaker at a professional conference, your goal should be the same: to give eloquent expression to the shared beliefs and values of your group or community.

The After-Dinner Speech

Sometimes epideictic speeches are delivered after lunch or dinner, perhaps at a business meeting or conference. Although after-dinner speeches are often designed to entertain, they also may address more serious topics. If Federal Reserve chair Ben Bernanke is asked to deliver an after-dinner speech, for example, people expect him to say something significant about the economy. In other situations, an after-dinner speaker might be asked to pay tribute to a person or to deliver something akin to a "keynote" address. In these situations, the speaker also is expected to say something significant yet still be entertaining or perhaps even amusing.

Not surprisingly, after-dinner speeches can pose quite a challenge. Not only have audience members just eaten a meal, but they may have been in meetings all day, with the dinner as their "reward." As a result, the after-dinner speaker must look for ways to enliven the speech, perhaps by telling anecdotes or stories or by delivering the speech in a more spontaneous and energetic style.

Humor, of course, is one way that speakers enliven after-dinner speeches, but humor can be tricky. Some people seem to have a knack for telling amusing stories;

others do not. Some seem to have good "comic timing," while others stumble over punch lines. The point is not that you should avoid humor in an after-dinner speech. But if you do aspire to be funny, you need to think carefully about what your audience might or might not find amusing.

Generally, an after-dinner speech should not be too long, perhaps no more than 10 or 15 minutes. Stay in touch with how the audience is responding during the speech. Build your speech flexibly, so that you can cut some material during the speech if the audience appears to be losing interest. The most common complaint about an after-dinner speech is that it was too long. One rarely hears people complain that an after-dinner speech was too short!

Finally, keep in mind that audiences expect to walk away from an after-dinner speech with something to think about, remember, or talk about with others attending the event. Some after-dinner speeches might even provide the basis for further discussion and action. However much your audience may enjoy themselves, it is important that they also get something meaningful out of the speech. Even a humorous after-dinner speech can be used to communicate a serious message, as when we pay sincere tribute to people by "roasting" them at a banquet.

Sermons

Sermons may or may not be epideictic speeches, depending on their purpose and audience. When we seek to convert somebody to our religion, we obviously are trying to persuade. But when we celebrate and reaffirm our audience's existing faith—when we "preach to the choir"—the sermon functions like other ceremonial speeches, reinforcing or strengthening existing beliefs and values.

The line between epideictic and persuasive speaking is sometimes blurred in sermons that urge believers to cleanse themselves of sin. In the early nineteenth century, for example, a revivalist preacher named Lyman Beecher delivered a series of famous sermons on the "evils of intemperance," elaborating on the "deleterious influence" of alcohol on both individuals and the nation. Most of Beecher's followers already agreed with him about the evils of alcohol. Yet tempted by sin, many still drank. So Beecher took it upon himself to warn the nation, in the metaphorical style of epideictic, that "our sun is fast setting" and "the darkness of an endless night is closing in upon us." At one level, of course, Beecher was trying to persuade his flock not to drink. At another level, however, his sermons were simply urging his followers to have the strength of their convictions and to resist the temptation to sin.[35]

Style and Delivery in Ceremonial Speaking

Preview. Speakers tend to sound more "poetic" on ceremonial occasions, as they strive to give eloquent expression to the significance of the occasion and the shared social values of the audience. This emphasis on "eloquence" focuses more attention on the speaker's language. When preparing a ceremonial speech, you should choose your language carefully, using vivid language and figures of speech to create memorable images and a poetic rhythm and cadence. And because of the emphasis on style, most ceremonial speeches are delivered word-for-word from a manuscript.

Throughout this chapter, we have emphasized how ceremonial speakers perform important educational and cultural functions, shaping listeners' identity as members of a community and reinforcing shared social values. Yet ceremonial speakers do more than honor our heroes or teach us about our traditions. They also *inspire* us with their eloquence, touching our hearts or motivating us to reaffirm our civic and cultural commitments. In Chapter 11, we discussed the resources of language, including some of the ways that you might make your language more lively and interesting. In the remainder of this chapter, we will revisit that discussion of style, focusing on how you might exploit the resources of language to make your ceremonial speeches more memorable.

Vivid Language and Imagery

The difference between a dull and lifeless ceremonial speech and one that we perceive as inspirational and eloquent often boils down to the speaker's choice of words. As we noted in Chapter 11, one way to make your speech more lively and interesting is to strive for *vivid* language, or language that is specific, concrete, and appeals to your listeners' physical senses. Specific, concrete words allow your audience to see, hear, smell, taste, or feel what you are talking about, and that sort of language can enhance the emotional impact of your speech. In the following passage, notice how Ronald Reagan used vivid, concrete language to recreate the scene on D-Day in 1944, as he commemorated the 40th anniversary of that fateful day in Pointe du Hoc, France:

> We stand on a lonely, windswept point on the northern shore of France. The air is soft, but 40 years ago at this moment, the air was dense with smoke and the cries of men, and the air was filled with the crack of rifle fire and the roar of cannon. At dawn, on the morning of the 6th of June, 1944, 225 Rangers jumped off the British landing craft and ran to the bottom of these cliffs. Their mission was one of the most difficult and daring of the invasion: to climb these sheer and desolate cliffs and take out the enemy guns. . . .
>
> The Rangers looked up and saw the enemy soldiers . . . shooting down at them with machine guns and throwing grenades. And the American Rangers began to climb. They shot rope ladders over the face of these cliffs and began to pull themselves up. When one Ranger fell, another would take his place. When one rope was cut, a Ranger would grab another and begin his climb again. They climbed, shot back, and held their footing. Soon, one by one, the Rangers pulled themselves over the top, and in seizing the firm land at the top of these cliffs, they began to seize back the continent of Europe. Two hundred and twenty-five came here. After two days of fighting, only 90 could still bear arms.[36]

So powerful were Reagan's images—so vivid was his recreation of the scene on D-Day 40 years earlier—that some of the grizzled old veterans in his audience actually broke down in tears during the speech.

President Ronald Reagan used a visually dramatic setting and vivid language and imagery to commemorate the 40th anniversary of D-Day at Point du Hoc, Normandy, in 1984. In his audience were many of the surviving U.S. Army Rangers who stormed the cliffs on that fateful day.

Imagery refers to the "word pictures" that our language creates, and Reagan painted a vivid one. So, too, did Theodore Roosevelt in a famous speech delivered at the dedication of a new federal office building in 1906. In "The Man with the Muck Rake," Roosevelt compared the irresponsible journalists of his day to a famous literary figure from Bunyan's *Pilgrim's Progress*—the man with the muckrake, who "could look no way but down." Refusing to see anything positive or "lofty," he instead fixed his eyes "with solemn intentness only on that which is vile and debasing." To Roosevelt's mind, that perfectly described those journalists who reported nothing but bad news and engaged in "hysterical exaggeration" of America's problems. "Hysterical sensationalism is the poorest weapon wherewith to fight for lasting righteousness," Roosevelt declared in summarizing the point of his speech. And the imagery stuck: to this day, we use the term "muckraker" to describe journalists who specialize in sensational exposés.

Ceremonial speakers often use *figurative language* or specific *figures of speech* to create imagery in their speeches. In his "I Have a Dream" speech, for example, Martin Luther King Jr. used metaphors to contrast the "dark and desolate valley of segregation" with the "sunlit path of racial justice." He began with an extended metaphor, comparing the March on Washington in 1963 to cashing a check:

In a sense we've come to our nation's capital to cash a check. When the architects of our republic wrote the magnificent words of the Constitution and the Declaration of Independence, they were signing a promissory. . . . This note was a promise that all men, yes, black men as well as white men, would be guaranteed the unalienable rights of life, liberty, and the pursuit of happiness.

It is obvious today that America has defaulted on this promissory note insofar as her citizens of color are concerned. Instead of honoring this sacred obligation, America has given the Negro people a bad check, a check which has come back marked "insufficient funds."

King used metaphors throughout his speech to create vivid imagery and to give more specific meaning to abstract terms, such as freedom, justice, opportunity, and equality. It would have been one thing for King to announce that blacks were unsatisfied with the progress of the civil rights movement. It was quite another for him to disavow the "tranquilizing drug of gradualism" and to declare, in biblical terms, that he and his followers would "not be satisfied until justice rolls down like waters, and righteousness like a mighty stream."[37]

You may not have King's gift of eloquence. Yet simply by using more specific, concrete words or a striking metaphor or two, you can enhance the imagery and eloquence of your ceremonial speeches. Writing a ceremonial speech is not like writing poetry, yet neither is it the same as writing a persuasive or informative speech. In a ceremonial speech, you should pay closer attention to language and choose your words carefully to achieve a more eloquent tone. Not all epideictic speeches are flowery or poetic, but all should reflect careful attention to language and style.

Rhythm and Cadence

As you prepare your ceremonial speech, you should pay special attention to its rhythm and cadence. That is, you should write the speech with a view toward how well it will "flow" when delivered. In general, you should strive for a smooth, balanced rhythm, paying special attention to the length and structure of the speech's phrases and sentences. You also might employ stylistic devices that contribute to a more "poetic" rhythm, such as antithesis, parallelism, or simple repetition.

When writing an epideictic speech, keep in mind that you are writing for oral delivery. It is crucial that your speech *sound* good when delivered out loud. Generally, this means that you should strive for shorter sentences, perhaps even using phrases or sentence fragments that might be inappropriate in a written essay. You want a speech that you can deliver smoothly, without stumbling over words that are difficult to pronounce or sentences that are awkwardly constructed. It is always a good idea to practice your speech out loud before you deliver it.

We remember some of the most famous ceremonial speeches in history not only for their imagery but for their rhythm and cadence. In his inaugural address, for example, John F. Kennedy made effective use of antithesis, most notably in the best-known line of the address: "Ask not what your country can do for you—ask what you can do for your country." Yet that was not the only example of antithesis in the speech. Kennedy also used a complex, extended antithesis to open the speech: "We observe today not a victory of party but a celebration of freedom—symbolizing an end as well as a beginning—signifying renewal as well as change." Midway through the speech, he employed antithesis again: "Let us never negotiate out of fear. But let us never fear to negotiate." Finally, he concluded by echoing the most famous line of the address, directing a similar antithesis to "citizens of the world": "Ask not what America will do for you, but what together we can do for the freedom of man."[38]

King's "I Have a Dream" speech is also noteworthy for its rhythm and cadence, primarily because of the repetition and parallelism toward the end of the address. While striking for its imagery, the speech is perhaps even better remembered for King's repetition of the phrase that gave the speech its title, "I have a dream today!" King repeated that phrase to punctuate a series of longer statements about his vision of the future—a future when the sons of former slaves and slaveholders would "sit down together at the table of brotherhood" and "not be judged by the color of their skin but by the content of their character." Then, in closing, King used parallelism to build to a dramatic climax, imagining the ultimate triumph of justice and freedom:

> So let freedom ring from the prodigious hilltops of New Hampshire. Let freedom ring from the mighty mountains of New York. Let freedom ring from the heightening Alleghenies of Pennsylvania. Let freedom ring from the snow-capped Rockies of Colorado. Let freedom ring from the curvaceous slopes of California. But not only that. Let freedom ring from Stone Mountain of Georgia. Let freedom ring from Lookout Mountain of Tennessee. Let freedom ring from every hill and molehill of Mississippi, from every mountain side, let freedom ring.[39]

Again, you may not possess King's natural eloquence, and not every ceremonial occasion calls for a speech so poetic in tone. In preparing your own ceremonial speeches, however, you *should* strive for a more eloquent style, and that means paying close attention to the language, rhythm, and cadence of your speech.

Speaking from a Manuscript

On most occasions, you will deliver your ceremonial speech from a manuscript rather than from an outline or brief notes. That is, you will take care to present the speech exactly as written. This is not to say that you should stand before your audience, eyes glued to your manuscript, and simply read the speech. To the contrary, you should have the same concern with delivering your ceremonial speech effectively as you would any other speech.

The reason most ceremonial speeches are delivered from manuscript should be obvious: because of the emphasis on language and style, it is important that we deliver the speech precisely as written. That is not to say that you should never diverge from your manuscript or "ad lib" a few lines. Yet when you invent that memorable turn of phrase or come up with the perfect metaphor—that is, when you carefully craft the language of your speech—you want to deliver those lines exactly as written. In his first inaugural address, Franklin Roosevelt knew exactly what he wanted to say: the "only thing we have to fear is fear itself." Imagine if FDR had delivered that line extemporaneously, concerned only with the idea behind it. Instead of that famous line, he instead might have said: "Let's not be paralyzed by our fears." Or even just: "Don't be scared!"

Unfortunately, delivering a speech from manuscript poses special challenges. Most speakers find it more difficult to maintain eye contact, use physical movement

Franklin Delano Roosevelt delivering his first inaugural address behind the symbol of an American Eagle with its wings spread. Roosevelt went on to win re-election to an unprecedented four terms and would deliver three more inaugural addresses, none quite as memorable as the first.

and gestures, sustain the appropriate rate and volume, and react to audience feedback while reading from a manuscript. Delivering a speech from manuscript requires that you write the speech in a good oral style, using words and sentence constructions that you will not stumble over as you speak. It also requires that you make a special effort to maintain a slow, deliberate pace that allows you to stay connected to your audience. In Chapter 12, we offered some other tips for delivering a manuscript speech, including ways to move and gesture and use your voice effectively while speaking from a manuscript. But perhaps the best advice for delivering a manuscript speech is simple: never forget that you are delivering a *speech*, not simply reading out loud.

Summary

- Ceremonial speeches perform important cultural functions in a free society.
  - They help us to remember the past.
  - They honor our heroes.
  - They celebrate shared beliefs and values.
  - They provide inspiration and encouragement.

- Ceremonial speeches articulate and reinforce shared social values.
  - Most ceremonial speeches affirm existing values and traditions.
  - Some ceremonial speeches promote social reform or encourage groups to re-assess their values and priorities.
- There are many different forms of ceremonial speeches, each unique but all with the same basic mission: to celebrate a special person or occasion.
  - Speeches of introduction should be brief and focused on the featured speaker.
  - Speeches of welcome or farewell often offer instruction or guidance.
  - Presentation and acceptance speeches may focus on the virtues of an award recipient or the significance of the award itself.
  - Commemoration and commencement addresses mark special dates or events.
  - Tributes and eulogies honor people and teach us about character and personal virtue.
  - Inaugural and keynote addresses articulate the "vision" of a new leader or the key principles of some group.
  - After-dinner speeches combine entertainment and a serious message.
  - Sermons may be considered *epideictic* speeches when they celebrate and reinforce the faith of believers.
- Ceremonial speeches should be written with careful attention to language and typically are delivered from manuscript.

QUESTIONS FOR REVIEW AND REFLECTION

1. What are some of the main purposes of ceremonial speeches in a free society?
2. Suppose you learn that you are going to receive an award and have to give a brief acceptance speech. Would you talk more about yourself, other people, or the award itself?
3. Do you remember any of the commemorative or commencement speeches you have heard in the past? What made those speeches memorable?
4. Think of an important public figure, celebrity, or other notable person, living or dead, whom you admire. If you were to deliver a tribute or eulogy to that person, what character attributes or personal virtues would you emphasize?
5. What are the major differences between an inaugural address and a keynote address?
6. Do ceremonial addresses always reinforce *traditional* social values? Can you think of speakers who have delivered ceremonial addresses that challenged traditional values?
7. Define *eloquence* and discuss what you think makes some speeches more eloquent than others.
8. What are some of the stylistic devices that contribute to vivid imagery or create a poetic rhythm and cadence in a ceremonial speech?

ENDNOTES

1. Dale L. Sullivan, "A Closer Look at Education as Epideictic Rhetoric," *Rhetoric Society Quarterly* 23 (1993): 71–72.

2. George Kennedy, *The Art of Persuasion in Greece* (Princeton, NJ: Princeton University Press, 1963), 160.

3. Rudolph Giuliani, "2004 Republican National Convention Address," *American Rhetoric*, www.americanrhetoric.com/speeches/convention2004/rudygiuliani2004rnc.htm (Accessed July 7, 2006).

4. See Celeste Michelle Condit, "The Functions of Epideictic: The Boston Massacre Orations as Exemplar," *Communication Quarterly* 33 (1985): 284–99.

5. John Hancock, "Boston Massacre Oration," in *American Rhetorical Discourse*, ed. Ronald F. Reid and James F. Klumpp, 3rd ed. (Long Grove, IL: Waveland, 2005), 103.

6. Henry W. Grady, "The New South," in Reid and Klumpp, *American Rhetorical Discourse*, 494–95.

7. Robert F. Kennedy, "Remarks on the Assassination of Martin Luther King, Jr.," *American Rhetoric*, www.americanrhetoric.com/speeches/robertkennedyonmartinlutherking .html (Accessed July 24, 2006).

8. Ronald Reagan, "State of the Union, 1982," *From Revolution to Reconstruction . . . and What Happened Afterwards*," a hypertext on American history from the colonial period to modern times, Department of Humanities Computing, University of Groningen, The Netherlands, www.let.rug.nl/usa/P/rr40/speeches/su82rwr.htm (Accessed July 10, 2006).

9. John F. Kennedy, "Inaugural Address," in Reid and Klumpp, *American Rhetorical Discourse*, 789.

10. Dwight D. Eisenhower, "Second Inaugural Address: The Price of Peace," in *The Presidents Speak*, ed. Davis Newton Lott (New York: Henry Holt, 1994), 310.

11. Winston Churchill, "We Shall Fight on the Beaches," speech to the House of Commons, June 4, 1940, www.winstonchurchill.org/i4a/pages/index.cfm?pageid=393 (Accessed July 20, 2006).

12. See Nicole Loraux, *The Invention of Athens: The Funeral Oration in the Classical City*, trans. Alan Sheridan (Cambridge, MA: Harvard University Press, 1986).

13. Sullivan, "A Closer Look at Education as Epideictic Rhetoric," 76–79.

14. Writing in the late 1950s, for example, scholars Chaim Perelman and Lucie Olbrechts-Tyteca observed that epideictic speeches were typically delivered by "those who, in a society, defend the traditional and accepted values, those which are the object of education, not the new and revolutionary values which stir up controversy and polemics." Chaim Perelman and Lucie Olbrechts-Tyteca, *The New Rhetoric: A Treatise on Argumentation*, trans. John Wilkinson and Purcell Weaver (1958; Notre Dame: University of Notre Dame Press, 1969), 51.

15. Cynthia Miecznikowski Sheard, "The Public Value of Epideictic Rhetoric," *College English* 58 (1996): 755–56.

16. Frederick Douglass, "What to the Slave in the Fourth of July?" in Reid and Klumpp, *American Rhetorical Discourse*, 343.

17. Jabari Asim, "Did Cosby Cross the Line", Washington Post, March 24, 2004, www .washingtonpost.com/wp-dyn/articles/A51273-2004May24.html (Accessed July 21, 2006).

18. George E. Curry, "Bill Cosby Stands behind Critical Comments," *Atlanta Daily World*, July 9, 2006, www.zwire.com/site/news.cfm?newsid=11810453&BRD=1077&PAG= 461&dept_id=237827&rfi=6 (Accessed July 21, 2006).

19. "Cosby Stands His Ground," *CBS News*, July 2, 2004, www.cbsnews.com/stories/2004/07/02/national/main627156.shtml (Accessed July 21, 2006).

20. See the speech and the biography of Gehrig at *Lou Gehrig: The Official Web Site*, www.lougehrig.com/about/speech.htm (Accessed July 14, 2006).

21. Dwight D. Eisenhower, "Farewell Address," in *Great Speeches for Criticism and Analysis*, ed. Lloyd Rohler and Roger Cook, 316–19 (Greenwood, IN: Alistair Press, 1988).

22. "His Holiness the Dalai Lama's Nobel Prize Acceptance Speech, University Aula, Oslo, 10 December 1989," *Government of Tibet in Exile*, www.tibet.com/DL/nobelaccept.html (Accessed July 15, 2006).

23. Colin Powell, "Commencement Address," in Rohler and Cook, *Great Speeches for Criticism and Analysis*, 343.

24. Qtd. in Mortimer M. Caplan, "Commencement Address," University of Virginia, May 18, 2003, Office of Major Events, University of Virginia, www.virginia.edu/majorevents/speeches/03speech.html (Accessed July 12, 2006).

25. John F. Kennedy, "American University Commencement Address," *American Rhetoric*, www.americanrhetoric.com/speeches/jfkamericanuniversityaddress.html (Accessed July 12, 2006).

26. "Detailed John Williams Kennedy Center Honors Coverage," *SpielbergFilms.com*, http://www.spielbergfilms.com/general/514 (Accessed July 24, 2006).

27. Donald H. Rumsfeld, "Lucky Us: A Tribute to Milton Friedman," *National Review Online*, www.nationalreview.com/nrof_document/document073102.asp (Accessed July 17, 2006).

28. Oprah Winfrey, "Eulogy for Rosa Parks," *American Rhetoric*, www.americanrhetoric.com/speeches/oprahwinfreyonrosaparks.htm (Accessed November 24, 2005).

29. Lyndon Baines Johnson, "Let Us Continue," *American Rhetoric*, www.americanrhetoric.com/speeches/lbjletuscontinue.html (Accessed July 17, 2006).

30. In a survey of rhetorical scholars to determine the top 100 speeches of the twentieth century, FDR's First Inaugural and Kennedy's Inaugural Address were ranked third and second, respectively, behind another epideictic speech, Martin Luther King Jr.'s "I Have a Dream." Jefferson and Lincoln's Inaugural Addresses were not part of the ranking, of course, since they were delivered in the nineteenth century. But their reputations are testified to by their inclusion in almost all major anthologies of American public address. See "Top 100 Speeches," *American Rhetoric*, www.americanrhetoric.com/top100speechesall.html (Accessed July 7, 2006).

31. Thomas Jefferson, "First Inaugural Address (1801)," in *American Voices: Significant Speeches in American History, 1640–1945*, ed. James R. Andrews and David Zarefsky (New York: Longman, 1989), 115–16.

32. Franklin D. Roosevelt, "First Inaugural Address," in Reid and Klumpp, *American Rhetorical Discourse*, 749.

33. John F. Kennedy, "Inaugural Address," in Reid and Klumpp, *American Rhetorical Discourse*, 788–90.

34. Barbara Jordan, "Keynote Address," in Rohler and Cook, *Great Speeches for Criticism and Analysis*, 53–55.

35. Lyman Beecher, "The Evils of Intemperance," in Reid and Klumpp, *American Rhetorical Discourse*," 278–85.

36. Ronald Reagan, "Remarks at the U.S. Ranger Monument, Pointe du Hoc, France, June 6, 1984," *Ronald Reagan Presidential Library and Foundation*, www.reaganlibrary.com/reagan/speeches/dday_pdh.asp (Accessed July 21, 2006).

37. Martin Luther King Jr., "I Have a Dream," in Rohler and Cook, *Great Speeches for Criticism and Analysis*, 350–52.

38. Kennedy, "Inaugural Address," in Reid and Klumpp, *American Rhetorical Discourse*, 788.

39. King, "I Have a Dream," in Rohler and Cook, *Great Speeches for Criticism and Analysis*, 351–52.

JOHN McCAIN

After labeling the Reverend Jerry Falwell an "agent of intolerance" during the 2000 presidential campaign, Senator John McCain (R-Arizona) accepted an invitation to deliver the 2006 commencement address at Falwell's Liberty University. McCain used the occasion to talk about humility, patriotism, tolerance, respect, and forgiveness. He also celebrated free speech in America and urged his listeners to devote themselves to a cause greater than themselves.

May 13, 2006

Thank you. Thank you. Thank you. Thank you, Dr. Falwell. Thank you, faculty, families and friends, and thank you Liberty University Class of 2006 for your welcome and your kind invitation to give this year's commencement address. I want to join in the chorus of congratulations to the Class of 2006. This is a day to bask in praise. You've earned it. You have succeeded in a demanding course of instruction. Life seems full of promise, as is always the case when a passage in life is marked by significant accomplishment. Today, it might seem as if the world attends you.

But spare a moment for those who have truly attended you so well for so long, and whose pride in your accomplishments is even greater than your own—your parents. When the world was looking elsewhere your parents' attention was one of life's certainties. So, as I commend you, I offer equal praise to your parents for the sacrifices they made for you, for their confidence in you and their love. More than any other influence in your lives they have helped you—make you the success you are today and might become tomorrow.

Thousands of commencement addresses are given every year, many by people with greater eloquence and more original minds than I possess. And it's difficult on such occasions to avoid resorting to clichés. So let me just say that I wish you all well. This is a wonderful time to be young. Life will offer you ways to use your education, industry, and intelligence to achieve personal success in your chosen professions. And it will also offer you chances to know a far more sublime happiness by serving something greater than your self-interest. I hope you make the most of all your opportunities.

When I was in your situation, many, many years ago, an undistinguished graduate—barely—of the Naval Academy, I listened to President Eisenhower deliver the commencement address. I admired President Eisenhower greatly. But I must admit I remember little of his remarks that day, impatient as I was to enjoy the less formal celebration of graduation, and mindful that given my class standing I would not have the privilege of shaking the President's hand. I do recall, vaguely, that he encouraged his audience of new Navy ensigns and Marine lieutenants to become "crusaders for peace."

I became an aviator and, eventually, an instrument of war in Vietnam. I believed, as did many of my friends, we were defending the cause of a just peace. Some Americans believed we were agents of American imperialism who were not overly troubled by the many tragedies of war and the difficult moral dilemmas that constantly confront our soldiers. Ours is a noisy, contentious society, and always has been, for we love our liberties much. And among those liberties we love most, particularly so when we are young, is our right to self-expression. That passion for self-expression sometimes overwhelms our civility, and our presumption that those with whom we may have strong disagreements, wrong as they might be, believe that they, too, are answering the demands of their conscience.

When I was a young man, I was quite infatuated with self-expression, and rightly so because, if memory conveniently serves, I was so much more eloquent, well-informed, and wiser than anyone else I knew. It seemed I understood the world and the purpose of life so much more profoundly than most people. I believed that to be especially true with many of my elders, people whose only accomplishment, as far as I could tell, was that they'd been born before me, and, consequently, had suffered some number of years deprived of my insights. I had opinions on everything, and I was always right. I loved to argue, and I could become understandably belligerent with people who lacked the grace and intelligence to agree with me. With my superior qualities so obvious, it was an intolerable hardship to have to suffer fools gladly. So I rarely did. All their resistance to my brilliantly conceived and cogently argued views proved was that they possessed an inferior intellect and a weaker character than God had blessed me with, and I felt it was my clear duty to so inform them. It's a pity that there wasn't a blogosphere then. I would have felt very much at home in that medium.

It's funny, now, how less self-assured I feel late in life than I did when I lived in perpetual springtime. Some of my critics allege that age hasn't entirely cost me the conceits of my youth. All I can say to them is, they should have known me then, when I was brave and true and better looking than I am at present. But as the great poet Yeats wrote, "All that's beautiful drifts away, like the waters." I've lost some of the attributes that were the object of a young man's vanity. But there have been compensations, which I have come to hold dear.

MAJOR THEME OF THE ADDRESS: THAT IN OUR "NOISY, CONTENTIOUS SOCIETY," WE SHOULD NOT LET OUR "PASSION FOR SELF-EXPRESSION" OVERWHELM OUR "CIVILITY" TOWARD OTHERS.

We have our disagreements, we Americans. We contend regularly and enthusiastically over many questions: over the size and purposes of our government; over the social responsibilities we accept in accord with the dictates of our consciousness [conscience] and our faithfulness to the God we pray to; over our role in the world and how to defend our security interests and values in places where they are threatened. These are important questions worth arguing about. We should contend over them with one another. It is more than appropriate: It is necessary that even in times of crisis, especially in times of crisis, we fight among ourselves for the things we believe in. It is not just our right, but our civic and moral obligation.

Our country doesn't depend on the heroism of every citizen. But all of us should be worthy of the sacrifices made on our behalf. We have to love our freedom, not just for the private opportunities it provides, but for the goodness it makes possible. We have to love it as much, even if not as heroically, as the brave Americans who defend us at the risk and often the cost of their lives. We must love it enough to argue about it, and to serve it, in whatever way our abilities permit and our conscience requires, whether it calls us to arms or to altruism or to politics.

HERE, McCAIN CELEBRATES FREE SPEECH, CALLING IT OUR "CIVIC AND MORAL OBLIGATION" TO SPEAK OUT ON IMPORTANT ISSUES, BUT ALSO REMINDING US OF OUR DUTY TO SERVE THE LARGER GOOD THROUGH MILITARY SERVICE, CHARITABLE WORK, OR POLITICS.

I supported the decision to go to war in Iraq. Many Americans did not. My patriotism and my conscience required me to support it and to engage in the debate over whether and how to fight it. I stand that ground not to chase vainglorious dreams of empire; not for a noxious sense of racial superiority over a subject people; not for cheap oil (we could have purchased oil from the former dictator at a price far less expensive than the blood and treasure we've paid to secure those resources for the people of that nation); not for the allure of chauvinism, to wreck [wreak] destruction in the world in order to feel superior to it; not for a foolishly romantic conception of war. I stand that ground because I believed, rightly or wrongly, that my country's interests and values required it.

War is an awful business. The lives of the nation's finest patriots are sacrificed. Innocent people suffer. Commerce is disrupted, economies damaged. Strategic interests shielded by years of statecraft are endangered as the demands of war and diplomacy conflict. Whether the cause was necessary or not, whether it was just or not, we should all shed a tear for all that is lost when war claims its wages from us. However just or false the cause, however proud and noble the service, it is loss—the loss of friendships, the loss of innocent life, the innocence—the loss of innocence; and the veteran feels most keenly forevermore. Only a fool or a fraud sentimentalizes war.

IN THESE PARAGRAPHS, HE TACKLES A CONTROVERSIAL ISSUE: THE WAR IN IRAQ. HE DEFENDS HIS OWN SUPPORT FOR THE WAR, BUT HE ALSO DECLARES WAR AN "AWFUL BUSINESS" AND CONCLUDES: "ONLY A FOOL OR A FRAUD SENTIMENTALIZES WAR." FINALLY, HE CALLS FOR MORE, NOT LESS, DEBATE OVER THE WAR, DECLARING IT THE RIGHT AND OBLIGATION OF THOSE OPPOSED TO THE WAR TO "STATE THEIR OPPOSITION" AND "ARGUE FOR ANOTHER COURSE."

Americans should argue about this war. They should argue about it. It has cost the lives of nearly 2500 of the best of us. It has taken innocent life. It has imposed an enormous financial burden on our economy. At a minimum, it has complicated our ability to respond to other looming threats. Should we lose this war, our defeat will further destabilize an already volatile and dangerous region, strengthen the threat of terrorism, and unleash furies that will assail us for a very long time. I believe the benefits of success will justify the costs and the risks we have incurred. But if an American feels the decision was unwise, then they should state their opposition, and argue for another course. It is your right and your obligation. I respect you for it. I would not respect you if you chose to ignore such an important responsibility. But I ask that you consider the possibility that I, too, am trying to meet my responsibilities, to follow my conscience, to do my duty as best as I can, as God has given me light to see that duty.

Americans deserve more than tolerance from one another; we deserve each other's respect, whether we think each other right or wrong in our views, as long as our character and our sincerity merit respect, and as long as we share, for all our differences, for all the noisy debates that enliven our politics, a mutual devotion to the sublime idea that this nation was conceived in—that freedom is the inalienable right of mankind, and in accord with the laws of nature and nature's Creator.

We have so much more that unites us than divides us. We need only to look to the enemy who now confronts us, and the benighted ideals to which Islamic extremists pledge allegiance—their disdain for the rights of Man, their contempt for human life—to appreciate how much unites us.

Take, for example, the awful human catastrophe under way in the Darfur region of the Sudan. If the United States and the West can be criticized for our role in this catastrophe it's because we have waited too long to intervene to protect the multitudes who are suffering, dying because of it.

Twelve years ago, we turned a blind eye to another genocide, in Rwanda. And when that reign of terror finally, mercifully exhausted itself, with over 800,000 Rwandans slaughtered, Americans, our government, and decent people everywhere in the world were shocked and ashamed of our silence and inaction, for ignoring our values, and the demands of our conscience. In shame and renewed allegiance to our ideals, we swore, not for the first time, "never again." But "never" lasted only until the tragedy of Darfur.

Now, belatedly, we have recovered our moral sense of duty, and we are prepared, I hope, to put an end to this genocide. Osama bin Laden and his followers, ready, as always, to sacrifice anything and anyone to their hatred of the West and our ideals, have called on Muslims to rise up against any Westerner who dares intervene to stop the genocide, even though Muslims, hundreds of thousands of Muslims, are its victims. Now that, my friends, is a difference, a cause, worth taking up arms against.

It is not a clash of civilizations. I believe, as I hope all Americans would believe, that no matter where people live, no matter their history or religious beliefs or the size of their GDP, all people share the desire to be free; to make by their own choices and industry better lives for themselves and their children. Human rights exist above the state and beyond history—they are God-given. They cannot be rescinded by one government any more than they can be granted by another. They inhabit the human heart, and from there, though they can be abridged, they can never be wrenched.

This is a clash of ideals, a profound and terrible clash of ideals. It is a fight between right and wrong. Relativism has no place in this confrontation. We're not defending—we're not defending an idea that every human being should eat corn flakes, play baseball, or watch MTV. We're not insisting that all societies be governed by a bicameral legislature and a term-limited chief executive.

We're insisting that all people have a right to be free, and that right is not subject to the whims and interests and authority of another person, government, or culture. Relativism, in this context, is most certainly not a sign of our humility or ecumenism; it is a mask for arrogance and selfishness. It is, and I mean this sincerely and with all humility, not worthy of us. We are a better people than that.

We're not a perfect nation. Our history has had its moments of shame and profound regret. But what we have achieved in our brief history is irrefutable proof that a nation conceived in liberty will prove stronger, more decent, and more enduring than any nation ordered to exalt the few at the expense of the many or made from a common race or culture or to preserve traditions that have no greater attribute than longevity.

As blessed as we are, no nation complacent in its greatness can long sustain it. We, too, must prove, as those who came before us proved, that a people free to act in their own interests will perceive those interests in an enlightened way, will live as one nation, in a kinship of ideals, and make of our power and wealth a civilization for the ages, a civilization in which all people share in the promise and responsibilities of freedom.

Should we claim our rights and leave to others the duty to the ideals that protect them, whatever we gain for ourselves will be of little lasting value. It will build no monuments to virtue, claim no honored place in the memory of posterity, offer no worthy summons to the world. Success, wealth and celebrity gained and kept for private interest is a small thing. It makes us comfortable, eases the material hardships our children will bear, purchase[s] a fleeting regard for our lives, yet not the self-respect that, in the end, matters most. But sacrifice for a cause greater than yourself, and you invest your life with the eminence of that cause, your self-respect assured.

All lives are a struggle against selfishness. All my life I've stood a little apart from institutions that I willingly joined. It just felt natural to me. But if my life had shared no common purpose, it would not have amounted to much more than eccentricity. There is no honor or happiness in just being strong enough to be left alone. I've spent nearly fifty years in the service of this country and its ideals. I have made many mistakes, and I have many regrets. But I've never lived a day, in good times or bad, that I wasn't grateful for the privilege. That's the benefit of service to a country that is an idea and a cause, a righteous idea and cause. America and her ideals helped spare me from the weaknesses in my own character. And I cannot forget it.

When I was a young man, I thought glory was the highest attainment, and all glory was self-glory. My parents had tried to teach me otherwise, as did my church, as did the Naval Academy. But I didn't understand the lesson until later in life, when I confronted challenges I never expected to face.

In that confrontation, I discovered that I was dependent on others to a greater extent than I had ever realized, but neither they nor the cause we served made any claims on my identity. On the contrary, they gave me a larger sense of myself than I had had before. And I am a better man for it. I discovered that nothing in life is more liberating than to fight for a cause that encompasses you but is not defined by your existence alone. And that has made all the difference, my friends, all the difference in the world.

Let—let us argue with each other then. By all means, let us argue. Our differences are not petty. They often involve cherished beliefs, and represent our best judgment about what is right for our country and humanity. Let us defend those beliefs. Let's do so sincerely and strenuously. It is our right and duty to do so. And let's not be too dismayed with the tenor and passion of our arguments, even when they wound us. We have fought among ourselves before in our history, over big things and small, with worse vitriol and bitterness than we experience today.

Let us exercise our responsibilities as free people. But let us remember, we are not enemies. We are compatriots defending ourselves from a real enemy. We have nothing to fear from each other. We are arguing over the means to better secure our freedom, promote the general welfare, and defend our ideals. It should remain an argument among friends; each of us struggling to hear our conscience, and heed its demands; each of us, despite our differences, united in our great cause, and respectful of the goodness in each other. I have not always heeded that injunction myself, and I regret it very much.

I had a friend once, who, a long time ago, in the passions and resentments of a tumultuous era in our history, I might have considered my enemy. He had come once to the capitol of the country that held me prisoner, that deprived me and my dearest friends of our most basic rights, and that murdered some of us. He came to that place to denounce our country's involvement in the war that had led us there. His speech was broadcast into our cells. I thought it a grievous wrong then, and I still do.

A few years later, he had moved temporarily to a kibbutz in Israel. He was there during the Yom Kippur War, when he witnessed the support America provided our beleaguered ally. He saw the huge cargo planes bearing the insignia of the United States Air Force rushing emergency supplies into that country. And he had an epiphany. He had believed America had made a tragic mistake by going to Vietnam, and he still did. He had seen what he believed were his country's faults, and he still saw them. But he realized he has—he had let his criticism temporarily blind him to his country's generosity and the goodness that most Americans possess, and he regretted his failing deeply. When he returned to his country he became prominent in Democratic Party politics, and helped [elect] Bill Clinton President of the United States. He criticized his government when he thought it wrong, but he never again lost sight of all that unites us.

We met some years later. He approached me and asked to apologize for the mistake he believed he had made as a young man. Many years had passed since then, and I bore little animosity for anyone because of what they had done or not done during the Vietnam War. It was an easy thing to accept such a decent act, and we moved beyond our old grievance.

We worked together in an organization dedicated to promoting human rights in the country where he and I had once come for different reasons. I came to admire him for his generosity, his passion for his ideals, and for the largeness of his heart, and I realized he had not been my enemy, but my countryman, my countryman, and later my friend. His friendship honored me. We disagreed over much. Our politics were often opposed, and we argued those disagreements. But we worked together for our shared ideals. We were not always in the right, but we weren't always in the wrong either, and we defended our beliefs as we had each been given the wisdom to defend them.

David [Ifshin] remained my countryman and my friend, until the day of his death, at the age of forty-seven, when he left a loving wife and three beautiful children, and legions of friends behind him. His country was a better place for his service to Her, and I had become a better man for my friendship with him. God bless him.

And may God bless you, Class of 2006. The world does indeed await you, and humanity is impatient for your service. Take good care of that responsibility. Everything depends upon it.

And thank you, very much, for the privilege of sharing this great occasion with you.

Speaking and Deliberating in Groups

CHAPTER SURVEY

Understanding Public Deliberation

Group Structures That Encourage Dialogue and Deliberation

Factors That Influence Effective Group Deliberation

Group Presentations

Guidelines for Deliberating in Groups

CHAPTER OBJECTIVES

After studying this chapter, you should be able to

1. Explain the role and importance of public deliberation.

2. Describe the fundamental steps in the deliberative process.

3. Provide illustrations of specific group structures that promote deliberation and dialogue.

4. Describe those factors that influence the effective functioning of deliberative groups.

5. Explain the attitudes and communication behaviors that characterize successful participation in group presentations.

6. Participate effectively in a group deliberation, following the guidelines explored in this chapter.

One of the chief ways that we may function as advocates for those causes we believe in is by speaking out in public settings—articulating our convictions and appealing to those who have assembled to hear us speak. As citizens in a democratic society, we speak out because we hope to influence our fellow citizens and because we care passionately about working with others to right wrongs, to build stronger communities, and to co-create a world that is safe, peaceful, and just.

Although we tend to associate this kind of advocacy with the presentation of formal public speeches, we often have the opportunity to speak out in other settings within our communities and places of work. In those instances, our listeners are less likely to resemble a formal "audience" and are more likely to belong to groups of which we are a part. In these settings, there are plenty of opportunities for advocacy, but "speeches" are less formal, with speakers and listeners frequently exchanging roles. In addition, these deliberative sessions may focus as much on consensus building, information sharing, or conflict exploration as on advocacy.

All of us participate in countless formal and informal group deliberations. Professionally, we may put in hundreds of hours attending staff meetings or meeting with clients or customers. In civic settings, we may participate in panel discussions, attend committee meetings, or work on task forces designed to tackle the community's problems. As we interact in these groups, we learn from each other, form friendships, and contribute knowledge and skills vital to the success of the community. Deliberating in a group is not the same as dealing individually with one other person or solving a problem alone. A group is both dynamic and complex. Group work may lead to long-term, productive relationships and inspire innovative decision making. Or it may lead to prolonged tensions and delayed action. This chapter identifies ways to promote the former and avoid the latter.

The frequency with which you deliberate in groups is in itself reason enough to read this chapter carefully. Your effectiveness in any organization or community will be influenced significantly by how well you communicate in groups. As businesses and nonprofit organizations have become increasingly team-based, their leaders are seeking employees and volunteers who feel comfortable working in a group-oriented environment. Thus, knowing how to be a team player, how to interact effectively with others to complete projects, and how to provide group leadership are increasingly valued skills in the twenty-first century.[1]

Group communication skills learned in one setting are quite applicable to others. Whether you are deliberating as a board member of a nonprofit agency, as a citizen in a community group, or as member of your work team, you will be more effective if you prepare carefully, thoughtfully analyze the problem, maintain an open and flexible attitude, and listen respectfully. When you communicate effectively in a group, you are likely to exert more influence and rise to positions of leadership. You also will have the *opportunity* to help maintain a civil and respectful dialogue and to collaborate with others in making decisions that contribute to the greater good. The more involved you become as a citizen in your community, the more frequently you will work in groups dealing with such issues as education, crime and public safety, or environmental policy. Your ability to contribute constructively to groups will affect your community's chances of successfully resolving its problems. For all these reasons, developing skill in group participation is vital to the short- and long-term well-being of your organization and your community. We begin by examining one of the most important contexts for group work, public deliberation, as an increasingly common form of civic engagement.

Understanding Public Deliberation

Preview. *Deliberative forums may vary in size and specific purpose. Even so, many overarching principles of deliberative discourse ideally govern them. Public deliberation is no panacea. At its best, it can lead to diverse tangible and intangible outcomes. Its potential benefits, however, are influenced by contextual factors. Under ideal circumstances, deliberation will be characterized by a spirit of dialogue.*

The notion of public deliberation grows out of democratic theory. According to Simone Chambers, the theory of deliberative democracy focuses on the communicative processes of opinion formation that precede voting.[2] Although the act of voting itself is a personal decision, the process of deliberation is concerned with public "account giving"—how people articulate, explain, and justify their political opinions and policy preferences to their fellow citizens. In other words, the theory of democratic deliberation is talk-focused. In a sense, then, public deliberation is the process through which democracy is enacted.[3]

Communication scholar John Gastil defines public deliberation as "judicious argument, critical listening, and earnest decision making."[4] Gastil echoes educational philosopher John Dewey, who described *full* deliberation as a careful examination of a problem or issue, including the identification of possible solutions, the establishment of evaluative criteria, and the use of those criteria in identifying the best solution.[5] Of course, deliberation in the real world does not always work so neatly. But by striving to deliberate as fully and completely as possible, citizens can improve the process and the outcomes.

Public deliberation, then, focuses on discourse among citizens—as they engage in dialogue, explore ideas, and strive to reach some common understandings and agreements about the legitimacy of specific courses of action. This discourse is a very real measure of civic engagement—as much so as voting, attending meetings, working for a political party, participating in voluntary organizations, and so forth. Deliberating with others in public provides the opportunity for citizens to develop and express their views, learn from the positions of others, identify shared concerns and preferences, and come to understand and reach judgments about matters of public concern. These kinds of exchanges are a "central way of clarifying and nego-tiating deep divisions over material interests and moral values."[6] At the same time, they can be critical for airing disagreements that have *not* been articulated, perhaps because so many citizens have become disengaged from public life.

As we consider public deliberation, we must recognize that its forms are varied. Sometimes it occurs in formal, larger settings, such as town hall meetings between political representatives and their constituents. On other occasions, it may occur more privately, in homes, schools, churches, libraries, and community centers. It can also involve face-to-face exchanges, phone conversations, e-mail exchanges, and Internet forums. Finally, it may be focused on local, national, or international issues of public concern.

Engaging in Dialogue

Whether the goal of public deliberation is viewed as education, consensus seeking, conflict exploration, or advocacy,[7] the deliberative process is more likely to be suc-cessful if the participants seek to engage one another in a respectful dialogue, or what we have previously referred to as arguing in good faith. As award-winning author Daniel Yankelovich points out, dialogue is most easily understood by contrasting it with the kind of debate whose only goal is to *win* an argument.[8] *Highlighting Dialogue* that follows summarizes the contrast.

Highlighting Dialogue

Making Deliberation Work

Debate	Dialogue
Assuming that there is a right answer and you have it	Assuming that many people have pieces of the answer and that together they can craft a solution
Attempting to prove the other side wrong in a combative manner	Working together toward a common understanding in a collaborative manner
Emphasizing winning over finding common ground	Emphasizing discovering common ground over winning
Listening to find flaws and make counterarguments	Listening to understand, to find meaning and agreement
Defending assumptions as truth	Revealing assumptions for reevaluation
Critiquing the other side's position	Reexamining all positions
Defending one's own views against those of others	Admitting that others' thinking can improve one's own
Searching for flaws and weaknesses in others' positions	Searching for strengths and value in others' positions
Seeking a conclusion or vote that ratifies your position	Discovering new options, not seeking to win

Source: Daniel Yankelovich, *The Magic of Dialogue: Transforming Conflict into Cooperation* (New York: Touchstone, 1999), 39–40.

Journalist Scott London points out that deliberative dialogue differs from other forms of public discourse because its objective is to *think together*, "not so much to reach a conclusion as to discover where a conclusion might lie."[9] Thinking together involves listening deeply and with empathy to other points of view. In many discussions, participants bat ideas back and forth, but they seem more interested in articulating their *own* views than truly identifying with others' perspectives or striving to understand what others are saying.

Participants need to approach deliberative dialogue with a spirit of equality. Even if status differences exist among those deliberating, they must be set aside so that each person is treated as an equal. As Yankelovich maintains, "In genuine dialogue, there is no arm-twisting, no pulling of rank, no hint of sanctions for holding politically incorrect attitudes, no coercive influences of any sort, whether overt of indirect."[10] Mixing people of unequal status and authority does not preclude dialogue, but it does make it more challenging to achieve. Those of higher rank must take the initiative in creating a safe space for trust building and the open airing of diverse views.

The deliberative process usually revolves around a pressing question that needs to be addressed, rather than a problem that can be efficiently solved. London notes that the Greeks believed that individuals uncover the truth for themselves by reasoning with others. He inventories what they envisioned, writing:

> By questioning and probing each other, carefully dissecting and analyzing ideas, finding inconsistencies, never attacking or insulting, but always searching for what they could accept between them, they could gradually attain deeper understanding and insight.[11]

In this spirit, deliberative dialogue is aimed at establishing a framework for mutual understanding and a common purpose that transcends individual ideas and opinions. While it may not produce consensus, it *can* produce collective insight and judgment that reflects the thinking of the group as a whole. When the deliberative process works well, it links people's private ideas and interests with what we might think of as *public values*—values that are clarified and corroborated through the process of group inquiry.

Understanding How Deliberative Dialogue Works

While there is no fixed procedure for organizing a deliberative dialogue, certain steps or stages are fairly typical. To begin, a facilitator welcomes participants, invites self-introductions, and quickly reviews the guidelines for dialogue. If participants have questions about the guidelines, the facilitator will address those before proceeding.

Participants then enter into *exploratory* dialogue—a potentially awkward time when some sit back and watch or express their views tentatively, perhaps sizing up others in the group or scrutinizing the procedures. As individuals begin to relate personal stories of their relationship to the issue at hand, a more comfortable group dynamic begins to unfold. Through the exploratory phase, group members may begin to establish trust and cohesiveness. They also grapple with "naming" the issue—a process that may take them in new and perhaps unanticipated directions. They may discover, for example, that the issue they thought they had come to discuss is only a part, or a symptom, of a deeper and more complex issue. So, a community group may initially come together because they are concerned about neighborhood crime, but as they deliberate, they may end up focusing on a broader set of concerns, such as poverty or at-risk youth.

Later, the dialogue will shift from inquiry and exploration to *purposeful deliberation*, as the group begins to wrestle with what may look like competing choices. Conflict and disagreement is almost certain as the group seeks to identify core group values that may transcend individual differences. Participants help generate productive dialogue when they indicate that their ideas are tentative, not cast in stone, and signal their willingness to listen, to grow, and to change. Participants also advance a spirit of dialogue when they are respectful of turn-taking norms, so that no one dominates the conversation. They also show their commitment to dialogue by establishing a supportive communication environment, where mutual respect is the norm.[12]

Deliberative groups come together for different reasons and with different outcomes in mind. Some are content to set directions for further study or to arrive at a shared sense of how best to address an issue. Others use that collective judgment to arrive at decisions about what course of action to pursue. Either way, the deliberative process comes to an end when the facilitator sums up what has been said (or asks group members to do so), points out areas of agreement and lingering disagreement, articulates the overarching concerns that are shared, allows for final comments, and points to "next steps," if appropriate.

Based on his studies of a number of deliberative groups, London argues that what distinguishes an ordinary from an extraordinary dialogue is the "presence of some transforming moment, or critical turning point." At this crucial point, participants shift out of identifying solely with their own point of view and entertain the possibility of developing a collective understanding of the issue at hand.[13]

Compelling personal narratives may trigger this kind of turning point, making abstract and ideological views more concrete and understandable. When individuals in the group recount their personal struggle with drug addiction, their experience of living on the streets, their battle with mental illness, or their anger and despair at being the target of racist or homophobic remarks, others in the group may be moved, perhaps for the first time. Personal narratives give the problem a human face.[14]

Benefits of Public Deliberation

The potential benefits of public deliberation are many. Among the most consistently cited are:

- Citizens will become more engaged and active in civic affairs.
- Tolerance for opposing points of view will increase.
- Citizens will improve their understanding of their own preferences and will be able to better justify those preferences with arguments.
- People in conflict will set aside their "win-lose" approach as they begin to perceive some sense of interdependence.
- Faith in the democratic process will be enhanced as citizens grow to feel empowered.
- Political decisions will become more considered and informed by relevant reasons and evidence.
- Collective decision making will grow in frequency and quality.[15]

There is considerable evidence that public deliberation can, under the right circumstances, produce impressive results. Gastil, for example, has documented numerous real-world deliberative initiatives, including a community "visioning process" held in Chattanooga, Tennessee. This deliberative process involved 50 community activists and volunteers who met over a 20-week period. Their deliberations produced a list of priorities and solutions, including a shelter for abused women and a riverfront park. The organizers next developed a series of neighborhood associations and new nonprofit organizations. Eight years later most of the solutions that had emerged from the forums had been implemented.[16]

Participants often also emerge "changed." Research on the National Issues Forums has reported that deliberative forums can produce an array of positive results, including increasing the participants' sense of community identity, enhancing their interest in politics, and making them more "deliberative" in their political conversations.[17] An extensive survey of small-group participants reported that, as a result of their deliberations, they subsequently donated money to charitable organizations (57 percent), became more interested in politics or social issues (45 percent), volunteered in the community (43 percent), changed their mind about a political or social issue (40 percent), and participated in a political rally or worked for a political campaign (12 percent).[18]

Potential Problems

Public deliberation does not always yield such positive outcomes. Much depends on participants' expectations, the deliberative format used, the facilitator's skill, and whether the groups feel that their deliberations have any real impact. For example, one study reported on the feelings of frustration experienced by members of a deliberative group who had made specific recommendations for health-care reform and environmental regulation. Later, they felt their deliberations had been in vain when the federal government failed to enact any sort of reform.[19] In general, when participants feel that they are "just talking" and that their talk will not have any measurable impact on policy making, they tend to experience post-deliberation frustration.[20]

It is also possible that participating in deliberative forums may increase participants' sense of *self*-efficacy while reducing a sense of *group* efficacy. One study found that participants left a challenging forum more confident in their own ability to take effective individual action but more skeptical of the efficacy of group-based political action. However, the reactions of participants seemed to depend on the nature of their experiences in the forums. Those who engaged in relatively successful forums—with well-prepared participants, clear guidelines, effective facilitators, and adequate time devoted to deliberation—reported greater attitude changes and more positive feelings about the group experience.[21] Facilitators must be well trained, capable of providing adequate structure while allowing plenty of room for the exploration of diverse perspectives, and able to help group members achieve a sense of closure. Either too much intervention (so that the group members are not really experiencing the hard work of deliberation) or too little (so that the group rambles out of control and often reaches agreement too early) tends to lead to poor outcomes and dissatisfaction.[22] In the next section, we turn our attention to some discussion structures that provide a potentially helpful context for deliberative dialogue.

Group Structures That Encourage Dialogue and Deliberation

Preview. *Some organizations have sought to create group interaction formats that are intended to encourage open, constructive, and engaged dialogue. The format a group should use depends on its size and intended purpose.*

Although the list of deliberative formats is extensive and includes citizen juries, roundtables, and public hearings, we focus here on two of the more widespread deliberative formats: study circles and National Issues Forums.

Study Circles

The Study Circles Resource Center (SCRC) was created by the Topsfield Foundation in 1989 to advance deliberative democracy and improve the quality of public life in the United States. Its goal is to develop communication tools to involve a large number of people, from every background and way of life, in face-to-face dialogue and action on critical issues.[23]

A study circle typically consists of 8 to 12 participants who are guided by an impartial facilitator. Study circle members are encouraged to consider many perspectives, rather than advocating for a particular point of view. Ground rules set the tone for a respectful, productive discussion. Participants are encouraged to listen attentively to one another and to work at building trusting relationships. A typical study circle will meet over multiple sessions, with members sharing personal experiences initially, examining diverse points of view, seeking common ground (while respecting individual differences), and ultimately devising creative strategies for action. Facilitators remind group members that they *can* make a difference.

Following the SCRC model, individual study circles often function as part of a community-wide effort in which a number of study circles meet simultaneously all across a community to address an issue of common concern. These groups contain people of all races and ethnic backgrounds, men and women, and people of all income levels. They also involve individuals and organizations from different sectors of the community, such as the Chamber of Commerce, the faith community, the media, local government, the United Way, the police department, the YMCA, the Urban League, and various neighborhood associations. Each brings unique tools, knowledge, and grassroots connections to the partnership.

Community-wide study circles are designed to be an inclusive program that invites the whole community to get involved in public dialogue and problem solving. At the end of the process, members of diverse study circles assemble in a community-wide meeting in which they learn how others are working to make a difference. They may begin to discern how their contribution might fit into the larger picture. Some groups may decide to join forces and work together, whereas others will choose to remain independent. In either case, everyone will have the chance to exchange ideas with public officials and other community members about public policy and discover ways to collaborate.[24] The *Focus on Civic Engagement* that follows highlights the story of one successful study circle.

National Issues Forums

National Issues Forums (NIF) is a nonpartisan, nationwide network of locally sponsored public forums for the consideration of public policy issues. NIF is rooted in the simple notion that people in a democracy need to come together to reason and to talk—to deliberate about common problems.[25] The NIF network has grown to include thousands of civic clubs, religious organizations, libraries, schools, and many other groups who meet to discuss critical public issues. Scholars have described the NIF process as the most pervasive model of small-group deliberation in the United States, used yearly by as many as 15,000 groups.[26] Forum participants range from teenagers to retirees, from prison inmates to community leaders, and from literacy students to university students.

NIF formats are varied and may include small groups, such as study circles, or large-group gatherings similar to town hall meetings (see *Focus on Civic Engagement* on page 481). NIF does not advocate specific solutions or points of view. Rather, it provides citizens of diverse views and experiences with the opportunity to carefully study an issue, consider a broad range of choices (weighing the pros and cons of each), and meet with each other in a public dialogue to identify the concerns they hold in common while seeking to identify common ground for action.

Although all forum activity is locally organized, moderated, and financed, the materials they use are produced by the Kettering Foundation and promoted by the National Issues Forums Institute. Prior to a typical NIF discussion, organizers encourage participants to read an "issue book" published by the NIF Institute. Each book provides factual information and outlines three or four broad policy choices for addressing an issue. During the forums, trained moderators encourage participants to consider the nature of the issue being discussed, the pros and cons of each, and the values underlying the choices. Forum moderators are trained to maintain

---

Focus on Civic Engagement

A Study Circle Success Story

Jackson, Minnesota—Concerned about the growing problem of poverty in their community, citizens turned to study circles. These circles included senior citizens, town leaders, citizens living in poverty, and church members. At the end of the process, an action forum led to such concrete outcomes as the creation of a community foundation aimed at

eradicating poverty and the establishment of a resource room where citizens can drop off donations or pick up basic life necessities. In addition, volunteerism has soared.

Source: Brad Rourke, "Talk That Leads Somewhere: Study Circles in Jackson, Minnesota," www.studycircles.org/en/Article.428.aspx (accessed December 28, 2006).

Focus on Civic Engagement

Planning the Town Meeting

The Democracy 2000 Civic Engagement Project believes that if all segments of the community become actively involved in searching for solutions, a community's conflicts can be turned into agreements that win wide public support. They suggest the following guidelines for organizing a productive town meeting:

- *Assemble an organizing committee*—make sure that the organizers will be seen as neutral or represent all major shades of opinion. The more points of view the committee encompasses, the more successful the project is likely to be.
- *Define the issue or goals*—the committee will have to agree on exactly what issue to tackle and what the meeting is expected to accomplish.

- *Attract broad participation*—seek endorsements for the meeting from groups and individuals who have large followings in the community and span a wide range of opinions.
- *Maximize public and media interest*—the meeting will have the greatest impact on the community if it draws a big turnout and is covered by local media. Prepare and distribute a press kit that explains how the meeting could lead to resolving an issue that greatly concerns the community.

Source: "The Civic Engagement Project: Planning an Interactive Town Meeting," www.democracy2000.org/meetingplan.htm (accessed November 30, 2006).

neutral positions and to steer participants away from digressions, logical pitfalls, indecisiveness, and disruptive arguments.[27] Recent NIF issue books include:

- *Terrorism: What Should We Do Now?*
- *Crime and Punishment: Is Justice Being Served?*
- *Money and Politics: Who Owns Democracy?*

Town Hall meetings promote active participation in deliberating issues important to a community.

- *The Environment at Risk: Responding to the Growing Dangers*
- *The Health Care Cost Explosion*
- *Public Schools: Are They Making the Grade?*[28]

These topics can be adapted to the local level, or addressed as part of larger problem that may involve citizens in diverse communities.

Whatever form the deliberating groups take, nearly 60 years of group communication research have taught us that there are specific factors that may determine whether or not they are likely to be effective.

Factors That Influence Effective Group Deliberation

Preview. *As groups work to complete tasks or grapple with difficult problems, they may interact in ways that enhance the quality of the decisions they make and the bonds they form, or they may deliberate less effectively because they fail to recognize some of the complex dynamics of group communication.*

A good place to begin is by examining those factors that influence the effectiveness of group deliberation across communication contexts. How groups handle these factors may determine whether they struggle or function in an empowering and productive way.

Conflict

Whenever people interact in groups, particularly if they are deliberating about an important, controversial, or complex issue, conflict is nearly inevitable. Conflict can emerge over differences in opinions, values, goals, competition for scarce resources, personal incompatibilities, status differences, cultural differences, or misinformation, misunderstanding, or communication breakdowns.[29]

In public life, conflict is inevitable. It is difficult to imagine any community—especially a diverse society—in which there are no differences of interests or opinion. In fact, the freedom to express our differences is fundamental to the process of effective deliberation. Through the ages, democratic ideals have revolved around finding participatory ways to live with, work through, and resolve our conflicting ideas and interests. Making conflict productive is an essential aspect of a democratic society. Although study circles and National Issues Forums are a good start, we need to do more to create democratic arenas in which everyday people can engage in a productive exploration of differences and learn to work together.

We could better manage conflict during deliberation. Public conflict is often treated as a zero-sum game, in which a win for one side means an automatic loss for the other. Antagonism overshadows our willingness to search for common ground and decreases the potential for collaboration.[30] We may also grow to underestimate the ability of the community and society as a whole to solve public problems. The media, too, play a role—covering public concerns as arenas of intractable conflict and often reporting on extreme positions. The nuances and areas of ambivalence are frequently ignored in favor of what will make a good story.

Often in these situations there is little room or reason for citizen involvement. Instead of involving large numbers of people in addressing an issue of shared concern, a few people who have an exceptional zeal for the issue enter into the public debate to battle for their side. Those who see the issue as important but feel ambivalent or uncertain about how best to proceed are left out of conversations about such critical public issues as education, poverty, jobs, youth issues, immigration, and much more.[31]

Whether conflict functions in a positive way depends on how it is viewed and managed. Although many of us are conflict avoidant, we must recognize that conflict *can* lead to enhanced creativity, a deeper understanding of complex problems, and the generation of better solutions. Conflict is not so much to be avoided or feared as *managed* constructively.[32]

Tolerance of Dissent

Sometimes citizens lose patience with the deliberative process—perhaps because they want to make a decision quickly. Some may feel that they have been grappling with a problem for a long time, with no emerging consensus on a course of action. Others may feel annoyed by those who raise objections or suggest a different way of viewing things. When an individual or a small minority expresses a dissenting opinion, the majority may react with particular intolerance. If the majority of citizens decide that they want to move on, they may begin to exert pressure on those who stand in the way.

Group pressure for uniformity can be quite powerful. One early study found that even if those in the majority simply stated their opinions *without* exerting any kind of pressure, individuals (who privately disagreed with them) would often pretend to agree with the majority view.[33] Giving in to group pressure can be especially tempting for those who really value their group membership or strongly identify with the group.[34]

Situational factors may play a significant role, too.[35] In general, we are more likely to conform to group pressure when we are in situations that are ambiguous or confusing, when other group members are unanimous in their views, or when the group contains those of higher status than our own. We may also feel a lot of pressure when the group is highly cohesive, or if a state of crisis or emergency exists (so that the group is being pressed by external factors to reach a unanimous decision).[36]

Those in the majority may use a variety of tactics to pressure minority members into yielding—ranging from incessant and sometimes hostile questioning or arguing to teasing or ridiculing to simply rejecting those who stand in the way of consensus.[37] In some cases, how the group responds to a dissenter may depend on his or her status in the group, sometimes tolerating more "deviation" from those of higher status.[38]

How does one respond to group pressure? Both individual and situational variables play a role. For instance, some of us tend to "go with the flow," preferring to fit in with the group rather than risk being perceived as "making waves." Others may grow to agree with the group's perceptions—either because we are, in fact, genuinely persuaded, or have begun to question the validity of our own views. Finally,

Expressing dissent in an articulate, well-informed way promotes dialogue and enhances group decision making.

some of us may respond to group pressure by refusing to yield. Challenging the group's authority in this way can result in a variety of outcomes, including rejection or punishment. Organizational communication scholar Phil Tompkins recounts the story of the engineer who unsuccessfully argued against launching the ill-fated space shuttle *Challenger*. Even though several other engineers had expressed reservations about the launch, they eventually went along with the management team. The lone dissenting engineer lost his job and was socially ostracized.[39]

If a group tolerates, or even encourages dissent, those who disagree may run few risks. In some cases, they may be quite persuasive. The *way* those in the minority articulate their views can make a huge difference. Much depends on being well informed and articulate and engaging in debate in a spirit of respectful dialogue.[40]

The Role of Cohesiveness

As citizens deliberate in groups over time, they may become quite cohesive. Although cohesiveness *may* function positively, it can also lead to intolerance of dissent and impaired decision making. One of the most extensive investigations of the potentially negative impact of cohesiveness on a group's ability to make intelligent decisions was conducted by Irving Janis.[41] Janis examined the decision-making processes leading to several historic military and political fiascoes, including the decision to cross the

38th parallel in the Korean War, the Kennedy Administration's decision to invade the Bay of Pigs, the choice to escalate the war in Vietnam, and the decisions surrounding the Watergate cover-up. More recently, others have used his framework to examine the U.S. decision to go to war with Iraq.[42]

To explain how poor decisions may be made, Janis introduced the concept of *groupthink*, which he defined as "a model of thinking that people engage in when they are deeply involved in a cohesive in-group, when the members' striving for unanimity overrides their motivation to realistically appraise alternative courses of action."[43] He also pointed out that although most deliberative groups strive for agreement over time, those who are caught up in groupthink seek consensus "prematurely" so that full and free discussion of alternative courses of action simply never occurs.[44] Janis identified a number of negative qualities that commonly lead to groupthink, including an illusion of invulnerability, an unquestioned belief in the group's inherent morality, a shared illusion of unanimity, self-censorship, and, of course, direct pressure exerted on dissenters.[45]

Janis does *not* argue that all highly cohesive groups fall prey to groupthink. Rather, he points out that strategies exist for counteracting it. Janis believes that the group's leader is in a position to insist on the open-minded pursuit of alternative courses of action. Specifically, he suggests that the appointed leader should:

A Senate committee investigated the administration's belief that Iraq possessed weapons of mass destruction, a belief that may have been reinforced through the "groupthink" process.

- Assign to everyone the role of critical evaluator.
- Avoid stating personal views, particularly at the outset.
- Bring in outsiders representing diverse interests to talk with and listen to the group.
- Play the devil's advocate and ask specific others to take turns in that role.
- Let the group deliberate without the leader from time to time.
- After a tentative decision has been made, hold a "second-chance" meeting, at which each member is required to express as strongly as possible any residual doubts.[46]

When those who lead deliberative groups insist on and groups endorse these kinds of norms, cohesive groups should function extremely effectively. Cohesiveness need not doom a group. On the contrary, with appropriate vigilance, cohesiveness can contribute to constructive, satisfying group outcomes.

Role Structure

The norms that develop in deliberative groups typically suggest (or require) appropriate modes of conduct for all group members (such as coming to the group as an informed, thoughtful citizen, engaging in respectful dialogue, and maintaining an attitude of open-mindedness). At the same time, however, these groups need considerable role diversity among their membership to function effectively. Individuals perform different, although often interdependent, functions as they work together on varied tasks. In addition, most will play multiple roles over time.

Roles are behaviors that perform some function in a specific group context. For instance, a group member may use humor during a meeting. Her humor, however, may function in diverse ways—to relieve tension, to diminish someone else's ego (especially if the humor is sarcastic), to get the group off track by distracting members from the task at hand, or to build group cohesiveness. Similarly, asking a question can function as a simple request for information, as a strategy for changing the subject, as a vehicle for introducing a new topic, or as a put-down or challenge ("What would *you* know about working in a minimum-wage job?").

Determining whether any one of these behaviors has functioned positively or negatively will depend on the context. So, if a discussion has become bogged down for an extended period of time and someone asks a question that moves the group beyond the sticking point, the question likely functioned constructively. But, if a group is still legitimately grappling with a complex problem, a subject-changing question (if pursued) might result in inadequate exploration of the problem under consideration.

Various classification schemes have been developed to describe the roles that group members enact. Typically, these roles fall into one of two main categories: group task roles and group building and maintenance roles.[47]

Task roles involve the communication functions necessary for a group to accomplish its task, such as problem solving, decision making, information exchange, or conflict resolution. One man who serves on the board of a nonprofit organization, for example, excels at offering financial data, explaining the budget, and providing clarification for anyone who is confused. Another listens thoughtfully to everyone, probes for additional information and opinions, and then is able to integrate what others have said into a coherent statement. Sometimes, he offers suggestions for new ways of approaching a problem. Both of these men are playing important task roles on this board that advance the board's ability to make effective decisions.

The other major roles are those that build and maintain the group—helping it to develop and sustaining interpersonal relationships within it. Group members who play these roles help others to feel positive about the task and to interact harmoniously and respectfully. On the same board mentioned above, one woman excels at mediating conflict and reconciling differences of opinion. She also encourages reticent group members to speak. Another man does an exceptional job of praising ideas that he finds creative or interesting. By performing these building and maintenance roles, these board members are encouraging cooperation among others and building a spirit of solidarity within the group.

In contrast to the positive roles, there are some roles that rarely function constructively in groups—those that tend to further self-interests over group interests and goals. One group member, for example, might try to dominate the conversation, with little regard for turn-taking norms. Another might be consistently critical of nearly everyone's ideas. Still another might attempt to drop names or brag about his children's accomplishments. These self-serving roles can get the group off track and lead to tensions.

In general, when positive roles are enacted and shared in deliberative groups (with negative roles minimized), they contribute to constructive outcomes, such as enhanced morale and sound decision making.[48] Moreover, those who perform the positive roles are actually serving as group leaders insofar as their behaviors assist the group in accomplishing its goals.

Status and Power

While much research on group roles has taken place in laboratory settings, enacting roles in real-life civic or professional settings is more complex. When individuals deliberate in task forces, committees, study circles, or teams, they bring to the meeting their professional identity as well as their status within the community. For example, one of the authors of this book recently joined a community group, the "social entrepreneurship" committee. The committee's task is to pool community resources and seek ways to help nonprofits become more self-sustaining by starting their own businesses and generating a portion of the revenue needed to advance their mission. The committee consists of the executive directors of several prominent nonprofits (including two who are already running successful businesses), the director of the United Way, a well-known judge, a member of the city council, a representative of the mayor's office, the president of the chamber of commerce, the director of the local university's new Center on Social Entrepreneurship, and a few concerned citizens who have varying connections to local nonprofits.

In nearly any real-life group, group members will vary in their status (the value, importance, or prestige associated with their given position) and power (their potential for controlling resources and/or influencing others). In general, members of the social entrepreneurship committee members possess high status. Yet, there are significant differences. Some bring success stories to the group. Others have labored with social justice issues in the community for more than three decades. Still others bring impressive academic credentials and strong ties to potential sources of financial support. A few are new to their positions or are simply eager to pick up ideas for action. Who will function most influentially as this group deliberates over time? Who will help the group advance its goals? Will those with less experience or knowledge participate actively? Much will depend on how those with the *greatest* power and status conduct themselves.

The bases of power are many.[49] Some are powerful because they have the capacity to reward or punish. The United Way director, for example, can influence which nonprofits are invited into the United Way circle (leading to financial gains or losses). Others, those with compelling success stories, are held as experts or as role models. Still others have the connectional power to make things happen because of their placement in crucial political networks (the judge and the social justice leader). Some possess many dimensions of power. The program director from the university, for example, is charismatic, is able to place interns at nonprofits of his choice (a valuable resource), is knowledgeable about successful entrepreneurship models throughout the United States, and is politically well connected.

Whenever deliberative groups are composed of those with varying degrees of power and status, group members do not communicate as equals, and this inequality can serve as an obstacle to effective interaction and decision making.[50] In general, when communicating with someone of higher status, one is likely to communicate supportively and cautiously, to attempt to seek approval, to downplay "bad" news, and to act deferentially. Of course, much depends on the nature of the relationship between the parties. If the person of higher status is someone who is genuinely respectful of others' views, those with less status are better able to communicate openly and accurately. In fact, actively encouraging the expression of other ways of seeing or other courses of action may be well advised.

All group members must be concerned with the effectiveness of the group's problem-solving ability. By virtue of their power or status, some group members are in strategic positions for greatly influencing the quality of the group's decision-making process. The judicious use of authority to encourage the free expression of ideas and to reward initiative and innovative thinking can go far in eliminating the doubts and skepticism of less powerful group members.

As we have noted throughout this chapter, group members may deliberate in private settings as part of a committee or task force, or they may deliberate in public spaces as part of a community forum. There are also occasions, however, when individuals will speak in public as part of a formal group presentation.

Group Presentations

Preview. *When we deliberate in public as part of a community meeting, we typically come to communicate and think together with other citizens. We want to deepen our understanding of issues we view as important. We do not view ourselves as experts. Occasionally, however, we are called on to speak in public as part of a group presentation given for the benefit of an audience that has come to hear us speak.*

Public discussions often bring together representatives from several different organizations, all of whom share some expertise on the discussion topic, but each of whom possesses a different perspective. For example, a recent community forum on hunger and poverty in Bloomington, Indiana, brought together the executive directors of five local agencies: Martha's House (a transitional housing unit for those experiencing homelessness), Mother Hubbard's Cupboard (a food pantry for those living in poverty), the Community Kitchen (an agency that provides free daily dinners to anyone in need of a hot meal), the Shalom Community Center (a daytime shelter and resource center for those experiencing poverty and homelessness), and the Hoosier Hills Food Bank (a food pantry that provides most of the food used by the agencies that feed those in need). Each director made a brief presentation, followed by an extensive question-and-answer period with the audience.

As you begin to establish some expertise in areas related to your profession and become increasingly passionate and knowledgeable about issues within your community, you will be asked to participate in panels and symposia. In addition, your instructor may ask your class to form groups to discuss issues of concern to your local or university community. While these presentations share some similarities with public speaking, there also are some special considerations that you will want to think about.

Panel Discussions

Public discussions can occur in several different formats or patterns of discussant interaction. A panel discussion is a format in which the participants interact directly and spontaneously under the guidance of a moderator. No participant has a planned speech. Instead, each speaks briefly, rather frequently, and within the realm of courtesy, whenever he or she desires. Here are some guidelines for preparing for and participating in panel discussions:

- *Know the group.* Find out who the other panel members are and what organizations or positions they represent. Having this information, as well as anticipating the group's size, will help you tentatively plan what you want to say and how much you want to talk.
- *Obtain an agenda for the discussion.* The moderator should have some plan for how he or she wishes to organize the panel discussion. Having an agenda gives you some idea of what to expect and what issues the panel will address. Use the agenda as your guide to prepare for the discussion. Your goal is to be able to make a substantive contribution. Make a few notes, although most of your remarks should be fairly spontaneous.
- *Participate actively while sharing the floor with others.* The moderator may start with a brief statement or open question, and you can feel free to jump in and comment whenever you are ready. Make your comments succinct. Take turns with other panel members. The best panel discussions are lively and dynamic.
- *Use good interpersonal communication skills.* Listen to others attentively. If you do need to interrupt, do so politely and tactfully. Build on others' comments, if appropriate. Establish good eye contact with listeners while also communicating directly with other panelists. Cooperate with the moderator.

Symposium Presentations

A more formal mode of public discussion is the symposium, in which discussants prepare brief speeches representing their viewpoints. Each group member speaks in turn without interruption or interaction. The symposium leader usually

In a symposium, each member of the group speaks in turn, without interruption; typically, a discussion and/or question-and-answer period follows.

introduces the group members and provides a summary at the end of the discussion. During the actual discussion, however, there is no need for moderator intervention or guidance—except for providing transitions between speakers. The poverty presentation described previously is an example of a symposium. Here are some guidelines for preparing for a symposium:

- *Know your assigned topic.* Understand what you are expected to talk about as well as the topics of other symposium members. Make sure you do not cover ground that others will cover. Once you understand your role, prepare your symposium presentation just as you would any other speech.
- *Respect group norms.* Stay within the time limits you have been given so that everyone will have a fair chance to speak. When you are not speaking, listen attentively to others. You are part of the group but also part of the audience. If reasonable, adapt your style of delivery to that of others in the group. If others remain seated while they speak (and if you are comfortable doing so), remain seated as well, unless you have a compelling reason to deliver your remarks standing.
- *Maintain a cooperative attitude.* Being asked to speak as part of a group can raise competitive feelings. Although the tendency to wonder who is going over best with the audience is understandable, it is better to stay focused on communicating as effectively as you can and to hope that everyone in the group makes an effective presentation so that the whole symposium is a success.

Both the panel discussion and the symposium are nearly always followed by a question-and-answer period during which members of the audience are encouraged to ask questions and express opinions. The forum is generally guided by the moderator, and questions may be directed to individual members or to the group as a whole. In either type of presentation, it is important that you anticipate responding to listener questions.

Regardless of the discussion format, whether you are deliberating in private or in public, as part of a more formal presentation or as part of a more spontaneous community group, there are certain kinds of behaviors that will serve you well. In this final section of the chapter, we will focus on these behaviors and offer some useful guidelines.

Guidelines for Deliberating in Groups

Preview. *Regardless of the context in which you are deliberating with others—whether it is part of a study circle, a National Issues forum, or a departmental team within an organization, there are certain kinds of behaviors that group members should display throughout the discussion.*

A group deliberation is only as good as its participants. Informed, participative members contribute to a deeper understanding of the issue or task before the group and enhance the chances that good decisions will be made. Uninformed, uninvolved, or unskilled participants virtually guarantee the group's failure. In this section, we will lay out some behaviors we have found effective in promoting positive group outcomes.

Prepare Carefully for Each Meeting

Every group member needs to be as knowledgeable as possible regarding the subject of discussion or deliberation.[51] It is probably inevitable that some members of your group will be better informed on certain aspects of the discussion subject than you are. But you will have knowledge and experience to contribute as well. Do your homework. Reflect on important issues that are likely to arise.

Approach the Deliberation with a Group Orientation

We previously noted the importance of approaching the group interaction with a spirit of collaboration. Avoid making irrevocable judgments in advance. Rather, each person should be group-oriented throughout—allowing for common ground and consensus to develop as the group deliberates over time. Each person shares some responsibility for the success or failure of the entire group. Whenever anyone allows personal ambitions to replace commitment to the objectives of the group, he or she is functioning in a manner detrimental to the group's success.

Participate Actively

Every group member must take an active part in the discussion and activities of the group. If you sit back silently during group meetings, you contribute nothing to the group or to your own credibility in the group, the community, or the organization. On the other hand, if you participate actively and make positive contributions to the group, you will help the group achieve its goals, improve your own standing within the group, and build a reputation as someone who is a valued asset in group situations. This perception may lead to other opportunities for you to become involved in deliberation and problem solving.

Maintain an Attitude of Open-Mindedness

Closely related to a group-oriented attitude is one of open-mindedness. Group members should enter the discussion as open-mindedly as possible and strive to maintain an attitude of open-mindedness throughout the decision-making process. Encourage the expression of all points of view. State your own views with some degree of tentativeness. If others persuade you, do not hesitate to change your mind.

Listen Carefully, Constructively, and Critically

When someone else is talking, listen to that person with the intent of seeking an understanding of his or her point of view. Even if you do not agree with it, give it fair consideration. At the same time, do not hesitate to question someone whose information seems vague or whose ideas are not clearly articulated. Research has shown that effective groups are careful and rigorous in the way they explore ideas and evaluate alternatives.[52] Good group members take each other seriously, have a healthy respect for each other, are not afraid to challenge each other, and expect to be challenged in return.

Play Several Different Roles

As we discussed earlier in the chapter, group communication scholars have identified nearly 20 constructive roles that group members can play, ranging from information giver to harmonizer. It is easy to get in a rut and perform only 1 or 2 roles. For instance, a well-informed or dominant participant might primarily provide ideas and information and control the flow of the conversation. That person should develop a more balanced approach, perhaps by *also* seeking others' ideas and offering appreciation when someone comes up with a good plan of action. When roles are shared in deliberative groups, everyone benefits.

Pay Attention to Nonverbal Communication

Often when we think of people working together in groups, we focus on what they say. But it is important to watch how they are acting.[53] Lack of eye contact may signal disengagement, poor preparation, or interpersonal tensions. Folded arms could suggest dissatisfaction with what others are saying, or the course of action that is being pursued. A group that meets around a round table demonstrates a desire for equal participation and a shared opportunity for mutual influence. Of course, when a group is culturally diverse, differences in cultural norms and practices will need to be taken into consideration, as addressed in *Highlighting Diversity* that follows.[54] As a sensitive group member, you will want to be attuned to how the group is behaving nonverbally, as well as to what they are verbalizing. If some group members seem uncomfortable or disengaged, you or the facilitator may want to take some action so that everyone is able to function constructively and have an impact.

Focus on Matters of Substance—Not Personalities

Every group member should strive to concentrate on substantive concerns. Every decision-making or deliberative group has a task before it. The individuals composing the group, however, are human beings who possess personalities that occasionally conflict. Severe personality clashes can damage the group's ability to establish common ground and move in the direction of good decision making.

As a mature group member, you should realize that it is impossible to be equally attracted to every other member. It stands to reason that some of your fellow discussants will seem insensitive, uninformed or unintelligent, domineering, or rude from time to time. Even so, the important consideration from the viewpoint of the group's welfare is to assist *all* members, regardless of personality peculiarities or irritations, to contribute their best effort to the group's deliberations. In *Highlighting Ethics*, we conclude this section by emphasizing the importance of ethical group communication.

Highlighting Diversity

Recognizing Cultural Differences in Nonverbal Communication

As groups have become increasingly multicultural, we must improve our skills in perceiving one another. Rather than interpreting others' behavior in terms of our own cultural norms, we must be respectful of cultural differences. Here are a few examples:

- North Americans prefer to maintain a greater personal distance with other parties than do those from the Middle East or Latin America. Many Arabs and Latin Americans see North Americans as distant and cold, while North Americans see the others as invading their personal space.
- Americans expect others to look them in the eyes as a way of exhibiting trust, openness, and sincerity, while other cultures consider this kind of eye contact to be impolite or even insulting. Africans, for example, are taught to avoid eye contact when listening to others.
- Arabs tend to use elaborate and ritualized forms of communication, especially during greetings. Wide gestures and animated faces may come across as boisterous, loud, and unprofessional to Americans.
- While the Japanese are very comfortable with silence, and may even close their eyes when they are deeply concentrating, others (including Arabs and Americans) may perceive silence as a sign that something is wrong.

Sources: Michelle Le Baron, *Bridging Cultural Conflicts: A New Approach for a Changing World* (San Francisco: Jossey-Bass, 2003); and Richard D. Lewis, *When Cultures Collide*, rev. ed. (London: Nicholas Brealey, 2000).

Highlighting Ethics

Communicating Ethically in Groups

Embedded in all the other guidelines presented in this chapter is an overarching concern for ethical deliberation. Here are some guidelines:

- Show concern for others' ideas, respect for their feelings, and willingness to give them time to reflect on new information.
- Develop an attitude of being less interested in winning an argument than in achieving common ground or consensus based on mutual understanding and respect.
- Refuse to use the group as an arena for promoting special interests or advancing your own status at the expense of others.
- Remain as eager to learn from and listen to others as to offer them your opinions and advice.
- Approach others in a spirit of dialogue.

- Be willing to take extra time and put up with extra meetings for the sake of a better, more fully informed decision.
- Develop a sense of responsibility for the good of the group as a whole while remaining mindful of the relationship between the group and the rest of the organization or community.
- Demonstrate the maturity to realize that other legitimate groups may have different priorities and perspectives.
- Recognize that no matter how hard your group deliberates or how excellently it performs, others work hard as well and have legitimate needs to be fulfilled.

Thus, the ethical discussant is a good thinker, a good listener, a hard worker, and a responsible member of the community.

Summary

- Deliberating in groups is a common occurrence in our professional and civic lives. In deliberating, we share information, gain new perspectives, seek common ground, and make decisions.

- Organizations are increasingly team-based, and citizens encounter many opportunities to help solve problems in their communities by deliberating with others in all kinds of groups.

- In community settings citizens often gather together to deliberate about important public issues.
  - Ideally, these deliberations will lead to positive outcomes such as increased civic engagement, deeper understanding of the issues, increased tolerance for opposing points of view, and enhanced faith in the democratic process.
  - Whether these positive outcomes are realized will depend on such contextual factors as the facilitator's skill, participant expectations and preparation, and whether the groups' deliberations have any practical impact.
  - The more citizens are able to interact in a respectful spirit of dialogue, the better their chances of having a successful experience.

- Certain group structures and formats can help, too, such as working together in study circles or deliberating as part of a National Issues Forum.

- Many factors influence the effectiveness of a group's deliberations.

  - Learning to manage conflict constructively will play a huge role in any group's comfort levels, creativity, and productivity.

  - Welcoming diverse views and tolerating dissent is another key factor. If majority group members pressure those with differing views to "go along with the group," their ability to make judicious decisions may be impaired.

  - Highly cohesive groups whose members are strongly bonded may be vulnerable to "groupthink"—leading them to seek agreement before fully exploring alternative courses of action and listening to dissenters. Group leaders can do much to discourage groupthink through the example they provide.

  - In healthy groups, members tend to play a variety of task and maintenance roles, with self-serving behaviors minimized.

  - Power and status differences must be carefully managed. The burden is on those of higher status to establish an environment of trust.

- On occasion, you may be called on to make public presentations as part of a group.

  - Some of these group presentations take the form of a panel (complete with spontaneous interaction under the guidance of a moderator), while others are organized more formally in the form of a symposium (with each group member making a short speech).

  - After group presentations are made, listeners usually ask questions. The question-and-answer period often leads to an extensive sharing of ideas and information and a great deal of interaction between speakers and members of the audience.

- In all group settings, public or private, small or large, participants should seek to be well prepared, embrace a group orientation, participate actively, maintain an open mind, listen thoughtfully, play different constructive roles, pay attention to nonverbal communication (including cultural variations), focus on matters of substance, and communicate with the highest concern for ethics.

QUESTIONS FOR REVIEW AND REFLECTION

1. Why is it important for you to be knowledgeable about deliberating effectively in groups?
2. Explain your understanding of "public deliberation." Have you ever witnessed or participated in any kind of event or meeting that you would characterize as public deliberation? If so, describe how it worked.
3. What are the benefits and potential pitfalls of public deliberation?
4. What does it mean to communicate in a spirit of "dialogue"? Be sure to contrast dialogue with debate.
5. Compare and contrast study circles with National Issues Forums as group structures that encourage dialogue and deliberation. What are some topics in your community that might be fruitfully explored through one of these formats?
6. How might the following factors influence the effectiveness of any deliberative group? Think of concrete examples from your own group experiences.
   - Conflict
   - Intolerance of dissent

- Group cohesiveness
- Group role structure
- Status and power differences among group members

7. Compare and contrast a panel discussion with a symposium as particular forms of group presentations. How would you prepare for participating effectively in each of these? If you have ever presented as part of a panel or symposium, describe your experience.

8. This chapter describes a number of guidelines for effective participation in deliberative groups. Which of these do you think are especially important? Why? Can you think of any others that might also matter in particular contexts? If so, explain.

9. Have you ever worked in deliberative groups whose members were culturally diverse? If so, how did cultural differences impact the way you communicated with others and the overall effectiveness of the group?

10. What does ethical group deliberation mean to you? You can use the discussion here as a foundation, and then add your own perspective and experience.

ENDNOTES

1. See David A. Whetten and Kim Cameron, *Developing Management Skills*, 6th ed. (Englewood Cliffs, NJ: Prentice Hall, 2005), 390–450.

2. Simone Chambers, "Deliberative Democratic Theory," *Annual Review of Political Science* 6 (2003): 307–26.

3. Michael X. Delli Carpini, Fay Lomax Cook, and Lawrence R. Jacobs, "Public Deliberation, Discursive Participation, and Citizen Engagement: A Review of the Empirical Literature," *Annual Review of Political Science* 7 (2004): 315–44.

4. John Gastil, *By Popular Demand: Revitalizing Representative Democracy through Deliberative Elections* (Berkeley and Los Angeles: University of California Press, 2000).

5. See Randy Y. Hirokawa and Kathryn M. Rost, "Effective Group Decision-Making in Organizations," *Management Communication Quarterly* 5 (1992): 267–88.

6. Carpini, Cook, and Jacobs, "Public Deliberation," 319.

7. Mark Button and Kevin Mattson, "Deliberative Democracy in Practice: Challenges and Prospects for Civic Deliberation," *Polity* 31 (1999): 612–13.

8. Daniel Yankelovich, *The Magic of Dialogue: Transforming Conflict into Cooperation* (New York: Touchstone, 1999).

9. Scott London, "The Power of Deliberative Dialogue," www.scottlondon.com/reports/dialogue.html (accessed July 6, 2006). This essay was adapted from an essay by the same name, published in *Public Thought and Foreign Policy*, ed. Robert J. Kingston (Dayton, OH: Kettering Foundation, 2005).

10. Yankelovich, 41–46.

11. London, "Power of Deliberative Dialogue."

12. Jack Gibb, "Defensive Communication," *Journal of Communication* 11 (1961): 141–48; and Sharon Ellison, *Don't Be So Defensive* (Kansas City, KS: Andrews McMeel, 1998).

13. Connie Gersick, "Time and Transition in Work Teams: Toward a New Model of Group Development," in *Small Group Communication: Theory and Practice*, 8th ed., ed. Randy Y. Hirokawa et al. (Los Angeles: Roxbury Publishing, 2003), 59–75. Gersick points to the transformative potential and power of "transitional moments" in determining successful or unsuccessful group outcomes.

14. London, "Power of Deliberative Dialogue"; and David M. Ryfe, "Narrative and Deliberation in Small Group Forums," *Journal of Applied Communication Research* 34 (2006): 72–93.

15. Both Gastil, *By Popular Demand*, and Carpini, Cook, and Jacobs, "Public Deliberation," do an excellent job of summarizing the arguments in favor of public deliberation.

16. See Gastil, *By Popular Demand*, 149–60.

17. Michael K. Briand, *Practical Politics: Five Principles for a Community That Works* (Urbana: University of Illinois Press, 1999); and Michael Delli Carpini, "The Impact of the 'Money + Politics' Citizen Assemblies on Assembly Participants," report to the Pew Charitable Trusts, Philadelphia, 1997.

18. Robert Wuthnow, *Sharing the Journey: America's New Quest for Community* (New York: Free Press, 1994).

19. Mark Lindeman, "Opinion Quality and Policy Preferences in Deliberative Research," in *Research in Micropolitics: Political Decisionmaking, Deliberation, and Participation*, ed. Michael X. Delli Carpini, Leonie Huddy, and Robert Y. Shapiro (Greenwich, CT: JAI Press, 2002), 195–221.

20. Button and Mattson, "Deliberative Democracy in Practice," 609–37.

21. John Gastil, "The Effects of Deliberation on Political Beliefs and Conversation Behavior" (paper, International Communication Association, San Francisco, 1999).

22. Ryfe, "Narrative and Deliberation," 72–93.

23. Catherine Flavin-McDonald and Martha L. McCoy, "What's So Bad about Conflict? Study Circles Move Public Discourse from Acrimony to Democracy Building," www.studycircles.org/pages/artabout/conflict.html (Accessed June 27, 2006).

24. Martha L. McCoy and Patrick L. Scully, "Deliberative Dialogue to Expand Civic Engagement: What Kind of Talk Does Democracy Need?" *National Civic Review* 91, no. 2 (Summer 2002), www.ncl.org/publications/ncr/91-2/ncr91-2_article.pdf (Accessed June 21, 2006).

25. John Gastil, "Adult Civic Education through the National Issues Forums: Developing Democratic Habits and Dispositions through Public Deliberation," *Adult Education Quarterly* 54 (2004): 311; and National Issues Forums, "Public Policy Institutes," wwwnifi.org/ppi.html (Accessed July 4, 2006).

26. Keith Melville, Taylor Willingham, and John Dedrick, "National Issues Forums: A Network of Communities Promoting Deliberation," in *The Deliberative Democracy Handbook: Strategies for Effective Civic Engagement in the Twenty-first Century*, ed. John Gastil and Peter Levine, 35–58 (San Francisco: Jossey-Bass, 2005).

27. See Gastil, *By Popular Demand*, 116–17.

28. See, for example, the website of the New England Center for Civic Life at Franklin Pierce College, www.fpc.edu (Accessed July 3, 2006).

29. See Whetten and Cameron, *Developing Management Skills*, 390–450.

30. Joseph P. Folger, Marshall Scott Poole, and Randall K. Stutman, *Working through Conflict*, 3rd ed. (New York: Longman, 1997).

31. Several books have addressed the need for communities to handle conflicts constructively. See, as examples, Daniel Yankelovich, *Coming to Public Judgment: Making Democracy Work in a Complex World* (Syracuse, NY: Syracuse University Press, 1991); *Civic Index: Measuring Your Community's Civic Health* (Washington, DC: The National Civic League, 2003); and Linda Ellinor and Glenna Gerard, *Dialogue: Rediscover the Transforming Power of Conversation* (New York: John Wiley and Sons, 1998).

32. Robert R. Blake and Anne A. McCanse, *Leadership Dilemmas-Grid Solutions* (Houston, TX: Gulf, 1991).

33. Solomon E. Asch, "Studies of Independence and Conformity: A Minority of One against a Unanimous Majority," *Psychological Monographs* 70 (1956).

34. George Cheney, "On the Various and Changing Meanings of Organizational Membership: A Field Study of Organizational Identification," *Communication Monographs* 50 (1983): 342–62.

35. Patricia Hayes Andrews, "Ego-Involvement, Self-Monitoring, and Conformity in Small Groups: A Communicative Analysis," *Central States Speech Journal* 36 (1985): 51–61.

36. For a more extended discussion of social pressure and conformity, see Patricia Hayes Andrews, "Group Conformity," in *Small Group Communication: Theory and Practice*, 7th ed., ed. Robert S. Cathcart, Larry. A. Samovar, and Linda D. Henman (Madison, WI: Brown and Benchmark, 1996), 225–35.

37. Carl L. Thameling and Patricia Hayes Andrews, "Majority Responses to Opinion Deviates: A Communicative Analysis," *Small Group Research* 23 (1992): 475–502.

38. Dennis S. Gouran and Patricia Hayes Andrews, "Determinants of Punitive Responses to Socially Proscribed Behavior: Seriousness, Attribution of Responsibility, and Status of Offender," *Small Group Behavior* 15 (1984): 524–44; and Edwin P. Hollander, "Conformity, Status, and Idiosyncrasy Credit," *Psychological Review* 65 (1958): 117–27.

39. Phillip K. Tompkins, *Organizational Communication Imperatives: Lessons of the Space Program* (Los Angeles, CA: Roxbury, 1993). Also see Dennis S. Gouran, Randy Y. Hirokawa, and Amy E. Martz, "A Critical Analysis of Factors Related to Decisional Processes Involved in the *Challenger* Disaster," *Central States Speech Journal* 37 (1986): 119–35.

40. See, for example, Andrews, "Group Conformity," 225–35; and Renee Meyers et al., "Majority-Minority Influence: Identifying Argumentative Patterns and Predicting Argument-Outcome Links," *Journal of Communication* 50 (2000): 3–30.

41. Irving Janis, *Groupthink*, 2nd ed. (Boston: Houghton Mifflin, 1982), 3.

42. Senate Intelligence Committee Report on the War in Iraq, July 9, 2004, MSNBC News, "Full Text: Conclusions of Senate's Iraq Report," www.msnbc.com/id/543731 (accessed December 6, 2004).

43. Janis, *Groupthink*, 9.

44. Rebecca Cline, "Detecting Groupthink: Methods for Observing the Illusion of Unanimity," *Communication Quarterly* 38 (1990): 112–26.

45. Janis, *Groupthink*, 197–98.

46. See Cline, 120–26; and Irving Janis, "Vigilant Problem Solving," in *Crucial Decisions: Leadership in Policymaking and Crisis Management*, ed. Irving Janis, 89–117 (New York: Free Press, 1989).

47. Kenneth D. Benne and Paul Sheats, "Functional Roles of Group Members," *Journal of Social Issues* 4 (1948): 41–49.

48. Michael E. Mayer, "Behaviors Leading to More Effective Decisions in Small Groups Embedded in Organizations," *Communication Reports* 11 (Summer 1998): 123–32.

49. John R. P. French and Bernard Raven, "The Social Bases of Power," in *Studies in Social Power*, ed. Dorwin Cartwright, 65–84 (Ann Arbor, MI: Institute for Social Research, 1959).

50. Dennis S. Gouran and Randy Y. Hirokawa, "Counteractive Functions of Communication in Effective Group Decision-Making," in *Communication and Group Decision-*

Making. Randy Y. Hirokawa and Marshall Scott Poole, (Beverly Hills, CA.: Sage, 1986), 81–90.

51. Hirokawa and Rost, "Effective Group Decision-Making"; and Randy Y. Hirokawa and Robert Pace, "A Descriptive Investigation of the Possible Communication-Based Reasons for Effective and Ineffective Group Decision Making," *Communication Monographs* 50 (1983): 363–79.

52. Randy Y. Hirokawa, Larry Erbert, and Anthony Hurst, "Communication and Group Decision-Making Effectiveness," in *Communication and Group Decision-Making*, ed. Randy Y. Hirokawa and Marshall Scott Poole (Beverly Hill, CA: Sage, 1986), 269–300.

53. See, for example, Mark L. Knapp and Judith A. Hall, *Nonverbal Communication in Human Interaction* (Belmont, CA: Wadsworth, 2005).

54. William Gudykunst, *Cross-Cultural and Intercultural Communication* (Thousand Oaks, CA: Sage, 2003).

acronym Letters that stand for names or titles, often derived from the initial letters or parts of a series of words.

active listening Channeling our energies and efforts so that we actively concentrate on the speaker's complete message.

actual example A real-life case or specific instance.

adaptation Connecting one's message to the interests and needs of the audience, at a level appropriate to their knowledge and experience, and in a style that they find comfortable.

aerobic exercise Physical activity that increases one's heart rate and respiration and, as a result, lessens tension.

after-dinner speech A ceremonial speech designed to entertain while still saying something significant.

alliteration A repetitive pattern of initial sounds in a sequence of words, used to gain attention and reinforce an idea.

analogical reasoning Inferring that what is true of one case will be true of another, similar case.

antithesis Placing two images together that have sharply different meanings.

appeal to ignorance (*ad ignorantim*) A fallacy of reasoning in which a speaker claims that because his or her argument has not been proven wrong, it must be right.

appeal to popular beliefs (*ad populum*) More commonly called a "bandwagon" appeal, this fallacy occurs when a speaker urges listeners to accept something simply because so many others accept it.

appeal to tradition (*ad verecundiam*) The fallacy that occurs when an advocate claims we should or should not do something simply because that is or is not the way we've always done things in the past.

argument A series of ideas, each one supported by evidence, used to advance a particular position about an issue.

assertion A claim that one advances with an insistence that it is truthful.

attack against the person (*ad hominem*) The fallacy that occurs when an attack on the person substitutes for refutation of that person's argument.

audience centered Focused on one's audience, their characteristics, needs, and well-being.

audience-centered communication Thinking about one's audience throughout the process of communicating, from topic selection to message delivery.

bar graph A graph in which a series of bars depict comparative amounts of certain features or elements.

begging the question The fallacy that occurs when a speaker makes a claim that assumes the very thing he or she hopes to prove, thus arguing in a circle.

belonging needs Identified in Maslow's hierarchy as the need to be loved, accepted, and wanted by others.

brainstorming The process of thinking creatively and imaginatively, temporarily suspending critical judgments of ideas advanced.

burden of proof The standards or expectations that define a "reasonable argument" in a particular situation, or the proof necessary to warrant serious consideration and further debate over an advocate's claims.

campaign   A series of messages aimed at moving listeners closer to a specific position or course of action.

captive audience   An audience who is required to attend a presentation.

categorical pattern   An organizational pattern in which several independent, yet inter-related, categories are used to advance a larger idea.

causal pattern   An organizational pattern in which ideas focus on causes or effects, or are arranged to reveal cause-to-effect or effect-to-cause relationships.

causal reasoning   Reasoning that aims to prove relationships between effects and causes.

chronological pattern   An organizational pattern in which ideas are arranged in a logical, time-based order.

citizen-critic   A citizen educated to critically evaluate the claims, reasoning, and evidence she or he encounters in public deliberations.

civic engagement   Actively participating in community or public affairs, not only by voting, but also by keeping up with the news, discussing issues with fellow citizens, and participating in civic and volunteer activities.

civic virtue   The attitudes and behaviors of good citizenship in a democracy.

claims   The debatable assertions put forward by a speaker.

climactic order   An organizational pattern in which the points being made in a speech are arranged so that they build in intensity.

closed question   A question that encourages a limited response.

coherence   The logical and orderly relationship of information and ideas to develop or support a larger point.

cohesiveness   A group characteristic that results in groups sticking together over time, holding similar views, and being inclined to put pres-

sure on any group member who disagrees with the majority.

commemorative speech   A ceremonial speech marking an important date or event.

commenting modifiers   Modifiers that attempt to boost the meaning of a word but reveal nothing new.

communication apprehension   The feeling of anxiety that a speaker experiences before and/or during a public presentation. *Note:* This term is used interchangeably with communication anxiety and speech anxiety.

competence   The audience's perception of a speaker's intelligence, experience, and education or training relevant to the speech topic.

connotative meaning   The subjective or emotional meaning associated with a particular word or phrase.

critical listening   Listening analytically, carefully evaluating all that is said.

cumulative ethos   The audience's accumulating perceptions of a speaker's credibility.

deductive reasoning   Reasoning from an accepted generalization to a conclusion about a particular case.

deep breathing   Expanding the diaphragm to increase one's intake of air, to assist with relaxation and enhance vocal support.

defining modifiers   Modifiers that provide new, needed information.

definitions   Meanings provided for words that are unfamiliar to listeners or technical in nature.

deliberating "in good faith"   Debating and discussing controversial issues with fellow citizens in a spirit of mutual respect, telling the truth as you see it, backing up your arguments with sound reasoning and evidence, and remaining open to persuasion by compelling arguments on the other side of a debate.

deliberative dialogue   A respectful exchange aimed at establishing a framework for mutual understanding and a common purpose that transcends individual ideas and opinions.

demagoguery   Deceptive or manipulative speech, often relying upon the charismatic ethos of the demagogue and appealing to "dark" emotions like hatred or fear.

denotative meaning   Meaning that is considered objective or universally agreed upon.

descriptive statistic   A statistic that describes what actually happened, based on observation.

Dewey's reflective thinking system   A problem-solution pattern that takes the audience through a thorough exploration of the problem and its causes before considering possible solutions and identifying a preferred course of action.

dynamism   The audience's perception of a speaker's enthusiasm, energy, and genuine interest in the issues being discussed.

empathetic listening   Listening supportively to another with the goal of understanding his or her point of view.

empty words   Words that add length but no additional meaning.

epideictic speech   The ancient Greek term for a ceremonial speech, or speeches presented on special occasions.

esteem needs   Within Maslow's hierarchy of needs, the need to feel important, respected, and admired.

ethical communication   Speaking honestly and truthfully with a thoughtful and genuine concern for the well-being of the audience and the community.

ethical delivery   Speaking authentically, with the utmost respect for listeners and concern for their well-being.

ethical emotional appeals   Emotional appeals that are backed up with strong evidence and sound reasoning.

ethical listeners   People who listen open-mindedly to a speaker before reaching any final conclusions about the integrity and value of the speaker's message.

ethics   A set of behavioral standards viewed by some as universal and by others as relative.

ethos   The ancient Greek term for ethical proof, or the audience's perception of the speaker's credibility.

eulogy   A ceremonial speech paying tribute to a recently deceased person.

evidence   The statistics, examples, testimony, or comparisons that we offer in support of our claims.

exemplum   A narrative pattern organized around an inspiring proverb or quotation and grounded in a value shared by speaker and listeners.

expert testimony   Testimony based on those whose expertise and experience make them especially trustworthy.

extemporaneous speaking   The presentation of a thoroughly prepared speech using an abbreviated set of speaking notes, often in the form of a keyword outline.

facts   Data that can be verified by observation.

fallacy   A flaw in reasoning or evidence that renders an argument logically unsound.

false cause *(post hoc ergo propter hoc)*   The fallacy that occurs when a speaker assumes that because one event precedes another, it must have caused it.

false dilemma   The fallacy that occurs when a speaker suggests that we have only two alternatives, when in fact more than two alternatives exist.

faulty analogy   The fallacy of analogical reasoning that occurs when speakers compare things that are not, in fact, similar.

feedback   Nonverbal and verbal reactions to another's message.

fidelity   Narratives that seem authentic to listeners because they ring true with their own life experiences.

figures of speech   Special uses of language that heighten the beauty of expression to make it clearer, more meaningful, and more memorable.

flip chart   An oversized writing tablet that speakers can place on a tripod for use during a presentation, interactive workshop, or brainstorming session.

formal outline   Outlines in which ideas and their development are articulated completely and precisely, usually using full sentences.

forum period   The question-and-answer period following a speech that allows for a dialogue between speaker and audience.

gendered language   Language that perpetuates traditional gender stereotypes.

general purpose   What the speaker generally hopes to accomplish by speaking, such as gaining audience understanding, agreement, conviction, or action.

ghostwriting   Writing a speech for another person to deliver as his or her own speech.

group pressure for uniformity   The pressure exerted by majority group members on those in the minority in an attempt at getting the minority to conform.

groupthink   A group mindset that hinders the group's ability to critically appraise ideas and express lingering concerns; seeking agreement on a course of action before the group has thoroughly and thoughtfully analyzed the problem and allowed everyone to express their points of view.

guilt by association   The fallacy that occurs when an advocate judges an idea, person, or program solely on the basis of its association with other ideas, persons, or programs.

hasty generalization   The fallacy that occurs when a speaker generalizes from too few examples.

hate speech   Language that demeans or degrades whole classes of people based on their race, ethnicity, religion, or other characteristics.

hypothetical example   An example that describes an action or event that could easily or plausibly occur.

imagery   The use of language to create "word pictures."

immediate audience   Those who constitute a speaker's audience at the speaking event.

impromptu speaking   Casual, off-the-cuff delivery used when a speaker has little or no time for preparation.

inaugural address   A type of ceremonial address given upon assuming a new office or position.

incorporation   Determining if and where specific information and ideas belong in a speech.

inductive reasoning   Reasoning from particular instances or examples to a general conclusion.

inferential statistics   Statistics that generalize from a small group to a larger population, based on probability.

information literacy   Understanding when information is needed and knowing how to locate, gather, and evaluate information and use it responsibly.

informational listening   Listening in order to learn.

informative oral report   An informative presentation intended to assist a group's performance or decision making.

informative speech   A presentation intended to help an audience gain understanding.

internal preview   A quick look ahead at what will be covered while developing a particular point of a speech.

internal summary   A brief review of what one has presented in one or more areas of a speech, offered before moving on to the next area.

irony   The use of language to imply a meaning that is the total opposite of the literal meaning of a word or expression.

isometric exercise   Tensing a muscle and holding it for a short time, followed by complete relaxation of the muscle.

key word outline   An abbreviated outline that serves as a speaker's notes during the delivery of a speech.

keynote address   A ceremonial speech designed to set the tone and sound the key themes of a meeting, conference, or other formal gathering.

lay testimony   Testimony based on the experiences of ordinary men and women whose direct experiences make their testimony compelling.

line graph   A graph in which one or more lines depict a trend or trends over time.

listening   Actively attending to and processing the verbal and nonverbal elements of a message.

listening critically   Analyzing what the speaker is saying in terms of whether it is accurate, reasonable, fair, and of good consequence.

listening for appreciation   Listening with the simple goal of enjoying what is being said.

logos   Logical content that influences our belief or action.

manuscript speaking   Presenting a speech from a prepared text, often in formal ceremonial settings.

margin of error   Possible error or miscalculation associated with inferential statistics.

Maslow's hierarchy   A scheme for considering human needs in terms of levels, moving from the very basic physiological needs to the highest level need for self-actualization; based on the assumption that basic needs must first be fulfilled before others can be satisfied.

mean   The mathematical average.

median   The number representing the midpoint between the largest and the smallest numbers within a particular set of numbers.

memorized speech   A prepared speech presented from memory, without the assistance of speaking notes.

mental argument   Mentally formulating rebuttals to the speaker's ideas and, in the process, losing track of the speaker's message as a whole.

metaphor   An implicit comparison in which two dissimilar objects are compared.

mode   The most frequently occurring number within a particular set of numbers.

monotone   Use of the same vocal pitch without variation.

motivated sequence   An organizational pattern for a persuasive speech that is based on psychological studies of what engages people's emotions and motivates them to act.

name-calling   Language that discredits or demeans others.

narrative example   An extended example that tells a story, either based on true experiences or on symbolism, perhaps in the form of proverbs.

narrative pattern   An indirect, organic organizational pattern that often uses a coherent series of stories to convey the main ideas of the speech.

National Issues Forums   A nonpartisan, nation-wide network of locally sponsored public forums for the consideration of public policy issues.

noise   Any interference that distorts or interrupts message flow.

non sequitur   A fallacy that occurs when a conclusion simply does not follow logically from the arguments and evidence that precede it.

nonverbal communication   Facial expressions, vocal qualities, and physical movements that reinforce or contradict one's verbal messages.

objectivity   The audience's perception of a speaker's openness and fair-mindedness in considering diverse points of view.

open question   Questions that encourage a detailed response and elaboration.

oral style   Language that is chosen with a listener in mind, characterized by short, simple, straightforward sentences and familiar word choices and repetition; generally more informal/conversational than a written style.

orator-statesman   Woodrow Wilson's term for the ethical, civic-minded public speaker.

oxymoron   An expression that presents, in combination, seemingly contradictory terms.

panel discussion   A public discussion format in which the participants interact directly and spontaneously under the guidance of a moderator.

parallelism   The use of a series of sentences with similar length and structure to signify the equality of ideas.

paraphrasing   Summarizing or restating another person's ideas in your own words.

passivity syndrome   Denying one's accountability as a listener and assuming that the burden of effective communication resides wholly with the speaker.

pathos   Emotional content that influences our belief or action.

personal testimony   Testimony based on your own personal experiences and beliefs.

personification   A description of an inanimate form or thing as if it were human.

persuasive definition   A definition that reflects the speaker's way of looking at a controversial subject.

persuasion   The chief mechanism through which citizens in a democracy select their leaders, determine their civic priorities, resolve controversies and disputes, and choose among various policies.

persuasive speech   A speech that seeks to influence the beliefs, values, or actions of others or "make the case" for a new policy or program.

physiological needs   The need to be physically secure, identified as the lowest level of Maslow's hierarchy.

pictograph   Graphs that rely on a set of self-explanatory icons to depict growth or decline over time or between situations.

pie graph   A graph, in the shape of a circle, where segments of the circle (cut into slices, like those of a pie) depict the relative size of a particular feature or element within the whole.

plagiarism   Taking all or part of your speech from a source without proper attribution.

presentational aids   Visual or audio-visual materials that help clarify, support, and/or strengthen the verbal content of a speech.

prestige testimony   The views of a popular or famous person who, though not an expert, expresses a genuine commitment to the cause.

preview   A glimpse of the major areas/points one will be treating in a speech or in a section of a speech.

primacy effects   Placing the most compelling information or arguments first in a speech.

problem-solution pattern   An organizational pattern in which a problem is identified and one or more specific solutions are proposed.

process perspective   Communication viewed as a reciprocal exchange between speaker and listener in which meanings are negotiated.

productive anxiety   Nervous energy that can be channeled into contributing to a more dynamic speech.

promiscuous audience   In the nineteenth century, an audience consisting of both men and women.

prop   Visual or audio material that enlivens a presentation but is not a necessary element.

public controversy   A controversy that affects the whole community or nation and that we debate and decide in our role as citizens in a democracy.

public deliberation   The discursive process through which people in a democracy articulate, explain, and justify their political opinions and policy preferences to their fellow citizens.

public values   Values that are clarified and corroborated through the process of group inquiry.

qualifiers   In the Toulmin model, the words or phrases that indicate the level of confidence we have in our claims.

question of fact   A question about existence, scope, or causality.

question of policy   A question about what policy or program we should adopt, or what course of action we should take.

question of value   A question about whether an idea or action is good or bad, right or wrong, just or unjust, moral or immoral.

racism   The denial of the essential humanity of persons of a particular race.

reasonable person test   A standard used in law courts and in public debate to judge whether an argument is complete, meets the tests of sound reasoning and evidence, and fulfills its burden of proof.

reasoning   Reaching a conclusion on the basis of supporting evidence.

recency effects   Saving the strongest argument or the most important information until near the end of the speech.

red herring   A fallacy in which the speaker attempts to throw an audience off track by raising an irrelevant, often highly emotional issue that prevents critical examination of an argument.

reflection   Cognitively processing and testing information and ideas.

repetition   Repeating, word for word, key elements presented in a message.

reservations   In the Toulmin model, the stated exceptions to our claims, or the conditions under which we no longer hold to our claims.

restatement   Restating, with slightly different language or sentence construction, key elements presented in a message.

rhetoric   The ancient scholarly discipline concerned with the techniques and ethics of speech.

rhetorical criticism   The modern discipline focusing on the critical analysis of public discourse in all of its various forms.

rhetorical question   Questions posed by a speaker that are intended to stimulate thought and interest, not an actual oral response.

safety needs   The need to have a safe and predictable environment as identified in Maslow's hierarchy.

search engine   A software robot (such as *Google*) that one can use to search the World Wide Web via keywords.

self-actualization needs The desire to achieve to the full extent of our capabilities; the highest need level identified by Maslow.

sensory appeals Vivid language that attempts to evoke one of our five senses: seeing, hearing, smelling, tasting, or feeling.

sequential pattern An organizational pattern in which the various steps of a process or phenomenon are identified and discussed, one by one.

sexual identity The roles and attitudes we think are appropriate for ourselves and others with regard to gender.

sexual orientation One's "emotional, romantic, sexual or affectionate attraction to individuals of a particular gender" (as defined by the American Psychological Association).

signposts Words that alert listeners to where you are in your speech, particularly in relation to the speech's overall organization.

simile A figurative comparison made explicit by using the word *like* or *as*.

slippery slope The fallacy that occurs when a speaker claims that some cause will inevitably lead to undesirable effects, ultimately resulting in some worst-case scenario.

source credibility The degree to which a source of information is perceived as reputable.

spatial pattern An organizational pattern in which ideas are arranged according to their natural spatial relationships.

specific purpose A precise statement of how the speaker wants the audience to respond to her or his message, which serves to direct the research and construction of the speech.

speech codes Rules that define and prohibit "hate speech" and other sorts of unacceptable speech on college campuses.

speech of demonstration An informative speech intended to teach an audience how something works or how to do something.

speech of description An informative speech intended to provide a clear picture of a place, event, person, or thing.

speech of explanation An informative speech intended to help an audience understand complicated, abstract, or unfamiliar concepts or subjects.

spin doctor A political operative who twists or distorts the truth in order to manipulate public opinion.

spiraling narrative A narrative pattern that builds in intensity from the beginning to the end of the speech.

statistics A numerical method of interpreting large numbers of instances to display or suggest such factors as typicality, cause and effect, and trends.

stereotyping Making assumptions about someone based upon such factors as race or gender without considering the person's individuality.

straw man fallacy The fallacy that occurs when a speaker attributes a flimsy, easy-to-refute argument to his opponent, then proceeds to demolish it, in the process misrepresenting the opponent's real position.

study circles Diverse, small groups that are guided by an impartial facilitator and that meet over several sessions to tackle community problems and devise creative strategies for action through respectful deliberation.

style A speaker's choice and use of language.

subscription database Immense, searchable collections of indexes, abstracts, and full-text materials compiled by private vendors (such as *EBSCOhost* or *ProQuest*) existing in the private sphere of the Internet, accessible by subscription.

supporting material Information that you present in your speech to substantiate and strengthen your main ideas.

symmetry Using a balanced approach to developing and presenting ideas in a speech, so that each idea is developed with a similar level of elaboration.

symposium A public discussion in which each group member speaks in turn without interruption or interaction, with the moderator providing introductions, transitions, and closure.

target audience Those whom the speaker would most like to influence with the message.

technical language Any language that has very precise meaning within a particular field or endeavor.

temporal context Previous, current, and anticipated events that affect what can or should be said and how it might be received.

thesis statement A single, simple, declarative sentence that expresses the principal idea of a speech that the speaker would have the audience understand or accept.

toast A typically short, abbreviated speech of tribute and celebration.

Toulmin model A visual depiction of the various components of an argument, including claims, warrants, and evidence or data.

town hall meetings A community-wide meeting that is highly organized and media-covered, and that brings together a wide array of citizens representing diverse and often conflicting interests to seek common solutions to community problems.

transactional dialogue An exchange in which speaker and listener are viewed as equal partners in the creation of meaning.

transitional devices Words and phrases that help listeners understand and follow the flow of ideas in a speech.

transitions Words, phrases, or sentences that help the audience perceive the relationship of ideas and the movement from one main idea to another.

tribute A type of ceremonial speech honoring a person, group, event, organization, town, or community.

trustworthiness The audience's perception of a speaker's reliability, honesty, sincerity, and goodwill.

uniform resource locator (URL) The specific address of a website that allows a user to travel directly to that site.

values Those things that we consider good and desirable.

verbal messages Messages created via language or code.

visualization Using language that creates "word pictures" and helps your audience "see" what you are talking about.

warrants In the Toulmin model, the general assumptions, rules, or principles that connect evidence to claims.

washout The reduction in brilliance of an image being projected onto a screen due to interference by light.

Wikipedia A free, online encyclopedia to which anyone can contribute information, and whose accuracy cannot be effectively monitored.

working outline Early drafts of your speech outline, representing your work in progress.

working thesis A tentative thesis, formulated to guide one's investigation and writing.

WorldCat An electronic catalog of the holdings for over 53,000 libraries from around the world.